JAZZ DANCE

Other books by Marshall Stearns:

ROBERT HENRYSON

THE STORY OF JAZZ

JAZZ DANCE

The Story of American Vernacular Dance

MARSHALL and JEAN STEARNS

SCHIRMER BOOKS
A Division of Macmillan Publishing Co., Inc.
NEW YORK

Collier Macmillan Publishers
LONDON

Schirmer Books
A Division of Macmillan Publishing Co., Inc.
866 Third Avenue, New York, N.Y. 10022

Collier Macmillan Canada, Ltd.

Schirmer Books Paperback Edition 1979

Library of Congress Catalog Card Number: 79-2531

Printed in the United States of America

Paperback printing number

1 2 3 4 5 6 7 8 9 10

Library of Congress Cataloging in Publication Data

Stearns, Marshall Winslow.
Jazz dance.

Reprint of the ed. published by Macmillan Co., New York.
Bibliography: p.
1. Dancing--United States--History. 2. Jazz dance--History. I. Stearns, Jean, joint author.
II. Title.
GV1623.S67 1979 793.3'0973 79-2531
ISBN 0-02-872510-7

Acknowledgments

IT IS A PLEASURE to be able to acknowledge our great indebtedness to the following dancers—as well as others interested in the dance—for the valuable time and effort they contributed in numerous interviews and correspondence. Meeting and learning from them was a thrilling experience: Arthur S. Alberts, Richard Allen, Maceo Anderson, Muzzie Anderson, Carlos Arroyo, Fred Astaire, Cholly and May Atkins, Bob Bach, Bill Bailey, John Baker, Marguerite Banks, Paul Barbarin, Philip Barber, Danny Barker, Mae Barnes, Helen Barnett, James Barton, Andy Bascus, Catherine Basie, Jo Bergstrom, Warren Berry, Eubie Blake, Rudi Blesh, Ken Blewitt, Ben Botkin, Carrie Boute, Carroll Bowen, Deighton Boyce, Perry Bradford, Buddy Bradley, Rose Brandel, Bunny Briggs, Ernest Brown, Reuben Brown, Willie Bryant, John Bubbles, Conrad Buckner, Johnny Budden, Dan Burley, Vivian Campbell, Nick Castle, Lon Chaney, Chappy Chappelle, Sam and Ann Charters, Honi and Marian Coles, Chink Collins, Nettie Compton, Frank Condos, Ben Cook, Charles Cook, Harold Courlander, Willie and Florence Covan, James Cross, Walter Crumbley, Cuban Pete, Charlie Davis, Mura Dehn, Maya Deren, Harland Dixon, Roger Pryor Dodge, Paul Draper, Teddy Drayton, Warren Duncan, Sammy Dyer, Sidney Easton, Jodie and Susie Edwards, Duke Ellington, Mercer Ellington, Bobby Ephraim, Mrs. Dena Epstein, Emory Evans, James Evans, Leonard Feather, Ida Forsyne, Gentleman Peppy, Ralph Gleason, Willie Glenn, Coot Grant, Chuck Green, Johnny Green, Rufus Greenlee, Groundhog, Adelaide Hall, John Hammond, Don and Jane Hanson, Herbie Harper, Gene Harris, Sheldon and Gladys Harris, Dan Healy, Mary Healy, Eric Hobsbaum, William Hogan, Bill Hollins, Susie Beavers Howard, Langston Hughes, Leon James, Willis Laurence James, Hansi Janis, Leticia Jay, Andy Jerrick, Charles Johnson, Joe Jones, George Kay, Raymond Kendall, Henry Kmen, Leonard Kunstadt, Jerry Kurland, Baby Laurence, David Leddick, Hal Leroy, Avon Long, Charlie Love, James Maher, Pigmeat Markham, Will Mastin, James Matthews, Billy Maxey, Catharine Miller, Flournoy Miller, Irving C. Miller, Norma Miller, Al Minns, Billy Mitchell, Sonny Montgomery, James Mordecai, Jack and Lynn Morris, Alan Morrison, Arthur and Janet Morrison, Tom Mosley, Leroy Myers, Ray Nance, Fayard Nicholas, Mrs. Ulysses Nicholas, Pete Nugent, Aaron Palmer, Terry Perez, Joe Peterson, Killer Joe Piro, Bill Pittman, Bernadine Pitts, Tommy Powell, Joe Price, Sam Price, Mike Ramos, Alice Ramsey, Charlie Randalls, Tiny Ray, Eddie Rector, Don Redman, Leonard Reed, Harry Reif,

Rhythm Red, Danny Richmond, Max Roach, Luckey Roberts, Phace Roberts, Clarence Robinson, Nipsey Russell, William Russell, Willie Sandberg, Sandman, Frank Schiffman, Baby Seals, Noble Sissle, Charles Edward Smith, Wilhelm Smithe, Shorty Snowden, Edmond Souchon, Harry Souchon, Victoria Spivey, John Steiner, Rex Stewart, Meave Sullivan, Wilbur Sweatman, John Thomas, Robert Farris Thompson, Ulysses S. Thompson, Slim Thompson, Sinclair Traill, Lorenzo Turner, Elizabeth O'Neill Verner, Ruth Walton, Archie Ware, Clay Watson, George Wein, Dewey Weinglass, George Wendler, Eddie West, Tom Whaley, Leigh Whipper, Alberta Whitman, Alice Whitman, Essie Whitman, Al Williams, Ethel Williams, Rubberlegs Williams, Louis Williams, Edith Wilson, Berta Wood, Mrs. Alice Zeno.

We should like to thank Paul Myers and Dorothy Swerdlove of the New York Public Library; Rae Korson of the Library of Congress; Cora Eubanks, Jean Hudson, and Ernest Kaiser of the Schomburg Library; the library staff of the British Museum, Cambridge (England), Harvard, Tulane, and Yale Universities.

We are especially grateful to Nadia Chilkovsky and Ernest R. Smith for their appendices.

We should also like to thank those magazines in which some of the chapters (since revised) in this book originally appeared: *Down Beat Yearbook, Esquire, Jazz, Keystone Folklore Quarterly, New York Folklore Quarterly, Show, Sounds and Fury, Southern Folklore Quarterly, Southwest Review.*

Finally, for faith and encouragement that can move mountains, we thank our editor, Bob Markel.

C O N T E N T S

PART FOUR Tin Pan Alley and Song Lyrics

PART FIVE Broadway and the Reviewers

PART SIX Technique: Pioneers, Innovators, and Stylists

PART SEVEN Specialties

PART EIGHT Acrobatics

PART NINE The Class Acts

PART TEN The Jitterbug

PART ELEVEN Requiem

MARSHALL WINSLOW STEARNS

An Appreciation by James T. Maher

INSIDE the classroom and out, in everything he did, Marshall Stearns served his contemporaries, young and old, as a whole-hearted guide and provocative teacher. As a faculty member at the University of Hawaii, the University of Indiana, Cornell University, and Hunter College; in lecture halls, on improvised platforms, or in whatever living room was handy; at jazz festivals and conferences on American civilization; on network television; and, perhaps above all, at his typewriter, he "taught." He undertook many public-service assignments, such as music consultant to the State Department and director of Dizzy Gillespie's goodwill tour of the Middle East. To each such project he brought the special illumination of his urge to teach. It was a natural reflex for him to share his knowledge, his insights, and his pleasures.

For twenty-seven years he taught college English, eventually specializing in Chaucer. He wrote what may have been the first serious essay published in the United States on the poetry of Dylan Thomas. Many years later, at the time of his death, he was making notes for an extended analysis of the Welsh poet's work. His doctoral thesis on Robert Henryson, the standard reference on this fifteenth-century English poet, had only recently been reprinted in a new edition. And ahead, he had hoped, lay a study of Chaucer and a novel.

As an undergraduate at Harvard he played a C-melody sax, an instrument that any really hip college man preferred to a uke. He knew where the action was: in jazz, the medium/message of the twenties. He started a record collection that ultimately grew into the extraordinary library of recorded jazz that he assembled (mostly with his own money) for the Institute of Jazz Studies. He was the principal founder of the Institute, and as its director he was always enthusiastic and patient, qualities that were severely tested as one foundation after another turned down his appeals for funds to carry out a broad program of scholarly research by jazz experts. (Jazz hadn't become a lady after all—at least not an academic lady.)

When jazz lovers were still few, he took the time to write for the "little magazines" in England and America devoted to this deliberately misunderstood music. No one was paid for such acts of love in the pioneer years. These affectionate pieces led him into a second career that evolved slowly over several decades. He became a forthright propagandist for jazz—a man with a message. He wanted people to listen with open minds and hearts to the music that had been created out of the Negro experience in White America. His message was simple: Discover the complex beauty of this rich music, then, if you must, judge it, but judge it *on its own terms,* not as "classical music." Enjoy, enjoy . . . without bias.

It was probably inevitable that as a young teacher in the depression years he would become an activist in the turmoil of inequity that confronted America. He helped a group of Negro students in their effort to enter and use the student center at the mid-Western university at which he was then teaching. Years later, he recalled the police sirens that accompanied the governor's car when the supreme Hoosier drove to the campus "to straighten out these guys." At another university he joined the union movement for a more equitable salary for teachers, who were, of course, expected to live on a small salary and some fringe *prestige.* He collaborated on a twelve-bar blues, "The Teacher's Blues," that rallied his colleagues with a wry final line: "You can't feed your kids on *noblesse oblige.*"

In 1949 he was invited by New York University to teach "Perspectives in Jazz," an evening course started by his old friends John Hammond and George Avakian that first met at Café Society–Downtown. Then, his great private scheme gathered momentum. Out of the long years of listening, exchanging views, arguing, interviewing, and article-writing came the substance of his superbly organized lectures, in which he frequently shared the platform with some of the finest jazzmen then performing—he numbered some of the most creative figures in jazz among his friends.

A man of easy dignity, he was a courteous and good-humored host. On successive Friday evenings at his home one might find Charlie Parker and the poet and teacher Sterling Brown. The novelist Ralph Ellison addressed his pupils. One of his enduring friendships was with Duke Ellington. Jazz historian Rudi Blesh enjoyed the generosity of his table, argued certain differences, then came back again and again as a fruitful affection grew from their common concern for jazz. From such encounters Stearns was able to bring to his lectures firsthand excitement and vitality.

At length he sat down and wrote what has become the standard book in its field, *The Story Of Jazz,* a fine and thoughtful work that is notable for its broad embrace of all aspects of this native music. He then discovered another story in the Negro experience that he felt must be told—the story of "jazz dance." For seven years he devoted every day and week he could muster, this time in partnership with his wife, Jean, to the search for facts that could be gathered only from that most fugitive of sources, the human memory. The search took him and his wife across the United States and to

England. They interviewed dozens of dancers, Negro and white, forgotten and remembered.

Finally, the manuscript for the new book was completed. Then, at five o'clock in the morning on December 18, 1966, in Key West, Florida, he was stricken with a fatal heart attack. He was only fifty-eight years old. His first jazz book had been translated into twelve languages, and he had shared with many thousands of people around the world the gifts of a generous teacher: knowledge, insight, and pleasure.

Jazz Dance is his legacy to his "students" everywhere.

INTRODUCTION

"ALL BALLETS' FUNDAMENTAL STEPS," writes Dame Ninette de Valois, Director of the Royal Ballet of England, "are derived from the folk dances of Western Europe." [1] Indeed, all dance may be said to derive ultimately from the folk.

The creativity of the folk, however, varies in time and place. "Since 1850 there has been little change in Europe," says Agnes de Mille. "All further innovations have come from the United States, Cuba, or South America, and all broke with previous tradition." [2] The chief source of these innovations—particularly the rhythms—is Africa.

This book deals with *American dancing that is performed to and with the rhythms of jazz*—that is, dancing that *swings*. It can, of course, be performed without any accompaniment, but even then it makes jazz rhythms visible, creating a new dimension. The subtitle, "American Vernacular Dance"—*vernacular* in the sense of native and homegrown—points to a second and no less important characteristic.

The phrase *jazz dance* has a special meaning for professionals who dance to jazz music (they use it to describe non-tap body movement); and another meaning for studios from coast to coast teaching "Modern Jazz Dance" (a blend of Euro-American styles that owes little to jazz and less to jazz rhythms). However, we are dealing here with what may eventually be referred to as *jazz dance,* and we could not think of a more suitable title.

The characteristic that distinguishes American vernacular dance—as it does jazz music—is *swing*, which can be heard, felt, and seen, but defined only with great difficulty. Jazz, as we all know by now, is different from the music that people from the Old World brought to the New, and the dancing that goes with it is different, too.

Jazz dance evolved along lines parallel to jazz music, and its source is similarly a blend of European and African traditions in an American environment. In general, European influences contributed the elegance, African influences the rhythmic propulsion. This is an oversimplification, of course, for the process is complicated and varies widely in time, place, and intensity.

Most of the material in this book is taken from more than two hundred interviews with dancers and individuals associated with dancing, many of whom are now dead. We owe a great debt to all of them.

The information we obtained, relying as it must on the memories of those we interviewed, is fallible and sometimes downright contradictory. In many cases we have presented more than one point of view—by direct quotation if possible—and in every case we have tried to weigh the evidence, including the scanty and unreliable information in print, and come to a sensible conclusion.

Further, jazz dance, like other arts, has its rival factions, its heroes and legends, its fashions and trends—in a word, its own unique history. This history is closely linked to the economics of show business, the changing status of the American Negro, and the evolution of jazz. Accordingly, we have attempted the similar but more difficult job of arriving at valid conclusions concerning over-all developments and traditions.

It would have been easier to edit a series of interviews, as others have done with roughly similar material, and let the reader wander among a welter of shifting detail and opinion. We felt, however, that one of our most important objectives should be to analyze the evidence and come to some viable synthesis, some evaluation of the subject in all its complexity.

In addition to a selected bibliography, an index, and footnotes, two important appendices have been included: an exhaustive list of films in which vernacular dancing may be seen (the best documentation of the subject) compiled by Ernest R. Smith, and a valuable analysis and notation of basic Afro-American movements by Nadia Chilkovsky.

The subject of vernacular dance is so vast that, after six years of research, we gave up all idea of telling the whole story. Nevertheless, as we proceeded we found that certain dancers were consistently singled out for specific accomplishments, and certain major trends were mentioned repeatedly. So we limited ourselves to tracing major developments and describing the careers of dancers who created styles and established traditions.

The aim of the book, therefore, is to chart the main currents in the stream of American vernacular dance.

Referring to the popularity of the Lindy Hop, or Jitterbug, Roger Pryor Dodge writes:

> Sadly enough, out of this whole dance mania, none of it developed into the professional stage dance . . . while Lindy Hoppers stood on the side lines, a new breed of dancer, fortified with ballet and modern dance training, took over show business and danced to some form of jazz music.
>
> The new dance has none of the style, refined or not, of the Negro

> dance. With its few movements derived from jazz it became a choreographer's idea of what dancers with ballet and modern training should do to jazz.[3]

Unfortunately, much the same thing happened to all vernacular dance. By the mid-sixties a great era seemed to be coming to a close.

Jazz dance is a thrilling art that deserves study. We enjoy it very much and regret its passing—it is perhaps too much to hope for a revival. Others will no doubt add and correct details, enlarge and modify generalizations in this book. That is as it should be, and we will welcome it. As with the pioneer studies of jazz itself, the surface has barely been scratched.

1 Prologue

FOR BETTER OR WORSE, rock-and-roll brought back popular dancing. In the twenties, the average dancer replaced European-derived dances with the Fox Trot and its marchlike footwork; in the thirties he replaced the Fox Trot with the Jitterbug, or Lindy, and its syncopated box step; and in the early sixties he replaced the Lindy with the Twist—and from then on the hips have been permanently involved.

The direction of this revolution is toward Afro-American styles and rhythms. The swaying motion of the Twist was employed long ago in Africa and by the Negro folk in the South. This movement was used in the 1913 routine of a dance called Ballin' the Jack (as a youth in New Orleans, pianist Jelly Roll Morton sang of "Sis' . . . out on the levee doin' the double Twis'"); blues shouters of the twenties used it as they raised their arms to belt out a tune; and in the thirties it was inserted during the breakaway (where partners separated) of the Lindy.

When the swing era faded in the forties, a blackout of about ten years intervened—from 1945 to 1954—with little or no dancing. Big-band devotees—gray-haired in the 1960's—are still arguing about what caused it: the federal tax on dance floors; the new and "undanceable" kind of jazz (bop); the recording bans of 1942, most of 1943, and again in 1948, which brought hitherto unknown composers and vocalists such as Johnnie Ray into prominence; and the consequent disappearance of ballrooms along with the expensive big bands that played them.

In any case, by 1955 the youngsters were beginning to dance to rock-and-roll. The music was a throwback, or rather a dilution by white musicians of the kind of music recorded for the Negro market over the past fifty or so years. Originally known as "race" in the 1920's, then "rhythm-and-blues" in the 1930's and 1940's, the tag rock-and-roll became popular in the fifties. It was all the same music, tailored for the jukebox and preeminently danceable.

For the first time, white teen-agers in large numbers danced in their homes and at record hops to music Negroes had been dancing to for decades. Much of it was blues. It was played by economical jazz combos with a honking tenor saxophone, and characterized by a big (and often mushy and monotonous) off-beat. As far as popular music was concerned, however, the beat was new and a widespread rhythmic revolution had begun.

Rock-and-roll was put on the market by record companies, popularized by some three thousand disc jockeys, and purchased and danced to almost exclusively by adolescents and preadolescents. Eighteen million teen-agers, it has been estimated, spend ten billion dollars a year. The key to the market, however, consists of thirteen to fifteen-year-olds. They still move in herds, and when they decide to buy a recording or adopt a dance, it sells in great quantities and becomes a hit overnight.

What do adolescents get out of rock-and-roll? Their world is in conflict say the psychiatrists: Dad urges them to be independent ("Get a job!"), and Mom wants them dependent ("Now finish your milk"). They are expected to grow up early and get married later. It is all very confusing, but they try to follow both commands at once. So while waiting to belong, they rebel, drinking their milk—so to speak—on the job.

Rock-and-roll supplies a temporary solution whereby the teen-ager has his cake and eats it. As a fan he protests as loudly as his phonograph will permit, or as grotesquely as the latest dance suggests (he knows his parents are unfamiliar with both the music and the dances), and at the same time, he belongs to a group with identical tastes in music and dance. He is both dependent and independent—he belongs and rebels simultaneously.

(Parents who are irritated by the dances of their youngsters need not take it locked up in the bedroom. By learning all the latest dances themselves—the more energy and enthusiasm the better—they have a good chance of shocking their children back into ballet.)

The radio program *Make Believe Ballroom* went the way of swing music and real ballrooms in the late forties. By 1951 in Cleveland, Allan Freed hit upon "ethnic" music—he played nothing but rhythm-and-blues, pounding on a phonebook next to the microphone. The sound was new to white audiences, but many of the younger ones loved it. In 1952 his listeners were mostly black, but by 1954 so many whites had begun to listen that they outnumbered his original audience.

In 1955 "Rock Around the Clock," by Bill Haley and his Comets, had sold three million copies, rock-and-roll was big business, and a new flock of disc jockeys rode the sound waves.

Then, in the fall of 1956, Elvis Presley arrived. The music underwent a gradual transformation. It became truly integrated. Establishing a guitar accompaniment with a sharecropper sound, Presley blended four distinct styles into an attractive whole: hillbilly music, gospel music, blues, and popular music. Some called it "rockabilly." The lyrics (if you could hear them) were simple, the melodies recognizable, and the rhythms engaging. New York's Tin Pan Alley, to put it mildly, was unsettled, and Nashville, the headquarters of what had become known as "country" music, took the lead.[1] By 1965 Presley had sold 100 million records.[2]

Dancing changed, too. Presley created a crisis on television. Hard-nosed executives reacted like frightened rabbits. After one debacle, the camera men on the next show were ordered to photograph Elvis from the chest up only. It looked silly. On Steve Allen's program they trussed him up in formal evening clothes—white tie and tails—and made him stand still. Nothing at all happened. "I gotta move," said Elvis patiently, "when I sing." [3]

After three appearances on TV, Presley was signed by Ed Sullivan, who announced that he had reviewed the performances on other shows and found them not too obscene for his own program. In fact, they were perfectly all right. Elvis was turned loose at last, and the skies did not fall. The show's ratings reached an all-time high and—hips or no hips—Presley was family.

At the height of the uproar John Crosby, in the New York *Herald Tribune*,[4] and Jack Gould in the *Times*,[5] criticized Presley savagely. Elvis was genuinely upset and, in all sincerity, asked his mother if she thought his motions were obscene. Her reply should have made her Mother of the Year. "Son," she said, "you're working too hard." [6]

The merciless criticism continued—Presley was considered fair game for anyone with a typewriter—in spite of the fact that he was unfailingly polite and well-mannered. "I never made no dirty body movements," [7] he insisted to an interviewer. He meant it. "Hormones flow in him as serenely as the Mississippi past Memphis," wrote the Baxters in *Harper's*, "and the offense lies in the eye of the beholder, not in Elvis' intentions." [8]

Elvis Presley was not exactly doing the Twist, but as did the hula hoop craze, he helped light the fuse. Professionals called it "eccentric legomania." He may have been copying one of his idols, the Negro blues singer Bo Diddley, who comes on stage in a crouch, playing guitar, waving his knees, and stamping his feet like a Haitian *rara* dancer. (Bo Diddley himself says it may be so and remembers Elvis asking for an autograph.) [9] But Presley was his own man. Actually his motions were a relatively tame version of the ancient Snake Hips of the Negro folk, popularized in Harlem by dancer Earl Tucker during the twenties.

Rock-and-roll and television grew up side by side. As the music became popular, the dancing spread, accelerated by a few quickly assembled movies and such disc jockeys as Dick Clark, who jumped from radio to television in 1957 with *American Bandstand*. It was the beginning of a highly successful combination.

In the foreground, these programs presented a group of authentically awkward dancers with whom any teen-ager could identify. The girls danced like girls, and unlike professional TV dancers, the boys really danced like boys. Back at stage center the disc jockey introduced singers who performed in "lip-sync" with their own recordings (it cost less), plugged various discs (in which he sometimes had a financial interest), and sold, among other products, quantities of medicated cream for adolescent blemishes.

Before and during Presley's initial success, the first wave of dances became popular. Group dances such as the Madison and the Birdland arrived first—then came the deluge: the Bop, Jet, Roach, Wobble, Locomotion, Choo-Choo, Fight, Freeze, and many others.

The best were unrealized revivals: Something strongly reminiscent of the Charleston emerged as the Mashed Potato and the Charley-Bop; bits of the old Eagle Rock returned in the Fly; an unintentional parody of the Lindy became known as the Chicken; a version of the Camel Walk survived in the Stroll; the Jig Walk came back (to Brooklyn) as the Slop; and some of the Slow Drag showed up in the Fish. (The Crawl was manufactured in Hollywood.) The youngsters, however, had never seen any of it before.

When the Twist finally hit in 1960, the teen-agers were already through with it. Cholly Knickerbocker (Igor Cassini) saw an inebriated dowager attempting the Twist at the Peppermint Lounge in New York, they say, and wrote about it in his column in the *Journal-American*. The tune—what there was of it—had been composed and recorded by Hank Ballard in the mid-fifties without causing a stir; in 1960 it was rerecorded and plugged by Chubby Checker on Clay Cole's TV show. That did it: Chubby was summoned to demonstrate the dance for cafe society.

"It caught on among adults," says disc jockey Murray "The K" Kaufman, because it was the only dance they could do." [10] True, anybody could perform the Twist. Arthur Murray nevertheless advertised "6 Easy Lessons for $25." Overnight the dance became an international fad, a worldwide craze, and hips came into their uncontrollable own. On a tour of inspection, dance critic Walter Terry reported carefully: "They never touch . . . just face to face . . . a rather tenuous partnership . . . when the female strikes out in the Twist, the movement originates . . . in the hips.[11]

A second wave of dances crashed over American dance floors during and after the Twist: the Monkey, Bug, Pony, Frug, Hitchhike, Watusi, Hully-Gully, Jerk, Boogaloo, and so on. Several of them showed traces of ancient lineage: The Frug harked back to the Shimmy, the Bug and the Monkey borrowed from the old Heebie-Jeebies, and the Pony employed bits of the Slow Drag. In fact, their debt to earlier dances was the chief thing that made them distinguishable.

But something was missing: As the dances multiplied, the quality deteriorated. Many such new "dances" as the Swim, the Woodpecker, the Hitchhike, and the Monkey were simply charades, pantomimes with hand-and-arm gestures and little body or footwork. Some dancers inserted motions anyway, chiefly hops or shuffles. Advertisers invented dances to sell their products. (The rumor that Thumbing-the-Nose would be promoted as a new dance, for example, turned out to be exaggerated.)

Of this second wave the Jerk and the Dog went back via Presley to Little Egypt of the Chicago Worlds Fair more than a half-century earlier and included variously modified bumps and grinds. On TV, *Hollywood a Go-Go* created a stir with the Jerk. With the inevitable toning-down on television and the glassy-eyed innocence of the dancers, it soon lost whatever shock value it possessed and adolescents went on to other dances.

The immense popularity of the Beatles speeded up the spread of dancing. In accents of rural Tennessee, they sang songs which sounded as if they were blending "Rock Around the Clock" with "Greensleeves." (The similarity of the *Credo* of Gounod's "St. Cecelia" and "I Want to Hold Your Hand" has been pointed out.[12]) New York's Tin Pan Alley was caught off balance again and danceable music with a new lyric feeling, aided by the films *A Hard Day's Night* and *Help!*, spread far beyond the teen-age market.

Back in the teens, dance-song routines from the Negro folk such as "Walkin' the Dog" had been popular. These songs had directions in the lyrics on how to dance them. Later, dance-songs were concocted for many musical shows in the twenties and thirties and the directions became pretty vague. Once again, in the sixties, the same formula was attempted but it did not seem to help. Repeated pleas to "Do the So-and-So" simply became a minor part of no-move dances.

When dancing at discotheques became popular—for years it was known in the South as "jukin'" and you inserted your own nickel in the juke box—night clubs made money again. There were about five thousand discotheques by 1965, but the dancing was erratic. No one could dance with finesse in such crowded darkness, even if he wished, and many patrons were older people who, although they liked the darkness, emphatically did not wish. The only way to attract attention was to go ape with more energy than skill, achieving a very disordered effect.

Frantic attempts were made to cash in on the craze. Tin Pan Alley and the big record companies in New York were at their wits' end: Now

Houston, Detroit, and the West Coast were competing successfully with Nashville while New York worried. "Nobody knows," said one harried executive, "what those damn teen-agers will go for next." The best single recordings, singers, and dances appeared and disappeared in a week. Only dance studios seemed sure of a steady income.

The indestructible Frank "Killer Joe" Piro survived handily. A Lindy Hopper in the thirties, teacher of Afro-Cuban dances at the Palladium in the forties and fifties, he became the favorite instructor of the jet set in the sixties. He was in the *avant-garde* of the ballroom tradition, and although more expert dancers viewed his success with a mixture of envy and alarm, Piro knew what he was doing.

In 1965 lush, full-page advertisements appeared from coast to coast (a double-page in *Life*) announcing that Killer Joe Piro had created his "wildest, wackiest dance"—the Mule—to go with a brand of vodka and a soft drink. In one of several shots, Piro is on top of a baby grand, looking desperately alert, while some unnamed model furnishes the action, and Skitch Henderson, who recorded an album of *Mule Music*, appears justifiably ashamed.

The implication is clear that the Mule is best enjoyed when drinking, if not when drunk. As for the choreography, Piro must have inserted a kick to go with the title, so it could have been an improvement on the dances of the time. (There is no truth to the rumor that Piro had been commissioned to create another dance to go with a tie-in advertisement for Scott Tissue and Tabu perfume.)

Television, too, was busy flattening out the new craze to produce a broader appeal and a steady income. The formula consisted of a series of hit songs and singers, from the early and less expensive *Lloyd Thaxton*, *Clay Cole*, and *Dick Clark* shows to the later big productions: *Where the Action Is*, *Hollywood a Go-Go*, *Hullabaloo*, *Let's Go-Go*, *Shivaree*, and the fast-paced model for most of them, *Shindig*. Again Ed Sullivan jumped on the bandwagon—later—with the current groups from England.

The result was to "professionalize" the dance by conforming to past formulas. A choreographer and a chorus line of regular TV dancers were hired. True, there were differences. A couple of girls usually danced in cages, hopping up and down in one spot and tossing their straight hair recklessly. Sometimes there was a bit of self-satire. The authentic teen-age dancers disappeared, however, and the boy dancers became once more indistinguishable from girls.

Soupy Sales, the unpretentious emcee of a TV kiddie show, plugged his new dance on *Hullabaloo:* the Mouse. The viewer's impulses were short-circuited, for Soupy stood anchored to one spot while the big beat boomed invitingly. "It's simple," he announced, which nobody could deny, for he merely made a face and stuck his thumbs in his ears. "Do the Mouse" he requested happily over and over, adding occasionally "in the house," which rhymed but might cause parental resentment. A chorus of six girls scrambled around him, gyrating in a style no amateur would attempt.

In midsummer, 1965, *Hullabaloo,* which started strong from Hollywood, featured hillbilly hoe-downs and country polkas along with the big beat. *Shindig,* although it made such an initial splash even among the college crowd that it was programmed twice a week on prime time in the fall, was featuring such guest emcees as Jack E. Leonard, Mickey Rooney, Hedy Lamarr, and Jimmy Durante among even less suitable celebrities in a desperate attempt to stay afloat. In spite of their early promise, the big rock-and-roll productions on TV did not sell and were fading as 1965 ended.

By November, Dick Clark was quoted as saying "English Sound's dead, Folk Rock's dying, the Rolling Stones are slipping badly, the Dave Clark Five's hurtin' so much it's working at home. There's nothing left big and hot but the Beatles. Way things are going, pretty soon singers will be getting haircuts." [13] The dancing was losing all its character, too.

But even with the predictions of doom, a revolution in popular dance had taken place. Out of 130 million single recordings sold in 1965, for example, 90 per cent were rock-and-roll,[14] eight hundred recordings were issued each week, and new dances popped up almost as frequently. Adults purchased a big share of the recordings, formed a large part of the radio and TV audiences, and performed many of the dances. These dances had, in the words of Walter Terry, "the peculiar quality of eliciting participation." [15]

A new and rhythmically sophisticated generation had grown. The exposure was instant, the activity tremendous, and the potential limitless (see Chapter 45). The influence of the Twist and related dances is still with us, and world dance will never be the same.

PART ONE

Prehistory

2 Africa and the West Indies

IN THE EARLY 1950's, during the first years of a summer resort in the Berkshire Mountains called Music Inn, we tried an experiment. Our aim was to entertain—quite informally—a handful of guests in the lounge after dinner, but our host Philip Barber was carried away with his theory of instantaneous talent combustion. "Throw gifted performers together," he said, "get one of them going, and watch them all discover talents which they didn't know they had." With various jazzmen of supposedly separate eras, the idea had worked well.

That evening we had dancers from three different countries: Asadata Dafora from Sierra Leone, West Africa; Geoffrey Holder from Trinidad, West Indies; and Al Minns and Leon James from the Savoy Ballroom, New York City. All of them were alert to their own traditions and articulate, eager to demonstrate their styles.

So we began with the Minns-James repertory of twenty or so Afro-American dances, from "Cakewalk to Cool," asking Dafora and Holder to comment freely. The results were astonishing. One dancer hardly began a step before another exclaimed with delight, jumped to his feet, and executed a related version of his own. The audience found itself sharing the surprise and pleasure of the dancers as they hit upon similarities in their respective traditions. We were soon participating in the shock of recognizing what appeared to be one great tradition.

Certain trends emerged. American dances of predominantly British and European origin, such as the Square Dance, seemed to go back only as far as the West Indies—if at all. The Cakewalk turned up no worthy African counterpart (Minns and James omitted improvised steps), although Holder demonstrated its general relationship to the Bel Air of Trinidad. The basic

Mambo, however, was immediately identified with a Congo step from Africa and a Shango step from Trinidad. (The Cuban scholar, Fernando Ortiz, is convinced that *mambo* is a Congo word.)

An American dance, the Shimmy, produced an immediate response from Dafora. "That is only the beginning of the Shika dance of Nigeria," he asserted and illustrated his point by vibrating his shoulders and then gradually shaking down and throughout his entire body. Minns and James were almost grieved: "You're doing our Shake dance!" Whereupon they produced their own version, throwing in a few grinds and quivers. Both Little Egypt and Elvis Presley, it now appeared, were standing still, and the Twist, Frug, and Jerk were simple-minded substitutes. We learned that the Shake is known as the Banda in Trinidad and the Oleke in West Africa.

Other American dances led to other parallels. The Charleston proved similar to a dance called the King Sailor in Trinidad (the title may have been taken from an American movie) and an Obolo dance of the Ibo tribe in West Africa. Another, Pecking—a neck and shoulder movement which begins with an imitation of chickens—was found to be similar to a Yanvallou dance in Trinidad and a Dahomean dance in West Africa. Elements of the Lindy, or Jitterbug, were noted by Holder in a Shango dance, and by Dafora in an Ejor tribal dance.

And thus the evening passed quickly. A rather sensational routine known as Snake Hips (a specialty of loose-jointed Earl Tucker at the Cotton Club in Harlem in the late 1920's), in which the loins are undulated in a very un-European fashion, brought a quick response from Holder: "That's called the Congo in Trinidad." Dafora, who was fiercely proud of his native land, seemed embarrassed, but agreed that it was called the Congo in Africa.

When Minns cut loose with the Fish Tail as a climax to the Snake Hips routine (accompanied by Duke Ellington's recording of "East St. Louis Toodle-Oo"), a movement in which the buttocks weave out, back, and up in a variety of figure eights, both Holder and Dafora were silent. Holder could not seem to place it, but Dafora finally observed with some asperity that although the Fish Tail came from Africa, dancing in the European fashion with one arm around your partner's waist was considered obscene. ("The African dance," writes President Senghor of Senegal, "disdains bodily contact." [1]) He was caught between two cultures and their almost opposite attitudes toward hip movement.

The evening at Music Inn gave us insights that are borne out by other evidence. Like music, the dance is found everywhere in Africa—"a fundamental element in aesthetic expression" [2] in the words of Melville Herskovits—and there seems to be no limit whatsoever to the movements employed.

"Ranging from the walk and all its variations," writes Pearl Primus, "the technique of the African dance embraces the leap, the hop, the skip, the jump, falls of all descriptions, and turns which balance the dancer at the most precarious angles to the ground." [3]

Perhaps the most clear-cut survival of African dance in the United States is the Ring Shout, or Circle Dance, with its combination of African elements from the counterclockwise movement of the group, through the stiff shoulders and outstretched arm and hand gestures, to the flat-footed Shuffle. Not so obvious is the survival of the Cross Over in the Charleston; the Congo hip movements in the Slow Drag, Snake Hips, and other social dances of the Negro folk; the African style of the subtly bouncing Shuffle performed by the dancers in a New Orleans street march; and the African acrobatic dances in the Jitterbug and earlier professional acts. Of course, the original African impulse, so to speak, has often been reinterpreted and diluted.

At the other extreme, several "American" dances have been observed in what was probably their original form in Africa. Take the Charleston, which first destroyed the distinction in the United States between a dance to watch and a dance to perform—everybody seemed to be doing it around 1925. Among the Ashanti, Herskovits recognizes a "perfect example of the Charleston;" [4] A. N. Tucker notes "the 'Charleston-like' step which is common to all Bari-speakers"; [5] and Frederick Kaigh writes: "The children of Africa were doing the Charleston before Julius Caesar had so much as heard of Britain, and they still are." [6]

A few years ago, watching films of West African dancing taken by Professor Lorenzo Turner of Roosevelt University, the present writers saw the Ibibio of Nigeria performing a shimmy to end all shimmies, the Sherbro of Sierra Leone executing an unreasonably fine facsimile of the Snake Hips, and a group of Hausa girls near Kano moving in a fashion closely resembling the Lindy, or Jitterbug.

Again, in her analysis of African dance films, the director of the Philadelphia Dance Academy, Nadia Chilkovsky, found close parallels to American dances such as the Shimmy, Charleston, Pecking, Trucking, Hucklebuck, and Snake Hips, among others.[7] Indeed, most films of African dancing —in and out of Hollywood (fortunately, no director knows how to commercialize the native dances)—are honeycombed with resemblances to American popular dance. The resemblances are strongest, however, to the Afro-American *vernacular,* that is, such basic dances of the Negro folk as the Strut, Shuffle, Sand, and Grind.

The evidence of eyewitnesses is also available. Folklorist Harold Courlander has seen dances in South Africa, Ghana, and Nigeria which were "virtually indistinguishable" from the Cakewalk, Shuffle, and Strut.[8]

The pioneering Negro dancer Thaddeus Drayton, who was born in 1893, remembers meeting an African student named Moleo in Paris during the 1920's. Moleo was putting himself through school by dancing. "He was from German South Africa, and was doing—barefoot—a complicated flash step, which we called Over the Top. We believed that an American Negro, Toots Davis, had invented it, but when I asked Moleo what American had taught him, he laughed and said, 'That step came from my tribe in Africa.' " [9]

"The dance itself," says Herskovits, "has . . . carried over into the New World to a greater degree than almost any other trait of African culture." [10] In fact, it is just possible, as Africanist Robert F. Thompson of Yale University has suggested, that certain basic movements can be associated with certain African tribes.[11] Thus, the Pygmies are famous for their footwork, the Dahomeans for their head and shoulder motions, and the Congolese for their hip and loin movements. We may some day be able to specify the tribal origins of various movements in American popular dance.

As time goes on, the influence of Afro-American dance on American popular dance is increasing. Today the Latin-American dances such as the Rumba, Conga, Samba, Mambo, Cha Cha, Pachanga, and so on, which have been imported from areas where a merging of African and European styles has already taken place, show the greatest African influence, both in quantity and quality. At the same time, these dances are still assimilating elements from such earlier Afro-American dances as the Charleston and Jitterbug. Although the time and speed of blending varies, the very ease of blending suggests a common source.

The matter of style is important. While comparing films of African dancing with social dancing of the twenties and thirties, Chilkovsky, who is an expert at dance notation, found it necessary to formulate a new "signature," that is, a symbol indicating the *style of movement,* to distinguish both African and American dancing from the dancing of the rest of the world.[12] She feels that the styles of African dancing and American popular dancing have become so similar that they differ in the same way from all other dancing.

Similarly, American social dancing—like the jazz to which it is often performed—has taken on an African-like rhythmic complexity. Chilkovsky discovered dance cadences in 6/4, or even 5/4, for example, executed to musical measures of 2/4 or 4/4—a fairly sophisticated rhythmic combination. These intricate steps were performed in ordinary social dancing of the ballroom variety, not in virtuoso jazz and tap dancing which, like the solo of a great jazzman, is much more difficult to notate. "In current rock-and-roll dancing," she observed in 1961, "the African component is even greater."

West Africans "dance with a precision, a verve, an ingenuity that no other race can show," [13] writes Geoffrey Gorer. It is far too complicated to be described in every detail, but six characteristics of African dance—they are not infallible—can help us identify African influence in the United States. First, because it is danced on the naked earth with bare feet, African dance tends to modify or eliminate such European styles as the Jig and the Clog in which the sound of shoe on wooden floor is of primary importance; the

African style is often flat-footed and favors gliding, dragging, or shuffling steps.

Second, African dance is frequently performed from a crouch, knees flexed and body bent at the waist. The custom of holding the body stiffly erect seems to be principally European. (The Flamenco style, it has been suggested, goes back to an imitation of a man on horseback; African dancing to a hunter crouched for the kill.) "The deliberately maintained erectness of the European dancer's spine," writes critic John Martin, "is in marked contrast to the fluidity of the Negro dancer's." [14]

Third, African dance generally imitates animals in realistic detail. Although by no means unique to Africa, animal dances portraying the buzzard, eagle, crow, rabbit, and so on, form a large part of the repertory. (The tales of Uncle Remus form a literary parallel.)

Fourth, African dance also places great importance upon improvisation, satirical and otherwise, allowing freedom for individual expression; this characteristic makes for flexibility and aids the evolution and diffusion of other African characteristics.

Fifth, African dance is centrifugal, exploding outward from the hips. This point is crucial. "The leg moves from the hip instead of from the knee, the arm from the shoulder," writes musicologist Rose Brandel, while the motion of the shoulders and head "often appear as the end result of a motion beginning at the hips." [15] John Martin adds that the "natural concentration of movement in the pelvic region is similarly at odds with European usage." [16]

The same point is made by Nadia Chilkovsky, who declares that African dance and much of American dancing to jazz rhythms "begins with the hips and moves outward, employing the entire body." Starting with the hips tends to make the dancing looser. Brandel notes that these movements are "markedly missing from the Oriental dance world." She might have added that they are almost as markedly missing in Europe, where they are a continuing embarrassment to Western notions of propriety and have often short-circuited any understanding or appreciation of African dance.

Sixth and most significantly, African dance is performed to a propulsive rhythm, which gives it a swinging quality also found—usually to a lesser degree—in the music of jazz and in the best dancing performed to that music. Here again, John Martin refers to the Negroes' "uniquely racial [sic] rhythm." [17]

African dancing gives the impression of "a completely civilized art," wrote Edwin Denby, reviewing the African Dance Festival, staged and danced by Asadata Dafora at Carnegie Hall in 1943, " . . . the lucidity of the style was remarkable—the way the body kept clear to one's eye, the feet distinct from the legs, the legs from the trunk, the shoulders, the arms, the head, each separately defined . . . and when the torso turned or bent it seemed to move from the hips."[18] Eight months earlier, he had written about Dafora: "I thought I recognized as the basis of the style, the dance carriage we know from our own Negro dancing."[19]

A helpful comparison of African elements in Haitian dancing with the dancing of Southeast Asia is made by Harold Courlander.[20] He feels that Indian dancing (which has had a considerable influence on "modern dance") conveys a feeling of poised balance and suspended movement, while African dancing communicates "an attitude of strong frontal assault against natural forces such as gravity, or direct submission to those forces."

"There is almost always a feeling of solidarity between the body and the earth," Courlander adds, concerning African dances in Haiti, "but the total effect is dynamic." For Haitian dancing implies "an intimate understanding of nature," while Indonesian dancing suggests a relationship with the supernatural. Perhaps the reason East Indian dancing tends to be static—in a frequently beautiful sense—while African dancing is dynamic can be found in the accompaniment: Unlike Indian music, African music is often polyrhythmic and propulsive and the dancing swings with it.

An example of what might be termed cultural feedback occurred during the 1940's with the appearance of American-style tap dancing among the Makwaya of Northern Rhodesia. "Choirs" donned shoes and retired to indoor stages, according to the English missionary, the Reverend A. M. Jones, where they put on "an exceedingly clever imitation of Western tap dancing"—inspired by American films.[21] While they gave the effect "of the fast footwork and syncopated accented taps of the conventional white man's practice," Jones insists that it was much more complicated rhythmically, "using a mixture of duple and triple times and staggering the main beats. . . ."

Jones does not realize the complexity of American tap dance. His understanding of the conventional white man's practice is no doubt based on performances in music halls, that is, English vaudeville, and seems to be limited to an old style of tap. Among American tap dancers—and even in ballroom dancing—the typically African blend of "duple and triple times" is a commonplace. Like attracts like. No wonder Africans are intrigued by a style of American dancing which owes so much to Africa.

In the old days, during the voyage from Africa, slaves were forced to dance on shipboard to keep them healthy. Before they reached the United States, however, many had absorbed something of British-European dance. Ships stopped over in the West Indies, leaving the slaves to become acclimatized before taking them to the mainland: The stopover increased the rate of survival, and consequently, the rate of profit. Many of the slaves were purchased then and there, staying on the islands and obtaining their first contact with British and European dances.

At first, because of the initial conquest of the islands by Spain, the blending consisted chiefly of Spanish folk and African tribal dance. But from 1800 on, fashionable dances from the courts and elegant salons of Europe—Spanish, French, and English—became popular and were imitated by the slaves. "Every island of the Caribbean," says the folklorist Lisa Lekis, "has some form of quadrille, reel, jig, or contradance . . . greatly transformed in style and function, but still recognizable." [22]

"At present, the societies are dying out . . . but the dances, *Cocoye, Masson, Babril, el Cata* and *el Juba* are still performed with grace, dignity and elegance," she writes of African cults in Cuba, "using steps and figures of the court of Versailles combined with hip movements of the Congo." [23] The addition of Congo hip movements to the dances of the court of Versailles is rather like serving rum in a teacup.

The Quadrille has been preserved in the Virgin Islands, too, but something new has been added: "The quadrille dances are still regularly performed by organized groups who strut elegantly through the measures of *Lanceros, Rigodon,* and *Seven Step,*" Lekis notes. "The slow, stately style of the original has been replaced by a rapid shuffling step with hips waving and shoulders jiggling, but the traditional figures are faithfully reproduced." [24] Thus, African shoulder and hip movements—as well as the Shuffle, which became the foundation of several jazz steps—are blended in the European Quadrille.

Similarly, Katherine Dunham, after participating in a Jamaican dance, writes that "gradually it dawned on me that this was a Maroon version of the Quadrille," and as the dance became wilder and wilder, she observed an increase in improvisation with "unveiled hip movements." [25]

It can even happen to a waltz. In Curaçao, Lekis comments, "when seen in informal occasions the waltz loses its decorous manner and the same type of hip movement used in the *Tumba* (an African hip dance) appears." [26]

Conversely, Dunham joined a Koromantee war dance in Jamaica that, she notes, "could easily be compared to an Irish reel." [27]

And of Cuba's Cha Cha Cha, Lekis says that "it combines African style steps with a hopping pattern typical of European schottische dances." [28]

"Africa," said André Malraux at the 1966 Festival of Negro Arts in Dakar, "has transformed dancing throughout the world. . . ." [29] For the merging of African body movements with formal European set dances, aided by the African emphasis upon improvisation, produced a new style of dancing.

Speaking of the blending taking place in the West Indies today, Lekis concludes: "The future of the mixed dance and musical forms is in a sense the future of the Caribbean. It seems inevitable that the blending process now moulding a new race of people will continue. And the final stages of acculturation will produce a new form, not African, not European, but fused from the meeting of two races in the New World." [30] The blending has already produced new forms of dance in the United States—American forms—which evolved years ago in the Afro-American vernacular.

3 New Orleans and the South

ON A FIELD TRIP TO New Orleans, in the fall of 1959, we went "back o' town" one morning to hear a marching band. Rain began to fall as the club members headed toward a meeting place, and we straggled along behind a silent band for endless blocks. Eventually a halt was called, and the paraders held a conference in a church. For several hours we waited, drenched and impatient, and finally decided to go back to our hotel. Then we discovered that we had a walk of two or three miles, since no taxis could pick up white people in that part of town.

Half way home, footsore and weary, we were resting on a wall in the railroad yards when suddenly the band came swinging around the corner in full blast. In an instant, our day became glorious. The numbing fatigue vanished, the sun came out, and we half walked, half danced all the way to town. (At one point we noticed the words "Rampart Street" on a signpost.) It was not just the music—we had heard the same or better on recordings—it was the dancing, a fascinating variety of walks, shuffles, grinds, struts, prances, and kicks, improvised by the marchers—official and unofficial—as the residents rushed out of their houses to join the parade. The dancing gave the music a new dimension of joy and vitality.

Our experience was by no means unique. Something quite similar happened to dancer-choreographer Roland Wingfield, who also ran into a New Orleans parade. He describes the predominant steps with the accuracy of a specialist: "The dancers moved with pelvis thrown forward, the upper body slightly tilted back, loose and responding freely to the rhythm, legs slightly apart and propelling a shuffling step with a subtle bounce—a step characteristic of Africa and found often in Brazil and the West Indies." [1]

New Orleans is a special case. The blend of dancing, like the blend of music, was early and influential. Because of lack of segregation in town, large plantations in the country, urbane Latin-Catholic traditions, and economic prosperity, New Orleans produced a blend with sharp contrasts. On the one hand, unlike the rest of the United States, the Creoles of Color—aristocrats of French or Spanish and African descent—devoted themselves to European culture and dance. On the other, large numbers of slaves, again unlike the rest of the United States, lived on the big plantations, where African dance had a good chance to survive.

Thus, while the Creoles of Color were sending their children to Paris to be educated and dancing quadrilles at country balls, their darker brothers were enjoying African dances on the surrounding plantations and at Congo Square in the heart of New Orleans—a tourist attraction that had the sanction of the city government. The dances of Negro domestics were a mild mixture of both, and the presence of many Africans from the West Indies, who had already achieved blends of their own, added a powerful yeast to the brew.

"Congo plains," writes an observant contemporary, G. W. Cable, "did not gather the house servants so much as the field hands." [2] To European eyes, the dancing was chaotic if not degrading, and the more sensational aspects attracted attention. Visiting New Orleans in 1819, the architect B. H. B. Latrobe considered the dancing "brutally savage" and "dull and stupid." [3]

In 1853, Henry Didimus describes the activities in Congo Square with some distaste, giving a general impression of uncontrolled frenzy. He mentions "patting," and then proceeds to give a fair description of a basic step in the Afro-American vernacular, the flat-footed Shuffle: "The feet scarce tread wider space than their own length; but rise and fall, turn in and out, touch first the heel and then the toe, rapidly and more rapidly . . ." [4] Patting and the Shuffle were to play an important role in the history of vernacular dance.

In 1886, putting together his impressions of many years, Cable painted a more general picture with overtones of shocked fascination. He names eight dances—the Calinda, Bamboula, Chacta, Babouille, Counjaille, Juba, Congo, and Voodoo—all of them well known in the West Indies. A Voodoo dance attracted him, probably because it was forbidden. "The contortions of the upper part of the body, especially of the neck and shoulders, are such as to threaten to dislocate them," [5] he writes and in another article, after noting the presence of slaves from both Dahomey and the Congo, remarks that the dance is "not so much of the legs and feet as of the upper half of the body, a sensual, devilish thing tolerated only by Latin-American masters." [6]

Finding nothing recognizable in the footwork—the activity that most Europeans associate with dancing—Cable turns to the African movements, which seem strange to a white person, accustomed to an erect posture. In the Dahomean shoulder movements (voodoo came from Dahomey), he was witnessing antecedents of the Quiver, Shake, Shimmy, and similar dances. Why he concludes that the dance is a "sensual, devilish thing" is not entirely clear. Perhaps it is as near as he cares to come to suggesting the simultaneous motions of the lower half of the body—the pelvic movements of the Congo—which surfaced in such dances as the Grind and most recently, and clumsily, in the Twist of 1960 and later rock-and-roll dances.

Cable's sensibilities seem rather delicate, his moral superiority to "Latin American masters" (whatever they may tolerate) unfounded. The French missionary Pere Labat describes the Calinda danced on Martinique in terms that might have given Cable courage, although much depends on the translation. Thus, Lillian Moore's version reads, "striking the thighs one against the other," [7] while Gilbert Chase translates the same passage as they "strike their bellies together." [8] Miss Moore appears to be slightly more accurate, but it hardly matters in the light of Labat's frank comments on the "absolutely lascivious gestures" and his conclusion that "one easily sees . . . how indecent this dance is." [9]

Cable's description gives us a limited view. As historian Henry Kmen of Tulane University points out, a large amount of blending had already taken place.[10] Kmen found references in New Orleans newspapers to the dancing of jigs, fandangoes, and the Virginia Breakdown among the slaves in Congo Square *before* 1837. What is more significant, he discovered that mixed dances with both black and white people in attendance were very common in New Orleans between the years 1800 and 1850. "They were the leading recreational institution," he states.

"The white Quadroon Balls were only a small part of the dancing in New Orleans, and even there, because of the repeated ordinances to keep them out, we know that many Negro slaves attended. From about 1800, Kmen adds, "African and European dancing was blending in New Orleans at mixed, white-and-colored dances, not only at Cocage's Ballroom but also in less respectable places such as taverns. Notices of them start to become rare around 1850."

The darker, city Negroes had their own dances, too, and Kmen notes "the music and dances were often the same as at the white balls." In 1841, for example, a Negro dance was raided, interrupting "a Cotillion in one room, a Virginia Breakdown in another, and a country dance in yet another." The country dance was perhaps less courtly and more African than the others, although a "breakdown" could be almost anything in the Afro-American style.

Gradually, mixed dances with both white and black people disappeared. In the 1830's, when Nat Turner's slave revolt occurred in Virginia and the *Liberator* was first published in the North, attitudes in New Orleans began to change. After the Civil War, race prejudice grew swiftly, spurred by the arrival of Northern carpetbaggers, until the caste system of the South became the dominant code of New Orleans. By that time, however, the mixing and merging of African and European dances was well under way.

Negro society, increasingly segregated, patterned itself on white society, with similar dances on similar levels—from the highest society down—with this difference: At the folk level Negroes were reinvigorated by elements from Afro-American dance, an influence that surfaced slowly.

While in New Orleans in 1959, we were invited (at the kind suggestion of William Russell) to visit Mrs. Alice Zeno, the ninety-five-year-old mother of clarinetist George Lewis. Light-skinned and spry, she prided herself on speaking several languages, especially Parisian French, which she had learned while employed as a companion for an aristocratic white lady. "I heard of dancing in Congo Square," she sniffed, "but *that* kind was considered common." [11] Mrs. Zeno belonged to the cream of Negro society.

She tossed her head disapprovingly at the idea of racially mixed dances (they had occurred much earlier) and remarked: "As a girl, let me see, back around 1878, I believe I danced the Mazurka, the Polka, the Waltz, and of course, the Quadrille. I don't remember the Irish Reel, and I certainly never danced the Slow Drag." (In a tactless moment, we had mentioned the Slow Drag, which is danced with Congo hip movements.) "We had many lovely Creole dances and we danced in ballrooms by invitation only. Brass bands played for us—cornet, clarinet, and trombone—but no strings. My, but those Creole dances were elegant." By Creole dances, she meant courtly French dances—without raggedy fiddles in the accompaniment.

That was part of the picture. Darker-skinned cornetist Charlie Love, born later in 1885, remembered playing for "high-toned" dances around 1903 in the town of Plaquamine, some eighty miles west of New Orleans, but he also recalled playing a different kind of music—"more raggy"—for less fashionable groups in town, where the Eagle Rock, the Buzzard Lope, and the Slow Drag were the favorite dances. "They did the Slow Drag all over Louisiana," said Mr. Love; "couples would hang onto each other and just grind back and forth in one spot all night." [12]

North of New Orleans, in the predominantly British-Protestant environment that isolated Negro from white more completely, the blending—as in the parallel case of jazz—was slower, later, less dramatic, and because of these factors, probably more stable. Dancing in the Afro-American style was even less understood and appreciated. (We learn about it as early as 1706 from Protestant clergymen who objected especially to dancing on Sundays—an objection seldom voiced in New Orleans.) [13] In 1774 a minister went to a "Negro Ball" in Maryland, where the music was supplied by a banjo. "Their dancing is most violent exercise," he notes, "but so irregular and grotesque, I am not able to describe it." [14]

In 1860, writing about the Richmond, Virginia, of "bygone days," Samuel

Mordecai mentions a famous Negro fiddler Sy Gilliat, and a Negro flautist London Brigs, who played at state balls dressed in courtly fashion. "To the music of Gilliat's fiddle and London Brigs' flute all sorts of capers were cut. . . . Sometimes a 'congo' was danced and when the music grew fast and furious, a jig would wind up the evening." [15]

This reference to the supposedly obscene Congo, as danced in polite white society, makes sense only in the light of Gilbert Chase's explanation: "The history of social dancing is full of instances in which a dance existed simultaneously on two levels, assuming a decorous form in polite society and manifesting a licentious character among the populace." [16]

Other, intermediate blends occurred in far different surroundings. Plantation Negroes were learning European dances—with a distinct difference. In 1960 eighty-year-old actor Leigh Whipper, a former president of the Negro Actors Guild in New York City, recalled the year 1901 when he returned to Beaufort, South Carolina, to attend his mother's funeral.[17] He was surprised to see his old nurse, who had walked five miles into town: "She was past seventy then, and as straight as an arrow. We had a nice visit. I said 'Well, your back didn't get bent working in the fields, did it?' 'No,' she said, 'I was a strut gal.' " Then she explained that back in the 1840's, when she was quite young and "full of bounce," slaves received special privileges if they were good dancers.

"Us slaves watched white folks' parties," she added, "where the guests danced a minuet and then paraded in a grand march, with the ladies and gentlemen going different ways and then meeting again, arm in arm, and marching down the center together. Then we'd do it, too, *but we used to mock 'em,* every step. Sometimes the white folks noticed it, but they seemed to like it; I guess they thought we couldn't dance any better." After a while she was taken from one plantation to another and entered in dancing contests with other slaves, while her owner wagered on the outcome with other owners. "I won a lot of times. Missy gave me a dress and my partner a suit."

The use of satire here is significant—"we used to mock 'em"—and it opens up a richly creative vein, although there must have been a limit to what could be improvised. Rotating the hips in Congo style while performing a minuet or a grand march might not be appreciated. Yet the Negro was frequently embroidering upon the mask of what was expected—making oblique fun of white folks. It was both satisfying and stimulating, since it was risky, and at the same time, called for subtle improvisations.

The same point was made in the late 1940's by ninety-year-old Shep Edmonds, discussing the origins of the Cakewalk: "They did a take-off on the high manners of the white folks in the 'big house,' but their masters, who gathered around to watch the fun, missed the point." [18] Maybe the point was not missed. What exactly could the masters do about it? Any reprimand would be an admission that they saw themselves in the dance, and they would be the only ones—apparently—to whom such a notion had occurred.

"Near about everybody you see around them dances could near about play for them," says Lightnin' Hopkins, speaking of Saturday nights many years later in Centerville, Texas. "Be old sets you know, them ole square dances. All you had to do was to rap on your git-tar and they'd pat and holler. Ole sister would shout, 'You swing mine and I'll swing yours!' and all that." [19] The folk dances of the whites were being adopted and transformed over a long period of time.

In urban surroundings, white and Negro danced in the same river-front dives. As a young reporter for the Cincinnati *Commercial* in 1876, Lafcadio Hearn describes a roustabout dance to the music of a fiddle, banjo, and string bass. "The dancers danced a double quadrille, at first, silently and rapidly . . . sometimes the men advancing leaped and crossed legs with a double shuffle . . . the music changed to an old Virginia reel . . . men patted juba and shouted . . . once more the music changed—to some popular Negro air . . . terminating with . . . stamping of feet, 'patting juba,' shouting, laughing, reeling." [20] The evolution is clear: As the music becomes more rhythmic, the dancing progresses from the Quadrille through the Virginia Reel to the Afro-American Juba with a "popular Negro air."

Well-to-do Negroes outside of New Orleans mastered European dances—again, with a difference. Clarinetist Wilbur Sweatman played for quadrilles at a Negro dancing school in St. Louis around 1901: "They danced quadrilles, lancers, polkas, and things like that, and you didn't have to call the steps—everybody knew them by heart." [21]

In Atlanta composer Perry Bradford went to dancing school around 1905: "We had dancing school every Wednesday afternoon; the admission was ten cents, and it included lemonade. Frank Rachel played the piano, and there was a banjo player, too. We called the Square Dances 'set' dances in Atlanta, and we did quadrilles, lancers, and polkas." [22]

But these "set" dances, according to dancer Sidney Easton, born in Savannah in 1886, were different from British square dances. "The colored people used a four-four, not a six-eight tempo, four couples at a time, with lots of solo work and improvised breaks by each dancer putting together steps of his own." [23] (Easton says that in 1924 he made a film of a set dance for *The Chronicles of America Series* at Yale University entitled "Dixie.") The original European dances were transformed.

On a semiurban level, the Slow Drag spread far and wide. "Up and down the Santa Fe tracks in those days was known as the barrel-house joints," says pianist Buster Pickens, " . . . they danced all night long . . . people that attended them were working at the mill . . . it would take a couple of rooms, maybe a store . . . the Dirty Dozens was the openin' number . . . it settled down to the slow low-down blues and they'd 'slow drag'. . . ." [24]

The blend with the strongest component of Afro-American dance occurred in less-well-to-do urban surroundings, where the Negro folk, in the course of adjusting to city life, were less inhibited and more footloose. Born in Birmingham, Alabama, in 1893, Coot Grant, of the team of *Coot Grant and Sox Wilson,* remembers vividly the dances she saw in the back room of a honky-tonk owned by her father: "I guess I was kind of smart for my age, because when I was eight years old—that would be 1901—I had already cut a peephole in the wall so I could watch the dancers in the back room." [25]

In 1960, Coot Grant, short, plump, and in her late sixties, could still execute just about any step she could remember, and she remembered many: "They did everything. I remember the Slow Drag, of course, that was very popular—hanging on each other and just barely moving. Then they did the Fanny Bump, Buzzard Lope, Fish Tail, Eagle Rock, Itch, Shimmy, Squat, Grind, Mooche, Funky Butt, and a million others. And I watched and imitated all of them."

When asked to describe the Funky Butt, Coot Grant hesitated and then explained: "Well, you know the women sometimes pulled up their dresses to show their pretty petticoats—fine linen with crocheted edges—and that's what happened in the Funky Butt." Her eyes lit up: "I remember a tall, powerful woman who worked in the mills pulling coke from a furnace—a man's job. And I can call her name, too. It was Sue, and she loved men. When Sue arrived at my father's tonk, people would yell 'Here come Big Sue! Do the Funky Butt, Baby!" As soon as she got high and happy, that's what she'd do, pulling up her skirts and grinding her rear end like an alligator crawling up a bank.' The Funky Butt, Squat, Grind, Fish Tail, and Mooche—needless to say—are all performed with hip movements.

By 1913 similar dances were popular in New York City. Playing at the Jungles Casino—"officially a dancing school"—pianist James P. Johnson knew all the favorites. "When they got tired of two-steps and schottisches . . . they'd yell: 'Let's go back home!' . . . 'Let's do a set!' . . . or 'Now put us in the alley!' I did my 'Mule Walk' or 'Gut Stomp' for these country dances." [26] Although the dancing school was on 62nd Street, the dancers were from the Deep South. "I saw many actually wear right through a pair of shoes in one night," adds Johnson. "They danced hard."

Thus, as the dance evolved, the Afro-American elements became more formal and diluted, the British-European elements more fluid and rhythmic, but the over-all trend was one way—Afro-American dance exerted an increasingly strong influence on the dance as a whole. This trend reverses the usual pattern described by anthropologists in which the culture of an early majority swallows up the culture of later minorities. Coming as it did from people who arrived late in the United States as slaves, the Afro-American vernacular demonstrated a rare vitality.

4 The Pattern of Diffusion

WHEN AFRICAN DANCES reached the United States, what happened to them? Did they change and spread, and in the same way? If we knew the answer we could analyze the extent of African influences more easily. Enough evidence can be found to make a start, however, and to suggest general trends based upon a brief discussion of a few key dances in this country.

A dance known in the South as the Buzzard Lope, for example, has just about disappeared. It may have been quite similar to a West African buzzard dance, since the buzzard is common in both Africa and the South, and the dance is a close imitation of the bird. In Africa the members of the tribe "went about in a circle," according to Melville and Frances Herskovits, "moving with bodies bent forward from their waists and with arms thrown back in imitation of the bird from which their spirit took its name." [1]

In the United States the Buzzard Lope turns up as part of a dance-story —with a running commentary—in which a turkey buzzard quite realistically goes about eating a dead cow. Mrs. Lydia Parrish saw the dance performed by the Johnson family on isolated Sapelo Island, Georgia, where it had existed for many years. They supplied their own *dramatis personnae:* "Of the twins, Naomi did the patting while Isaac did the dancing; an older brother rhythmically called out the cues in a sharp staccato, and another one lay on the floor of the wide veranda representing a dead cow." [2]

March aroun'!	(thc cow)
Jump across!	(see if she's daid)
Get the eye!	(always go for that first)
So glad!	(cow daid)
Get the guts!	(they like 'em next best)

Go to eatin'! (on the meat)
All right!—cow mos' gone!
Dog comin'!
Scare the dog!
Look aroun' for mo' meat!
All right!—Belly full!
Goin' to tell the res'.

"Mr. Herskovits tells me," adds Mrs. Parrish, "that he has seen a similar dance in Dahomey."

Mrs. Parrish observes that the performance offered "a combination of the old dance form with rather more modern steps than the African original pantomime warranted." In other words, Isaac is improvising, adding a few "modern steps" of his own, and achieving a new blend. Of religious origin, the dance is now entirely secular, rural, and swinging with the combined accents of the hand-clapping and the "sharp staccato" directions of the older brother, "rhythmically called out."

The transition to a solo dance takes place early. The Buzzard Lope was discovered (and later recorded) in the little town of Sunbury, Georgia, when WPA researchers asked some old Negro women about harvest festivals. The women replied (in the overwrought phonetic approximation used by the interviewers): "We do git together an hab dance an pahties an big suppuhs . . . we does duh *Snake Hip* and duh *Buzzard Lope* . . . an addalas [at the last] dance we did duh *Fish Tail* and duh *Fish Bone* and duh Camel Walk."[3] This interviewer adds that "all efforts failed to persuade the women to describe these dances"; and for good reason. Snake Hips and the Fish Tail are compounded of Congo pelvic movements that would probably have shocked the white interviewers.

The shift from country to town occurred a little later. Around 1901 Coot Grant saw the Buzzard Lope in her father's honky-tonk in Birmingham and could still describe and demonstrate it sixty years later:[4] "That dance had arms high and wide like the wings of a bird, along with a cute shuffle and hop; why, I remember one little ol' girl did it all the time, spread her arms and yelled 'C'mon and grab me, Papa!'" As she performed the dance, Coot Grant retained the original arm movements and supplied a birdlike hop, but there was no conscious attempt to imitate a buzzard.

Why did the Buzzard Lope vanish? A partial explanation is that the Eagle Rock, another dance with winglike arm movements, body rocking from side to side, took its place. City folk looked down on the Buzzard Lope because it was associated with plantation life. "The Buzzard Lope was old fashioned," says New Orleans cornetist Charlie Love, "we danced the Eagle Rock to Buddy Bolden's music."[5]

The Eagle Rock was named after the Eagle Rock Baptist Church in

Kansas City, according to Wilbur Sweatman: "They were famous for dancing it during religious services in the years following the Civil War." [6] The dance may well have been much older, but like the Buzzard Lope and a religious dance known as the Shout (which later popped up as part of the Big Apple), it has the high arm gestures associated with evangelical dances and religious trance. In any event, the Eagle Rock spread north and south, discarded the hop for a shuffle that could be performed at a crowded house-rent party, and also died out—in turn—among the city folk during the early twenties. White people seldom if ever danced the Buzzard Lope, Eagle Rock, or Shout.

A small but ubiquitous detail from another African dance has shown considerable powers of survival. In Africa scratching is part of a dance to Legba, Guardian of the Crossroads, who was identified with St. Peter by Negro folk in New Orleans because both are depicted carrying a bunch of keys. "Each went round and round in the circle," write Melville and Frances Herskovits of a Winti dance in Suriname, "arms crossed from time to time over his breast, the fingers tugging at the clothing, as though scratching to relieve an itching sensation." [7]

This gesture became a standard routine known as the Itch in Negro dancing, accompanied by eccentric footwork. "Bull Frog Hop," a song published in 1909 by Perry Bradford, describes the Itch as part of its routine, and Butterbeans of the team of Butterbeans and Susie used it in the teens to the tune of "Heebie Jeebies" as the climax to his vaudeville act. "I borrowed it from a great dancer named Stringbeans," [8] says Butterbeans.

The Itch is described by Elise Marcus as "a spasmodic placing of the hands all over the body in an agony of perfect rhythm." [9] It is the rhythm, of course, that makes the motions effective.

Other and later dancers adapted the Itch to suit their own purposes. Clarence "Dancing" Dotson, who played the Keith circuit, combined elements of the Itch and the Quiver with singular success to create what he announced as "Throwing a Fit." James Barton's "Mad Dog" act also utilized the Itch. By the late 1940's at the Savoy Ballroom, the Itch was incorporated in the breakaway of the Lindy as part of the improvisation, and turned up again at the Palladium Ballroom in the fifties and sixties as an improvised addition to the Mambo. Indeed, the gesture has a universality that could lead to its appearance—with or without syncopated rhythms—almost anywhere.

Another dance, the Giouba, was changed radically in the United States, losing most of its African characteristics before taking on new movements, some of which outlived the original and survived in popular dance. "The *guiouba* [*sic*] was probably the famed Juba of Georgia and the Carolinas," [10] writes G. W. Cable; while dance critic Marian Hannah Winter observes that "the juba dance (simplified from giouba) was an African step-dance which somewhat resembled a jig with elaborate variations, and occurred wherever the Negro settled, whether in the West Indies or South Carolina." [11] (This is a little misleading, for the Irish Jig is not flat-footed, moves only from the waist down, and relies on taps.)

The Juba is found in Cuba, as we have seen, "using steps and figures of the court of Versailles combined with the hip movements of the Congo." [12] It is called the Martinique in Haiti and described as "a set dance of several men and women facing each other in two lines." [13] (This form is apparently the temporary result of European influence, since in Africa and the United States it is usually a circle dance.) "Known throughout the Antilles," writes Harold Courlander, "Juba is also remembered in New Orleans and other Creole communities of Louisiana." [14]

Among the Negro folk of the South, Juba soon took on the classic Afro-American pattern. " 'Juba' itself was a kind of dance step," writes Thomas Talley in a careful description, "two dancers in a circle of men . . . while the following lines are being patted:

Juba circle, raise de latch
Juba dance dat Long Dog Scratch
—Juba! Juba!

The dancers within the circle described a circle with raised foot and ended doing a step called 'Dog Scratch.' Then when the supplement 'Juba! Juba!' was said, the whole circle of men joined in the dance step 'Juba' for a few moments." [15]

The Juba step itself is described as going around in a circle with one foot raised—a sort of eccentric shuffle—and it is danced by the surrounding circle of men before and after each performance of the two men in the center. Both the words and the steps are in call-and-response form, and the words must ring out as rhythmically as a drummer's solo. The two men in the center start the performance with the Juba step while the surrounding men clap, and then switch to whatever new step is named in the call, just before the response "Juba! Juba!" sounds and the entire circle starts moving again.

In the given verse, the two featured dancers in the circle, after starting with the Juba step, switch to the "Long Dog Scratch," which has just been called out in the manner of a square dance. After this the surrounding chorus of dancers goes back to the Juba step. In other verses other steps are introduced: "Yaller Cat," "Jubal Jew," "Blow Dat Candle Out," and "Pigeon Wing." (Only the Pigeon Wing, a scraping—and sometimes shaking—from one foot to the other with fluttering arm and hand motions like a bird trying to fly, managed to survive for any length of time.)

The result is a completely choreographed, continuous group dance, combining the call-and-response pattern, dancing in a circle (generally counter-clockwise), the Shuffle, improvisation, and the rhythms of calling and clapping. These characteristics are a fair list of the major Afro-American traits in the blend of vernacular dance.

In minstrel days the name Juba was used for dancers as well as the dance, and the Negro pioneer William Henry Lane, called "Juba," received higher billing than his white colleagues before the Civil War. At this time the Juba dance was spoken of as a jig, indicating the direction in which minstrelsy would go, and many dancers began their careers featuring it.

Patting Juba, which started as any kind of clapping with any dance to encourage another dancer, became a special routine of slapping the hands, knees, thighs, and body in a rhythmic display. (In Africa, of course, this function would be performed by drums, but in the United States, where drums had frequently been forbidden for fear of slave revolts, the emergence of patting seems to have been inevitable.) Patting was known from Dutch Guiana to New Orleans and the Cincinnati levees, where Lafcadio Hearn found it in the 1870's.[16]

Mark Twain describes raftsmen on the Mississippi in the 1840's: "Next they got out an old fiddle, and one played, and another patted juba, and the rest turned themselves loose on a regular old-fashioned keelboat break-down."[17]

By the 1890's a minstrel and vaudeville team known as *Golden and Grayton*—white men in blackface—performed Patting Rabbit Hash to the tune of "Turkey in the Straw." According to Douglas Gilbert, it consisted of "patting and slapping the hands on the knees, hips, elbows, shoulders, and forearms, producing triple time and rolls almost like a snare drum."[18]

A minor detail attached itself to Patting Juba in the course of its evolution into a display piece, and then became a part of the more pretentious style of Charleston: crossing and uncrossing the hands on the knees as they fan back and forth. Encouraged by Joan Crawford's example as a Charleston-dancing flapper in *Our Dancing Daughters,* most teen-agers of the twenties mastered this trick. Thirty years later, the same thing turned up in a rock-and-roll dance named the Charley-Bop, a revival of the Charleston.

Patting still has the power to attract popular attention. In 1952 a tune named "Hambone," with patting by a group of children, was recorded by Chicago drummer Red Saunders. The youngsters, led by eleven-year-old Sammy McGrier of Evanston, Illinois, were also a success on television, working up a fine, swinging rhythm—Patting Juba. Sammy told *Ebony* magazine that he got the idea from a new kid at school who had just arrived from the South.[19] The trade press called it a novelty hit.

Perhaps the best-known example of an African survival in the United States is the Ring Shout, derived from the African Circle Dance. It survived partly by accident. The Baptist Church prohibited drumming and dancing, which ruled out most African religious observances. But the Ring Shout happened to employ clapping and stamping instead of drumming, as well as a shuffle step in which the legs did not cross. Since the Baptists defined dancing as a crossing of legs, the Ring Shout was considered acceptable.

We are not dealing here with a dance that disappeared long ago. The present writers have seen it quite recently in South Carolina, and John and Alan Lomax saw it—and recorded it—in Louisiana, Texas, and Georgia. "The song is 'danced' with the whole body," they write, "with hands, feet, belly, and hips . . . with a focus on rhythm. This 'shout pattern' is demonstrably West African in origin." [20] The Ring Shout exists in various nooks and crannies of the South to this day.

How was the Ring Shout danced in the early days? We have a few brief descriptions. "This step . . . is something halfway between a shuffle and a dance," writes H. G. Spaulding. "At the end of each stanza of the song the dancers stop short with a slight stamp on the last note, and then, putting the other foot forward, proceed through the next verse." [21] Here, a shuffle is combined with a pause and a stamp.

They begin "first walking and by-and-by shuffling round, one after the other, in a ring," according to an unsigned article in the *Nation* in 1867. "The foot is hardly taken from the floor, and the progression is mainly due to a jerking, hitching motion which agitates the entire shouter." [22] This observation is quite accurate, as any amateur who has tried to execute the Shuffle—or Truck—knows. The step seems to combine so many contrary movements that the usual result is a frustrating "jerking, hitching motion," although the seasoned performer does it with fluid ease.

"I shall never forget the night at the Hall of the Queen of the South Society when I first saw the ring-shout," writes Lydia Parrish of her adventures on the isolated Sea Islands of Georgia. "Little had I suspected, when Margaret took care of my room at the Arnold House years before, that she could outdo the Ouled Nail dancers of Biskra—if she wished. . . . She wriggled her hips shamelessly, held her shoulders stiff—at the same time thrust them forward—kept her feet on the floor, and with the usual rhythmic heel tapping, progressed with real style around the circle." [23]

Margaret's stance closely resembles what Courlander calls the "Congo pose." The "tapping" of the heels, according to the present writers' observation, is heavy, more like a stamp than a tap, while the stiff shoulders and flat-footed Shuffle are typical. The phrase "with real style" covers a multitude of intangible, improvised movements, which reveal a dancer's skill and personality.

Like Lomax, Mrs. Parrish is one of the few who mention hip movements, a basic part of the Ring Shout, which later spread far and wide. Early authors were hesitant about mentioning pelvic motions. Writing about the dancers on a Georgia plantation, actress Fanny Kemble notes "certain outlines which . . . they bring into prominence and most ludicrous display," [24] and H. R. Sass, describing dances on a Carolina plantation in the 1850's, mentions a "swaying motion of the hips." [25]

While it originated and continued as a religious dance, the Ring Shout also contributed at an early date to the Walk Around of the minstrel show, where it was employed as the closing number and performed by the entire company singing and dancing. At this point the Ring Shout has become a secular group dance. (Krehbiel calls the Walk Around a "secular parody" of the Ring Shout.) During the long popularity of minstrelsy, the Walk Around received considerable exposure and became a great influence on later styles.

"The Northern towns had a holdover of the old Southern customs," says pianist James P. Johnson, who heard shouts when he was a youngster in Brunswick, New Jersey, around 1900.

> I'd wake up . . . and hear an old-fashioned ring-shout going on downstairs . . . somebody would be playing a guitar or a Jew's harp or maybe a mandolin, and the dancing went to "The Spider and the Bed Bug Had a Good Time," or "Suzie Suzie."
>
> They danced around in a shuffle and then they would shove a man or a woman out into the center and clap hands. This would go on all night and I would fall asleep sitting at the top of the stairs in the dark.[26]

The pattern of forming a circle around a dancer or dancers and clapping occurred in the previously discussed Juba (the setting is now urban rather than rural) and may be found to this day in the less genteel ballrooms from coast to coast.

By 1913 one of the first all-Negro revues, *The Darktown Follies,* which was produced in Harlem, employed the entire cast, shuffling in a circle counterclockwise across the stage, around behind the scenery, and out front again to a tune called "At the Ball." Ziegfeld saw it, bought the entire number, and added it to his show on the roof of the New Amsterdam Theater. The Ring Shout had made Broadway.

Almost anything can happen to an Afro-American dance in the United States. It can vanish almost without a trace, like the Buzzard Lope, giving way perhaps to similar dances; it can persist as a minor detail in a variety of surroundings, like the Itch; it can take on new characteristics that survive alone, like patting in the Juba; and it can splinter and spread into popular dance while still retaining its original form, like the Ring Shout.

Nevertheless, certain changes in most of the dances seem to take place more or less consistently. Religious dances become secular, group dances become solo, rural dances become urban, and the literal style of the dance is lost in individual expression. These changes are wrought in part by the influence of the British-European tradition on African dance in the United States. At the same time, certain basic characteristics of Afro-American dance persist and grow; improvisation, the Shuffle, the counter-clockwise circle dance, and the call-and-response pattern (in voice, dance, and rhythm).

Because they are a fairly reliable sign of African influence, and at the same time, the source of confused responses, Congo hip movements are another characteristic of great importance. They may be found almost anywhere, from the dances of rural women of Sunbury and the urban honky-tonks of Birmingham, through the movements observed by Fanny Kemble and Lydia Parrish, to the celebrated performances at Congo Square in New Orleans. Perhaps one of the greatest single influences in the spread of these movements is the Ring Shout.

The one common and constant factor in all these Afro-American characteristics is a powerful, propulsive rhythm, which can appear in the singing, the stamping, the clapping and the dancing all at one time. This is the rhythm that is found in the music of jazz.

The over-all pattern of diffusion is certainly unusual, and may be unique. Writing about "the law of regeneration in the dance," Curt Sachs points out that "when the dance in a too highly refined society becomes anemic," it turns first to "the peasantry of the country." If it cannot find nourishment there, it turns to "foreign peoples, who are more primitive in their way of life and superior in physical mobility and expressiveness." [27] In the case of American vernacular dance, Negroes have been the equivalent of "foreign peoples" and the "peasantry" at one and the same time, which gives their dances double force and effectiveness. Perhaps this is the reason why their style of dancing is so vital and enduring.

PART TWO

Beginnings

5 From Folk to Professional

ON A FIELD TRIP to South Carolina with the folklorist Arthur Alberts in 1951, we spent two weeks searching for music which might have something to do with the beginnings of jazz. We were attracted to that area, where the Gullah or "Geechee" dialect is spoken, because it represents a cultural pocket, a place where several hundred words from African languages have survived by historical accident: During the Civil War, when a Yankee gunboat appeared off the island of Hilton Head, the white plantation owners departed hurriedly, leaving the slaves to shift for themselves. To this day many of the descendants of these Negroes remain isolated in the area.

In our search for origins we drove through the backwoods coastal area, making inquiries as we proceeded (and frequently having trouble understanding the answers) until we found ourselves on the ruins of an old plantation near a tiny village named Frogmore. We were tracking down Sam Jenkins, a guitar-picker, who was born on the Mary Jenkins plantation of St. Helena Island in 1893. When we finally found him, we discovered to our chagrin that he had lived for a time in New York City and his playing was quite modern.

Sam Jenkins decided that the place to make recordings was the Chicken Shack, a tumble-down two-room store at the end of a dirt road. As we were setting up our equipment, a small crowd assembled to watch us. Then Sam sang a few songs into the microphone, and we played them back. The effect on the crowd was miraculous—everybody wanted to perform—and we proceeded to record each of them. In the midst of the melee we wandered into the rear room and found an old jukebox loaded with the hits of the day. That was the last straw.

Nevertheless, something happened which—in retrospect—throws light on

American vernacular dance. As the afternoon wore on, the recording session developed into a party, with everyone expressing himself in his own way. We had walked outside the shack for a breath of air when suddenly we heard the beat of African drums. (We had studied African drumming with Asadata Dafora, and this sounded like the real thing.) We rushed inside, and there, in the middle of the creaky wooden floor, were two young men dancing.

They were wearing hobnailed boots, and the splinters flew as they stomped on the floor, first alternately and then together. It was a competition and the rest of the party, attracted by the resounding rhythms, left whatever they were doing and crowded around the dancers. Sam Jenkins produced a washboard and began to accompany the dancers, while somebody else added a rhythmic counterpoint by tapping a gin bottle with a knife.

The rhythm was more or less duple, that is, you could march to it—if you concentrated—but it was also complicated, polyrhythmic, with offbeat accents and bursts of staccato sound which gave it tremendous swing. The dancers were humming snatches of melody as they danced. Their bodies were bent at the waist, knees flexed, and arms out at the sides. The emphasis was on the rhythmic thunder they were creating with their feet.

Later we learned that the two dancers were Frank Chaplin and Evans Capers, that the name of the song they were humming was "Blow Gabriel, Hallelu," and that they were local men who had never even visited nearby Savannah, the goal of most citizens of the neighborhood. They had no idea where the dance came from—"I seen my Daddy do it," said Chaplin—and they had clearly improvised part of it. The rest of the crowd took it for granted.

Was any part of that stomp African? It was certainly no shuffle, and although stomping dances such as the Mahi of Haiti can be traced back to the Dahomeans of West Africa, the emphasis is not upon the sounds produced by the feet, and the dancers do not stand in one spot, but move around in a circle. Perhaps this dance at Frogmore was already blended with British folk dances such as the Jig and Clog—at least to the extent of standing in one place and concentrating on the sounds produced by shoes on the floor. Non-European body movement and rhythms had certainly been added. (Some old-timers recollect a similar dance called the Mobile Buck—"That dance came along before tap," says Leigh Whipper. "All they did was stomp.")

Jigging was the general term for this kind of dancing. The word jig was originally used to describe an Irish folk dance, of course, but it soon became associated in the United States with the Negro style of dancing (and even as an epithet for Negro), perhaps because whites confused any kind of Negro dancing with the lowly Irish Jig. "Jig dancing," according to a statement attributed to the famous minstrel-man Charles White, "had its origin among slaves of the southern plantations . . . it was original with them and has been copied. . . ." [1]

Describing a "jigging contest" on an old plantation, B. A. Botkin quotes an ex-slave James W. Smith, who was born in Texas around 1850: [2] "Master . . . had a little platform built for the jigging contests. Colored folks comes from all around, to see who could jig the best . . . on our place was the jigginest fellow ever was. Everyone round tries to git somebody to best him." The dance is strikingly similar to the dance we witnessed at Frogmore: "He could . . . make his feet go like triphammers and sound like the snaredrum. He could whirl round and such, all the movement from his hips down."

The contest, combined with the feat of balancing a glass of water on the head—we have seen acrobatic dancers from Sierra Leone do similar tricks—builds to an exciting climax:

> There was a big crowd and money am bet, but Master bets on Tom, of course. So they starts jigging . . . they gits faster and faster, and that crowd am a-yelling. Gosh! There am 'citement. They just keep a-gwine. It look like Tom done found his match, but there am one thing yet he ain't done—he ain't made a whirl. Now he does it . . . the other fellow starts . . . but just a spoonful of water sloughs out his cup, so Tom is the winner.

Here Negroes, while still retaining African rhythms, are beginning to assimilate the solo style of white dancers.

Modern tap dancers use the term *jigging* to describe a style of dancing that is considered both old-fashioned and humiliating. "That jumping around," says one dancer, "is nowhere," and points out the resemblance to those tin toys of dancers—now manufactured in Japan—that wind up and clatter spasmodically.

Rhythmic footwork had another source, which must have existed since the earliest times in the South. As described by Bill Bailey: "Father was a preacher in a Holy Roller church, I guess that's where I got my start dancing. The congregation stamped its feet and clapped its hands, and I'd sit there and use my heels in an off-beat rhythm to what they were doing—we worked up a lot of swing." [3]

At the opposite extreme and at an earlier date, white dancers, who were in a better position to attract audiences and make a living at it, were picking up ideas from Negroes. The original conception of the Negro, before slavery became a large and profitable business, was as romantic as it was unrealistic. In the popular novelette, *Oroonoko* (1688) by the English author Aphra Behn—as well as in the later play based upon it—the Negro was delineated as a mixture of the "regal slave" of Colonial fiction and the "noble savage" of Rousseau. Neither stereotype bore much resemblance to the real Negro.

While these attitudes were still current, one of the first American dancers about whom we have any information was born in Lancaster, Pennsylvania. John Durang was white, but he knew something about Negro dances. He became an actor, author, manager, and dancer—one of whose specialties was the Hornpipe—and in 1789, at the Southwark Theatre in Philadelphia, he played the leading role of "Friday" in blackface in Robert Brinsley Sheridan's pantomime of *Robinson Crusoe, or Harlequin Friday.* By inserting the Hornpipe in the course of the play, Durang was the predecessor, as Lincoln Kirstein observes, of white dancers in blackface who became so popular thirty years later.[4]

What appears to be Durang's own choreography of the Hornpipe—step by step—has been preserved:[5]

1. Glissade round (first part of tune).
2. Double shuffle down, do.
3. Heel and toe back, finish with back shuffle.
4. Cut the buckle down, finish the shuffle.
5. Side shuffle right and left, finishing with beats.
6. Pigeon wing going round.
7. Heel and toe haul in back.
8. Steady toes down.
9. Changes back, finish with back shuffle and beats.
10. Wave step down.
11. Heel and toe shuffle obliquely back.
12. Whirligig, with beats down.
13. Sissone and entrechats back.
14. Running forward on the heels.
15. Double Scotch step, with a heel Brand in Plase [*sic*].
16. Single Scotch step back.
17. Parried toes round, or feet in and out.
18. The Cooper shuffle right and left back.
19. Grasshopper step down.
20. Terre-a-terre [*sic*] or beating on toes back.
21. Jockey crotch down.
22. Traverse round, with hornpipe glissade.

The terminology is strongly influenced by French ballet, which was popular at the time, but seven of the twenty-two steps incorporate some kind of shuffle—"double shuffle," "back shuffle," "side shuffle," "heel and toe shuffle,"—and so on—and a footnote adds that "there are a variety of other shuffles, but the above are the principal, with their original names."

Among many dancing masters, the word *shuffle* had a special meaning, and Durang's use of it is not entirely clear. "With both feet 'tap,'" writes Henry Tucker, illustrating the Shuffle, "making the sounds at nearly the same time."[6] Tucker is writing about clog dancing in wooden shoes and the flat-footed, dragging step that most people know today as the Shuffle is not specifically described. ("Sure, I've heard of so many taps to a shuffle," says Pete Nugent, "but that's dancing-school stuff; no modern dancer ever did it." [7]) Durang twice adds "beats" or taps specifically to his shuffles (Steps Nos. 5 and 9); he may intend the more common meaning.

"A good dancer with imagination could easily reconstruct much of John Durang's hornpipe from this simple description," Lillian Moore remarks, commenting on Durang's list, "for many of these phrases are still familiar or recognizable: the *double shuffle, the pigeon wing,* and the *heel and toe haul,* for example."[8] Lillian Moore might have added other of Durang's steps to this list, which suggest movements that may be found in the Afro-American vernacular—especially in improvised passages—such as "cut the buckle," "wave step," "running forward on the heels," "parried toes round, or feet in and out," "grasshopper step," "beating on toes," and "jockey crotch."

By Durang's day the Hornpipe was danced in duple meter—the rhythm of jazz—and although he probably could not have achieved the rhythmic complexity that later became a fundamental element in American dance (we may be sure it did not exist in his accompaniment), he was quite possibly trying something different. French tightrope and ballet dancers were the fashion at the time, and an art lover who signed himself "Amateur" in the New York *Journal* (1793) complained of Durang's "agility".[9] Perhaps any imitation of Negro steps was considered too energetic to be graceful.

Spurred by the example of Durang and others, various imitations of the Negro gradually became popular on the American stage. In 1799 a "Song of the Negro Boy" was presented between the acts in a Boston theater. As Marian Winter observes, "The Negro dancer on the American stage was originally an exotic, much the same as blackamoors in a Rameau ballet opera." [10] Then she adds: "By 1810 the singing and dancing 'Negro boy' was established. . . . These blackface impersonators simply performed jigs and clogs of Irish and English origin to popular songs with topical allusions to Negroes in the lyrics." By 1820, white dancers in blackface imitating Negroes—accompanied by banjo, tambourine, and clappers—were all the rage and beginning to create a new blend.

An early example of a professional white dancer "borrowing" from the Negro folk with phenomenal success may be found in the career of Thomas Dartmouth Rice, known professionally as Daddy "Jim Crow" Rice. Rice's borrowed song and dance set the course of minstrelsy. A professed eyewitness, Edmon S. Conner, writing in *The New York Times,* gives the only version that describes the dance itself. The incident occurred in the years 1828-1829: [11]

> N. M. Ludlow took a Summer company to Louisville. Among the members were Sol Smith . . . and Tom Rice. It was the first regular theatre in the city.
>
> Back of the theatre was a livery stable kept by a man named

> Crow. The actors would look into the stable yard from the theatre, and were particularly amused by an old decrepit negro, who used to do odd jobs for Crow. As was then usual with slaves, they called themselves after their owner, so that old Daddy had assumed the name of Jim Crow.
>
> He was very much deformed, the right shoulder being drawn high up, the left leg stiff and crooked at the knee, giving him a painful, at the same time laughable limp. He used to croon a queer old tune with words of his own, and at the end of each verse would give a little jump, and when he came down he set his "heel a-rockin!" He called it "jumping Jim Crow." The words of the refrain were:
>
> *"Wheel about, turn about*
> *Do jis so,*
> *An, ebery time I wheel about,*
> *I jump Jim Crow!"*
>
> Rice watched him closely, and saw that here was a character unknown to the stage. He wrote several verses, changed the air somewhat, quickened it a good deal, made up exactly like Daddy, and sang it to a Louisville audience. They were wild with delight, and on the first night he was recalled twenty times.

Most accounts of this legendary meeting are concerned with the tune, probably because such songs eventually became great money makers by themselves, as well as establishing the name of the singer. Rice's version of the tune has been preserved and sounds to the present authors like a British play-party or fiddle song.

But what was the dance like? Instructions are built into the lyrics: He wheels, he turns, and each time he "jumps Jim Crow"—but these directions are not much help. Marian Winter refers to T. D. Rice as the "blackface performer who first definitely used a Negro work song" and describes the step as a "jig and shuffle." [12] As usually notated, the refrain is too long, the melody too diatonic for a work song, but the dance might be a blend of Jig and Shuffle, with the jump coming from a jig, and the arm and shoulder movements from a shuffle.

In 1840 a New York editor quoted by George C. D. Odell attended a performance by Rice and remarked among other things "such a twitching-up of the arm and shoulder." [13] This agrees with Conner's description of the old Negro: "He was very much deformed, the right shoulder being drawn high up, the left leg stiff and crooked at the knee, giving him a painful, at the same time laughable limp." The shoulder movements of the Shuffle are indicated here, and the cramped footwork is perhaps implied.

Again, a young lady "jumped Jim Crow" by "throwing her weight alternately upon the tendon Achilles of the one (*i.e.*, the heel), and the toes of the other foot," according to a description of the dance in 1855 unearthed by Hans Nathan, "her left hand resting upon her hip, her right . . . extending aloft, gyrating as the exigencies of the song required, and singing Jim Crow at the top of her voice." [14]

Nathan writes:

> While singing the first four measures . . . Rice probably moves cautiously along the footlights. In the refrain . . . he began to dance . . . in windmill fashion, he rolled his body lazily from one side to the other, throwing his weight alternately on the heel of one foot and on the toes of the other. Gradually, he must have turned away from his audience, and, on the words, "jis so," jumped high up and back into his initial position. While doing all this, he rolled his left hand in a half seductive, half waggishly admonishing manner. Imaginative though he was, he was undoubtedly inspired by the real Negro.

Nathan is drawing heavily on the description of the footwork of the young lady who "jumped Jim Crow," as well as the famous illustration of Rice dancing Jim Crow on the sheet music, but his timing can be improved. The jump comes, as Conner says, and as the lyrics indicate, at the end of the stanza: "I jump Jim Crow!" The earlier phrase "jis so" simply calls attention to the all-important style—the cramped yet rhythmic circling *before* the jump, which is a syncopated hop in the flat-footed Shuffle manner rather than a jump "high up" as Nathan suggests.

This interpretation is strengthened by the first half of the two alternate choruses listed by Thomas W. Talley:

Now fall upon yō' knees
Jump up an' bow low . . . etc.
Put yō' han's upon yō' hips,
Bow low to yō' beau . . . etc.,

in each case followed by the refrain "An' ebry time you tu'n 'round, you jump Jim Crow."[15] In other words, the recurring hop or jump of the title is preceded by a variety of maneuvers.

In fact, Jump Jim Crow, although it often consisted of revolving in one spot, resembles a popular dance of the late thirties: Trucking. In Trucking, the shoulders are often hunched up, one above the other, the hips sway in Congo fashion, and the feet execute a variety of shuffles while the index finger of one hand wiggles shoulder-high at the sky. The movement tends to be more or less straight ahead.

Trucking is a highly individual dance with as many fine versions as there are dancers. Everybody has his own style, although the dance is usually based on short steps forward, turning the heel in after each step. Thereafter, almost anything goes. Every good dancer who "trucks" recognizably is trying to create a unique impression. Out of an endlessly contorted and even tortured manner, each conflicting motion nevertheless dovetails with some cross-rhythm (heard or unheard), and the whole exploding combination somehow miraculously flows together and moves—a triumph of rhythm over the unorganized human condition.

We are faced here with what Winter calls "the intangibles of performance," at which, she adds, the Negro excels. In Daddy Rice we are also dealing with a virtuoso dancer whose individual flair escapes definition. A few hearings of the tune, however, make it reasonably clear that the dance, not the melody, made Jump Jim Crow a national craze. The first of many Afro-American dances to become a worldwide success, Jump Jim Crow's appeal was universal—the fascination of rhythmic tensions set up and neatly resolved.

In Washington, D.C., Rice introduced a four-year-old partner, Joseph Jefferson (the famous actor), doing a juvenile version of the step. Rice traveled abroad and performed with great success in London and Dublin, while the tune became "London's greatest song hit of the century," according to Carl Wittke, and Rice soon "commanded the highest salary of any minstrel performer." [16]

Rice was not alone in his borrowings. Billy Whitlock, for example, the banjo player with the pioneering *Virginia Minstrels,* made a point of keeping in close touch with the Negro folk. "Every night during his journey south, when he was not playing," says the New York *Clipper,* "he would quietly steal off to some Negro hut to hear the darkies sing and see them dance, taking with him a jug of whiskey to make them all the merrier." [17]

Once and for all the attention of professional white entertainers became riveted upon the Negro as a source of material. "'Negro specialists,'" as Wittke observes, "everywhere were much in demand." White men in blackface performed in theaters, in the "lecture" room of Barnum's Museum in New York City, and in various circuses—several years before the first minstrel show was organized sometime in 1843 by the *Virginia Minstrels* and the presentation worked out the following year by E. P. Christy.

In general the mixture of British with Afro-American dance was a two-way blend. It first surfaced in the United States, however, as a borrowing from the Negro folk by white professionals who were in a better position to profit by it, and the first dances to show the effect of a new merging were white performances of the Jig, Clog, and Hornpipe.

In time it became easier for Negro to borrow from white, although the Negro folk retained a feeling for rhythm which continued to be both the joy and despair of many white imitators. Yet as far as the general public was concerned, the first sign of what was taking place occurred in blackface performances by white men on the professional stage, twenty or so years before the advent of minstrelsy.

6 Early Minstrelsy

THE STORY OF MINSTRELSY is the story of the increasing influence of the Afro-American style of song and dance in American life. Minstrelsy was the most popular form of entertainment in the United States for more than half a century—from 1845 to 1900 approximately—and it soon spread to many parts of the world. Bayard Taylor, according to Carl Wittke, heard the song "Jump Jim Crow" sung by Hindu minstrels in Delhi,[1] and a minstrel troupe enroute to California via Cape Horn, according to Gilbert Chase, turned up in Santiago de Chile in 1848.[2] Minstrelsy and the dancing that went with it circulated far and wide.

What accounts for the great appeal of minstrelsy? The time was ripe for it, says the fine historian and critic Constance Rourke:[3]

> The rise of the Negro minstrel coincided with a marked change in his place within the nation. Little Jim Crow appeared at almost the precise moment when the *Liberator* was founded; and minstrelsy spread over the land and grew in popularity as the struggle for emancipation gained in power through the '40s and '50s. The era of course was the turbulent era of the Jacksonian democracy . . . when many basic elements in the national character seemed to come to the surface.

From her reading of early American almanacs, joke books, theatrical posters, memoirs, travel accounts, tracts, sermons, and pamphlets, Rourke concludes that the American people tended to identify with certain aspects of the Negro, who became a sympathetic symbol "for a pioneer people who required resilience as a prime trait."

Audiences all over the country enjoyed minstrelsy because it reflected something of their own point of view. Jim Crow, Zip Coon, and Dan Tucker

—originally characterizations of the Negro, both the dandy and the plantation hand—were portrayed as devil-may-care outcasts, and minstrel men played them with an air of comic triumph, irreverent wisdom, and an underlying note of rebellion, which had a special appeal to citizens of a young country. One of the most effective delineations of these characteristics occurred in minstrel dance.

In general, professional Negro minstrel companies did not come into existence until after the Civil War (although a lonely quartet appeared in New Hampshire in 1858 [4]), and then they usually had white managers. One Negro dancer stood out before minstrelsy even began; William Henry Lane, billed as "Master Juba." "The world never saw his equal," writes Edward Le Roy Rice.[5] Negro historians have ignored him, perhaps because, unlike the Shakespearean actor Ira Aldridge, he did not excel at an art which had prestige.

Lane was a free-born Negro and Michael B. Leavitt writes that he was from Providence, Rhode Island.[6] Promoters often billed dancers as born in the city where they were appearing, but Lane is often associated with the Five Points district of New York City. He learned his dancing, according to Marian Hannah Winter, from a Negro jig-and-reel dancer named "Uncle" Jim Lowe, "whose performances were confined to saloons, dance halls, and similar locales outside the regular theaters." [7] By 1845, as minstrelsy was becoming world famous, he was acknowledged the greatest dancer of them all.

In the 1840's, performances by Negro dancers, as contrasted to white dancers in blackface, occurred mostly in low-class dives, and in several contemporary reports Lane is described as performing in the notorious "dance houses" of the Five Points district. This area was formed by the intersection of Cross, Anthony, Little Water, Orange, and Mulberry streets, which converged on a park named Paradise Square in lower Manhattan. (Today, Baxter, Worth, and Park streets intersect at the same spot.)

"For almost fifty years," writes Herbert Asbury, "the thoroughfare was lined with brothels and saloons . . . and scores of dance houses soon appeared on the streets surrounding Paradise Square." He points out that the entire area was occupied, "for the most part, by freed Negro slaves and low-class Irish." [8] Among the dilapidated tenements that crowded the section, the "Old Brewery" was perhaps the most notorious. In a missionary's notebook, published in 1854, one entry reads: "I went and found a house (the Old Brewery) full of negroes and Irish citizens." [9]

This building, according to Asbury, "housed more than 1,000 men, women, and children, almost equally divided between Irish and Negroes." The Irish had just arrived from Ireland in the first great wave of immigration, while the Negroes were trying to support themselves in the uneasy status of freemen. Both groups were thrown together by crushing poverty.

"The Negro," says Rourke, "seemed to pick up the Irish musical idiom with facility."[10] He also picked up the dance that went with it—the Jig—and improvised upon it, which was no small accomplishment, for the Jig requires considerable skill. (According to E. A. Little, good Jig dancers execute fifteen taps a second.)[11] Lane lived and worked in the Five Points district in the early 1840's, and in such surroundings a blending of Afro-American vernacular with the Jig was inevitable. He was described as a dancer of "jigs" at a time when the word was adding to its original meaning, an Irish folk dance, and being used to describe the general style of Negro dancing. In fact, Lane probably hastened the change.

"Those who passed through the long hallway and entered the dance hall, after paying their shilling to the darky doorkeeper, whose 'box office' was a plain soap box . . . saw this phenomenon, 'Juba,' imitate all the dancers of the day and their special steps," said the New York *Herald* describing a dance hall in the Five Points district. "Then Bob Ellingham, the interlocutor and master of ceremonies, would say, 'Now, Master Juba, show your own jig.' "[12] Lane was performing at a time and place where the Irish Jig was well known and his own improvisations must have been exceptional to receive such attention.

In 1845 Lane achieved the all-time "first"—and last, because as far as can be ascertained it never happened again—of receiving top billing with four white minstrel men. The handbills tell the story:[13]

> Great Attraction! Master Juba! The Greatest Dancer in the World! and the Ethiopian Minstrels! Respectfully announce to the Citizens of this place that they will have the pleasure of appearing before them . . .

After six parts in which singing, dancing, and playing the banjo and tambourine alternate—including a song and statue dance by Lane—the program ends with "Master Juba's Imitation Dance":

> . . . in which he will give correct Imitation dances of all the principal Ethiopian Dancers in the United States.
>
> After which he will give an imitation of himself—and then you will see the vast difference between those that have heretofore attempted dancing and this WONDERFUL YOUNG MAN.

A little later, on tour with the *Georgia Champion Minstrels* in New England, Lane was billed as:[14]

> The Wonder of the World Juba, Acknowledged to be the Greatest Dancer in the World. Having danced with John Diamond at the Chatham Theatre for $500, and at the Bowery Theatre for the same amount, and established himself as the King of All Dancers.
>
> No conception can be formed of the variety of *beautiful* and intricate steps exhibited by him with ease. You must see to believe.

This was high praise indeed—even for a handbill—since, as Winter points out, the word "beautiful" was seldom used to describe minstrel dancing.

The white dancer John Diamond, Lane's competitor, is described by Edward Le Roy Rice as "one of, if not the greatest jig dancers that the world ever knew," [15] and beginning in 1844 a series of challenge matches took place between them. The custom of using three sets of judges became popular at this time: Style judges sat in the orchestra pit, time judges sat in the wings, and judges of execution sat under the stage.

Lane's victories over Diamond did not come without a struggle, for in an undated reference to a "jig dancing tournament" in which Lane was a contestant at Boylston Gardens, Boston, Leavitt notes that it was won by "John Diamond of Boston." [16] (Diamond was born in New York City in 1823, and the reference to Boston was the promoter's idea.) This contest must have taken place at a fairly early date, since in various matches with Diamond after 1845 Lane is consistently listed as the victor.

Perhaps because his dancing was almost entirely without precedent abroad, descriptions of Lane's performance by English writers are more detailed and perceptive. Charles Dickens describes a visit to the Five Points district where he was fascinated by a dancer who almost surely is Lane himself:[17]

> Single shuffle, double shuffle, cut and cross-cut; snapping his fingers, rolling his eyes, turning in his knees, presenting the backs of his legs in front, spinning about on his toes and heels like nothing but the man's fingers on the tamborine; dancing with two left legs; two right legs, two wooden legs, two wire legs, two spring legs—all sorts of legs and no legs—what is this to him?

The emphasis here upon the variety of leg movements, with no mention of body movements, suggests the influence of the Irish Jig. On the other hand, references to the Single and Double Shuffle may indicate the addition of Afro-American elements. The comparison of Lane's dancing to "fingers on a tamborine," moreover, furnishes the best clue to what made the performance outstanding: rhythm.

In 1848 Lane joined *Pell's Ethiopian Serenaders* in London. The reviewers were ecstatic. "The dancing of Juba exceeded anything ever witnessed in Europe," wrote an English critic. "The style as well as the execution is unlike anything ever seen in this country. The manner in which he beats time with his feet, and the extraordinary command he possesses over them, can only be believed by those who have been present at his exhibition." [18]

The same observation is amplified by a Liverpool critic, who compares Lane's dancing to the rhythms of the banjo and bones: ". . . this youth is the delight and astonishment of all who witness his extraordinary dancing; to our mind he dances demisemi, semi, and quavers, as well as the slower steps." [19] (A "demisemi" is the British word for a thirty-secondth of a whole note and implies *very* fast execution.) The intricate rhythms of Lane's dancing were consistently singled out for special comment.

These critics were all familiar with British dances such as the Jig, the Reel, the Hornpipe, and the Clog. What made them write about Lane's dancing as if it were altogether different? The answer seems to be, in the words of the London critic, "the manner in which he beats time with his feet." For in the person of William Henry Lane, the blend of British folk with American Negro dance in the United States had, by 1848, resulted in a striking new development. So foreign observers, who were in a position to view its emergence objectively, treated it as an original creation.

"The performances of this young man are far above the common performances of the mountebanks who give imitations of American and Negro character;" wrote a critic in the London *Theatrical Times,* adding a further point: "There is an ideality in what he does that makes his efforts at once grotesque and poetical, without losing sight of the reality of representation." [20] Lane's dancing had a rare authenticity. He was apparently *swinging* —relatively speaking—naturally and effortlessly. At a time when white men in blackface were making fortunes imitating the Negro, the real thing must have been a revelation.

In 1852, at about the age of twenty-seven, Lane died in London. His influence was decisive. "Because of the vast influence of *one* Negro performer," says Winter, "*the minstrel-show dance retained more integrity as a Negro art-form than any other theatrical derivative of Negro culture* [*authors' italics*]." [21] She adds that William Henry Lane was "the most influential single performer of nineteenth-century American dance," while "the repertoire of any current tap dancer contains elements which were established theatrically by him."

Lane founded a school of dancing. The white dancer, Richard M. Carroll (1831-1899?), was noted for dancing in the style of Lane and thus earned the reputation of being a great all-around performer. Another dancer, Ralph Keeler, who starred in a riverboat company before the Civil War, reveals that he—like many others—learned to dance by practicing the "complicated shuffles of Juba." [22]

At the same time Lane's example renewed the search by white dancers for inspiration among the Negro folk; thus, a dancer in blackface named David Reed (1830-1906) emerged in the fifties with a new step, which he learned "from the Negroes when he used to dance on the steamboat *Banjo* on the Mississippi." [23] The step became a hit, and the New York *Herald* described it as ". . . certain comical and characteristic movements of the hands, by placing his elbows near his hips and extending the rest of his arms at right angles to his body, with the palms of the hands down." [24] This stance is very similar to the Congo pose of the Buzzard Lope and Ring Shout (see Chapter 4).

The music that accompanied minstrel dancing eventually contributed to jazz, but at first it consisted predominantly of British folk, and increasingly, American popular music into which the rhythm and style of the American

Negro began to blend. Later the rhythms of tap dance influenced jazz. In the dancing, Constance Rourke concludes, "a strong individualism appeared," and African elements began to surface: "The climax of the minstrel performance, the walkaround, with its competitive dancing in the mazes of a circle, was clearly patterned on Negro dances in the compounds of the great plantations, which in turn went back to the communal dancing of the African."[25]

After Lane's death, minstrelsy went on to bigger but not better things. The pioneering *Virginia Minstrels,* who had started in 1843, soon changed their program. Hans Nathan writes:

> The ragged, Southern plantation type of Negro was frequently relegated to the second part of the show, while the more formal, Northern type, the dandy, was introduced into the first part . . . In consequence the Negro atmosphere of the first part of the show paled during the forties and led eventually to the use of sentimental ballads and the addition of a flashy middle section, the olio, which was characterized by musical virtuoso acts. Thus, in the fifties it was mainly the last (third) part which retained a pronounced and genuine Negro atmosphere.[26]

About forty white troupes are listed by Wittke as touring in 1850, and he adds that "these and many other minstrel companies . . . were in the heyday of their success in the middle of the nineteenth century."[27] It was the beginning of the end of its contribution to the dance, for while Lane's achievement was still a living influence, minstrelsy reached its peak in the fifties and sixties.

7 Minstrel Dances and Dancers

THE JIG AND THE CLOG were perhaps the two most influential dances from the Old World in early minstrelsy. The Jig came from Ireland, the Lancashire Clog from England, and both were on the American stage by 1840.

The Soft Shoe, often referred to as Song and Dance—the kind of act in which it usually appeared—evolved from a blend in the United States. "A man danced clog or 'song and dance' (soft shoe)," writes song-publisher Edward B. Marks of minstrel days at the turn of the century.[1] The Jig gradually lost its popularity (the word itself was soon used to describe almost any kind of early Negro dancing) and Marks is distinguishing—for one thing—between dancing in shoes with wooden soles (Clog) and leather soles (Soft Shoe).

The influence of the Irish Jig persisted, however, for it had a well-established tradition of its own, which outlasted minstrelsy. It consists of very rapid leg and footwork, tapping with both toes and heels, with the arms held close to the sides, and the upper half of the body stiffly erect. It also demands exceptional skill, as the present authors noted when they interviewed the champion jig dancer Mary Healy during the summer of 1963 in Sligo, Ireland. To this day the Jig is performed unchanged both in Ireland and the United States.

"Possibly clog did not originate in America," writes Douglas Gilbert, "but America made it its own." [2] To illustrate his point, Gilbert tells the story of the American clog dancer Johnny Queen during the 1880's in England. Suspected of trickery because of his phenomenally fast dancing, Queen made his entrance in slippers and passed his dancing shoes around to be examined by the audience "as proof that he used no clappers or other Yankee gadgets." The Clog had evolved so rapidly during its forty years in the United States—new styles such as the Hornpipe, Pedestal, Trick, Statue, and Waltz Clog soon appeared—that Queen's version made a deep impression in the land of its origin.

Until late in the day, all these dances lacked one thing. In the words of James McIntyre, of the team of *McIntyre and Heath*: "None of these . . . had syncopated rhythm." [3] In other words, they all lacked *swing* in the jazz sense.

The swinging rhythm came later, with the Buck and Wing, and upset the old-timers. The celebrated clog dancer Barney Fagan "believed that the buck and wing, a combination of clogs and jigs and song and dance (i.e. soft shoe), had hurt the original clog dance." [4] Dancer Tom Barrett is more outspoken. The Buck and Wing, he says, is a "bastard dance, with a little of this and a little of that all mixed, and now there is no dancing left, only acrobatics." [5] (The identical criticism would be raised again—a little more accurately—a half century later.)

Indeed, the Lancashire Clog and the Soft Shoe—as danced in white minstrelsy—seemed pretty much the same to most Negro performers, since they were both equally deficient in swing. In the teens, Negro dancers such as Willie Covan added both punch and elegance to the Clog and early Soft Shoe, which resulted in a new blend that continued to be called the Soft Shoe among Negro dancers.

McIntyre, however, was a pioneer who prided himself on having introduced a syncopated buck-and-wing on the New York stage around 1880 (it did not become popular until later), and he told a reporter that he learned it "by watching Negroes in the South soon after the Civil War." [6]

Minstrelsy's most famous dance, The Essence of Old Virginia, came from the Shuffle and led to the early Soft Shoe. The Essence was "based firmly on Negro source material," [7] says Marian Winter, and a performance by Dan Bryant in 1858 is described as "a dance characteristic of the rude and untutored black of the old plantation." [8] Bryant was a leading exponent of this dance and excelled, as Carl Wittke observes, in "shaking up a grotesque essence." [9]

As performed by Eddie Girard after 1872, the Essence is described by Gilbert as "slow tempo, made up of old-fashioned darkey steps, a kind of bastard clog, danced to Southern tunes." [10] The Essence was the first popular dance—for professionals—from the Afro-American vernacular.

The Essence evolved rapidly. Ragtime composer Arthur Marshall said "if a guy could really do it, he sometimes looked as if he was being towed around on ice skates . . . the performer moves forward without appearing to move his feet at all, by manipulating his toes and heels rapidly, so that his body is propelled without changing the position of his legs." [11] That was only part of it. To illustrate the Essence, which he called "a combination of shuffles," James Barton did a series of walking steps for us, progressing rapidly and intricately forward.

Old-time Negro entertainers associate the Essence with Billy Kersands, the most famous of all the genuine Negro minstrels. Both Leigh Whipper and Willie Covan remember him singing "Wait till the Clouds Roll By" and peeling off a dozen vests as he danced a great Essence. "Kersands did the Virginia Essence perfectly," says Arthur Marshall, "so much so that when he did it before Queen Victoria he had her laughing heartily over it." [12] Kersands was famous for doing a monologue with his mouth full of billiard balls. "Son, if they hate me," he once told Flournoy Miller without a smile, "I'm still whipping them, because I'm making them laugh." [13] He lasted a long time, making a comeback on the Loew's circuit in 1911, and died two years later.

In time, the more graceful and less eccentric part of the Essence evolved into the Soft Shoe. "Both the Essence and the Soft Shoe were danced to tunes in 6/8 tempo like 'Narcissus,' but are now danced to a mild 4/4," says Harland Dixon. "The Soft Shoe is a *refinement* of the Essence." [14]

It emphasized grace and elegance. "The delicacy and ease with which you execute the steps," says Sammy Dyer, "make it good or bad." [15] The Soft Shoe combined with light and tasty taps became known as "picture dancing," and an important dance in the repertory of the class acts of the 1930's and after.

The leading exponent of the Soft Shoe—both white and Negro dancers agree emphatically upon it—was George Primrose. Because he lasted well past the turn of the century and appeared in vaudeville—sometimes on the same bill with Negro acts—as well as in minstrelsy, Primrose was seen and admired by many young dancers. (He is supposed to have been Bill Robinson's idol.) "Every motion of George Primrose," says Willie Covan who was expert in the same style, "made a beautiful picture." [16] From one dancer to another, this is a high compliment.

"For me the big moment would not arrive until George Primrose would step out on the stage," writes dancer Jack Donahue. "The orchestra would strike up 'Suwanee River' and the old master would go into one of those beautiful soft shoe routines." [17] "Everybody," says dancer Billy Maxey, who was born in 1883, "was influenced by Primrose." [18]

An Irishman whose real name was Delaney (minstrel men often adopted stage names—sometimes for the worse), George Primrose was born in London, Canada, in 1852. At the age of fifteen, he joined *McFarland's Minstrels* in Detroit and danced a solo billed as "Master Georgie the Infant Clog Dancer." [19] Later, he joined the *New Orleans Minstrels, O'Brien's Circus, Skiff and Gaylord's Minstrels,* and *Haverly's Mastodon Minstrels* ("Forty—Count 'Em—Forty") where he was presented as the "Ne Plus Ultra of Song and Dance." In 1871 he formed a partnership with William H. West, which lasted almost thirty years as they danced together in their own and other shows.

After the *Primrose and West Minstrels* broke up, Primrose joined Lew

Dockstader for a few years and then formed his own company of forty performers, playing one-night stands across country. It was a battle for survival. "It must have been disheartening," writes Harlowe Hoyt, who was shown Primrose's accounts later on, "to enter receipts of $30, $60, and $70 a night, with an occasional $100 or better." [20] After several lean years, Primrose was forced into vaudeville. He died in San Diego in 1919 (according to Wittke), far away from his Mount Vernon, New York, home.

"Prim was the greatest *stylist* of them all—not necessarily the greatest technician—with the finest Soft Shoe I ever saw in my life. When he died, he took it with him," says Harland Dixon, who got a job with the *Primrose Minstrels* in 1906 and at once adopted Primrose as his lifetime model. "He was of medium height, weighed a little over a hundred and ten, and could wear clothes like Fred Astaire; he smoked cigars but he didn't drink; I never heard him raise his voice or swear; I never saw him practice a step and yet I never saw him perspire—even during the minstrel street parades on the hottest summer days. He wore a high, stiff collar and looked up over the audience as he danced; he had a flat stomach, beautiful legs, and fine hips and shoulders—and just the way he walked was poetry."

Around 1900, before the vaudeville circuits, minstrelsy was the only way to make a song a national hit in one season, and E. B. Marks was busy plugging his songs: "I made it a point to pal with the minstrel kings. Prim, particularly." Referring to Primrose as a "peerless dancer," Marks adds, "Prim used to rehearse all his dances and keep fit between seasons in his Mount Vernon barn . . . his whole face was lined from the cork make-up of many years . . . the deep lines were not ugly, but attractive and strangely pleasing." [21] Marks likens Primrose's facial expression to the mask of Greek comedy—to which the grin of a leprechaun should be added.

Primrose "talked white out of black"—that is, although he used blackface, he made no attempt to fake a Negro dialect—and was known for his dry sense of humor. When someone reported that a rival dancer Eddie Leonard, notorious for milking the audience by stealing bows, was playing a nearby theater, Primrose observed in his slight brogue: "I hope he doesn't stop the show with his bowing entirely." [22] (Eddie Leonard's Soft Shoe was imitated more widely than Primrose's, because it was easier.) Primrose also had a reputation as a tight-fisted business man. "When my partner and I showed up," says Harland Dixon, "Prim hired us for $15 a week and fired two others who had been getting $25."

After the turn of the century, a few sparks were struck in minstrelsy before what had been a conflagration flickered out altogether. And the minstrel dance, perhaps because it was impossible to cheapen it drastically without destroying it completely, was one of the last things to go. (Since minstrelsy was traditionally masculine, the obvious substitution of a hootchy-kootchy dance from the lowly carnival would have been a double disgrace.)

"George H. Primrose and Billy West, Lew Dockstader, Barney Fagan, the Gorman brothers, George Wilson, Dick Jose, were as well known as talkie stars today," writes E. B. Marks about conditions at the turn of the century. "They were annual events from New York to the Pacific Coast—like the circus." [23] Four out of the seven celebrities that Marks names—Primrose, West, Fagan, and (George) Gorman—were fine dancers.

In 1963, seventy-eight-year-old Harland Dixon could vividly recall the performers he saw as an eager youngster in 1906-1912, when vaudeville was taking the place of minstrelsy. Dixon has his favorites, of course—a professional dancer's favorites, some hitherto "unknown"—but he saw the best white dancers of those days. "While I was with Primrose, a dancer named Joe Bennett joined for about two weeks. He had legs like iron and could really move, going from one side of the stage to the other with his body held as if he were sitting in a chair. He only had a few routines, but they were gifts from heaven—the greatest comedy dancer I ever saw but he never became famous."

Dixon has reservations about the well-known Barney Fagan. "He was a great technician and one of the first to syncopate the Clog, but his steps were so intricate that the audience and even other dancers couldn't follow what he was doing." Dixon chuckled. "Fagan wanted to be a comedian, but the results were sad." Eddic Leonard, according to Dixon, was not much of a dancer: "He had a nice backward-shuffle exit, but he was more of a singer and personality."

Dixon remembers other dancers for their specialties: Max Ford was a fine Wing dancer; Jimmy Monahan did a very expressive jig down at Inmans on Coney Island with a glass of beer on his head; Johnny Boyle was a great teacher but lacked style and a personality (he taught James Cagney the routines for the film *Yankee Doodle Dandy*); George White was a good buck-and-wing dancer; Tom Smith did a wonderful eccentric dance in tramp costume (his accompanist announced formally that Mr. Smith had been detained just before Smith entered "in the most gosh-awful suit you ever saw"); and always, George Primrose was far and away the best.

Others he remembers because they were historic firsts: Al Leach was doing the Stair Dance in the 1880's—long before Bill Robinson—and he kept the rest of the act, the chorus girls, billed as "The Six Rosebuds," off stage so the audience would watch him; Harry Pilser "ran up to the wall and kicked over just like George M. Cohan did later." And still others he remembers because they copied somebody else: Bernard Granville, who was featured later in Broadway shows, "got all his stuff from Doc Quigly," an eccentric dancer who nevertheless had some "fine twisting steps that nobody could copy" (wine and women were said to have interfered with Granville's successful use of the stolen steps); "Milton Berle copied Eddie Cantor, and Jack Donahue took all he could from me." And finally, Fred Stone was "no dancer at all—he did stunts."

Dixon remembers only one Negro dancer in those days: Bert Williams.

He saw him in a white show, the *Follies*. "He had a beautiful speaking voice and a trick step I'll never forget—he'd raise one knee waist high with his foot back underneath him, and then hitch the other foot up to it, traveling across the stage." Dixon admired Williams especially for his pantomime and remembers one short five-minute skit which caused a lot of trouble. "While the show was on the road, that skit lengthened to almost twenty minutes because the audience demanded it. The manager had to wire Ziegfeld to come out and cut it down so the show could continue."

As far as the general public was concerned, the Negro performer had never appeared on the stage, and his white imitator in blackface disappeared with minstrelsy, with a few scarcely understood exceptions like Al Jolson. It was almost as if nobody knew that the Negro could be a fine entertainer and an even finer dancer, so that when the Negro appeared on Broadway around 1900 in the persons of Williams and Walker, he seemed like a delightful discovery. The Cakewalk was soon to ignite a new and more general interest in Negro-rooted dance, and it was followed by a series of social dances, launched at first with the aid of Vernon and Irene Castle, which were to sweep the ballrooms of the country.

8 Late Minstrelsy

"THE MOST AUTHENTIC or 'classical' period of minstrelsy was from 1830 to 1850" [1] writes Gilbert Chase—and he does not need to add that he is speaking of white men in blackface. But why, if minstrelsy is based upon an imitation of the Negro, were not the Negro companies (formed after the Civil War) the best or at least the most authentic? Perhaps the simplest answer is that big-time minstrelsy was virtually a white monopoly.

After the Civil War minstrelsy mushroomed into a huge and tasteless business. In 1869 the first transcontinental railroad was completed, supplying swift and convenient transportation for the ever-expanding minstrel troupes, which were swallowing all other kinds of entertainment. "Minstrel programs were cluttered up with such utterly incongruous acts," writes Carl Wittke, "as sentimental Irish ballads, silly 'Dutch' comedy of the slap-stick variety, and the variety (i.e. vaudeville) features of the olio." [2] About the same time, white managers were beginning to organize a few Negro companies.

Complaints that the minstrels had lost the desire and ability to portray Negro character were widespread before the Civil War. Comparing what she had seen on a Georgia plantation in 1838-1839 with a Northern minstrel show, Fanny Kemble writes: "all the contortions, and springs, and flings, and kicks, and capers you have been beguiled into accepting . . . are spurious, faint, feeble, impotent—in a word, pale Northern reproductions of that ineffable black conception." [3] By the fifties Boston critics were saying the same thing.

In spite of the boom in minstrelsy, even the lot of a white minstrel man was far from easy. "It was usually a life of drudgery, with long railroad jumps, long hours, and small salaries," [4] writes Edward B. Marks who knew all about the minstrels because he kept after them to plug his tunes. Minstrel men started as apprentices at $8 or $10 a week and lived in fear of being fired without notice or stranded with the show in some small town.

The famous parade which began every morning at 11:45 promptly, although it dazzled newcomers, became a daily disaster to minstrel men. "The boys would drag their aching heads and topsy-turvy stomachs from straw pallets in small-town hotels and trot down to the rendezvous at the theater without breakfast," Marks explains. Minstrel men like to stay up and sleep late. The complaint of the cornetist with a bad hangover is typical: "Mister, a cornetist blows from his stomach, and if you have ever tried pumping hard with your stomach when you are not sure that you have one at all . . ." [5]

Toward the end, P. T. Barnum added the singer Lillian Russell to his minstrels to jack up the box office and the distinction between a minstrel show, a carnival, or even a circus became vague. Only a few minstrel men were really successful. "The hundreds who failed to achieve distinction remained in this *monde* of their own, bright-eyed and toothless japes," writes Marks, "hocking their watches after poker games and performing their slightly stiffened capers to please some small-town filly, until some day they remained behind in South Norwalk, Connecticut, or Waukegan, Illinois, to grin in death." [6]

What killed minstrelsy? In 1902, when asked why minstrelsy had slipped, the successful promoter-performer Lew Dockstader replied that the essential Negro qualities had become dated and lost—a point upon which everyone now seems to agree. E. B. Marks also points out that minstrelsy was "masculine musical comedy"—in other words, no sex appeal—and that the big combines gave the minstrels inferior bookings compared to the growing musical-comedy companies (with women) in which they had a direct interest. "When the leading minstrels entered the better-paid field of vaudeville," he concludes, "minstrelsy went with them." [7]

But where were the Negro minstrels and why were they not heard from? "Encyclopedists and historians of the American stage," says W. C. Handy, "have slighted the old Negro minstrels while making much of the burnt cork artists who imitated them." [8] Professional Negro entertainers did not appear until the late 1860's after the Civil War, and they were few and limited almost entirely to the minstrel stage. "Kersands, Weston, the Hunn brothers, and some few others," writes Marian Winter, "were actually the only Negroes on the stage who had steady employment." [9]

There was no question of their talent. "These performers brought a great deal that was new in dancing," says James Weldon Johnson, "by exhibiting in their perfection the jig, the buck and wing, and the tantalizing stop-time dances." [10]

But they had to work within certain limitations. "By the eighteen-seventies there was a relentless, and impalpable, pressure to stereotype the stage Negro completely," says Winter. "The Negro performer found that unless he fitted himself into the mold cast for him as typical, he could get no work." [11]

In 1906 George Walker of the famous team of *Williams and Walker* wrote with a backward look at old minstrel days: "There were many more barriers in the way of the black performer in those days than there are now; the opposition on account of racial and color prejudices and the white comedians who 'blacked up' stood in the way." [12] The same thing happened during the teens to the pioneering New Orleans jazzmen who were opposed by entrenched white musicians when they arrived in Chicago.

The conflict was clear. White entertainers who worked in blackface imitating the Negro fought to preserve their jobs by keeping the Negro out of work. The result was doubly disastrous. "Blackfaced white comedians used to make themselves look as ridiculous as they could when portraying a 'darky' character," says George Walker. "The one fatal result of this to the colored performers was that they imitated the white performers in their make-up as 'darkies.' Nothing seemed more absurd than to see a colored man making himself ridiculous in order to portray himself." [13]

One of the great Negro companies—and a partial exception to the overall trend—was the *Georgia Minstrels*, organized in 1865 by Charles Hicks, a Negro.[14] The *Georgia Minstrels* became so famous that the name was used later by many imitators. Because of his color, Hicks encountered so many difficulties that he was forced to sell in 1872 to the wealthy white impresario, Charles Callender. The show was then billed as "Callender's Original Georgia Minstrels." Minstrelsy was at its commerical peak, and partly because Hicks knew his talent and had already hired actor Sam Lucas and Billy Kersands, Callender became a success.

In 1878 Jack Haverly bought the show, increased its size, changed the name to "Haverly's European Minstrels," and went abroad on a grand tour, where a good Negro troupe was always well received. His manager, Gustave Frohman, one of the few whites who favored Negro performers at the time, not only retained Lucas and Kersands but also hired James Bland, the composer of "Carry Me Back to Old Virginny," Billy Speed, Irving Sayles, Tom McIntosh, and the Bohee brothers—all Negro artists of the first rank. Kersands excelled at the Virginia Essence, and the Bohee brothers, at the Soft Shoe.

In 1882 Frohman decided to organize the greatest of all Negro companies—the trend was to mammoth and stupendous shows—and purchased the entire troupe, to which he added a few more acts. This company was billed as "Callender's Consolidated Spectacular Colored Minstrels," resurrecting Callender's name because it had been associated with the original *Georgia Minstrels*. It was the last, gigantic gasp, and after three years of indifferent business, Frohman quit and went on to better but not bigger things.

By 1893 three large Negro companies—as compared to dozens of "colossal" white troupes—were still on the road: the *Hicks and Sawyer Minstrels,* the *Richards and Pringle Minstrels,* and the *McCabe and Young Minstrels* —with white owners and managers. Their best business was done abroad, and to a lesser extent, in the South, but they had arrived late, were few and far between, and conformed increasingly to the white stereotype, which meant that the comedy and the dancing suffered.

If the white minstrel man led a life of drudgery, he was nevertheless fortunate compared to the Negro minstrel man. W. C. Handy gives a remarkable account of "the nightmare of those minstrel days" when he was working from 1896 to about 1900 in the Negro troupe of the Irishman William A. Mahara. "Minstrels were a disreputable lot in the eyes of a large section of upper-crust Negroes," says Handy, "but it was also true that all the best talent of that generation came down the same drain. The composers, the singers, the musicians, the speakers, the stage performers—the minstrel shows got them all." [15]

During his four years with *Mahara's Minstrels,* Handy advanced rapidly on his own indisputable merits as an arranger, conductor, and cornet soloist, becoming the leader of the band. At the same time he went through some searing experiences. A good friend, the talented trombonist Louis Wright, was lynched in Missouri shortly after their ways parted. A gang of cowboys in a Texas town nearly broke up one morning parade "just for fun" by lassoing the band leaders, and Handy's refusal to play his cornet under such circumstances almost got him killed. In Orange, Texas, "their conception of wild he-man fun was to riddle our car with bullets as it sped through town." [16] Handy and his friends lay flat on the floor.

And so it went, this so-called glamorous career as a minstrel man. In Murfreesboro, Tennessee, Handy stopped a white man from murdering a fellow trouper, knocked him down, and hid in the "bear-wallow" or secret compartment of the Pullman car until the sheriff and his posse gave up the search. In Tyler, Texas, when a member of the company came down with smallpox, the local doctor seriously suggested lynching the whole troupe as a health measure. In his deceptively pleasant way Handy adds that afterward many members of the company went to live abroad permanently—"perhaps they found it hard to erase from their minds the nightmare of those minstrel days." [17]

"The last of the big minstrel shows aimed at the splendiferous," says Marks. "They went in for elaborate scenes and theatrical effects, and the casts kept growing . . ." [18] Minstrelsy was suffering from galloping elephantiasis, and the genuine Negro minstrels simply could not compete. They were the real thing, but at best they were trying to imitate an imitation under impossible conditions. In 1894 Buffalo Bill's agent Nate Salisbury produced *Black America* in Brooklyn with (among other things) cabins, mules, washtubs, a meeting-house, and a preacher—an entire "Negro village"

—featuring "African tribal episodes and a war dance." How could a mere minstrel show compete with this predecessor of Disneyland?

Certainly there were great dancers in the last large Negro companies—we know the Bohee brothers and Billy Kersands were with the earlier *Georgia Minstrels*—but information is scanty. White minstrelsy finally splintered into other forms of entertainment: variety, farce, burlesque (in the literal nonstripping sense), revue, operetta, and the beginnings of vaudeville, carrying with it a few vestiges of the vernacular dance, spiritless and dilute. "The Negro element remained primarily in the rhythmic treatment of the material," writes Winter, "the 'intangibles of performance,' and a phenomenal virtuosity in 'trick' dances." [19]

Small nondescript Negro minstrel shows, along with thousands of medicine shows, gillies, and carnivals, persisted nevertheless in the South and lasted well into the 1940's and even later (see Chapter 9–10). These shows were of, by, and for Negroes, and although they were gradually disappearing, the dancing of their comedians was based squarely on the Afro-American vernacular of the folk, varied by improvisation and invention. Their dances surfaced later, and several became national fads.

The memory of the sheer corny fun and games of minstrelsy, and the dances that go with it, has not vanished entirely. During the 1960's, a group of hale and hearty oldsters plus a few ringers—average age, sixty-five—put on, in and around New York City, several minstrel revivals staged by dancer Dewey Weinglass and written and produced by Noble Sissle and Eubie Blake. The results were frequently hilarious. It was also a revelation to audiences that had never seen minstrel shows.

These revivals seem to have taken place whenever the group was invited to perform and wherever they could find a hall. "The rehearsals," says Mercer Ellington, "were even funnier than the performances." [20] They had appeared at the Harlem YMCA before we saw them in Collins Hall at Fordham University on September 25, 1964, where they were sponsored by an astonished and enthralled undergraduate organization. The performers seemed to enjoy it more—if possible—than the students.

In deference to militant contemporaries the production was entitled "The Grass Roots of American Folklore" and opened with a lecture by Sissle on the history of Negro show business, concluding with the announcement that this program was to be a recreation of the famous *Georgia Minstrels.*

A cast of eighteen strutted noisily on stage playing tambourines and singing. They were dressed in garish red-striped jackets and wore boaters. As they sat down in a half circle facing the audience, Sissle stood in the center as interlocutor, and Sidney Easton and Willie Glenn, clad in suits with blindingly large blue and white checks, took their positions as end men.

Two dozen or so numbers followed—songs, dances, skits, instrumental solos—alternating with jokes so ancient that, delivered with reckless assurance, they seemed new-minted from another world. (The most *modern* jokes were in the question-and-answer pattern: Sissle, "Who was that lady I saw you last night?" Easton, "That was no lady. . . .")

Then the acts pyramid: Willie Glenn steps and sweeps in rhythm with a broom; Sissle sings "Lucinda Lee"; Reuben Brown does an elegant tap routine; Luckey Roberts plays his own composition, "Moonlight Cocktail"; Sidney Easton sings a wildly sentimental song; Frisco Bowman takes a drum solo all over the stage; sixty-four-year-old Dewey Weinglass does cartwheels; and Don Redman and his band, with Joe Thomas, Tom Whaley, and Teddy Benford, supply a swinging background for everybody.

And always the cheerfully idiotic jokes. Eighty-four-year-old Walter Crumbley, champion dancer of legomania, has his own technique. Whaley vamps on piano, and the group sing "We Want Crumbley" to the tune of "We Want Cantor." Then Crumbley sings a catchy song—the hoarse voice is off-pitch but the syncopation is infectious—with many solo verses, while the rest of the gang come in loudly and rhythmically on the chorus with "What a time! What a time!" backed by the band.

With the expression of a horn-rimmed owl, Crumbley intones:

I once knew a doctor, his name was Beck,
He fell in a well and broke his neck,
Serves him right, he should have stayed at home,
Take care of the sick and leave the well alone.

And the group answers "What a time! What a time!" Meanwhile, Crumbley transfixes the audience with his angular stance and quizzical stare. He makes each verse funnier than the last. Finally, having run out of breath, he simply pantomimes his verse—no words—pointing around the auditorium on the off beat. It brings down the house.

After intermission, the olio follows, with a brief concert by the Redman band, a tear-jerking song, a comedy violinist, and a medley of favorites by Noble Sissle and Eubie Blake. The show ends with a lively Walk Around—struts, twists, prances, taps, rubberlegs, and even splits—and exit.

PART THREE

The Vernacular

9 Medicine Shows and Gillies

"IN THE OLD DAYS," says Dewey "Pigmeat" Markham, "show business for a colored dancer was like going through school. You started in a medicine show—that was kindergarten—where they could use a few steps if you could cut them, but almost anything would do. Then you went on up to the gilly show, which was like grade school—they wanted dancers. If you had something on the ball, you graduated to a carnival—that was high school—and you sure had to be able to dance. College level was a colored minstrel show, and as they faded out, a vaudeville circuit or even a Broadway show. Vaudeville and Broadway sometimes had the best, although a lot of great dancers never got out from under the rag, never left the tent shows." [1]

Dewey Markham was born in Durham, North Carolina, in 1903, and clawed his way by sheer talent and tenacity to the Nirvana of Ed Sullivan's television shows. Pigmeat (the nickname was supposed to refer to young and tender meat) was called "Black Rock"—a more accurate description—until he joined the *Gonzell White Minstrels* and made a hit with a new song-and-dance number: "I'm sweet Papa Pigmeat, I've got the River Jordan in my hips, and all the women is rarin' to be baptized."

Around 1900 the popularity of medicine shows, gillies, and carnivals with the increasing influence of circuses and the diminishing influence of minstrelsy, helped the Negro dancer establish himself as a small but necessary cog in the wheel of tent-show business. These shows provided the seeds on a grass-roots level for the growth of a professional style of dancing.

The influence of minstrelsy was still quite strong. Negro dancers performed in blackface before Negro audiences and continued to play the role of knockabout comedians, but now they were frequently hired on their own merits as entertainers and given the freedom to create anything that might attract an audience. Most important, they held down reasonably steady jobs, and if they were good enough, received better offers from bigger shows. Here was a new avenue of advancement with, as the folk phrased it, "every tub on its own bottom."

The path to fame and fortune was seldom clear-cut, for the operations of medicine shows, gillies, carnivals, and minstrel shows overlapped. On the lowest level, a medicine show could range from one or two self-constituted salesmen calling from door to door with a bottle of alleged medicine or "Snake Oil," to a hundred-man organization traveling by railroad with an embryonic minstrel show and a variety of nostrums.

Pianist Ferdinand "Jelly Roll" Morton attempted the door-to-door approach with one of his gambling friends, selling a mixture of salt and Coca Cola as a cure for consumption, until he was run out of town. The famous white "Doctor" Ferdorn toured the mid and far West with a big company and a small minstrel show, renting an impressive office in each city and selling a different medicine for each ailment. "He was the best known of all," says Pigmeat.

The average medicine show, however, was a small hit-and-run affair traveling by wagon with a "Doctor" and two or three "assistants," sleeping in bunks and cooking on a portable stove. They stopped wherever they could find an audience. The show centered around the doctor, who made his living "spieling," or giving sales talks to sell the medicine, while his assistants were valued according to their ability to attract anybody's attention, anywhere, and at any time. One of the best ways was to sing and dance.

Ulysses "Slow Kid" Thompson, born in Prescott, Arizona, in 1888, ran away from home at the age of fourteen, and after working as a cook with a circus, landed a job dancing with a medicine show.[2] (Thompson got his nickname from a remarkable slow-motion dance he performed.) "His name was Doctor Randolph 'Somebody'—I can't remember it," says Thompson with an astonished smile (nobody had ever asked him about it) "and we hit all the dirt roads in Louisiana. We had a canvas tent in back where we dressed and a small platform out front where we danced—any step was okay—clapping our hands for accompaniment. Then the doctor went into his sales talk." Slow Kid was promised room and board and ten dollars a week, but was lucky if he got room and board. "If Doc didn't make any money, we didn't, so I quit when I got a chance to join a carnival."

A change from medicine show to carnival did not always mean a better job. Stranded with a carnival in Lexington, Kentucky, in 1921, Pigmeat Markham went back to Doctor Andrew Payne's medicine show. "We just played hick towns, ol' Doc, a banjo-harmonica player, and two dancer-comedians, but us two dancers had a ball outshining each other." The assistants mixed the medicine during the day—"it wasn't nothing but Epsom salts and coloring," says Pigmeat—and opened the show at night.

"Before Doc's spiel," he continues, "we came out and did a little comedy dancing, mostly Buck—no Wings yet—with plenty of eccentric stuff while the banjo backed us up, loud and for laughs, to put the yokels in a buying mood." After the doctor's sales talk, his assistants jumped into the crowd and sold the medicine, usually pocketing a little something for themselves.

One-time production manager at Harlem's Apollo Theater, Leonard Reed, born in Nowata, Oklahoma, in 1906, recalls his first job with a medicine show.[3] "Doctor Howard Clark was making a mint in the early twenties selling some terrible stuff mixed with turpentine—the dose was four drops on a teaspoon of sugar."

The doctor was a high-pressure salesman, and he made his assistants work as salesmen, too. As he warmed to his sales talk, the assistants would hustle around in the crowd exclaiming, "Now don't be impatient, there's a few more bottles, and you can have yours." "We'd jingle a few coins in our pockets as if we were making change and yell 'Thank you, sir,'" Reed adds. "We hadn't sold a bottle yet, but we'd wind up selling a couple of dozen, depending on the crowd."

Doctor Clark was talented—he played fine guitar and furnished accompaniment for his own dancers, sitting on the platform with a ten-gallon hat on the back of his head. "As a come-on before his spiel," says Reed, "Doc would play some great down-home guitar while three of us banged away with tambourines and shouted. We didn't get a chance to do any real dancing because he liked to feature himself." The doctor did not trust any of his assistants to go into the crowd with more than six bottles at a time, but they outsmarted him by stuffing a few extra bottles in their pockets or shirts.

Some medicine shows invaded the big cities of the North. Around 1919, according to the late journalist-musician Dan Burley, one of the most successful hucksters in Chicago was known as "Poppa Stoppa."[4] "He came to town in a wagon," says Burley, "stopped at a convenient corner on the South Side, and went into his spiel. The dancers would do their stuff on the sidewalk right in front of you—real crazy jumping around, but funny." Burley adds that the man in charge of collecting the money for the medicine was always white. One brand of medicine, "Kickapoo Snake Oil," helped to make these shows big business.

The dancing in medicine shows was minor and sporadic, yet many of the great dancers-to-be served their apprenticeship there. The style of dancing was based on a crazy-quilt blend of folk material such as shuffles, struts, hops, twists, and grinds, with a touch of the flat-footed Buck—in short, the early vernacular dance. The emphasis was on eccentric dancing, that is, highly individual and inventive movements following no set pattern, but rather exploring new ways of capturing attention. "It was," says Leonard Reed, "a comic, exaggerated, almost grotesque style."

Graduating from a medicine show to a gilly could be the most crucial of all promotions for a dancer. Although his ability as a comedian was still important, he became a true professional, hired for his skill as a dancer, a part of established show business, which offered steady employment and better pay. In the mid-teens, a dancer-comedian might earn fifteen dollars a week (although three dollars of it went for company meals), and if he doubled as a barker—a light skin was essential—he could earn five dollars more. Working in a gilly might be the start of a dancing career.

"Little carnivals and 'gillie' shows. Aw . . . rough going *that* was," says pianist Jesse Crump who started out singing and dancing, ". . . they be up today and down tomorrow and you play to all kind of little towns in the South—sometimes you have to borrow a garage to play out there . . . we used to call it the big time when you played in theaters." [5]

The size of gillies varied, too, but several in the early days employed as many as fifty or more people, traveling from one small town to another—thirty or so miles at a hop—in specially equipped trucks known as gillies, which were sometimes festooned with decorations and plastered with advertisements. The show offered two or three rides—a Merry-Go-Round, a Ferris Wheel, and perhaps a Whip—and three or four tents—one each for the Freaks, the Hula Dancers (with sometimes a taxi-dance platform), the Strong Man, and the Negro performers. At strategic points in between were small stands with "Games of Skill and Chance."

The tent occupied by the Negro entertainers was called the Jig Top. A small and closely knit island of Negroes in a sea of white people, the Jig Top consisted of six or seven performers: a three-or four-girl line, which included an ingenue; a musician who played tambourine, drums, or piano; a straight man who danced a little and set up jokes for the comedian; and finally the comedian, who was the featured dancer.

The entertainment was a combination of medicine-show salesmanship and minstrel-show formulas. "Half the battle was conning the hayseeds into paying the price of admission," says Pigmeat Markham. This was the barker's job, and he made frequent use of the performers in the course of the ballyhoo, which could go on for an hour while he filled up the tent.

Marking time—and sometimes eating meals—behind the front curtain, the company rushed out on the platform at the barker's command of "Bally, everybody!" to give the lagging customers a taste of the wonders inside. "A dancer cut his craziest capers at that point," says Slow Kid Thompson. The rest of the group clapped, stamped, and shouted a tune such as "Raise a Ruckus Tonight."

"On the Fourth of July one year, starting at nine-thirty in the morning," says Leonard Reed, who was employed as a barker on the strength of his fast talking and light complexion, "we did *forty-eight shows*."

Inside the tent a rope was stretched down the middle to keep white and Negro customers apart, and a small, curtained stage stood at the far end. The program usually consisted of three parts: first, the comedian and his straight man in front of the curtain cracking jokes—working in local topics if possible—punctuated with bursts of eccentric dancing; then a series of specialties by the members of the company, singing, talking, dancing, with a few "blackouts"; and, finally, the afterpiece, sometimes called "Eph and Dinah."

Audiences loved Eph and Dinah. The curtain parts on a plantation scene with a quartet off-stage singing "Old Black Joe." Front center, Uncle Eph lies snoring through his false whiskers. The role of Uncle Eph is played by the dancer-comedian, who is dressed as an ancient farmer. Then young Rastus walks on, wakes up the old man, and pantomimes a story. They are soon joined by Aunt Dinah, wearing a sun-bonnet, a pillow for a bustle, and bent double with years. She is another dancer disguised as a creaky-voiced farmer's wife.

The plot is unimportant—they play it by ear—but it usually turns out to be Eph and Dinah's Golden Wedding anniversary. As the festivities begin, the entire company tries to persuade Eph and Dinah to dance. Just to be agreeable, the old people hobble around a bit and sit down exhausted. Then, suddenly, Eph gets interested. "Eph starts with the Possum Walk," says Pigmeat, "two or three steps forward and then two or three quick jumps back." The audience is astonished by the old man's agility. Mightily pleased with himself, Eph tries another step, and another, limbering up swiftly, transformed into an exciting, virtuoso dancer.

Eph then grabs the squeakily protesting Aunt Dinah, and before she seems to know what is happening, they are dancing expertly together. "That's when they do the Slow Drag," says Pigmeat, "with plenty of grinds, and after that, the Pull It, leaning back and arching their bodies like the breakaway in the Lindy." By the end of the skit Eph and Dinah are executing wildly acrobatic steps, skirts and whiskers flying, while the audience screams with shocked delight. The Jig Top with its Eph and Dinah afterpiece was often the most popular attraction of the gilly.

Working the South in the Jig Top of a gilly show—or any tent show, for that matter—was not a restful occupation. Just keeping the tents up could be a problem. "I was in a place in Kentucky they call Dawson Springs, when a cyclone came through," says Norman Mason who played clarinet with "Ma" Rainey's show, "and the tent blew down and it was really somethin' trying to get out of the tent . . . with those poles and the trees fallin' down and you could hardly see your way through because it was so dark out there, and the wind throwing you about." [6]

"In addition to everything else," says Pigmeat, "the crowds came looking for a fight. I remember one time in Hollow, Kentucky, the coal miners tried to date the hula dancers, and this made all the white fellows in the carnival jealous. When we heard the war cry 'Hey, Rube!' we knew a rhubarb was gonna jump off, wailin' heads with iron stakes, and we'd run for our lives."

Members of the Jig Top simply disappeared—it wasn't their war. "A Negro is a target for everybody in a fight," adds Pigmeat, "most of the corpses was miners."

Nevertheless, unlike a medicine show, the Jig Top gave a Negro dancer more range and scope. He was able to portray a real character, employing more subtle and dramatic steps as he built to a climax. In the course of many improvised performances he could, in fact, choreograph his role. It was still comedy, but the potential was much greater, and he would gain applause and recognition for any step he might invent. Best of all, a Negro dancer in a gilly worked in front of a consistently large audience and could establish a reputation in the business.

10 Carnivals, Circuses, and Negro Minstrels

IN THE SOUTH, during the early teens, a switch in jobs from gilly to carnival meant belonging to a bigger and more stable organization at better pay. Unlike gillies, carnivals sometimes had a few animal acts, along with rides, sideshows, and games of chance. They usually traveled by railroad instead of wagon, and often played one-week stands at state fairs. Some of the larger carnivals combined a circus and minstrel show on a small scale—the distinction between a dirt-road circus and a large carnival was never very great. A few of them carried bands that could play ragtime, and by the twenties, jazz.

The social status of carnival performers was definitely low. When her act was stranded in Cincinnati during the teens, Ethel Waters did "what lots of Negro acts do when hard-pressed for eating money: we got jobs with a carnival." She joined *Bob White's Greater Shows* in Lexington, Kentucky. "The colored people in Lexington wouldn't let carnival show girls into their homes . . . we of the stage were considered not much better than cattle by respectable Negroes." Miss Waters had no professional trouble. "I could sing, dance, and do the split . . . I was also known as the champion hip shaker, the best in the world." [1]

In the teens, Ulysses "Slow Kid" Thompson jumped from a medicine show to a series of carnivals: [2] the *Pa Patterson Carnival* in Texas, *Parker's Mighty Show* in Kansas, and *George J. Loose's Carnival* in Florida. "They had colored minstrel shows in all those carnivals," says Slow Kid, "as well as animals, Shake dancers, and even a weight lifter, but the big attraction was the rides." Thompson's tap dancing, plus his acrobatic specialties, made such a hit that he climbed out of the South and up to the Keith vaudeville circuit by 1920.

Before joining Doctor Andrew Payne's medicine show in 1921, Dewey "Pigmeat" Markham had worked for a season in *Jeff Murphy's Carnival*, touring from Cuthbert, Georgia, through North Carolina, Alabama, and Tennessee.[3] "We put on a regular minstrel show with a semicircle of performers, two end-men and an interlocutor or emcee—we also had a good five-piece band," says Pigmeat. "The hit of the show was a dancer-comedian named Joe Doakes, who was a very funny man, and he left me with my mouth open. He had an eccentric routine with one trick I'll never forget: He'd shake his head from side to side so hard and fast that the make-up on his lips dotted his ears, and he didn't have a big mouth, either."

The late Henry "Rubberlegs" Williams, born in Atlanta in 1907, got his start singing the blues and dancing in Lizzie Murphy's sporting house.[4] (The nickname "Rubberlegs" described his style of dancing, also known as legomania.) "When I was just a kid, I'd climb out the window at home and sneak over to Lizzie's, where Nob Derricot played low-down piano, and I'd sing and dance for tips. I used to see my father there. When that 'ol' bad house,' as my mother called it, closed for the night, Nob would bring me home."

By the age of sixteen, and big for his years, Rubberlegs was a veteran. He went North with Bobby Grant's female impersonators (female impersonators had been a regular feature in minstrelsy); won a Charleston contest in Atlanta, accompanied by the legendary Eddie Heywood, Sr., on piano; and had his own act on the Negro T.O.B.A. circuit (Theater Owners' Booking Association), dancing and featuring the song "Home Again Blues." He resembled a gigantic and many-talented Billy de Wolfe.

Canceled out of a bankrupt theater in Birmingham in 1922, Rubberlegs joined a carnival, *The Sunshine Exposition Show*. "They had a 'plant,' that is, a plantation show in the Jig Top, and they were still doing a cakewalk for a finale," says Rubberlegs. "That's when I worked up a strut—I was considered a pretty good cakewalker—and won the cake most of the time; never did get to eat it." The show toured the South, and in New Orleans, Rubberlegs first thrilled to jazz. "I caught Papa Celestin at the Lyric Theater and some wonderful music in Pete Lala's club. I never heard anything like it before."

Leonard Reed joined a small carnival—the *Silas B. Williams Show*—in Kansas City around 1925.[5] When the white barker in front of the Jig Top asked for volunteers, Reed ran up barefoot, did a Charleston, and got the job: "Inside the tent, we put on 'blackouts,' that is, jokes acted out, something like burlesque did later," he recalls. "For example, a burglar breaks into a house while the husband is away and takes advantage of the wife. Then the husband walks in and the wife tells him someone broke in. 'Did he steal anything?' asks the husband, and the wife answers 'Yes, but I thought it was you.' " Reed worked in the summer only, returning to Kansas City to attend school in the winter.

The Orpheum Theater in Kansas City staged a Charleston contest—strictly for whites—while he was still in high school, and Reed, passing as "pure" white, entered and won it. "On closing night, the manager approached me with the prize money in a box and an evil glint in his eye," says Reed. "Two of the colored usherettes had given away my secret. I grabbed the box and ran out into the crowd with the manager yelling 'Catch that n——!' close behind me. So I yelled 'Catch that n——!' too, and made my getaway while everybody was trying to help me find the thief."

In 1902 Nettie Compton, later billed as "The Bronze Eva Tanguay," was doing a cakewalk in the *Ponsell Brothers Circus*.[6] Mrs. Compton, born in Iowa in 1879, had joined the circus at the age of sixteen as part of a vocal quartet in a sideshow. "The circus was all white except for us," she says, "and we had two quartets at the entrance of the freak tent—four boys and four girls—singing songs like 'Carry Me Back to Old Virginny' and 'Sweet and Low.' "

The management decided to introduce a cakewalk after the main show—"Stay and see the concert," announced the ringmaster, "only twenty-five cents!"—and discovered that only the Negro singers could do a creditable job. Six couples were assembled, the girls dressed in fancy frocks and the boys wearing top hats and flourishing canes.

"I can still see it—the girls kind of flirted, and the boys strutted and pranced," says Mrs. Compton. "You used a lot of strut in the Cakewalk—lots of fellows walked like that just for notoriety—and they could really show off. The girl would stop and applaud her partner, while he made up four steps of his own, sometimes regular tap steps, and then he'd end it, maybe with a somersault. We had some nice dancers and a good band."

In 1902, when Slow Kid Thompson joined a small circus, the *Mighty Hagg*, with headquarters in Shreveport, he got a job as cook, but was soon called upon to do the Cakewalk. "The featured dancer-comedian," Thompson reminisces, "was a white man named Spider, but they needed a grand-entrance parade in the ring. So six or eight of us kitchen help doubled as cakewalkers, wearing huge *papier-mâché* heads with top hats, carrying canes, and strutting and prancing around the ring in time with the music. Even the horses cakewalked."

Dancer-musician Sidney Easton recalls working with *Thompson's Wild West Show* in 1909.[7] A small, white company that featured four horses, the show had a Jig Top, where Easton and a few others did the Buck and eccentric dancing as well as the Cakewalk. Cakewalking in a white circus was a step up for Negro dancers, but it did not last, and as the Cakewalk lost popularity in the teens, the circuses dropped it.

While the large white minstrel companies exploded into gigantic irrelevancies, Negro minstrelsy persisted on a smaller scale in the South. Luckily, it was forced to do precisely what it could do best. With dancing talent but without the financial resources to imitate the excesses of the white companies, Negro minstrelsy tailored its entertainment to rural audiences in the South and kept its size and format as a small carnival or gilly with a Jig Top.

Susie Beavers, who later married bandleader Paul Howard, was born in Atlanta in 1888 and ran away to join Pat Chappell's *Rabbit Foot Minstrels* at the age of fifteen.[8] "I sang—one of my songs was 'Find Another Tree to Build Your Nest'—and I did what you'd call Buck dancing. Grace and Billy Arnte got me the job and taught me the Time Step." After two years with the *Rabbit Foot Minstrels,* she joined *Funny Folks,* a show owned by the same people and employing the same format.

Around 1906 *Funny Folks* toured the South—"Texas was awful," says Susie Beavers. "When we crossed the line into the next state, we got out and kissed the ground"—traveling as far North as Pennsylvania and closing for the winter in Tampa. The troupe numbered about sixty, including a brass band, and went to work at noon with a parade to drum up trade for the evening performance.

"Mr. Chappell and the spieler—you'd call him the master of ceremonies today—rode at the head of the parade in high style, followed by the minstrel men or 'walking gents' doing some fancy stepping," says Susie Beavers. "Then eight of us girls came in little carts, two to a cart. The band—mostly brass—came loud and last." The parade marched around the residential area and stopped in front of the city hall, where the band gave a brief concert. (In *Father of the Blues,* W. C. Handy, who was bandmaster in *W. A. Mahara's Minstrels,* describes the same kind of parade.) After touring with *Funny Folks,* Susie Beavers joined other minstrel shows —*Douglas and Worthy's Florida Blossoms* (they boasted that they had purchased a railroad Pullman from Billy Kersands, the famous Negro minstrel) and *W. A. Mahara's Minstrels.*

In 1925 *Florida Blossoms* was still staging the same kind of parade, according to Pigmeat Markham. "When the noon whistle blew at the factories, letting the workers out, we came right off the train and started the parade," he says. "I played bass drum then, but I wanted to be a walkin' gent—they were the dancers and comedians—wearing a cape or frock-coat of many colors." Carrying banners advertising the evening performance, the paraders marched down streets lined with people on their lunch hour. "We played real jazz," says Markham.

Like the gillies and carnivals that set the pattern, the *Florida Blossoms* show was divided into three parts: a dancer-comedian act, a series of specialties (including a juggler and a hoop roller), and a playlet. An "after concert" consisting of a few acts from the regular show and a cakewalk finale was added with an extra admission fee.

The specialty numbers were becoming more varied and the dancing more than merely comic. With the *Florida Blossoms*, Pigmeat and his partner Enoch Baker had a top-notch Sand Dance: "We kept a pile of sand in the 'possum belly' of the railroad car—a compartment for tools—and spread some of it on the stage for our dance. The music stopped while the audience listened to our feet scraping in tempo." The Sand Dance, an audible and syncopated shuffle, was a perennial favorite.

"We were called the *Florida Cotton Blossoms* but we had never been to Florida," says Charlie Love, who joined in 1931. "We used to parade the brass band at twelve o'clock . . . some feller'd sing and dance . . . another feller used to clown—you know, he'd do eccentric dancing . . . Foots Robinson was one of the comedians; a feller named Perry was another and a feller by the name of Sapp used to dance and tell tall tales. That's about six comedians . . ." [9]

The period during which tent shows nurtured great dancers was in the teens and twenties. "When you joined a big minstrel show," says Pigmeat, "you ran up against the best." Pigmeat's experiences with minstrel shows took place in the early twenties, when he worked with five organizations: "I jumped around from *Gonzell White's Minstrels* to the *Florida Blossoms, Silas Green's Minstrels, A. G. Allen's Mighty Minstrels, Huntington's Minstrels,* and back to the *Florida Blossoms*—everybody was colored except the boss—and I saw dancers who were so good you wouldn't believe it."

Around 1923, when he was with *A. G. Allen's Mighty Minstrels,* Pigmeat remembers the dancing of Foots Robinson and Jim Green, who was the stage manager of the show: "Green and Robinson had a dance number that stopped the show every time. They were the end men and had to be versatile. Green had a specialty I'll never forget: He'd dance awhile and then fall on the floor and spin around on his backside in time with the music—he called it the Black Bottom years before a dance of that name became popular."

As it turned out, Jim Green was not good enough. "One day a hayseed who said his name was Cliff Pettiford came walking along the railroad track and allowed as how he could dance some," Pigmeat continues. "We put him on as a joke after Jim Green, but our laughter froze—he had the wildest personality and the craziest eccentric dance you ever saw. Nobody could follow him.

"The next night they put him in the olio and nobody could follow him there, either. Then they put him in the afterpiece and he broke *that* up. So finally, they had him close the show, but then the audience wouldn't leave. He was fired."

Pigmeat recalls others: Kid Neal, King Nappy, Kid Sapp, Peg Lightfoot (the first of the one-legged dancers), and still others, who spent their lives dancing in tent shows, known only to their colleagues in the South.

Negro dancing in tent shows had a gradually emerging influence on a wide variety of dancing that followed. The tent shows developed their own stars, who blended struts, shuffles, grinds, spins, twists, and what-not into endlessly new creations, which in turn helped set the style of dancing—both amateur and professional—which crowded the stages and ballrooms of the twenties and thirties.

Perhaps because it was isolated and "outdoors," tent-show dancing evolved rapidly and radically during the teens and is still being assimilated. Carnivals were "definitely shot," say Abel Green and Joe Laurie, Jr., "by 1928." [10] The decline of tent shows was inevitable, although some of them —without great dancers—are still touring the South. ("A few make it as far North as New Jersey every spring," said Pigmeat Markham in 1965). Films, radio, and television took their place. Today the Jig Top with its dancer-comedians is virtually extinct.

11 Roadshows, T.O.B.A., and Picks

WHILE TENT SHOWS were playing outdoors to country audiences in the South, a more sophisticated kind of show was playing indoors to urban audiences in both the North and South. Some were called "Tom" shows because they presented some version of *Uncle Tom's Cabin;* others were referred to as "Plant" shows because they were staged as plantation scenes; and many of them were spoken of as "Tab," or tabloid, shows because they were abbreviated vaudeville shows. These types often overlapped, of course, but they were all known as roadshows.

Three shows were outstanding: *In Old Kentucky, The Smart Set,* and *Black Patti's Troubadours. In Old Kentucky* was perhaps the best known. Organized around 1900, it was white with the exception of the musicians and dancers, who worked together. The show had a flimsy plot about horse racing and a black horse named Queen Bess, who wins the Derby. "The great moment came," says dancer Earl "Tiny" Ray who played the jockey in one company, "when the Old Man told us: 'If Queen Bess loses, you play "Massa's in the Cold Cold Ground." If she wins play as you've never played before!' Then, when Queen Bess won, the famous pickaninny band went to town." [1] (The racing scene was adapted later in the film *Wunderbar.*)

The great importance of the show to Negroes consisted of the Friday night dance contests, which anyone could enter. Winning the prize was a major triumph. *In Old Kentucky* (usually shortened to *Old Kentucky*) gave each contestant a number, and placed two judges under the stage, in the wings, and out in front. The only accompaniment was the stop-time banjo —one plunk at the beginning of each bar—by Charles "Old Man" French, who played Uncle Neb in the company. "It was the best stop-time rhythm I have ever heard," writes Tom Fletcher, who began his career as the bass-drum player in the pickaninny band, one of the celebrated features of *Old Kentucky*.[2]

Playing in the pit band for two weeks, while the company toured from New York to Richmond in 1902, pianist-composer Eubie Blake says that the star dancer with the show at that time was Harry Swinton: "He came out in roustabout clothes with a paper cone full of sand and did more dancing just spreading the sand than other dancers could do with their whole act." [3] "Spreading the sand," of course, was merely a preliminary to his dance.

Bill Robinson is supposed to have defeated Swinton once, according to Tom Fletcher, who adds that the contest was not exactly fair. When *Old Kentucky* was playing the Bijou Theater in Brooklyn, Swinton took a low number and came on early, generously giving the later and better spots to lesser men. "That left the field to Bill. He took charge and won the prize"—and never let his friends forget it. Eubie Blake is not impressed: "When you mentioned Swinton's name," he says, "Bill Robinson shut up."

By 1915 a dancer named Kid Checkers was supposed to be the star of *Old Kentucky*, but a cornet player in the band, who is remembered only as "Mose," had taken up dancing overnight and was defeating all comers. Sixteen-year-old Willie Covan had been practicing and waiting patiently in Chicago. "That Willie never stopped dancing," says acrobat Archie Ware. "I don't know how his parents kept him in shoe leather." [4] When the show arrived, Covan hastened to sign up for the Friday night contest.

"I was all set for *Old Kentucky*," says Covan matter-of-factly. "I'd been working up new ideas all year." [5] Assigned a late number, he watched his predecessors begin with the traditional Time Step and run short of time on their routines. A contestant was allowed no more than five or six minutes, and Covan decided that the Time Step took too much time. Besides, he had some steps to try.

"So I came jumping out with a Wing, a Grab Off, and a Roll," says Covan, "and managed to get in a lot of new stuff before my time ran out." The judges gave Covan the prize and the audience came backstage after the show and carried him out on its shoulders. From then on, everybody in Negro show business knew about Covan.

The second of the three roadshows, *The Smart Set*, was also organized around 1900 by white producer Gus Hill with a Negro cast. (There were numerous imitations, including Tutt-Whitney's *The Smarter Set*, which usually played the South.) Featuring a play called "The Black Politician," *Smart Set* was held together by another flimsy plot about horse racing and politics, intermixed with singing, dancing, and comedy. "I was supposed to dope the horse before the race," says dancer-comedian Walter Crumbley, who played the villain on the first Southern tour and did not enjoy it. "It was one of those Simon Legree plots where all the colored people *suffered*." [6]

"*Smart Set* wasn't as classy as *Old Kentucky*," adds Crumbley, "but they were both doing good business." Gus Hill booked *Smart Set* from New York—no Negro circuits existed then—signing up various places in different cities, wherever an indoor stage could be found. Opening in Newark in the fall, they traveled South during the winter by private railroad car, passing through North Carolina, South Carolina, and Georgia. (*Chappelle and Stinnette*, a top-drawer singing act in the show, had their own private car.) *Smart Set* played to white audiences, although Negroes were sometimes permitted in the balcony.

"The show opened with everybody singing," says Crumbley, "then one scene after another, according to the story, not like vaudeville acts, with a chorus line of girls and lots of comedy and dancing." The featured singer was Marian Smart, who specialized in songs of the Stephen Foster variety, but the dancer-comedian was the star. Over a period of four or more years the leading dancer-comedians were Ernest Hogan, Tom McIntosh, and Sherman H. Dudley.

Ernest Hogan, who changed his name from Reuben Crowder to cash in on the popularity of Irish comedians, was the most famous, and indeed, some old-timers think he was more gifted than Bert Williams. "He could walk on stage all by himself," says Eubie Blake, "and make the audience laugh one moment and cry the next." Tom McIntosh was a knockabout comedian, a member of the *Original Georgia Minstrels*, who did exhibition drumming. And Sherman Dudley was famous for his comic skit with a mule named Pat, and his characterization of a millionaire from Honolulu. The line "I'm proud of the fact that I came *from* Texas *and I'm going to stay away*," is generally ascribed to him.

On his first trip with *Smart Set*, Ohio-born Walter Crumbley was thoroughly unhappy. In Spartanburg, South Carolina, a gang of white roughnecks picked a fight with members of the company who had been talking to some light-skinned Negro girls. The roughnecks claimed the girls were white. "I hated that trip and quit the moment I got back. Still, I learned a lot about dancing." By 1901, *Smart Set* was also staging its own buck-and-wing contests on Wednesday nights for all comers.

The third roadshow, *Black Patti's Troubadours*, had the most prestige. Black Patti's name was Sissieretta Jones (her first name was originally Sissie Etta) and she made a great reputation as a concert artist touring Europe, soloing with Patrick Gilmore's band, and performing for President Harrison.

"Negroes were proud of Black Patti," says Professor Willis Laurence James of Spelman College, who grew up in Jacksonville and remembers the excitement caused by the arrival of the *Troubadours*.[7] "In a sense, she was a kind of 'racial' heroine because she was so outstanding as a singer, even by white standards, and white people came to hear her, too."

As a youngster, Eubie Blake lived near Sissieretta Jones in Baltimore: "I never heard anybody with a voice like hers—and I heard the original white Patti, too—when she sang 'The Prison Song,' first in the original key and then an octave higher, it was like she had a wonderful bird in her throat. She had a range like Yma Sumac and a fine operatic voice." Young Blake ran errands for her: "She ate more ginger snaps than the boxer, Joe Gans."

Black Patti's Troubadours were organized by white managers in 1895 and offered a departure from the usual minstrel format. The show was divided into three parts: The first closed with a Buck-dancing contest; the second was an olio, or series of specialties, ending with a cakewalk; and the third, billed as an "Operatic Kaleidoscope," brought on Black Patti accompanied by the entire cast singing selections from various operas.

The show toured the South for seven years. In 1898, when she was fifteen, Ida Forsyne joined *Black Patti's Troubadours.*[8] "A girl in the show was sick, so I went down and did my number, 'My Hannah Lady,' and got the job at $15 a week. I was the only young girl in a company of twenty-six. For my specialty, I pushed a baby carriage across the stage and sang a lullaby, 'You're Just a Little Nigger but You're Mine All Mine,' and no one thought of objecting in those days."

Nobody in the company had operatic training, but they were told to sing loudly behind Black Patti. "We all stood in a row behind her and yelled our heads off," says Ida, "belting out our own version of how each opera should go, and I used to think the sound was wonderful."

"The spirit and musical finish displayed in the choruses," wrote A. L. Howard, the New York correspondent for the London *Era*, "are exciting nightly enthusiasm." [9]

The dancing-comedian Bobby Kemp was also featured. Dressed in Zulu costume, he sang "Under the Bamboo Tree" with Nettie Compton and then went into his buck-and-wing specialty. (The legendary Buck dancer King Rastus Brown was with the show for a time.) Ida Forsyne learned to dance with the *Black Patti* show. "I could do any step I saw and there was plenty to see." In 1902, just as she was raised to $25 a week, the show folded.

Unlike the tent shows and roadshows, Negro vaudeville had its own chain of theaters, which evolved slowly and late in the day. During the middle teens comedian Sherman Dudley retired to Washington, D. C., where he began to lease and buy theaters. Combining with various white and Negro theater owners in the South, he helped to form the Theater Owners' Booking Association (T.O.B.A.), also nicknamed "Toby" or "Tough on Black Artists", which expanded until, by the twenties, it had penetrated most of the South as well as the Southwest and several Northern cities.

The Chicago *Defender* notes in 1921 that the T.O.B.A. reached from Galveston to Jacksonville and from Cleveland to Kansas City. The itinerary of a T.O.B.A. company originating in Chicago is outlined by Clarence Muse: St. Louis, Nashville, Chattanooga ("a dead town"), Memphis, New Orleans, Durham, Norfolk, Newport News, and Baltimore.[10]

Some of the old-time dancers never played T.O.B.A.—it came too late—and a few were great enough to get a job with a well-known act up North, skip T.O.B.A., and rise swiftly to the Keith circuit. *The Whitman Sisters,* however, played the T.O.B.A. circuit, where they were a top attraction, by preference, and some of the best dancers served their apprenticeship on this circuit: Bill Robinson, Jack Wiggins (with blues-singer "Ma" Rainey), Eddie Rector, *The Berry Brothers,* and many more. T.O.B.A. was eager for new acts and a tryout was not difficult to arrange. "You found out if you could dance on T.O.B.A.," says Pete Nugent, "and if you couldn't you were fired on the spot." [11]

What were the T.O.B.A. shows like? "The shows playing the Toby time were tabloid editions of musical comedies," writes Clarence Muse. "Three shows were given nightly, each of about forty-five minutes duration. The company for these revues constituted about thirty-five people."

Dancer-producer Ernest "Baby" Seals had his own show on T.O.B.A.[12] His wife, Emma, who sang ballads and blues, was the leading lady. "We started with eighteen performers in 1924," says Seals, "and gradually built up to twenty-five by 1931." The show carried four sets of scenery and an eight- to ten-piece jazz band, with Sammy Price playing boogie-woogie piano ("I tried out as a comedian," says Price with rare modesty, "and failed").[13] Bill Jackson, working in blackface, was the featured dancer-comedian. "We were always discovering new talent on the road," says Seals.

Each year of a successful seven-year run, the show opened in Chattanooga, touring down to Miami by way of Wilmington, Winston-Salem, Charlotte, and Macon, and back again by a different route. "The Florida theaters for colored were fine," says Seals, "Palm Beach, Jacksonville, and Miami—and we did good business with all-Negro audiences." If you didn't make money on T.O.B.A., you were through in a week.

Seals's show lasted an hour and fifteen minutes and was divided into eight parts, alternating comedy skits, chorus numbers, solo specialties, and—always—plenty of dancing. (The fourth part featured the headliner, and the last part was a *finale* with the entire company.) Anything could change on a moment's notice, however, depending on the inspiration and talent available. "I made up some material, we'd see things on the road, other guys had ideas—we'd try anything," says Seals.

The comic "bits" were not notable for their high moral purpose, although "blue" material was carefully censored in certain towns. A typical routine consists of a raffish comedian bragging to the straight man, who has his collar turned around to give the impression of ministerial respectability, that his buddy knows the Bible backwards.

When the buddy enters, dressed like a tramp and tongue-tied with ignorance, a bet is wagered, and the straight man addresses three questions to the tramp to test his knowledge. "Who created heaven and earth?" Non-plussed until stuck in the backside with a long pin by his pal, the tramp yells "Great God Almighty!" The next question, "Who brought down the Ten Commandments from the mount?" is answered when the tramp is stuck again and hollers "Holy Moses!" The last question is "What did Eve say to Adam?" and the tramp, finally catching on, cries "Hey, watch what you're doing!"—or something far worse. Luckily, dancing was the mainstay of the show.

"Well, you didn't get no money, and you didn't want any," concludes Sammy Price, remembering. "You joined the show, and in one week's time you friendly with everybody, and you're like one big happy family . . . it could be tough, but there were good times too." [14] Guitarist Lonnie Johnson agrees: ". . . on T.O.B.A. you *work*—you do five, six shows a day; you got little money, but everybody was happy . . . I went as far as T.O.B.A. can carry you, from Philadelphy to New Orleans." [15]

T.O.B.A. outlasted white vaudeville, disintegrating slowly in the thirties. In 1929, eighty theaters remained in the circuit, but by 1932 most of them were showing films only.[16] Thereafter, a surviving roadshow, such as the indestructible *Silas Green from New Orleans*, which never came North, traveled by automobile and booked itself.[17] The era of homegrown dancing on T.O.B.A. was over, and with it a great source of talent.

From the beginnings of white vaudeville a few Negro acts existed on the strength of their extraordinary talent, but they had to put up with the usual humiliations, which increased noticeably from 1900. "If the bill is weak, add a Negro act," the head of a great vaudeville circuit is supposed to have commanded, "and if that don't do it, hire some Negro kids." Actually, the quickest way to land an early and steady job—with low pay—was to work as a "pick" with a white star in vaudeville. You could start young, have few responsibilities, and play the top circuits. All you had to do was sing and dance—"sensationally," as they say. It was less risky and difficult than trying to organize your own act on T.O.B.A., which more than deserved its reputation for being rough and tough. Very few played the deep South by choice.

"In the 1900's many of the so-called single women carried 'insurance' in the form of pickaninnies, or 'picks,' as they were called," writes Joe Laurie, Jr. "After singing a few songs of their own, they would bring out the picks (a group of Negro kids that really could sing and dance) for a sock finish . . . I never saw any picks flop." [18] ("Pickaninny" probably comes from the Portuguese *pequeno*, which means "little one.")

Headliners such as Sophie Tucker, Eva Tanguay, Blossom Seeley, Nora Bayes, and many more carried what amounted to juvenile dance troupes in their acts. "It wasn't really a single act, but nevertheless they were so classified," adds Laurie, who lists his top ten: Grace LaRue, Phina & Her Picks, Ethel Whiteside, Laura Comstock, Mayme Remington, Josephine Saxon,

Emma Kraus, Louise Dresser, Canta Day, and Carrie Scott. The custom of using Negro youngsters was so general that when "Canta Day and Her *White* Picks" appeared, the act was a novelty.

In Mayme Remington's act at one time or another for example, were Bill Robinson, Coot Grant, Dewey Weinglass, Luckey Roberts, Archie Ware, Eddie Rector, Lou Keane, and Toots Davis. "She was a former French burlesque dancer," says Coot Grant, who joined her in 1901 as one of fifteen picks, "and her specialty was a Hawaiian dance which sure looked like what they call the Shake in Birmingham." [19] The kids did special dancing for various "Hawaiian," "Indian," and "African" numbers, which turned out to be some variation of the Strut, Grind, or Shuffle.

Dancer Tiny Ray, who became the leader of an early class-and-flash act, *The Three Eddies*, feels that he danced with the best pick act on the stage: "We worked for a white actress named Gussie Francis, and there were four of us—Jimmy Walsh, Pop Bennett, Clarence Wesley, and myself," he says. "We played all kinds of circuits and wore opera hats, tuxedo jackets, short pants, and black silk stockings." As for the act, Miss Francis sat in a swing and "swung" while the picks did a soft shoe and then sat on the stage, watching her and singing "Won't You Come Down, Rainbow Queen." "We worked out all our own routines, too," adds Ray.

White headliners often scouted for their own picks. Dancer Susie Beavers remembers Sophie Tucker dropping in at Maps, the one Negro club on San Francisco's Barbary Coast, sometime around 1915.[20] "She was so jolly—she gave us all silver dollars—and watched the show." The temporary master of ceremonies was a youngster named Earl Dancer, who later became a good friend of Ethel Waters and a well-known producer. At the time, however, his talents had not fully developed.

Animated by the presence of Miss Tucker, who was well regarded by Negro performers because she gave them credit whenever possible, Dancer outdid himself. "He did a sloppy slide and half a Wing," says Susie Beavers, "and sang 'Ain't Nobody's Business' as if he was crawling with ants. Sophie just leaned back and laughed and laughed and said: 'Come here, Sonny, what's your name?' He said his name was Earl. 'Earl what?' she asked and he told her. 'Well, Earl,' she said, 'you just keep up the good work—you can't sing worth a damn and you can't dance but you're sure a jumpin' S.O.B.'" Earl Dancer never worked as a pick for Sophie Tucker.

After a job as a pick on the Keith circuit with a famous star, a Negro youngster had a difficult adjustment to make when he grew too large and was no longer "cute" enough for the job. If he was exceptionally talented, he might form his own act on Loew's or some lesser circuit, but this was aiming high. The problems involved are illustrated by the experience of Dewey Weinglass, who became a great Russian-style dancer.

Weinglass was born in Georgetown, South Carolina, in 1900, and moved to New York with his family when he was six.[21] At the age of fifteen and small for his years, he got a job as a pick with a Negro singer and dancer in an act billed as "Mattie Phillips and Her Jungle Kids." He was earning $12.50 a week on the lowly Gus Sun circuit. "Miss Phillips was *very* tall and a fine dancer," says the diminutive Weinglass in a gravelly voice. "She got a big hand turning cartwheels 'way over our heads while we worked at a routine underneath and in back of her, accompanied by piano and drums. We did a challenge dance for a finish, each of us doing his stuff in turn while the rest clapped and stamped."

For his own solo Weinglass tapped and started experimenting with Russian steps, which came easy to him. (He imitated the Russian dancer Ivan Bankoff, whom he watched at the Palace Theater on Broadway.) After four months he discovered that he could make more money working in his father's shoeshine parlor. "I could make nearly $18 a week just shining shoes," he says, "and once I shined the shoes of Bert Williams' *father*." So he quit.

At this time, picks were in demand and Weinglass was developing a business sense. Because he loved to dance, he went back to work as a pick with a white singer, Gertie LeClair, at $15 a week, and when he was refused a raise, quit and joined *Georgette Hamilton and Her Picks* at $18 a week. "We toured Cuba and came back in 1915 after the war had started." During the tour Weinglass was a hit doing the Cakewalk and got a raise to $20 a week.

Early in 1916 Dewey Weinglass did not have to look for a job—Mayme Remington called him. His reputation as a pick had grown swiftly. "I asked for $22," says Weinglass with a chuckle, "and after a long pause she said 'All right, you be at the Bushwick Theater in Brooklyn tomorrow.'" They opened on the same bill with the Marx Brothers. "Us picks wore Dutch wigs and clogged, while Miss Remington sang her songs and did her little dance." Weinglass was hired for the finale, where he performed his Russian steps and was the hit of the show.

The career of Dewey Weinglass ground to a halt when he attempted to form his own act. "When I told Miss Remington that I was going out for myself, she couldn't believe it," he recalls. "She just laughed at me." But he persisted with his revolutionary plan.

With another boy and two girls, Weinglass rehearsed an act which they decided to call *The Dancing Demons*. One of the girl's mothers sewed the costumes, and they asked for and received permission to play the Alhambra Theater's Sunday concert in Brooklyn—without pay. This led to the offer of a week's job in Newark.

All the other acts on the Newark bill were white, and at the end of the week these acts were paid. Weinglass was invited up to the manager's office, congratulated, and offered a drink. Gradually Weinglass realized that he was not going to be paid. "I took the drink—although I'd never had one before—and another, and became violently sick all over that nice office," says Weinglass placidly. "I must have been nervous and upset." It was the end, for a time, of *The Dancing Demons*.

Weinglass soon organized another act, persuading a new group to rehearse without salary. After many fruitless auditions they landed a week at the Keith Theater on 24th Street and Fifth Avenue. At the opening the audience kept applauding Weinglass and his group after his act was over, ignoring Nora Bayes, who tried to come on with the next act. "That was when Nora Bayes refused to follow us and walked out," says Weinglass. "To keep the peace, the management fired us."

"Going on T.O.B.A.," Weinglass observes, "never entered my head." For a Negro dancer raised in the North, the idea of going South—even with an act of his own—was almost unthinkable. He pulled up stakes, and with a new and congenial partner, headed for the West. On the lesser-known circuits out there, he soon became a headliner, and in a few years returned to New York on the Keith circuit as the star of *The Dancing Demons*. By 1921 the group was a sensation in London. Dewey Weinglass had made the jump from pick to a top act of his own in five years.

The practice of white stars hiring Negro children lasted a long time. In 1926, nineteen-year-old Henry "Rubberlegs" Williams was still a pick on the Keith circuit with *Naomi Thomas's Brazilian Nuts*.[22] "She had a boy named Rastus who was sensational," says Rubberlegs. "He jumped down from a high drum into a split and came up dancing the Charleston."

Nora Bayes and Her Picks were on the same bill. "She'd sing 'Mississippi Mud,'" says Rubberlegs, "and when she came to the line 'the darkies beat their feet,' her six picks would do the Pasmala around her." As late as 1929 Charles Cook, later of *Cook and Brown*, was working on the Keith circuit with *Sarah Venable and Her Picks*.

Picks disappeared with the decay of vaudeville. No doubt the practice provided a fine schooling and developed a youngster's ability, as well as teaching him show business. But the profits were one way. The employer was white and adult, while the pick was Negro and a child—so picks never got rich. It was child labor, theatrical style. Many dancers started as picks only because it was one of the few ways for a Negro to get into show business.

All in all the Negro style of dancing in various kinds of tent shows, road shows, and vaudeville—especially T.O.B.A.—was in the Afro-American tradition, which stresses two characteristics: continual improvisation and propulsive rhythms. These qualities became energizing factors in American vernacular dance.

From this Afro-American tradition, much that came later surfaced—from the tasty tapping of Bill Robinson and Fred Astaire (to name but two), through the naïve Shimmy of Gilda Gray and social dances such as the Charleston, to the Lindy (or Jitterbug) and other ballroom dances, up to, including, and after, the Twist. Most of the dancing we see today on stage and screen, in ballrooms and night clubs, at discotheques and on television, owes what vitality it has to this barely tapped reservoir of American vernacular dance.

12 *The Whitman Sisters*

THE WHITMAN SISTERS troupe was by far the greatest incubator of of dancing talent for Negro shows on or off T.O.B.A.[1] From about 1900 to 1943 they owned their show and traveled over the United States, usually playing a full two weeks in the big cities. Before the act broke up, they had appeared in every state in the Union. At the start, the Whitman sisters worked various theaters and circuits but eventually, in spite of many other offers, they stayed with T.O.B.A., because they were headliners and could command top prices.

Other competing all-Negro shows were touring the country. *Black Patti's Troubadours* (she retired in 1918) had more prestige, since Black Patti herself came close to beating the white concert-singers at their own game; and *The Smart Set* (which lasted until 1920) had prettier chorus girls—it was known as The Ebony Ziegfeld Follies. *The Whitman Sisters* outlasted them all, however, changing with the times, and consistently featuring fine dancers. Wherever and whenever they saw a talented youngster on their tours, they collared him—with his parents' permission—and literally raised and educated him in their family troupe.

The Reverend Whitman, father of the girls, was born in Kentucky, graduated from Wilberforce College, and became a Bishop of the Methodist Church, first in Lawrence, Kansas, and later in Atlanta, where he was also Dean of Morris Brown College. According to his daughter Essie, the Reverend Whitman and the poet Walt Whitman were first cousins.

When they were little girls in Kansas, their father taught them the Double Shuffle—but insisted that it was "just for exercise." (Later, when they went into show business, Clarence Muse writes that their father disowned them.) [2] George Walker of the *Williams and Walker* team was a neighbor of the Whitmans in Lawrence, and Essie recalls cooking greens for him. "He was the greatest strutter of them all," she says.

A neighbor, Susie Beavers, recalls the Whitman family in Atlanta. "We kids used to sit up in the balcony of the Big Bethel Church and listen to Reverend Whitman preach. At socials Essie sang 'Mr. Johnson, Shet That Door' while Mabel played the piano. Later on, Alberta joined them and the youngest daughter, Alice, won a lot of cakewalk contests."[3] Perry Bradford, also from Atlanta, says the Whitman sisters introduced the Cakewalk locally at Jackson Field around 1908.[4]

The two older Whitman girls, Mabel and Essie, helped raise money for the church by singing at benefits. Then they formed an act and hired a local hall. "At first they were jubilee singers," says dancer-comedian Walter Crumbley. "Later they did 'harmony' songs like 'Adam Never Had No Mammy' and 'Little Black Me.'"[5] With their mother as chaperone they toured abroad, and upon their return, Alberta joined them. In the summer of 1904, when they were in New Orleans, they organized a company called *The Whitman Sisters' New Orleans Troubadours.* The featured entertainer in this show was the famous pianist-singer Tony Jackson, composer of "Pretty Baby," who traveled with them for a while.

By July 23, 1904, the troupe was appearing at the Jefferson Theater in Birmingham and *Stage* magazine observed:

> This is the first time in the history of Birmingham, Alabama, that the colored people have been allowed seats in the dress circle and parquet. Credit is due to the clever management of Mabel Whitman who can safely say that she is the only colored woman managing her own company and booking them continuously in the leading Southern houses. . . . The singing of Tony Jackson was much appreciated. . . . Mabel, Essie and Alberta are decided favorites throughout the Southland. . . .[6]

For a time the Whitman sisters toured the West on the Pantages circuit. A tinted photograph taken around 1900—considerably retouched—dominates one wall in the living room of their Chicago home. The picture shows three beautiful, fair-complexioned young ladies in pale yellow dresses with leg-of-mutton sleeves; their blonde hair is arranged in high, fluffy pompadours. The over-all impression is of fashionable Gibson Girls.

The sisters' light skin led to some confusion. Slow Kid Thompson remarked casually that "they sometimes worked as a white act," and Essie herself told us a story of how, in the early days when they were singing jubilees in churches, Hammerstein signed them to sing in his theater with the proviso that they wear blackface and wigs at first, and then as a finale, take off the make-up and the wigs, let their blonde hair down, and come back on stage. "The audience was always puzzled," says Essie, "and someone was sure to ask, 'What are those white women doing up there?' Then they would recognize us as the performers and laugh in amazement."

After their mother died in 1909, the youngest sister, Alice, joined the group and soon became a favorite with audiences. By 1911 the Whitman sisters were so popular that Perry Bradford, playing on the same bill at Minsky's Theater in Pittsburgh, found it almost impossible to follow them on stage. The audience would not let them go. "They already had some wonderful dancing kids from Charleston—Aaron Palmer, Samuel Reed, Julius Foxworth, and Tommy Hawkins—along with Alice, who was just a little girl."

"Alberta stood to one side, patting and stamping a Charleston rhythm—they didn't have the tune yet—and those kids stopped the show cold," Bradford recalls. "The manager told us to go on, but we wouldn't. We just waited while they went back for encores until they were worn out, and then we went into the meat of our act—no time to fool around and build it up. Those kids were great."

The Whitman sisters took their cue from the famous white singers who bolstered their acts with picks, but they could do a better job of it because they had the inside track—the trust and cooperation of their own race.

Aaron Palmer joined the Whitman sisters in 1910, when he was thirteen, staying with them for twelve years.[7]

> I was working in Atlanta with two other kids—Julius Foxworth and Samuel Reed—when they came through and saw our act. They followed us around trying to find out where we were from and they finally went to our home town, Charleston, and got permission from our parents to let us join their show.
>
> A little while after we joined, Sister May took out her pick show, called *Mabel Whitman and the Dixie Boys*. We toured all over, even Germany and Australia, and the other sisters just stayed home and lived off the money we made. Maxie McCree was in the show, too.

(McCree later appeared in vaudeville and George White's *Scandals*.) According to Palmer, May Whitman sang and the boys danced. "She could really put a song over and was a wonderful business woman. May Whitman was just like a mother to me."

After May's tour, *The Whitman Sisters* was reorganized as a regular roadshow. The sisters made an impressive team. May took care of the booking and all the business; Essie designed and made the costumes; and Alberta, better known as Bert, composed the music for the show and acted as financial secretary.

May was a formidable woman. Once, when the act was about to play the Regal Theater in Chicago, the management decided to pay them less than the agreed-upon amount. May walked across the street to the Metropolitan Theater, which lacked a stage, had a new stage built, opened with a different show, and ruined the Regal's business for two weeks.

May soon quit performing, but Essie was featured as a comedian in a drunk act and as a singer performing numbers such as "Some of These Days" in a resonant contralto that made Sophie Tucker sound like a soprano. "Essie was a real coon shouter," says Aaron Palmer, "and I guess she can still sing. There's always a good tune in a real violin." "When I was ten years old," says Essie, "I won a prize at a Kansas City theater for singing 'God Won't Love You If You Don't Be Good' so loud that they could hear me clear in the fifth balcony."

Essie took great pains with her appearance and Alice remembers the problems that arose when Essie was supposed to follow her act on stage: "I'd take a dozen encores waiting for Sister Essie to make that one spit curl backstage. 'Fess' would be going 'Doo-dee-doo-dee-doo' on the piano, vamping for her, until she finally came out." ("Fess" is an abbreviation of *professor,* the customary title of the piano player.) Alice gives a good imitation of how Essie wiggled her hips as she entered. Essie retired in Chicago in the late twenties, where she became a lay preacher at the Metropolitan Church—a profession for which she had more than ample presence.

Alberta cut her hair short, dressed as a man, and became one of the best male impersonators. "I did flash dancing," says Bert, "throwing my legs every way there was, and I never saw anybody do a strut until after I had already started it." (Bert was married for a time to Maxie McCree.) The most popular white male impersonator of the day was Vesta Tilley. "Miss Tilley was supposed to follow Bert on one bill," says Essie with stern loyalty, "but when she saw Sister's act, she ran out of the theater and wouldn't come back. Sister Bert was the best in the business."

Many years younger than her sisters, Alice was billed as "The Queen of Taps" and deserved the title—"the best girl tap-dancer in the country—bar none," says Willie Bryant, who worked with *The Whitman Sisters* in the twenties.[8] For many, Alice was the star of the show. "As a kid I'd be 'Georgia Hunchin' up and down Auburn Avenue in Atlanta," says Alice with a twinkle in her eyes, "just a little shuffle with taps, but you could move along. I even used to do it after Sunday School in front of the church, and the people would shake their heads disapprovingly and say, 'Oh, look at Alice!' "

Later, on stage, she did Ballin' the Jack, Walkin' the Dog, the Sand, and the Shimmy. "In Ballin' the Jack I'd stop in the middle of the song, squeal, and make my kneecaps quiver—I used to have dimples on them, but I don't know what you'd call them now." Dancer Bill Bailey remembers her as "the prettiest thing in show business." [9]

When Alice came on stage, she walked out to the center, tossed off a tricky little step, and inquired of the bandleader in the pit: "How's this, Fess?"

"What is it?" asked the bandleader.

Alice replied, "I don't know what you call it but it sure feels good." When the chorus line went off before her specialty, Alice sang with a voice something like Helen Kane's.

"I'd make my exit with the Shim-Sham-Shimmy, mostly from the waist down—along with more squeals—wearing a shawl and a little flimsy thing around my middle with a fringe and a bow on the back. If I ever lost that bow, they used to say, I'd sure catch cold." Alice has no false modesty. "I could swing a mean . . ."—and she whistled to indicate the part of her anatomy and the general effect—"around."

Other dancers admired Alice unreservedly: "She had a fabulous figure," says Pete Nugent, "and clear, clean taps." [10]

Alice married Aaron Palmer, and in 1919 they had a son named Albert, who became the last member of the family to join the show. By the time he was four years old, he was performing the Charleston in a miniature tuxedo. Nicknamed "Pops," he developed into one of the first great acrobatic tap dancers, a master of cartwheels, spins, flips, and splits—swinging with the rhythm. During his brief life (he died in 1950), Pops teamed with a series of highly talented dancers, beginning with Billy Adams (who later married blues singer Victoria Spivey) and ending with Louis Williams (see chapter 33).

Touring with *The Whitman Sisters* in the early thirties, Pops, Louis, and a legendary youngster known as Groundhog were the runaway hit of the show. Later on, Pops and Louis went out on their own as a team, danced with many of the big swing bands, toured Europe, and returned to make a film in Hollywood. *Pops and Louis* were better known to white audiences than *The Whitman Sisters*.

Sometime in the twenties the sisters discovered a talented midget and adopted her. Billed as "Princess Wee Wee," she became one of the chief attractions of the act. In 1926, when Willie Bryant was sixteen, he did a song-and-dance with Princess Wee Wee. He was tall for his age, and the top of her head reached his waist. "She'd sing in a cute, high-pitched voice," says Bryant, "and then she'd dance around and between my legs."

In their day *The Whitman Sisters* were the royalty of Negro vaudeville and the highest paid act on T.O.B.A. The size of their troupe fluctuated between twenty and thirty performers. They featured dancing comedians (Willie Toot-sweet, Gulfport and Brown, "Sparkplug" George, and Billy Mitchell were the best known), various girl singers (Doris Rewbottom, Bernice Ellis, and others), a chorus line of twelve or fourteen girls, a fine five- or six-piece jazz band (Lonnie Johnson was with them for nine years), and always a few superb dancers.

But first and foremost it was the Whitman sisters' show, featuring the family, and they kept it strictly that way—even if it meant soft-pedaling the talents of their young discoveries. "I've seen Pops' first partner Billy Adams, break down and cry," says Pete Nugent, "because they cut out all his best dancing."

The format of the show varied—"They had six or eight different programs at any one time," says Willie Bryant, "and it was the fastest paced show on the road. If you tried to take it easy, you were fired."

In the early days May ran the show with a rod of iron. "Sister May hired and fired everybody," says Catherine Basie, who joined the show in 1930 when she was fifteen.[11]

"Sister May coached the dancers," says Essie, with obvious satisfaction, "and if there was any mother's child with talent, and we had them, they did their best. 'Get those feet *up* there,' May would order during rehearsals. 'What the hell do you think you're doing? Get those feet moving!' "

When silent movies became popular, the Whitman sisters simply shortened their act to fit between the showing of films, and continued to prosper. The average stage show ran about an hour and fifteen minutes, starting with a band overture, and running through a dozen fast numbers.

"Sometimes the first scene was a plantation number," says Alice, "Mammy peeling potatoes and the kids singing and dancing around her; then came the specialty numbers." Solo singers, dancers—with Pops featured—and comic skits alternated until the big production number: "The chorus did a Tiller dance, something like the Rockettes," says Catherine Basie, "kick to the left, kick to the right, kick straight up, and so on, to the tune of 'Stardust.' Then we always did a Shake dance to 'Diga Diga Doo.' "

After the next comic skit, or perhaps Princess Wee Wee's number, Bert and Alice did a boy-girl song-and-dance, backed by the chorus line. (Willie Bryant made this a trio for a time.) Then Alice sang her number, the chorus line going off when she started her tap solo. A blues singer or comedy act followed, leading into the finale headed by Bert doing her Strut. As an encore Pops sometimes came out by himself and closed the show. "All the top colored bands played for the show at one time or another," says Catherine Basie. "I met Bill [Count Basie] when he was playing for *The Whitman Sisters* with Bennie Moten's band, at a theater in Baltimore."

The fast pace and freshness of *The Whitman Sisters* act was partly due to the careful management of the stream of young talent that passed through the show. "Any mother could tell you that if your daughter was with *The Whitman Sisters,* she was safe," says Catherine Basie. "Sister May telegraphed my mother and got her consent to take care of me. We couldn't drink or smoke, and each of the young girls had to travel by car with one of the sisters—they wouldn't let us ride in the bus."

Clarence Muse takes a more cynical view: "They always carried a bunch of clever kids with the show. These, they explained to their audiences, were friendless and homeless orphans. They'd picked them up in their travels and were trying to provide for them after God's commandment . . . the orphan gag and their so-called charitable efforts to care for them was a tremendous sympathy-getter and helped their business."[12]

Every Thursday night after the last show, when the troupe was getting ready to move on to the next town, May gave a lecture—some called it a sermon—to the entire cast as they stood on the front of the stage with the curtain down: "Now when we get to Cuthbert, the married couples will live together and the unmarried couples will not. It's a mortal sin, and I don't want to catch any of you young girls staying with any boys. Is that clear?" May had a stentorian voice and a powerful frown—"She looked like a stern school principal," says Catherine Basie—and she stalked back and forth chewing gum as she put the fear of hell-fire and brimstone into her protégés. Sister Bert was the only one who dared question May's authority—in hair-raising language.

Dancer Joe Jones, later one of the *Three Little Words*, joined *The Whitman Sisters* in 1922, when he was seven years old.[13] "We had a private tutor, Uncle Dave Payton, who was married to Sister May, and both Sister May and Sister Essie kept us in line. They had deep voices like men and could really spank—I was scared to death of them." Jones still looked a little frightened at the memory. He worked with Pops, who was four years old at the time: "He could do a beautiful cartwheel, but he did it crooked. I showed him a spin and a twist and we started doing flips together."

Leonard Reed joined the show in 1926, when it was playing in Cleveland. "I argued with Sister Essie so much that I quit after three months." Bunny Briggs summed up the life of a youngster with *The Whitman Sisters*: "You sang one week, danced the next, sold peanuts the next, and if you got caught breaking any of the rules they shipped you home in a hurry." [14]

When May died in 1942, the show never fully recovered, although it managed to keep going another year. After the show disbanded, *Pops and Louis* went out under the aegis of Joe Glaser's booking office. In 1962 Essie and Alice were living in the family home, a fine stone house on the South Side of Chicago, around the corner from the Regal Theater, scene of their former triumphs. Bert had just come back to stay with them after living in Arizona for several years. Their home was headquarters for some of their former protégés who were playing engagements in Chicago. By June, 1964, Essie and Bert were dead; Alice took them to Atlanta for burial.

"The Whitman sisters stood for something," says Louis Williams.[15] "They were the ones I was going to build a monument for on Broadway—they knew talent when they saw it and gave hundreds of dancers their first big break." More specifically, the Whitman sisters not only employed comedians who were Buck dancers in the old tent-show tradition, they also featured dancers *as dancers*—a hint of what was to come on Broadway—and sold the show to the public largely on the strength of this dancing. By 1936 the little-known surge of Negro vaudeville was almost ended, but its influence continued undiminished for many years, as a growing number of Negro dancers on Loew's and other circuits adapted material that had first evolved in roadshows, on T.O.B.A., and especially, with *The Whitman Sisters*.

PART FOUR

Tin Pan Alley and Song Lyrics

13 Ballroom Origins

"THE DECADE BETWEEN 1910 and 1920 can be identified primarily," writes Sigmund Spaeth, "as the period in which America went dance mad."[1] Tin Pan Alley never lagged far behind in its exploitation of trends, and if the public wanted dances, it was ready and able to produce innumerable songs "adapted to the ballroom." Among the thousands published in the teens, a few of what might be called "dance-songs with instructions" indirectly aided the survival of vernacular dance because they were derived in part from folk sources and sometimes described how to perform a specific dance.

Before 1910 popular music consisted chiefly of two standard types, happy and sad—"Hail, Hail, the Gang's All Here," or "She's Only a Bird in a Gilded Cage"—and they were not particularly danceable. As Spaeth remarks:

> After 1910 the publishers of popular music became more and more insistent that a song must be danceable in order to achieve real success. In time this became an absolute rule of the industry, and even if a ballad happened to be printed in the free vocal style, it was immediately supplied with a dance orchestration in strict time.[2]

"From 1912 through 1914," according to Sylvia Dannett and Frank Rachel, "over one hundred new dances found their way in and out of our fashionable ballrooms."[3]

None of these dances, however, added much to dancing as an art. During this period a few vernacular dances surfaced, diluted and fragmented, and were adopted by a part of white society. The titles had a significant flavor: Turkey Trot, Grizzly Bear, Monkey Glide, Chicken Scratch, Bunny Hug, Kangaroo Dip—and the lesser known Possum Trot, Bull Frog Hop, The Buzz (like a bee), Scratchin' the Gravel, and so on. Some of these had folk roots. Other kinds appeared, of course, but the animal dances were prominent, as if Uncle Remus had joined high society.

Spurred by war hysteria, people went slumming for their dancing. "Dances that had been going on in the West and South for years invaded and rapidly became popular in the East," writes Tom Fletcher. "Dances that had hitherto been performed mainly in honky-tonks, dance-halls on the levee and in tenderloin districts began to be seen regularly in New York." [4] (The Texas Tommy, for example, traces at least as far back as a Negro cabaret on San Francisco's Barbary Coast.) The "primitive" West led the cultured East.

The Cakewalk, like the earlier Polka and Schottische, had been a strenuous and far from easy dance. Not so the animal dances—they were simple to the point of awkwardness, and for the first time, they permitted what was denounced as "lingering close contact." (In the old-fashioned Waltz you whirled so rapidly that you were fortunate if you simply kept in touch with your partner.) The animal dances spread among a more general public.

One of the earliest of these dances was the Turkey Trot. It varied from city to city and seemed to change weekly, but in general it consisted of a fast, marching one-step, arms pumping at the side, with occasional arm-flappings emulating a crazed turkey. In 1910 the dance reached New York in a show from San Francisco called *Over the River,* accompanied by a tune entitled "Everybody's Doing It." The lyrics contain the repeated phrase, "It's a bear!" at which point the dancers are supposed to lurch like a grizzly bear—another dance from the West which became a hit a year later in the *Follies of 1911.*

Whether or not the Turkey Trot owed anything to the Buzzard Lope of the Southern Negro, the dilution had gone too far to afford much of a resemblance. The name itself was not new, for it appears in the lyrics of the transitional "Pas Ma La" of 1895, where the dancer is advised to go to the World's Fair "and do the Turkey Trot." Nor was the reaction of sober citizens new. "A Paterson, New Jersey, court imposed a fifty-day prison sentence on a young woman for dancing the turkey trot," write Dannett and Rachel. "Fifteen young women were dismissed from a well-known magazine after the editor caught them enjoying the abandoned dance at lunchtime. Turkey trotters incurred the condemnation of churches and respectable people, and in 1914 an official disapproval was issued by the Vatican." [5]

By 1910 *Harper's Weekly* published an article entitled "Where Is Your Daughter This Afternoon?" implying that she might be trotting to hell at an afternoon tea in some hotel—the latest location for dancing.[6] The Turkey Trot was even spreading to the lower echelons of society, for in 1910 the *New York Committee on Amusement and Vacation Resources of Working Girls* condemned the dance as vicious.[7] The hired help were having too much fun.

In a very real sense ballroom dancers Vernon and Irene Castle capitalized on the uproar. In 1907 the smash hit *The Merry Widow* (with Franz Lehar's "Merry Widow Waltz" at the close of the second act), glorified ballroom dancing, and as Cecil Smith observes, "opened the way for Vernon and Irene Castle." [8]

By 1913 the Castles were featured on Broadway, performing the Turkey Trot in *The Sunshine Girl.* "Castle is an acquired taste," wrote one critic about Vernon, "but once acquired, his fantastic distortions and India-rubber gyrations exert a decided fascination." [9]

By 1914 the Castles had discarded the Turkey Trot as lacking in elegance. "They started Castle House, which was sponsored by several important people in New York," say Dannett and Rachel, "and its announced purpose was to turn the tide against 'the orgy that the world indulged in during the vogue of the Turkey Trot.'" [10] Castle House was a studio for instruction in the more genteel varieties of popular dance—a high-class predecessor of "Killer Joe" Piro's busy studio in the 1960's.

The Castles also gave exhibitions for society (a film of their brittle but energetic dancing is available at the Museum of Modern Art in New York City) and promoted a few dances of their own, such as the Castle Walk, which Spaeth describes as "a refinement of the plebian Toddle." [11] (The lady bounced backward, however, a maneuver which some of the more sophisticated Negroes of the day considered ill-mannered.)

The Castles were good ballroom dancers, who substituted a hectic elegance for the easy rough and tumble of the animal dances. In the course of their teaching at Castle House, they formulated certain commandments, which were printed in a book of instructions: "Do not wriggle the shoulders. Do not shake the hips. Do not twist the body. Do not flounce the elbows. Do not pump the arms. Do not hop—glide instead. Avoid low, fantastic, and acrobatic dips . . . Drop the Turkey Trot, the Grizzly Bear, the Bunny Hug, etc. These dances are ugly, ungraceful, and out of fashion." [12] Dancing became much safer with the Castles.

The Castles helped to popularize dancing by making it a fad in high society—a pattern which recurred in 1960 with the Twist. Actually, they enjoyed and danced the animal dances, occasionally learning specific steps from Negro dancers. "A lot of us gave private lessons at homes on Park Avenue," says dancer Ulysses S. Thompson, "during the late teens and twenties—our steps seemed new to white people." [13] Vernon was an amateur jazz drummer, and they both preferred to dance to the accompaniment of James Reese Europe's Negro band with drummer Buddy Gilmore, the admitted source of much of their inspiration. (One of the side effects was that a few Negro musicians were steadily employed by white patrons.) The animal dances continued to flourish.

The Castles left their mark on social dancing. They popularized and may even have "invented" the imperishable Fox Trot—and no dance could be easier to invent or to perform. W. C. Handy tells one of many versions of its creation: "Jim Europe, head of the local Clef Club, was the Castles' musical director. The Castle Walk and One-Step were fast numbers. During breath-catching intermissions, Jim would sit at the piano and play slowly the Memphis Blues. He did this so often that the Castles became intrigued by its rhythm, and Jim asked why they didn't originate a slow dance adaptable to it. The Castles liked the idea and a new dance was introduced. . . ." [14]

Irene Castle is quoted as saying, "It was Jim Europe . . . who suggested the foxtrot to us, and for all I know he invented it." [15] The Fox Trot outlasted all the other dances of the period. By the time Vernon Castle died in 1917 (he enlisted in the Air Force and was killed in the early days of World War I), a new kind of semi-syncopated social dancing was established among many white people in the United States.

Other and perhaps more significant dances were becoming popular, too, on a different level. It is no coincidence that the perennial favorite, "Ballin' the Jack," which was a hit in the Ziegfeld *Follies* of 1913, was composed and written by two Negroes, Chris Smith and Jim Burris, and published in Harlem. "It became so popular," writes E. B. Marks, "that I remember a vaudeville soprano's singing "Come, Come, I Love You Only'—and balling the jack." [16]

The phrase *ballin' the jack,* according to Professor Willis Laurence James, is a railroad expression. *Jack* is the name given to the locomotive by the Negro folk, on the analogy of the indestructible donkey or jackass, while *ballin'* comes from *high balling,* the trainman's hand signal to start rolling. Hence, "ballin' the jack" means traveling fast and having a good time.[17]

The Negro folk had been dancing the various steps incorporated in "Ballin' the Jack" for many years, and Negro professionals had picked them up long before the song was published. "Why, I used to do that dance as a kid," says Eddie Rector. "They wrote a song afterwards." [18] Perry Bradford says he first heard the name around 1909 in Texas.

In any case, by the time it arrived in New York, the dance was considered pretty rough, as the lyrics to James P. Johnson's later tune "Stop It Joe" suggest: "I don't mind being in your company," says the young lady to Joe, "but don't you Eagle Rock or Ball the Jack with me . . . this ain't no hall room, it's a ballroom."

Happily, the song writers revived an ancient formula that helped to make the number a success: The lyrics give instructions on how to dance the steps. Thus, the words of "Ballin' the Jack" constitute capsule choreography:

First you put your two knees close up tight
Then you sway 'em to the left, then you sway
'em to the right

Step around the floor kind of nice and light
Then you twis' around and twis' around with
all your might
Stretch your lovin' arms straight out in space
Then you do the Eagle Rock with style and grace
Swing your foot way 'round then bring it back
Now that's what I call 'Ballin' the Jack'

In performance of course, everything depended upon the ability of the dancer.

The reason Ballin' the Jack was considered better suited to the hall room than the ballroom is clear in the fourth line, where the dancer is told to "twis' around and twis' around" with all his might. In practice, these directions were interpreted—and meant to be interpreted—as rotating the protruding pelvis in a circle (usually with a bounce on the beat), a common Afro-American hip movement.

As James Barton says, "They just put the Georgia Grind into Ballin' the Jack."[19] Afro-American hip movements occur frequently in vernacular dance and turn up under many names, but "Grind" is one of the most widespread. "I am told that the action employed in 'Snake Hip,'" writes Lydia Parrish gently, "is similar to that used in 'Ball the Jack'"[20] and she describes the movements that she witnessed (brought to St. Helena Island, Georgia, "about fifty years ago"), as a "flow of undulating rhythm from chest to heels, with a few rotations of the hip region," adding that she had seen the same dance in the Bahamas and in a film about the Congo entitled *Saunders of the River*.

As for the remaining lyrics in "Ballin' the Jack," the Eagle Rock—as we have seen—goes back to the Negro folk and appears to have been too well known to need description (it consists of thrusting the arms high over the head with a variety of shuffle steps). The further instructions about knee-swaying and foot-swinging suggest movements characteristic of many dances, including the Boogie Woogie—a step that also goes back in time and is associated with an early style of piano playing that surfaced in the thirties. Ballin' the Jack is a well-sustained sequence of vernacular steps.

The tune itself has been revived off and on—with and without words—since its publication in 1913, and has become a standard in the repertory of Dixieland bands. The steps are known, too, by many professional dancers of the old school—but not, until recently, by the coast-to-coast dance studios. "I did Ballin' the Jack for them at the Dancing Masters Association in California a while ago," said Willie Covan in 1960, "and the first thing I knew, every dancing teacher in the country seemed to be teaching it."[21] The appeal of the dance is strong.

At an early date lyrics were created to go with the dances. "The Dance Rhyme was derived from the dance,"[22] wrote Thomas W. Talley in 1922 and—as in the similar example of the Juba discussed in Chapter 4—illustrates his point with a dance called Jonah's Band:

> First of all be it known that there was a 'step' in dancing, originated by some Negro somewhere, called 'Jonah's Band' step . . . The dancers formed a circle placing two or more of their skilled dancers in the middle of it. . . . Some dance leaders, for example, simply called in plain prose—'Dance the Mobile Buck,' others calling for another step would rhyme their call.

The chorus of the song consists of a repetition of the line: "Setch a kickin' up san'! Jonah's Ban'!" to a Charleston rhythm at which point all the dancers execute the same step.

Before each of three choruses other steps are introduced:[23]

Raise yo' right foot, kick it up high,
Knock dat Mobile Buck in de eye . . .

Stan' up, flat foot, Jump dem Bars!
Karo back'ards lak a train o' kyars . . .

Dance 'round, Mistiss, show 'em de p'int;
Dat Nigger don't know how to Coonjaint.

The Karo and Jump Dem Bars seem to have disappeared without a trace, although the latter is self-explanatory, and a flat-footed bar-jump is typically Afro-American. Old-timers say the Mobile Buck is an ancestor of the common Buck, which evolved into the Time Step, while the prolific Coonjaint—once a rhythmic shuffle performed by roustabouts loading riverboats and a dance observed in Congo Square—later became identified with the tune of a children's play-party song ("I love coffee, I love tea . . .").

In its early folk form the dance-song with instructions is a *group* dance performed in a circle with a few "experts" in the center—and the emphasis is upon what they do. An apparently unlimited number of locally known steps are inserted and improvised upon by the experts. The entire performance is held together by the chorus of dancers forming the circle and executing the step that gives the dance its title. The description of inserted steps is brief if it occurs at all (in the Juba, the inserted steps are merely named), and little editorializing occurs as to its purported origin, nature, or popularity—gimmicks that became common later, when the dances were commercialized.

A transitional dance-song entitled "La Pas Ma La" (Isaac Goldberg says that the phrase comes from the French *pas mêlé*, or mixed step) was published in 1895—perhaps the dance introduced by Ernest Hogan and his *Georgia Graduates* as the Pasmala. As one of the early efforts to combine folk steps with topical dances of the time, the "Pas Ma La" describes its title step in the chorus:[24]

Hand upon yo' head, let your mind roll far,

Back, back, back and look at the stars,
Stand up rightly, dance it brightly,
That's the Pas Ma La.

Old-timers recall the step clearly. "It was a comedy dance," says Walter Crumbley. "You walked forward and then hopped back three steps with knees bent" [25]—as the directions "back, back, back" indicate. The hand on head and mind-rolling appear to be optional variations.

The "Pas Ma La" was sometimes confused with an animal dance, which may have aided its survival, for by 1898 a song entitled "The Possum-a-la" was published, one of a series of dance-songs that popped up with titles such as the "Possum Trot" around 1910. "The Possum Trot," says Perry Bradford, "was a dance which consisted of a series of fast, flat hops." [26] Here the folk tradition which favored a flat-footed style, seems to have become stronger, while blending with the Tin Pan Alley version.

Again, other steps are introduced before each chorus in four verses of the "Pas Ma La":

Fus yo' say, my niggah git yo' gun
Shoot-a dem ducks an' away you run,
Now my little coon come-a down the shute
With the Saint-a Louis pass and Chicago Salute.

The literal directions in the first two lines in which the dancer acts out the shooting of a duck is typical of many vernacular dances and finds an analogue in a rock-and-roll dance of the early nineteen-sixties: The Peter Gunn, emulating a fast-shooting private eye on television. The St. Louis Pass and Chicago Salute are apparently topical concoctions of Tin Pan Alley referring to the World's Fairs.

Another introductory quatrain contains references to three more dances, which are better known:

Fus yo' say, my niggah, Bumbishay
Then turn 'round and go the other way
To the World's Fair and do the Turkey Trot
Do not dat coon tink he look very hot.

The variously spelled Bumbishay (mentioned along with the Eagle Rock, the Mooche, and Hootchy-Ma-Cootch—which is the Congo Grind—in pianist Jelly Roll Morton's "Animule Ball") was known in New Orleans, according to Paul Barbarin, as the Fanny Bump [27]—which needs no explanation. Going to the World's Fair was a strut ("you put both feet together and move forward on your toes," says Ida Forsyne [28]), while the appearance of the Turkey Trot here, about fifteen years before it became a hit in New York, suggests that it came from the folk.

In spite of the atrocious dialect and Jim Crow sentiments, the lyrics of the "Pas Ma La" reveal the nature of the change taking place in the dance-song as it became commercialized. It is clearly no longer a *group* dance with improvising soloists, but rather a *couple* dance with fixed steps in definite order. Although the verse names new steps, and the chorus describes the main step, the aim is simply to sell the dance.

During the early teens and after, the dance-song with instructions multiplied rapidly, and a few, chiefly by Negro composers, drew upon folk sources. These few became more influential than their numbers indicate, for although their popularity was limited at first to the Negro public, they gradually—as in the case of "Ballin' the Jack"—reached a white audience. This led the way to the more enduring dances of the twenties and thirties that are often named and sometimes described in the earlier dance-songs. Tin Pan Alley was contributing indirectly to the surfacing of vernacular dance movements.

14 The Song Writer: Perry Bradford—I

THE LYRICS to the tunes of pianist-composer Perry Bradford furnish outstanding examples of the contribution during the teens of Negro dance-songs to popular dance.[1] His songs had instructions in the lyrics on how to perform many dances of the folk.

Born around 1890 and raised in Atlanta, Bradford toured the South and parts of the North from 1908 to 1919 in a song-and-dance act billed as "Bradford and Jeanette." At first he says he booked the act himself and later, along with another act, *Stringbeans and Sweetie May,* became one of the highest paid attractions—always excepting *The Whitman Sisters*—on T.O.B.A. After 1920, when he hit the jackpot with Mamie Smith's recording of his "Crazy Blues," Bradford concentrated mainly on composing more blues.

Bradford came by his composing of dance-songs naturally enough. "Touring the South, I saw a million steps in a million tonks," he says. "The dancers had all kinds of names and no names for them, and I just took over the steps I liked and put them in my act. Once in a while, if the step went over big, I'd work up a tune and lyrics that explained how to do it, have it printed, and sell it to the audience after my act." In this way, elements of vernacular dance surfaced in sheet music.

Like W. C. Handy, Bradford was smart enough to write his tunes down and try to get them published. And again like Handy, he had an uphill climb. "The publishers wouldn't take no songs from colored people then," says Bradford, "so I had them printed up privately and sold them for a nickel apiece in theaters."

At the same time Bradford, who was nothing if not persistent, haunted the music publishers' offices night and day. (His nickname, "Mule," came from his piano-vocal specialty in vaudeville, "Whoa, Mule!" but the title fit in other ways.) When the popular dance craze arrived with the Castles, and "Ballin' the Jack" demonstrated that numbers by Negro songwriters could make a profit, the song publishers literally changed their tunes. Bradford never made big money with his dance-songs—some of them never caught on at all—but he was far ahead of his times and pioneered in a *genre* which became popular in the late teens and after that.

The lyrics of Bradford's dance-songs read like a rollcall of vernacular dance. He dates one of his first numbers, "The Bullfrog Hop," around 1909 and recalls the lyrics:

First you commence to wiggle from side to side
Get 'way back and do the Jazzbo Glide
Then you do the Shimmy with plenty of pep
Stoop low, yeah Bo', and watch your step
Do the Seven Years' Itch and the Possum Trot
Scratch the Gravel in the vacant lot
Then you drop like Johnny on the Spot
That's the Bullfrog Hop

"I closed my act with that dance when I was playing burlesque," he adds. Lean and wiry in 1962, Bradford could still demonstrate the routine with agility.

Of the steps mentioned, the Jazzbo Glide is a simple couple step with fingers snapping, a favorite of Bradford's which never got off the ground; the Shimmy consists of shaking the shoulders—at the very least—and became a national craze in 1922, when Gilda Gray introduced it in the Ziegfeld *Follies;* the Seven Years' Itch—an ancient and universal gesture that consists of scratching the body in rhythm—is still used in "new" dances today, like the Mambo; the Possum Trot is a series of "fast, flat hops," says Bradford, who used it as the title of another dance-song in 1915; and Scratching the Gravel is the ancient Sand, according to Willie Covan, although Bradford employed it in 1917 as the title of a new dance-song with a routine all its own.

Of course, in "The Bullfrog Hop" the big hit-to-be is the Shimmy. Both Mae West and Gilda Gray have eagerly confessed that they invented it, and their claims have been repeated until they have become a part of the folklore of "show biz." Mae West's version, as she takes pains to point out, antedates Gilda Gray's by eight months: She introduced it in Arthur Hammerstein's *Sometime* on the fourth of October, 1919—precisely ten years after Bradford's use of it. In her autobiography she says that she had seen a crude version called the Shimmy-Sha-Wabble on a slumming trip to Chicago's South Side—"big black men with razor-slashed faces, fancy high yellows and beginner browns . . . we were terribly amused by it"—and perfected the movement herself just for fun. The result was—and still is—literally unbelievable. "I had suddenly started a great new dance fad in respectable circles." She gave it up because, as she writes, "Who wants to make a career of the shakes?" [2]

Gilda Gray's version is sweeter, and at the same time, more ambitious. "The shimmy is really a sacred dance dedicated to Cupid," [3] she once explained, while *The New York Times* states that the dance was her own "spontaneous invention in John Letzka's Saloon in Cudahy, Wisconsin."[4] (This would have been sometime in 1916 when she was fourteen years old and billed as Maryanna Michalska.) *Time* magazine retails the standard version: "I was just shaking my chemise," Maryanna explained to a popeyed customer, but her pronunciation was a little awkward, and the Shimmy got its name." [5]

In an interview in *The Dance* magazine, Miss Gray denies that the Negro had anything to do with it—and she may be right in the wrong sense—"There weren't any Negroes in Milwaukee," she states, shifting the location of her invention.[6] In any event, Sophie Tucker changed Maryanna's name, but not the name of the dance, and brought her to New York in 1919, where three years later she started a new dance craze among the white middle classes.

To the Negro folk, Gilda Gray's success—if they heard about or saw it—could only have been cause for wonder why "white folks" had suddenly become enamoured of an old dance, especially in such an awkward version. There is good evidence that the Shimmy—and the Shake and the Quiver—trace as far back as the Shika of Nigeria (see Chapter 2), aided in its surfacing in the North by the popularity of the European Hootchy-Kootchy, or belly dance, which Little Egypt made famous at the Chicago World's Fair in 1893.[7]

The evidence for the earlier appearance of the Shimmy in the South is overwhelming. Wilbur Sweatman thought the name had been coined around 1900 by the legendary New Orleans pianist, Tony Jackson. Coot Grant saw it in a Birmingham honky-tonk in 1901; Perry Bradford says, "In Atlanta they called it the Shake, and I saw it for several years before 1909, when I put it into 'Bull Frog Hop' "; dancer Nettie Compton says, "We did the Shimmy in San Francisco in 1910 and later called it the Shimme-Sha-Wobble—most dancers put a tremble in it and some shook everything, but I never exaggerated those things"; [8] and Spencer Williams finally capitalized on its popularity by incorporating the dance into a dance-song called "The Shim-Me-Sha-Wabble" in 1917: "I can't play no piano, can't sing no blues, but I can Shim-me-sha-wabble from my head to my shoes."

Ethel Waters writes that she used "Shim-Me-Sha-Wabble" at the time of its publication as one of her specialties: "When the boys played that I'd put my hands on my hips and work my body fast, without moving my feet." In the true folk tradition, Miss Waters seems to have incorporated the

Shake and the Quiver into her performance. Her "fast and furious wrigglings" were so good that when she temporarily lost her voice she kept her job at Barney Gordon's saloon in Philadelphia "because I could shimmy so good." [9] The Shimmy had been around a long time.

When he was working with the *New Orleans Minstrels,* Bradford says he composed another dance-song, "Rules and Regulations," which he had printed in 1911. The lyrics of this tune furnish an additional insight, since narrator "Slewfoot Jim," as social arbiter, enumerates the dances which are forbidden:

The first rule was now you can Jazzbo Glide
You must do it neat and have a gal by your side,
Scratchin' the Gravel and Ballin' the Jack
If you do them rough dances you mustn't come back,
If you Shimmy inside you will Wabble outside
If you break these rules now Jim will break your hide. . . .

The next rule was you can Stew the Rice
Do the Bullfrog Hop and you must do it nice,
On the Puppy's Tail so neat and slow
Get 'way back and do the Georgia Bo-Bo,
No Shimmy dancing on the inside
Or there will be some cryin' and a mighty slow drive,
No rough dancing, smile and grin,
Rules and Regulations, signed Slewfoot Jim.

Of the permissible dances, the Jazzbo Glide is Bradford's favorite failure, plugged in his earlier "Bullfrog Hop"; Stewing the Rice he cannot quite remember, although he made it into a routine and published it in 1914; Stepping on the Puppy's Tail is performed by moving each foot alternately backward "like a horse pawing the ground"; and the Georgia Bo-Bo is a grind with vernacular hip movements—which make some of the forbidden dances seem tame.

On the other hand, the Shimmy, although unknown on Broadway at the time this dance-song was composed, eventually became the most popular of them all. Presumably in 1908, when Bradford composed "Rules and Regulations," the Ballin' the Jack routine included hip movements, which survive in the line "twis' around with all your might," while the Shimmy was performed in the South with hair-raising quivers and shakes. Bradford did not know—or care—how innocuous the average white dancer could make these steps appear. Others subsequently made their fortunes with Ballin' the Jack and the Shimmy.

In 1912 Bradford scored his first small success, when a young and slender Ethel Waters sang his new song "Messin' Around" on T.O.B.A. This dance consists of one fairly complex step instead of a routine, and the verse attempts to explain in some detail where and how the step originated. "A gal called Mojo Queen [*mojo* is a voodoo charm], the Shimmyn'st gal I ever seen," went down to the Virgin Islands and "learned the native style." The chorus describes the step:

Now anyone can learn the knack
Put your hands on your hips and bend your back,
Stand in one spot, nice and light
Twist around with all your might,
Messin' round, they call that messin' round

Here, as in "Ballin' the Jack," which came a year later, the key word is "twist": Hands go on hips, the pelvis—and backside—move in a wide horizontal circle while the body bounces on the toes with each beat.

"Messin' Around," partly because it was a twelve-bar blues with a catchy melody, became quite popular with Negro audiences. (Bradford knew blues and tried to sell them before the twenties with less success than W. C. Handy.) It also became a standard selection in the repertory of Negro jazz bands.

In 1926—fourteen years later—the dance is incorporated but not described in the routine for DeSylva, Brown, and Henderson's big hit, "The Black Bottom." Messin' Around is referred to in *The Dance* as "The Louisiana Mess Around," where Elise Marcus in a series on "Low Down Dancing" (illustrated by Buddy Bradley) gives the inside information that it is performed: ". . . with hands on hips. Rock on heels, hips moving in a circle. This keeps the center region of the body moving, while the rest must remain quiet." [10] Such careful control of "the center region" was difficult for many dancers who had never heard of the step, and Miss Marcus failed to point out that a steatopygic performer has a distinct advantage.

"Ballin' the Jack," by Smith and Burris, became a hit in the *Follies of 1913,* a year after the appearance of "Messin' Around." The market for dance-songs began to boom. In the same year Bradford composed "The Baltimore Buzz," based on a dance step he had seen in Baltimore (not the more popular Buzz, which imitated a bee). During the next two years Bradford also had "Stewin' the Rice" (1914) and "The Possum Trot" (1915) printed, steps used in his earlier dance-songs. "It cost about eight dollars to get a song printed up then," says Bradford.

In 1917 the Negro composer Shelton Brooks published "Walkin' the Dog," which became almost as popular as "Ballin' the Jack" and a standard with Dixieland bands. "He got that from me," says Bradford with unusual equanimity. "I saw the step in Kansas City around 1909—everbody who went West at that time must have seen it—and put it into my act with Jeanette Taylor; we called it C'mon Hon and Walk the Dog with Me. Later, Shelton Brooks was on the same bill with us, saw it, and put into a song—although he left out our ending, where Jeanette did the Quiver." Since the dance was ancient, well known, and he had not published a version, Bradford had no valid objections, and again, no luck.

The lyrics to "Walkin' the Dog," including the phrase "It's a bear," which appeared in the Tin Pan Alley hit "Everybody's Doing It" (1910), describe a combination of much older steps. In cheerful disregard of the facts, the verse stresses the sudden popularity of the dance, "originated for about ten days," and the chorus describes the routine:

Get 'way back and snap your fingers
Get over Sally one and all,
Grab your gal and don't you linger
Do that Slow Drag 'round the hall
Do that step the Texas Tommy
Drop, like you're sittin' on a log
Rise slow, that will show
The dance called Walkin' the Dog.

Backing up and snapping fingers is more of a gesture than a step, as is dropping and rising, but Get Over Sally is a jump to the side, arms down, and fingers pointing at the floor; the Slow Drag—a shuffle—is the ancient and close couple dance, which traces back to New Orleans and beyond; and the Texas Tommy, a hit around 1910 at Lew Purcell's Negro cabaret on the Barbary Coast, is a "kick and a hop about three times on each foot followed by a slide"—according to Ethel Williams, who helped to make it popular in New York in 1913.[11]

With "Walkin' the Dog," the gradual divergence from the early dance-songs of folk origin becomes clearer. It is definitely a *couple* dance, rather than a group dance, with a full routine leaving little or no room for improvisation. In order to sell it, every step is specified. Most of the movements must have been new to the white public. This could be an advantage, however, since instruction was necessary, and the dance studios could supply it. What brands it as Tin Pan Alley once and for all, however, is the assumption in the verse—and as it turned out, a correct one—that the public would want to be in on the latest craze.

15 The Song Writer: Perry Bradford—II

THE YEAR 1917 was a big year for successful dance-songs. Spencer Williams's "Shim-Me-Sha-Wabble" was published and another Negro composer and arranger, W. Benton Overstreet assembled a number entitled "The Jazz Dance" (subtitled "Song and Foxtrot") which named the Texas Tommy, the Eagle Rock, the Buzz, and the Shimmy-She (it had to rhyme with *bee*) in a lengthy routine. All of these steps had been used before, and Overstreet was apparently improving his chances by calling it a fox-trot.

In the same year Perry Bradford sold his "Scratchin' the Gravel" to publisher Charles K. Harris, whom he admired because Harris was always available to Negro song writers.[1] "I sang the song and did the dance and Mr. Harris said, 'Man, that's great!' and called in Jack Yellen to make it commercial. Yellen added a few words to my lyrics and I sold it to Harris for twenty-five dollars." Yellen was just starting his career at the time, and although he had a contract, Bradford doubts if Yellen was paid very much, either.

The verse of "Scratchin' the Gravel" takes the form of an announcement: This is the dance that Slewfoot Jim introduced at a jazzband ball down in Johnson's Hall, and the chorus outlines a routine:

First you Mooch to the left and you Mooch to the right,
You do the Shimmie to your heart's delight,
And then you whirl yourself around and 'round
Goin' down, goin' down, till you're near the ground,
Now you sway at the knees like a tree in the breeze
Then buzz around just like the bumblebees,
Then you do the Sooey around the hall,
That's nothin' but Scratchin' the Gravel, that's all.

The basic step in Scratchin' the Gravel is the Sooey, a short sliding motion alternately on each foot ("I'd call it a two-step with a dip," says Ida Forsyne [2]), and in performance just about any step could be added as long as the performer returned to the Sooey at the end of each chorus. "I first heard that name," says Bradford, "in Louisville."

Of the other movements in the number—the Shimmy has already been discussed—the most important is the Mooche, which is a variation of the Congo Grind combined with a forward step. In *The Dance* eleven years later, Elise Marcus gives the following directions for the Mooche: "Shuffle forward with both feet. Hips come first, feet follow"—and then she adds with a hint of desperation, "Be sure not to lose the rhythm." [3] The Buzz, often used as an exit step, is a shufflelike predecessor of Trucking, in which the arms are held out horizontally but bend straight down at the elbows, with fingers fluttering in imitation of a bee. The rest—whirling, swaying, and sinking—are perhaps too common to have special names.

The germ of the last of Bradford's dance-songs, "The Original Black Bottom Dance" printed in 1919, came from "Jacksonville Rounders' Dance," which he composed in 1907. "It was a dance they were doing in Jacksonville 'way back," says Bradford, "but people didn't like the title because 'rounder' meant pimp, so I wrote some new lyrics in 1919 and renamed it 'The Original Black Bottom Dance.'" (The Jacksonville Rounders' Dance may have been one of the earliest-known versions of the Pimp's Walk used in *West Side Story*—shoulders hunched, fingers popping.)

The Black Bottom was a well-known dance among semiurban Negro folk in the South long before 1919. Both Henry "Rubberlegs" Williams and Jodie Edwards of the *Butterbeans and Susie* team are sure that the name came from a Negro section in Atlanta. "That dance is as old as the hills," says Rubberlegs, "done all over the South—why, I remember doing it myself around 1915." [4] A similar dance with many variations had been common in earlier tent shows, and before they reached T.O.B.A. in the early teens, *Bradford and Jeanette* were using it as a finale.

The Black Bottom became a craze, second only to the Charleston, when it was introduced by Ann Pennington in George White's *Scandals of 1926.* (Miss Pennington never claimed to have invented it, perhaps because there was truth in the widespread belief that a Negro dancer, Freddie Taylor, taught it to her. "I introduced Ann Pennington to Freddie Taylor," says Mae Barnes, "and she gave him a Cord automobile.") [5] According to Bradford, George White saw the dance in a Harlem show, *Dinah* (1924), produced by Irving C. Miller, bought it, and hired three white composers to write a song for it. The result was the DeSylva, Brown, and Henderson hit.

Bradford's lyrics and the lyrics of DeSylva, Brown, and Henderson contrast sharply. Unlike the later version, Bradford's directions are explicit:

Hop down front and then you Doodle back,
Mooch to your left and then you Mooch to the right
Hands on your hips and do the Mess Around,
Break a Leg until you're near the ground
Now that's the Old Black Bottom Dance.

Now listen folks, open your ears,
This rhythm you will hear—
Charleston was on the afterbeat—
Old Black Bottom'll make you shake your feet,
Believe me it's a wow.
Now learn this dance somehow
Started in Georgia and it went to France
It's got everybody in a trance
It's a wing, that Old Black Bottom Dance.

This is essentially the professional Black Bottom routine ("Doodle" means slide) with Break a Leg (a hobbling step) instead of the more obvious slapping of the backside.

By contrast the DeSylva, Brown, and Henderson song ("They didn't know no dances," says Bradford) proclaims in the verse that the dance "will soon be renowned"—a prophecy that for once proved to be correct—and adds that the dance originated on the mud flats of the Swanee River, a statement that seems to have been accepted thereafter. In the chorus the dance is described as a "new twister," a "raggedy trot," with a movement "just like a worm"—these are the entire directions, except for a wild misstatement toward the end, referring to the dance as a "new rhythm." The rhythm of the Black Bottom is based solidly on the Charleston.

"Like the Charleston and all the other dances that were too abandoned in their early phases," write Sylvia Dannett and Frank Rachel—repeating and often-voiced comment—"the Black Bottom went through a refining stage in which the movements and steps were modified until it finally emerged as a dance suitable for the ballroom." [6] Unfortunately, this is true. The chief gesture that survived on the ballroom floor was a genteel slapping of the backside, along with a few hops forward and back.

Bradford's "Original Black Bottom Dance" mentions the Charleston as already out of fashion, and underlines the reference with a strong Charleston accent in the melody. (His tune is actually a twelve-bar blues, approximately twenty years before the name and form were recognized by white musicians as basic to jazz.) Although many people have claimed they invented it, there is general agreement that, four years after Bradford's dance-song, the Charleston first reached a fairly large public in the all-Negro show, *Runnin' Wild* (1923), where the chorus line danced to James P. Johnson and Cecil Mack's celebrated tune, while the rest of the cast clapped and stamped out the accents (see Chapter 20).

Here again, the evidence for the African origin and early appearance of the Charleston in the South is convincing. LeRoi Jones says it comes from an Ashanti ancestor dance, and there is evidence to support this statement.[7] Thaddeus Drayton, born in Charleston, saw the dance when he went back home for a visit in 1903. "They dolled it up later," he says.[8]

"It's a real old Southern dance," says Noble Sissle, "I remember learning it in Savannah around 1905." [9]

Coot Grant saw it upon her return from Europe in 1909,[10] and by 1911 the Whitman sisters were using the Charleston in their act.

They were using it around 1913 as "a regulation cotillion step," according to James P. Johnson; "it had many variations—all danced to the rhythm that everybody knows now." [11]

Dancer Billy Maxey saw it in 1917 and was giving lessons to movie stars out on the West Coast by 1919.[12] "The first contest I ever won was a Charleston contest," says Rubberlegs Williams. "It was in Atlanta in 1920."

Various night clubs and stage productions, on and off Broadway—including the Negro musicals, *Liza* (1922) and *How Come* (1923) with *Chappelle and Stinnette,* as well as the Ziegfeld *Follies of 1923*—featured the dance, but *Runnin' Wild* put it across. Later, George Raft at Texas Guinan's night club ("The fastest dancer in this sort of thing I've ever seen," said Fred Astaire [13]; "feet of mud," said Shirley "Snowball" Jordan, the fine Lindy dancer from New Jersey [14]), Ginger Rogers, billed as "Queen of the Charleston," and Joan Crawford in the film *Our Dancing Daughters* started their careers as Charleston dancers, as did many others.

In the history of American popular dance, the Charleston marks two new departures: For the first time a step was taken over generally by men (the Shimmy had been considered too effeminate) and again, as Abel Green and Joe Laurie, Jr., observed: "the distinction between popular dances to watch, and popular dances to dance, was wiped out." [15] For the first time, too, ballroom and tap dancing merged on the professional level as tap dancers worked out a tap Charleston.

Dance critic Roger Pryor Dodge, who remembers a policeman in St. Louis at the height of the craze directing traffic and doing the Charleston, feels that the Charleston was one of the great folk contributions to American dance. "Out of what may be hundreds of steps a few . . ." he says, "have been taken up. . . . The greatest step was the Charleston; it is truly generic in character. When done to a Charleston rhythm in the music it could be infinitely varied without losing any of the quality . . ." [16]

The Charleston didn't last very long in the twenties—it was soon superseded by the Black Bottom—but unlike the Black Bottom, it has been revived many times. Something about the outgoing exuberance of its gestures, a kind of kicking over the traces, has a continuing appeal.

As a description of the dance, the "Charleston" lyrics are not very helpful: "Some dance, some prance . . . Lord, how you can shuffle." The brief mention in Bradford's "Original Black Bottom Dance," which describes it as "on the afterbeat," is not much better, although it gets to the heart of the rhythm. After all, Bradford was not trying to describe the Charleston —to his lasting regret—and although he knew the dance well and could easily have put it into a dance-song, he never did.

The days of the dance-song with folk material were passing. (A recording by Claude Hopkins and orchestra entitled "Music of the Early Jazz Dances," 20th Century Fox 3009, documents a wide variety of these tunes.) It had never been more than a thin thread in a huge musical tapestry, where a catchy melody was always more successful. The teens were an age of song-pluggers who struggled to persuade some stage, vaudeville, or cabaret entertainer to sing their songs. If Sophie Tucker, Blossom Seeley, Nora Bayes, Belle Baker, or any one of a number of performers adopted a song, the composer might have a hit. But the composers who knew folk-based dances—and most of them were Negroes, a fringe group who lacked money and connections—could not compete successfully in Tin Pan Alley.

Further, as the dance craze moderated—or perhaps as people became accustomed to taking dancing lessons—the demand for dance-songs faded. The practice of including instructions in the lyrics of a song dwindled and gradually hardened into a meaningless formula. Every show opening on Broadway wanted a hit dance of its own and usually paid someone to construct it. The description of the dances became less exact—there frequently wasn't much to describe—while the emphasis was placed on the fancied origins, novelty, and popularity of the yet-to-be-presented number.

Thus, "down on your heels, up on your toes" is the sum total of instructions offered in "The Varsity Drag." The optimistic lyricist of the mid-thirties hit, "Truckin'," begins: "They had to have something new, a dance to do, up here in Harlem—so, someone started Truckin'." His optimism was well founded, but since the step was as ancient as the Shuffle, his information was faulty.

In the thirties Don Redman and his orchestra recorded "Shakin' the African" in which Redman himself whispered an effective vocal panning other dances and stressing the sudden popularity of this new dance in Harlem—"It's really *in* there," he sings hoarsely, which wasn't quite true. "As a matter of fact," he said, "I never saw anybody dance it—some writer brought in the tune, and I just recorded it. A little later, the *Amsterdam News* printed an item to the effect that I had just composed a new hit, 'The Joe Louis Truck.'" (This was before "Truckin'" became popular.) "I was on the road with my band at the time," says Redman, "I didn't know anything about it—so I wrote the tune and nothing happened." [17]

With the popularity of the phonograph, and around 1920, the discovery of a Negro market for the blues, Negro composers broke into the business and even started their own publishing houses. Perry Bradford's "Crazy

Blues," sung by Mamie Smith—who was unknown to the white public—sold in great quantities in Negro neighborhoods. Dance-songs were forgotten as it became clear that the road to success was paved with songs that, as W.C. Handy demonstrated, contained a tinge of blueness in the melody.

The link with the folk became strongest in the music and message of the blues, while the dance withered. And yet the vernacular dances that had surfaced—the Shimmy, the Charleston (and later on, the Lindy, or Jitterbug)—whether performed by white or Negro dancers, survived and prospered through innumerable variations, reinterpretations, revisions, and revivals. (White professionals still had difficulty with vernacular hip movements—although a few who mastered some part of them, like Mae West, Gilda Gray, and Ann Pennington, created a sensation.) Perhaps because they allowed room for improvisation and at the same time had real character and style when performed to jazz rhythms, the vernacular dances survived, while other dances disappeared.

The vernacular dances, however, had to battle public opinion. In a typical dispatch to the New Orleans *States* in 1922, the Morality League denounced the "cherry pickers, tack-hammers, cheek-pressers, hip-swingers, and lemon-rollers of the fierce jazz dance invaders," and pressed for an "anti-vulgar dance ordinance." Generalissimo Leslie Schroeder, president of the league, urged boys and girls to sign a pledge and dedicate themselves to bringing about the death of jazz. At the time he had enrolled one girl.[18]

On Broadway a dance might be linked to a new tune—especially in musicals—and the lyrics might attempt some description of the dance, but the over-all message was merely a feverish recommendation. The listener is no longer urged to participate—he is merely a spectator whose fantasies are perhaps nudged. In the film *Flying Down to Rio* (1933), the "Carioca" tells the audience that it is "a new rhythm, a blue rhythm that sighs." As directions for performing the dance, the lyrics are meaningless, and besides, Ginger Rogers and Fred Astaire are already executing steps that the audience would never dream of attempting.

PART FIVE

Broadway and the Reviewers

16 *Williams and Walker* and the Beginnings of Vernacular Dance on Broadway

"BERT WILLIAMS doesn't exactly dance, that is, in the orthodox style," wrote a critic in the Boston *Traveller* in 1909, "he just wiggles his legs, crooks his knees, falls over his feet, bends his back." [1]

"The fact is that Williams is awkward on his feet," theorized another critic in the *Green Book* of 1912, ". . . by sheer hard work he evolved a series of grotesque slides and glides, the very awkwardness of which constituted their chief merit." [2]

In those days, critics were hard-pressed in commenting upon American vernacular dances—the Shuffle, the Strut, and especially the hip movements of the Grind—and resorted regularly to the word *grotesque* as well as elaborate theories to explain it. They even managed to suggest that Bert Williams was a great dancer because he could not dance.

Actually Williams was what became known as an "eccentric" dancer, performing in the catch-all style of Southern tent-show comedians, whose one and only aim was to attract attention. "He was doing a lazy grind, or Mooche," says the great actor-dancer James Barton, who idolized Williams and later startled Broadway with his own version. "It was popular among Negroes in the South, with rotary hip-slinging and maybe a hop or shuffle." [3] At the time and to white audiences, the dancing of Bert Williams seemed to be a clumsy but endearing mistake.

Vernacular dance took a long time surfacing on Broadway, which was becoming the center of show business in the United States toward the end of the nineteenth century. In the early days groups of Negro dancers had been inserted in various white productions: Harrigan and Hart's *Cordelia's Aspirations* used several in a number entitled "Sam Johnson's Cakewalk" in 1883; the *Passing Show*, one of the first revues, included "a dozen colored youths" in a plantation dance in 1894.[4] Broadway shows were still dominated by European models, however, and when Negroes appeared, they were also forced into the usual stereotypes of minstrelsy.

Musical comedy was the path through which Negro talent found its best opportunity for expression. A blend of American farce-comedy with British comic opera and burlesque, musical comedy was born in 1894, according to Cecil Smith, when the English production of *A Gaiety Girl*, with its own line of chorus girls, opened in New York. In addition to plot and characterization, musical comedy began to employ "vernacular types of song, dance, and subject matter"—an area in which Negro entertainers had much to offer.

"In 1897 a brilliant period for Negro entertainment, lasting something more than a brief decade, was inaugurated," writes Marian Hannah Winter. "It produced musical comedies or extravaganzas which assembled the talents of Will Marion Cook, Ernest Hogan, Will Vodery, Paul Laurence Dunbar, Ada Walker, Jesse Shipp, Bob Cole, and many others. The bright particular stars were the famous team of Williams and Walker."[5] This period was sparked by ragtime and the worldwide popularity of the Cakewalk.

The break with the minstrel pattern had begun a few years earlier. In 1889 *The Creole Show*, one of the first productions to discard blackface makeup, opened in Boston and played several seasons in New York at the old Standard Theater on Greeley Square. A Negro cast, organized by white manager Sam T. Jack, featured a line of sixteen chorus girls—thus anticipating one of the chief attractions of *A Gaiety Girl*—plus a minstrel circle of women including the interlocutor.[6]

One practical result of adding women to the show was the new emphasis on dancing in couples. The beautiful Dora Dean made her first hit in this show, doing a cakewalk. There she met her future husband-partner, Charles Johnson, with whom she went on to become one of the few Negro acts on the Keith circuit.

Meanwhile, a few Negro shows still cast in the minstrel mold were arriving in New York. *The South before the War* came North from Louisville in 1891 with twelve-year-old Bill Robinson in a bit part, and played the burlesque houses for a few seasons.[7] (At that time true burlesque consisted of a travesty on some well-known romance, play, opera, or legend.) In 1895 *The Octoroons*, organized by white manager John W. Isham in New York City—where most shows thereafter were assembled—featured girls in the leading roles.[8] The show closed with a "Cakewalk Jubilee."

Then, in 1896, Isham's *Oriental America* broke away from the burlesque houses and became the first production with a Negro cast to open on Broadway.[9] Spurred by the success of singer Black Patti, this show introduced a medley of operatic selections in the third part, instead of the usual cakewalk finale. The cast sang solos and choruses from *Carmen, Martha, Il Trovatore, Faust,* and *Rigoletto,* and cut out the dancing—which may help to explain why the show soon closed.

By 1898 several pioneering efforts bore fruit. Bob Cole, who had written the book for the traveling company of *Black Patti's Troubadours,* produced his own show, *A Trip to Coontown,* which ran for three seasons. Besides being the first show owned and operated entirely by Negroes, *A Trip to Coontown* had characterization and plot and was, in the words of James Weldon Johnson, "the first Negro musical comedy." [10]

There is strong disagreement here. Bandleader Noble Sissle, who saw the show, states flatly that *A Trip to Coontown* was an operetta based on European models, and Cole's later productions—*The Shoofly Regiment* (1906) and *The Red Moon* (1908)—bear Sissle out.[11] In any event, the customary Cakewalk was omitted, and the show was a moderate success. Cole and his partner, J. Rosamund Johnson, soon became headliners in big-time vaudeville, went abroad, and collaborated on the writing of still more operettas in which they were featured.

The summer of 1898, however, did produce some remarkable dancing. It occurred in a sketch, with music by Will Marion Cook and lyrics by Paul Laurence Dunbar, entitled *Clorindy—The Origin of the Cakewalk,* which appeared on Broadway at the Casino Roof Garden.[12]

Clorindy featured the Negro actor-comedian-dancer Ernest Hogan, whose real name was Reuben Crowder (he changed it because Irish comedians were popular at the time). Born in Kentucky, Hogan came up the hard way, playing in various "Tom" (that is, *Uncle Tom*) and minstrel shows in the South, where his fame as a comedian obscured his reputation as a dancer.

During the early nineties, in a minstrel troupe named *The Georgia Graduates,* he scored a success introducing a dance step, the Pasmala—a walk forward plus three backward hops with incidental gestures. "Hogan was a fine eccentric dancer," says author-actor Flournoy Miller, who wrote skits for him. "Among other things, he did a wonderful imitation of a crab and a fish." [13] At one time or another, Hogan played with the best-known roadshows, including *Black Patti's Troubadours* and *The Smart Set.* He reached stardom in *Clorindy.*

Many old-timers who saw Hogan say that he was the best dancing-comedian who ever lived, although Bert Williams was the idol of the era. "Hogan was a notable exception among blackface comedians," writes James Weldon Johnson. "His comic effects did not depend upon the caricature created by the use of burnt cork and a mouth exaggerated by paint. His mobile face was capable of laughter-provoking expressions that were irresistible, notwithstanding the fact that he was a very good-looking man." [14]

Flournoy Miller says flatly: "Hogan was the greatest of all colored showmen," and composer Eubie Blake agrees enthusiastically. "The greatest performer," says Luckey Roberts, "that I ever saw." [15]

In 1896 Hogan committed what proved to be the unpardonable sin of composing the hit, "All Coons Look Alike to Me," which was sung again and again by entertainers—black and white alike—of the nineties and later. It helped start the "coon-song" craze during the depression of the nineties and gave employment to many singers. As objections to the epithet "coon" gathered momentum, and the song continued to be popular, Hogan was savagely criticized.

"Poor Hogan!" writes the composer and publisher E. B. Marks.

> As his race rose in the world, they became as sensitive to slights as the Irishman who egged *The Playboy of the Western World,* or the rabbis who believe all entrance examinations are specially directed against Jews. The verse of "All Coons Look Alike to Me" was forgotten. The refrain became a fighting phrase all over New York. Whistled by a white man it was construed as a personal insult. . . . Hogan . . . died haunted by the awful crime he had unwittingly committed against the race.[16]

In 1907, after starring in the *Memphis Students* and *Rufus Rastus,* Hogan opened in *The Oyster Man,* with book by Flournoy Miller and Aubrey Lyles. He became ill during its run and retired to a small home in Lakewood, New Jersey, where he died in 1909.

During his last days Hogan was deeply troubled by the increasing hostility of other, younger Negroes, and when pianist-entertainer Tom Fletcher came to visit him, he could not stop talking about it. "Son, . . . with nothing but time on my hands now, I often wonder if I was right or wrong . . . we have been called every name under the sun, so I added another. The coon is a very smart animal . . . this song caused a lot of trouble in and out of show business, but it was also good for show business . . . we came along in leaps and bounds after weighing the good with the abuse." [17]

Hogan was no "Uncle Tom." Although he was forced to hide during the New York race riots of 1900, in New Orleans, while with the *Black Patti* show, he knocked down a white man during an argument and left town secretly to avoid a lynch mob.

Getting *Clorindy* staged on the Casino Roof Garden in the summer of 1898 was quite an accomplishment. It took Will Marion Cook considerable time and effort—and by his own testimony, a little skullduggery—to inveigle white producer Edward E. Rice into backing it.

On opening night, Cook writes:

> When I entered the orchestra pit, there were only about fifty people on the roof. When we finished the opening chorus, the house was

> packed to suffocation . . . the show downstairs in the Casino Theatre was just letting out. The big audience heard those heavenly Negro voices and took to the elevators . . . My chorus sang like Russians, dancing meanwhile like Negroes, and cakewalking like angels, black angels! When the last note was sounded, the audience stood and cheered for at least ten minutes.[18]

It is hard to realize today what the success of *Clorindy* meant to Negroes of that time, especially Negroes in show business. "Negroes were at last on Broadway, and there to stay," wrote Cook over-optimistically. "Gone was the uff-dah of the minstrel . . . we had the world on a string tied to a runnin' red-geared wagon on a downhill pull." [19] Unfortunately, Cook's next musical sketch, *Jes Lak White Folks*, produced the following summer at the New York Winter Garden without Hogan, was a failure.

In 1898 Bert Williams and George Walker, during a forty-week run at Broadway's top variety theater, Koster and Bials, brought the Cakewalk to its peak of popularity. They had met during the early nineties in San Francisco, and still in their teens, put together an act at the Midway Theater billed as "The Two Real Coons." Although the title smacks of minstrelsy, the emphasis was upon the "Real" and not the "Coons," for they were consciously rebelling against minstrel stereotypes.

"My partner, Mr. Williams, is the first man that I know of our race," wrote Walker, "to delineate a 'darky' in a perfectly natural way, and I think his success is due to this fact." [20] The progress achieved by Williams and Walker—and it was very real—shows how low minstrel stereotypes had sunk, for their delineation of the Negro in "a perfectly natural way" consisted—in part—of Walker playing the role of the strutting dandy and Williams the role of the shiftless, shuffling "darky" whose shoes pinch his feet. Today, both are considered stereotypes.

Before their successful run at Koster and Bials, Williams and Walker made their New York debut in *The Gold Bug* (1896), which was a failure. Subsequent appearances in London and two roadshows, *A Senegambian Carnival* and *The Policy Players*, also flopped. Their first success was a musical farce *The Sons of Ham* in 1900, and in 1902 they produced *In Dahomey*, the first Negro show to open on Times Square and one of their greatest hits.[21]

In Dahomey played London for seven months in 1903, where it made the Cakewalk an international fad. Before Walker's retirement in 1907—he died in 1911—he and Williams produced and starred in two more shows, *In Abyssinia* (1906) and *Bandana Land* (1907). Shortly thereafter Bert Williams joined Ziegfeld's *Follies* and was featured until his death in 1922, building up a considerable following among white audiences. "No Negro comedian ever reached his heights, and no white comedian ever surpassed him,"[22] writes E. B. Marks, who compares Bert Williams favorably with Charlie Chaplin.

The dancing of Williams and Walker, with the not inconsiderable addition of the Cakewalk, Buck and Wing, and eccentric dancing by Walker's wife, Ada Overton, contributed largely to their great appeal. "Williams and Walker, the immortal colored team, were also comedy dancers," wrote dancer Jack Donahue, who saw them at the Howard Theater in Boston: "Walker did a neat cakewalk, much like the strut of today, and Bert Williams would follow behind him doing a slow loose-jointed mooch dance."[23] The Williams Mooche, or Grind, while employing movements similar to the Twist and later dances of today, had a subtle flow that would have made our rock-and-roll devotees look like mechanized monkeys.

"George 'Bon-Bon' Walker was the greatest of the strutters, and the way he promenaded and pranced was something to see," says dancer Walter Crumbley. "One of the things I remember best is his beautiful white teeth and the trick he had when he forgot his lines of just opening his mouth and grinning until they cued him from the wings—he even made that seem hilarious. He had a white tailor downtown and all his clothes were made there. Oh, he was a fashion-plate."[24]

"Walker was the man who turned the Strut into the Cakewalk," says singer Thomas "Chappy" Chappell, "and made it famous."[25]

The impact of the Cakewalk at the turn of the century was tremendous. "The Cakewalk was really one of the great dance crazes, not only on stage but off as well," writes Joe Laurie, Jr. "There were hundreds of cakewalk contests throughout the country."[26]

The first cakewalk contest in New York, according to song-writer Perry Bradford, was sponsored by Richard K. Fox at Madison Square Garden in 1897. (Others date it around 1892.) "They also had cakewalk competitions at Coney Island on Saturday nights and paid six dollars a couple if you entered," says dancer Willie Glenn. "When one of us dancers was out of work, we'd get a girl and go down there and pick up a little cash."[27]

Tom Fletcher, society's favorite Negro entertainer, was hired to teach the Cakewalk to Mr. and Mrs. William K. Vanderbilt. When Williams and Walker heard about it, they made a formal call at the Fifth Avenue mansion of the Vanderbilts and left the following letter:[28]

> Dear Sir:
>
> In view of the fact that you have made a success as a cake-walker, having appeared in a semi-public capacity, we, the undersigned world-renowned cake-walkers, believing that the attention of the public has been distracted from us on account of the tremendous hit which you have made, hereby challenge you to compete with us in a cake-walking match, which will decide which of us shall deserve the title of champion cake-walker of the world.
>
> As a guarantee of good faith we have this day deposited at the

office of the New York World the sum of $50. If you propose proving to the public that you really are an expert cake-walker we shall be pleased to have you cover that amount and name the day on which it will be convenient for you to try odds against us.

Yours very truly,
Williams and Walker

No reply was ever recorded, but by 1898 the Cakewalk needed no further publicity.

"All of the big colored shows featured the Cakewalk," writes Tom Fletcher, "the *Black Patti Troubadours*, Sam T. Jack's *Creole* Company, Williams and Walker Company, *South before the War* company, and all the big colored minstrel companies." [29]

John Phillips Sousa, on his European tours from 1900 to 1904, carried ragtime and the Cakewalk to London, Paris, Moscow, and elsewhere, making a point of featuring a drummer who could "syncopate" while the band played "At a Georgia Camp Meeting" as an encore. (Stravinsky's "Ragtime for Eleven Instruments" and Debussy's "Golliwog's Cakewalk" testify to Sousa's influence abroad.)

As usual, there was plenty of opposition. In 1899 the *Musical Courier* editorialized: 'Society has decreed that ragtime and cake-walking are the thing, and one reads with amazement and disgust of historical and aristocratic names joining in this sex dance, for the cakewalk is nothing but an African *danse du ventre*, a milder edition of African orgies." Criticisms of dancing the Twist and later steps to rock-and-roll are just as heated but not as perceptive: Elements of the Cakewalk *do* go back to Africa. (It is doubtful, however, if they could have been recognized in the dancing of Mr. Vanderbilt.)

Although there are innumerable stories of how it was "invented," the Cakewalk has a long history and was popularized much earlier in the Walk Around, the grand finale of minstrelsy in which couples dance, promenade, and prance in a circle, improvising fancy steps in competition. The Walk Around, in turn, is indebted to the Ring Shout of the Southern plantations, which as critic-historian Constance Rourke observes, traces back directly to the African Circle Dance.

Of course, something new has been added. The circular form is retained, but the Strut takes the place of the original Shuffle, and topical satire crops up in the improvisations. During its origin the Cakewalk, as performed by plantation Negroes, was a satire on the fine manners of the Southern gentleman. Hence the Strut. With its emphasis on humorous improvisation, the Cakewalk added other steps that were readily adapted to minstrelsy.

In addition to making the United States dance-conscious, the Cakewalk furnished a springboard for the rash of dances to come, for during the competitions stress was placed upon individual invention. "In a cakewalk you could do anything,"says Willie Glenn. "You could even do some tap or a Russian dance—but at the finish you grab the girl and strut and prance off." It was an incubator of talent, a framework for new steps, which helped to prepare the way for ballroom dances.

The Cakewalk put the Negro back before the public. It was "a great exhibition dance with such superb theatrical potentialities," writes Marian Hannah Winter, "that it served as a Negro re-entry permit to the stage." [30] Fortunately for Negro performers there were few white dancers at the time who could compete with them. Further, as Winter adds, the Cakewalk furnished "an authentic American note at a period when imported operetta and extravaganza were eclipsing most of our indigenous theatrical forms"—and the Cakewalk profited by the comparison.

George Walker never lived to enjoy and Bert Williams gained little from the vogue that they helped to popularize. They were professionals and had little in common with the dilute ballroom dances that soon deluged the public. Yet the part they played was crucial. The music and dances they helped to create "were unfettered by past conventions," as Miss Winter says, "and the raw elements of twentieth-century popular music acquired a style that would supersede the schottisches, waltzes, and cotillions of the nineteenth." [31] The form of the blend was largely European, but the music, and especially the dances, were in the American grain.

17 Early Harlem

"WE HAD SOME wonderful dancers, a featured dance called the Texas Tommy, and a fine cakewalk for the finale, but the most fun was a circle dance at the end of the second act. Everybody did a sort of sliding walk in rhythm with their hands on the hips of the person in front of them," says Ethel Williams, one of the stars of *Darktown Follies*, which opened at Harlem's Lafayette Theater in 1913, "and I'd be doing anything but that—I'd 'Ball the Jack' on the end of the line every way you could think of—and when the curtain came down, I'd put my hand out from behind the curtain and 'Ball the Jack' with my fingers." [1]

For the Circle Dance the entire company formed an endless chain, dancing across the stage and off on one end, then around behind the curtain and back on stage at the other end—circling continuously, snapping fingers with a "tango jiggle," a "moochee . . . slide," and a "Texas Tommy wiggle" (as the lyrics suggested) and singing J. Leubrie Hill's "At the Ball, That's All."

Organized originally in Washington, D.C., around 1911, *Darktown Follies* was a success in New York, and the Circle Dance, the hit of the show. "This was the beginning," writes James Weldon Johnson, "of the nightly migration to Harlem in search of entertainment." [2] Within a few months Florenz Ziegfeld had purchased the song and dance for his own Broadway show on the roof of the New York Theater.

Although musical comedy with a line of chorus girls and a bit of plot and characterization had appeared earlier, no dancing—or music for that matter—had arrived on Broadway with what might be described as swinging or propulsive rhythm. With the possible exception of Bert Williams, a solo act in the *Follies*, the few Negroes who could dance in the vernacular had vanished. "Ernest Hogan and George Walker were dead, and Bert Williams had been swallowed up," says actor Leigh Whipper. "All the great performers were gone." [3]

In 1900 the Negro population of New York City was centered around West 53rd Street—San Juan Hill—but by 1910 the trek to Harlem had begun. (Before that time Harlem had been an exclusive white neighborhood that was then shaken up by a real estate boom and bust.) In 1913, just before *Darktown Follies* opened at the Lafayette, the theater was integrated, and Negro patrons were welcomed. A competing theater, the Lincoln, had already opened its doors to Negroes.

"The Lafayette was considered higher class," says dancer Ida Forsyne, who returned to New York from abroad in 1914 and attended both theaters. "Society people went there, and the management didn't present off-color blues singers, comedians and Shake dancers from T.O.B.A. like they did at the Lincoln." [4] The real thing was more likely to appear at the Lincoln Theater—where Bessie Smith sang the blues—but there was more than enough talent to go around.

At first the Lincoln and Lafayette formed stock companies—like the earlier Pekin Theater in Chicago—sometimes presenting versions of Broadway hits with the choice running to melodrama. Bit by bit, comedy and variety were introduced, however, and the need to tailor material for white audiences lessened. As he had always done with Negro audiences in the South, the Negro performer began to modify minstrel stereotypes and to improvise with a new freedom.

The pioneering spirit behind *Darktown Follies* was John Leubrie Hill, with the assistance of Alex Rogers on the book and Will Vodery arranging and conducting the music. Hill helped write the book, and having composed the songs, designed the costumes, constructed the scenery, assembled the cast, and located a theater, he went downtown to raise the money, and in the show itself, played the leading role of the formidable wife, Mandy Lee. "He was an all-around businessman," says Ethel Williams, "and a fine actor." J. Leubrie Hill, as he billed himself, was known as the colored George M. Cohan.

Born in Cincinnati around the eighteen-eighties, Hill learned about show business writing and acting in the Williams and Walker company at the turn of the century. By 1911 he had put together his own group of thirty to forty performers, which he directed in a two-act musical comedy, *My Friend from Dixie.*

"Leubrie was way ahead of his time," says author-actor Flournoy Miller, "and he knew just what he was up against." [5]

"Our race made a wonderful showing on the musical stage for a few years," Hill told an interviewer from the Columbus (Ohio) *Dispatch* in 1911, referring of course to *Williams and Walker*, "but look at us now." [6]

The years from 1910 to 1917 are quite accurately described by James Weldon Johnson as "the term of exile of the Negro from the downtown theaters of New York," [7] but J. Leubrie Hill never stopped trying, and with *Darktown Follies*, gained some measure of success in spite of numerous obstacles.

At that time, for example, love scenes between two Negroes were strictly taboo. "White audiences wouldn't stand for it," said white producers, and the few Negro producers found it advisable to agree. Not Leubrie Hill. He not only considered the prevalent "African operetta" ridiculous, but also tried to present "the real Negro."

When *Darktown Follies* moved downtown to white audiences and the Grand Opera House on 23rd Street at Eighth Avenue, a Negro tenor sang to a Negro soubrette in what James Weldon Johnson describes as "a most impassioned manner," [8] and the only response was applause.

Some confusion regarding the title occurred when the show moved downtown. A later program reads: "J. Leubrie Hill and his *Darktown Follies of 1915* in a three-act musical comedy entitled *My Friend from Kentucky.*" "It was first called *My Friend from Dixie,* then it opened in Harlem as *My Friend from Kentucky,*" says Alice Ramsey, who sang "Rock Me in the Cradle of Love" in the first act, "but we always thought of it as *Darktown Follies.*" [9]

The plot of *Darktown Follies* concerns a young wastrel, Jim Jackson Lee, who, misled by bad company, mortgages the plantation of his father-in-law and flees to Washington, D.C., in search of high society and the presidency of the Colored Men's Business League, as well as escape from his six-foot wife, Mandy Lee. Mandy Lee, played by Leubrie Hill, follows Jim Jackson Lee and brings him back alive and kicking feebly.

Darktown Follies exploded with a variety of dancing, some of it topical and much of it new to the New York stage. Two pioneering tap dancers who later became famous, Toots Davis and Eddie Rector, started as chorus boys in the show and worked up their own specialties. "When I saw *Darktown Follies* in 1916, it was the talk of the town," says Ida Forsyne. "Eddie Rector was featured in his smooth military routine, and Toots Davis was doing his Over the Top and Through the Trenches—they were *new* steps then."

Rector helped perfect a new style of tap dancing (perhaps derived from white minstrel star George Primrose) in which he traveled across the stage with superb grace and elegance, a style that transcended the stereotypes of the strutting or shuffling "darky" and culminated in the suave "class acts" of the 1930's and later.

Davis popularized two flash, or air, steps that became the traditional finale of dancers when the accompaniment drowns out the taps, or when they need something that looks, and is, strenuous to spark applause—or both. Over the Top consists roughly of a figure-eight pattern in which the dancer jumps up on one leg and brings the other around and forward beneath it with an almost self-tripping effect; Through the Trenches is a more or less stationary running step, bending at the waist with arms flailing as the outer sides of the feet scrape alternately from front to back.

The Texas Tommy also helped make *Darktown Follies* a success. In 1910, when San Francisco was having a shipping boom, this dance, usually performed by teams of four to six pairs of dancers, became popular at Lew Purcell's, the only Negro cabaret on the Barbary Coast. "All the new dances came from Purcell's, which hired the best colored entertainers from coast to coast," says impresario Gene Harris, who worked at the Thalia, a nearby cabaret. "They wouldn't admit Negro customers, though." [10] (A few years later Lester Map took over the cabaret and the legendary stride-pianist Sid La Protte led the band.)

"When I danced at Purcell's in 1912," says Nettie Compton, "everybody was working out his own variations on the Texas Tommy. They told me that Johnny Peters brought it up from the South." [11]

Susie Beavers is more certain: "Johnny Peters brought the Texas Tommy to San Francisco in 1911 and then went east with the Al Jolson troupe of eight youngsters. His partner was Mary Dewson, and they were a sensation in Chicago and New York." [12]

A few years later, dancer-producer Will Mastin went east with his own group of Texas Tommy dancers, billed as "The California Poppies," featuring the fastest dancer of them all (according to legend), Pet Bob Thurman. "'Tommy' meant prostitute," says Mastin, "and when we presented the dance at a San Francisco theater, the place was jammed—lots of cops, too, expecting a riot—but nothing happened because there wasn't anything bad about it, just a kind of acrobatics, with every step you could think of added to it." [13]

Johnny Peters's partner, Mary Dewson, became ill after the Jolson troupe arrived in New York, and Ethel Williams took her place. In 1912 Johnny Peters and Ethel Williams formed a team, dancing the Tango, Maxixe, One Step, Waltz, and—as a finale—the Texas Tommy, at Bustanoby's cabaret on 39th Street and Broadway. They won a series of contests in and around New York City. "Mrs. Irene Castle called at my home," says Ethel Williams proudly, "and asked me to teach her some steps."

Ethel Williams had begun her career in 1897 as a pick first with Buddy Gilmore and then Viola DeCosta, with whose company she traveled to Cuba. "Dance director Lawrence Deas discovered me, and Will Vodery organized the act," she says. "Then Leubrie Hill hired me and Johnny for his *Darktown Follies*. It was my first big break."

"The Texas Tommy had a different first step than the Lindy, or Jitterbug," dancer Willie Covan says, "that's all." [14]

"I saw the Texas Tommy around 1914," says dancer Willie Glenn. "It was like the Lindy Hop." [15]

"It *was* like the Lindy," Ethel Williams agrees, "but there were two basic steps—a kick and hop three times on each foot, and then add whatever you want, turning, pulling, sliding. Your partner had to keep you from falling—I've slid into the orchestra pit more than once."

In 1912 Caroline and Charles Caffin described the basic movements of the Texas Tommy: [16]

> The Texas Tommy dancers are perhaps more acrobatic than eccentric . . . the whirl which spins his partner towards the footlights with such momentum that without aid she must assuredly fly across them, must be nicely adjusted so that in neither force nor direction shall she escape the restraining grasp of his hand outstretched just at the right moment to arrest her . . . Poise and gentleness of handling must regulate the seemingly fierce toss of his partner, first in the air, then toward the ground . . .

This is the earliest example that we have found in the vernacular of a couple-dance incorporating, as did the Lindy fifteen or more years later, the breakaway, or the temporary and energetic separating of partners—a distinctly unwaltzlike and non-European maneuver.

Although the Texas Tommy was a great success in *Darktown Follies,* the Circle Dance, in which the entire cast shuffled across the stage ("a moochee . . . slide") in various improvised styles, singing "At the Ball, That's All," received the most attention. "Anything Broadway has ever seen" was surpassed said the New York *World*,[17] and *Variety* described it as a number done in "snake fashion . . . the best put on song ever seen in New York." [18] (*Variety* also noted with surprise that white people were attending a theater in Harlem.)

At the time—and later—the Circle Dance was thought to be "one of those miracles of originality which occasionally come to pass in musical comedy" (in the words of James Weldon Johnson), but its origin is clear.

"It was a serpentine dance which goes back to the Ring Shout and Africa," says Leigh Whipper, "and its immediate inspiration was church 'Watch Meetings,' the custom with which colored people watch the old year out and the new year in. A little before midnight, someone starts shuffling and singing 'Tearing Down the Walls of Zion, Goin' to See My Lord,' and everybody puts his hands on the hips of the person in front of him and inches forward in a circle with a rocking motion."

Here again, Ethel Williams caused considerable and highly favorable comment. "When they finished throwing each other around in the Texas Tommy," singer-bandleader Noble Sissle explains, "the whole cast went into the Circle Dance—except Ethel, who was so winded or something that she just faked crazy steps that brought down the house. Josephine Baker did the same thing in *Shuffle Along* eight years later." [19]

Miss Williams's explanation differs: "I never could work in a chorus because I kicked too high—I would kick my head with my foot—and I couldn't seem to stay in line." So she clowned around at the end of the chorus line, pretending to be out of breath and unable to keep in step, while adding movements from the current dance-song hit, "Ballin' the Jack" (see Chapter 13). The perennial gag of the chorine who just cannot keep in step was given new impetus.

At the conclusion of the show the entire company got together again for a cakewalk—parading, bowing, prancing, strutting, and high-kicking with arched backs and pointed toes. "The last big company to do the Cakewalk as a feature of the grand finale," [20] wrote pianist-entertainer Tom Fletcher, but it was done with such vitality that it seemed new-minted.

"Why, I was amazed," says aristocratic Leigh Whipper, who according to a contemporary, came to scoff and remained to praise, "it made Broadway dancing look tame." As an ensemble finale, the Cakewalk was unbeatable, and it brought *Darktown Follies* to a triumphant dancing conclusion.

The critics, too, were impressed by the dancing. "It is stimulating to find a company whose members, especially the chorus, show intelligent interest in their work," wrote a reporter from *Current Opinion.* "A refreshing spontaneity pervades the entire performance." [21]

"The prevailing complexion of colored players is pink," wrote the reviewer from the New York *Dramatic Mirror*, to whom seeing a Negro company perform without burnt cork must have been a new experience. "The dances in particular are handled with much originality and grace." [22]

The cast of *Darktown Follies* was never well paid, but nobody objected. Leubrie Hill was an inspired leader and shared a dream with them. " 'We're fighting to get on Broadway,' he told us, 'and we all have to put our shoulders to the wheel.' Everybody knew he meant it," says Luckey Roberts, who later became a well-known stride pianist and composer. "We were all young and crazy to work anyway."

"I gave up a job playing piano in a Washington cabaret," he continues, "to join a quintet of chorus boys singing and dancing in the show." Luckey's specialty was tumbling, and he wrecked the beds in a series of boarding houses, practicing. "Leubrie Hill gave us plenty of food, a place to sleep and carfare—but no money," he adds cheerfully. "You'd have to do a jig to get a quarter from him, and we never did make Broadway." [23]

When Florenz Ziegfeld purchased the "At the Ball" routine, he made no mention of J. Leubrie Hill in the program. "I went down to the New York Theater and showed the cast how to dance it," says Ethel Williams. "They were having trouble. None of us was hired for the show," she adds a little sadly, "and at that time I was supposed to be the best woman dancer in the whole country."

The drought of vernacular dance in musical comedies on Broadway continued for seven years (in spite of *Darktown Follies*) until the miracle of *Shuffle Along* in 1921. The great Negro dancers were in vaudeville, many of them on Southern circuits where they remained unknown. Perhaps the chief reason Broadway lagged behind was that nobody realized that money could be made with native, homegrown dancing.

For the most part the heavy feet of what Cecil Smith describes as the "gigantic chorus ladies with their Amazonian marches and drills" [24] were still literally tripping over the Broadway stage. Producers sent to England for the *Tiller Girls*—predecessors of the Radio City *Rockettes*—who jumped a phosphorescent rope in the *Follies of 1924* while the lights flashed off and on. In the finale of the *Vanities of 1924*, Earl Carroll presented one-hundred-and-eight Vanity Girls on a revolving staircase. Broadway wanted show girls, not chorus girls who could dance.

Writing in the Pittsburgh *Courier* in 1927, Negro journalist Theophilus Lewis took a backward glance:

> The tendency to borrow from the colored stage openly . . . began . . . when J. Leubrie Hill produced his 'Darktown Follies' . . . Hill's production marked the turning point in the relations existing between the white stage and the colored stage.
>
> Before that time the Negro theater had borrowed its materials and methods from the white stage. Our comedians had accepted the minstrel tradition without questioning its merit or authenticity . . . he [J. Leubrie Hill] turned aside from Indian themes and South Seas motifs when he wrote the music and arranged the dances for the show, and *it was the singing and dancing that carried it over* [*author's italics*].[25]

18 Shuffle Along

WHEN *Shuffle Along* BROKE through to Broadway, a new trend was set, a new legend born. Negro musicals were in demand thereafter, and dancing in musical comedy finally took wing.

Opening at New York's Sixty-Third Street Theater on May 21, 1921, *Shuffle Along* was still fighting for its life. Weeks of struggling to survive preliminary tryouts were over, but months of battling to obtain adequate theaters on road tours lay ahead. Fortunately, nobody realized the difficulties to come, and opening night went off without a hitch—except for the lack of first-string critics. They thought Sixty-Third Street was too far off Broadway.

The show was conceived, organized, and personally presented by four talented gentlemen: Flournoy Miller, Aubrey Lyles, Noble Sissle, and Eubie Blake.

Miller and Lyles were author-actor-comedians who had served an apprenticeship writing and acting in the Pekin Repertory Theater in Chicago, graduating to the Keith circuit and tours abroad. "They were the first Negro comedians who could do more than dance," says producer Irving C. Miller, Flournoy's brother. "They also succeeded as writers and actors." [1] During their days in vaudeville *Miller and Lyles* were often compared with the top teams of *McIntyre and Heath* or *Williams and Walker*.

Sissle and Blake were more than a song-writing team. Sissle, a handsome vocalist and writer of lyrics, had sung with Jim Europe's famous military band during and after World War I, and the diminutive Blake was a professional composer, conductor, and pianist from Baltimore. They had an act in Philadelphia when Miller and Lyles, at the suggestion of

Jim Europe, came to see them. Miller proposed that they join forces and put together a musical comedy.

Miller and Lyles furnished the plot: an election race for the job of a small-town mayor, with complications arising from the social aspirations of the candidates' wives. Sissle and Blake supplied the tunes: "I'm Just Wild about Harry," "Gypsy Blues," "Love Will Find a Way," "In Honeysuckle Time," "Bandanna Days," and "Shuffle Along."

Sissle sang and Blake conducted. "Sissle in action and Blake at the piano," wrote Gilbert Seldes, reviewing the show in *Vanity Fair*, "were wholly satisfying and expert." [2] Miller and Lyles acted the parts of the two would-be mayors, introducing a dancing fight—with tumbling—which became one of the hits of the show.

"The fight lasted about twenty minutes," says Flournoy Miller. "We wrote it out and then *ad libbed*, too. Lyles would fuss at me until we both began swinging—at one point I knocked him down, and he jumped over my back—Jack Benny once told us that our timing was the best he'd ever seen." [3] Miller was tall; Lyles, short.

"For a finish they would be doing some Time Steps and a little buck-and-wing," says Sissle, "as Miller kept one hand on Lyles' head while Lyles with his short arms kept swinging and missing." [4] This bit was Fiorello LaGuardia's favorite.

"When we were starting out in the early teens," says Miller, "Negro acts only sang and danced. We had to black up to get a job—to make audiences think we were two white men blacked up. Lyles had straight hair and my skin was light, so I left my wrists uncovered." People who inquired were told they were white. Later, in *Shuffle Along*, Miller and Lyles used burnt cork because it had become a standard part of their act, a predecessor of the *Amos 'n' Andy Show*, for which Miller later wrote scripts.

Shuffle Along made its own stars. A cast was assembled from all over the country, whose talents were known chiefly to Sissle, Blake, Miller, and Lyles: four singers from a chautauqua circuit; several performers from cabarets in San Francisco, New Orleans, and Memphis; and a few members of the former Pekin Stock Company.

Florence Mills, who replaced Gertrude Saunders ("Hertig and Seamon," says Miller, "hired her away from us") became a star overnight. "As a pantomimist and a singing and dancing comedienne," writes James Weldon Johnson, "she had no superior in any place or race." [5] Later, she left for Lew Leslie's *Plantation Revue* at a higher salary, but by then another girl was causing a sensation in the chorus.

Josephine Baker, who exploded rather than emerged, was sixteen years old when she was hired as end-girl on the chorus line. The second act opened with dancer Charlie Davis, dressed as a policeman, directing traffic and singing "Shuffle Along." The chorus line came on to back him up, singing and doing a routine while he danced, with Josephine at the end of the line.

"That was when she started doing some crazy things," says Blake, "no routine—just mugging, crossing her eyes, tripping, getting out of step and catching up, doing all the steps the rest were doing, but funnier." [6] The audience always cheered. She was paid $125 a week on the road, an astronomical sum in those days and for that show, and she stayed in the chorus line as long as she was with *Shuffle Along*.

The two dancers originally featured were Charlie Davis and Tommy Woods, although others soon got into the act. Charlie Davis was a fast tap dancer who concentrated on Buck and Wing. "I could do all variety of dances," Davis recalls, "but my own was strictly Buck and Wing and flash." [7] He knew Toots Davis of *Darktown Follies* fame and admired him unreservedly: "Toots started Over the Top and Trenches, two of my biggest assets in *Shuffle Along*." On stage, the sheer speed and endurance of Charlie Davis staggered the audience. Later he danced in other shows, toured abroad, choreographed a few specialties for George White's *Scandals*, and financed by Carl Van Vechten, opened his own studio where he taught many white dancers.

Tommy Woods did a slow-motion acrobatic dance. "Everything he did was in tempo," says Sissle. "He'd start with a Time Step and go into a flip, landing right on the beat." Although this kind of acrobatic dancing was beginning to be known in vaudeville, it seemed new to the audiences of *Shuffle Along*. Woods was a full year ahead of the popular *Crackerjacks*, a team who made acrobatic dancing that swings to jazz rhythms an important part of the vernacular tradition.

"Tommy Woods twisted all over the stage," says Eubie Blake, "in perfect rhythm."

Two dancing stars emerged by accident. One of them, Bob Williams, played trombone in the pit band until they discovered that he was humming through the instrument instead of blowing. "He was a braggadoccio kind of fellow," says Sissle. One night when one of the six chorus boys became ill, Bob Williams volunteered to take his place. "We all retreated to the dressing room," Sissle adds, "because we didn't want to watch the disaster."

When the audience started to roar applause, Sissle returned to see what happened. Williams, having missed his cue to follow the rest into the wings, was stranded in the center of the stage. Whether or not he had planned it that way, he was not at all flustered. "He just did an eccentric dance and then a strut off," says Blake, "shaking his head and his straw hat the way Eddie Jackson and Jimmy Durante did later." (Old-timers say George Walker originated it. A part of the Cakewalk, Bob Williams's Strut—prancing and high-kicking with back arched and toe pointed

—became a regular part of the show, winning encores at every performance.

Other dancers—and singers—appeared at one time or another in *Shuffle Along.* Ulysses S. "Slow Kid" Thompson played the porter in the mayor's office: "I did eccentric, the Soft Shoe, and legomania," he says, "and that line of chorus girls backed me up." [8] (The husband of Florence Mills, he left with her to appear in *Plantation Revue.*) Blues singers Eva Taylor, who was also a fine dancer, and Lucile Hegamin were stars of road companies, while Mae Barnes was doing the Charleston in another, long before the dance became a hit. The show was revived in 1932 and again in 1952.

Getting to New York had been an uphill climb. Miller, Lyles, Sissle, and Blake had plenty of talent but no money. First they approached promoter Al Mayer, who had booked *Miller and Lyles* on the Keith circuit. Mayer was broke but promised to talk to young Harry Cort, son of John Cort, the prominent producer.

On a cold winter day, each of the four chipped in a dollar and twenty-five cents to finance Mayer's luncheon with Harry Cort. "Flournoy Miller had a good-looking new overcoat that he loaned to Mayer," says Eubie Blake, "so he'd make the right impression. It was too big, it came to his ankles, but it looked expensive. Al Mayer worked night and day for us. It's funny, but the only people who ever helped us were Jewish. I owe them a great debt." After considerable delay John Cort agreed on a trial run.

The quartet was ambitious—they aspired to put on their show at white theaters that were playing serious drama, frequently second-rate melodrama—and no Negro shows. This meant that they must interest white theater owners in the show, and of course, prove that it could make money.

The best they could do for initial tryouts was the Howard, a Negro theater in Washington, D.C., and then some of the cast nearly missed the opening because they lacked carfare from New York.

Shuffle Along made just enough money during a successful two weeks in Washington to go on to the Dunbar, another Negro theater in Philadelphia. At this point John Cort was persuaded to come down from New York with his friend Abe Erlanger to see the show. "Mr. Cort and Mr. Erlanger laughed themselves sick," recalls Sissle, "and then pointed out that we had a colored audience and that a white audience wouldn't enjoy it." By way of a compromise Cort agreed to send the company on a "graveyard tour"—three weeks of one-nighters in rural Pennsylvania—to see if it could survive.

The one-night audiences were small because nobody had ever heard of the show, and when rave reviews came out the following morning, the company had already moved to the next town. The cast had to stay in Negro homes because no hotels would take them. This was not a total loss, since they paid their landlords in tickets whenever they could. Al Mayer perfected a technique of paying for his meals at various restaurants by giving the waitresses passes to the show.

"You learn a lot of tricks on the road," says Miller. "Sissle and I would visit people who were boarding some of the cast—always at mealtime—and I would take a bite of everything on the table and insist that Sissle taste it, too, because it was so delicious. Then we'd go to another house and do the same thing—we usually had plenty to eat."

"Blake and Lyles were always playing poker and kidding around, while Sissle and I took care of business," says Miller. "Everything we made, we gave to the cast right away. One night everybody only got two dollars, and Eubie Blake—we called him Mouse then—nearly cried he was so disappointed. So I said, 'Sissle, give him your two dollars, Lyles, give him yours,' and I gave him mine. That made him happy. A few minutes later we all borrowed the money back, and then Mouse felt like a big shot."

"We never could pay all our bills on the spot," says Sissle, "so we signed checks and made them good from our receipts at the next town." At one time the cast was owed some $17,000 in back salaries. It was a rough shakedown cruise, but they returned with a fistful of fine notices.

Then they discovered that no New York theater was available. With the exception of the Williams and Walker productions (and the partial exception of *Darktown Follies*) Negro musicals had never appeared on Broadway, and their absence had hardened into a tradition that theater owners somehow felt duty-bound to maintain. John Cort had become infected with enthusiasm for *Shuffle Along*, however, and finally located a broken-down music hall on Sixty-Third Street. "It violated every city ordinance in the book," says Blake.

The carpenters went to work. They extended the apron out into the audience, covering up the front boxes, which continued to be obstacles getting on and off stage, erected a gridiron, and planned dressing rooms. Remodeling went on during performances, but the dressing rooms never were completed during the run of the show. "You could hear hammering during the performances," says Miller, "and we had to run out to the men's room to wash up."

"White show people," says Sissle, "spread the word." Although the Sixty-Third Street Theater was not on Broadway, it was reasonably close, and Alan Dale, one of the best-known theater critics of the day, soon made it official by including it on his beat and writing a highly complimentary review.[9]

Thereafter, reviews were a study in admiring confusion. Most of them agreed that the show pioneered by having something to do—here they disagreed on what—with jazz. A rather mild kind of jazz had been around for some time, but the reviewers found the music in *Shuffle Along* remarkable, particularly in combination with the dancing.

Sooner or later the critics got around to the dancing and the chorus girls, although their comments made little sense. "Syncopated singers and steppers," said the *Evening Journal*, "speed the action to ragtime rhythms . . . with a well-drilled chorus." [10]

The *Mail* went further: "The principle asset is the dancing . . . the chorus was exceptionally well drilled." [11] Actually, the chorus was anything but well drilled. They made up for it with their energy, rhythm, and blazing talent. Burns Mantle summarized: "Everybody dances." [12]

"Society people felt that their guest tours were incomplete unless they brought their friends to *Shuffle Along*," says Blake. Midnight shows had been inaugurated on Wednesdays (a procedure adapted from the southern custom of putting on midnight performances for whites only), so that show people could drop by after their own shows, and soon white celebrities packed the theater. "Then Negroes came to see the celebrities," says Miller.

"LaGuardia came three nights in one week," says Blake, "and the traffic commissioner finally had to make Sixty-Third a one-way street."

The second half of the battle for survival began in August, 1922, when the Broadway run was ending, and the time for a road tour was drawing near. Out-of-town producers were skeptical: "New York is a freak town which can take to a freak show," they said, "but other towns won't go for it." A Negro musical was a new departure. "Shubert and Erlanger wouldn't touch us," says Sissle, "but finally Cort persuaded Selwyn to let us have his Boston theater during the last two weeks in August, when nobody else wanted it because of the stifling heat and no business." Air conditioning, of course, did not exist.

"Before we left for Boston, they brought in a white dance director named Walter Brooks to give the show 'that Broadway touch,'" says Eubie Blake with indignation. "He got two per cent of the production, and Lawrence Deas, who had done all the work, was paid off with a small amount of cash and dropped. The same thing happened in *Chocolate Dandies* [1924], when Julian Mitchell got all the money and credit, while Charlie Davis did the real work."

Instead of two weeks, *Shuffle Along* played to land-office business at the Selwyn Theater in Boston for almost four months. "Negroes came down to the box office to buy tickets," says Blake, "and the management was scared to death that the audience would be top-heavy with colored people. Then they discovered that the Negroes were buying tickets for their white employers."

The show left the Selwyn Theater because of a law suit: Julia Marlowe and E. H. Southern, the Shakespearean actor, had been set to open after the original two weeks of *Shuffle Along*, and when they were left dangling for over three months, threatened to sue Selwyn, who reluctantly let *Shuffle Along* go. "While we were at the Selwyn," says Sissle, "the *Follies* and

Scandals both opened at other theaters and ran out of business after a couple of weeks."

In spite of its unqualified success in New York and Boston, *Shuffle Along* still had trouble finding theaters in which to play. "We had to jump all the way to Chicago—nobody else would take us," says Blake. At the last minute they were let in by a lady who owned the Olympic, a rundown burlesque house. "The audience was peeking around a lot of posts to see the show," says Sissle, "but we filled the house in Chicago for four months."

The next engagement took them to Milwaukee, where with the assistance of Erlanger and a little subterfuge, they found a good theater, the Davidson. "The manager, Mr. Brown, was out of town, and Erlanger pressured his assistant to take us," says Sissle. "When Brown returned and found that the deal had been signed, he left town in disgust." The show sold out before it opened, and Brown, hearing rumors of success, came back only to discover his private box occupied. He was forced to stand in the rear.

Shuffle Along forged steadily ahead, breaking new ground and attendance records: St. Louis, Indianapolis, Cincinnati (three unprecedented weeks), Pittsburgh, Philadelphia, and Atlantic City. And it was making money: Producer Cort took half the profits and the other half was divided among Miller, Lyles, Sissle, and Blake. Toward the end Miller and Sissle were increasingly at odds over the management of the show: Miller wanted the show to remain untouched, and Sissle wanted to add new material.

The show closed for the summer in June, 1923, when Miller and Lyles left to work on a new show, *Runnin' Wild.* Lew Payton and dancer Johnny Hudgins took their places for the next road tour with Sissle and Blake. (Road tours usually made more money.) Two other road companies continued until 1924. "Each manager still objected, saying that maybe the show was a hit somewhere else, but it wouldn't be a success in *his* town," says Sissle, "not until the very end were we welcomed on arrival."

As time went by, favorable opinion of *Shuffle Along* gathered momentum. A year after its Broadway opening, Heywood Broun, reviewing another show, wrote in the New York *World:* "The first reportorial responsibility of any reviewer who goes to a Negro musical comedy is to say whether or not it is as good as *Shuffle Along.*" [13]

In 1924 columnist C. B. Zittell, reviewing still another show, observed: "To many minds, colored shows may come and go, but there will always be only one *Shuffle Along.*" [14]

And in 1927 Van Dyke was still writing about the show in the New York *Telegraph:* "New Yorkers take their colored shows by one standard, the success of *Shuffle Along.*" [15] It took time, however, for the Broadway critics to realize exactly what *Shuffle Along* had accomplished.

The most impressive innovation of *Shuffle Along* was the dancing of the sixteen-girl chorus line. When not dancing on stage, they sang in the wings to keep things moving. "Besides being superb dancers," says Sissle, "those chorus girls were like cheerleaders." They started a new trend in Broadway musicals.

Shuffle Along was the first outstanding Negro musical to play white theaters from coast to coast. It also made money. Thereafter, producers and backers were eager to finance another such show, and Negro musicals flourished on Broadway for a decade or so. Attention was focused on the talents of the Negro in vernacular comedy, song, and dance, and jobs opened up for Negro performers. Above all, musical comedy took on a new and rhythmic life, and chorus girls began learning to dance to jazz.

"We have, recently, learned a vast amount from negro dancing," wrote Gilbert Seldes in his pioneering discussion of *The 7 Lively Arts*, "[it has been] an active influence for the last fifteen years at least, touching the dance at every point in music, and tending always to prevent the American dance from becoming cold and formal." [16]

19 Broadway: The Early Twenties

THE CUMULATIVE IMPACT OF *Shuffle Along* became the yardstick by which dancing in all other musicals was measured—at least in memory. By 1925 the over-all effect was clear to at least one critic. Referring to the influence of the eight or more Negro shows that had appeared on or off Broadway, the New York *American* pointed out that "all stage dancing underwent a change—steps became more intricate, daring, perilous." [1] Dancing became more rhythmic, and jazz drummers were getting ideas from tap dancers.

Paradoxically, Negro musicals offered dancing that was superior to the dancing in white musicals but at the same time, made little use of their best dancers. As far as can be determined, innovators such as King Rastus Brown, Kid Checkers, Harry Swinton, Jack Wiggins, and Clarence Dotson, never appeared in Broadway musicals, while such equally great dancers as Willie Covan, U. S. Thompson, Maxie McCree, Eddie Rector, and John Bubbles appeared now and then like migrant workers. When they did reach Broadway, they were seldom starred.

No Negro dancer became well enough known to the Broadway public in the early twenties to constitute a strong drawing card, and in any case, Negro shows could not meet the salaries paid to Negro stars by vaudeville. In 1922 vaudeville was flourishing. There were approximately 368 Negro theaters in the United States, according to *Billboard*, and they employed around six hundred acts.[2]

"They wanted us to dance in *Shuffle Along*," says Rufus Greenlee, "but they couldn't afford to pay us anywhere near what we were getting in vaudeville, so we turned them down." [3]

"Being in a Broadway musical," writes Ethel Waters, "always builds up your prestige and future earning power" [4]—at a cut in salary. Meanwhile, unknowns were often good enough to make the Broadway critics rejoice.

Shuffle Along was able to create its own stars, such as Florence Mills and Josephine Baker, but the success of its dancing was due to a group effort, which although energetic and enthusiastic, pioneered few steps new to Negro vaudeville. Further, since many of these musicals had something that passed for a plot, an increasing demand for eccentric, comedy, and character dancing occurred. "Grab a role to play in the story," a dancer was advised, "and do your dancing on the side."

The pattern had long been established in white musicals and revues. George M. Cohan, Fred Stone, Leon Errol, George White, and others were all dancers, but incidentally. Their popularity was based upon their personalities, which they projected, in part, by acting. Thus, dancing for its own sake began to lose ground the moment it stepped on the Broadway stage. Broadway did not encourage plain hoofers, although whoever appeared might receive attention in the press.

From 1921 to 1924, while *Shuffle Along* was still on the road, at least eight Negro musicals opened on Broadway. "Let one colored show make money," says Leigh Whipper, "and everybody wants to get in on it." [5]

Florenz Ziegfeld's *Follies of 1922*, the sixteenth annual production of what Noble Sissle calls "glorified minstrelsy with girls," presented a number that documented the new development. Dressed in a costume that turned black or white according to the lighting, Gilda Gray lamented that "It's Getting Dark on Old Broadway," describing how all the cabarets high-lighted their "dancing coons" and "chocolate babies," who "shake and shimmie" while the "darktown entertainers" monopolize the stage. She advised anyone who wanted to be the "latest rage" to don blackface.[6]

A little more than three months after the arrival of *Shuffle Along*, Cora Green and Hamtree Harrington appeared in *Put and Take,* which opened at Town Hall, with music by Perry Bradford and Spencer Williams. The critics loved the chorus line. John Martin stated flatly that it surpassed any "chorus of white girls on Broadway this season or for many seasons past." [7]

The *World* was favorably distressed: "They never stop dancing . . . how can a girl croon a love song when she's gasping for breath?" [8]

"After viewing the blasé slouch of many of our Broadway queens," said the *Globe*, "it is a relief to see . . . real snap and verve." [9]

The dancing star of the show was unknown to the critics who praised "Maxie," but never mentioned his last name. Even *Variety* had no idea who he could be. Maxie McCree (see Chapter 33) was a gifted pioneer in various styles from straight tap, through legomania and Russian to acrobatic dancing, with the added distinction of being a formative influence on the class acts. He died in 1922.

Three Negro musicals of note arrived on Broadway in 1922: *Strut Miss Lizzie*, the *Plantation Revue*, and *Liza*. Produced originally in Chicago and then on Houston Street, *Strut Miss Lizzie* presented few great dancers, with the exception of Grace Rector, when it opened at the Times Square Theater in June. The dancing of the chorus, nevertheless, startled the reviewers. "Gilda Gray's intrepid whirlpoolings in the Follies," wrote Percy Hammond, "are but chaste inertia by comparison." [10]

The Plantation Club, a restaurant over the Winter Garden Theater, was the incubator of a fine show. In a sense, the *Plantation Revue* was not all-Negro, since the owner-director-producer—as was frequently the case—was a white man, Lew Leslie, the husband of vaudeville star Belle Baker. He later produced the annual editions of *Blackbirds*. Although the debate as to how well Leslie treated his employees continues, he made it possible for many Negro entertainers to become better known. He was a pioneer in his belief that Negro shows could make money, and it made him wealthy.

As entertainment for his restaurant, Leslie put together a floor show from Negro vaudeville. (The more prosperous white revues had been raiding vaudeville for several years.) In 1921 he persuaded Florence Mills and her husband, dancer Ulysses S. Thompson, to entertain at his restaurant each night after *Shuffle Along*. Within a year they were both working for Leslie full time. "He offered Florence three times as much as she was getting from *Shuffle Along*," says Thompson, "and then he had to take me to get her." [11]

Hiring Thompson was one of the best bargains Leslie was ever forced into making. "That's when the Plantation Club began to get popular," says Noble Sissle.[12]

The *Plantation Revue*, billed as "A Colored Chauve Souris" (*Chauve Souris* was then a hit on Broadway), opened at the Forty-Eighth Street Theater in July, 1922. Will Vodery's pit band featured cornetist Johnny Dunn, who danced as he played. The show consisted of the best acts from the Plantation Club with Shelton Brooks as master of ceremonies. Four fine dancers appeared: U. S. Thompson, Lou Keane, and the team of *Kelly and Palmer*.

Leslie had an exceptional eye for talent. "I was with *The Whitman Sisters* when Lew Leslie saw me, told me to find a partner, and hired us for his review," says Aaron Palmer. "We worked up a class act—top hat and tails like *Greenlee and Drayton*—and I added spins and pivots while Kelly did Russian and acrobatics." [13] Palmer was noted for his elegance; Kelly, for his versatility. Lou Keane and U. S. Thompson were both first-rate tap and acrobatic dancers. "We teamed together on a soft-shoe to 'Swanee River,'" says Thompson, "and then did our own specialties."

The reviews were as mixed as the reviewers. The *Globe* felt that all three shows—*Shuffle Along, Strut Miss Lizzie,* and the *Plantation Revue*—were "about equal in quality";[14] the *Post* dissented strongly, criticizing the *Plantation Revue,* which "resembles *Shuffle Along* as chalk does cheese";[15] while the *Telegram* called it a "conglomeration of unrelated acts."[16]

Several of the critics, however, observing the dancing of U. S. Thompson, seemed to feel that something unusual was taking place, even if they could not describe it. Two metropolitan dailies mentioned him: The *Times* called him "a jumpin' Jack,"[17] and *Women's Wear* noted that "Thompson throws himself around the stage in splendid fashion."[18] In a revue, a dancer got a chance to concentrate on his dancing.

The Negro hit of the year, with book by Irving C. Miller and music by Maceo Pinkard, opened at Daly's 63rd Street Theater in November. "The dressing rooms, which were being built for *Shuffle Along,*" says Eubie Blake, "were completed just in time for *Liza.*"[19] A few months later *Liza* moved to the Nora Bayes Theater on 44th Street, and became the first Negro show to play Broadway proper during the regular season. (Only the summer months had been available for Negro productions heretofore, while the critics wondered why the shows were presented at such a hot time of year.) *Liza* ran for 172 performances at a time when a run of one hundred was considered good.

"When they talk of the Negro in show business," said Thaddeus Drayton sadly in 1963—forty-one years later—"I can't understand why they never mention *Liza.* It was a great show with great tunes."[20]

At the time, the critics agreed wholeheartedly—especially about the dancing. One of the most perceptive, Heywood Broun, who was almost unique in his ability to transcend the stereotypes of the day, observed: "After seeing *Liza* we have a vague impression that all other dancers whom we ever saw did nothing but minuets."[21]

There is some confusion as to who was the featured dancer. The critics, in addition to inevitable praise for the chorus, singled out Johnny Nit for special mention. Alexander Woollcott described him as possessing "as talented a pair of clogging feet as ever danced in our time."[22]

Nit was a tap dancer, however, not a clogger, a style associated with early minstrelsy. "Let some of the dancers on Broadway who think they can really dance compare their dancing with his . . ." asserted the New York *World.* "We can recall no other male dancer in town who can equal him."[23]

Yet one of the great dancers whose influence was far-reaching, Eddie Rector, claims that he closed *Liza* with his own number, and producer Irving C. Miller agrees, adding that Rector performed a waltz clog and his own rhythmic speciality. Eddie Rector is neither mentioned in the program nor by the reviewers. "Rector substituted for Nit at the last minute," says Miller. "Nit never appeared in *Liza.*"[24] The critics were praising the wrong man.

Reviewers of *Liza* also mentioned the team of *Greenlee and Drayton,* who carried canes, wore monocles, and sang and danced the Virginia Essence in top hats and tails (see Chapter 36). "It was the first time that any Negro dancer had done those steps in anything but overalls," says Drayton.

"Before our act," adds Greenlee, "it was always a blackface comedian and a straight man, like *Williams and Walker.*" *Greenlee and Drayton* were the direct predecessors of the class act.

Although the dance that became known as the Charleston had been around in the South for a long time, and a later show made it popular, *Liza* first presented the step on Broadway—without attracting much attention. "In that show," says Greenlee, "Maude Russell and I danced the Charleston."

By 1923 signs of diminishing returns were beginning to appear. A Negro musical, *How Come,* opened in April at the Apollo Theater on 42nd Street and lasted for thirty-two performances. It was written by comedian Eddie Hunter, who starred, while the soon-to-be-famous jazzman, Sidney Bechet, played the role of chief of police. In addition to the beautifully costumed singing and strutting act of *Chappelle and Stinnette* (old-time favorites on the Keith circuit), *How Come* presented one dancer of note: Johnny Nit.

Dancers who knew and worked with Johnny Nit have no doubt of his talent. "He trained like a prize fighter," says Buddy Bradley, "and could do high-speed Wings for hours and execute all kinds of taps sitting down." [25]

"He was a good buck-and-wing dancer," says Charlie Davis, "and a better showman." [26]

"Nit was on the order of a nontalking Bill Robinson," says U. S. Thompson, "but not quite as good. He had real personality—a broad smile and big ivory teeth."

"He could take a little step," says Thaddeus Drayton, "and when he added that grin of his, the audience went crazy—a real entertainer." Johnny Nit seems to be the first Negro tap dancer to be recognized and celebrated as such by the Broadway critics. From 1922 on, his appearance in a show usually meant high praise for the dancing.

Several critics liked only Johnny Nit. The *Telegram* thought the entire cast too well dressed; [27] the *Commercial* called the show "the most pretentious yet"; [28] and Burns Mantle worked out a retrospective scorecard with *Shuffle Along* at the top, *Liza* a poor second, and the rest—including *How Come*—at the bottom of the list.[29] Perhaps Heywood Broun put his finger on the trouble: "We found much of *How Come,*" he wrote, "rapid and strident rather than exhilarating." [30]

Apparently the cast fell into the error of trying to be what they thought the white public wanted them to be, namely, energetic, happy, and talented children—with unfortunately brassy results. They worked too hard at it and lost much of the relaxed spontaneity that made the white musicals appear so artificial by comparison.

Conversely, when John Cort, who had helped produce *Shuffle Along*, opened an all-white show, *Go Go*, in early 1923 at the 63rd Street Theater, it never got off the ground. The show was modeled on *Shuffle Along* (with a score by Luckey Roberts) and featured Bernard Granville. Granville was a singer and eccentric dancer who derived his style from Doc Quigley and the minstrel tradition. "His personality," according to dancer Harland Dixon, "never quite got across the footlights." [31]

The critics recognized *Go Go* as "a white edition of *Shuffle Along*," [32] offered mildly favorable comments, and ignored Granville.

Runnin' Wild, a Negro musical, was produced by George White and opened at the Colonial Theater on 62nd Street in October, 1923. The atmosphere of the show was a definite improvement—there were no crap-shooting scenes, as the *Times* observed, and "ham replaces chicken as the most desirable of all dishes." [33] Singer Adelaide Hall starred, along with the comedy team of *Miller and Lyles*. Acrobatic tapper Tommy Woods and George Stamper, who did a Lazy Man's Dance in slow motion—including splits—were the featured dancers, along with the later addition of two excellent women tappers, Lavinia Mack and Mae Barnes.

A dance, rather than any dancer, was the hit of *Runnin' Wild*, for James P. Johnson composed his hit, "Charleston," for this show (see Chapter 15). It was presented by the chorus boys—billed as "The Dancing Redcaps"—to the simple accompaniment of hand-clapping and foot-stamping, the way it had been danced for many years in the South. (The chorus line included several dancers who became well known later: Pete Nugent, Chink Collins, Sammy Dyer, and Derby Wilson.) "The effect was electrical," wrote James Weldon Johnson, who saw the show. "Such a demonstration of beating out complex rhythms had never before been seen on a stage in New York." [34]

During rehearsals of *Runnin' Wild*, Flournoy Miller had gone uptown to see a midnight show at the Lincoln Theater. He found three youngsters dancing on the sidewalk for pennies, entertaining the waiting customers. That night the producer at the Lincoln, Irving C. Miller, decided to eliminate the competition by bringing the youngsters in and putting them on stage. They were a success.

"The leader of the trio was Russell Brown," says Flournoy Miller, "but all we knew then was his nickname 'Charleston.' He had another little colored boy with him and an Italian kid named Champ." Equipped with the lids of garbage cans and a tub on which they drummed, the youngsters took turns dancing, trying to outdo each other—a procedure known as challenge dancing. "Champ wore boots," adds Miller, "and did a little Camel Walk which the audience loved." [35]

The next afternoon, Miller brought the trio to a rehearsal of *Runnin' Wild*. "I had them dance for the cast, asked Jimmy Johnson to add some music to the beat, and convinced our choreographer, Lida Webb, that it would make a fine number for the chorus." Willie Covan and his partner

Leonard Ruffin, who were watching the rehearsal, agreed to develop the step into a routine. "The kids only had that first little step and a sort of Camel Walk," says Covan, "so we added an Airplane and a slide." [36] The youngsters never did their dance in the show.

One more obstacle remained. Producer George White did not like the dance and went out of his way to say so. "He brought his friends around to show them—in front of us—that the Charleston was nothing," says Miller, "and he tried everything but cutting the dance, which would have made us quit." On opening night in Washington, D.C., the Charleston chorus came on first. It was politely received. A few nights later, in New York City, it was a smash hit. "I found out later," says Miller, "that White wanted the dance for his *Scandals*."

As time went on, Negro musicals—with the well-meant urging of white owner-producer-directors—tended to become "sophisticated," which usually meant imitating white musicals. "They'd say 'It needs that Broadway touch,'" says Eubie Blake, "which always meant hiring a white dance director."

Producer George White, for example, was continually trying to make Negro dancers forget their own styles "and leap around like ballet dancers," according to Harland Dixon, who coached a few of White's shows. The models were the *Follies, Scandals,* and *Vanities,* which except for infrequent bits of humor, attained annual peaks of pretentiousness.

Meanwhile, at least two more Negro shows appeared on Broadway while *Shuffle Along* was still on tour: *Chocolate Dandies* and *Dixie to Broadway. Chocolate Dandies,* with Josephine Baker, opened at the Colonial Theater in September, 1924, and ran for ninety-six performances. Eubie Blake and Noble Sissle collaborated with Lew Payton to put together a musical comedy about a horse race with a plot similar to *In Old Kentucky*. The featured cornetist in the pit was Joe Smith.

Three years had passed since the struggle to keep *Shuffle Along* alive and conditions had changed dramatically. "B. C. Whitney, who produced *The Chocolate Soldier,* asked us to do the show," says Sissle, "and we had no trouble getting a theater."

Everybody was willing to help. "We played deluxe houses," says Blake, "and were booked by William Morris—the fight we had to get *Shuffle Along* on the road seemed like a bad dream."

Josephine Baker became a featured star in *Chocolate Dandies.* The dancers were Charlie Davis, who was listed as "Dancing Master" in the program, and Bob Williams, both of whom had appeared in *Shuffle Along,* plus a new eccentric dancer, Johnny Hudgins. A former stagehand from Baltimore, Hudgins was a comic pantomimist in blackface, using Chaplinesque hand and arm gestures along with slides reminiscent of burlesque. (Like Josephine Baker and many other Negro performers, Hudgins later became a hit in Paris.)

The precision work by the chorus line was a new departure. For the first time the chorus danced closely together with a swinging rhythm. Dancer (later coach) Charlie Davis took the tame routines of the *Tiller Girls,* who were imported from England for white musicals, and added complex ensemble tapping. "I just took out the kicks and put in taps," says Davis, "and then drilled them until they could all do it together." The reviews were favorable, but "the imitation of Ben Turpin's eyes" by Josephine Baker won the highest praise.

An anonymous reviewer in the New York *Sun* dissented sharply. Although he admired the dancing in spite of the plot, "these people can dance themselves quite *out* of the Broadway sophistication of their parts," he added. "Lamentably, the show is not funny . . . the negro patter is flatly theatrical. It seems absurd to tell the negro cast . . . that negroes do not talk that way, but they really don't." [37] The ill effects of imitation were becoming evident, while the dancing, which did not need to imitate, remained outstanding.

Dixie to Broadway opened at the Broadhurst Theater a month later, starring Florence Mills. It was a revue in two acts and twenty-four scenes from Lew Leslie's *Plantation Club Revue,* after it had combined with a white revue for a successful tour of England. This combination was called *Dover to Dixie.* "Half of this show was white—that was the Dover Street part, then Dixie was colored," says U. S. Thompson. "They did the first half, and we did the second." *Dixie to Broadway* was a transitional show in which both white and Negro (although segregated) were equally represented.

The show was enlivened by fine dancers who joined and left the cast with disconcerting frequency. The revue format lent itself to such substitutions, and no one dancer seems to have proved indispensable. The critics played it safe by praising the well-known Johnny Nit. The *Post* made the accurate comment that "he of the wide, white teeth . . . is no acrobat" but a "buck and wing versifier," [38] while Woollcott observed that "the dark Mr. Nit with the toothful smile . . . is the high point of the evening." [39]

In one skit Willie Covan impersonated George M. Cohan; U. S. Thompson and Henry Rector (Eddie's brother) imitated Gallagher and Shean; U. S. Thompson copied Bert Williams; and Snow Fisher, a strutter, impersonated George Walker. In another skit Byron Jones, Lou Keane, and Johnny Nit were chained together and executed a clever tap in convict suits. Such other fine dancers as Sammy Vanderhurst, Billy Mills, and Charlie Walker appeared at various times.

Near the finale U. S. Thompson and Willie Covan did their acrobatic specialties while a chorus line of eight girls ("The Chocolate Drops") and eight boys ("The Plantation Steppers") backed up the acts. The chorus lines also presented a satire called "Darkest Russia," making fun of the *Chauve Souris* to the tune of "The Parade of the Wooden Soldiers."

Heywood Broun was carried away by a tiny youngster who led a dance ensemble. "When I see a Negro child two or three years old come out and dance a little better than anybody at the New Amsterdam or the Winter Garden, I grow fearful that there must be certain reservations in the theory of white supremacy." [40] He concluded that "*Dixie to Broadway* is the most exciting of all the musical comedies now current in New York"—a group that included *Lady Be Good,* with tunes by Gershwin and dancing by the Astaires.

The critics, however, were revealing a growing discontent with Negro musicals. Speaking of an increasing tendency "to make-up white," Alan Dale remarked: "I think that a pity"; [41] and Percy Hammond concluded that *Dixie to Broadway* was "just black performers in a white play." [42] Something essential was slipping away. Whether the critics were beginning to miss the old stereotypes or the new spontaneity, whether the shows were trying too hard to conform or to imitate, Negro musicals were becoming more pretentious and theatrical. Only the dancing remained.

These nine Negro shows from 1921 to 1924—from *Shuffle Along* to *Dixie to Broadway*—had a decisive impact on all Broadway musicals. Dancing was given new life and vitality. During this revolution no Negro dancer achieved stardom. That came later. The great Negro dancers were ahead of their times, for the Broadway audiences and critics had difficulty understanding and appreciating the subtleties of their art.

Although it paved the way for the eventual recognition of a dancing star such as Bill Robinson, this burst of creative activity did not last. By the middle of 1924 a business slump was in full swing, record sales fell off 85 to 90 per cent according to *Variety,* Hollywood was fighting bankruptcy with rumors of "talkies" to come, and the curtain was falling fast on vaudeville. Financing musicals became very difficult, and no notable Negro shows appeared on Broadway again until 1927.

20 Broadway: The Late Twenties

AFTER A DEARTH during the middle twenties, Negro musicals came back in time to ride the boom into the bust of the Depression, and before fading away altogether, establish a dancing star and personality around whom a Broadway musical could be built and film roles written: Bill Robinson (see Chapter 23). Bojangles led the way in breaking down a variety of economic and social barriers while creating a new and much larger public for vernacular dance. Other and perhaps more gifted Negro dancers were available, but only Robinson succeeded on such a grand scale.

At that time and for some time thereafter the advice "be yourself" was often addressed by white critics to Negro performers. It generally meant to be what later became known as a stereotype, and Negro musicals ran headlong into problems created by this attitude. During the period, nevertheless, Negro musicals reached a three-year peak from 1928 to 1930. In these years the critics became more knowledgeable about dancing; the talking film became a great success, drawing Broadway talent—mostly white—to Hollywood; and a few minority attitudes about the Negro began to see print without causing too much alarm.

The mid-twenties were disastrous for Negro productions. *Lucky Sambo,* appearing in 1925, with dancers Lou Keane, Mae Barnes, and Johnny Hudgins, lasted for nine performances. In the following year *My Magnolia* —with no notable dancers—came and went, hastened by poor reviews.

The still-prevailing attitude is indicated by a would-be liberal article in the same year by the young bandleader, Ted Lewis.[1] He states with *avant-garde* abandon that "the real jazz dance can only be done to jazz rhythm" and praises "colored choruses." But then he rules out acrobatic, eccentric, ballroom, and even tap dance, concluding that "the pure jazz styles" are three: "the blackface or Charleston, the shimmy or Gilda Gray, and the thumb-licking Pennington type." All Negro dancers are lumped in the Charleston category, and although he is trying to sound liberal, his careful but superficial distinctions between individual white dancers contrast with his references to black dancers as a faceless mob. At that, his remarks were—comparatively speaking—a step in the right direction.

In Harlem the first edition of *Blackbirds* (1926) opened at the Alhambra Theater, ran for several weeks, and set out for London, where the star, Florence Mills, became an international celebrity. Harlem was off the beaten track, and few reviewers saw the show. The New York *World,* however, declared *Blackbirds* better than *Dixie to Broadway* (1923-1924).[2]

By 1927 Negro musicals began to gather momentum. *Bottomland,* with singer Eva Taylor and music by Clarence Williams—but no prominent dancers—lasted for twenty-one performances. The title tune and "Shootin' the Pistol" were recorded by Clarence Williams (Paramount 12517) with among others, trumpeter Ed Allen and trombonist Charlie Irvis.

The general climate of critical confusion is indicated by the *Tribune's* comment that the show is "neither racial nor exclusively imitative of white shows, so has no form at all." [3] By "racial," the reviewer meant watermelons, crap games, chicken stealing, and the minstrel stereotypes—but imitating a white show would scarcely give it "form" either. *Africana,* a musical starring Ethel Waters, was also staged in 1927. "It was a good, fast show," writes Ethel Waters, "and gave the theater-going ofays of Broadway their first long look at me." [4] Dancers were well represented: *Baby and Bobby Goins* appeared in an "athletic-aesthetic" number, *Glenn and Jenkins* did a shoeshine routine with eccentric dancing, *Eddie and Sonny* had a "speedy routine," *The Two Black Dots* (*Taylor and Johnson*) executed a Black Bottom tap routine, and strutters Snow Fisher and Pickaninny Hill led a rousing ensemble cakewalk.

Ethel Waters sang "Shake That Thing," "Dinah," and "Take Your Black Bottom Outside," and recorded the hit of the show, "I'm Coming Virginia," on Columbia 14170 with the orchestra of Will Marion Cook. The critics all praised her: "The first good Negro comedienne," said Richard Watts, "since Florence Mills." [5]

An early and vociferous champion of the Negro, Carl Van Vechten, appeared in the reviews, too. Sitting in back of Van Vechten on opening night, Bide Dudley of the *Mirror* wrote: "He'd clap his hands with resounding smacks each time Ethel appeared, and in the midst of her second act specialty he began yelling things . . . I became uneasy for fear the assembly would think I was yelling at Ethel." [6]

Van Vechten remained unintimidated, and Miss Waters stopped the show with her "shimmy and shake" about which she writes cheerfully, "I sure knew how to roll and quiver, and my hips would become whirling dervishes." [7] In a later comment she adds, "I never shimmied vulgarly but only to express myself." [8]

In 1927, *Rang Tang* ran for 119 performances with comedians *Miller and Lyles* and music by Ford Dabney, while critics made jokes about the predominance of Negro musicals on Broadway. The reviews were mixed, from the Brooklyn *Eagle's* "all the native sparkle of *Shuffle Along*," [9] to the *Herald Tribune's* subheading: "The Colored Folks in Another Childlike Imitation of Dull White Extravaganza." [10] Unfortunately, the chorus imitated the *Tiller Girls*, in spite of the precedent of *Shuffle Along*.

Once more dancing carried the show. "Some of Harlem's friskiest hoofers," wrote Percy Hammond, "dance more skillfully on one foot than most palefaces do on two." [11] Mae Barnes, known as the "Bronze Ann Pennington," formed a trio with Byron Jones and Lavinia Mack and received long-overdue praise. *Rang Tang* was "a personal triumph" for her, said the *Eagle* [12] and the *Evening World* analyzed her charm: "a pudgy, shuffling little figure . . . who accompanied her sleepy jog trot with an absent-minded whine that was evidently a secret between herself and the footlights." [13] Reviewers commented upon her self-possession and seasoned talent in contrast to the rest of the cast. (With a mixture of conservatism and confusion, the Boston *Transcript* hailed the show as a blow for good old tap dancing and against the wicked Charleston.) [14]

Toward the end of 1927 a white musical named *Weather Clear–Track Fast* opened and closed without much comment. Yet the *Times* and, later *Theater* magazine noted "a pair of darkies" who furnished "the best moment in the play" and were "enthusiastically and justly applauded." [15] The names of the dancers in the program were "Joe Buck the Chicken Man" and "Jim Bubbles the Baltimore Sleeper." Already headliners in vaudeville, *Buck and Bubbles* had to wait another four years to be truly appreciated on Broadway in the Ziegfeld *Follies of 1931*.

Blackbirds of 1928, a revue with Adelaide Hall, opened at the Liberty Theater on May 9, 1927, and ran for 518 performances. This was the show that "discovered" Bill Robinson. Bojangles, whose Stair Dance was now acclaimed, became the first Negro dancing star on Broadway. Already fifty years old, Robinson had hit the top circuits in vaudeville before the nineteen-twenties and had danced professionally since the 1890's.

Bill Robinson achieved his lone success in spite of *Blackbirds*, for the sets were a series of stereotypes with Negro children eating watermelons and so forth. The critics said the skits were poor: The show was "a duplicate of Times Square's usages," according to the *Tribune*, "bound up in the red tape of its monotonous traditions"; [16] and it was "just a third-rate Broadway musical show, tinted brown . . ." in the words of Alexander Woollcott, ". . . with the Congo memories and plantation melodies of Tin Pan Alley." [17]

Robinson, along with a few others such as Snake Hips Tucker, nevertheless made the show a resounding success. With his appearance the critics began to show some understanding of tap. Bojangles had the showmanship to make the audience pay attention. In their enthusiasm the critics began to examine exactly what Robinson did with his feet—starting with the Stair Dance—and although innocent of technical terms, they noted that his taps were clean and clear.

Keep Shufflin', a Negro musical of 1928, was a moderate success. It opened in February at Daly's 63rd Street Theater with actor-comedians *Miller and Lyles*. Fats Waller and James P. Johnson wrote the tunes, Will Vodery arranged the music and conducted the orchestra. The show ran for a respectable 104 performances while the *New Yorker* noted "the tempestuous dancing for which the race is unsurpassed," [18] without mentioning a dancer. Both the *Post* and the *American* remarked that the chorus girls were too light-skinned.[19] Presumably they expected what they referred to as "darkies," although in Harlem only light-skinned girls had been hired since the teens.

The year 1929, just before the Depression, was a banner year for Negro shows on Broadway. Five notable revues or musicals and one important play were produced. After a successful run uptown, *Deep Harlem* opened at the Biltmore Theater in January with a new approach. Salem Tutt-Whitney and J. Homer Tutt wrote, staged, and acted in a portrayal with song and dance of the Negro from Africa to Harlem. In *Deep Harlem* they were swimming against the stream, for whites had a low opinion of African culture, and most Negroes had been taught to feel ashamed of it.

The critics arrived expecting watermelons on the ol' plantation and were puzzled. The *Telegram* panned it without conviction,[20] the *Sun* announced that *Deep Harlem* was "too self-conscious . . . too refined . . . weighted down with a Message or whatever it was," [21] and the *Post* pointed out that the show improved "after tracing of the history brings the Negroes to Harlem"—when the stereotypes began—and added that it "showed a tendency toward satire . . . Harlem, according to one of the characters, is built on a bluff." [22] At the time, this brand of humor was obscure to many whites.

One reviewer labeled the show "a combination of *The Emperor Jones* and *Shuffle Along*," and although he didn't care for it, noted that "two boys named Cutout and Leonard knew how to dance." [23]

Cutout and Leonard were Maceo Ellis and Leonard Reed. They could tap, but they specialized in eccentric dancing. "We didn't exactly fit in except as a kind of dancing relief," says Reed, "but that show was years ahead of its time." [24]

The cliché that the Negro was "a man without a past" survived *Deep Harlem*, for as Noble Sissle observed, "People expected a colored show to *romp*." [25]

Such expectations were rudely thwarted a month later when *Harlem*, a play by William Rapp and Wallace Thurmond, opened at the midtown Apollo Theater. In a rent-party scene, the Slow Drag hit Times Square, and Broadway was staggered by a glimpse of the authentic roots of Negro dance. Unlike most musical-comedy dancing, the Slow Drag was social dancing—Negro folk variety—and beyond registering alarm, nobody knew what to make of it.

In the play's rent-party scene fifteen or more couples danced the Slow Drag, each couple improvising their own variations. They were "writhing lustily through their barbaric dances," [26] wrote Alison Smith in the *World;* "steaming couples," wrote Arthur Pollack (who was usually sympathetic) in the Brooklyn *Eagle,* "undulating with a great unholy violence never seen before." [27] In the *News,* Burns Mantle prophesied that the police would stop the "orgiastic exhibition." [28]

Richard Lockridge in the *Sun* liked it and went a little deeper. He spoke of "the slow sensual deeply felt rhythms which the negro has brought to the white man and which the white man, however he may try, is always a little too self-conscious to accept." In spite of the inherent bow to the "noble savage," he puts his finger on an underlying cause of many a critic's response: "Men and women who dance like that have the strength for violence." [29]

Inevitably, groups in Harlem objected, the dance was toned down at the request of the authorities, and the play did not have a long run. Although it would probably have passed unremarked in the 1960's, the rent-party scene dipped so far back into the Negro tradition that it seemed entirely new. On the other hand, it appears that more recent dances like the Jerk and the Frug, which came forty years later, still have a long way to go.

A second musical, *Messin' Around,* opened at the Hudson Theater in April with "a huge cast of unknowns," as one reviewer stated. After a brief interval, the *New Yorker* called it third rate [30] and *Theater* magazine described it as fourth rate.[31] No dancers of note appeared in it.

A quick casualty the following month was *Pansy,* which lasted for three performances. It was so bad that, according to the *Tribune,* "hisses were to be heard for the first time in the annals of Broadway premieres." [32]

Nevertheless, *Pansy* has a claim to fame: Bessie Smith, described at the time as "the Aunt Jemima of the radiolas and dictaphones . . . a dusky and bulky song shouter," [33] was judged to be the best part of a poor show and, according to the *Post,* executed "sundry dance steps at intervals." [34] Bessie Smith was not a great dancer, but she could do a reasonably good shimmy and shake.

For several years such Harlem night clubs as Small's Paradise, the Cotton Club, and Connie's Inn had been staging annual revues. Following the lead of Lew Leslie's Plantation Club, from which *Blackbirds* was assembled, the revue at Connie's Inn came downtown in 1929. *Hot Chocolates* opened June twentieth at the Hudson Theater on Broadway. Singers Baby Cox and Edith Wilson starred in a cast of some eighty-five entertainers and Leroy Smith's orchestra played in the pit. By mid-July, Louis Armstrong, and later Fats Waller, were playing during intermissions.

"What the show does go in for and perfectly grandly," wrote the *World*, "is dancing," [35] and the critics noticed a new dancer: Jazzlips Richardson. Used as a filler-in on opening night, Richardson, who had been a carnival comedian, became one of the show's hits. He combined eccentric and acrobatic dancing (plus a few contortions) with blackface comedy. The *Sun*, carried away with this combination of techniques, began talking about "side-splits" [*sic*] and "back-flips" [36]—perhaps the first time a Broadway critic had shown such a technical interest and ignorance—while the *Post* noted that "an eel-like gentleman named Jazzlips" [37] was the hit of the show.

The critics were slightly off target. As acrobatic dancer U. S. Thompson mildly observed: "Jazzlips was an eccentric dancer, not an acrobatic dancer. His specialty was blackface comedy." [38] Pictures of Jazzlips in the program bear out Thompson's statement. Jazzlips wears a frock coat, white gloves, floppy tie, and a tiny hat. He uses black cork with a huge white mouth—the costume of a minstrel comedian. The critics failed to mention the swinging acrobats billed as "The Six Crackerjacks" (see Chapter 32), who joined the show later, and must have made Jazzlips's acrobatics seem amateurish.

Hot Chocolates could not obtain the services of Bill Robinson, since he was tied up in vaudeville, but by October, eighteen-year-old Roland Holder, inaccurately billed as Robinson's protégé,[39] was performing an elegant soft-shoe, dressed in top hat and tails.

"He did a great schottische to 'Swanee River' in a minor key," says Harland Dixon, "and it was really clean cut." [40]

Pete Nugent agrees and adds, "He did a soft-shoe with a lot of action and body movement." [41] At the time, few dancers knew that Holder had learned most of his routines from Buddy Bradley (see Chapter 21).

For the rest, Baby Cox presented a Snake Hips dance that shook the Brooklyn *Eagle* reviewer: "a dance . . . which it is to be hoped will never get to be a ballroom pastime." [42] And Shake-dancer Louise "Jota" Cook reminded another reviewer of Little Egypt.[43]

Before the end of 1929 *Bomboola* opened at the Royale Theater, where it lasted for about a month. Two reviewers noted the appearance of a new dancer: "It has . . . a tap dancer called Derby," said the *Journal*, "who gives an imitation of Bill Robinson that should cause the imitated to pause and contemplate the fact that when he is gone there will be others to follow after, close on his tapping heels." [44]

A month later *Commonweal* referred to "some superlative tap dancing by a dusky gentleman named Derby." [45]

Derby Wilson, who along with Bill Bailey was a disciple of Bill Robinson, appeared and disappeared on Broadway without a last name. Although they never achieved the showmanship of Bill Robinson, both Wilson and Bailey could do more with their feet, a state of affairs that Bojangles acknowledged by insisting that they copy none of his steps, especially the ancient Stair Dance. By 1965 Bailey was in temporary retirement, while Derby Wilson was still active abroad.

The last good year for Negro musicals was 1930. *Hot Rhythm* was billed at the Times Square Theater as "A Sepia-Tinted Little Show," and in spite of poor reviews, survived for sixty-eight performances. Everyone liked the dancing, but otherwise the *Sun* called it "mediocre," [46] the *Times* "tasteless," [47] and the *World* "stale," [48] with the increasingly repeated criticism that it was copying white imitations of Negro shows. "These colored revues," stated the *World*, "are reflecting not the native Negro product but the white Broadway reflection of it."

In *Hot Rhythm*, Mae Barnes and Eddie Rector (who played the role of master of ceremonies), had the same hard luck that dogged both of them for most of their careers: They never appeared in a musical good enough to establish them as popular stars. They carried *Hot Rhythm*, however. "Mae Barnes, who possesses a real sense of comedy . . . and an effortless dancer by the name of Eddie Rector," reported the *Times*, "are outstanding." [49] The critics were becoming more competent—the adjective "effortless" is right for Rector. The length of time a Broadway show could be kept going by dancers, however, was diminishing.

Perhaps the most important Negro musical, with the exception of the original *Shuffle Along*, was *Brown Buddies*, which opened at the Liberty Theater on October 7, 1930. The show was built around Bill Robinson and ran for 113 performances. Also in the cast were Adelaide Hall, Ada Brown, Putney Dandridge, and a comedy team called *Red and Struggy*. The popularity of tap dance was never higher.

The plot, songs, and jokes of *Brown Buddies* were all described as poor. The *Tribune* called it "a cheaply pretentious . . . imitation opera," [50] and the *World* voiced a common objection: "how near they are to a Broadway which used to copy them, but which they now copy in return." [51] Yet the applause for Bill Robinson, reported the *Tribune*, "has not been equalled since the first night of *The Merry Widow*" [52]—an historic occasion. *Brown Buddies* was a personal triumph for Bill Robinson.

The education of the reviewers continued. Critic after critic was delighted by the manner in which Bojangles watched his feet: "He croons with his feet and laughs with them and watches them in wide-eyed amazement," wrote Lockridge in the *Sun*, "as they do things which apparently surprise him as much as they do the rest of us and please him, if possible, even more . . ." [53]

"He has a trick of watching his feet as he dances," wrote Skinner in *Commonweal,* "as if he were talking to them gently and coaxing them to do the impossible. When they obey him, as they always do, he beams with delight . . ." [54]

The effect was to make the audience—and the critics—watch Robinson's feet. With their eyes riveted where the action was taking place, the critics took a lesson in tap, becoming interested in the finer points, absorbing a standard for future comparison, and gaining confidence in their own judgment. After they had seen Robinson a few times, the competence of drama critics reviewing tap dance improved noticeably. Robert Benchley wrote in the *New Yorker:* [55]

> Dancers come and dancers go, they twist their bodies and they work their feet to a double, triple, and even quadruple tempo in an attempt to do something new to the old-fashioned tap. But Bill Robinson just goes right ahead—one-two-three-four-one-two-three-four—in the regulation beat, slow measured, and indescribably liquid, like a brook flowing over pebbles, and . . . satisfies every craving for rhythm. . . . It is very simple, once you realize that it isn't speed and that it isn't complexity and that it isn't acrobatics that make a satisfying tap. All you have to have is a God-given genius and take your time.

Both Percy Hammond and George Jean Nathan pointed out that Robinson was a fine actor. To cap the climax, Bojangles was breaking down long-standing prejudices. "Many of the most uppity white folks," noted Gilbert Gabriel in the *American,* "—Fred Stone and family, for instance—have taken lessons from his nimble feet." [56]

Almost ignored because of Robinson's triumph were the eccentric and comedy hoofers *Red and Struggy.* A good example of a satiric tradition tracing back to carnival days and before, they amazed Broadway. "What the audience liked best last night," said the *Eagle,* "were the crazy antics of two inspired black imbeciles." [57]

John Mason Brown thought them a match for Robinson.[58] "This Red gets a big hand for a sort of freak, eccentric bit of hoofing," said the *Interstate Tattler.* "He is a weird looking chap who works along the lines of his looks." [59] Red was a freckled blond and a fine pantomimist (see Chapter 30), famous among dancers as a "cool cat"—twenty or so years before it became fashionable.

The repeated criticisms of *Hot Rhythm, Brown Buddies,* and other Negro musicals as imitations of white musicals copying Negro musicals finally drew fire from a Negro who had been through the mill. "Most of our shows are financed, staged and directed by white men," wrote Salem Tutt-Whitney in the Chicago *Defender,* "and most of these white men arrogate the right to tell us when and how. Under the circumstances I don't see how we miss being colored so often." [60]

Pointing out that many people think the white entertainers *Amos 'n' Andy* as well as *Moran and Mack* (*The Two Black Crows*) are more like Negroes than real Negroes, Tutt-Whitney observed: "Just how the imitation can surpass the original is difficult for many to understand." As for a critic who pines for the ante-bellum Negro: "Not one out of every hundred of the boys and girls who try to be 'colored' on Broadway ever saw a log cabin or a cotton field. They are likely not to be as familiar with these properties as the reviewer. . . . Every day in every way it is becoming more difficult for Race actors to be 'colored.'" [61]

Thirty years later Howard Taubman announced an "indisputable trend" in which, as the headline stated, the "Negro *Begins* [*author's italics*] to Speak for Himself on Stage." [62]

Another musical, *Change Your Luck,* appeared in 1930 at the Cohan Theater and sank almost at once. The *Sun* reported a "bad plot, awful acting, shouting of directions from the wings." [63] Alberta Hunter was in the cast, however, and a team of acrobatic tappers named *The Four Flash Devils* were the highlight of the show. *The Four Flash Devils* were part of a new trend: teams instead of a solo dancer and hair-raising acrobatics such as slides, flips, and splits in addition to tap. Audiences seemed to be losing interest, and dancers were trying to recapture attention with new stunts.

Blackbirds of 1930, which ran for sixty-two performances at the Royale Theater and starred Ethel Waters, was the last notable musical of the year. Critics agreed that the show was too long—"they came back for encores even if it was only a dropped program or a sneeze" [64]—and disliked the blackface makeup, the "darkey dialect," and the stale humor. (Robert Benchley thought Ethel Waters's songs too smutty.) [65] But they loved the dancing, which was well represented by Jazzlips Richardson, *Buck and Bubbles,* and *The Berry Brothers* (see Chapter 34). "The whole show stops," said the *Telegram,* "when there isn't any dancing." [66]

The humor of Jazzlips was beginning to pall, but *Buck and Bubbles* received favorable mention, and the Berrys became one of the hits of the show. "Together they do one of those acrobatic dances," said the Boston *Transcript* where the show tried out, "in top hats and faultless evening attire as if to show how easy it is for them after all." [67] Their act lasted about four-and-a-half minutes. The brothers combined "picture" strutting with precise acrobatics, a seemingly relaxed blend that was over before anyone knew what was happening.

Several critics were very impressed by the team. "Ananias Berry stops the show," said the Brooklyn *Eagle,* perceptively. "No one, black or white, can dance as he does. A kid, he has gone further already than most dancers ever get." [68]

In spite of all this, a note of disenchantment was slowly appearing.

"These darkies, like most darkies, simply go on repeating the one or two little tricks they have, and get pretty tiresome after you've been looking at them for a number of years," wrote George Jean Nathan. "The dancing is still as hot as ever, though it follows the rapidly becoming stale pattern . . ." [69] Nathan's comments, although uninformed, were typical of a growing attitude toward vernacular dance on Broadway.

By 1931 most Negro musicals were folding rapidly. The best, Lew Leslie's *Rhapsody in Black,* tried to be different by featuring choirs singing Jewish and Russian songs. In between, Ethel Waters, who was feuding with Leslie over salary, sang and delivered monologues. There were fine dancers, too: Eddie Rector, *The Berry Brothers,* and Snake Hips Tucker, although by cutting down on the time allotted to each dancer, the show overdid the attempt to be different. It had a respectable run, but most of the reviewers wanted more than "brief glimpses."

Times and attitudes were changing. Robert Benchley tried to explain the mood:

> Up until three or four years ago, I was the Peer of Tap-Dance-Enjoyers . . . it didn't seem as if I could get enough tap-dancing. But I did. More than enough. With every revue and musical comedy offering a complicated tap routine every seven minutes throughout the program, and each dancer vying with the rest to upset the easy rhythm of the original dance form, tap-dancing has lost its tang.[70]

Tap dancing could no longer carry a musical.

For the rest, *Singin' the Blues,* a "musical melodrama," employed *The Four Flash Devils* and a group of Lindy Hoppers—John Mason Brown called it lively and "an honest attempt to do something different"; [71] *Sugar Hill,* although it featured an anonymous "old man who sprinkles sand before he performs" [72] (perhaps Chappy Chappelle, who was in the cast), brought on accusations that the chorus was imitating a satire by Ray Bolger; [73] and *Fast and Furious* led to the observation that "the so-called colored show is going definitely out of fashion." [74]

In 1932 *Blackberries of '32* and *Yeah Man* with Eddie Rector vanished overnight, while an ill-fated revival of *Shuffle Along* with *The Four Flash Devils* and a new plot, based on the Depression—"waitin' for the whistles to blow"—lasted about a week.

In 1933 Bill Robinson, in a new edition of *Blackbirds,* lasted one month, and another show, *Hummin' Sam,* survived for one performance. Four years passed before the WPA produced *Swing It* in 1937, which prompted *Variety* to observe that the "vogue of colored musicals which came in with *Shuffle Along* passed from favor years ago . . . *Swing It* will not revive it." [75]

Beginning with *Flying Down to Rio* with Ginger Rogers in 1933, Fred Astaire made a more personal style of dancing popular in the movies, and a few Negro teams, preceded by Bill Robinson, were occasionally employed in Hollywood well into the forties. As for night clubs, the two annual Cotton Club revues, which had featured just about every dancer of note during the twenties and thirties in Harlem, came down to Broadway briefly in the late thirties before the club closed permanently.

The last years of Bill Robinson were some of the best during the decline of tap. A hit in *The Hot Mikado* (1939), he flopped in a white show, *All in Fun* (1940), and staged a comeback in a movie *Stormy Weather* (1943) and a Broadway show *Memphis Bound* (1945). Bojangles died in 1949 when the great years of vernacular dance on Broadway were ended.

What killed the Negro musical, and more specifically, what killed vernacular dancing on Broadway? The immediate causes were careless presentation, overexposure, and the Depression. The most crushing blow came from within. In 1936 *On Your Toes* featured the widely acclaimed ballet sequence "Slaughter on Tenth Avenue," choreographed by George Balanchine, and any comeback that tap dancing might have staged was nipped in the bud. With the appearance of *Oklahoma* (1943), the process was irreversible. Ballet was the rage, and "ballet," says George Balanchine, "is woman." [76]

An interesting incident took place at the second—and also unsuccessful—revival of *Shuffle Along* in 1952. "The show was trying out in Philadelphia, and the chorus 'girl-boys' were doing a mournful ballet to the tune 'I'm Just Wild about Harry,'" says Noble Sissle, "so Flournoy Miller found Eddie Rector and told him to do one of those old-time Sand dances. When the ballet boys saw Rector, they yawned and said 'What's this old man gonna do?' Rector took his little tin of sand, spread it carefully on the stage, and stopped the show cold. The chorus boys nearly popped their eyes out." During the short time that the *Shuffle Along* revival lasted, Rector was the dancing star.

21 Choreography: Buddy Bradley

THE MUSIC BOX THEATER curtain parts on the most-talked-about scene in the *Little Show of 1929.* Sprawled on a sagging bed in a shabby room is Clifton Webb, dressed in the flashiest zoot-suit of the twenties—no jacket—and an oily pimp's wig with long sideburns. Libby Holman enters, and as Webb ignores her, conceals a few bills in her stocking. She hands the rest of her earnings to Webb.

Momentarily interested, Webb rises languidly and starts to dance with her. As he dances, he makes love until he comes upon the hidden money. He tears away the money with a curse, throws Holman violently to the floor, and saunters to stage front and center. This is the cue for the song—and the dance which caused consternation.

While Libby Holman sings "Moanin' Low" in the background, Clifton Webb counts the money expertly and goes into an imitation of Earl Tucker's Snake Hips dance, facing the audience. The usually dapper Webb becomes a one-man Laocoön, writhing in rhythm and tossing his pelvis about in figure-eights like a cowboy's lasso. As the song ends, Webb slithers out, slamming the door as Holman throws herself against it.

The press reported the hysteria that followed the dance, the *Telegraph* noting, "Its execution seemed . . . to be assailed by panic,"[1] the *Telegram* observing, "the way Webb turned elastic in this scene caused an uproar out beyond the lights."[2] The boy-and-girl duet, scheduled to follow, waited while Holman and Webb returned for bow after bow.

A page of photographs with instructions on how to perform Clifton Webb's routine "High Yaller" from the "Moanin' Low" number in *The Little Show* appeared in 1929 in *The Dance* magazine, posed by Webb in full costume.[3] Interviewed sixteen years later by a New York paper, Clifton

Webb remembered "the story of the 'Moanin' Low' number" perfectly. He had wanted to use Libby Holman in a dance. "I was inspired by a book I'd been reading . . . Carl Van Vechten's *Nigger Heaven,*" he said. "I told Dwight [the producer] I wanted to do a 'high-yaller pimp' . . . we rehearsed the number in the toilet of the Music Box Theater because I didn't want anyone to see it until we were finished. . . ." [4]

Did Webb remember Buddy Bradley? He did not mention him—but then, neither would many others in the same position. In those days a musical comedy had its dance director, who "grouped" the scenes (the title of choreographer came later), and the stars had their private coaches (they still do). When a star performed a routine which he had been carefully taught by a coach—down to the slightest gesture—the public naturally thought it was his own and gave him all the credit. Nobody saw anything wrong in such an arrangement. The coach had been paid.

"Clifton Webb came to me hunting ideas for himself in the *Little Show,*" said choreographer Buddy Bradley when we interviewed him in London during the summer of 1963, "and I worked up the entire scene for him, using Earl Tucker's Snake Hips dance, and called it High Yaller." [5] At the time Webb was a musical-comedy dancer who had been influenced by the ballroom dancing of Vernon and Irene Castle. As a result of the *Little Show,* however, he was forthwith regarded, even among Negro dancers, as a highly talented performer.

"Buddy Bradley is the greatest teacher of them all," [6] says Pete Nugent flatly. Although his name is seldom mentioned, Bradley created dance routines for many of the Broadway musicals in the late twenties and early thirties. He coached Mae West, Ed Wynn, Gilda Gray, Pat Rooney, Ann Pennington, Eddie Foy, Betty Compton, Clifton Webb, Ruby Keeler, Jack Donahue, Adele and Fred Astaire, Tom Patricola, the Lane Sisters, Will Mahoney, Lucille Ball, Joe Laurie, Jr., Eleanor Powell, Paul Draper—to name some of the best known—creating one or more dance routines, sometimes complete scenes, for each of them.

In one edition of George White's *Scandals,* he coached Tom Patricola in a tap Black Bottom, Ann Pennington in a "cute" Black Bottom ("I always had her do things that accentuated her dimpled knees"), and Frances Williams singing "Black Bottom." Again, he coached Adele Astaire in a Ziegfeld show, which featured Fred Astaire and Marilyn Miller dancing together. "It was the first time Fred danced with another partner," says Bradley, "so they gave Adele a solo dance. She came to me instead of Fred for a routine, and although the show didn't last long, she was very pleased with it."

Another time Bradley danced at the Palace with Joe Laurie, Jr. As an encore, Bradley recalls, Laurie announced: "I've been learning a new routine from a fellow on 46th Street who is the greatest teacher in the world—do you want to see it?" When the audience applauded, Bradley came out and did the dance himself.

Bradley never choreographed a white show as long as he remained in the United States. "They called me in to patch them up," says Bradley, "when they realized how bad the dancing was." Well paid, but well known only within show-business circles, he received no public recognition. "I never saw half the shows my stuff appeared in," he adds with an amused grin. "I wasn't invited, and besides I was too busy teaching."

Buddy Bradley had the talent and diplomacy to crack the mold. His keeping all those stars happy and coming back for more testifies to his tact and ability. In 1933 Charles Cochrane, "the Ziegfeld of England," hired him to choreograph the London production of *Evergreen,* which became a hit. "In all modesty," says Bradley, "no colored person had ever been given so much responsibility." He was in charge of sixty-four people—sixteen regular dancers, sixteen Tiller girls, sixteen show girls, and sixteen chorus boys. As far as can be ascertained, it was the first time a Negro choreographed an entire white show and received credit for it on the program.

He stayed on happily in London, working with the Cochrane musicals. "I was doing exactly what I should have been doing in New York," he says. Over the years he has worked in France, Italy, Switzerland, and Spain. He created a cabaret act for Vera Zorina and Anton Dolin; joined forces with Massine, Balanchine, and Frederick Ashton in several productions; directed the dancing in films and television shows abroad; and wrote and choreographed *High Yellow,* in which Markova starred for Sadlers Wells.

"Bradley is the Gauguin of the dance," declared the *Manchester Guardian.* Jessie Matthews, whom he coached in many of her films, compared him to Busby Berkeley—apparently unaware of the irony that Berkeley had little or no sense of rhythm—and concluded that he could have been the top dance-director in Hollywood. Unfortunately, she was wrong.

Clarence "Buddy" Bradley was born in Harrisburg, Pennsylvania, in the early teens. When Buddy was quite young, his father died, and his religious mother brought him up strictly—"she insisted that I mind my manners, whatever I did." Still, he managed to see Dancing Dotson (whom he calls One-Eye and means no disrespect) and Jack Wiggins at the local theater, learning to do the Time Step on one foot by the time he was eight years old. He preferred the Charleston, however, along with the vast assortment of Afro-American vernacular dances from the deep South —the Strut, the Drag, the Shuffle, and all the rest.

At the age of fourteen, when his mother died, Bradley went to live with a brother-in-law in Utica, New York, and worked as a hotel busboy. Three months later, escaping to New York City, he wound up at Mrs. Douglas's

133rd Street boarding house, a place full of show people—especially dancers. "Engagements were not too plentiful," says Bradley, "and most of the boarders had day jobs." He soon found a job as an elevator boy.

"I remember 'One-String Willie' of the *Tasmanian Trio,* who lived at that boarding house," Bradley adds. "He came from Georgia. His real name was George 'Tosh' Hammid, and he could stand on a phone book in his overcoat with a briefcase under his arm and do a front flip—a forward no-hands somersault—and land right back on that phone book."

With a group of youngsters, including Derby Wilson, Bradley practiced dance steps in a blind alley next to Connie's Inn. "The competition at the Hoofers Club, the unofficial headquarters of tap dance, was too fast," he notes, "although later on I was practically a charter member." Bradley soon learned the Time Step on both feet and then an Off to Buffalo with Scissors.

The real stars of Mrs. Douglas's boarding house, however, were *Greenlee and Drayton* the elegant "class act." One afternoon downtown Bradley ran into Thaddeus Drayton on his way to meet Leonard Harper, who was choreographing Negro revues at the downtown Kentucky Club and at Connie's Inn uptown. He needed more chorus boys, and when Drayton recommended Bradley—"Buddy was a fine, hard-working chap," Drayton recalls—Harper hired Bradley then and there.

Bradley had never danced professionally, but he soon mastered the routines and served an apprenticeship of a little over a year in the Connie's Inn chorus. "Bradley learned quickly," says Drayton, "but I think chorus work bored him." [7]

During the year Bradley learned to do Wings, flips, knee-drops, and other tap and acrobatic steps ("I never could do splits") and gradually became known as one of the best young dancers in Harlem. Most important of all he was in the same show as the dancer who was to become his idol: Eddie Rector. Well aware of Rector's grace, Bradley was most impressed by his inventiveness. "At a time when everybody else was just hoofing," says Bradley, "Eddie was traveling across the stage with his own free-flowing style."

Around 1928 Bradley met Billy Pierce, the impresario who had been trying to effect a liaison between the white and Negro show worlds. White show business needed new dances and was beginning to realize that the Negro was an inexhaustible source. Sensing the trend, Pierce, who had been a taxi driver in Chicago, opened a small office and dance studio in a 12-by-16-foot room on the third floor of a building at 225 West 46th Street. A screen around the battered desk separated the office from the studio. He also worked as janitor to help pay the rent. Pierce was not a dancer himself ("he couldn't lift a foot," says Pete Nugent), but he had hired Negro dancers to coach white clients without much success.

Pierce tried once more when he met Bradley. "I hear you're a good dancer," he said. "I have a client who needs a routine—will you teach her?" The scheme was to charge fifty dollars for the routine and take twenty-five dollars apiece. Bradley had never coached anyone, but he cheerfully agreed. The client turned out to be Irene Delroy, a singer and dancer in the *Greenwich Village Follies of 1928,* which according to Bradley, had been running at the Imperial Theater for about four months, with Busby Berkeley as choreographer.

Irene Delroy was an attractive person, but not much of a dancer. Ready to teach her Wings and complicated tap steps, Bradley was brought up short by the fact that she simply could not execute them. "She had a solo dance to a medium-tempo tune with a Charleston beat," says Bradley, "two choruses of thirty-two bars, sixty-four bars in all—it was her big moment." On an impulse Bradley worked out a compromise: "I put a few easy taps to the Charleston beat and worked them into traveling movements which she could handle." He was aided by his feeling that "a lady dancer should look cute and appealing, not like a regular hoofer."

Irene Delroy was so pleased with the new routine that she memorized it from entrance to exit in four days and introduced it with tremendous success. The following afternoon six other girls from the show came to Bradley for lessons, and a few days later, producer Morris Green asked Bradley to rechoreograph the entire production. (Busby Berkeley's name remained on the program as dance director.) "From then on," Thaddeus Drayton recalls, "nobody needed to teach Bradley anything."

Prosperity had arrived. "Ned Wayburn was our only competition," says Herbert Harper, one of Bradley's assistants, "and he was square." [8] The Pierce Studios with Buddy Bradley as "Director," took over the entire first floor of 225 West 46th Street, putting in showers, dressing rooms, and private studios. "Billy Pierce had private peepholes through which he watched the lessons as they were being given," says Harper, "and he fired a couple of instructors for being too friendly with their pupils." "I worked from ten A.M. to ten P.M. every day except Sunday, giving two private lessons every hour and running back and forth between them," says Bradley. He soon had a staff of five instructors, charged $250 a routine, and made over a thousand dollars a week.

Early in 1931, photographer Cecil Beaton had a date with Adele Astaire.[9]

> I went down Broadway to see Adele Astaire at a Negro dance school where she is taking lessons. Adele looked her best in a pair of pale blue drawers that revealed witty legs. She smiled like a little monkey and said, "Oh, Buddy has taught me such marvelous, new, *dirty* steps. . . . [*authors' italics*]"

> An atmospheric place, this dance school: a rather "high" smell of stale sweat and face powder predominated. Gramophones ground away in competition from every room, accompanied by a frenzied tapping of steel-toed shoes. . . .

As for the "dirty steps," Adele Astaire was simply reflecting the common attitude of professional white dancers to the traditional hip movements of Afro-American vernacular dance.

Day after day, with consistently impressive results, Bradley tossed off foot-tailored routines for a variety of dancers, some of them already top-notch performers. Others were gangsters' molls. The demand was ceaseless, but Bradley was filling it with no apparent effort. How did he do it? He was a born teacher with a fine personality, of course, but the real key to his success was a new blend, a revolutionary simplification.

In Bradley's day dancers in Broadway shows fell into three overlapping categories: Buck and Wing, Soft Shoe, and musical comedy. This third category, musical comedy, was used to describe the combination of simple steps employed by the ingenue and juvenile—before Bradley and others made their influence felt. These steps were the lowest common denominator of professional dancing, taught—along with courses in makeup, costume, diet, singing, and deportment—at the large and immensely successful Ned Wayburn Dance Studios.

At the same time, uptown, Negro dancers who were largely unknown to Broadway were concentrating on tap and being driven by competition among themselves to create intricate steps, which no one else could do. This led to great emphasis on technique as well as complex rhythms, and in the process, non-tap steps—the Afro-American vernacular—fell into disrepute. "We thought nothing of the fact that everybody in and out of colored show-business seemed to know a million old jive steps," says Bradley, "endless variations on the Shuffle and so on—they were corny."

Bradley and his friends laughed at the gyrations of Dynamite Hooker for example, although Hooker always brought down the house. "We all knew those movements as kids," says Bradley. "They were a part of our life that we took for granted—and it was some time before I realized that they were pretty new to Broadway and that most white people couldn't begin to do any of them." They turned out to be the magic ingredient in the blend he created.

Further, even the tap dancing of his peers had a limited appeal to Bradley. "It seemed to me that there were about forty or so tap steps with variations, which just about everybody knew and repeated over and over," Bradley says, "and the sound of most of those steps was pretty ricky-tick."

As an example he points out what Bill Robinson could do with the simplest rhythms—"he made them *look* great"—and adds: "Jack Wiggins's

Tango Twist was a pretty thing to watch, but the sound was elementary." The exception to the rhythmic monotony of tap, as Bradley heard and saw it, was Eddie Rector. "He put together new combinations, used his whole body, and traveled." Rector opened up new vistas for Bradley.

Thus, faced with the problem of creating a routine for Irene Delroy, Bradley developed a blend of easy tap plus movements from the Afro-American vernacular, put together with an over-all continuity and rising to a climax. "I like to finish out a step with a graceful movement," says Bradley, explaining how he combines steps into routines that form an artistic whole. Compared to the tap dancing of the day, the result was simpler in sound (although it had eccentric accents), and more interesting visually.

Bradley had the ability to create a routine with a beginning, middle, and end—and then break it down into component parts and teach it. In a sense, he parallels the achievement of W. C. Handy in having the impulse and ability to "get it down," if only for a few moments, so that his ideas could be transmitted to others. He had no system of dance notation, however, nor any way to copyright his steps. Unlike Handy, Bradley made a living on the first and only sale of a product he had to create anew each time.

The source of Bradley's inspiration is surprisingly logical. He went directly to jazz recordings. "I bought rafts of records and listened carefully to the accenting of improvised solos," he says, "at first, to musicians like Trumbauer, Beiderbecke, Lang, and Rollini." He remembers using a solo by Miff Mole on a Red Nichols recording of "Riverboat Shuffle"; later, a solo by guitarist Charlie Christian on the Goodman Sextet's "Flying Home"; and still later, various solos by Dizzy Gillespie.

"In those early days I couldn't use Duke Ellington," Bradley says. "Duke was too far out for my pupils. He was blues-oriented and his soloists used glissandos, slurs, and smears, while I needed sharp, clear accenting." (Later, he used Ellington's "Old Man Blues" and "Rockin' in Rhythm" for ensemble routines.)

"I preferred white soloists in those days because they played like drummers, hitting every note on the head," says Bradley. "They were easy to follow." One of Bradley's assistants, Frank Harrington, was enamored of Rollini's booming saxophone solos and adept at copying them on the piano. "He'd play the low-pitched instruments with his left hand, the high-pitched with his right." Bradley took it from there to his students.

Bradley had great talent for translating the *accents* of improvising jazz soloists into dance patterns that were new to Broadway. "I didn't have my pupils copy a jazz solo note by note, but worked it all out myself first, using the solo to give me a notion of what I wanted to do. I had to get a picture in my mind of how a dance should look, and those accents always gave me new ideas." Bradley ignored the melody and followed the accenting of the soloist, gaining a fresh rhythmic pattern, which he filled in with body movements from the Afro-American vernacular.

Buddy Bradley was not a great solo dancer, but his ideas spilled over into Harlem. "One of my assistants was Roland Holder," says Bradley. "Whenever he saw me teaching a routine he liked, he would ask me to teach it to him." Short, bandy-legged, and immaculate, Holder took a soft-shoe-and-rhythm routine which he had learned from Bradley to a midnight show in Harlem and created a sensation. "We never had swapped steps with Holder on the street corner as we did with other dancers," says Pete Nugent. "He appeared on the scene all of a sudden and knocked us out—of course, he never mentioned Buddy Bradley."

Herbie Harper, who took over after Bradley left and stayed on until Pierce died in 1934 (he was paid the low salary of $15 a week because he wanted the job so badly), coached his share of celebrities, too. He worked with Adele and Fred Astaire—"I'd teach her first, and he'd get it from her"—as consultant to Reuben Mamoulian to pep up *Porgy and Bess* (John Bubbles was in the cast), and as assistant to George Balanchine for *On Your Toes*—"I was supposed to help him get used to working in America." In the course of this last job he taught rhythm dancing to Ray Bolger for the "Slaughter on Tenth Avenue" number. "Bolger knew his ballet but not his jazz toe and heel work," says Harper. "He had to come down out of the air for this new blend."

Paradoxically, some of the best choreography in those days was accomplished by white producer, Lew Leslie, who directed Negro shows. The reason is simple. "At rehearsals Leslie would ask a dancer what he had done last time," says Bradley, "and then announce: 'Okay, that's what you'll do this time.' " The dancer then did pretty much as he pleased and it was usually something new. When Cochrane took over the British edition of *Blackbirds,* he hired Bradley as choreographer and gave him credit in the program. Leslie objected, saying he never needed a choreographer, to which Bradley says Cochrane replied: "Well, you're going to have one this time because the last *Blackbirds* was just a re-hash."

Once in a while Leslie had a great idea, or at least, took over something that turned into a big hit. One such was a rhythmic version of the *Chauve Souris'* "Parade of the Wooden Soldiers," which had become popular in the early twenties. "It was a scandal among dancers," says Bradley, "because Leslie took the whole idea from Eddie Rector, had him teach it to the chorus, and then put Florence Mills out front as the leader and Rector back in the chorus."

Bradley was not alone as a Negro choreographer—he simply was one of the best. Before and after his time, other talented choreographers were employed, among them Charlie White, Frank Montgomery, Charlie Davis, Addison Carey, Sammy Dyer, Willie Covan, Leonard Reed, Clarence Robinson, and Leonard Harper—to name the best known. They worked with Negro shows, in night clubs, vaudeville, and theaters, and now and then coached white stars, privately.

At least two Negro director-producers, Irving C. Miller and Addison Carey, who choreographed their own and other shows, could not dance a step according to other performers; they followed the general practice of hiring Negro dancers who could do the job. Again, dance-director Clarence Robinson ("He couldn't dance to pass a fly," says Bill Bailey [10]) had the enterprise to borrow ideas from Roxy's productions downtown—chorus girls with bells and bicycles, for example—and stage them with great success in Harlem. It was a case of the hydrant turning on the dog.

Once in his career Bradley came close to becoming a Hollywood dance director. In 1939 the head of the Fox film studios in England, having seen several British films choreographed by Bradley, signed him to direct the dances in the forthcoming Hollywood production of *Alexander's Ragtime Band.* Bradley had two months before he was due back to work on another Jessie Matthews film.

"I arrived in New York and discovered that the writers were hopelessly tied up with the script. They couldn't get to the dances for several months," says Bradley, "so I had to go back to London to get ready for the Matthews film." On his return he found Jessie Matthews ill and plans for the film postponed indefinitely. "I lost both jobs," says Bradley, "but if the Hollywood plan had gone through, I think I would have been the first colored person to choreograph an all-white American movie."

In 1966 Buddy Bradley was living and teaching in London where he is happy and respected. "I still use the same basic movements, and they still seem new to white dancers, although the dancers pick them up more easily," he says. "At the same time, I see more colored dancers who can't do them naturally—they've been studying ballet." He is working up routines from the improvisations of modern musicians now, and experimenting with waltz tempos for Afro-American vernacular dances.

His opinions are stated mildly but firmly. "Agnes de Mille did a fine job of making the dance advance in the plot in *Oklahoma,* but she turned her back on real American dance and everybody followed her example." It was Miss de Mille who once accused her male dancers of acting "like virgin butterflies," [11] a state of affairs for which many dancers feel she was partly responsible. He does not care for Gene Kelly or Fred Astaire "as jazz dancers" nor does he enjoy the work of Jerome Robbins in *West Side Story,* which he considers "too mannered." He thinks the choreography of Jack Cole is clever and that Peter Gennaro has the best feeling for jazz. He likes Katherine Dunham very much. "I think both jazz and the dance are trying to break through into something new," he concludes.

The essence of Bradley's philosophy was expressed years ago by Earl "Snake Hips" Tucker when someone asked him why he gave away his secrets by teaching. "Listen," Snake Hips is supposed to have hissed, "there's only one Snake Hips, and every time I teach somebody my stuff it only goes to show everybody how much better the original is." [12]

PART SIX

Technique: Pioneers, Innovators, and Stylists

22 King Rastus Brown and the Time Step

DURING THE NINETEEN-TWENTIES, thirties, and into the forties, the unacknowledged headquarters of American dance—tap variety—was a small cellar room next door to the Lafayette Theater on 131st Street and Seventh Avenue in New York City's Harlem. A back room, this space was an afterthought, an adjunct to the Comedy Club—one of Harlem's better gambling joints—where a man could play poker or blackjack any time of the day or night; it soon supplied the name for the entire establishment: the Hoofers Club.

To reach the Hoofers Club, a patron walked up Seventh Avenue past the stage entrance of the Lafayette Theater, in front of which stood a majestic elm called the Tree of Hope (he patted it and prayed "Hope to get a gig," that is, a job), and two doors beyond, descended the stairs into a big, smoke-filled room crowded with two leather-covered gambling tables and two pool tables. Maneuvering carefully through the crowd—some of the customers were known to be both touchy and tough—he arrived at a doorway in the back. Beyond was a 15-foot square room with benches, maybe one chair, and a battered upright.

Here, for more than two decades, anybody could practice any dance step he pleased for as long as he pleased. The proprietor, Lonnie Hicks, was a piano-playing patron of the dance from Atlanta, who never made a penny on the kids who jammed his backroom to practice and watch and learn. He had the extra room and he liked dancers; besides, the gambling up front paid the bills. "He was a big-hearted guy," says Pete Nugent, "but strict." [1]

Considerable action took place at the Hoofers Club, and every six or eight months Hicks put in a new floor over the splinters of the old. He permitted no outright sleeping on the benches, although the club stayed open around the clock, and during the Depression a dancer out of work could combine instruction with relaxation by napping with his eyes open, subway style, as he sat against the wall.

On a good night a young dancer learned a lot at the Hoofers Club. Working as a newsboy in 1926, Maceo Anderson, who later became a member of *The Four Step Brothers,* spent every spare moment in that backroom. "The minute we had any free time, we'd stuff our tapping shoes in our pockets, hang the shoelaces around our necks, and sprint over to the Hoofers Club," [2] says Anderson. When they hit that front door they came to a dead stop, sidled innocently to the rear, and leaned their heads in the doorway of the back room, their mouths shut and eyes open, watching the footwork. "Do one or cut one" was the cry if you happened to be noticed, and then you had to dance or leave.

"Sometimes one of the greats would saunter in," he adds. "We'd do anything for him, get him ice cream or hot dogs from the stand upstairs with our last penny and then beg him to show us a step." Left to themselves, the youngsters practiced incessantly, some clamoring for attention, a few oblivious of the rhythmic barrage from all sides—until a great dancer appeared.

When King Rastus Brown strolled in, the hubbub stopped short. Everyone scrambled for the benches and sat at attention. "Boy, give me some stop-time," the King commanded, and the first aspirant to reach the piano started a simple tune with one finger known as "The Buck Dancer's Lament," his body twisted sideways so that he could watch the old man's feet.

A simple eight-bar tune, "Buck Dancer's Lament" furnishes a frame for six bars of the Time Step, plus a two-bar "break" for an improvised solo step. Anybody can play it with one finger. Starting on Middle C, the melody ascends five white keys to G every two bars—after a while, the third note was flatted to give it a blue feeling—until the seventh bar where it stops for the break, leaving two bars silent until the last beat. (Another tune, "Buck Dance," which was popular during the 1940's, would do as well—both are constructed to showcase tapping.)

For the first six bars King Rastus tosses off his own versions of the Time Step, and then during the two silent bars, taps out a rhythmic miracle. As he walks out, the room becomes a beehive of imitation. "Look, he did this," says one scrub, attempting a demonstration. "No, it went like this," says another, spelling it out with his feet. Others crowd around with their interpretations. Within a half-hour the youngsters reconstruct King Rastus's performance, tap by tap, until most of them know it by heart. Eight bars of improvised dancing have been choreographed.

Unlike many of the big shots, Brown enjoyed showing the youngsters a few steps. "He taught me a Cross Step," says Al Williams, another member of *The Four Step Brothers,* "and then, later on, showed me how the step originated and ten new ways to do it." [3] He helped Bill Bailey, too. King Rastus became justly popular with several younger generations of tap dancers whom he never ceased to dazzle with fresh footwork.

Legends of other old-time giants exist—King Nappy, "Mose," Romeo Washburn, Clarence Bowens, Jim Dukes, Harry Swinton, Henry Williams, and Kid Checkers among them—but King Rastus Brown was the greatest, Mister Tap himself. Conflicting stories about him still circulate. Slow Kid Thompson says Brown was born in Louisville; Luckey Roberts says Boston; Muzzie Anderson says he came to New York as a grown man in 1903; Willie Glenn thinks he made his headquarters in Baltimore; comedian Billy Mitchell associates him with Philadelphia; and Eubie Blake says that he died during the 1940's in New Haven. More than one dancer remembers hearing about a Buck-dancing contest held in the old Madison Square Garden around 1910, which King Rastus won. If so, it was the climax of his career, for except among Negro dancers and show folk, Brown is unknown.

He was seen by men who were still alive in 1962. "He was a brownskin," says dancer Eddie Rector, "about five-foot nine and thin, with medals he won in Europe all the way down his front." [4] Others agree that he always performed in a derby, wore spats, and smoked long cigars. Some say he was very unreliable and never worked without a jug of "lightnin'" or corn whiskey within easy reach. "It was gin that he drank," [5] says Rufus Greenlee, who worked with Rastus at Huber's Museum in New York around 1906. "He was known as the Coast Defender," says Willie Glenn, who was a sturdy seventy-nine years old in 1965, "and if a show was short an act, he was always ready to go on—trouble was, you couldn't get him off." [6]

"He did the Sand," says Al Williams, "and a Cane Dance with a cakewalk strut." He could execute a fine Irish jig, according to Slow Kid Thompson. Some say he did no imitations, just his own steps. "He could imitate anything," says Glenn, "whatever the audience called for: a train, a drunk, and different nationalities—Irish, Dutch, Jewish, Scottish. Then he'd say 'Now I'll go for myself' and top them all." By general agreement, King Rastus could dance for an hour standing up (the usual solo dance lasted about ten minutes) then dance for another hour sitting down (a more difficult feat)—without repeating a step.

Dancer-comedian Dewey "Pigmeat" Markham recalls the first time he saw King Rastus Brown, who was playing a Negro theater in Cincinnati: "A saloon was located across the street from the theater, and the King danced all over the stage, down the aisle, across the street, where they had a drink waiting for him, and then tapped back to the theater, up the aisle, and onto the stage, while the audience cheered." [7] Brown's preeminence is defined by dancer Willie Covan, who treasures the memory that the King once gave him a pair of dancing shoes: "He could do everything and keep it up forever." [8]

The highest compliment that can be paid any dancer, according to the versatile James Barton, is to be called a real hoofer—a phrase that he defines as "a good Buck dancer." [9] King Rastus Brown represents a high point in the evolution of Buck dancing. "He danced flat-footed, close to the floor, moving from the hips down, and swinging," says Willie Covan. "Buck dancer" has become a term of mild derision among modern tap dancers, but old-timers rightly insist upon the fundamental importance of the step itself, with its basic blend of Shuffle and tap.

One afternoon in May 1961 we saw a barefoot Negro doing a step on the sidewalk in front of New York's Astor Hotel. Although the weather was warm, he wore a huge coachman's overcoat with a high collar and a dented derby. His name, he announced, was "Hot Foot Sam from Alabam." He played a harmonica strapped around his neck and accompanied himself with thimble-covered fingers on a ridged tin can filled with jingling coins. He was a one-man band—plus a dance act. At each break in the music, he performed something like a Buck with feet that looked like pancakes. The step was conspicuously flatfooted but he stamped—no real taps—a shuffle in the process of becoming a Buck.

A simple version of the Buck gradually became standardized in show business as the Time Step. To synchronize with the accompaniment and each other, tap dancers begin with it. To say of a tap dancer: "He doesn't even know the Time Step" or conversely: "He makes even the Time Step look good," is the worst and best that may be said.

The Time Step is executed in as many ways as there are tap dancers. The late Jack Donahue, a fine dancer who starred with Marilyn Miller in *Sunny* (1925), writes: "In the good old days every hoofer had his own time step by which he was recognized by the rest of his profession. . . . This was done to help the musicians in the pit to play his music in the same tempo to which he was going to dance. The one that was used the most frequently is called the time step today." [10]

The rhythm of the simplest Time Step is basic but not exactly easy. Discussing Time Steps in his manual, Beale Fletcher notes: "All of the buck time steps employ a form of syncopation that is unusual and requires mental concentration to master." [11]

Back in 1925 Ned Wayburn wrote: "Most any 2-4 march number is suitable for buck dances, but they must be syncopated rhythm . . . and not what is called straight marches." [12]

The difficulty lies in the fact that most of us are conditioned by European march rhythm, which accents the first and third beats in a four-beat measure. Jazzmen refer to this as playing *on* the beat and consider it "square." They begin by syncopating, that is, stressing the second and fourth beats, and build on top of that. (Gospel singer Mahalia Jackson, disturbed by audiences clapping *on* the beat, occasionally interrupts her song and shows them how to clap on the *off* beat.)

Tap dancers have their own ways of remembering the correct rhythm. They use mnemonic devices: the phrase "*Thanks,* for the Bug-*GY* Ride" repeated as in informal speech with an unexpected accent on the second syllable of "Bug-*GY*" is the rhythm of the single Time Step. The conventional first and third beats are accented to emphasize the syncopated beat—the *Thanks* and the *Bug*—with a pause after *Thanks.* (The right pauses are just as important as the right accents.) The trick consists of accenting the *off* beat—the "*GY*" in "Bug-*GY*"—between the third and fourth beats.

In actual execution this single Time Step may vary infinitely in appearance. An early flat-footed version consists of a preliminary shuffle leading into a Brush, in which one foot is moved forward, out, and around and back, followed by a quick Catch Step, in which the weight is transferred from one foot to the other with a stamp on the *off* beat. A good tap dancer alternates feet and spells out the accents with sounds that are clean and distinguishable. (Jack Donahue had two tap steps—probably a Cramp and a Wing—which he memorized with the rhythm of the phrases "Cover the *Buck*le" and "Croppy *Lie* Down [*authors' italics*]."[13])

Before the 1920's tap dancers were performing regularly to popular tunes of the standard thirty-two bar length and it became customary to break the thirty-two bars down into four units of eight bars each. Each eight bars was further subdivided into six bars of the Time Step and a two-bar break, or solo improvisation.

Although a built-in spot for creative tapping was thus a part of the formula, an uninspired dancer could repeat the same Time Step throughout most of a tune—or all of it, by ignoring the breaks entirely. The established routine for a good dancer, however, is to introduce four different breaks—one for each subdivision—and sometimes four different Time Steps, in the course of one chorus of a thirty-two-bar tune.

The Time Step had become so standardized by 1915 that when *In Old Kentucky* arrived in Chicago with its weekly competition in Buck dancing, all the contestants—except Willie Covan—began their dance with it.

Several variations—and complications—of the single Time Step have become well established. Perhaps the most common is an unemphasized, introductory tap called a Pick Up, preceding the Time Step and creating the rhythm "AND *Thanks,* for the Bug-*GY* Ride." The Pick Up *and* came to be a standard preliminary to the Time Step, adding a weak tap between each combination, which throws more emphasis upon the first beat and thus accentuates the following syncopations. (It is common in African drumming.)

The rhythm of the double Time Step is actually more regular though perhaps more difficult than that of the single Time Step—because the pause is omitted: "AND *Thank YOU* for the Bug-*GY* Ride." It has one more tap.

The triple Time Step has two more taps, placed between the first and second beats: "AND *When* WILL WE Take a Bug-*GY* Ride." The double triple Time Step separates the men from the boys, adding three extra taps in two different places, so that two taps occur between both the first and second, and the second and third beats: "AND *What* 'LL I DO with the Bug-*GY* Ride."

These mnemonic devices, of course, are only formulas—a kind of spoken diagramming. And they are the most simple of steps compared to many entire eight-bar routines, which dancers telegraph to each other by a kind of "scat" singing, or series of rhythmic nonsense syllables. "I'll never forget how surprised Albert Gibson was," says Pete Nugent, "when I told him there were some tap dancers who couldn't duplicate with their feet any combination of accents you could make with your mouth."

What cannot be diagrammed is the essential artistry in performance, for these rhythms can be executed precisely but lifelessly. Much depends upon how the dancer moves his body and such intangibles as his presence and timing. A great tap dancer can make the simple Time Step a thing of beauty that flows on top of the beat with compelling clarity and momentum.

Of all American vernacular dances, tap, with its immense variety of rhythmic sound and movement, is the most complex and has proved to be one of the highest artistic achievements—partly because, like the frosting on the cake, it can be incorporated effectively into almost any combination of steps, if the dancer is talented enough. The true professional looks upon most other dances as unfinished approximations. "Tap," says Willie Covan with utter conviction, "is the *master* dance."

King Rastus Brown was extraordinarily gifted as a tap dancer but in onc area—and a very important area for an early dancer—he was an abject failure. The King was no comedian. Around 1917 Jesse Shipp, who had helped stage the pioneering Williams and Walker shows at the turn of the century, organized an act called *The Tennessee Ten* for the Keith-Orpheum vaudeville circuit. The act, which ran about twenty minutes, starred Florence Mills. As an added attraction, a jazz band—in part—from Johnson's *Creole Band of New Orleans,* with Horace Eubanks, Ed Garland, and Freddie Johnson, played a comic concert on the stage. (*The Original Creole Band,* with trumpeter Freddie Keppard, had been previously signed by Shubert for a competing show.)

Shipp's act opened with the traditional plantation scene as Florence Mills sang "Darling Nellie Grey," followed by the entire company doing a cakewalk to "Waiting for the Robert E. Lee," whereupon the jazz band marched on stage and, conducted by Ulysses S. "Slow Kid" Thompson, who was billed as "The Black Sousa," blundered into a comedy rehearsal. Getting the band to tune up was the problem. After a lot of fussing, conductor Thompson brought down his baton: "The band would hit a horrible chord," says Thompson, "and I would do a front somersault as if I was surprised out of my skin." [14]

When Thompson was drafted in World War I, they sent for King Rastus Brown to take his place. The King simply could not handle it. "He didn't have much conception of comedy," says Thompson, who returned to the act in 1918. And like most of the old-timers, King Rastus took a dim view of the growing trend toward acrobatics. He was a hoofer—the best of the hoofers—and this jumping around the stage seemed a waste of time.

But that was not the worst. According to all reports King Rastus Brown was loudly and insistently grieved by a young upstart named Bill "Bojangles" Robinson, who stole his Stair Dance. The fact that King Rastus borrowed the dance from one of *his* predecessors made no difference; Robinson had the opportunity and showmanship to make it famous, and that hurt. King Rastus Brown never became resigned to obscurity.

23 Bill Robinson: Up on the Toes

ALTHOUGH KING RASTUS BROWN continuously and vociferously challenged Bill Robinson to a cutting contest on any stage, anywhere, anytime, Robinson kept uncharacteristically silent. "Robinson never seemed to be around," says Al Williams, "when King Rastus was in the back room of the Hoofers Club." [1] Bill Robinson came to shoot pool in the front room. A skillful player who hated to lose, he insisted on silence during his turn. For a particularly difficult shot, the story goes, he took out his gold-plated pistol and placed it on the edge of the table. Everyone walked wide and carefully while he was playing.

Robinson made a point of being available for police benefits and was proud of being an honorary member of the force in several big cities. He had a permit to carry a gun, and once broke up a robbery with it. On another occasion he was accidentally shot in the shoulder, when he insisted upon running ahead, coming between the police and a fleeing thief. That was in Pittsburgh in 1930, while Robinson was in the tryouts of a show called *Brown Buddies*. When it reached Broadway, Percy Hammond panned it unmercifully in the *Herald Tribune*—but praised Robinson: "Mr. Robinson was especially popular last evening because his right arm was in a sling, wounded wrongfully by a Pittsburgh policeman, who thought he was a culprit when he was a knight." [2]

Born in 1878 in Richmond, Virginia, Bill Robinson began his career as a pick with Mayme Remington at fifty cents a night. At the age of twelve, he was touring with a show called *The South Before the War*, featuring dancer Eddie Leonard, whose specialty was the Virginia Essence. According to his childhood friend James "Muzzie" Anderson, Robinson came to New York in 1898 and got a job at Minors Theater in the Bowery.[3] Later he danced at various restaurants in Coney Island, played vaudeville with partner George Cooper, and toured abroad.

Robinson eventually found his place in vaudeville, taking time out to win the famous Buck-dancing contest in *Old Kentucky,* and over a period of thirty years fought his way to the top. He became one of the few Negro dancers who performed solo on the leading Keith circuit (Henry Williams preceded him and Robinson shared the distinction with Dancing Dotson). At his peak, Robinson was making $6,500 a week in vaudeville.

Yet Bill Robinson did not become well known to the New York theater critics until he was fifty years old. In a review of the Palace bill in August, 1921, a critic in the New York *Dramatic Mirror* described all the acts except Bojangles's, noting only that "Bill Robinson follows." [4] Vaudeville had been fading, and Broadway shows were becoming more and more influential. In 1928 producer Lew Leslie hired Bill Robinson as an "Extra Attraction" for his *Blackbirds*—three weeks after it had opened to lukewarm reviews. A glorified night club revue, *Blackbirds* needed new talent for each edition. Robinson was assigned a late spot in the second half of the show to sing "Doin' the New Low Down" and perform his dance on a set of stairs to which several steps had been added. (A recording of Bill Robinson singing and dancing to this number with Don Redman's band exists on Brunswick 6520 and on LP "Great Moments in Show Business," Epic LN 3234.)

Robinson's success was instantaneous and overwhelming. The weekly gross jumped from $9,000 to $27,000. He was "discovered" and hailed as the greatest of all dancers by at least seven of New York's newspapers. In the *World,* Alexander Woollcott did not much care for the show as a whole, but warned his readers, "If you stray into the Liberty Theater at all, do not leave before eleven o'clock"; then the audience is treated, he adds, to "as expert and tickling and delightful a tap dance as you may ever hope to see." [5]

In the *Times,* Brooks Atkinson wrote that "the most accomplished tap dancing of the evening is exhibited by Bill Robinson on his pair of stairs." [6]

In the *Herald Tribune,* Percy Hammond was moved to compose a non-rhythmic metaphor, equating Robinson's "xylophonic footsteps" with the "music of raindrops on a tin roof." [7]

In the *Mirror* Robert Coleman was more perceptive—after praising Robinson to the skies, he adds, "And get this, he manages to inject a sense of humor into the proceedings. Just imagine a hoofer with a sense of humor, with laughing pedal extremities." [8]

In the *News* Burns Mantle joined the chorus of praise: "Bill is among the two or three great tap dancers of the day. For a quarter of an hour last night the show was absolutely his and his alone." [9]

To his annoyance Robinson was not the only dancing success in the show. Among later comments at least three reviewers mentioned a non-tap dancer, who never became famous except among other dancers: Earl "Snake Hips" Tucker (see Chapter 29). Two months later Rockwell J. Graham reviewed the show with a more professional touch, speaking of Robinson as "one of the finest tap dancers in the country" with "barely audible, but crystal-clear taps." [10]

Stereotypes of the Negro were accepted without question in those days. Most of the critics disliked the comedy scenes, but none—with the exception of Heywood Broun in another instance—objected to the portrayal of the Negro as a happy-go-lucky, shiftless fool. The printed programs of *Blackbirds of 1928* carry cartoons of "darkies" in supposedly comic poker and graveyard scenes, while a photograph of the chorus displays a backdrop with a grinning Negro child eating a huge slice of watermelon.

The only dissenting opinion came from a Negro newspaper with little or no circulation among whites: the Baltimore *Afro-American. Blackbirds* toured abroad in 1929, and a group from Fisk University went to see it in Paris. In his dispatch L. K. McMillan liked the dancing but felt that "all in all, *Blackbirds* is probably doing more harm than good." [11]

The posters advertising the show in Paris were the usual stereotypes, "hideous signs that one finds in towns like Baltimore, Richmond. . . ." and the show was full of "graveyard scenes . . . card games . . . together with little acts of dishonesty, razors, pistols, and policemen." (In the same issue S. H. Dudley, the old-time Negro comedian, who helped to found the T.O.-B.A. circuit, had nothing but flowery praise for producer Leslie and the entire show.[12])

In the spate of interviews that followed his sudden and great success in *Blackbirds of 1928,* Bill Robinson, with his customary directness, made some points that must have sounded revolutionary at the time. In the *World Telegram* he is quoted as saying that "protracted exposure to hot jazz-band music" is the way to learn to dance,[13] while W. A. Roberts writes that Robinson, after showing him "some very complicated steps," stated: "all these have been supposed to be white tap dances which I adopted and ragged . . . but the truth is . . . I never consciously imitated a white performer." [14]

As we look back now, this statement seems to be a courageous lapse into the simple truth, but thereafter, at testimonial dinners and various celebrations with "white folks," Robinson, when called upon to say a few words, always gave credit for his skill to various white dancers. He would seldom have been invited, if besides being a fine raconteur, he had not made this disclaimer.

For example, Bojangles quite consistently asserted that he owed a great debt to the versatile actor-dancer James Barton (see Chapter 25), but once, at a banquet in honor of another dancer, Jack Donahue, he got carried away and bestowed all the credit on Donahue. This caused some hurt feelings—Barton never forgot it—although Robinson actually owed little or nothing to either dancer. His real idol, according to Ed Sullivan, was the great minstrel dancer George Primrose,[15] which just might be true.

On the other hand Robinson liked to claim that he had taught younger dancers. "He said that he taught us but he didn't," says Fayard Nicholas. "He just showed us one of his soft-shoe routines so that when we met at benefits he could say: 'My boys are here—*The Nicholas Brothers*—come on up and we'll do a dance together.' We never had any lessons." [16] Willie Covan still remembers with a trace of annoyance how one summer day someone in a long Deusenberg stopped in front of his Hollywood studio while he was working for MGM. "Then Bill Robinson hopped out and presented me with a big picture of himself to hang over my desk." [17]

Two or three critics went out on what must have been a very unpopular limb. W. A. Roberts declared that the United States had made two contributions to the dance: Isadora Duncan, "who liberated costumes and the use of the body"; and Negro-American jazz dancing, in which "the entire body is employed as a medium of expression." [18] The best exponents of this, he adds, "are found in the colored race." "Taps," added Gilbert Gabriel, "that's really all that's worth blowing about in modern dance." [19]

Reviewing *Blackbirds of 1933* in the *Herald Tribune,* Richard Watts caused lifted eyebrows among devotees of terpsichore. "This veteran tap dancer," he wrote, referring to Robinson, "is one of the great artists of the modern stage and is worth in his unostentatious way several dozen of the Mary Wigmans, Charles Weidmans, Martha Grahams . . . who are more pompous in their determination to be Artists." [20]

In 1930 Robinson starred in a Broadway musical, *Brown Buddies,* which in spite of strongly adverse criticism of much of the show, was kept alive by Bojangles's dancing and personality. Comedy dancers *Red and Struggy* were praised in passing, but it was the first time since *Williams and Walker* that a Negro dancer had headlined an entire show on Broadway—and Robinson was only one man.

Bill Robinson was on his way. In 1932 he went out to Hollywood, and by 1935 costarred with Shirley Temple, whom he coached in *The Little Colonel.* During his career he made fourteen films in Hollywood, and two of them—*Stormy Weather* and *One Mile from Heaven*—broke away from the reigning stereotypes. He was featured in several Cotton Club shows, and in 1939 became a hit in the *Hot Mikado* at the New York World's Fair. That was the peak of his career. In the following year Robinson starred in an all-white show, *All in Fun,* which lasted—through no fault of his—only three performances. In 1945 he had a moderate success in *Memphis Bound,* a "jive version" of *Pinafore.* Divorced and remarried, Bojangles seemed to have run out of luck.

More than any other Negro in show business at the time, Bill Robinson, with the constant help of his wise and tactful first wife, Fannie, surmounted the barriers of racial prejudice. Although uneducated, he was accepted in high places previously beyond the reach of most Negroes, he became close friends with influential white people, and he commanded the respect due a highly gifted artist. He seemed indestructible, and indeed, often boasted that he would dance forever. In 1949, at the age of seventy-one, he died in debt.

To his own people Robinson became a modern John Henry, who instead of driving steel, laid down iron taps. Their attitude toward him, however, was ambivalent. The cocky sparkle of his stage personality was produced, in part, by the driving ego, which sometimes made him a problem to his friends, while the public figures in the white world who enjoyed and admired him never saw the salty side he took no trouble to conceal at the Hoofers Club. ("Bill was so easy to get along with," says James Barton. "Why, we even used each other's music.")[21]

Ethel Waters and Bill Robinson never got along. Both were strong and outspoken personalities, and Miss Waters seemed to be suspicious of Bill's ability to socialize with white people—"they used a different language and I didn't understand it." Her opinion of his dancing is frank and reasonably accurate: "I wasn't knocked over because I had seen other great Negro dancers who could challenge Bill Robinson or any other hoofer, including Fred Astaire . . . two of these men were King Rastus and Jack Ginger Wiggins . . . White people never saw them, but that's the white folks' loss."[22]

Most of the time Robinson seemed to make little attempt to be friendly or to offer help to younger Negro dancers, who were understandably in awe of him. "I soon learned not to take any favors from Bill," says Pete Nugent, "because he'd embarrass you by proclaiming the fact loudly in public and insisting that you admit it. For example, standing on the corner with a bunch of show people, he'd yell 'Come here!' and then start in. 'Now, when you were broke in L.A.,' he'd shout, 'didn't I loan you $50 and carfare to get back east and a suit to wear because you were so raggedy?' And you had to stand there and take it."[23]

"Adored as he was by the white audiences of his time," writes Rex Stewart, "Robinson was pretty hard to take among his own people, especially the younger ones."[24]

Robinson's billing as "The Dark Cloud of Joy" was accurate in more ways than one—the darkness of mood sometimes outweighed the joy. His very nickname, "Bojangles," is still something of a mystery. A common explanation is that it comes from the African custom of tying decorative bells to the ankles, but Tom Fletcher says it means *squabbler*.[25] *Jangle* is a perfectly good word meaning to quarrel or wrangle—an activity for which Robinson was sometimes noted—while the prefix *bo* may be the folk pronunciation of *boar*, signifying the strength and power of this animal. (Professor Willis L. James points out, for example, that the name of Negro pugilist Beau Jack owes nothing to the French, but rather combines the shortened names of two powerful animals: the wild boar and the jackass.[26]) *Bojangles,* then, may simply mean a powerful squabbler.

"Only my close ones knew I had a bad temper," writes George Jessel in a poem entitled *Bill "Bojangles" Robinson,* "one night in Cincinnati . . . I had an argument with a man, a bad man, and I whipped out my pistol and shot him. And the police came and took me away." [27]

As Robinson became a legend, stories—some of them verifiable—clustered around him.[28] Bo had a nasty disposition," says one dancer. "He came back-stage after Bill Bailey's act one night and slapped him for doing the Stair Dance." Another dancer tells a similar story, but it is Derby Wilson who gets slapped. Since both Bailey and Wilson, who were partners at one time, modeled much of their dancing on Robinson's, both of these stories could be true—or untrue. Bill Bailey, for one, denies it.

Eddie Rector asserts that he was doing the Stair Dance in Paris at the request of the management—a routine which he does not consider difficult —when Robinson cabled him to stop it or die. When Rector returned to the States, Robinson had forgotten about it.

Another story concerns an incident that took place at the Keith Theater in Boston. Waiting to go on, Bojangles overheard a conversation between two white girls in the preceding act. "Hey, Sis!" said one to the other, "let's watch—I hear this n——'s good." Robinson picked them both up and dumped them in the wings on his way to the stage. Tension mounted during his act because the husbands of the girls were present and swore immediate revenge. They ran up to Robinson's dressing room after his performance, kicked open the door, and found themselves staring up the barrels of two pistols.

Robinson was a masterful story teller, but he would bully his audience if he knew he could get away with it. A younger Negro dancer recalls that "with us, when he laughed, everybody else laughed, or he'd say 'Don't you think that's funny?' and you were in trouble." Youngsters did not say hello to Robinson unless they knew him pretty well, and he clearly enjoyed the reputation of being a tough guy.

Bit by bit Robinson earned the respect if not the affection of the younger generation. A Harlem newspaper, the New York *Age,* once published a piece accusing him of being an Uncle Tom—a Negro who bowed and scraped to white people. Brandishing his pistol, Robinson set out for the newspaper office, arriving in a taxi at three o'clock in the morning. He saw a light upstairs, banged on the bell, and swore to kill whoever opened the door. When an old scrubwoman appeared, he subsided.

He had his generous moments, too. "Every now and then," says Pete Nugent, "he'd take me aside with a great air of secrecy and say 'Get this!' showing me some little fly step so cute that he must have known he was the only one who could do it." Honi Coles remembers Robinson grabbing the microphone and helping to put across Coles's dancing act when they were competing on the same bill, and Hal Leroy, one of the few white dancers who saw the inside of the Hoofers Club, says it was Bojangles who took him there.[29]

Whatever else he may have been, Bojangles was always alive and usually kicking. (One of his claims to fame: He could run backward faster than most men could run forward.) At a benefit a highly-dignified Negro celebrity who was delighted by Robinson's performance threw his arms impulsively around him. "Don't you kiss me, you sissy!" roared Bojangles in genuine alarm. In Seattle, at the opening of the new Albee Theater, headlining Sophie Tucker, Robinson turned up in the audience and could not resist running up on the stage. "I know Mr. Albee didn't mean to open this theater without me," he announced, then stole the show.

Robinson preferred to do his good deeds secretly or on a high level. "During the Depression he'd be walking down Seventh Avenue in Harlem," says Leigh Whipper, "and see some furniture on the street—people he didn't even know, being dispossessed—and he'd go in and pay the back rent." [30] During World War II he heard that the Army planned to quarter white troops at Atlantic City and segregate Negro troops at the Hotel Theresa in Harlem. Picking up Leigh Whipper on the way, Bojangles taxied down to City Hall where Mayor LaGuardia greeted him with "How's the Mayor of Harlem?" Robinson told him what he had heard. "The next thing I knew," says Whipper, "LaGuardia had President Roosevelt on the phone and the Army's plans were changed then and there."

One of the most persistent and unverified legends about Bill Robinson concerns a challenge contest after hours at a Broadway theater. Conflicting accounts exist, and indeed, one of the alleged participants does not remember it at all. Three famous white dancers—James Barton, Will Mahoney, and Jack Donahue (in another version, Ray Bolger, Fred Astaire, and Barton)—competed with Robinson while six judges, two in front, two in the wings, and two beneath the stage, rendered a verdict for Robinson.

That was just the beginning. Bojangles then wagered that the judges beneath the stage could not tell when he shifted from one foot to the other doing the same step. He won again. Then he asked the musicians in the pit band for an eight-bar introduction, synchronized to a metronome and followed by silence. Without hearing the metronome, Robinson danced for three-and-a-half minutes all by himself, and then when the band started up again—cued by the metronome—came out exactly on the beat. This is the sort of legendary event, stressing clarity and precision, which seems to attach itself to Bojangles in the folklore of tap dancing. True or not, he probably could have done it.

Bill Robinson's contribution to tap dancing is exact and specific: He brought it up on the toes, dancing upright and swinging. (Clogs, jigs, and reels had been danced on the toes, but they did not swing.) The flat-footed wizardry of King Rastus Brown, although some old-timers still prefer it, seemed earthbound compared to the tasty steps of Bojangles, who danced with a hitherto-unknown lightness and presence.

"When I first saw Bill Robinson at the Lafayette Theater in 1929," says Bill Bailey, "I thought it was the prettiest thing I'd ever seen, and I tried to live as clean as he did ever after—you know he didn't smoke or drink, only ate huge amounts of ice cream." [31]

Robinson invented no new steps; rather, he perfected and presented them. "He was a *Buck* dancer who didn't change his style for sixty years," says his old friend Muzzie Anderson. "He didn't need to." His Stair Dance, up and down a set of steps, with each step reverberating at a different pitch, was the most famous, but he had other favorites. "He always did things in eight bars," says Lindy dancer Al Minns, who worked with Bojangles in the *Hot Mikado* and learned Robinson's routines, "and he loved those breaks." [32] At the same time, Robinson would often ignore breaks, repeating the same step and maintaining clear continuity.

Sandwiched between a Buck or Time Step, Robinson might use a little skating step to stop-time; or a Scoot step, a cross-over tap, which looked like a jig: hands on hips, tapping as he went, while one foot kicked up and over the other; or a double tap, one hand on hip, one arm extended, with eyes blinking, head shaking, and derby cocked; or a tap to the melody of a tune such as "Parade of the Wooden Soldiers"; or a broken-legged or old man's dance, one leg short and wobbling with the beat; or an exit step, tapping with a Chaplinesque waddle. (He names and illustrates several of his steps on a 78 rpm recording entitled "Keep a Song in Your Soul," Columbia 30183.) "Every tap," says Nick Castle, "was a pearl." [33]

The step itself didn't seem to matter much. "Robinson was the absolute tops in *control*," says Pete Nugent. "The toughest thing about imitating him is to get that perfect balance which seems so natural."

Like the older dancers, Robinson did not make much use of his hands, nor did he employ body motion to any great extent—most of the action was from the waist down. A younger but retired dancer who went in for acrobatics in the 1940's remarked: "That's why Bo lasted so long. He didn't knock himself out doing flash stuff."

Again, Robinson selected his accompaniments with great care, and sometimes, nerve. He liked such melodies as Massenet's "Elegie," played very softly so that it did not obscure the clarity of his footwork. He used flutes and oboes and had Will Vodery and Charles Cook make his arrangements. "Why, he even did a great soft-shoe dance to 'God Bless America'— nothing seemed out of place," says Pete Nugent, "and then he tiptoed off stage sideways to 'The Bells of St. Mary's,' while the bells faded in the distance."

Robinson's career is proof that a tap dancer with technique and personality can make relatively simple tap dancing an exciting art.

To top it off, Bojangles was a first-rate entertainer who, while he danced, recited an endless stream of amusing anecdotes and comments—some of them offensive to the younger generation. His timing, as might be expected, was perfect, and the sheer vivacity of his personality enthralled the public. He was a competent singer, too. "In a sense," says Honi Coles, "Bo's face was about forty per cent of his appeal." Robinson had the power to project his personality with irresistible effect across the footlights.

Bill Robinson's memory is kept fresh in a manner he would have approved. On September 5, 1949, the Copasetics Club was organized in New York by a group of his friends in show business ("Everything is copasetic" was one of Bojangles's favorite expressions, meaning better than okay. Ethel Waters writes that the expression was current at an early date "all over the South.")[34] The big event each year is a September "cruise," a benefit for charity, at which the top dancers of the club—and it includes the best—put on several of Robinson's routines as part of the entertainment.

Beneath it all Bojangles had his own dreams of glory. Explaining how he happened to do the Stair Dance, he once told a contemporary: "I dreamed I was getting to be a knight, and I danced up the stairs to the throne, got my badge, and danced right down again." Like Ferdinand "Jelly Roll" Morton, the pioneering jazz pianist who sang of himself as "Mister Jelly Lord," Robinson also equated real success with royalty. Perhaps the fact that royalty—like equality for the Negro—does not exist in the United States has something to do with it.

A short while before he died, Robinson and James Barton planned to do a play called *Two Gentlemen from the South.* According to the script Barton is the master and Robinson the servant until the middle of the show, whereupon they swap roles, don masks of each other, and in the words of Barton, "do each other's steps and wind up doing a dance together." Here is the goal for which Bojangles always fought: complete equality. As an artist and as a human being, he deserved no less.

24 Frank Condos: Wings and the Expanding Repertory

"MATTIE OLVERA and me were great dancers from the waist down," says Frank Condos, speaking of the famous team of *King and King*, "but from the waist up we didn't have much personality—we were just two homely looking guys, and neither of us could be called a ladies' man." [1] What *King and King* could do from the waist down, however, made them a legend among dancers: five-tap Wings.

To explain a five-tap Wing, it is important to note what is *not* happening. One leg (the legs alternate) is bent at the knee and raised up and back —out of the way. *This leg does nothing*—or something additional. With the other leg, the dancer jumps up in the air, and on the way up and down, *makes five clear and distinct sounds on the floor with his foot.* "It's no use jumping higher to gain more time to tap because then your foot won't reach the floor," says one old-timer, "and jumping lower gives you no time to tap at all—that jump has to be just right." And he might have added that the taps have to be in perfect rhythm.

Tap dancers employ a staggering assortment of steps, body movements, and combinations of both—and sometimes agree on the names for them. Some steps are strictly tap, others may or may not use taps, depending upon the skill and inclination of the dancer, and still others dispense with tap entirely.

During the teens, tap dancing was evolving away from the original concept of the Irish Jig—that is, movement from the waist down only—toward a more flexible style. Specifically, tap was assimilating body movements from vernacular dance, putting them together in new combinations, and inventing steps of its own—including air steps, which employed the upper half of the body, too.

The rhythms could and would become more complex and swinging, but before this took place, tap dancing began to utilize the entire body and open up more possibilities for expressiveness. With this expanding repertory, new categories of steps evolved that any respectable tapper was supposed to be able to execute.

Dancers often distinguish between two classifications: "jazz" and "flash" steps, and combine them into standard routines with special names. "Jazz" steps consist of body movement in which taps are not essential. Originating among the folk, and later in the eccentric dancing of tent-show comedians after the Civil War, these steps surfaced gradually, blending with Clog and tap in minstrelsy and vaudeville. Some of the more easily performed movements, like the Shimmy and Charleston, eventually became "social" dances and were performed in the ballroom. To many of them—including the Charleston—taps were occasionally added. Many of the steps that tap dancers adopted, however, were too difficult for the ballroom and were called stage steps.

Versions of two jazz steps became a standard part of a tap dancer's repertory: Falling Off a Log, and Off to Buffalo. Off to Buffalo consists of a shuffle, with one foot crossing and recrossing in front of the other as the dancer edges sideways, usually toward the exit. Falling Off a Log employs a similar and alternate crossing of the feet, plus a leaning pause before the performer moves into his next step. (Joe Frisco, who billed himself inaccurately as "The First Jazz Dancer," used Off to Buffalo as his trademark.)

"Flash" steps consist of acrobatic combinations with expanded leg and body movements. Again, with one exception, taps are not essential. Besides being impressive—and sometimes startling—they serve a definite function. "You have to open and close with something that catches the eye," says Pete Nugent. "With the music *fortissimo*, nobody can hear taps." [2] Flash steps are primarily visual and tap dancers use them to close their acts.

Two flash steps, or more accurately, combinations of body movement, became a standard part of the tap dance repertory in the late teens and early twenties: Over the Top, and Through the Trenches. (Their titles, of course, came from World War I, when they became popular.) Unlike most blended movements from the vernacular, these steps are generally credited by other Negro dancers to Toots Davis, who was performing them as early as 1913 in *The Darktown Follies* at the Lafayette Theater (see Chapter 17). "They are fundamental," says Charles "Cholly" Atkins, "and when done with real punch can wear you out fast." [3]

Over the Top consists of bending forward, springing up, and bringing each leg, in turn, around from the back and across the front of the other leg—a figure-eight pattern that had previously been performed flat-footed—giving the impression of elaborate and energetic self-tripping. The audience often applauds because the dancer does not fall on his face.

Through the Trenches consists of long backward slides on the outside edge of the foot, alternating each leg, while the body is bent forward at the waist and the opposite arm flails the air. "It came from the old running step," says James Barton, "held down to one spot." [4] All of these jazz and flash steps can be faked—or executed with consummate skill.

The most important step of all, the Wing, became a standard part of the tap-dancers' repertory at an early date, although it was not fully extended until the thirties. It is based on a paradox. Unlike most tap, it is an air step; and unlike most jazz and flash steps, taps are essential. Actually the Wing is a dynamic compromise, a transitional blend of vernacular body movements and taps, executed mainly in the air.

The Wing, with its combination of taps with an upward spring, holds two opposing impulses in balance, creating a dramatic fusion which can be thrilling. "The Wing has everything," says Cholly Atkins, "jazz, tap, and flash."

Aside from the Pigeon Wing, an early folk step taken over and expanded into a kind of foot-shaking by the minstrel dancers, the word *Wing* was used to describe a combination known as Buck and Wing—the general designation for tap dance (and almost anything else) at the turn of the century. Introduced on the New York stage in 1880 by James McIntyre, the Buck and Wing began to swing—unlike the Clog, which preceded it—and launched a new style of Negro-derived dancing. As it surfaced in those days, the Buck was close to a Time Step and the Wing was a simple hop with one foot flung out to the side.

Dancers began to develop the Wing around 1900. Old-timer Willie Glenn first noticed it in 1902 and did not think much of it. "Now King Rastus Brown, he didn't do any 'winging' or jumping around," he observes. "He stayed on the ground and tapped." [5] Throughout the early teens, the Wing remained more of a tap step than an air step. "They called it Buck and Wing, says Charles "Honi" Coles, "but there was no elevation, no *real* Wing in it." [6]

By the twenties, the three-tap Wing was becoming established: On the way out and up a dancer's foot made one tap or scrape, and on the way down, two more. The number of taps inserted became crucial. Yet some great dancers still ignored Wings. "Bill Robinson wasn't much of a Wing dancer," says Pete Nugent, "but he'd stick one in occasionally." Other dancers, like Frank Condos, however, practiced Wings incessantly.

A variety of Wings began to emerge in the thirties: the Pump (the "winging" foot goes up and down—in the back), the Pendulum (from front to back), the Saw, the Fly, Rolling, Stumbling, the Double Back, and so on. Many dancers worked up their own Wings and the variations in performance became endless. Few dancers, however, considered a five-tap Wing possible, and even fewer attempted it.

"Around 1922 when I was with the *Dan Fitch Minstrels*," says Frank Condos, "an old-time singer asked me if I had ever seen a five-tap Wing and showed me his idea of how it could be done—that put me on the track." Condos was sixteen years old at the time and had already run away from home with his partner, Mateo Olvera. By the mid-1920's they were famous as the team of *King and King*. "Condos and Olvera sounded terrible," says Condos, who was born in Greece and brought to the United States when he was a year old, "so we changed it to *King and King*, which sounded good in Greek, too."

Condos was the spark-plug of the team. His father owned the Standard Restaurant opposite the Standard Theater in Philadelphia, where many Negro acts were booked, and as a freshman in high school, Condos worked in the restaurant after class, carrying meals to the performers, who soon became his idols. His father wanted him to be a lawyer, but young Frank watched the dancers and was fascinated. He saw some of the best. As a teen-ager he studied *Covan and Ruffin*, Eddie Rector, Jack Wiggins, *Buck and Bubbles*, and a team that gave him the idea for an act of his own, *The Three Eddies* (Chick Horsey was the outstanding Wing dancer in this group). "The best dancers," says Condos flatly, "were colored."

With boundless energy and determination, Condos began to practice upstairs in his bedroom while his father worried downstairs in the restaurant. "I went for those three-tap Wings and I said to myself, I'm going to try to do this step even better." One day, while practicing, he jumped too high and hurt his knee. "I told my father I slipped on the ice." Condos learned the hard way. "I practiced all the time, night and day, and I danced very, very hard. It just about wore me out."

By 1925 Condos and Olvera found a job in Chicago. "In those days," says Condos, "all you had to do was work up a soft-shoe routine and top it with a challenge dance—competing with each other—and you were in business. "If you were any good, one circuit would hire you away from another and pay you more." *King and King* earned a reputation for sheer speed and energy and were soon referred to as "the fastest legs in the business."

Working everlastingly on the Wing, they began to execute it on the ball of the foot while throwing the foot up and out five or six inches (a mere three-inch "lift" had been considered sensational), and they added a mat of wooden strips, which helped on rough floors and accentuated the taps. In time they worked up their five-tap Wing, in which one foot scraped out and up and—in the process of coming back down—made four additional and distinct taps. "There wasn't many teams copying Mattie and me," says Condos, "because we did those Wings faster than anybody else. We had shoes with steel plates, and you could always hear our taps."

Timing is the crucial problem in any Wing, and with the five-tap Wing, timing the spring upward is excruciatingly difficult. "The hardest part after you've jumped up—with a tap—is getting those four taps on the way down," says Condos, "and *then going up into another Wing right away*." The upper part of the body must be elevated before the feet begin to move or the result is a flat Wing, and the split second it takes to fling out a foot with one tap and bring it back with four more must be calculated precisely. "Those five taps come so fast—ta-ta-ta-ta-ta—it sounds like a machine gun," says Condos.

Condos's admiration for other dancers is unbounded, and his estimate of his own abilities, modest. Nor is he under any illusions about the act's limitations: "We got pooped out. Other guys would be fresh after sixteen bars. We were exhausted trying to give our act more flash." Condos is convinced that if they could have talked like Bill Robinson or sung like John Bubbles, they would have been a much bigger hit and lasted far longer. On the other hand Negro dancers are unanimous in their praise of Condos. "He had legs of iron," says Pete Nugent. "I've seen him do the impossible—a five-tap Wing without a mat *from a low crouch.*"

At first *King and King* wore black trousers and white shirts with long puffed sleeves in the early Eddie Rector style, but they soon switched to business suits, which made them look more prepossessing. Their usual act consisted of a soft-shoe to "Tea for Two," a clog to "Three O'Clock in the Morning," and their specialty—a challenge dance—to a fast-tempo "June Night." We nearly killed ourselves trying to out-dance each other," says Condos, "and at the end of the act, my heart would be pounding like a trip-hammer."

When *Artists and Models* opened at the Winter Garden on November 15, 1927, *King and King* were the featured dancers. "We did mostly Wings," says Condos. The New York critics seemed to have no comprehension of the kind of dancing they were witnessing. Gilbert Gabriel in the *American* called them "soft-shoers," [7] Robert Coleman in the *Mirror* described them as "buck and winging," [8] and Burns Mantle in the *News* made an extra effort, calling them "tap dancers, or step dancers, or high-schooled ankle-twisters of some particular classification" [9]—and then gave up. *Variety* reached a new high in poverty-stricken jargon by labeling them "tap steppers." [10]

At least all the critics agreed that *King and King* were great. Referring to them inaccurately in the *Times* as "clog dancers," Alexander Woollcott documented the nature and extent of their impact on the audience: "Then a team named King and King (one of whom looks like a Chinese Sam Harris and each of whom shakes a mean foot) danced such clogs . . . as brought down the Winter Garden and spilled so much applause into the next scene that a prima donna, all squared off to sing some fearful ballad, was in no end of a pet." [11] Dancers themselves simply refer to *King and King* as "the greatest of all Wing teams."

As the years passed, the act inevitably slowed down. "In the early days the audience loved it when you repeated a hard step three times in eight bars, and they would applaud as we piled on the Wings," says Condos, "but later dancers began to consider it corny—no matter how difficult the step was—so we changed to three or four difficult steps every eight bars, and that made it tough for us to show off our specialty."

In 1929 Condos and Olvera split up their act. Olvera started a trio with his brothers, billed as *King, King, and King* (who got rave reviews in *Broadway Nights* the same year and were lampooned hilariously by Ray Bolger shortly thereafter), while Frank Condos added his younger brother Nick and changed the billing to *The Condos Brothers.* "We took out some of the hard dancing which was wearing us down," says Frank, "and used just one tough step at the end of each chorus." Young Nick soon learned to do a five-tap Wing on either foot, too.

The Condos Brothers danced in *Earl Carroll's Vanities* in 1932. "At the audition for Earl Carroll," says Condos, "we did our soft-shoe number, and he started to walk out when our agent said 'Wait, they have another number,' and we hurried into our Wings. Carroll yelled with surprise and said, 'Why didn't you show me this right away?' " In the *Vanities* their act consisted mostly of Wings with a mixture of other flash steps.

Later in 1932 they toured Europe, where they met with mixed reactions: The English loved them and the French seemed puzzled. "We were booked into the London Palladium for two weeks and stayed two years," says Frank, "and then we went to Paris and it was weird—they liked eccentric and body movements, but they just didn't understand tap at all." *The Condos Brothers* stopped doing the Wings with complicated taps, at which they were unequalled, and substituted simpler flash steps.

For about eight years Frank and Nick danced as *The Condos Brothers.* Then the youngest brother, Steve, took Frank's place. Frank worked for a while as a single, appearing twice at the Music Hall in Radio City before retiring in 1937 to become a dance director. Since 1952 he has worked as a welder in a shipyard.

King and King employed the standard steps—both jazz and flash—in the tap repertory, building up routines with various combinations. "Sure, we did Falling Off a Log, and Off to Buffalo," says Condos, "but we worked them in early. Towards the end of the act we used Through the Trenches and sometimes combined Over the Top with Wings—a Wing on the right foot, left foot in back, and then Over the Top—but Wings were our specialty."

Speaking of routines, Sammy Dyer, who choreographed floor shows at the Club DeLisa on Chicago's South Side during the forties, observes: "In my experience four steps are basic: Falling Off a Log, Off to Buffalo, Over the Top, and Through the Trenches—you can put together anything you need from combinations of these four steps." [12] Dyer is thinking of routines he created for his well-drilled group of chorus girls, known as *The Dyerettes*, and has assembled the lowest non-tap denominator.

Chorus girls could not always be expected to execute flash steps with great skill. They had their standard routine called The B. S. Chorus (some chorines thought it stood for "Boy Scout"), which combined the clichés of tap and non-tap and could be performed as a background for any soloist —with varying vigor. The B. S. Chorus is called a "chorus" because it lasts for the duration of a standard thirty-two-bar tune such as "Tea for Two." It is a "routine" because the thirty-two bars are divided into four parts of eight bars apiece, with each part devoted to a different step.

Thus the B. S. Chorus consists of eight bars of the Time Step, eight bars of the Cross Step (a step to the side with one leg crossing the other), eight bars of the Buck and Wing (employing the simplest of hops with little or no tapping), and four bars each of Over the Top and Through the Trenches, reduced to an easy pantomime. With a little luck and competent chorus girls, this often coincides—as it should—with the end of one thirty-two-bar chorus of the tune.

The average chorus line, with such notable exceptions as *The Dyerettes* and the Cotton Club girls, offered a pretty limp version of the real thing. Each of these steps (except Through the Trenches) can be performed with taps, and the performer who puts in taps quite justifiably feels superior, since he or she is executing a far more complicated maneuver. The acid test, therefore, is the number and quality of inserted taps, since like any other dance step, the B. S. Chorus can be a thing of beauty or a mess.

Not that there were no fine women tap dancers. If they were good, however, they usually performed alone, as soloists. Before 1920 and for at least fifteen years, Alice Whitman was tops. "She had clean, clear taps, something like Bill Robinson's," says Pete Nugent. Dancer Rufus Greenlee thinks that Etta Gross, one of the early women tap dancers, was as good as Alice Whitman.

As a youngster, Mae Barnes, who did the Charleston in the second road company of *Shuffle Along*, was an excellent tap dancer before she turned to singing. "In those early days," she insists, "a few of us chorus girls knew more flashy steps than the dance directors or choreographers." [13]

Other women tap dancers—among many—were greatly admired: old-timers Katie Carter and Muriel Ringold; Lavinia Mack featured in *Runnin' Wild*; Cora LaRedd who danced in Cotton Club shows; Maud Mills, the sister of Florence Mills, nicknamed "Hardfoot Maud" because she hit the deck with such force; and later, Louise Madison of Philadelphia, who could cut a five-tap Wing like a man. On Broadway and especially in Hollywood, a series of white tap dancers had the chance to attain far greater fame: Ruby Keeler, Eleanore Whitney, Dixie Dunbar, Ann Miller, and Eleanor Powell—perhaps the best.

A second slightly more complicated combination of tap and body movements, known as the Shim Sham, became a standard routine in show business around 1931. (A third, called the Dip, is not as well known). The Shim Sham's origin is disputed: Both Willie Bryant and Leonard Reed, who were working together at the time, say that they had a comedy dance, "an old-man shuffle to a fast 'Goofus' rhythm," which they presented at the Lafayette Theater. An act named *The Three Little Words* saw it, slowed it down, and presented it at Connie's Inn as the Shim Sham. "We worked it out," says Leonard Reed, "and they got credit for introducing it." [14]

On the other hand, flash-dancer Joe Jones, one of *The Three Little Words,* says he helped invent the routine during a rehearsal: "I had been practicing something like a Time Step and we just changed it a little." [15] Actually, there is every reason to believe that Bryant, Reed, *The Three Little Words*—and other dancers—all helped to create this routine, since it contains elements of various older steps.

In any event it became popular in 1931 when *The Three Little Words* were dancing at Connie's Inn in Harlem. "We'd close the show at Connie's doing the Shim Sham and inviting everybody to get aboard," says Joe Jones, "and the whole club would join us, including the waiters. For awhile people were doing the Shim Sham up and down Seventh Avenue all night long."

The Shim Sham consists of a one-chorus routine to a thirty-two-bar tune, with eight bars each of the Double Shuffle, the Cross Over, the Tack Annie (an up-and-back shuffle), and Falling Off a Log. Conceived as a tap routine, the Shim Sham became so popular that it evolved into a quasi-ballroom dance without taps—the movements can easily be faked—and survives to this day in the finale of television and other shows when the cast lines up to wave goodbye. Even Milton Berle, for example, can do a dilapidated version of it, but a good dancer prides himself on putting the taps back into it.

In 1933 Willie Bryant took over Lucky Millinder's old band at a salary of $45 a week—the sidemen got less—and opened at the Lafayette Theater. Teddy Wilson, Benny Carter, Ben Webster, and Cozy Cole were in the band. "I taught all the musicians to do the Shim Sham," says Bryant, "and it was a big hit. It was the first time a band brought musicians off the stand to do a dance routine." [16] Shortly thereafter Jimmie Lunceford's band staged a similar show.

Today, Wings, along with many lesser steps and the routines that evolved from them, are a lost art. "Some dance instructor worked out directions for doing my five-tap Wing," says Frank Condos wonderingly, "but I never heard of anyone learning it that way." Condos established no new tradition—a dancer might equal but he could go no further along those lines—while the demand for such dancing was swallowed up by the fast-growing popularity and prestige of ballet and modern dance. "Taps today certainly aren't what they used to be," says Condos. "Now they have what I call move-around dancing, with lots of ballet and no punch."

Gene Kelly is more specific: "Dancing is a man's business, altogether," he said in an interview, "but women have taken it over." [17]

25 James Barton: Versatility

WITH HIS FATHER an interlocutor in the *Primrose and West Minstrels* and his mother a ballet dancer, James Barton, born in Gloucester, New Jersey, in 1890, got off to a fast start. "My Uncle John taught me my first step when I was two years old," he says, and demonstrates the step. "I was part of the family act by the time I was four, and I starred as 'The Boy Comedian' when I was seven." [1]

Because of his rare ability to dance any step he saw and make it his own, Barton developed rapidly and without any conscious attempt to copy anyone. Yet he remembers what a deep impression Bert Williams and George Walker made upon him. At the Howard Theater in Boston in 1898, when Barton was eight years old, he was on the same bill with them. "I can see it now," says Barton. "Walker did a great strut, and Williams brought down the house with a terrific Mooche or Grind—a sort of shuffle, combining rubberlegs with rotating hips." Twenty-five years later Barton astonished the Broadway critics with his own Strut and Grind.

From 1898 to 1902 Barton traveled in a knockabout comedy act with his family; from 1907 to 1915 he played anything he could get—North or South—in stock and vaudeville, with side excursions into ice-skating, bicycle racing, and baseball; and from 1915 to 1919 he was on the Columbia burlesque chain as a dancing comedian in a show called *Twentieth Century Maids*. "That was before the strippers came in and killed it," says Barton, "but there was plenty of slapstick." By the time he was thirty, Barton had played the Morris, Fox, Lubin, Sun, Orpheum, Loew's, Pantages, Columbia, and Keith circuits in everything from *Uncle Tom* shows—he was cast in all the roles except that of Little Eva—to repertory theater.

Although burlesque and vaudeville reached a large, nationwide audience, New York theater critics ignored it, and Barton received little or no attention until he arrived on Broadway. At that, his discovery was an accident. During an Equity strike, while Barton was rehearsing a small part in *The Passing Show of 1919*, a benefit was staged at the Lexington Opera House with Ed Wynn and Ethel Barrymore (in a bit from *Camille*). Barton was backstage among a host of others. Alexander Woollcott reviewed the performance: [2]

> . . . it was announced that Ed Wynn had suffered a slight injunction and would be unable to appear. A Mr. Barton had kindly volunteered to take his place. No one knew Mr. Barton. Silent groans throughout the house. And then he ambled on and danced a few steps and owned the audience to a man.

In 1923 a critic in *The New York Times* was still writing ironically about the "Equity strike show" when James Barton "burst forth into Broadway prominence from the obscurity of burlesque shows, in which he was only known to several hundred thousand people . . ." [3]

The pattern of Barton's rise is clear. Whenever he was allowed to dance and improvise his own steps, the impact was tremendous, the recognition immediate. Again and again, alone and unassisted, he literally stopped any show in which he appeared. He reached a peak of critical acclaim in the musical *Dew Drop Inn*, which opened at the Astor Theater on Broadway in 1923. Taking over the role written for Bert Williams, who had died before the show reached Broadway, and donning blackface, Barton was a smash hit.

Dew Drop Inn was not much of a musical, but Barton's performance brought high praise from New York critics. *Variety* noted that Barton "stopped the show ten times by actual count," adding that "Barton dances the show into success." [4]

The New York *News* observed that "whenever the book failed him, he shuffled into one or more of his eccentric dances. And whenever the book failed any of his associates he shuffled again." [5]

The New York *Mail* added: "James Barton's nimble legs . . . just about carried *Dew Drop Inn*." [6]

The program lists only four numbers featuring Barton: "Porter, Porter," "The Struttinest Strutter," "Travesty," and "You Can't Experiment on Me"—but before the show ended each evening, Barton recalls, he came up with at least fourteen different routines, inserting them to fill dead spots or as encores. "I did a strut, a Mooche, a knock-about dance, a military drill, a dying-swan burlesque (my mother gave me the idea for that), a ballroom shiek, a skating act on a pedestal, a mad-dog act, an acrobatic bit, a challenge dance, a burlesque waltz, and some others I can't remember."

The critics singled out the pantomime Waltz as the hit of the show. Dancing with an imaginary partner, Barton satirized the genteel Waltz offered in a preceding number in the same show by Miss Evelyn Cavanaugh and Mr. Richard Dore. (This couple's comments have not been recorded.)

The New York *World* called it "burlesquing the emotional dancing of the restless set," adding that "although this was done without a partner, it left nothing to the imagination." [7]

Theater magazine added: "Theatergoers who have never seen Barton . . . imitate a society high stepper have missed the treat of their lives." [8]

Barton made merciless fun of high society's posturings on the dance floor. "I even pretended to pull my partner through my legs," he recalls with a loud laugh.

Barton's take-off on "The Parade of the Wooden Soldiers" from *Chauve Souris* (1922), according to another reviewer, "seemed new even to the members of the company, and Balieff himself would have been stricken speechless." [9] The achievement of Barton's Strut, an involved and energetic version which took incredible stamina, escaped the critics. "I 'walked' for seventy whole bars, using this special step," says Barton proudly, "but only other dancers knew how difficult it was." His skating routine on top of a pedestal drew raves, although the critics seemed unaware that he was performing without skates. "One night I lost one of my skates," says Barton, "so from then on I did it without them."

Barton's Mooche, or Grind, drew mixed responses. Describing his earlier act in vaudeville and burlesque, Barton says, "I wore a mohair tux and a big shiny belt buckle right in the middle of my stomach; when they turned the spotlight on me, that buckle reflected beams in circles all over the theater." In *Dew Drop Inn* Barton did his Grind in a flannel shirt and baggy trousers. One unidentified New York critic was fascinated: [10]

> Perhaps the most extraordinary number he performed was that in which the upper part of his body remained utterly still, while the lower part, led by the region around his belt, went through striking gyrations. . . .
>
> The upper half of him seemed intent upon leading a calm and carefree existence, while the lower half was determined to be up and doing, so that quite a fierce struggle ensued where they met. . . .
>
> Muscle dancers from the Orient couldn't twist and squirm more intriguingly. . . .

A more antiseptic and yet wide-eyed description of Afro-American pelvic motions in vernacular dance would be hard to find. "His movements were all fresh," another critic remarked, "one of them perhaps too fresh." [11]

In general the critics were confused but ecstatic. Most of them, having seen *Shuffle Along* and other Negro revues, made the clear-cut connection with Negro dancing. The New York *Telegram* announced with considerable insight that Barton was "as negroid as Bert Williams used to be." [12] Others wrote of him as "truly Nubian," while still others described him as "a true levee darkey."

A few critics attempted to describe Barton's footwork. "He dances lying down or sitting or standing," said the New York *Mail*. "He dances with his toes, his legs, his hands, his eyes. . . ." [13]

Another critic observed: "Sometimes he was gay with a levity of step that went with his blackface. Sometimes he weakened at the knees and came towards his audience like a very tired and dejected old negro. Sometimes he fairly chortled across the stage. . . . He would stand on one foot in one spot while he watched the motions of the other foot with the most intense interest." [14]

Alexander Woollcott tried a different approach, comparing Barton to more famous performers: [15]

> He is a far more crafty and amusing black face comedian than Jolson or Tinney or Cantor . . . he has a magnificent physical precision that Deburau must have had. . . .
>
> Such exploits as his should not be described in terms of the ordinary hoofers of the two-a-day. When you talk of Barton as a dancer and a pantomimist, you should mention him in the great company of Nijinski and Charles Chaplin.

For a man who was proud to be known as "a good hoofer," this is high praise indeed.

Heywood Broun, concluding with his usual perception that Barton was a dancing genius—"Here is a performer meant to dance and do nothing else"—made an effort to get at the essence of his appeal: "He manages to be sublime and grotesque at the same time. . . . Broad strokes and infinitely subtle ones are combined in the complete interpretation of the cosmos step by step." [16]

An anonymous critic in *The New York Times* added, "When he dances, he reduces to absurdity all the philosophical schools in the world." [17]

The quality of Barton's dancing, which critics were struggling to pin down, appears to derive from a combination of his experience as a burlesque comedian with his observation of Negro dancers. He was using this flamboyant mixture before the critics knew much about either. "Barton was a great tapper," says Pete Nugent, "but he was more fun to watch than to listen to." [18]

The rubbery anarchy of Barton's dancing, its irreverent vulgarity—he could and would try anything—cut through the conventional concept of "The Dance" and many other genteel attitudes of the day like a meat axe, and he made the most of it. "Barton," says Nick Castle, "made sensational use of his body." [19] At the same time, his uninhibited earthiness, which made him seem irrepressibly common, was new to Broadway, fascinating reviewers and audiences alike. The chief criticism at the time—and it came from the cast—concerned his "strong language" backstage.

Later the reviewers became more fastidious. By 1926, when Barton was starred in *No Foolin'*, *Variety* had one word for a blackface skit written by Barton himself: "brutal"—adding that he stayed on too long.[20]

The New York *Sun* summed it up: Barton has brought "burlesque's coarse-grained humor along with him . . . let him forget to be funny and just keep on dancing." [21] Unfortunately, the broadly explicit and satirical pantomime that overlay his dancing obscured the perfection of his footwork. Viewers concluded that Barton should be an actor, not a dancer, and he was in and out of Broadway shows (both musical and legitimate) and Hollywood for the rest of his long career.

Incidentally, the relationship between James Barton and Bill Robinson illuminates the comparative roles of white and Negro performers during the twenties and later. The lines were clearly drawn. "Though I liked many of the white vaudevillians," writes Ethel Waters, ". . . I didn't fraternize with them . . . and I had the sense to know I was colored. The white actors and I didn't eat together, we didn't sleep together, and I thought it wisest to keep everything on a casual 'Nice day, isn't it?' basis." [22]

Barton and Robinson lived in two separate worlds. Yet because their paths crossed professionally, they grew to respect each other's talents and eventually became friends of a sort; that is, Barton took Robinson's friendship for granted, and nobody knows exactly what Robinson thought, although he frequently (and untruthfully) announced that he got all his stuff from Barton.

Barton's world was almost completely white. When interviewed in 1960, he had never heard of King Rastus Brown or the Hoofers Club. He was genuinely puzzled when asked about the early influence of Negro dancers, and after a moment's thought, observed: "You know, I can't remember any colored hoofers in vaudeville when I started out; later, Bill Robinson came up on the Keith circuit and he was just about the only colored solo dancer."

"Years ago," Barton continued thoughtfully, "they used to say the Negro was a flat-footed dancer, but Bill Robinson sure tapped on his toes." Barton had been brought up in an Irish theatrical family where everyone danced jigs, clogs, and reels as naturally as walking. "We all danced both on our toes and heels," says Barton, "but I added a little more swing." It was the added rhythmic complexity borrowed from Negro performers that made his dancing distinctive.

Similarly, a good friend of Barton's, Dan Healy, who produced Cotton Club shows in Harlem during the late 1920's and 1930's, says: "Towards the end of the twenties, Negro dancers became as good as anybody, but at first they just did a kind of shuffle step." [23] Healy is right about early dancers doing the Shuffle, wrong about their comparative skill and the date. King Rastus Brown and others were putting together taps of hitherto unknown intricacy and momentum before 1900.

Healy's observation points up the lack of communication and the consequent misunderstanding—which often still exists—between the two worlds. The same kind of uninformed mistake occurred in jazz during the 1920's: White jazzmen repeated the erroneous cliché that the Fletcher Henderson band played out of tune simply because it sounded strange to them. Due to lack of familiarity, white ears were not adjusted to the "blue" tonality of the Henderson band, just as white feet remained unaware of the complicated rhythms of Negro dancing.

Healy, who directed and admired many Negro dancers including Maxie McCree, Eddie Rector, Snake Hips Tucker, Bill Robinson, and John Bubbles, concludes: "The main contribution of the colored dancers were Wings, personality, and lots of enthusiasm." "Wings, personality, and lots of enthusiasm" hardly describe Snake Hips Tucker's routine or the class act of Eddie Rector, but they are the characteristics for which most Negro dancers were praised in the 1920's—no matter what they did. The stereotypes died hard.

Although he spent most of the latter half of his life acting, James Barton was a jack-of-all-steps and master of them, too. He thought of himself as a drummer and loved to dance to the music of a swinging band—on one condition: The volume had to be down so the taps could be heard. "I can dance a lot better with a good jazz band," he says. His customary trick with a noisy pit band was a "*Sh-sh-sh*" with his forefinger to his lips, followed by the admonition, "Not now—I'll tell you when." "When" never arrived. Best of all, he liked a solid rhythm section—piano, drums, bass, and guitar—with maybe a clarinet "capering" in the background.

On the subject of tap dancing, Barton is explicit. "I like a normal floor—no resin—I carried around a six-foot square mat on which I did all of my routines." He had a definite approach: "A lot of dancers will do a Time Step, then a step of their own, then back to the Time Step, while they talk to the audience and so on." (This is a fair description of much of Bill Robinson's tapping.) "But I always start with three kinds of Time Steps—single, double, and triple—and never go back. From then on I'm doing my own stuff without repeating." Audiences did not always realize what was happening, but other dancers did.

Barton is unique in that most other dancers, white and Negro alike, agree that he was tops for sheer versatility. He had his matchless triumphs, too. The Palace Theater on Broadway, goal of all performers in the days of vaudeville, had an iron-clad rule: once the asbestos curtain comes down on an act, it stays down. Barton changed that. After his act the management was forced to raise the curtain a few more times or have the theater wrecked. "When I played the Palace," Barton says, "the boys would turn up in the audience and then disappear in the men's room after my act to practice my steps."

To be a dancer and not use something of Barton's was just about impossible. "Both Jack Donahue and Johnny Long used a lot of my stuff," says Barton with just a trace of bitterness, "while Ben Blue borrowed my dying-swan act and Red Skelton took over my mad-dog routine." Toward the end of his career Barton became a little annoyed at the wholesale borrowing. Like King Rastus Brown he had taken steps from a now-forgotten source and felt they were his own. Although he became famous as an actor, his reputation as a dancer meant more to him.

From 1934 to 1939—for five-and-a-half years—Barton quit dancing to star in *Tobacco Road* on Broadway. Taking Henry Hull's place, he played the turnip-eating role of Jeeter Lester 1,899 times, without dancing a step. "I never could look at a turnip without shuddering after that," he says. The part of a slovenly hillbilly was something that Barton, with his burlesque background, could get his teeth into. He was in too much demand for theatrical roles to concentrate on his dancing and remained a legendary dancer's dancer.

Dan Healy is convinced that Barton could have been a first-rate Shakespearean actor. Like Charlie Chaplin, to whom Alexander Woollcott compared him, Barton was a master of pantomime, a superb clown. (Barton's Uncle John was a big hit in England when Chaplin was starting his career, and as Barton points out, Chaplin may have learned something from him.) In 1926, when he attended a performance by Barton at the Palace, Chaplin stood up and applauded vigorously, stamping his cane. "One of the few performers I ever impersonated," says Barton proudly, "was Chaplin."

Back in the 1920's Harlem's Cotton Club was one of the few places where white and Negro dancers could meet and perhaps learn from each other. (The management discouraged all but the most famous Negro customers.) On Sunday or "Celebrity" nights, after their own Broadway shows were over, Barton and his friends went uptown to see Dan Healy. "We loved to dance to Duke Ellington or Cab Calloway," says Barton. "Eddie Rector was in the floor show, and Bill Robinson was often in the audience, and we'd all do a challenge dance, competing in a friendly way." On such nights the audience saw some fine dancing.

James Barton died in 1962 at the age of seventy-one. His obituary in *Variety* made one crucial point: Barton was invariably and wrongly identified with *Tobacco Road*—"this was like Bill Robinson being famous for running backwards." [24] Barton was, first and foremost, a dancer. And yet Barton is often remembered today for his "souse act," or drunk scenes, the one routine that Bernard Sobel selects for special praise.[25] Barton also played the leading role of Hickey in O'Neill's *The Iceman Cometh.* In 1961 he appeared briefly in a barroom scene with Marilyn Monroe and Clark Gable in a film entitled *The Misfits*, as a drunk, not a dancer.

In his day Barton was preferred by critics to Jolson, Cantor, Bojangles, Astaire, Bolger—as *Variety* reports—"whoever anybody was inclined to mention as a master." [26] A few movie shorts such as *After Seben* and *The Whole Show* (filmed by Mentone) survive and dimly document Barton's superb dancing. He was an original who, aided by an Irish background of jigs and reels, absorbed the rhythms and movements of Negro dancers early in his career and added an earthy, uninhibited genius for satirical pantomime. Sidetracked into legitimate theater, Barton nevertheless remains one of the great pioneers who brought a new and shamelessly vital blend of vernacular dance to the notice of Broadway critics and thence to the rest of the country.

26 Harland Dixon and Character Dancing

AT A WEDNESDAY MATINEE of *Tip Top* in April 1919 Fred Stone broke the little toe of his right foot coming out of an acrobatic stunt called a Coffee Grind. Only one man could take his place on Broadway without derailing the entire production: dancer Harland Dixon. Not that Fred Stone was a great dancer—he was more of an acrobat—but Harland Dixon had the well-deserved reputation of being able to pantomime anybody or anything.

Unfortunately, Dixon was in Cleveland with his partner, Jimmy Doyle, dancing in *Hitchy-Koo,* which starred Raymond Hitchcock and Julia Sanderson. "My wife and I were having dinner," Dixon recalls, "when our dyspeptic road manager burst into the hotel dining room announcing that I had to go to New York—he forgot to say why." [1] Everything had been arranged by Charles Dillingham, who owned both shows, and the Dixons entrained at eight o'clock that night.

Arriving at nine the next morning, Dixon went straight to Dillingham's office in the Globe Theater building. It was Thursday, and Dixon was to open the show the following Monday night. "For four days I rehearsed from nine A.M. until a lunch break at one; from two to five-thirty in the afternoon, and from seven-thirty to eleven-thirty at night," says Dixon, "alternating one hour for lines, one hour for music, one hour for dancing—that was the easiest—until the curtain went up." On Monday night, he played the lead without a mistake.

Dixon made the Italian-style dance in *Tip Top* his own with great success, and at the last minute, added a few eccentric steps to an Indian routine which brought down the house. The cast, which included *The Duncan Sisters,* Dorothy Stone, and *The Brown Brothers,* helped in every way, overjoyed at the possibility that the show would not fold. The following Sunday young George S. Kaufman wrote a four-column review in *The New York Times,* raving about the dancer who single-handedly saved a show.

Harland Dixon's career covered the entire spectrum from minstrelsy through vaudeville to Broadway, where he appeared in some two-dozen shows over a period of fifty years. The names of the shows read like a history of musical comedy: *Broadway to Paris* (1912), *Honeymoon Express* (1913), *Stop, Look and Listen* (1915), *Century Girl* (1916), *Jack O'Lantern* (1917), *Hitchy-Koo* (1917), *Chin Chin* (1917-18), *The Canary* (1918-19), *Tip Top* (1919), *Good Morning Dearie* (1922), *Ziegfeld Follies* (1923), *Kid Boots* (1923), *Oh Kay* (1926), *Manhattan Mary* (1927), *Rainbow* (1928), *Heads Up* (1929), *Top Speed* (1930), *Better Times* (1932), *Dilly Dally* (1933), *Life Begins at 8:40* (1934), *Anything Goes* (1934), *Marinka* (1945), *A Tree Grows in Brooklyn* (1951), and *Old Bucks and New Wings* (1962).

He was eighty-one years old in 1966 and could still execute almost any step he had ever learned. Although never the highest paid or most famous dancer on Broadway, Dixon was by far the most durable and adaptable, and he pioneered a new and difficult *genre.*

"I learned my first bit of dancing in gym class, when I was about twelve," says Dixon, who was born in Toronto in 1885. "The kid in front of me was doing a Slap Step as we hopped up and down in line during calisthenics, so I had to imitate it and add a few flourishes of my own." One of his pals returned from Buffalo with a traveling step derived from the Cakewalk, which he called the Jennie Cooler, and Dixon learned that, too. "For about a year I made a real nuisance of myself wherever they'd let me dance."

Dixon became a dedicated dancer when, having paid ten cents to sit in the balcony of Toronto's Grand Theater, he watched Johnny Ford and Mamie Gerhue in a musical called *Lovers and Lunatics.* Ford had just won the Fox medal for Buck dancing offered by the owner of the *Police Gazette.* "He was a fine Buck dancer, and Mamie did some Wings," Dixon recalls.

Around 1903 Dixon won second prize and three dollars in the contest staged by the traveling show *In Old Kentucky* (Austrian-born George White, who later became a producer, won first prize and five dollars). With a partner, Jimmy Malone, Dixon began to earn pocket money dancing at stag "smokers." At first they danced without pay, passing the hat, and later charged three or four dollars for gigs outside of town. "We had a schottische which lasted forever," Dixon remembers, "and a beginner's buck-and-wing."

Then he saw the dancer who was to become the greatest single influence in his career: George Primrose (see Chapter 7). "He was the greatest *stylist* of them all," says Dixon, choosing his words carefully. The *Primrose Minstrels* came to Toronto, and at four o'clock in the morning after the first show, Dixon and Malone managed to crash Primrose's room in the King Edward Hotel and get him out of bed to arrange for an audition. "He was quite pleasant and treated us very courteously." Dixon is still astonished. The audition next day was a failure—"we danced too much and too long"—but Primrose told them to look him up in New York.

Dixon promptly ran away from home, worked as a busboy in Buffalo, a checkroom attendant in Boston, and landed in New York without a penny. "I remember looking through advertisements that said 'Singers, Dancers, and Musicians Wanted—No Dope Fiends—Mustn't Play Cards or Smoke.'" His best hope was Primrose. Arriving at the office at 1550 Broadway, Dixon bumped into his old partner, Jimmy Malone, who was on a similar mission. They pretended to have come all the way from Toronto together, just to see Mr. Primrose.

Among other things George Primrose was an unsentimental businessman. He hired Dixon and Malone for fifteen dollars a week and fired two other dancers who were getting twenty-five dollars a week. "I think the old tightwad liked me," says Dixon, "although he never showed any personal interest. We had the same Calvinist background." Primrose sent them to Jimmy O'Connor, who was working out the chorus routines before the minstrel show opened on June 30, 1906, in Plainfield, New Jersey.

"I had trouble with the unsyncopated Lancashire Clog, which went 'diddely, diddely, diddely'—with no 'dum' at the end," says Dixon. "It took a lot of concentration to keep it from swinging." The chorus of eight dancers learned the simplest kind of Virginia Essence. It was dying out at the time, but still looked good when performed in unison by a group. They danced in back of a lady singer during a plantation scene. Neither Malone nor Dixon was permitted to dance solo—that was done by two old-time cloggers and the one-and-only Primrose.

Dixon and Malone worked with the *Primrose Minstrels* for a year-and-a-half, playing mostly one-night stands in the South. The show carried a fine ragtime drummer named Joe Wilson, who attracted crowds of youngsters—white and Negro—during the parades in Southern towns. Dixon, alert to every opportunity, was watching Primrose when he could and working out his own style. "I think he purposely scheduled his own dances while we were backstage changing costumes," says Dixon. "He wasn't giving anything away."

When he joined the *Primrose Minstrels*, Dixon was a hardworking hoofer—"I was doing eight difficult Wing steps in sixty-four bars"—but he began to change his style. "I got tired of digging a hole in the stage—the audience doesn't appreciate Wings anyway—so one night I decided to put in an easy step as a sort of rest, and the way I happened to do it got a bigger hand than anything else." So Dixon threw out Wings and put in his own brand of comic steps. "From then on," he says, with a twinkle in his pale blue eyes, "I never did Wings except in hotel lobbies when other dancers were around."

His rest steps were different, too. "I was copying Primrose, but it came out different; while he was all grace and elegance, I was more stiff and angular—in a humorous way." Dixon took pretty steps by Primrose and employed them in comic pantomime. Like Primrose, Dixon used the upper part of his body, especially the shoulders—in one instance holding his arms close to his sides "like a stick" and twisting his shoulders alternately forward. "The effect was funny but classy," says Dan Healy, "and many musical-comedy dancers imitated Harland's jaunty shoulder movements." [2] Dixon was evolving an eccentric, comedy version of his model, Primrose, and his buoyant pantomime had a sophistication of its own.

In August 1907 Dixon left Primrose to join *Lew Dockstader's Minstrels*, with which he worked for about nine months. "Old Dockstader was a moral guy and liked to lecture us about the perils of flirting during the street parades," Dixon recalls. "One day during a parade he was watching a pretty blonde leaning out of a window and walked right into a horse—the band was laughing so hard they had to stop playing."

While with Dockstader, Dixon met Jimmy Monahan, who had danced a jig at Inman's Coney Island restaurant, balancing a glass of beer on his head. "Monahan did the kind of jig that reflected the Irish temperament, the kind I like," says Dixon, "footwork plus hands on hips, head tossing, and shoulders rising and falling—it had character." Shortly thereafter Dixon was executing his own version of the same dance. "I stole it," he says cheerfully.

Dixon has a keen eye for characteristic gestures he can use. One day he saw Lew Dockstader, who was a monologist not a dancer, unconsciously doing a tight little strut during rehearsals. "It was a gem, and I adopted it then and there." Another time he was fascinated by "a little body twist" that Billy Rock employed. "He was famous for doing something with nothing. If he knew two more steps, he would have had six more routines." Dixon still treasures it. He learned something from everybody, including hand gestures from the vaudeville orator Henry E. Dixey.

In 1908 Dixon gave up wooden shoes for split soles, and with another partner, Jack Corcoran, accepted an offer of $40 a week as a blackface act on the Orpheum circuit. Dockstader, who was paying him $20, made a counter offer of $35 and tried to make him stay. It took a great deal of ingenuity—including a fake fight—to get away, trunk and all. When the new act reached Denver, the manager of the vaudeville house reacted with uncharacteristic enthusiasm: "We've had a million tap dancers here, but what are *you* doing?"

After a stint in burlesque, Dixon was ready in 1912 to make the leap to Broadway musicals. He had given up blackface, and with Jimmy Doyle as his new partner, was performing at a theater on Broadway and 34th Street. An agent offered them $25 apiece to appear at the Winter Garden on a Sunday night. "Al Jolson and Nora Bayes were on the bill, but I guess everybody *expected* them to be great. The audience quieted down when we came on because nobody knew us, and then, as we were finishing our act, they began to roar. By the time we were through, a dozen agents were waiting to sign us up."

Broadway went to vaudeville for its dancers and helped to revive a dying tradition that had its roots in minstrelsy. In the process the style of dancing began to change. The plots increasingly employed by musical comedy, no matter how superficially, called for eccentric dancing to fit the needs of a role in the story. Straight hoofers who soloed in one spot were no longer in demand. Just dancing—even the most expert—was not enough. Broadway wanted performers who could dance out their parts, fitting into some sort of role—in short, *character dancers*. Doyle and Dixon were dancing minor roles in *Broadway to Paris* within a month.

Describing *Doyle and Dixon* at the Palace—between musicals—in 1916, Dixon says: "We open fast in top hats and tails, alternately singing phrases from a song Gershwin gave us: 'I'm Crazy about You, Daffy about You, Can't Live without You,' which lasts about a minute; then forty bars of the Schottische—Soft Shoe—with a quick finish; I do a snap and he does one, I do a jump and he does one, and off we go, alternating snaps and jumps. Then we come back with a waltz. I point at him as he does a hard step, he points at me as I do an eccentric step—we're aiming for contrast—and exit arm in arm."

After that, several things can happen. They may swap top hats: "Doyle has his hat in his right hand, mine is in my left, and his head is much larger than mine," says Dixon. "I step over in front of Doyle and we exchange hats, unobserved, before we hit the floor in a split. When we come up, we don our hats graciously, but mine looks like a big stovepipe and Doyle's like a dime on a maypole as we stroll off stage."

At another point they pretend to be annoyed and insult each other with steps. "We'd each do a complicated step and then snap our fingers in each other's face—sort of a challenge dance, but very lofty and disdainful." One of their most effective finales employed a dummy cigarette as a prop. "After a bit of knockabout, Doyle offers me a cigarette from an elegant gold case by way of a truce. I take one and spill another on the stage. As Doyle bends scornfully to retrieve it, his back is horizontal and I suddenly go into a Side Roll over him with my head to the audience and land on the other side erect, and we both stroll off smoking, without a backward glance at the audience."

A good part of the act's success was due to contrast, produced by a mixture of startling action and suave aplomb. Above all, they established characterization—there was always a touch of plot as well as sophistication in the short stories they danced. "Doyle and Dixon," wrote Joe Laurie Jr., "were the classiest two-man hoofing act in show biz." [3]

In those days dancing imitations of different nationalities were in great demand: Irish, Scottish, Italian, Chinese, Russian, Dutch, Indian, and so on *ad infinitum*, as well as such stereotypes as the rube, hayseed, tramp, constable, Negro, or city slicker.[4] Dixon could and did do them all, working out revealing steps and gestures for each, and adding new humor and vitality. With Dixon's gift for spirited characterization, the stereotypes came back alive.

Doyle and Dixon worked together for nine years—until 1921—when Dixon went ahead on his own, fitting into any role in any setting in any act or show. Although the salary was not as high as in vaudeville, Dixon always enjoyed Broadway: "You never have to worry about the act that follows you." In *Good Morning Dearie*, which ran from 1920 to 1923, Dixon was earning $500 a week with no commissions or taxes to pay. "I never felt richer," he declares.

The reviewers warmed to Harland Dixon's dancing slowly and surely but without much understanding. Pantomimes of stereotypes, no matter how well done, are easy to enjoy but hard to analyze, and the reviewers were not dance critics. Nevertheless they sometimes came close. A reviewer of *Good Morning Dearie* wrote that "Mr. Dixon besides giving *real impersonation* [*authors' italics*] to his underworld character, delighted with his air of wondering how his dancing legs got that way." [5] (Reviewers were uniformly impressed by dancers who did not seem to know what they were doing.)

Reviewing *Kid Boots*, which featured Eddie Cantor and ran for sixty-five weeks on Broadway and three years on the road (1923-1926), Gilbert Seldes actually noticed "an entirely new pivoting stunt" [6]—a step Dixon describes as "a fast twist plus a slow turn" which he had been doing for some time.

Gordon Whyte, reviewing the same show in *Billboard*, wrote "he dances superbly, chants a ditty well enough and reads his lines with masculinity." [7] To praise a dancer for masculinity became increasingly rare.

By 1926, when he opened in *Oh Kay* with Gertrude Lawrence and the tunes of George Gershwin, Harland Dixon had become an established and welcome figure. Brooks Atkinson remarked in *The New York Times*, "Mr. Dixon becomes wooden or supple according to need in a gauche potpourri of eccentric steps" [8]—which hints at his fine particular talent; while Alan Dale in the *American* went back to safer generalities: "After Miss Lawrence I should say that Harlan [*sic*] Dixon was the most interesting feature. He danced till every inch of his flesh quivered." [9]

During his career Harland Dixon has put together countless routines for vaudeville, night clubs, and Broadway shows. "I think of the action I want first, and then add the rhythm," he says. "Sometimes I have a step all worked out before I find the music for it." His aim is always something more than just dancing, and the appeal of his routines is never based on the difficulty of a step but rather the manner in which it is performed—specifically, whether or not it communicates *character.*

"I think of myself as an entertainer first, and then a dancer," says Dixon. "Why, I've had jobs where all I did was talk." More often, he illustrates his stories with dancing, as in the tale of "Guppy and Fog" (two fictitious vaudevillians) or "The Tip Top Cavalry" (an old gag put to rhythm). Or again he works out wordless pantomimes portraying a nervous tap dancer in a dentist's office, using metal strips on the sides of his shoes; or an imitation of John Barrymore—"if he could dance."

"As a creator of eccentric with the greatest variety of steps," wrote Jack Donahue, "in my opinion Harland Dixon stands alone." [10] In addition to his shoulder twists, which were so widely imitated on Broadway, Dixon invented a knee-snap. "Dancers still ask me how to do it," he says. "And he used a cane," adds Nick Castle, "better than anyone in the world." [11]

Dixon was never at a loss for material. "I divide a dancer's art into four parts—appearance, personality, voice, and material—and the material comes last. Ralph Waldo Emerson says that out of the old comes the new, and I could always take an old step and work it into something else, something that nobody had seen before."

The number of dancers who gained recognition during the twenties and after is phenomenal. Joe Laurie, Jr., lists seventy-six "hoofers" and "eccentric dancers" of this period, not counting a much larger number of ballroom and specialty acts, toe, adagio, and hootchy-kootchy dancers, as well as "the real greats of years ago." [12] Among Dixon's contemporaries, for example, George M. Cohan favored a stiff-legged cakewalk step; Fred Stone performed a neat stop-time dance with his partner Dave Montgomery; Joe Frisco "combined a shuffle and a grind" and called it a jazz dance; Leon Errol specialized in rubberlegs—"he was more comedian than dancer"; and George White, who started his career as a straight hoofer, gave it up to produce his *Scandals.*

As the emphasis upon novelty and comedy increased, the amount of tapping decreased while the eccentricity and humor broadened. A new wave of dancers evolved on Broadway in the twenties: Jack Donahue, whose clowning and "lissome vaulting" was praised by reviewers—"he tried to copy everything I did," says Dixon without rancor, "but it came out looser and maybe not as clean-cut"; Tom Patricola, "a mop gone crazy," who played the ukelele as he danced; Will Mahoney, "the sawed-off gutta percha comedian," who was famous for his pratt falls and tap-dancing on a xylophone ("he didn't have much of a sense of rhythm," [13] says Clarence "Buddy" Bradley who coached him); and Ray Bolger, who soon eliminated much of the tapping to specialize in parodies and satires. "The zany is part of all our best men dancers," wrote Kenneth Macgowan in 1927. "Harlan [*sic*] Dixon has the least of this." [14]

By the mid-thirties it was no longer possible to fall back on vaudeville, which was being obliterated by radio and films. "In 1934 vaudeville's principal excuse for being was as a peg on which stars from other fields could hang their hats for brief personal appearances," [15] write Abel Green and Joe Laurie, Jr. "It seemed like everybody was out of work for a while," Dixon recalls, "and you took whatever you could get." (James Barton, for example, was in *Tobacco Road* from 1934 to 1941.)

Following the Depression and into the forties, eccentric dancers and even comedians ran into trouble on Broadway. Interviewed by the *New Yorker,* Bert Lahr remarked sadly: "In the thirties . . . suddenly the funny man was out. Everyone wanted ballet and dream sequences and schmalzy love stories with wholesome American backgrounds—operetta stuff." [16] The dancing comedians, especially those who used tap, were the first to go.

In the late twenties Dixon was on tour with *Showboat.* Then, like many dancers before him, he went into dance directing. "I was with the Winter Garden in 1933-1934; did some dance-directing for Warner Brothers' shorts at their Brooklyn studio off and on during 1935, 1936, and 1937, and danced in a few; then went out to Hollywood to stage a dance for James Cagney in *Something to Sing About* in '37. When I returned, I picked up odd jobs putting on things for hotels and night clubs in New York and New Jersey. For a while I joined the show at Billy Rose's Diamond Horseshoe."

In 1966, still dapper but slightly stooped and frail, Harland Dixon was entertaining and dancing wherever he could. "I've been reading C. Wright Mills," (he belongs to a Great Books study group) Dixon says, "and I've also worked up a new routine—three choruses with an eight-bar tag—to keep me from puffing; a sort of mixture of steps from the past, brought back from the attic of my memories. The whole act lasts about seventeen minutes, including the narration." Harland Dixon is a great character dancer who lasted as long as and longer than there was any demand for it.

27 John W. Bubbles and Rhythm Tap

THE HOOFERS CLUB in Harlem was the tap summit, and the code decreed that a fledgling dancer was not to bother the great ones, even with a question. If you were lucky enough to be inside when one of the kings arrived, you remained seated on the bench utterly motionless and "cool," although, curled up beneath you, your feet maybe moved as you watched, imitating a step. But your face was expressionless, and when the great man stopped dancing and sat down, you stayed glued to the bench, no matter how great the strain, until he left.

Not that the youngsters at the Hoofers Club were a quiet and colorless lot. With no idol to awe them, they expressed themselves in highly individual fashion. "Slappy" Wallace never finished a Time Step without inserting an unexpected slap somewhere along the line; "Piano" could not execute a step unless he held on to the battered upright with both hands; "Happy" had a step in which he leaned over and dusted off one shoe on the beat; and "Motorboat"—well, he was the self-proclaimed genius who appeared before his draft board during World War II in a cerise cutaway and proclaimed "Broadway *needs* me!" (He was rejected on other grounds.) Everybody had his own punch step, calculated to spark applause.

Around 1920 one of the future kings first visited the Hoofers Club. He was a cocky eighteen-year-old named John "Bubber" Sublett, a singer whose voice was changing, and who saw no reason why he should not be a dancer, too. He waited impatiently and needed no urging to perform. "I was only doing a strut and a turn then," he says, "while Eddie Rector, Dickie Wells, and a bunch of other experts were watching me. I did my little steps, and they laughed me out of the club—'You're hurting the floor,' they said. I just couldn't class with them." [1] Sublett left for California on the next train.

He continued his singing on the Orpheum circuit out west, where he stayed six months, but between songs he practiced tap. A year later he was back in New York full of ideas for new steps. "One night I started practicing about eleven o'clock; at three A.M. I took off my shoes and danced barefoot, and around six A.M. I had a new routine. I didn't look back after that. I kept multiplying to it all the time, changing steps so fast that each step was mounting the next."

Sublett took his creation to the Hoofers Club the next evening. "Man, I was really fortified, like a fellow with a double-barreled shotgun—who's gonna stop me?" His success was immediate, complete, and a new king was crowned.

John Sublett—he later changed his name to John W. Bubbles—was born in Louisville in 1902 and raised in Indianapolis. When he was eight years old, he worked up a routine of Walking the Dog with one of his seven sisters. At the age of ten he teamed with six-year-old Ford Lee "Buck" Washington in an act billed as "Buck and Bubbles." Bubbles sang, and Buck played accompaniments standing at the piano. Between local engagements they worked in a bowling alley, and later, while winning a series of amateur-night shows, sold candy in theaters.

In a short time they were playing engagements in Louisville, Detroit, and finally, New York City. The New York date, a Sunday afternoon benefit at the Columbia Theater on Broadway, led directly to a job at the Palace in 1922. Among the many dancers who came to watch them, according to Bubbles, was Fred Astaire. *Buck and Bubbles* bypassed T.O.B.A.

For over twenty years they had the same act. Buck Washington, who died in 1955, described it to Bernard Sobel: [2]

> I believe that we got our first laugh with the help of our costumes. The shoes are too big. The trousers are too short on one of us and too long on the other.
>
> Our first movements also create laughter, for I pretend that I'm an amateur. I watch Bubbles do a step, then I repeat it, but listlessly as if I were tired. The biggest applause comes when I stub my toe.

This mood of relaxed exhaustion furnished a sharp contrast to Buck's piano playing and Bubbles's dancing.

Incidental dialogue set the tone. Short and stocky, Buck sits at the piano, as Bubbles, tall and slender, walks on stage.

"You don't look so good," Buck observes.

"I don't feel so good," Bubbles replies.

"What's the matter?" asks Buck without much interest, and Bubbles goes into a slow-tempo song, "This Is My Last Affair," phrasing like a heartbroken Louis Armstrong. The moment Bubbles finishes, Buck announces with loud disdain, "You can't sing that song like that!" and starts banging furiously on the piano—with considerable power and drive—stomping out the tune up-tempo and scat-singing like a jubilant Cab Calloway.

At this point Bubbles decides to go along with the fast tempo, and he, too, sings a chorus, climaxing his vocal with some tricky steps: "I did some heel-and-toe taps, then a Cross Over while backing up, followed by coming forward on the heels—almost like a Roll—and ending with a floor slap with one foot." Having watched this exhibition from the piano, Buck rises slowly to his feet and asks suspiciously "What was that?" Bubbles replies "That's Harlem," whereupon Buck, not to be outdone, tries—without expending energy—to top the step.

Buck's performance is the kind traditionally described as eccentric. Starting with a lazy Charleston, he adds a slide and a Fall Off the Log, ending with a two-bar break in which he places one large shoe on top of the other and falls on his face. Yawning, he picks himself up and returns to the piano, where he plays a few self-congratulatory chords, confident that he has outdone Bubbles. For a moment the act seems to have gone to sleep.

Then comes Bubbles's solo dance. Paul Draper still remembers it: "Bubbles has a casual approach to the complicated steps he executes. His nonchalant manner contradicts the incredible things his feet are doing. You think he is just going to stroll around the stage, when presto, he'll toss off a burst of sight and sound that you just can't believe. At the same time, Buck plays stop-time on the piano in the laziest manner imaginable. He falls off the piano stool, remembering to reach up from the floor just in time to plunk one note every sixteen bars." [3]

To this somnambulistic accompaniment Bubbles's taps exploded in counterpoint. "I did every step four different ways," Bubbles recalls, "including a tap version of 'In a Little Spanish Town' to tango rhythm." An erroneous legend among dancers held that he was left-footed, which helped to explain why his steps were inimitable. "Nobody could take Bubbles's steps," says Frank Condos,[4] and Nick Castle adds: "I could never steal a step from Bubbles—he never repeats—he's the greatest *ad lib* dancer in the world." [5]

Bubbles, however, had little trouble adopting other dancers' steps. He had a reputation for being cagey, and his technique for extracting a step from a competitor became notorious.

Watching another dancer practicing at the Hoofers Club, Bubbles bides his time until he sees something he can use. "Oh-oh," he says, shaking his head in alarm, "you lost the beat back there—now try that step again." The dancer starts only to be stopped, again and again, until Bubbles, having learned it, announces, "You know, that reminds me of a step I used to do," and proceeds to demonstrate two or three variations on the original step. The other dancer usually feels flattered.

In 1921 the pioneers whom young Bubbles admired considered the Buck and Wing old-fashioned, although the general public loved it, and the Charleston, a "jazz" step which eventually penetrated many ballrooms, was beginning to catch on among professionals, especially those who could not tap too well. "When I first started dancing," says Bubbles, "performers tapped a little and then went into Wings, splits, and Russian kicks—anything to be flashy—and they did the Charleston and the Black Bottom. Body movement was the big thing, not taps." Going against the current, Bubbles made tap dancing popular all over again.

When he first conquered the Hoofers Club, Bubbles beat the competition at its own game. "I was very fast and energetic," he says, "and I'd get applause for my endurance." He had a routine to 164 bars of "Mammy O' Mine," which began with strenuous body movements—turn slides and four-way slides—and built up to thirty-two or even sixty-four bars of fast, complicated tapping.

"I remember a cutting session at the Hoofers Club," says Clarence "Buddy" Bradley. "A fellow named Detroit Red was scaring everybody to death doing variations on Over the Top. Then somebody said, 'Here comes Bubbles,' and there he was. Well, Bubbles started working out on the same step, and before he was through, Toots Davis, who was in the audience, said to me: 'I invented that step, but I never knew there were so many ways to do it.' "[6]

"When I got to Over the Top, I did a double Over the Top—alternate legs," says Bubbles, "but not the figure-eight pattern. I traveled backwards and forwards, and from side to side. Instead of making this the climax, I'd do the Trenches *backwards,* like a cakewalk slide, not a kick. I left nothing undone." Still he was not satisfied. "I kept thinking about when I got older, and then I wouldn't want to jump around."

The new style Bubbles created in 1922 soon became known as rhythm tap. "I figured I'd cut the tempo," says Bubbles off-handedly, forgetting to add that he also complicated the rhythm. In dancers' terminology, Bubbles changed from two-to-a-bar to four-to-a-bar, cutting the tempo in half and giving himself twice as much time to add new inventions.

For the jazz-oriented, the switch in rhythmic accenting may be described as the difference between Dixieland and the swing beat. "He was like Coleman Hawkins in sound,"[7] says Baby Laurence. Approximately fourteen years before the Basie band came east, Bubbles was dancing to the kind of rhythm that Count Basie called "four heavy beats to a bar and no cheating."[8]

To feel the difference between two-to-a-bar and four-to-a-bar, hum "Yankee Doodle" the way you have always heard it, fast and jerky, stressing the usual accents:

1 2 *1* 2 *1* 2 *1* 2 *1* 2 *1* 2 *1* 2
*Yan*kee / *Doo*dle / *went* to / *town* / *ri*ding / *on* a / *po*ny

To put the same tune into four-to-a-bar, hum it slowly, tapping your foot four times to each bar:

1 234 *1* 234 *1* 234 *1* 234 *1* 234 *1* 234 *1* 234 *1* 234
*Yan*kee / *Doo*dle / *went* to / *town* / *ri*ding / *on* a / *po-* / -ny

Notice that there are twice as many beats for the same number of words. By contrast, the over-all feeling is long-drawn-out, affording room for off-beat accenting. It can also be highly syncopated and swinging.

Tap dancers have a more concise way to count the two tempos. Taking "Tea for Two," a great favorite, they refer to the two-to-a-bar version as "fast" and count *1*,2; *2*,2; *3*,2; *4*,2 during the lyrics "Picture you upon my knee, tea for two and two for tea." Four-to-a-bar is spoken of as "slow," and the same lyrics would be counted *1*,2,3,4; *2*,2,3,4; *3*,2,3,4; *4*,2,3,4; *5*,2,3,4; *6*,2,3,4; *7*,2,3,4; *8*,2,3,4. Again, four-to-a-bar has twice as many beats as two-to-a-bar, with the same lyrics, and a good dancer uses that extra time to advantage.

The paradox is that dancing four-to-a-bar turns out to be more difficult than dancing two-to-a-bar. "Working with twos, you can't add much because the tempo is too fast, Charles "Honi" Coles remarks. "You just have time to do the traditional steps with as much skill as possible. With fours, a good dancer works just as fast, even though the tempo is slower, but he has to fill in with his own ideas as well as watch his balance. In fact, he has to learn to handle his entire body more gracefully." [9] The parallel to a jazzman playing a slow ballad is quite close—the more time for embellishment, the more obvious are the merits or defects of his improvisation.

As for the actual steps, Bubbles combined elements that had been around for a long time. "He started a new style," says Dan Healy, "by combining the Lancashire Clog with Buck dancing." [10]—and much more. In 1926 Pete Nugent worked on a bill with old-timer Barney Fagan: "Fagan tried to show me some of his clog steps, and do you know I just couldn't do them?" Nugent recalls. "He used his heels and toes in a way which was new to me, putting together combinations which were very complicated but didn't swing—they just kind of bounced. Later, when I saw Bubbles, I realized that he was doing stuff like Fagan's, but adding more material and making all of it swing." [11]

Bubbles verifies this. "When I was just a kid," he says, "I was on the same program with a fine Lancashire Clog dancer named Harland Dixon of the team of *Doyle and Dixon*, and I picked up a lot of ideas." Later, on a television program, Bubbles dedicated a dance to Harland Dixon (see Chapter 26). Getting extra beats by hitting the heels and toes together came from the Clog.

Of course, dancing four-to-a-bar is not new. The tempo of soft-shoe dancing is traditionally four-to-a-bar, and dancers gradually switched to two-to-a-bar for a whirlwind finish. History had repeated itself, for back in the early teens, Jack Donahue remembers when "things were beginning to speed up; the four-four dancer was being replaced by the two-four buck dancer," [12] who used more taps and less space.

Bubbles's contribution was unusual accenting, off-beats with the heels and toes in a variety of Cramp Rolls, which made for greater dynamics. "When he started dropping his heels," says Honi Coles, "he could get an extra thud whenever he wanted it." He did new things with his toes, too, adding taps behind and bringing them together for an extra accent in front. At the same time he worked out turns and combinations, or rhythmic patterns, some of which extended beyond the usual eight bars. In so doing, he anticipated the prolonged melodic line of "cool" jazz in a later era.

Bubbles has his own notions of what he was trying to do: "I thought I'd fix a step in a rhythm more in keeping with a person sitting out there in the audience. He doesn't really know what I'm doing—whether it's difficult or easy—but I can make it relaxed to suit the average rhythm of the average person. If a person is satisfied with walking, he don't want to run. Besides, I was sick of those fast tempos which are just a lot of noise. When an audience is sitting down, they're relaxed and they want to stay that way. So I fixed my dancing to keep them relaxed, and they liked it."

Bubbles is not afflicted with false modesty. "I can do anything with my feet," he says. "Why, I can dance 'Swanee River' and make you hear every word."

Bubbles's most important experience with a Broadway show was in the *Ziegfeld Follies of 1931*. Two better-known dancers were in the cast—Mitzi Mayfair and Hal Leroy—along with Harry Richman, Ruth Etting, Jack Pearl, and the Albertina Rasch troupe, all performing amid lavish surroundings. When their turn came, Buck and Bubbles simply walked out on the bare stage in front of a painted backdrop: "Just as if the emcee had announced 'Now you can go out and have a cigarette,'" says Bubbles, "'because we're going to give you a rest from the *Follies*.'"

During rehearsals the survival of the act seemed doubtful. Buck and Bubbles ran into problems from two sides. Bill Robinson advised them vehemently to insist on a better dressing room. "It didn't take a fortune teller to see that one squawk from us and we'd be fired," says Bubbles, "and Bojangles was positive that he should be dancing in our place anyway." Besides, the wisdom of quitting vaudeville and taking a salary cut from $1,750 to $800 a week, just for the privilege of appearing with "white folks" on Broadway, seemed questionable.

The show was ragged during dress rehearsal in Pittsburgh, and Buck and Bubbles were abruptly ordered to cut their act from fourteen to nine minutes just before opening night. Rehearsing all day, they chopped the act down to eight minutes. When they arrived for the show—a little late—all anybody wanted to know was whether they had cut their act.

"I decided to quit," says Bubbles. "I was so discouraged. When our cue came, we went into the act. Right in the middle, as I was dancing over to the wings, the manager yelled 'You're overtime!' and I knew he was going to turn off the lights. Buck didn't hear him, and I decided not to panic him with the news. We just went ahead and finished in exactly eight minutes. It was the longest eight minutes I ever lived." The audience sat as if stunned. After a few moments the applause began. It went on and on. "I think they're still cheering in Pittsburgh," [13] says Hal Leroy.

Harry Richman came out, and in order to get on with the show, made the gratuitous announcement that Buck and Bubbles had "left for a speak-easy." Someone in the balcony shouted "Then go get 'em!"

Eventually, they were brought up from their basement dressing room and took a few bows to quiet the audience. After that night, nobody in the show wanted to follow *Buck and Bubbles*—the audience was not interested in anyone else. "They changed our spot almost every night," says Bubbles. "Finally they put us next to closing—the feature spot—and kept us there."

When the *Follies* reached New York City, Buck and Bubbles doubled at the Lafayette Theater in Harlem. The contrast between the noisy informality of the Lafayette and the quiet solemnity of the *Follies* made a distinct difference. "I was doing the same steps in both places," says Bubbles, "but with a different feeling. Downtown, it was a battle among the acts; uptown, between the dancer and the audience. In Harlem the audience practically dared you to dance, and you had to swing. Downtown they just watched, and you couldn't fail. I danced loose and rhythmic uptown—flop and flang-flang; simple and distinct downtown." As in jazz, the audience exerted a crucial influence.

By 1935 Bubbles was acting, singing, and dancing the role of "Sportin' Life" in *Porgy and Bess.* He was Gershwin's choice for the part, although he could not read music and had to memorize his songs by ear. The original production ran eighteen weeks. Later he made several movies in Hollywood: *Cabin in the Sky, Varsity Show,* and *A Song Is Born* (with Judy Garland). During 1958 he appeared frequently on the Peter Lind Hayes television show, and in 1961 was interviewed on *American Musical Theater* (CBS-TV), giving a superb demonstration of his many talents.

In the summer of 1961, when an attempt was made to open the Carver House, a Negro night club in Las Vegas (with the exception of a few headliners, the town had a lily-white policy), Bubbles was hired, along with a chorus line, a girl vocalist, and an orchestra, to perform in a revue entitled "Le Jazz Hot." At the press conference the morning after opening night, the journalists—all but two were Negroes—objected to Bubbles's singing "Shine," a word sometimes used as an epithet for Negro. Bubbles was indignant and took it as a reflection upon his entire career. "Who's kidding? There really *are* people like that and at least it helps one colored man—myself—make a living." [14] When the reviews appeared, they were favorable.

In the past Bubbles visited the Hoofers Club frequently. He seldom took time out to instruct beginners, but he never ignored a challenge. "There's not a dancer who has been in New York—if he was colored—that I haven't watched, and if he thought he could dance, we've had it out." Dewey Weinglass remembers a legendary contest in the Hoofers Club, when Bubbles and Sammy Vanderhurst battled for hours.

Bubbles did have one pet—a sort of protégé—the fine bop-influenced dancer Chuck Green (of the *Chuck and Chuckles* team), to whom he taught the few steps of his own that Chuck had not already mastered.

In 1964, at the age of sixty-two, Bubbles made a comeback dancing and singing with Anna Marie Alberghetti. His earnings rose to $2,000-$3,500 a week, according to *Ebony*.[15] Later he became a frequent guest on the *Tonight* and other television shows, as well as a star of Bob Hope's Christmas show for the troops in Vietnam. A record album (with liner notes by Hope), entitled *Bubbles, John W., that is* (Vee-Jay 1109), to some extent captures the essence of his appeal. In 1967, he entered the hospital after suffering a stroke.

When old-timers gather of an afternoon in front of Tin Pan Alley's Brill Building on 49th Street and Broadway, they sometimes discuss great entertainers. A hundred names may be mentioned and violently debated, but agreement is never reached except on three or four. Bill Robinson is considered tops because, among other things, he broke through so many social barriers with his dancing. Sammy Davis, Jr., is mentioned with great respect. Peg Leg Bates, who can execute just about any tap step with one leg, is considered a marvel. On the subject of Bubbles, however, enthusiasm mounts and sparks fly. "As an all-around entertainer," they agree, "he is unbeatable." Merely to command agreement among these rugged veterans is perhaps the best proof of Bubbles's all-time greatness.

28 Fred Astaire

FRED ASTAIRE, the debonair dancer in top hat and tails, is the original "cool cat," who created an image of elegance that circled the globe.

"How," asks John O'Hara, pointing out that Astaire was the son of an Omaha brewer, had little or no formal education, and spent a third of his life playing straight man to Adele, his popular and older sister. "How did this guy metamorphose into a genuine, original artist; an accepted figure in upper-class society . . . a style setter . . . a living symbol of all that is best in show business?" [1]

Running true to form, Astaire's answer is the coolest. He replies, when an interviewer asks him about the origins of his style: "I just dance." He insists that he is *not* a ballroom, tap, or ballet dancer, although he studied all three.[2] He thinks of himself, if at all, as a "musical comedy performer" with no rules of dancing that he cannot break, and no limitations on what he may attempt. He has even written, "I don't know how it all started and *I don't want to know.*"

The answer to O'Hara's question lies in those long, formative years when Fred was playing second fiddle to his sister and biding his time—"cooling it." Those years of enforced apprenticeship also furnish a clue to his style of dancing.

Not until the mid-thirties did the talent of Fred Astaire fully emerge. In 1932 his sister Adele retired to become Lady Cavendish; in 1933, he switched to Hollywood; and in 1934 he was very happily married. These events led to the turning point in his life. "It was so perfect, the whole life," he writes about those days, "I often woke up in the morning saying to myself, 'I must be the happiest fellow in the world.' "

Before the thirties, things had been decidedly different. For over twenty-five years, Fred stayed in the background while audiences cheered his sister. "Dancing was merely something my sister did," he writes in *Steps in Time,* "I let it go at that and the hell with it." How would any sensitive boy feel playing the part of the girl, Roxanne, while his older and taller sister played Cyrano? Besides, the wig tickled his neck and the satin dress tripped him.

"Adele grew and blossomed, but I spoiled the act by refusing to grow fast enough, remaining plainly a kid, not quite tall enough to be the partner of a pretty girl in a dancing act." Fred had the humiliating experience of going through a part of his awkward age on stage. The reports of theater managers, which the boy was allowed to read, could have robbed anyone of self-confidence: "The girl seems to have talent but the boy can do nothing" or "They seemed to need rehearsals because the boy tripped the girl a couple of times and once nearly fell into the footlights."

In 1906, when Adele was nine and Fred seven years old, they were rated as "an important child act" in vaudeville. Two years later, although Adele continued to sparkle, Fred was no longer a "cute kid," but merely an awkward youngster. The act fell apart, and their parents mercifully gave them a two-year breather.

Then they went back to work. The wonder is that young Astaire found the courage and conviction to continue.

Under such discouraging conditions he did what even the best brought-up boy would do: *He rebelled*—but in his well-mannered way. The style of his rebellion was shaped by the same influences that gave him the determination not to quit: a closely-knit family and a capable and determined mother. ("We have," wrote Astaire years later, "a sensational mother.")

"It is no accident that Adele married an English lord and Fred a Back Bay aristocrat," wrote Lincoln Barnett in *Life*. "Their mother never let them forget that they sprang from one of Omaha's best families." [3] But it was more than that. Among other things, Fred was expected to act like a gentleman in *any* situation.

Even Adele set an example. "I was still a detriment to my sister," writes Astaire. "She practically had to 'carry me on her back' all through that period. I don't think she ever realized it, and if she did *she never let me know it* [*authors' italics*]." It was essential that Astaire revolt without being revolting.

So he developed an outward appearance of amused superiority, a pretense of nonchalant insouciance that was probably very irritating at the time. "I must have been a tiresome little boy," he recalls. As he danced he gave the impression of thinking, "Okay, Adele's the star, so I'll help her out, but I'm bored to death." And, of course, it influenced the development of his style of dancing: the fine art of understatement.

As early as 1916 reviews of the vaudeville act reflect this pose. Adele was over eighteen and Fred seventeen years old: [4]

> Fred and Adele Astaire, brother and sister, give a fine exhibition of whirlwind dancing, although it could be wished that the young man gave up the blasé air which he carried constantly with him. He is too young for it and deceives no one.

Three years later Alexander Woollcott still described Astaire's dancing as "lack-a-daisical,"[5] while more friendly critics commented on his gift for "wry" humor.

The strain was showing, but as time passed and Astaire became more successful he smoothed and polished the cool pose of polite unconcern into a mature and engaging style of carefree sophistication. Because of his very real talent, his rebellion was creative.

He rebelled in lesser ways and met with rebellion, too. Since Adele was the star, he became the pessimist at little emotional cost to himself, predicting flops continually and insisting upon lengthy rehearsals after a smash hit. (He really preferred to rehearse alone.) At this Adele rebelled and called him Moaning Minnie. Later, when he was on his own, this attitude evolved into an insistence on many rehearsals and the highest standards of performance *for himself.*

"I had never felt upset about the prospect of Adele's retirement," Astaire writes, "because I knew I'd have to face it sooner or later." His way of thinking is indicated by a comment about the time he was making the big switch, on his own, to Hollywood: "I did a great deal of listening and studying. I was pleased with lots of things but kept thinking of what I would like to try if I ever got in a position to make my own decisions."

Fred Astaire's training in ballet was early and brief. At the age of five he was studying toe-dancing, among other things, at the New York school of Professor Claude Alvienne, whose wife, La Neva, was a famous toe-dancer. Astaire's mother made sure that he also saw ballet, taking him to performances of the celebrated Danish ballet star, Adeline Genée, in *The Soul Kiss*—twenty-eight times. "We all studied it intensely," he writes, and one of his earliest solo dances was a weird compromise: a buck-and-wing on his toes.

"I never cared for it," says Astaire with a spark of the old rebellion. "I always resented being told that I couldn't point my toe in." Because they are trained to point their toes out, ballet dancers, according to some critics, often waddle like ducks. "Ballet," agrees Jerry Kurland of *The Dunhills,* "forces the body into unnatural positions."[6] Only twice in his career did Astaire attempt out-and-out "ballet-type" dances: in 1931 on Broadway with Tilly Losch in *The Band Wagon,* and in 1937 in Hollywood with Harriet Hoctor in *Shall We Dance.* In both instances he danced a literally supporting role.

Dancer Ann Miller referred to Astaire's ballet technique as "just about the world's worst." [7] This may be, but still his early ballet training opened up his style, helped him release the upper part of his body before elevation, and showed him that a dancer could use much more than his feet. "My regular style was to cover ground," he wrote later, "and also get off the floor and go up in the air a lot." Astaire's use of his arms and hands, and indeed his entire body, was one of his greatest contributions to American vernacular dance.

Fred Astaire did not study tap exhaustively, but he worked on it far more seriously than ballet. In preparation for a comeback after the two-year layoff, Fred and Adele were both enrolled in Ned Wayburn's fashionable dance-and-deportment factory in New York City.

In those days, "Professor" Ned Wayburn had a monopoly on just about everything associated with the dance. He operated the largest dancing school; he was "stage director" for Klaw and Erlanger, Ziegfeld, and the Shuberts (this meant he "grouped" the dance numbers); he wrote "vaudeville vehicles"—or acts—at a good price for beginning dancers; he advertised profusely with a portrait of himself looking like Norman Vincent Peale in *pince-nez;* and in the same trade papers, he sometimes reviewed the acts he had written ("Credit a sure-fire hit to Ned Wayburn. . . .").

On one occasion Wayburn brushed aside several assistants and personally demonstrated some steps to young Astaire, who was impressed because Wayburn looked more like a preacher than a dancer. It was Wayburn, according to Lincoln Barnett, who decided that "Freddie" should drop ballet and learn the manly art of tap.[8] "Fred based his tap on the clog dancing he learned with Wayburn," says the pioneer choreographer Clarence "Buddy" Bradley who worked with Fred and Adele, "which helps explain his highly selective use of tap." [9]

After the two-year layoff of the Astaire vaudeville act, Wayburn sold Mrs. Astaire a new act for one-thousand dollars. He had trouble writing it and apologized fretfully for the delay: "I completely exhausted my *nerve force* and experienced a case of *brain fag* of the worst kind. [*Wayburn's italics*]." [10] The act received raves (quite possibly Wayburn's) at a benefit but flopped the first time it was presented professionally. "It must have been awful," writes Astaire, "unbalanced and plain dull."

For two years, the Astaires played "every rat trap and chicken coop in the Middle West" as Fred worked his way out of the awkward age. "I didn't do any solo dancing in those days," he says. "Everything was with my sister."

In 1916 Fred and Adele jumped to Broadway musicals, never to return to vaudeville. But not until 1925, in the Gershwin musical *Lady Be Good,* did he work out a solo for himself—a tap routine that was promptly dropped. By that time, however, his reputation as a tap dancer was growing.

At a Buck-dancing contest for performers in Broadway musicals in 1928, Astaire tied for third place with Will Mahoney, while Bill Robinson and Jack Donahue won first and second.

Later on Astaire made considerable use of tap. In 1935, three years after Adele retired, he successfully emceed a radio show, *The Packard Hour,* on the strength of his own singing and dancing. Since leaps could neither be seen nor heard, he had to stick to "a lot of taps close together—a string of ricky-ticky-ticky-tacky-ticky-tacky steps." The job demanded considerable versatility.

Even the conscientious Astaire could not prepare a new rhythmic pattern for each of thirty-nine weeks, so he simply improvised on each program, tapping the way he happened to feel, and finished with one of "a dozen . . . exhibition tap steps." He mentions three: "a spinning tapping affair . . . a tapping and arm-waving gem, and . . . a half-falling, half-standing-up flash that sounded like a riveting machine."

He also used tap, along with all the rest, in some thirty or so movies but especially in *Broadway Melody of 1940* with Eleanor Powell. "She 'put 'em down' like a man, no ricky-ticky-sissy stuff with Ellie," writes Astaire. "She really knocked out a tap dance in a class by herself." Ironically, the numbers with Eleanor were not as successful as previous tap numbers with Ginger Rogers, because Eleanor had her own style, which she did not change, while Ginger copied Astaire exactly and fitted in more harmoniously. "We rather specialized in tap dancing," writes Astaire, characteristically throwing the line away, "for that film."

Fred Astairc developed a style of dancing, which although it did not employ the best tapping in the world, made good use of it in combination with other movements. "He uses a lot of old soft-shoe steps," says Charles "Cholly" Atkins, "like the Scissors." [11] He likes to write of himself as a "hoofer," which he decidedly is *not,* for the word usually designates the one-spot tapping of an old-timer who works only with his feet. "Fred dances beautiful," says James Barton, "but he's no hoofer." [12] The pose is harmless, the motive modesty. But his consistent use of tap reinforced the acute sense of rhythm on which all of his dancing is based. Astaire always dances with some sort of a beat.

Fred Astaire's training in ballroom dancing was continuous and sometimes intensive. All dancing schools include it in their curriculum, of course, but Fred and Adele received their first real coaching in ballroom—and a bit of acrobatic—dancing in 1913, when they studied with a top "musical and flash act" in vaudeville, *The Coccias.*

It was Professor Aurelio Coccia who threw out the corny Wayburn number and gave the Astaires a straight song-and-dance act that developed into a "streamlined show stopper." He also worked tirelessly with them on such ballroom rhythms as the Waltz and Tango. He may even have introduced Fred to some flash, or air, steps, which dovetailed with the open technique he had absorbed from ballet. And he taught them showmanship. "The most influential, as far as dancing goes," writes Astaire, "of any man in my career."

Vernon and Irene Castle were another major influence on the Astaires. During the winter of 1913-1914 Fred and Adele attended three Broadway musicals featuring the Castles: *The Sunshine Girl, The Girl from Utah,* and *Watch Your Step.* They saw *The Sunshine Girl* nine times. "They were a tremendous influence on our careers," writes Fred. "Not that we copied them completely, but we did appropriate some of their ballroom steps and style for our vaudeville act."

The Castles achieved a unique kind of success that appealed greatly to the Astaires. They "were received with such acclaim," as Astaire notes, "both professionally and socially that it seems almost impossible to describe it." In other words the Castles were a huge success both financially and among the leaders of society. Their dancing, like the Twist at the Peppermint Lounge in 1960, became a fad among the wealthy.

The social success of the Castles, aided by the tradition of European dancing masters, set a goal that musical comedy performers found harder to reach than ballroom dancers. Musical comedy, after all, was an upstart *genre* associated with the public stage. Nevertheless, within a decade the Astaires had attained a good share of acceptance, and eventually Fred, like the Castles, had his own (much more numerous) dance studios. In 1939, when *The Story of Vernon and Irene Castle* was being cast in Hollywood, Irene Castle chose Fred Astaire for the role of Vernon.

The Astaires observed other dance teams, too. Back in 1915 they were on the same bill with the famous Spanish dancers, Eduardo and Elisa Cansino (the parents of Rita Hayworth). "I watched Eduardo," says Astaire, "at almost every show." They could also have seen the DeMarcos, who were in George White's *Scandals* in the early twenties and remained popular through the forties. "I think Astaire got his style from Tony and Sally DeMarco," says Hal Leroy, "and built on that." [13]

The acid test as ballroom dancers occurred in 1926 when the Astaires agreed to dance at the Trocadero, a New York night club, for six weeks. Putting together special routines, they jammed the place for the first two weeks. Then business fell off and they took a voluntary cut in salary.

"Adele and I were not ballroom dancers particularly," Astaire concludes. "A night club was an atmosphere we had never worked in before, and we didn't like it." Trying to make a hit two or three times a night with a changing, noisy audience—these were Prohibition times—was nerve racking. "We were really out of our element," he writes. "Adele and I never would work another cafe."

In 1933 Fred Astaire left Broadway for Hollywood and never came back. He soon found that he preferred working in films. There was no live audience to worry about, and he could select the best of several "takes" of each dance, attaining a consistently better result. Best of all, his ingrained habit of understatement was highly effective in the narrow dynamic range and close-ups of films. As his career mushroomed, he became more and more of a perfectionist, and movies proved to be the ideal medium.

Astaire's thorough training in ballroom dancing served him well in Hollywood, where in one successful film after another, he coached and danced with a galaxy of stars from Joan Crawford in 1933 to Cyd Charisse in 1957. Ballroom dancing was the basic ingredient—each film had at least one ballroom number—and Astaire created an almost endless variety within that style.

Out of all three disciplines—ballet, tap, and ballroom—Astaire forged what he calls "a sort of outlaw style," a new blend of his own. He was particularly fond of abrupt transitions from flowing movements to sudden stops, posing for a moment before proceeding to the next step—stop and go, freeze and melt—a style adopted wholesale by later choreographers. "He used balletic turns," says Cholly Atkins, "but came out of them with a jazz kick and slide."

In achieving this blend, Astaire was aided from his earliest days in musical comedy by a series of dance directors, or (later) choreographers. The help of Jack Mason in *The Passing Show of 1918*, when Astaire danced costumed as a chicken, was not greatly appreciated, but for *Apple Blossoms* in the following year, Teddy Royce "put on an excellent number for us," says Astaire, and "he gave Adele one of her greatest comedy bits."

By 1922 in *For Goodness' Sake,* Astaire writes that he had started to "take hold at creating and choreographing dances." He developed rapidly thereafter as his own choreographer, employing only steps and movements that suited him. As time passed the art of choreography developed, too, and Astaire found some very able choreographers in Hollywood, among them Hermes Pan, who worked with him on a majority of his films.

Something of the give and take in working with Astaire is described by Nick Castle, who helped choreograph *Royal Wedding*: [14]

> We locked the doors and worked together all day. I'd have a step he liked and he'd say "Do it again," and I'd do it and he'd have me do it again and he'd say "I love it."
>
> He never said "No" to me—he just asked "Do you think that's right for me?" and sometimes I'd have to agree that it wasn't.

Between them—always subject to Astaire's veto—they worked out dances for a scene on a rocking boat where the floor tilts and furniture flies by, for a trick dance in which Astaire seemed to be performing on the walls and ceiling, and for a solo number with a hat rack for a partner.

The nature of Astaire's "outlaw style" is formed by the fusion of ballet, tap, and ballroom dancing, under the constant pressure of choreographing new dances. The process consists of arranging whatever styles and steps seem right—anything is right if it *works*—into an artistic whole according to Astaire's standards; the purpose, which shapes the standards, being simply to entertain by dancing some sort of "story."

To be successful, each dance must revolve around an "idea"—straight hoofing is not enough. (The ideas come to Astaire in the middle of parties, causing him to rush to the studio; or in the middle of the night, making him get up and write down a few steps.) The idea can range widely, from the realistic to the abstract: from plain characterization, through an evocation of situation, theme, or mood, to a trick dance (no story) with a stage prop such as a whisk broom, golf club, or hat rack.

Back in 1932, when Adele retired, Fred Astaire was an all-around performer who beneath the self-imposed and iron restraint was exploding with talent. "Just watching Fred with Adele in those early days," says Nick Castle, "got me started." Over a period of twenty-five years with Adele he had stored up enough material—with incidental assistance—to choreograph what turned out to be more than thirty highly successful films in Hollywood and several hour-long television programs. The same discipline helped him maintain his standards. "I have always tried," he writes, "to carry out my steadfast rule of not repeating anything in dance that I've done before."

At a meeting of the Copasetics Club, a group of top-notch dancers dedicated to the memory of Bill Robinson, proceedings were suddenly suspended when someone remarked that a television program with Fred Astaire was on the air. The entire membership remained glued to the television set with exclamations of admiration and delight until the program ended. They represented all kinds of dancing to jazz—several were far better tap dancers than Astaire—but they all admired him unreservedly.

What is it that makes Astaire's dancing universally admired? "I flap my legs out in a jerky figure-eight pattern and alternate between using my elbows with dangling hands and throwing my arms out like a windmill," [15] says another great dancer, Fayard Nicholas, who brings down the house with his impersonation of Astaire. This is, of course, the lowest common denominator. Bill Robinson has been quoted describing Astaire as an "eccentric dancer"—a rather unenthusiastic way of saying Astaire is no tap dancer but has a style of his own.

"Astaire sells body motion," says Charles "Honi" Coles, "not tap" [16]—a comment to which Cholly Atkins adds: "He's a *descriptive* dancer who works painstakingly with his musical accompaniment; he was the first to dance to programme music, describing every note in the dance." Thus, when Astaire heard "St. James Infirmary Blues" by Jonah Jones, he says he "flipped," and "began to block out in my mind the dance steps to go along with his singing and playing the number."

While the lyrics set the scene—a morgue—and Astaire is costumed as a devil-may-care gambler, the menacing vitality of Jonah's horn sets the mood with steps and, especially, body motion that follow accents in the improvised trumpet solo. The parallel is precise, the interpretation meticulous.

"Astaire," dancers declare, unable to find a better word for it, "has *class.*" By that they mean many things: poise, charm, nonchalance, grace, sophistication, elegance, and so on. He can communicate all these moods, but in spite of his real uneasiness about it, the almost-stereotype image of the debonair aristocrat in top-hat-and-tails has survived indelibly—without causing the slightest irritation. He remains indisputably masculine. His background and tastes fitted him perfectly for the role—"I'm putting on my top hat"—and combined with his shy diffidence, helped make it a success.

Almost any move Astaire makes is a joy to behold. And although he has many imitators—none of them very successful—he has no equals. His style is his own and has proved to be literally inimitable. "Astaire," says Nick Castle, "is the King."

For many years Astaire has treasured a remark of Jimmy Cagney's: "You know, you so-and-so, you've got a little of the hoodlum in you." (Astaire loves to dance gangster roles.) Without such impulses he would never have thrown out the traditional rules and created his own "outlaw style." In his cool detachment, Astaire paved the way for the James Bond generation to come.

PART SEVEN

Specialties

29 Eccentric Dancing

THE LIGHTS GO DOWN, the curtain parts, Duke Ellington and the Jungle Band swing into "Rockin' in Rhythm" at Harlem's Cotton Club, and a lurid spotlight picks out Jigsaw Jackson the Human Corkscrew. The audience gasps: Jigsaw has his face on the floor stage center, while the rest of his body seems to be running around with his feet tapping in rhythm.

Jigsaw's chin was about eight inches long, they said, because he used it as a base for his contortions, and he was known in the trade as a "freak dancer."

He was a dancer with a gimmick. Reviewing his act in Pittsburgh, *Variety* reported (1938): "Sock novelty . . . it takes a tough stomach to stand the things he does to his body . . . most unusal trick stuff, his midriff twisted in a knot while his head faces one way and feet another. Keeps his pedals doing a jig all of the time." [1] ("Jig" is *Variety's* pseudo-hard-boiled term, consecrated by years of misuse, for any dancing this side of ballet.) But more important, Jigsaw performed to jazz rhythms. "He did everything around the beat," says Charles "Honi" Coles, "and he had no imitators." [2] At the height of his success it was said that Jigsaw (his real name was Brady Jackson) insisted on being paid in one-dollar bills because he could not count larger denominations. In the 1950's he was long-retired and was working in Harlem as an iceman.

The story of American dancing includes various specialties performed to jazz rhythms. One of the most common and popular is known as eccentric, and it may include elements of contortionist, legomania, and shake dancing, although these styles frequently overlap with others, and a dancer can combine something of all of them. A few involve tap, for tappers are generally regarded as the dancing elite and imitated whenever possible. Jigsaw Jackson was a contortionist, an eccentric dancer *par excellence.*

The term "eccentric" is a catchall for dancers who have their own nonstandard movements and sell themselves on their individual styles. It has been used to describe a variety of highly personal performances by dancer-comedians on Broadway. Thus, George M. Cohan, Leon Errol, Joe Frisco, George White, Harland Dixon, Jack Donahue, James Barton, Tom Patricola, Hal Leroy, Buddy Ebsen, and Ray Bolger have all been labeled eccentric dancers at one time or another, although some are much more than that, and James Barton, for example, used eccentric movements along with a wealth of other and perhaps finer steps.

Regular hoofers were not impressed by Jigsaw's tapping, but they were forced to admit his spectacular success. They were more envious—and justly—of Clarence "Dancing" Dotson, who along with Bill Robinson, was one of the few Negro dancers who hit the top in the twenties, soloing on the Keith circuit. Dotson, after all, was a kind of eccentric tap dancer. "Call him a jive dancer," says Bill Bailey, implying that Dotson was kidding. "He didn't have much technique." [3] Dotson had a cast in his eye, which earned him the nickname of "One-Eye" and seemed to add to his appeal. He talked more than he danced and everything he said stopped the show. Dotson was an unqualified success until he retired in 1943; he died in 1954 at the age of seventy-three.

Most dancers had their own arrangements, which during rehearsal they presented to the pit band with detailed instructions. Not Dotson. As the piano player in the darkened theater went over the music of each act for the coming week, he would arrive at a gap where Dotson was supposed to appear. "Where's Dotson?" he would ask. After a pause, Dotson, sitting out of sight at the back of the theater, would drawl, "Here I come," and walk slowly down the aisle, handing the pianist a scrap of paper with the title of one tune written on it. "Play this till out," he would say softly.

Dotson, tall and thin, wore a swallowtail coat (minstrel men called it a walking coat because they wore it for parades) with striped pants, patent-leather shoes with white spats, a string tie—and a derby. His standard opening consisted of a quavering song: "My father's name is Dot and I'm his son, that's why they call me Dotson." Having identified himself, he then proceeded to entertain the audience with a monologue to an imaginary person offstage, recounting—among other things—the accomplishments of "a neighbor lady, who cooked so good that people came from miles around just to wipe their bread on her door."

Dotson had four or five numbers—it would be an exaggeration to call them routines—most of them pantomime. One of his first was an imitation of a corkscrew, dance and all. "From then on," says Pete Nugent, "the audience was rolling in the aisles." [4] Dotson then pointed dramatically across the stage and announced: "I'm gonna throw a fit, and it's gonna happen right over there." Starting with a jump and a headshake, which he called Jumpin'

Crow, Dotson's fit consisted of a combined Quiver and Itch as he shook and scratched in swinging counterpoint.

As a finale Dotson announced a dance entitled "Snow Time" featuring a "skating step." Turning solemnly to the conductor in the pit, he asked "May I have a little wintertime, professor?" The band started something like "Jingle Bells," only to have Dotson cut it short with the command, "That's cold enough." With his hands on his hips, he began to hop, roll, and slide in a crazy version of the Virginia Essence. As an exit Dotson disappeared with huge leaps on an imaginary pogo stick, leaving the theater a hysterical shambles. His act was a triumph of the eccentric over mere dancing.

Dotson was on the high-class Keith circuit; at the other extreme was an eccentric dancer who played T.O.B.A. billed as "Buzzin' Burton." In the twenties Burton made the Buzz his own, although a lesser-known dancer named Sparrow Harris featured the same step. As the climax to his act, Burton fell into the Buzz—long, sliding steps forward, knees bent and arms flung out alternately to the sides, with hands turned down at the wrist and fingers vibrating in imitation of a bee's wings. (The arm and hand motions are similar to the much earlier Pigeon Wing.)

For his exit Burton hunched his shoulders, wiggled his index finger toward the sky, and shuffled offstage—a combination of motions that became the standard ingredients of Trucking years later.

Like Dotson, Buzzin' Burton depended on patter and pantomime. He was an old man when Henry "Rubberlegs" Williams worked with him in a Southern carnival. "Buzz drank a mixture of Sterno, denatured alcohol, and Coca-Cola," says Rubberlegs with admiration, "and he did that Buzz like nobody else. He taught it to me, too, but it came out different, like Trucking." [5] (Everybody outside of the dance studios had his own style of Trucking. Rubberlegs's version, which was a hit when he played the Apollo Theater in Harlem, qualified as an eccentric dance in its own right.)

Perhaps because they had to be outstanding to get a job, Negro dancers were occasionally eccentric to the point of no return. A dancer billed as "Dynamite Hooker," whose style has been described as "*ad lib* Buck" or "tap Charleston gone mad," performed in the late twenties and thirties with the Lunceford, Calloway, Ellington, and other bands. Wearing white tails, Dynamite hit stage center to a very fast version of "Dear Old Southland" (with Lunceford) or "Black Rhythm" (with Calloway) and vibrated all over, holding his arms out like a jittery scarecrow, while his hands dangled uselessly—brute speed and energy. One of his pet steps was a straddle-legged stomp, in which he simply jumped up and down on the beat with his legs apart. After four or five minutes they banged a gong as a signal to quit.

Offstage, however, Dynamite was another "cool cat." He had a voice like a hoarse Louis Armstrong and a habit of bobbing his head to some unheard rhythms. As a youngster dancer James Cross of the team of *Stump and Stumpy* remembers being greatly impressed with Dynamite's knowing ways. "Why, he'd just stand in a doorway bobbing his head and looking cool, and everybody would tiptoe around him with the greatest respect. Then when he spoke in that gravelly voice, you *knew* he was something else." [6]

The eccentricity of the eccentric dancers sometimes carried over into their private lives. During a tour of England George Stamper, who was featured earlier in *Runnin' Wild* doing splits in slow motion and a routine called Lazy Man's Dance, decided he wanted to stay abroad, in spite of the fact that he had no working permit. However, he worked out a plan: On boarding the ship for home, he pretended to be an Armenian and refused to speak to anyone. "He figured that if he convinced the authorities he was a foreigner," says Slow Kid Thompson, "they would let him go back to Europe." [7] After a week on Ellis Island, Stamper became very talkative.

Another eccentric performer, Wilton Crawley, danced while he played clarinet, juggling the pieces as he dismantled it. He invented an "international language," which he spoke to anyone who would listen. Crawley was cured when he accidentally boarded a train taking some mental patients to an institution. "He started talking his international language with such success," says Chink Collins, "that they took him to the sanitarium, too." [8] Crawley abandoned his linguistic pioneering and was released after some delay.

Another specialty, legomania, is a limited type of eccentric dancing sometimes known by the even more restricted term, *rubberlegs*. As performed in Europe by the Majiltons, however, legomania consisted largely of a variety of high kicks, which became the trademark of such female impersonators as Julian Eltinge and the lesser-known Julian Costello, who worked on T.O.B.A. (The predecessors of minstrelsy had their own tradition of "wench" dancers as early as the 1830's.) By contrast, Alberta Whitman, of the famous *Whitman Sisters*, executed high-kicking legomania as a *male* impersonator.

Coming North in 1919 with Bobby Grant's troupe of female impersonators, Rubberlegs Williams brought a broad blend of eccentric dances. "He combined legomania with high kicks, wiggles, and shimmies," says Joe Price, who teaches acrobatics, "and then added other steps like the Boogie Woogie, Camel Walk, and so on—steps used later by chorus lines." [9] A giant of a man who was consistently pleasant but took no back talk from anybody, Rubberlegs sang with various shows, made a few fine recordings, and developed his own Strut and Trucking routines for vaudeville and night clubs.

The Shake dance, another specialty that qualifies as eccentric and even contortionist (among other things), traces back at least as far as the "Egyptian" belly dance and the Afro-American Grind, although it surfaced in varying times and surroundings. As performed by Little Egypt at the Chicago World's Fair in 1893, where it first received national attention as the Hootchy-Kootchy, the Shake dance was not particularly rhythmic. (George Walker's wife, Ada Overton, was the only Negro on the big time to have her own version of a Salome dance—around 1910—with a special string section added to Creatore's band.)

By the twenties and later in various revues and night clubs, such women dancers as Ola Jones, Louise "Jota" Cook ("What she did with her stomach," says trumpeter Ray Nance, "would make you seasick" [10]), Kalua, Bessie Dudley, Princess Aurelia, and Tondelayo were synchronizing their undulations to jazz rhythms. "Every chorus line had some kind of a Shake dancer," says Mae Barnes, "from *The Whitman Sisters* on T.O.B.A. to Florence Mills, who shook in *Dixie to Broadway.*" [11]

Up north, a musical-comedy tradition existed, however, whereby the chorus executed jazz steps or body movements but did not tap, while the stars tapped but did few jazz steps. This was based on both the assumption that tap was more difficult and the fact that early chorus lines were not very talented. With the overwhelming popularity of the Charleston, a new day dawned: Professionals had to learn it, sometimes adding taps, along with other jazz steps and body movements. Still there were distinctions: Men danced the Charleston, but not the Shimmy or the Black Bottom—they were for women.

The Shake began as a woman's dance, in the European tradition, but a few male dancers born and raised in the South gradually developed their own parallels to it. During the teens dancing comedians, of whom String-beans is perhaps the best known, were tossing off pelvic movements that would have made Little Egypt blush. The dances were performed in the course of in-group satire before Negro audiences, and their origin was probably African. The Shake hit Broadway late in the day. Thus, Bert Williams was doing a mild Mooche around 1903, James Barton upset the critics with his Grind in 1923, and Clifton Webb finally caused a furor with a synthetic Snake Hips in 1929.

In the mid-twenties Earl Tucker arrived in New York from the May Kemp show in Baltimore and blew the whistle. "I think he came from tide-water Maryland," says Duke Ellington, who employed Tucker to go with the band's jungle effects, "one of those primitive lost colonies where they practice pagan rituals and their dancing style evolved from religious seizures." [12]

According to one account, Tucker glided noiselessly backstage at the Lafayette Theater in Harlem, dressed in overalls, and leaned against the wall with an air of boredom as Irving C. Miller interviewed applicants for jobs. Finally, Miller decided to notice him: "What can you do?" "Lissen, man, my name is Snake Hips. I dance, and if I don't stop the show you can fire me," Tucker hissed. A brief demonstration convinced Miller. On the other hand, Miller himself says it did not happen that way. He thinks it might have occurred at Connie's Inn where, he says, Snake Hips got his first New York job.[13]

Snake Hips became a fixture in the show at Connie's Inn, dancing at the Cotton Club later to Ellington's "East St. Louis Toodle-Oo." (Ellington also composed the "Snake Hips Dance" for him.) He wore a loose white silk blouse with large puffed sleeves, tight black pants with bell bottoms, and a sequined girdle with a sparkling buckle in the center from which hung a large tassel. Tucker had at the same time a disengaged and a menacing air, like a sleeping volcano, which seemed to give audiences the feeling that he was a cobra and they were mice.

The impression Snake Hips transmitted so forcibly had a basis in fact. His contemporaries agree that he could neither read nor write, had a violent temper, which was continually getting him into trouble, and carried a razor, which he used with lethal effect.

Snake Hips liked to think of himself as a big gambler. On a good night at Connie's Inn, he might pick up $75 or $100 off the floor, thrown there by the audience, and gamble it away at the Hoofers Club after the show. "He was a real mean guy, not like these flittin' and floppin' faggots you see now," says Bill Bailey. "Even Bill Robinson didn't mess with *him*."

When Snake Hips slithered on stage, the audience quieted down immediately. Nobody snickered at him, in spite of the mounting tension, no matter how nervous or embarrassed one might be. The glaring eyes burning in the pock-marked face looked directly at and through the audience, with dreamy and impartial hostility. Snake Hips seemed to be coiled, ready to strike.

Tucker's act usually consisted of five parts. He came slipping on with a sliding, forward step and just a hint of hip movement. The combination was part of a routine known in Harlem as Spanking the Baby, and in a strange but logical fashion, established the theme of his dance. Using shock tactics, he then went directly into the basic Snake Hips movements, which he paced superbly, starting out innocently enough, with one knee crossing over behind the other, while the toe of one foot touched the arch of the other. At first, it looked simultaneously pigeon-toed and knock-kneed.

Gradually, however, as the shining buckle threw rays in larger circles, the fact that the pelvis and the whole torso were becoming increasingly involved in the movement was unavoidably clear. As he progressed, Tucker's footwork became flatter, rooted more firmly to the floor, while his hips described wider and wider circles, until he seemed to be throwing his hips alternately out of joint to the melodic accents of the music.

Then followed a pantomime to a Charleston rhythm: Tucker clapped four times and waved twice with each hand in turn, holding the elbow of the waving hand and rocking slightly with the beat. The over-all effect was suddenly childish, effeminate, and perhaps tongue-in-cheek.

The next movement was known among dancers as the Belly Roll, and consisted of a series of waves rolling from pelvis to chest—a standard part of a Shake dancer's routine, which Tucker varied by coming to a stop, transfixing the audience with a baleful, hypnotic stare, and twirling his long tassel in time with the music.

After this Tucker raised his right arm to his eyes, at first as if embarrassed (a feeling that many in the audience shared), and then, as if racked with sobs, he went into the Tremble, which shook him savagely and rapidly from head to foot. As he turned his back to the audience to display the over-all trembling more effectively, Tucker looked like a murderously naughty boy. The impression he gave was apparently intentional, for he appealed particularly to women, and by all reports, knew it. "Few men could move like that," says dancer Al Minns who can do a Snake Hips of his own. "Women were fascinated and even wanted to mother him." [14]

Snake Hips performed with deadly and what might have been artistic seriousness, but that did not lessen the impact. As a callow and puritanical undergraduate, one of the present writers, escorting an even less worldly Vassar sophomore, visited the Cotton Club to hear Duke Ellington in the late twenties. At midnight the floorshow came on, and Snake Hips went into his act. The writer distinctly remembers being unable to believe what he saw and spending most of his energy trying not to look shocked. At the end of the act, when his innocent date applauded on the well-meant assumption that as a visitor she should encourage the performers, it interrupted his search for a place to hide and struck him as a public endorsement of depravity.

Tucker staggered the Broadway critics when he appeared briefly, along with Bill Robinson, in *Blackbirds of 1928.* A majority played it safe by "discovering" fifty-year-old Bojangles and making no attempt to describe Snake Hips. In the *Evening World,* E. W. Osborn said only that it was "quite unbelievable," [15] while *Variety's* Ibee gave him more space than Robinson: ". . . a caution. Has he got snake hips—and how! . . . no such weaving of the hips has yet been shown." [16]

Two months later R. J. Graham reviewed the show in *The Dance,* noting that "a young chap by the name of Earl Tucker crashed the good notice of the house . . . with extraordinary acrobatics and control work thrown in." [17] ("Control work" was as close as he apparently cared to come to the Tremble and Quiver, while "extraordinary acrobatics" seems to be an anesthetic description of the Snake Hips.) Tucker, who had probably never been referred to as a "chap," did not know the correct terms for what he was doing.

By 1931 the critics were becoming more courageous. "Snake Hips stands head and shoulders above every one else in that line,"[18] wrote Vere Johns in the Boston *Chronicle*, without specifying *what* line, or indeed, why he referred to "head and shoulders." He did add, by way of tempering his approval—and apparently missing the point—that some of the "coarse suggestiveness" might well be eliminated.

When his contemporaries are asked where Tucker got his style, they shake their heads and retreat to the rationalization—which could be true—that he was "built different." "He was a torso dancer,"[19] says Dan Burley, and lets it go at that.

Butterbeans, who was no mean eccentric dancer himself, once persuaded Tucker to teach him Snake Hips: "But I never *could* learn it,"[20] he recalls.

"All he did," says Pigmeat Markham in a moment of over-simplifying optimism, "was bend and wiggle his knees while he mixed up variations on the Quiver and Grind."[21] Yes and no: Nobody equaled Snake Hips Tucker in his own specialty; nobody claimed to.

Tucker has been described as the first male headliner who did not tap—which does him less than justice. (He could do a tap Charleston.) "I don't think we would have had the nerve to do that kind of dancing in my time,"[22] says Willie Covan.

Mild-mannered Eubie Blake still disapproves: "I consider Snake Hips in bad taste, but nowadays they call it art, and I suppose it's all right."[23] Although his would-be imitators were legion, after Snake Hips's early death from "internal ailments" in 1937 (Ellington paid his hospital bills), the only dancer to carry on the tradition with anywhere near the necessary nerve and conviction was Freddie Taylor, who did not last. The tradition soon reverted to lady Shake dancers, and later, the rock-and-rollers.

Tucker's fantastic skill at pelvic movements was too early and convincing to influence the general surfacing of this element in vernacular dance. (In the film short *Rhapsody in Black*, with Duke Ellington, Earl Tucker appears briefly, but long enough to cause consternation among current viewers who can take Elvis Presley in stride.) In the last decade or so, such popular Afro-American dances as the Rumba, Conga, Mambo, Cha Cha Cha—with an added sway from the Polynesians—have helped to make pelvic movement less alarming, while rock-and-roll dances of the sixties have gone further with anesthetic results. Today Earl "Snake Hips" Tucker, the king of eccentric dancers, pantomiming the facts of life, would still be far ahead of the times.

30 Comedy Dancing

THE YEAR IS 1918 and World War I has just ended. Sweetie May "trucks" provocatively on stage at the Globe Theater in Jacksonville, Florida, cuts a neat buck-and-wing and sings a blues.[1] She is an outrageous flirt, and the men in the audience are shouting encouragement as Stringbeans strolls out of the wings. Tall and lanky, a flashing diamond in one of his teeth, he wears a dilapidated jacket with a huge padlock hanging way down in front of his tattered trousers. He stops, listens to the shouts, and gives a loud and contemptuous sniff. His presence is so powerful that the audience falls silent.

As Stringbeans concentrates on polishing his padlock, Sweetie May eyes him critically: "Stop cuttin' the fool, Beans," she commands. "Don't you see them intelligent peoples out front watchin' you?" Stringbeans explains: On the way to the theater a cop stopped him, noticed the padlock, and told him that he had been in jail often enough to know about locks and keep away from them. "So I tol' him the truth *an' he believed me,*" says Stringbeans with a grin that changes abruptly into an accusing glare at the audience: "I don't want no colored folks 'round this town stealin' *my* clothes." The cream of the jest, of course, is that the white policeman believed Stringbeans's explanation.

Stringbeans then lopes to the piano and announces "The Sinking of the Titanic," commemorating a famous event. Standing at full height, he reaches down to the keyboard as he sings like an early Ray Charles: [2]

Listen no-good womens
Stop kickin' us men aroun'
Cause us men gonna be your iceberg
And send you sinkin' down

Sinkin' like Titanic
Sinkin' sinkin' down
Oh you no-good womens, listen
You sure is bottom bound

White folks got all the money
Colored folks got all the signs
Signs won't buy you nothin'
Folks, you better change your mind

Sinkin' like Titanic
Sinkin' sinkin' down
If you don't change your way of livin'
You sure is bottom bound

Apart from the comment that "white folks got all the money, colored folks got all the signs" (that is, voodoo signs or superstitions), Stringbeans is threatening domineering women, who just like the people on the Titanic that refused passage to prize-fighter Jack Johnson (as the audience is well aware), are "bottom bound." He has broached an aspect of Negro life which he pantomimes at the end of the act.

As he attacks the piano, Stringbeans's head starts to nod, his shoulders shake, and his body quivers. Slowly, he sinks to the floor of the stage. Before he submerges, he is executing an undulating Snake Hips, shouting the blues, and as he hits the deck, still playing the piano, he is performing a horizontal grind that makes rock-and-roll dancers of the sixties seem like staid citizens.

The act proceeds with singing, dancing, and dialogue, until finally, at the end, Stringbeans stands on his head, turns his pockets inside out so that a few pennies fall on the stage, and pleads, "Don't, Baby . . . Don't, Baby . . . Don't Baby!" Sweetie May wants to know "Don't what?" and adds aggressively, "I ain't done nothing to you—*yet.*" Stringbeans continues to beg like a masochistic Milquetoast until he cuts short the refrain: "Don't —*leave me a damn cent!*"

Stringbeans is pantomiming the problem of a male in a matriarchy, the plight of the well-known "Monkey Man" in a moment of petulant rebellion. The Monkey Man is the servile mate who turns over his hard-earned money to some woman. His origin goes back more than a half century.

After the Civil War the Negro was free to earn his own living, a situation which gave the woman an advantage over the man. Considered manageable, she was in demand as a domestic; he was considered a potential troublemaker and lucky to get an ill-paid job as a manual laborer. Thus the wife was relatively independent, the boss who kept the family together—or tore it apart. The husband who put up with it was called a Monkey Man and became a standing joke.

Stringbeans is demonstrating a recipe for survival. He is not "laughing

The original stomp

Festival dance in South Carolina (circa 1800), blending African and American costumes and instruments. *(Abby Aldrich Rockefeller Folk Art Collection, Williamsburg, Virginia)*

Theatrical poster: "The Dancing Professors" *(The Bettmann Archive)*

Theatrical poster: "The Minstrel Parade" *(The Bettmann Archive)*

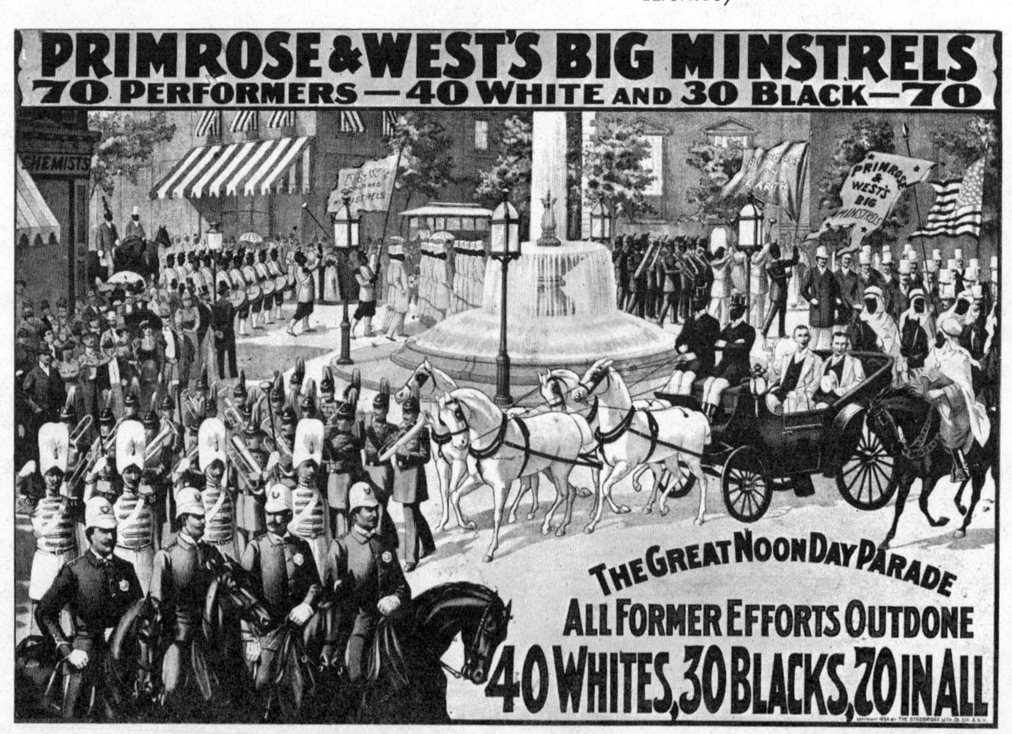

Walter Crumbley delivers a verse in the minstrel show
(Jack Bradley)

Dewey "Pigmeat" Markham Trucking at the Apollo
(Dewey Markham)

U. S. Thompson demonstrating the finish of the Georgia Hunch (1923) *(U. S. Thompson)*

Alberta and Alice Whitman *(Alice Whitman)*

ert Williams (*Schomburg Branch,*
ew York Public Library)*

urnoy Miller and Aubrey Lyles
Mirjian, courtesy C. P. Greneker)

Noble Sissle and Eubie Blake *(White)*

Buddy Bradley *(Rimis Ltd.)*

Robinson's double roll: Fig. 1—Jump up with double roll. Fig. 2—Right foot close to left. Two taps. Fig. 3—Jump up on left foot with double roll. Fig. 4—Right foot over top to left. Two taps. Then cross right and left until the finish. Fig. 5—To break at end of dance.

The Nicholas Brothers jump down into a split. Harold left, Fayard right.

Harland Dixon in blackface, 1908-9
(Harland Dixon)

Doyle (right) and Dixon (left) fake a high kick. *(Harland Dixon)*

Buck and Bubbles
(New York Public Library)

John Bubbles *(Jack Bradley)*

Earl “Snake Hips” Tucker

Chuck and Chuckles

Ida Forsyne

The Four Covans: Left to right, Mrs. Dewey Covan, Dewey Covan, Willie, Mrs. Willie Covan

Fayard (right) and Harold (left) Nicholas

Dora Dean and Charles Johnson
(New York Public Library)

Eddie Rector

Honi Coles (right) and Cholly Atkins (left) at the United Nations doing Robinson's "Scoot" step *(Jack Bradley)*

Shorty Snowden and Lindy Hoppers at Small's Paradise, 1936

Lindy Hoppers at the Savoy

Whitey's Hopper Maniacs (Leon James second from right)

Whitey's International Hoppers in Hollywood (Whitey at far left)

Bunny Briggs dancing with Duke Ellington, Fifth Avenue Presbyterian Church, New York City, 1965 *(Raymond Ross)*

Groundhog at the Village Gate (drummer Jo Jones in background) *(Fred W. McDarrah)*

to keep from crying"—although this cannot be too far from his true feelings—but rather ventilating the absurdities of a chronic situation in a manner that made him the favorite of Negro audiences in the South.

Stringbeans and Sweetie May played Negro theaters, and their act was created of, by, and for Negroes. They attracted so much business, according to legend, that manager after manager hired them for as long as they would play his theater. Off stage Stringbeans was a man of substance—his real name was Budd LeMay—and his wife a highly respected woman. "Stringbeans . . . was a fine man and a good buddy," writes Ethel Waters, who billed herself as "Sweet Mama Stringbean." "He never resented my taking over his professional name." [3] Audiences knew Stringbeans and Sweetie May were married, which gave their pantomime special relevance.

Stringbeans and Sweetie May was part of a great tradition. Early on, white minstrelsy adopted two characterizations of the Negro: the comedian and the straight man, or the shiftless clown and the dandy. They were played in a comic style that, as Constance Rourke points out, helped make minstrelsy overwhelmingly popular because of its appeal "for a pioneer people who required resilience as a prime trait (see Chapter 6). In minstrelsy, she observes, the Negro was portrayed as a devil-may-care outcast with an air of comic triumph, irreverent wisdom, and an underlying note of rebellion. These characteristics did not fade. As time went on, they were embroidered upon.

After the Civil War Negro minstrelsy adopted the same duo. Both danced; the dandy strutted and the clown shuffled. Later, Negro tent shows presented comedians—solo and in pairs—with a more rhythmic and eccentric style of dancing. These performers excelled at satiric pantomime, and along with everything else, made fun of each other as well as themselves.

At the turn of the century these characterizations made a hit on Broadway in the performances of *Williams and Walker*. With the aid of vernacular dance—George Walker did a strut or cakewalk, and Bert Williams, the Shuffle and a bit of a grind—they introduced a new kind of comedy (see Chapter 16). They were a great success, but the humor was relatively bland, and the blend was still evolving in the South.

By the teens such man-and-wife comedy teams as *Stringbeans and Sweetie May* were becoming popular on the embryonic T.O.B.A., the Negro vaudeville circuit. The inspiration for their acts came from the Negro folk, and they often, as we have seen, pantomimed the conflict between the henpecked husband and the domineering wife in a rough-and-tumble burlesque that white people sometimes enjoyed but frequently did not understand.

Comedy teams of various kinds proliferated rapidly. Theirs was perhaps the most ubiquitous of all vernacular styles and often the most original. A comic blend of knockabout eccentric dancing was perfected, which although the satire became more general as it came north and was performed before white audiences, nevertheless incorporated a brand of inside humor that often reflected a realistic appraisal of Negro life.

As the satire sharpened and zeroed in on Negro subjects—particularly before Negro audiences—a humorous strain of vilification in high style was added to the repertory and developed along new and personal lines. One of its sources was probably the West African song of allusion (where the subject pays the singer *not* to sing about him), reinterpreted in the West Indies as the political calypso, in New Orleans as the "signifyin'" song, and in the South generally as "the dozens."

The objective is iconoclastic insult, a hilarious heckling. Vestiges of it survived in the big Negro bands of the twenties and thirties. For example, as Ivie Anderson sang a sad blues in front of the Duke Ellington orchestra, drummer Sonny Greer, safely ensconced behind a mountain of percussion, talked back between pauses in the lyrics—rudely and with a straight face. "I got the blues," sang Ivie, and Sonny interjected, "That ain't the worst you gonna get, Baby!" This was one of the traditional ways to encourage a vocalist.

The tradition continues. In a 1965 concert pianist Billy Kyle, in Louis Armstrong's sextet, made rude remarks while the well-proportioned Jewel Brown sang. "I left my heart in San Francisco," she intoned, and Mr. Kyle observed loudly, "I see you brought the rest along." The predominantly white audience laughed nervously, but Miss Brown seemed to enjoy it, feeling no doubt that the remark called attention to certain indisputable facts.

The conflict between man and wife, with emphasis upon mutual insults, becomes more explicit with *Butterbeans and Susie* (Mr. and Mrs. Jodie Edwards), who at one time formed a trio with Stringbeans.[4] They are better known because they came north and made a series of successful recordings. (Their first "When My Man Shimmies," Okeh 8147, was issued in 1922; their last, an album, *Butterbeans and Susie*, Festival M-7000, in 1962.)

Between duets Susie sang the blues and cakewalked, while Butterbeans performed his eccentric dance. He was famous for his Heebie Jeebies, a dance routine known in the trade as the Itch, in which he scratched in syncopated rhythms. "That Butterbeans, he wore the tightest pants and kept his hands in his pockets and looked like he was itching to death," says dancer James Cross, who is Stump in the team of *Stump and Stumpy*, "and when he took his hands out of his pockets and started to scratch all around the beat, the audience flipped." [5]

Butterbeans and Susie spent little time pantomiming a male in a matriarchy (*they looked the part*), but made it verbally explicit—alternately singing, interrupting, and heckling each other. In one of their own numbers,

"Get Yourself a Monkey Man," [6] the forthright Susie describes exactly what she wants: "The man I got he's a hard-workin' man, he works hard all the time; and on Saturday night when he brings me his pay, he better not be short one dime."

Butterbeans's opinion of such a man is very low. "He's a bran' new fool and a Monkey Man." He believes in treating women rough: "I'd whip your head every time you breathe; rough treatment, Susie, is 'zactly what you need." This bloodthirsty declaration is contradicted by the baby-face and timorous bearing of Butterbeans, who is clearly indulging in delusions of grandeur. In fact, Butterbeans looks exactly like a Monkey Man.

In their version of a standard tune, "Until the Real Thing Comes Along," [7] Susie sings the original lyrics with feeling, swearing eternal devotion and establishing a more romantic mood than many popular singers. Then Butterbeans, apparently swept off his feet, carries on with lyrics of his own: "I'd fight all the animals in the jungle or even in the zoo, I'd grab a lion and smack his face and tear a tiger in two!" (Susie interjects an encouraging "Yeah" at this point.) "If that ain't love, it'll have to do," he continues, while Susie asks breathlessly "Till when, till when?" and Butterbeans answers: "Until another *fool* come along."

Butterbeans and Susie not only make the ignominy of the Monkey Man of Negro life clear as they heckle each other, but they also expose—as do the blues—the saccharine fantasies of Tin Pan Alley.

Not all the early man-and-wife teams were married. "Two-Story" Tom, so-called because of his height (and perhaps the floor of a house on which he liked to break and enter), picked up a partner in each town as he traveled the circuits.[8] Her part was not large. He was a fine Buck dancer with a genius for satirizing the stereotype of the "bad" Negro, who is supposed to flash a razor, shoot crap, and get into fights. "When I start after you," he roars, "you'll run so fast, you'll cut out a new street." The possibilities of embroidering upon the mask of the "bad" Negro who "don't take nothin' from nobody"—a mean and militant John Henry—are almost endless, and Two-Story Tom made the most of them.

At least one of the more notable man-and-wife teams lasted into the thirties: *Brown and McGraw*. "Brown, the husband, danced like Sammy Davis playing 'Sportin' Life' with a cane," says dancer Charles Cook, "and his wife came out dressed in feathery plumes, high kicking and shaking her backside—all for laughs." [9] They added a variety of acrobatic and flash steps, too, in spectacular disorder. "It was so fast and furious," adds Cook, "that after it was over, even dancers couldn't describe what they had done."

The lady in the act had a sharp tongue, and just before she retired—some say she *was* retired—made a remark that became a Harlem slogan. Switching her displeasure from her husband to the audience, she walked out on the floor of the Cotton Club, and hushed the band with an imperious gesture. "*I*," she said airily, "am Greta Garbo, and *you*," she added curtly, "can kiss my foot"—or words to that effect. The audience cheered.

Bit by bit, solo comedians and two-man teams came into popularity. One of the earliest to make the Keith circuit was *Glenn and Jenkins*, who dressed as street cleaners and pushed brooms as they performed comic steps. (Lonnie Johnson played guitar in their act for four years.) They were tops in the teens, and because they appeared so early, their humor had little to do with the real problems of Negro life.

The humor became more pointed on T.O.B.A., where two eccentric teams, *Bilo and Asher* and *Gulfport and Brown*, made their reputations. It was less pointed with such other teams as *Chilton and Thomas*, who headed north as they danced the Charleston, and *Baby and Bobby Goins*, with their jazz-Apache dance, who appeared on Broadway.

To a northern city audience—and especially to a northern Negro audience—the problems of a male in a matriarchy (although increasingly applicable to middle-class whites) held less appeal than satire involving immediate situations met by those who had migrated north, an experience they had all shared. The acts changed accordingly, and with the rise of solo comedians in vaudeville and theaters, an infusion of new and inside humor resulted.

Hundreds of country comics established themselves in urban night clubs, vaudeville, and local theaters, spicing their down-home characterizations with sophisticated comments on city life—and eccentric dancing. Many had graduated directly from tent shows. The inside nature of their humor made possible some extremely blue and bawdy remarks, which only those in the know could understand. The urban environment did not create this kind of humor, but it seemed to sharpen and coarsen it.

Many of these dancing comics remain semi-anonymous: "Yowse," a favorite at the Regal Theater in Chicago; "Sweet Papa Garbage" (Marshall Rogers), who contrary to his billing, dressed impeccably and performed like Bert Williams; Billy Mitchell, who sang unprintable parodies of popular songs and marched with his toes pointing backwards; and "Flink," a comedy dancer at the Club DeLisa and the Rhumboogie in Chicago, who dressed as a tramp and carried a bedpan and broom to sweep up coins tossed on the stage ("I wonder where them *green* ones is?" he hinted loudly, looking around for dollar bills). And there were many more.

Several of these solo comics became well known. "Pigmeat" (Dewey Markham) set the styles in eccentric dancing at Harlem's Apollo Theater; Dusty Fletcher popularized "Open the Door, Richard"; Timmie Rogers was still active on the Sammy Davis TV series in 1966; and Rochester (Eddie Anderson) became a fixture on the Jack Benny programs. (At one time Rochester featured a well-upholstered comedy dancer, Kitty Murray, in his troupe.) Each of them was expert in satirical pantomime.

The true peak of the comedy-dancing tradition arrived in the early thirties with the great two-man teams. They blended tumbling and acrobatics with superb dancing and developed satire on the human comedy to a new high as they played night clubs (mostly Negro), vaudeville, and once in a while, Broadway musicals. A few appeared in Hollywood films.

One of the finest teams was *Cook and Brown.* They began their career as a team with Ben Bernie's orchestra at the College Inn in Chicago around 1930. When they came east and opened at the Cotton Club in 1934, they met with no competition. Nobody could touch their frantic, knockabout style. "Later on," says Ernest Brown, "other comedy teams showed up." [10]

They had watched circus tumblers and the knockabout acts of Barto Mann, Russ Wise Jr., and the white comedian Buster West. (Barto Mann broke so many instruments sliding into the orchestra pit that he was fined for it.) "Buster West was the greatest," says Charles Cook. "He could stop any show." It was Buster West who showed Brown how to execute a five-tap Russian Wing.

Cook and Brown worked steadily through the Depression. "Why, we closed on Thursday at Loew's with Helen Morgan and Eddie Peabody," says Cook, "and opened the next day at the Roxy." Unlike some comedy teams, *Cook and Brown* had a reputation for being steady and reliable.

The act combined just about every kind of vernacular dance, including tap, with first-rate acrobatics. Brown, who is four-feet-ten inches short, and Cook, who is six feet tall, carry on an undeclared war. They have a routine, but the irrepressible Brown breaks out of it again and again to show off his own eccentric steps, whereupon the short-tempered Cook literally knocks him back into line.

"Brownie can fall like a champion," says Cook, and indeed he can—dropping into a split, sliding the length of the stage, and bouncing up at the other end thumbing his nose. It looks like bone-crushing mayhem, but it is actually carefully rehearsed dancing and acrobatics, with tiny Brown emerging triumphant at stage center in the finale doing a wildly satirical version of the Twist.

The success of the act is based on the universal appeal of the little guy who proves indestructible, but the underlying parallel of Gray Goose and Boll Weevil inevitably comes to mind. Cook and Brown appeared for a while on Broadway in *Kiss Me Kate* (1948) and were among the last comedy teams to be steadily employed in the sixties.

Other fine comedy teams followed *Cook and Brown*, but the comedy often obscured the high quality of the dancing. Among them were *Batie and Foster*: While Clarence Foster mugged, Walter Batie executed a walking tap pantomiming Harry Langdon. *Moke and Poke* managed to conduct their dialogue in hip rhymes: "We're Moke and Poke, it ain't no joke, that's all she wrote, the pencil broke." Fletcher Moke tumbled while Leon Poke executed top-notch rhythm tap.

One of the greatest teams, *Chuck and Chuckles*, has been described as a modern *Buck and Bubbles.* Chuckles (James Walker) played a ragged set of vibes and excelled at legomania, while Chuck (Charles Green) performed graceful and breathtaking rhythm tap in the style of John Bubbles, whose protégé he later became (see Chapter 43). Chuck Green was still dancing in top form in the mid-sixties.

Red and Struggy, who made Broadway but had to dance in the shadow of Bill Robinson in *Brown Buddies* (1930), were perhaps the keenest satirists of all. Long before it became the thing to do, they made fun of the hipsters of their own generation. Struggy was famous for a back-to split and pull-up, but their specialty was an excruciating burlesque of the Lindy: While the band went into an up-tempo flag-waver, and Struggy worked feverishly around him, the taller Red, playing the part of the (girl) partner, remained bored and "cool" to the point of sophisticated sleep walking. It was a triumph of understatement, and the contrast was shattering.

Red and Struggy pioneered a stance that is still with us. At the time, however, a white man-and-wife team, *Jerry and Turk,* copied the act, lock, stock, and barrel-rolls, and sky-rocketed to the top, far beyond the reach of *Red and Struggy.*

Then a trio, *The Chocolateers,* arrived from the West Coast with a barnyard novelty called Pecking that became a ballroom sensation. Clowning was emphasized as they ran all over the stage and up the walls, and it obscured the excellent dancing. Eddie West was a good acrobat, Paul Black could execute Chinese splits—straddling to the floor as he walked—and Albert Gibson was one of the great tappers. It was Pecking that sold the act, however, and took them back to Hollywood.

One more among many first rate teams, *Stump* (James Cross) *and Stumpy* (Harold Cromer), carried on the tradition of *Stringbeans and Sweetie May,* satirizing a well-known attitude of Southern Negroes. It occurred in a skit at the Apollo Theater in Harlem. Both dark-skinned, they are seated happily in a night club "up North." [11] Behind Stump and out of his sight stands a light-skinned and threatening bouncer-waiter, a napkin over his arm. His glowering presence sobers Stumpy, who is facing him. Stump, unaware of the threat, tries to cheer up his buddy: "Whatsa matter, man? You up No'th now, let's have a ball!" He is convinced that his troubles are over since he has left the South. Stumpy, watching the bouncer, tries to hush Stump, who is becoming noisier and noisier. "You up No'th, man!" Stump cries.

At last Stumpy catches Stump's eye and nods fearfully at the bouncer. Stump turns around, puzzled at first by the figure towering above him. For a moment his newly won confidence does not falter. He pulls his buddy's coat, points wildly at the bouncer, and commands: "Straighten that fool *out,* man, straighten that fool *out*!" Whereupon the bouncer picks him up, and as the audience screams with laughter, thrashes him unmercifully. The act is climaxed by some fine flash dancing.

The assumption of the Southern Negro that once you come north your troubles are over is widespread, and many in the audience recognize their own shattered illusions in the skit. As in the case of Stringbeans, another aspect of Negro life has been reduced to laughable proportions.

By the sixties the great comedy dancers had all but disappeared, although the humor survived and became popular in the form of stand-up comics (Bob Hope style) such as Slappy White, Red Foxx, Nipsey Russell, Dick Gregory, Flip Wilson, Godfrey Cambridge, Bill Cosby, Moms Mabley, and Richard Pryor. Several of them had been good dancers.

To the general public, which thought of Negro humor, if at all, in terms of *Amos 'n' Andy*, these comics sounded sparkingly new as another element in the Afro-American tradition surfaced. "I hope that Negro 'low' comedy persists," writes LeRoi Jones, "even long after all the gangsters on television are named Smith and Brown." [12]

31 Russian Dancing

IN 1911, in the middle of her Moscow dance program, tiny Ida Forsyne—she wore a size two shoe—suddenly inserted a series of improvised *kazotskys* and brought down the house. "When she finished," says dancer Rufus Greenlee, "there wasn't anything left to do." [1] Ida was hailed as the greatest Russian dancer of them all, and thereafter, as she toured Europe, closed her act—by popular demand—with *kazotskys*.

"I had seen a Russian troupe at Hammerstein's Victoria Theater in New York City long before, and then I saw two peasant women in Rostov doing *kazotskys*—you know, you start from a squat, your arms on your chest, and kick out first one leg then the other—I was fascinated," she says. "They must have weighed 150 pounds apiece, and I weighed less than 100, so I could move faster." [2] She practiced the step every day by herself, adding things to it, and finally tried it out in Moscow.

Russian dancers usually stand up between steps, but Ida could not wait. "I just changed steps and traveled across the stage in a crouch, working out new combinations." She flung both legs out in front and touched her toes with her hands before she came down in time with the music. "Then I'd mix it up with down-steps, up-steps, and cross-ankle steps—I never could spin—and as a finale, kazotsky all the way across the stage and return, backwards." The top theaters in Europe booked Ida Forsyne for nine years without a break.

The popularity of Russian dancing in the United States came after Ida Forsyne had pioneered in the style abroad. It lasted among professionals for about fifteen years—roughly from 1910 to 1925—primarily in vaudeville. The general public got a concentrated taste of it in 1922 and again in 1925 when the resplendent Russian company, the *Chauve Souris,* was the hit of Broadway. (The tune, "The Parade of the Wooden Soldiers," has been with us ever since.) By that time, however, other styles were taking over the stage.

Perhaps because the music to which it was performed did not swing in the jazz sense, Russian dancing was not very popular with Negro audiences and developed few great performers in this country. From the first, it was adopted in varying degrees as part of a performance, usually the acrobatic finale, and then endlessly modified. Eventually Russian dancing became a small but enduring component of American dance.

"I saw a Russian company on Broadway in 1905," says Ida Forsyne.

"When I started dancing in 1906," says dancer Thaddeus Drayton, "we all worked on our Russian dancing—the Shuffle and the Sand were going out, and tap hadn't come in." [3] His partner, Rufus Greenlee, recalls copying steps from the Alexander Russian Dancers at Coney Island in 1910. By 1914 Greenlee and Drayton were on their way to the top with an all-Russian finale employing spins, flips, and kazotskys. It made a fine climax, but their specialty was a soft-shoe, and they had already modified the steps and adopted a new accompaniment: ragtime.

In the transition to a swinging blend of taps, acrobatics, and Russian dancing, Ulysses S. Thompson was a pioneer. "We started to call Russian dancing legomania after World War I," [4] he says. Specifically, Thompson was combining somersaults, cartwheels, and tap dancing with knee-drops and kazotskys. The mixture was sometimes called eccentric dancing, and much depended on the individual style of the performer. By the twenties the versatile Willie Covan was leading the trend toward assimilation. "I threw in knee-drops and kazotskys along with everything else," he says, "and I was the first to work out a double Around the World, *no hands*" [5] (see Chapter 33).

The greatest male Russian dancer, however, was Dewey Weinglass (see Chapter 11). Starting as a pick, he fought his way to the top with a quartet billed as "The Dancing Demons," in which he starred. Weinglass had seen a family of Russian dancers at the Hippodrome and copied steps of Ivan Bankoff, Thaddeus Drayton, and Eva Taylor. (Eva Taylor was making a great reputation as a Russian dancer when she married Clarence Williams, the pianist, and retired.) "I did other things besides Russian, such as song-and-dance," [6] says Weinglass, referring to the Soft Shoe, "but the finale of our act was all Russian.

Combining Russian with legomania, Weinglass performed spins, squats, splits, as well as Around the Worlds—no hands—and a step he invented called the Flying Eagle, in which he kicked from a squat alternately to each side with each leg. "Your muscles have to be—good," says Weinglass, "and when I did a split, I always broke the falls with the calf of my leg, so I never had any injuries to my knees or feet."

"Dewey has a natural advantage," says John Bubbles with a chuckle. "He looks like he's sitting down when he's standing up." [7]

Like Ida Forsyne, Weinglass stayed low and never telegraphed his next step, rising to his full five feet only to fall at once into another squat. "Nobody was as fast as Dewey," [8] says dancer Willie Glenn. "He didn't have to move as far."

Dewey Weinglass had his own private crusade. "While I was playing the Poli circuit, I overheard the manager asking my agent what we were paid. Told it was $150, the manager said: 'If they were white, they'd be getting $500.' " Weinglass never forgot. He played the western circuits until his first partner, Dave Stratton, quit in 1917, and replaced him with Tommy Woods. They made a hit in Chicago and traveled all the way to Nova Scotia and back at $175 a week. In a short time, they were making $300 on the Columbia burlesque wheel, going back into vaudeville during the summers, when the Columbia circuit shut down. "I said to myself I'm going to make $500," Weinglass recalls, "and I won't be white."

The break came in 1921. While the act was filling in at the Audubon Theater in New York City, William Morris saw it. "The next day I got a telegram to come to the Putnam building, and when I arrived, Morris asked me how I'd like to go to England at 100 pounds a week." In those days 100 pounds was near enough to $500, and *The Dancing Demons* opened at the Victoria Theater in London with great success. The Flying Eagle was the hit of the show. "That was the high point of my career," says Dewey in his husky voice. "I was getting $500 a week, and I was still black."

Returning to the United States, Weinglass found that jobs were scarce. He worked in two Broadway shows, *Dixie to Broadway* (as a chorus boy) and *Liza* in 1923, but his specialty was no longer in demand. For a while he went back in vaudeville with decreasing success and then landed a job as producer at the Pearl Theater in Philadelphia. "A lot of great dancers came from that town," he says. "I booked *The Miller Brothers* when Honi Coles was with them, Lavinia Mack, and Bill Bailey at one time or another." In the late thirties Dewey Weinglass quit show business to become the manager of a bar and grill in Harlem.

While Thompson, Covan, and Weinglass were transitional figures in the evolution of vernacular Russian dancing in the United States, the first and foremost Russian dancer of them all was Ida Forsyne. In 1962, at the age of seventy-nine, she could still do a cartwheel. "My father disappeared when I was two years old, and Mother went into domestic service," says Ida, who was born in Chicago in 1883. "She didn't think I could dance, but I was picking up pennies dancing in front of the candy store when I was ten."

That summer she got a job as a pick, cakewalking at the Chicago World's Fair at twenty-five cents a day. "We went around in a wagon with a rag-time band to drum up trade." At home she sang "The Holy City" as she washed the dishes.

Ida and her mother lived over a saloon. "I learned my first real steps from Willie Mason, the sporting-house pianist downstairs, and picked up dimes dancing at house-rent parties." In those days, many shows originated in Chicago. She haunted the Alhambra Theater, by way of the fire-escape, watching the shows rehearse—including *The Coontown 400* and *The South before the War*—and then sneaked into a private house on 22nd Street and Wabash, where she discovered more rehearsals were taking place.

Ida ran away with a tab show when she was fourteen. "It was called *The Black Bostonians* and had a little plot, while everybody did their own specialties," says Ida. "I sang 'My Hannah Lady' and did a Buck dance." (By the phrase "Buck dance," she does not mean tap: "It was eccentric dancing and legomania.") The finale was a big plantation scene with the entire cast on stage.

On tour the show rented theaters in each town—"there were no theaters for colored; we played the same places as the *Follies*"—and then went broke in Butte, Montana. "I never wrote to my mother for help. I was a born hustler, and besides, I was having too much fun." Adopting a five-year-old boy as a prop, Ida sang her way home by walking down the aisles of rail-road coaches hand-in-hand and harmonizing "On the Banks of the Wabash" as she passed the child's hat and collected enough money to pay the fare and a little more.

Working with *Black Patti's Troubadours* (see Chapter 11) from 1898 to 1902, Ida received a raise from fifteen to twenty-five dollars a week before the show closed. "We had a cakewalking contest every performance, and my partner and I won it seven nights straight in a row," she says. "We added legomania and tumbling in the breaks." Ida could do any step she saw.

On her sixteenth birthday Ida and the Black Patti troupe of twenty-six performers arrived in San Francisco. "We all stayed at a fine white hotel and ate together at a long table," says Ida. "Everybody was so nice to us." That was in 1899, and Ida remembers talk about the dancing at the Barbary Coast, the notorious sporting district of San Francisco. "In those days I wouldn't even have thought of going to see it." When the show arrived in Los Angeles, it was a different story: "The people were so nasty—I guess they classed us with the Mexicans."

Returning to New York, Ida had no trouble getting jobs at Atlantic City and Coney Island. "All the colored people were working those places then —sort of like minstrel shows," she says, "and Henderson's big theater at Coney was showing two-a-day with famous acts like Eddie Cantor." Ida lost her voice at Coney Island when she was sixteen. "It was all song-and-dance then—you'd sing a verse, then a chorus, and then dance a chorus—you'd have to yell your songs in those crowded clubs. I was like a coon shouter until my voice gave out, and I used to have a wonderful alto." She learned to put a song across "by sort of talking it."

Ida joined the original *Smart Set* in 1902. A white producer Gus Hill financed the show. "Colored shows had no trouble finding a white backer then," says Ida, "and they generally made money." This show starred Ernest Hogan, Billy McClain, and the Hun Brothers. "Bert Williams just had one style, but Ernest Hogan was great—he was really *ingenious*." Among the performers was a girl who did a ragtime toe-dance, accompanied by a trio of two men and Maisie Brooks, who played the harp. Ida sang a song—or more accurately, talked a song—called "Moana." "I never did know what that song was all about." Then she did a solo dance, "all jazz steps and no Russian."

By 1904 Ida Forsyne's career was booming. "I was considered sensational," she says defensively, "before I ever did any Russian dancing." She danced a solo with Will Marion Cook's *The Southerners* on the New York Roof Garden and a mixed cast of thirty-five performers. "Mr. Cook never wore a hat and had long hair. He was very artistic-looking and wrote mainly for white shows," says Ida. "This show wasn't separated into half white and half colored—everybody worked together—there were a lot of integrated groups in those days." The star of the show was the white dancer famous for his soft-shoe routine, Eddie Leonard.

The following year she went abroad with *The Tennessee Students,* a troupe of seventeen performers, most of whom played some stringed instrument and sang. The music was in a transitional style between ragtime and jazz. The stars were Abbe Mitchell, Ernest Hogan, and Henry Williams, who did a Sand dance. *The Tennessee Students* grew out of *The Memphis Students* (who were New York musicians and neither students nor from Memphis) after they made a hit at Proctor's 23rd Street Theater with Will Dixon, "The Dancing Conductor."

Billed as "Abie [*sic*] Mitchell and Her Coloured Students" at the Palace Theater, London, in 1906, the show was a smash hit. Ida Forsyne, judging by a handbill printed at the time, was the star. Her photograph appears on the cover—full face, wearing a bandanna, with an infectious grin—over the caption: "Topsy, the Famous Negro Dancer." On the back the reader is warned, "Look out for 'Topsy,' the most fascinating negro dancer ever seen—the little lady who 'was not born but just grew.'" The same picture appeared on magazine covers and in London buses.

Describing a dancer as "fascinating," instead of the customary "show-biz" superlatives of "sensational" or "extraordinary," is rather unusual and hints at the kind of charm that Ida radiated. "Part of her personality," said Sophie Tucker years later, "is in her facial expression"—a real compliment for a dancer. The only quote from the press on the handbill refers to Ida: A reviewer in the *Daily Telegraph* wrote "If Topsy is not soon the talk of the town we are very much mistaken." [9]

When *The Tennessee Students* were ready to sail for home, Ida was flooded with offers. She accepted a long-term contract with the Marinelli Agency, the largest in Europe, and disappeared from the American scene for nine years. Although she did not know it at the time, those years were to be the peak of her career.

The entire first year Ida played the *Moulin Rouge* in Paris, singing and dancing her fast mixture of eccentric steps. Then she was booked throughout England. (She saw Bill Robinson and George Cooper for the first time there.) "They billed me as 'Topsy' in London," she says. Wearing a bandanna and a short gingham dress, she sang and talked "Lindy by the Watermelon Vine" and danced like a tiny tumbleweed. As she darted about the stage—"they described me as 'little, black, and cute' "—she filled the role of Topsy to perfection.

At the Alhambra Theater in London, Ida introduced her Sack dance to special music with a ballet company. "A stagehand brought me out in a big potato sack," she says, "and first I'd throw out one leg, then an arm, and so on until he dumped me in the middle of the stage." The line of ballet dancers backing her up was paid extra to appear in blackface.

"I wear a sack, too, with straws stuck to it, and I run around dancing like a wild woman, while the music roars, and then a shot rings out, and I fall and roll over and over dead—that was the act." It was a very "arty" production, of course, but Ida was improvising with all the jazz steps she knew. "I danced on the lawn at garden parties," she says, "and gave a command performance for the royal family."

On the way to her triumph in Moscow several years later, Ida had a Russian costume made for her in St. Petersburg, including fancy-stitched boots. "Oh, boy!" she exclaims, transfigured by the memory. "I was as fast as lightnin'—then." She practiced her Russian dancing secretly every day. "Some said I overpracticed, but that was the way European artists prepared." She danced for nine years without a vacation and loved it. "They treated me like a princess."

In 1914 Ida Forsyne returned to the United States and the end of her dazzling career.

World War I broke out while she was in Paris, and all aliens were directed to leave the country. Ida left for home by way of England, and a few days later arrived in New York. After several months making the rounds of theatrical agencies and asking for help from everyone she had ever known in show business, the truth finally dawned on her: "It seems that I couldn't get any work at all. I was too black—I literally starved."

Ida did not give up, however. She had the tenacity of a bulldog. And she was aggressively proud. "I wanted to be a little different from the average colored performer. Perhaps my success in Europe made me feel that way. I lived a clean life—you can't spend all night in a gin mill and then do a Russian dance—and I didn't know how to do a Shake dance and darned if I was going to learn."

Before she quit dancing, Ida Forsyne scuffled—taking whatever she could get—for fourteen years. She never stopped enjoying life, however, switching from one place to another if things became too difficult. Her first job was back in Coney Island, coon-shouting from twelve noon to twelve midnight. "I soon gave up any idea of doing what I wanted to do," she says grimly.

Later, she managed to stay a week at Harlem's Lincoln Theater. "Lincoln audiences were terrible and always booed anything artistic. All they wanted was bumps and Shake dancing, which I couldn't do, but somehow I lasted a week." Work at second-rate cabarets such as the DeLuxe in Chicago was torture. "You had to mix with the customers and all that goes with it." So she tried T.O.B.A., first with partner Billy Sells and her own act, which folded in Richmond, and then with other tab shows: Will Mastin's, Billy King's, and a troupe billed as "Over the Top."

"On T.O.B.A. you had to sing double-entendre blues—or else," says Thaddeus Drayton. Ida just danced. Most of these shows used the pit band at the various theaters. Will Mastin carried a contortionist, however, who played clarinet lying on the floor with a flaming lamp on his head. "His name was George McClellan," says Ida, "and he did his contortion work while he was playing, too." In addition, Mastin had a comedian, chorus boys, and chorus girls. "I was one of six or eight dancing girls."

Ida has mixed feelings about the Billy King show. "He was a nice man, and I think he appreciated the fact that I was doing something different with my Russian dance. I guess I felt that the old song-and-dance routine was beneath me." The audience in Cleveland disagreed violently. They booed, gave cat-calls, and someone yelled "What do you think you're doing?" Ida offered to let anyone come up on the stage and try it. That was in 1920, and she was so disgusted that on the way back to New York she sold her fine Russian boots for $20 to Ivan Bankoff, whom she happened to meet on the train. He wanted them for his partner, Girlie.

For two years—from 1920 to 1922—Ida worked as a personal maid, both offstage and on, for Sophie Tucker. She was paid $50 a week and they played the top circuits with their own pianist, Al Seeger. "Sophie sang thirteen songs, and she wanted a dancer to help whip up applause at the end," says Ida. "My colored friends objected that I was getting the applause and Sophie was taking the bows, but I didn't mind. She was a wonderful performer."

When the act came down to Washington, D.C., on the Keith circuit, new rules caused some difficulty: No Negro performers were allowed on the stage unless they were with a white performer, and in any case, they must wear blackface. Further, no Negro working backstage was permitted to watch the show. The Sophie Tucker act played havoc with the rules. When the manager informed Miss Tucker that it was customary to have picks black-up and that Ida would do better in blackface, Sophie refused in no uncertain language, and Ida, when she was not dancing, continued to watch the show from backstage.

By 1924 Ida was back on T.O.B.A. as one of six dancing girls with Mamie Smith's act. "Nobody went in for tap—we all did the same steps—Fall Off the Log, and so on," says Ida. "We wore black shoes and stockings, and white bloomers to the knee trimmed with yards and yards of lace—almost like Can-Can costumes—with a dress over it." The act carried its own comedian and used the pit band.

She toured the South in 1926 with a late version of *The Smart Set*, organized by the half-brothers Homer Tutt and Salem Tutt-Whitney. "Salem was the comedian and a real gentleman—but Homer!" says Ida. "And a dancer named Joe Jackson, who tapped sitting down, was wonderful." Ida hated the South. "Toilet facilities in some of those towns were unbelievable, and if you wanted a drink of water you had to send somebody out with a milk bottle," she says. "In the Memphis hotel where we had to stay, a rat took the food right off my tray." Her former career in Europe seemed like an impossible dream.

Meanwhile, night clubs were thriving in Harlem, and Ida tried for them, too. She never got inside the Cotton Club, Connie's Inn, or the Nest—"they all had light-skinned chorus girls and talent didn't seem to count"—but she did have an audition at Small's Paradise. "They put me on during intermission, and Danny Small said, 'You're good, and I'll use you in my next revue' but he never did." Ida didn't approve of the abbreviated costumes, anyway. "They were practically naked."

On two occasions Ida came close to a job in a New York show. While she was dancing at the New World Club in Atlantic City in 1927, Jack "Legs" Diamond, who fancied himself as a judge of talent, told her to see Jules Martin at the Frolic Club on 52nd Street and Broadway. The Happy Rhone band was playing there. "I knew everybody in the show, including Amanda Randolph, and I went home and made my own costumes," says Ida. "They all knew me, too, but I guess Legs was slipping, because Mr. Martin wouldn't give me a job."

Another time Clarence Williams, whom she asked for a job in Atlantic City, invited her to come up to New York for an audition. She arrived the afternoon before the opening and tried out. "I'd never heard the music before, but I could dance to it." They liked her, and she got the job. "That night, while I was waiting for my cue, the manager walked over and said 'We think it's best if you don't go on'—and that was that."

Ida was back again on T.O.B.A. in 1927 at $35 a week with Bessie Smith's show. The show carried pianist Fred Longshaw, who was making piano rolls on the side, and a few acts, including *The Hootens.* "They were a comedy team—Mrs. Hooten was very tall, and Mr. Hooten very short—and he did a preaching bit where he just recited the letters of the alphabet," says Ida. "It was a riot—and they were never vulgar."

Ida and Bessie got along well. "I worked in the chorus," says Ida, "but I also did my Russian specialty—the music would give a fanfare and I'd be standing there with my arms folded on my chest just like the Russians, ready to dance. Bessie stood in the wings and shouted 'Go on, Ida, show 'em!'" And Ida danced her heart out for an often-bewildered audience, which did not know what to make of it.

In 1928, when T.O.B.A. asked Bessie Smith to go on a southern tour, Ida quit. "I'd learned my lesson with *Smart Set* and vowed I'd never go south again." She arrived at home on New Year's day and decided to give up dancing altogether. "The good Lord knows I'd tried just about everything." She worked for three-and-a-half years as a domestic and then as an elevator girl.

What went wrong? "I was the best dancer around," she says with conviction. "Nobody had what I had." It could have been many things. Jobs were not plentiful in 1914 when Ida returned to the United States—James Weldon Johnson calls 1910 to 1917 the "term of exile" for Negroes on Broadway.[10] Then Ida, having lost her voice, did not fit readily into the song-and-dance formula. She was something special and just presenting her —especially on T.O.B.A.—was a problem.

Again, playing "Topsy" was no good because her own people considered it a stereotype, and Russian dancing—to Russian music, not jazz as in the case of *Greenlee and Drayton*—must have seemed energetic but unswinging to a sophisticated Harlem audience, which was enjoying the superlative dancing of Ethel Williams, Toots Davis, and Eddie Rector in *The Darktown Follies* (see Chapter 17). "Dancing to Russian music was all right for white audiences," says Drayton, "but colored audiences didn't care for it."

Ida has her own explanation. "Leigh Whipper and the others don't like me to say it, but I will—I couldn't get a job because I was black, and my own people discriminated against me." Ida's explanation is supported by considerable evidence. Contrary to the usually accepted view, racial prejudice began to mount rapidly in the early years of the twentieth century.

Thaddeus Drayton agrees: "In 1898 my family steamed north from Charleston to New York in an outside stateroom; five years later, in 1903, they couldn't get anything but steerage."

Ida makes the same point: "Why, I never heard of segregation in schools until recently in New York; when I was a little girl in Chicago, I sat right across from Marshall Field's daughter, Alice, and we all played together." Her early experiences in San Francisco and New York bear her out.

In any case, Ida was not finished. In 1930 she had a bit part with Helen Menchen in *Lily White*; in 1936 she played the part of Mrs. Noah in *Green Pastures*; in the same year she appeared with Rex Ingraham in *Emperor Jones*. As late as 1951 she helped a choreographer put on a cakewalk at City Center. She worked whenever she could. In the March 1944 issue of *American News*, published by the American Hotels Corporation, a correspondent from Schenectady writes: "We have in our midst a movie actress—Ida Forsyne Hubbard, our new elevator operator."

Ida Forsyne was still very much alive in 1965. "But I'm so stiff," she sighed, "and I've lost twenty-four pounds—I'm down to ninety-four." For years her spare time was occupied with visits to various hospitals, where she tried to cheer up her sick friends. "I guess I'm the only one who can still walk," she chuckled. By 1966 she was living in a rest home herself.

PART EIGHT

Acrobatics

32 Straight Acrobatics

A DOZEN little old men hobble on stage dressed as hayseeds with gray beards, each with one hand on his aching back, the other hand tapping with a cane, as if he were blind. In quavering tones they sing "Down Dere," promising that there'll be some changes made in the South. Suddenly the band takes off on "Jumpin' at the Woodside"—one of Count Basie's flag-wavers—and the little old men explode into acrobatic anarchy. It is organized; that is, they are all doing the same thing simultaneously, but the steps are wild, the effect frantic.

To top it off, Deighton Boyce catapults on stage dressed as a sweet old lady and throws himself into rows of cartwheels, flips, and spins, with wig, shawl, and skirts flying. He is tumbling in the traditional acrobatic manner, *but it is all precisely on the beat.* A semblance of order is restored as the dancers exit on an imaginary bus to the tune of "Alabamy Bound."

Other acts come and go. The featured speaker is Dick Gregory, who observes, among other things, that "Eisenhower is—er-uh, er-uh, er-uh—just a white Joe Louis." For the finale the old men are back in flannel shirts and overalls with an energetic challenge dance—each soloing in turn.

Once more Boyce shoots out from the wings with a front no-hands somersault over five dancers lined up on the floor and then, with a running start, slides the length of the stage on his stomach and off into the orchestra pit with a loud crash. The scramble of the musicians to get out of the way is genuine.

The occasion was the yearly celebration of the Copasetics at the jam-packed Riverside Plaza Ballroom in September 1963. A benevolent organization dedicated to the memory of Bill Robinson—"Everything is copasetic" meant everything is perfect to Bojangles—the Copasetics are a select group of fine dancers and entertainers whose annual "cruise" is a celebrated event. That year, in line with explosive political developments, they decided to draw upon the tradition of acrobatic dance.

Granted its preoccupation with improvisation and invention, American vernacular dance was bound to be influenced by acrobatics sooner or later. Before 1900, when minstrelsy and circus carnivals merged, and more specifically, when the popularity of the Cakewalk persuaded circuses to hire Negro performers, dancers and acrobats were thrown together and began to learn from each other. As vaudeville boomed, black and white followed each other on the same bill with predictable results.

The earliest and best-known Negro acrobats were tumblers, who worked *on the ground* performing somersaults, cartwheels, flips, and spins. Perhaps Negroes excelled at the art of tumbling because it required a minimum of props and a maximum of energy. Tumbling is geared-to-the-ground, do-it-yourself acrobatics, which anyone can afford. It also lends itself readily to the dance.

In the course of listing hundreds of acrobats in twenty-two different styles, Joe Laurie, Jr., mentions only three Negroes, all of them tumblers: "Henry Bolden . . . was considered the greatest Negro acrobat in show biz. Acott & Bailey were also great Negro acrobats. They played very little over here, but went to Europe, where they were a sensation, and stayed there." [1] Negro acts have generally done better abroad.

Old-timers disagree as to whether the Japanese, Arabs, or Germans are the best *straight* acrobats. (By "straight," they mean acrobats who perform the traditional European movements, and more particularly, do *not* synchronize with jazz rhythms.) The late Billy Maxey favored the Germans. He joined *The Sinclaire Sisters* in 1892, when he was nine years old. "That was in Indianapolis—they were acrobats and taught me stunts. My job was to come out ahead as The Rubber Boy and predict 'This is what they're gonna do,' and make fun of it with a back bend with my head between my legs, hopping around until they shooed me off." [2]

Thaddeus Drayton was favorably impressed by a troupe of Japanese acrobats, while Willie Covan liked the Arabs. "In the teens, they brought a lot of knockabout acts over here from Europe, just like Ed Sullivan does now," says Covan. "I got some ideas from a troupe of Arab acrobats called *The Seven Devils*." [3]

Choreographer Sammy Dyer, who once was an apprentice in Duke Ellington's sign-painting business in Washington, D.C., made a deal with some German acrobats: "This man had two daughters, and I taught them the Soft Shoe while he taught me acrobatics. In the early twenties, if you were on a bill with a white act from Europe, they seemed more interested in your work than you were." [4]

Other old-timers recall a few Negro troupes, but they could not be accurately classified as straight acrobatic: the *Toni Trio* of minstrel days, *The Gaines Brothers,* who also wire-walked in vaudeville, and *Rastus and Banks,* an early class act, famous abroad. *They worked in rhythm but they did not dance.* The first acrobatic *dancer* to be generally remembered is Sherman Coates of *The Watermelon Trust,* an act consisting of two men and their wives, who played top vaudeville spots around 1900. "One of the real great big acts," writes Laurie, "and also one of the first." [5]

"Grundy was older and the comedian," says Thaddeus Drayton. "Coates was the straight man who added acrobatic dancing—forward and back somersaults, flip-flops, forward cartwheels, butterflies, and a lot of other things." [6] In 1911 on the Poli circuit in New England, Harland Dixon, who later became a fixture on Broadway, played on the same bill with *The Watermelon Trust.* "What impressed me most," says Dixon, "was Coates, who tap danced during his acrobatics and *right with the beat.*" [7]

When Coates and Grundy broke up in 1914, Sherman Coates's wife, Lulu, a competent singer and dancer, organized an act billed as "Lulu Coates and Her Crackerjacks" that included three young dancers who aspired to be acrobats: Wilfred Blanks, Harry Irons, and Archie Ware. It was the beginning of a famous troupe.

Archie Ware, the spark-plug of the group, had served a rugged apprenticeship. Born in Topeka in 1892 and raised in Chicago, he was fascinated by the circus. "Flat-ground tumblers were what I loved," he says. "My pals and I, we watched what they did at the circus and went home and tried it." He never had any lessons. "I shiver when I think of the crazy stunts we tried to copy," he adds. "It's a wonder we didn't kill ourselves." [8]

Like many topnotch athletes, and especially acrobatic dancers, Archie Ware is short, almost tiny—a characteristic that helps to account for his lightning-fast coordination. When asked his height, he looks quickly at the questioner to see if he is being teased, and replies carefully: "Four feet, ten and *one-half* inches." It becomes clear, although he is too polite to argue about it, that he considers that last half-inch of great importance.

His father disapproved of show business and made Archie promise to finish grammar school. Archie managed to keep his promise without wasting a day. At the age of fourteen, just graduated, he joined an act billed as "Cozy Smith and Her Pickaninnies" and hit the worst road in vaudeville: George Webster's circuit in the Dakotas.

"I spent three seasons straight on this forgotten circuit playing to all-white audiences," he says, "and we worked towns where they had never seen or even *heard* of colored people." In the same troupe at one time or another were two youngsters who were to become famous dancers: Willie Covan and Maxie McCree. "We all did the Buck and Wing," adds Ware, "and I did a back somersault and a few flip-flops."

So young that he wasn't allowed to appear on the stage, Maxie McCree remained a puzzle to Archie Ware. "Why, he couldn't even tumble," says Archie. "I tried to teach him a back pitch, where you stand on someone's hands and they send you into a back flip, and he could hardly do it and never got any further." In the early twenties, when Maxie dropped around and told Archie how much money he was making, Ware, who is inclined to judge dancers by their tumbling, found it hard to believe. (McCree was earning $500 a week at the Lafayette Theater.) "When we knew him," Archie repeats, "all he could *really* do was sing."

Working with Cozy Smith's troupe could be fun. At one town in the wastes of North Dakota, the owner of the deserted Bijou Theater decided to try publicity. "He found a broken-down chariot abandoned by some carnival and hitched up a couple of mustangs," Archie Ware recalls. "Then he plastered signs on it saying 'We'll Be at the Bijou Tonight' and told us to go out and advertise the show." As the oldest performer in the act, fifteen-year-old Archie was handed the reins.

"When we turned into the main street, I thought we ought to speed up a little and look alive. Well, those horses had been hitched too close to the chariot, and when I slapped their backs with the reins and let out a whoop, they backed into the chariot first and then stampeded forward, kicking the chariot to pieces as they galloped through town." The local citizens ran for their lives, Archie tumbled off—acrobatically as it were—in front of Bijou, and the show was a sell-out that night.

In 1913 Ware left Cozy Smith to join Mayme Remington in a trip abroad, stayed on for a while with Belle Davis, playing Germany and Holland, and returned to the United States a few months before World War I. Back in Chicago, he worked briefly with comedian Andrew Tribble. The turning point came in 1914. "I met Mrs. Grundy of Coates and Grundy's *Watermelon Trust*, who told me that Lulu Coates was getting an act together," says Ware, "so I went to New York to join her."

For eight years Ware worked and learned under the most favorable conditions: Lulu Coates favored acrobatic dancing, his fellow dancers were all acrobats, and he had a chance to help with the business end as the act toured the length and breadth of the country.

In 1922 Mrs. Coates retired, and with her blessings *The Crackerjacks* were organized: Raymond Thomas, Clifford Carter, Harry Irons, and Archie Ware, *director*.

Over the years *The Crackerjacks* varied from four to six members, with occasional changes in personnel. Bobby Goins, Joe Chism, Tosh Hammid, Wilfred Blanks, Norman Wallace, Walter Humphrey, Lloyd MacDonald, George Staten, and Deighton Boyce were in the act at one time or another. "Of the dozen or so who worked with us during the life of *The Crackerjacks*," says Ware, "only four were not real acrobats, and they had special stunts of their own."

Deighton Boyce, for example, had some training in gymnastics. Born in Panama in 1913, where he became flyweight boxing champion as a teenager, Boyce came to the United States for his education. He studied at St. Augustine College in Raleigh, North Carolina, and went out for physical education. Excited by stories of the big city, Boyce could not wait. He quit school and headed for New York, where at Harlem's Hoofers Club, Bobby Goins discovered him rehearsing stunts. "Goins was with *The Crackerjacks* and took me to the rest of them," says Boyce. "They asked me to show them what I could do and then signed me up." [9]

Built "like a well-padded box car," according to a contemporary, Boyce took the place of Clifford Carter, who like so many other dancers, had strained his heart. The year was 1932, and the effects of the Depression were everywhere. "*The Crackerjacks* had played big shows before I joined them—the *Cotton Club* and *Hot Chocolates*—and we went right on as if times were booming," says Boyce. They had a five-year contract with Loew's circuit that took them from coast to coast each year. "We worked everything vaudeville had to offer, all the top night clubs and Broadway shows, such as *Hellzapoppin* and Ed Sullivan's *Harlem Cavalcade*." *The Crackerjacks* were the acknowledged tops in acrobatic dancing.

What made *The Crackerjacks* outstanding? "We weren't just acrobats," Archie Ware insists. "We had an acrobatic *variety* act—we tumbled in different costumes, we tapped, we sang, we danced, we featured lots of comedy—and our act was the fastest and *the first to do it in swinging rhythm*." At the same time *The Crackerjacks* were *true* tumblers in the European tradition, and they looked down on later stunts such as knee-drops and splits, which came to be called acrobatic.

Their act consisted of five numbers and lasted about ten shattering minutes. "The first number was a flash-tap ensemble," says Ware, "all of us dancing precisely together—but fast—and singing our theme, 'We Are the Crackerjacks.'" They raced through this number, wearing formal Eton jackets with flowing ties. The second number featured Bobby Goins's solo, in which he did an "acrobatic-contortionist chair dance" to a medley of "Rose Room" and "Deed I Do." "Goins was a real acrobat," says Ware. "He made a leap over a chair into a hand stand look easy." "He could bend over, around, and under chairs," adds Boyce, "and do a back snap-up, that is, jump *backwards* from his hands onto his feet."

The third number was known as the Old Man number and became the trademark of *The Crackerjacks*. At first only three of the troupe performed it. Clad in tattered Civil War uniforms and long gray beards, hands on aching backs and canes tapping to help them hobble on stage, they suddenly burst into tumbling pandemonium, filling the air with flying bodies and miraculously catching each other on the beat as the orchestra raced through an up-tempo "Alexander's Ragtime Band." "It was *real circus stuff*," says dancer Chink Collins, recalling the act vividly, "and it swung like mad." [10]

The fourth number, like the second, often varied: It might be Norman Wallace doing some balancing stunts—"he was a great acrobat"—or Joe Chism strutting in top hat and tails manipulating a cane as he inserted contrasting acrobatics or perhaps Walter Humphrey twirling two batons as he slid the length of the stage and then executed a row of somersaults *in slow motion*, a specialty that reminded Europeans of an overwrought Nijinsky.

The fifth and last number was a continuation of the Old Man number, an exercise in rhythmic mayhem. "We used to change to Spanish or Russian costumes for this," says Ware, "until the popularity of the old men became so great that we went back to the uniforms." Here *The Crackerjacks* did all the tricks they knew at once. "Boyce did a running front somersault over five of us as we lined up for a second on the floor; Wallace ran up and down the wall and the rest of us went into various specialties including cartwheels, flips, spins, and twists from one side of the stage to the other"—and all in jazz rhythms.

Touring Europe in 1936, *The Crackerjacks* had their greatest success in Germany, where tumbling is an old and honored art. "Those German acrobats were after Humphrey day and night to tell them the secret of his slow-motion somersaults," says Ware. And Boyce's running front somersault over five of his fellows caused consternation. "I forget the German word for it, but they wanted to know over and over how I got that 'elevation,'" says Boyce, "and I wasn't so sure myself."

Without a good manager *The Crackerjacks* might not have been such a success. "We were lucky," says Ware. "We found Morris Greenwald right at the start and stayed with him during our entire career." Those were the days when many white managers considered it quite ethical to overwork and underpay Negro acts. "Morris was a wonderful guy," adds Ware, "and honest as the day is long."

"Of course, he never got us into the Palace." This is one of Ware's little jokes. "As a matter of fact, he called us again and again to ask if we wanted to play the Palace— at half salary—but he never objected when we turned it down. The Palace had its policy, and we had ours."

" 'The top money I can get for you *Crackerjacks*,' Morris told us, 'is $800, but if you were white I could get $1,600.' " *The Crackerjacks* were steadily employed, but they never played the Palace, and they never got rich. The act broke up in 1952. During their career acrobatics had become an important part of dancing to jazz.

33 The New Acrobatics

MANY DANCERS in the mid-thirties turned to acrobatics for ideas. With Russian dancing almost dead, tap dancing fading, and *The Crackerjacks* with their straight acrobatics a great success, ruinous rivalry began. Acrobatics are highly visible, and audiences are greatly impressed by them. To old-timers it was the crippling way out, but in the course of competition, sensational new stunts evolved, which culminated in the great flash acts.

Straight acrobatics, of course, would not do. "A guy runs out of the wings," says a dancer who grew up in the thirties, "flips across the stage right on the beat into a somersault, and so what?—nothing happens." To keep up with—and sometimes to stay ahead of—the growing complexity of jazz rhythms, pioneering dancers needed steps that could be modulated, speeded, or slowed extemporaneously during execution.

Bit by bit, straight acrobatics were adopted and changed, a few Russian tricks retained, and ideas from circus, ballet, and even modern dance added. (Like jazz, vernacular dance seems able to absorb almost any influence without losing its individuality.) The result was a new, more difficult, and predominantly acrobatic blend. It started simply enough and just went up in the air. "If you take your feet more than one inch off the floor while you're doing rhythm tap," says the legendary Groundhog, "you're starting to do flash dancing." [1]

One of the pioneers in the blending was the short-lived Maxie McCree. While still in his teens—he started as a pick in Chicago and the West—McCree was a top attraction on T.O.B.A. "He could sing, too," says Dewey Weinglass, "one of his songs was 'Ten Baby Fingers and Ten Baby Toes.'" [2] McCree worked out a variety of new tap and acrobatic combinations long before they became common. John Bubbles, who is not given to lavish compliments, says "He could do anything." [3]

When he first came to New York, starring in *The Follies and Fancies of 1920* at the Lafayette Theater, the management framed McCree's contract instead of his picture out front. He was being paid the unheard-of sum of $500 a week. For a while, with a partner named George (no one seems to remember his last name), McCree put together what later dancers would call a class act, emphasizing his own natural grace—with the radical addition of acrobatics.

In 1921 he starred in *Put and Take*, a Negro show that opened at Town Hall, with music by Perry Bradford and others. The theater critics (there were no dance critics) were bowled over, and although they were never at a loss for words, seemed to have no idea what was happening. "Maxie romped in from Heaven ten minutes before the last shut-in," said *Variety* glibly, "tied the show into ribbons with his dizzy hoofing, and led the ensemble into a rabid mob scene of prancing, hopping, shimmying, eye-rolling, wiggling, leaping, and fit-throwing." [4] (Visualize that.) None of the critics knew Maxie's last name, either.

George White immediately signed McCree for the next edition of the *Scandals*. Like Bert Williams, Maxie was one of the very few performers featured in an all-white production. "When Maxie was drowned in Winona, Minnesota, in 1922," says Dewey Weinglass, "they say that White had to close the show temporarily." The rumor persists that McCree was in love with a girl in the show and the victim of foul play.

Maxie McCree's most celebrated achievement, among the wide variety of steps he executed brilliantly, was the knee-drop, or more particularly, the superb style in which he performed it. The knee-drop is probably a late and radically modified version of the Russian jack-of-all steps: the squat. (On Ed Sullivan's TV program in 1965 a troupe of Russian Raduga dancers were still executing a series of kazotskys, spins, and knee-drops to a nonswinging accompaniment.) Briefly, it is a way of hitting the floor. By scraping the side of the foot, the ankles, and the calf of the leg on the way down (often with feet crossed), the fall may be broken, more or less. In any case, the dancer finds himself quickly on one or both knees.

McCree used the knee-drop to punctuate cadences in his dancing—not unlike the bop drummer's "dropping bombs" many years later. That is the easy part. The hard part is rising gracefully—no hops or jerks—with or against the beat without using the hands and certainly no clumsy leaps upward from a kneeling position. The pressure is on the kneecap but the crossed legs help. Maxie rose from a knee-drop as if refreshed.

Like McCree, his cousin Willie Covan was truly versatile. As a youngster he worked out a variety of acrobatic stunts. As an established star, he performed an elegant soft-shoe with partner Leonard Ruffin, paving the way for the class acts. And as a seasoned performer he led an act called *The*

Four Covans, which combined all these styles—and more, becoming one of the best teams of the mid-twenties.

"Willie's a genius born," says Florence Covan, who married Willie in 1921 when she was a chorus girl in New York's Everglades Club. "He thinks dancing, eats dancing, dreams dancing—at night he'll be moving his feet in bed, and I'll have to kick him." [5] On the other hand Willie could never understand why Florence did not feel exactly the same way.

The Four Covans consisted of the Covan brothers, Willie and Dewey, and their wives. By 1927, after working with Lionel Hampton at the Sebastian Club in Los Angeles, the act jumped from the Orpheum to the Keith circuit and the Palace Theater in New York City. "*The Four Covans* were headliners in any league," says Pete Nugent, "and Willie was the star." [6]

Covan says that the secret of their success was "pace—all four of us never left the stage, we just kept pouring it on." [7]

The act opened with jazz dancing—no tap—by all four to a very fast "Nagasaki" that suddenly slowed to a graceful tap-waltz to "Russian Lullaby." The contrast was highly effective. Then came Covan's first solo, as the others fell back and clapped, building up through three-and-a-half choruses of the Buck and Wing to a medium-tempo "Rose Room." "Willie loved to tap best of all," says U. S. Thompson, "and nobody could beat him at it then." [8]

Toward the end of Covan's solo, the band cut to half tempo, and he topped it all with some breathtaking acrobatics: "some Rolls and Wings I worked out and a couple of double twists." This was followed by the quartet performing a precision tap ensemble with toy drums and Cossack hats, a tricky regimental drill to "Parade of the Wooden Soldiers," in which they danced together as one man, while the audience marveled and relaxed once more.

Then came some rousing kazotskys, to stop time, in unison. The finale was a challenge dance—each dancer soloing in turn—until Willie's second solo, which ended with sensational acrobatics and wrapped up the act. *The Four Covans* had something for everyone. "According to *Variety,*" says Florence Covan, "we wiped up more stages than anybody in show business."

Willie Covan claims—and nobody contradicts him—that he invented the Double Around the World, *no hands.* Akin to Russian dancing—from which it was probably adapted—the Double Around the World is a pretzel-like floor step, starting with a stride, but it is particularly difficult: Sitting on the stage, the dancer rotates his legs alternately beneath him, as he takes turns supporting himself with each hand and raising the other to wave as a leg passes under it. (In 1964, in a film entitled *Only One New York,* dancers at a Ukranian wedding were shown executing endless Around the Worlds—using both hands.)

"I was playing a matinee in Chicago in 1917, the floor was slick, and the band was racing, while I was trying to do a Double Around the World," says Covan. "I sort of lost my balance and got going too fast, and when I came off, my brother said, 'You were doing it no hands,' and I said, 'It can't be done no hands.'

"That evening at 31st Street and State, the corner where all the dancers used to hang out, my brother announced that I could do a step nobody else could do—a Double Around the World *no hands*—and bet $20 on it before I could stop him. So I had to try it right on the sidewalk and ruined a brand-new $65 suit, almost cut my pants off at the knees getting started, and won twenty bucks. It wasn't worth it."

For many years Willie Covan has been in Hollywood giving the stars private dancing lessons. Eleanor Powell recommended him to MGM, and at one time or another he has coached Signe Hasso, Polly Bergen, Elaine Stewart, Marilyn Maxwell, Pier Angeli, Vera Ellen, Jeanette McDonald, Robert Taylor, Mickey Rooney, Kirk Douglas, Gregory Peck, Shirley Temple (when she was eleven), Mary Tyler Moore, and Dick Van Dyke. His first pupil was Mae West, who encouraged him to open a studio; one of his last, Bobby Burgess, who taps on the Lawrence Welk TV show. He has never received any film credits.

When we phoned for an interview in 1960, he was coaching Debbie Reynolds and told us that he had one afternoon free in the next two months. In spite of his pioneering role as an acrobatic dancer, Covan does not care much for acrobatics. "That acrobatic stuff isn't real dancing," he says. "Tap is the real dance of the U.S.A."

By the mid-twenties another perilous stunt was beginning to circulate: the split. From a standing position, and usually in the middle of another step, the dancer drops suddenly—or by rhythmic degrees—*not* to a sitting position but rather to a front-and-back straddle, hitting the knee and "resting" on the inside of his thighs. "You need to develop a spread," says Cholly Atkins.[9] Splits look, and frequently are, excruciatingly painful, although sponge-rubber padding is used to cushion the shock (Covan wore knee pads), and the fall can be partially broken with the ankles, calves, and thighs.

Admirers of Louis Armstrong often witnessed a bone-shattering split during the forties and fifties, executed by his popular and overweight vocalist, Velma Middleton. With more courage than prudence, she usually crashed into a split at the end of her act. No doubt about it—the audience was always shaken and generally impressed. Getting up posed a problem. She solved it by considering her act over when she hit the floor, and scrambling to her feet after the spotlight died.

The split is like a knee-drop, carried to its most damaging extreme, and rising from it rhythmically is very difficult. All a performer has to do—his legs are out on a horizontal, pointing in opposite directions—is to rise, pulling his feet smoothly together.

The split probably came from early ballet, diluted past recognition in vaudeville. (Some think it originated among circus acrobats.) Writing about the high-kicking craze in 1894, with Charlotte Greenwood, Joe Laurie, Jr., observes that with the high kicks "came the splits and different forms of legomania that lasted for about four years and then gradually settled down to a standard form of vaudeville dancing." [10] During the nineties, however, a split consisted of a gentle sinking to a sitting position. In the heat of competition vernacular dancers had to make the split more dramatic.

"If I'd had any sense at all," says Joe Peterson who still has water on the knee, "I'd never have done a split." [11] Peterson organized one of the first trios, *The Three Browns,* who specialized in acrobatic stunts. They opened at the Plantation Club in Chicago in 1923, played the Balaban and Katz circuit out to the West Coast and back, and joined Duke Ellington at the Kentucky Club in New York.

"We did everything," says Joe drily, "eccentric, tap, the Soft Shoe, and acrobatic. Reuben Brown tapped, Russell Brown worked up a special knee-drop, and I had my own Around the World and a *real* split—I didn't fake it by doubling one leg under me." (Doubling a leg is cheating; the result is a "jive" split and even more dangerous.) Because of their strenuous acrobatics, *The Three Browns* qualified as a flash act—it lasted six minutes—and they maintained a pace that killed the act in three years and permanently lamed Peterson.

By the thirties most of the up-and-coming tap trios were featuring at least one member who specialized in the new acrobatics. The *Three Little Words,* an act that set a record for durability, worked from 1927 to 1942. (The billing came from the then-current song hit.) The team was composed of Charles Blackstone, Billy Yates (a fine tap dancer), and little Joe Jones, who began his career as one of the dancing wards of the Whitman sisters.

The *Three Little Words* opened with a mild soft-shoe ensemble, and then, just before the audience began to get bored, exploded into a frantic challenge dance to the tune of "Bugle Blues" for the rest of the act. Anything could happen, including eccentric acrobatics, as each member of the trio tried to top the next.

The climax of the act, according to Jones, who has the nervous energy of a lightning bug and a competitive spirit unafflicted by false modesty, occurs when he climbs up the wall and does a back-flip into a split and then bounces up on his feet again.

"I did work like 'Nias Berry," [12] says Jones breathlessly, comparing himself with the most legendary of all flash dancers [see Chapter 34]. In any case, a back-flip into a split—with or without hands—is a formidable stunt: It is an *air* step, leading into the split with a back somersault and thus prolonging the fall and increasing the distance uncontrolled by contact with the stage, as well as the impact upon landing. The split had come a long way from the mild vaudeville version of the 1890's.

In the depths of the Depression, the *Three Little Words* helped Dickie Wells open his night club in Harlem, where they later popularized the Shim Sham. "We sat at a table pretending to be customers—*that* was the best part—until a real sucker appeared," says Jones. "The boss would take the order and signal me, I'd run out and get the booze on credit, come back and wait for the customer to pay his check—meanwhile putting on our act—and then run out and pay the bootlegger."

Another acrobatic-tap act, *Tip Tap and Toe*, started in the late twenties and set the pace for several years. "That was one of the acts we had to compete with," says Pete Nugent, "and they were real good." The original members were Sammy Green, Teddy Frazier, and Raymond Winfield (for a while the much-admired Freddie James joined the group).

Tip Tap and Toe had been employed by Eddie Cantor at the Palace and played the Paramount Theater on their own, but the peak of their career arrived when George White "discovered" them in 1936 and put them in the *Scandals*. They were among the first to line up and tap the same sounds using different steps or the same steps making different sounds—and build on that.

Raymond Winfield contributed the act's innovation: slides—which later became very popular. Working on a small oval platform (like the old skating act on a pedestal), Winfield slid forward, backward, sideways, and around, as if he had buttered feet on a hot stove. "You've got to have perfect control of the body," says Cholly Atkins, "particularly the shoulders and the arms, although few people even notice they're being used." His slides were a miracle of gravity-defying balance with a maximum of activity on a minimum of space.

Another act, *The Four Bobs*, "sat in a Philadelphia theater all day," in the words of Honi Coles, "until they copied the entire performance of *Tip Tap and Toe*, including the mistakes." [13] Another dancer, Prince Spencer, who joined *The Four Step Brothers*, took Winfield's slides and developed them further until they became an outstanding part of the act.

Perhaps *Son and Sonny* (Roland James and Sonny Montgomery) illustrate the extremes at which acrobatic-tap arrived before the climax was capped by the top flash acts. Taught acrobatic stunts by his father, Sonny grew up in Chicago idolizing *The Berry Brothers* and the team began its career in the mid-thirties with Ben Bernie at the College Inn. When they arrived in New York in 1939, the act lasted only a strenuous and exhausting *four minutes.*

It was, however, spectacular. After a frantic three-or-more minutes of everything that acrobatic tap had evolved, *Son and Sonny,* at the climax, executed no-hand flips into splits—in the new style, that is, suddenly, without an anticipatory gesture. From a standing position they leaped forward, up, and over in a front somersault, without using hands (this is straight acrobatics) and then down sharply on the inside of the legs and thighs, feet and legs wide apart in a front-and-back straddle, into a "sitting" position. From here, they snapped back up, on the beat, and into another and another (this is flash).

Working at Robert's Show Lounge in Chicago in 1960, Sonny Montgomery, who is built like a hefty weightlifter, was not performing no-hand flips into splits anymore—he uses his hands and takes his time coming back upright. "I've quit those," he acknowledges. "Life's too short." [14]

For sheer durability, diversity, and flexibility, the thirty-eight year and continuing (in 1966) career of *The Four Step Brothers* takes the prize and illustrates the changing fashions among acrobatic-tap acts. They established themselves in the late 1920's as a trio, appearing with Duke Ellington at the Cotton Club. "Duke composed 'The Mystery Song' for us," [15] says Al Williams, the leader of the act, and Duke Ellington concurs, eyebrows raised in astonished recollection, as he adds, "I wrote it in 1928." [16]

By the 1930's *The Four Step Brothers* became a quartet and anticipated the trend to song, and later, acrobatics. They consistently incorporated comedy and latest developments in vernacular dance. At one time or another rhythm tap, Snake Hips, five-tap Wings, slides, Afro-Cuban movements, and the entire repertory of new acrobatics formed a part of the act. Like the Ellington band, which took advantage of the special skills of newcomers without changing its basic style, *The Four Step Brothers* retained a similar routine while featuring a series of dancers with different specialties. "We made fewer changes than most acts," says Williams, "and we tried to make every change an improvement."

In addition to the two regulars, Al Williams and Maceo Anderson, several fine dancers passed through the ranks, from Red Gordon, Sherman Robinson, Sylvester Johnson, and Freddie James, to Prince Spencer and Flash McDonald, who were still with the act in 1966.

Maceo Anderson dates a change in the unwritten dancer's code around 1930. "In the twenties it was a point of honor to change another guy's steps before you used them," he says, "but by the thirties the steal-and-change was out and the direct-steal was in. Guys would take your whole routine step by step and laugh in your face." [17]

The Four Step Brothers had a partial answer to this, a routine which became their trademark: the challenge dance. Each dancer solos in turn while the rest clap, "just like kids on the sidewalk," and since each varied his solos, the routine was never the same and therefore difficult to copy.

In 1936 they ran into trouble. They asked their manager, Irving Mills, for a long-overdue raise. "We were green kids and had been doing terrific business," says Williams, "so one night after warning Mills, we just didn't show up." Mills had them blackballed from coast to coast. "Nobody would hire us," says Maceo, "and we had to pick up odd jobs around Chicago to keep from starving." After a year or so MCA took them on, and they began to eat regularly.

In 1939 Freddie James joined the act and became its star for four years, while bit by bit *The Four Step Brothers* gravitated to comedy. The chubby and irrepressible Maceo became the clown of the act, heckling the rest of the dancers unmercifully and getting away with it because he and the audience enjoyed it. The other dancers were not so sure. On days when he didn't feel like dancing, Maceo faked so skillfully that the audience seemed to like it better than the real thing. "When Maceo does a split nowadays," said Fayard Nicholas in 1965, "he only goes down on his knees and Al helps him up." [18]

In the forties dance acts no longer needed singers. Prince Spencer joined *The Four Step Brothers in* 1941, replacing Sylvester Johnson and introducing slides. In 1943, after Freddie James became ill, Flash McDonald took his place, bringing with him the latest poses and gestures assimilated from Afro-Cuban dancing. These were the last changes in personnel, and in 1966 *The Four Step Brothers* were one of the few acrobatic-tap acts still employed.

The act that forms the transition into the flash acts, because except for its variety, it was almost a flash act itself, is *Pops and Louis*. Albert "Pops" Whitman had been dancing since 1923, when at the age of four, he performed in a miniature tuxedo with *The Whitman Sisters* on T.O.B.A. (Alice Whitman was his mother and Aaron Palmer his father.)

By the 1940's Pops Whitman and the last in a series of partners, Louis Williams, graduated from T.O.B.A. and went to work with the big swing bands: Lunceford, Goodman, Ellington, and so on, with a later tour of Europe and a Hollywood film, *Change of Heart*. Louis Williams was an eccentric dancer with a fine personality who could do a bit of everything—a reasonably accurate description of the act.

Pops and Louis never gave the same show twice. They improvised, with Louis coming up with whatever struck his fancy, and Pops topping it on the spur of the moment. "We were a little different from *The Nicholas Brothers* and *The Berry Brothers*, who were dancing at the same time," says Louis Williams. "We had a sort of *ad lib* song-and-dance act, singing duets together and doing whatever we felt like." [19]

Furthermore, they played instruments. "For a while they even worked as mascots for an NBC 'Kiddie Hour,'" says Leroy Myers, "singing and clowning around without hardly dancing." [20] They were a highly-talented pair of young showmen, who enjoyed every moment on stage.

The high point of the act was Pops's acrobatics. "I'm sure he invented a lot of flash steps," says "Baby" Laurence Jackson, "a front-and-back spin that looked effortless but was almost impossible—I tried it—and a Russian twist that was indescribable: He started spinning like a top and went down into a squat and up, over and over, and each time he came up, he was facing the audience with his ankles locked. In my book he was the greatest of all the acrobatic tap dancers." [21]

"Pops was a little king," says Louis Williams, remembering the old days with misty eyes, "he was born in a trunk, and he had all the savvy of show business at his fingertips. He was my inspiration. When I saw him, I saw all the dancing there was." And then Williams adds, almost gratefully, "Pops was proud of my talent, too." By 1950, at the age of thirty-one, Pops Whitman was dead.

Acrobatics had come to stay, hastening the final collapse of the tap acts. "When I came back from World War II, I found out that you didn't have to *dance* any more," says Pete Nugent. "I remember when dancers took pride in their steps and looked at you in surprise if you missed a tap, but now. . . ."

34 The Flash Acts

JUST ONCE in their meteoric careers *The Nicholas Brothers* and *The Berry Brothers* fought for supremacy on the same bill. The legendary confrontation took place at New York City's downtown Cotton Club—later becoming the Latin Quarter—in 1938. Dancers still remember that floor show as the greatest of Cotton Club productions.

Herman Stark was in charge of programming. "He also happened to be the personal manager of our rivals, the Nicholas brothers," says Warren Berry without rancor, "and he put us on last so we had to top the preceding acts or die." [1] When Ananias, the oldest of the three Berry brothers, approached Mr. Stark, wondering aloud about the order of events, Stark cut him short with "*You're* the Berry brothers, let's see what you can *really* do."

Fresh from a successful appearance in *The Big Broadcast of 1936* and a tour abroad, the Nicholas brothers already had a large following. They were the stars and they appeared all through the show, singing, tapping, and dancing with the Lindy Hoppers and the chorus girls. "We were real cool," says Fayard Nicholas. "We figured, let the Berry brothers prove themselves." [2]

The Nicholas brothers were scheduled near the middle of an overlong production and followed by a special routine backed by the chorus line in which they sang and danced one of the show's hits, "The Boogie-Woogie Dance." "Everybody in the audience loved the Nicholas brothers," says Al Minns, one of the Lindy Hoppers in the show. "Everything they did—singing, tapping, acrobatic dancing—was beautiful." [3]

Late in the evening the Berry brothers got their chance. Cab Calloway's orchestra was playing on an elevated platform at the rear of the stage.

About twelve feet above and behind this band platform was a balcony with stairs on each side where semi-draped chorus girls posed.

Ananias had a plan. Just before the end of their act Ananias and Jimmy Berry jumped up on the band platform and then sprinted further up the stairs (followed by spotlights) and took a running leap out, over the heads of the musicians—twelve feet through the air—and down to the stage, landing with their legs apart in a body-rending split on both sides of Warren Berry, who had just snapped out of a twisting back somersault into a split of his own at stage center—*all on the last note of the music.*

The grand finale with all the acts made little impression because it was drowned out by the applause of an audience, which could not stop screaming. "*That* was a flash act," says Pete Nugent, slipping into the role of spokesman for all Negro dancers anywhere, "the greatest flash act we ever had." [4]

The older Berry brothers, Ananias and Jimmy, were born in New Orleans, and Warren, the youngest, was born in Denver, as the family made its way to the West Coast. They landed in Hollywood on their gifted feet. Ananias and Jimmy entered an amateur contest around 1925 billed as "A Miniature Williams and Walker"—a clue to their future style—and Jimmy, who danced at parties given by Mary Pickford and Clara Bow, got a job with *Our Gang* comedies.

"Mother encouraged us from the first," says Warren quietly, "but Father, who was very religious, didn't care for show business." A family friend, eccentric dancer Henri Wessels, was their only teacher. "We just practiced at home until things began to hum, and then Father changed his mind. He was a great cakewalker, and he taught us the old-time, prancing Strut. He finally became our agent and did all the booking."

In 1929, when Ananias was seventeen and Jimmy fifteen, they opened as a duo with Duke Ellington at the Cotton Club in Harlem and stayed off and on for four-and-a-half years. Their fame soon spread. Between shows at the Cotton Club they went abroad with *Blackbirds* and appeared at the opening of Radio City Music Hall in 1932. When Ananias married trumpet-playing Valaida Snow in 1934 and left the act, Jimmy taught Ananias's routine to Warren, and *The Berry Brothers* still carried on. A year or so later, Ananias came back and for ten years all three danced together. In Hollywood, they made *You're My Everything* with Dan Dailey and choreographer Nick Castle. "I'd never seen splits before," says Castle. "They started it." [5]

The act was extremely short—four-and-a-half minutes—and consisted of two parts: first a strut and then a cane sequence. "If you drop a half dollar," wrote a dazzled Chicago critic, "don't reach down to pick it up or you'll miss them." [6] Every moment was strictly timed. "The secret of our act was tempo and precision," says Warren. "We did everything in syncopation." He might have mentioned dynamics, too, for the act sparkled with sudden contrasts between posed immobility and flashing action. (The expression for such contrasts, popular at the time, was "freeze and melt.")[7]

The first, or strut, sequence lasted about two minutes, using one thirty-two-bar chorus of "Papa Dee Da Da" for accompaniment. As the curtain parts, Ananias steps out in top hat and tails, a cane under one arm, and struts with aching elegance across the stage, inserting high kicks and "freezing and melting" like frames in a film strip.

The Strut of Ananias Berry, with his stiffly arched back, shoulder-high knee work, and toe-pointed kicks into space, has never been equaled. Dancers agree that, compared to him, the most flamboyant baton-twirling drum-major merely shuffles.

Then Jimmy enters singing while Ananias "poses," that is strikes a series of rocking "stills," concluding with a double turn to a sudden stop, fists on chest and legs snapped closed. Ananias joins Jimmy and they strut together, starting and stopping with lightning contrast. The contrasts fade out as the action speeds up with six bars of high kicks—and then an explosion of acrobatics.

As Warren, his eyes narrowed, remembering, describes it: " 'Nias does a cross step, turns, and goes into a split—throwing his cane to Jimmy as he glides back up—then dives into a somersault, a split, a turn, another split (in that order), and floats up just in time to turn around and catch the cane that Jimmy has thrown at his back during the last split." This takes only a few seconds.

Ananias then jumps over his cane into a spin. "Ananias didn't need to spot his spins—you know, stare at the same place each time around," says Honi Coles. "He had a phenomenal sense of balance." [8] He then falls into a split, coming up like a steel spring with his top hat in his hand and bowing in unison with Jimmy, who has just come out of his own split. They exit strutting, Jimmy backwards and Ananias forward, bending away from each other.

The second, or cane, sequence took a little over two minutes and combined tossing and catching canes with a riot of acrobatics. At one point, having tossed their canes into the wings, Warren jumps around Jimmy's neck, his legs locked, while Jimmy winds into a spin and then a split—the two boys glued together. At another " 'Nias takes a flying somersault over us both and drops into a split at the same instant that we drop into our own splits," says Warren, "and as 'Nias pulls up, he and Jimmy do a somersault, facing me, and we all take a bow together on the last note of the music."

In 1951 Ananias, slowed down by injuries, died suddenly at the age of thirty-nine, and the act fell apart.

The Berry Brothers, according to dance critic Roger Pryor Dodge, head the list of all jazz dancers. "The whole act was built around the extraordinary ability of Ananias Berry . . . his strut itself was marvelous." [9]

Dancer Cholly Atkins agrees and adds, "Jimmy was a showboat, selling what Ananias was doing, and Warren was a lesser copy of Ananias." [10] By some miracle they fused two widely separate eras of Afro-American vernacular dance, the Strut of the Cakewalk and the acrobatics of the flash acts.

The Nicholas brothers grew up in Philadelphia. "My parents were from New Orleans originally," says Fayard, "but by the time I was born, Dad played drums, and Mother, piano, in their own pit band at the Standard Theater in Philadelphia." At the age of three Fayard was planted in the front row of the theater while his parents worked. "I'd be bouncing up and down in my seat, digging all the comedians, singers, and dancers." Slim and gentle, Fayard still bounces with excess energy as he talks.

By the time he was ten, Fayard had seen most of the great Negro acts, especially the dancers—"I loved Alice Whitman, Willie Bryant, and Bill Robinson"—and had watched the acrobats at the circus. "They fascinated me." As early as he can remember, he was doing splits over the hedges in the neighborhood and clowning with crazy hand gestures for the kids in the gang. "I tried to do everything easy and graceful." Baby brother Harold, six years younger, watched and imitated. "But as soon as he learned to dance," says Fayard, "Harold was full of his own ideas."

Their success in Philadelphia was immediate. They were hired for a radio program—the *Horn and Hardart Kiddie Hour*—and then by local theaters, the Standard and the Pearl. "We had worked out three routines," says Fayard. Their reputation traveled fast, and while they were at the Pearl Theater, Frank Schiffman came down from New York and signed them for Harlem's Lafayette Theater. From the Lafayette they went into the Cotton Club on April 10, 1932, where they stayed for the best part of two years.

When *The Nicholas Brothers* opened at the Cotton Club, Harold was eight, and Fayard, fourteen years old. Dressed immaculately in top hats and tails, they played at being sophisticated in a way that delighted everyone, and they seemed to radiate astonished joy at being treated like grown-ups. Harold twinkled cherubically—"he was so cute the ladies didn't notice what he was doing," says dancer Leon James. "They just wanted to mother him" [11]—and Fayard shone with adolescent urbanity.

The two children strolled on stage and sang a song—Harold had a good soprano voice—and then took turns tapping. Their steps combined a little of everything put together with unifying punch and elegance. "I didn't know the Time Step then," says Fayard, "so we skipped it." He was one of the first to employ dramatic arm-and-hand gestures, which his father encouraged, contrasting effectively with his air of precocious sophistication. Nick Castle ranks Fayard as having "the most beautiful hands in show business," with Fred Astaire second, and Buddy Ebsen third.

Separately, then together, the Nicholas brothers slipped swiftly into a series of spins, twists, flips, and tasty taps, to the accompaniment of "Bugle Call Rag." It was as if a young Fred Astaire and his still younger brother had gone unaccountably acrobatic. As an encore Harold sang another song, while Fayard, still dancing, conducted the orchestra dramatically. "I always felt that Fayard exaggerated everything," says dancer Norma Miller, "but beautifully." [12]

During their two-year stay at the Cotton Club, they worked with the orchestras of Cab Calloway, Lucky Millinder, Jimmie Lunceford, and Duke Ellington. "I like Duke best," says Fayard. "His music makes you feel like you're floating."

Their abundant charm and undeniable talent made them an overwhelming success. Although Fayard was the better dancer, Harold, who did imitations of Cab Calloway and Louis Armstrong, received more attention. He was compared to Bill Robinson by Danton Walker in the *News* (the highest praise a critic could bestow), although there was little similarity in their dancing. During their first year at the Cotton Club the Nicholas brothers made their first movie short: *Pie Pie Blackbird,* with Eubie Blake and his orchestra.

Then the pace began to accelerate. From the Cotton Club they went to Hollywood in 1934 to make *Kid Millions* with Eddie Cantor. "We did our number just before the finale," recalls Fayard. Back to the Cotton Club again, out to Hollywood for *The Big Broadcast of 1936,* and on to Broadway in the Ziegfeld *Follies.* Their act in the *Follies* stopped the show so consistently that Fanny Brice, who followed in a skit with Judy Canova, was forced to fall back regularly on an *ad lib* at the first opportunity: "Do you think we can talk now?" It made the audience laugh and then quiet down.

The next job was a tour of England with *Blackbirds.* "Although they never had a lesson, the boys saw real ballet in London," says their mother, Mrs. Ulysses Nicholas proudly, "and whatever they saw, they could do." [13] Buddy Bradley, who choreographed the show, agrees that the brothers were very impressed by ballet: "I think they absorbed quite a bit of it." [14]

Back at the downtown Cotton Club in 1938, competing for the one and only time with the Berry brothers, who were doubling at Radio City, the Nicholas brothers were also doubling in the Broadway musical, *Babes in Arms,* with Mitzi Green. It was a high point in their careers, for George Balanchine, the celebrated ballet master, was choreographer of the show and they learned some new stunts.

"Mr. Balanchine watched us practicing for a long time and then got an idea—he *told* us, he didn't *show* us," says Fayard. "There were eight chorus girls bending over, and I started out running, doing cartwheels and flips and leaping over one, then two, and finally all eight girls and landing in a split. Then the girls lined up with their legs apart, and Harold slid into a split beneath all of them from the rear and snapped back up as he came out in front. We did it on each side of the stage." Many people assumed that the Nicholas brothers were trained ballet dancers.

Returning to Hollywood in 1940, the Nicholas brothers worked with dancer-choreographer Nick Castle, who has a strong feeling for jazz. For the first time, two years after their battle with the Berrys, they tried taking ten-foot leaps into splits. The film was *Down Argentina Way.* "Nick was glad to work with us because, up 'til then, he had only coached starlets." It was Castle who thought up their most difficult stunt (an idea borrowed in part from *The Mosconi Brothers*). "He had us take a long run," says Fayard, "climb up a wall for two full steps, and backflip, no hands, into a split, bouncing up from the split on the beat. We're the only ones who could do it, and we don't do it any more." Audiences in the darkened theater often broke into loud applause at this point in the film.

In *The Great American Broadcast* (1941) they danced on suitcases while *The Ink Spots,* dressed as redcaps, sang "Alabamy Bound," and then they jumped through the window of a moving train as the song ended, turning around to wave goodbye. ("That was a rush job that was put together, rehearsed, and filmed in two days.")

In *Sun Valley Serenade* (1941) they performed on and off the platform of a Pullman car in the "Chattanooga Choo Choo" number. "Nick Castle did a fine job with them at M.G.M.," says Al Williams. "They had good spots, and unlike the Berry brothers, appeared at their best in the movies."[15] In 1948 they appeared in *The Pirate,* which starred Judy Garland and Gene Kelly. "We had to tone down for him," says Fayard, "although he told somebody that I was the only dancer who danced like him."

The Nicholas Brothers alternated between night clubs, concerts, Broadway shows, Hollywood, and a series of long tours of South America, Africa, and Europe. "We've danced everything but opera," says Fayard, who has also done "modern" dance in a Los Angeles repertory theater, "all over the world." From 1958 to 1964 they were separated. Harold remained in Paris while Fayard returned to the United States and toured Mexico as a single. Back together in 1964, they played Las Vegas and later appeared many times on TV: *Hollywood Palace,* the *Bell Telephone Hour,* and the *Sammy Davis Show.* They were featured in Bob Hope's Christmas show for the troops in Vietnam in 1965.

The relative merits of the Nicholas and Berry brothers have been endlessly debated. Dancers agree that both were superb. If your taste runs to tap, you prefer *The Nicholas Brothers.* If you incline to the superdramatic, you elect *The Berry Brothers.* "The Nicholas brothers sang, tapped, and did acrobatics," says Cholly Atkins. "They were the best all-around talent. The Berry brothers did not tap, and their singing was only fair, but they were the greatest flash act of them all."

A technical detail in the execution of the split helps to explain why *The Nicholas Brothers* long outlasted *The Berry Brothers.* "A split should be executed with one leg in front and the other in back, as in ballet," says Atkins, "*not* with one leg doubled up underneath on one side—that's a jive split and it can cause serious injury."

The Nicholas brothers did their splits correctly—ballet style, while the Berry brothers did "jive" splits. "We wore rubber pads that protected our knees and legs," says Warren Berry, "but our hips and backs got hurt."

"They say Ananias had a corn right on his buttocks," says Fayard, "where he hit every time he did a split."

What did the flash acts contribute to vernacular dance? In ballet the movements are entirely choreographed; among straight acrobatic teams, the routines are set—the acrobats line up and bow after each stunt before getting ready for the next. The flash acts blow these customs sky high. They spice their routines with *ad lib* acrobatics. Without any warning or apparent preparation, they insert a variety of floor and air steps—a spin or flip or knee-drop or split—in the midst of a regular routine, and then, without a moment's hesitation, go back to the routine.

Flash dancers *compress* acrobatics and jazz dance together, creating a shock effect. By so doing, they communicate a feeling of desperate sophistication, a calculated impulse of *carpe diem,* reflecting a hot defiance that makes the rebellious movements of the Charleston seem low-key. This style of dancing evolved with the Depression and perhaps mirrors something of its mood.

Still, fashions were changing, and the demand for dance teams dying, although to this day, those that appear on TV guest shots are predominantly flash acts. Jazz music became respectable, but the dancing that went with it got lost. Nobody needed dancing that swung in the jazz sense, least of all ballet-inspired musical comedy and television.

PART NINE

The Class Acts

35 The Original Stylists

THE CLASS ACTS, among other things, were an expression of the Negroes' drive toward equality and respectability. Imitating and embellishing the formal elegance of the more sophisticated white acts, they ran headlong into an old stereotype: a Negro performer had always been an overdressed dandy or a shiftless plantation hand. Bit by bit they refuted the stereotype, first as individuals and then as teams, taking this characteristic here and that quality there and blending them into a dignified combination. Tap dance died before the example of the class acts could be strongly felt.

The standard class act generally included a soft-shoe in slow tempo with light taps, frequently the high point of the act. It traces back to minstrel days, when it was known as song-and-dance, and evolved from the more graceful motions of the Virginia Essence. Precisely because it stressed elegance, the Soft Shoe was adopted by the evolving class acts and became the featured routine.

The acknowledged master of the Soft Shoe was minstrel man George Primrose (see Chapter 7). For forty years or more, having begun his career in Detroit in the late eighteen-sixties, Primrose was the star dancer with his own and other minstrel companies. One of the few who transcended all ethnic barriers, he influenced white and Negro dancers alike, establishing "picture" dancing ("Every motion as pretty as a picture!") as a fine art.

The pioneering team *Johnson and Dean* was perhaps the first to break ground for the class acts. They were "the first to really do the professional stage cakewalk," [1] according to Joe Laurie, Jr. Acclaimed as "the originators of high-class Negro show business," *Johnson and Dean* established the roles of the genteel Negro couple on the American stage—the courtly gentleman and the gracious lady.

Charles Johnson attributed his success (in an interview in *Ebony* many years later [2]) to the inspiring stories that his mother, who had been a slave, told him: The moral was always "Be a real gentleman," and that became one of his goals. Born soon after Primrose started his career, Johnson joined *The Creole Show* when it came through St. Louis in 1889, and four years later married one of the chorus girls, Dora (Babbige) Dean. With the help of J. Leubrie Hill (see Chapter 17), they soon put together an act of their own.

The act set many records. According to Johnson he introduced the Soft Shoe in 1891, presented the Cakewalk on Broadway in 1895 (three years before *Williams and Walker* made their first hit at Koster and Bials), and wore full evening dress—top hat and tails (in several colors)—with a monocle, gloves, and cane, on the Keith circuit in 1897. When the *Ebony* interviewer questioned him about Fred Astaire, Johnson described him gently but firmly as "a sort of imitator."

Johnson and Dean sold themselves to audiences through their well-dressed elegance and impressive personalities. Johnson was not a tap dancer. He was a strutter in the cakewalk tradition and an eccentric dancer who employed legomania, a rhythmic twisting and turning of the legs. Neither of them could sing—they "talked" their songs, while Johnson inserted an occasional dance and Dora "posed."

Dora Dean had a stunning, plump figure and was the first Negro woman to wear thousand-dollar costumes on the stage. (A cigarette company obtained permission to print her picture on a card as "The Sweet Caporal Girl" and enclose it in packages of cigarettes.) A popular song of the day—written in her honor—asked "Have you met Miss Dora Dean, prettiest girl you've ever seen?" On tours abroad, according to dancers in the company, she had the crowned heads of Europe literally at her feet.

"Miss Dean had a fabulous personality," says Rufus Greenlee, who along with his partner Thaddeus Drayton, joined Johnson and Dean on a tour of fourteen European countries in 1913. "Whenever she encouraged us, it made us feel two feet taller." [3] On this tour the act carried "the first jazz band to play Europe," according to Drayton, "with drummer Peggie Holland and pianist Kid Coles—they created a sensation." [4] Johnson and Dean had their share of marital squabbles, and except for later "special appearances," broke up at the start of World War I. Their last performance together was a "comeback" at Connie's Inn in 1936.

In 1954 Charles Johnson, for many years a widower, was living alone in Minneapolis, visiting the public library on Friday nights and reading anything he could find on show business. He still wore a monocle, but he had to supplement it with a magnifying glass. "I always like to keep up with the news," [5] he told us. Although past eighty, he held himself stiffly erect and spoke with quiet formality. He died a few years later. "Charlie

Johnson," says Thaddeus Drayton, whose style of dancing was greatly influenced by Johnson, "was one of nature's noblemen."

The battle for dignity implicit in the class acts was first blended with vernacular dance before a different audience and in a different world—T.O.B.A. (the Negro circuit of the South). Other acts, like *Chappelle and Stinnette,* who sang but did not dance, and Sadie and Joe Britton, who originated the remark, "You ain't seen nothin' yet," carried on the *Johnson and Dean* tradition in the North. But the elegant Negro *dancer* appeared first on T.O.B.A., solo, several years after *Johnson and Dean,* and he was tailored in a way to impress the most flamboyant tastes of the audience.

On a circuit where eccentric dancers wore tramp costumes, "Ginger" Jack Wiggins broke all the rules and became a T.O.B.A. headliner. Tall and slender, with innate dignity in every step, he wore high-heeled patent-leather shoes and a series of dazzling dinner jackets with rhinestone lapels, and sequins which sparkled as he danced. To the southern folk, Wiggins transformed the stereotype of the "Darky Dandy" into a high-class gentleman.

At the age of six Nipsey Russell saw Wiggins at the Eighty-One Theater in Atlanta and never forgot it. "He was immaculate and had a commanding presence that was a revelation to me," says Russell. "I realized for the first time that a Negro could have *real class* in show business." [6] From then on, although he discovered that he was a better comedian than dancer, Russell was determined to make a living as an entertainer.

Jack Wiggins is credited with inventing, or more accurately, popularizing several complicated steps, among them the Pull It, the Bantam Twist, and the Tango Twist—which indicates the lasting impact that his dancing made upon others. Further, he is generally agreed to have executed his steps with new punch and vigor.

"Towards the end of his act, Wiggins would announce 'I'm going to do it,' and then when the audience yelled back 'What?' he'd say 'I'm going to Pull It,'" Dewey Markham recalls, "and then he'd go into a trick tap, ending with his right leg arched behind him as he leaned backwards—it looked just like something Fred Astaire did long afterward." [7] A diluted version later became standard among chorus lines. The Bantam Twist is an elegant reverse turn.

The Tango Twist is perhaps Jack Wiggins's most famous step: Starting with an undulation of the torso, he executes a floating half-turn with heel-and-toe taps, which achieves a balletlike, and at the same time, swinging effect. It is the epitome of elegance, and many other dancers tried unsuccessfully to copy it. (A lesser dancer named Midnight—of the team *Midnight and Daybreak*—followed Wiggins around and executed an inferior version of his routine on the sidewalk outside theaters where Wiggins was appearing.)

Wiggins, of course, did a soft-shoe, but the snap he put into it helped to bring about a crucial development in the late teens. "Until Jack Wiggins and then Willie Covan came along, the Soft Shoe was pretty much like a clog, and white dancers called it Lancashire style," says Pete Nugent. "Wiggins and Covan were more aggressive, they put in kicks and hand motions —and *they swung harder.*" [8] It was this more rhythmic version of the Soft Shoe that most Negro dancers came to know in the twenties.

Willie Covan, with his early partner Leonard Ruffin, first brought the class act (blended with vernacular dance) to the top circuits in the North, but not without a struggle. Ruffin had the reputation of being the better soft-shoe dancer, but Covan could do a soft-shoe and just about anything else, including a variety of acrobatic steps, with or without taps. Their act was subtitled "Every Move a Picture" and they performed a soft-shoe together, multiplying syncopated accents and giving the dance more flow and propulsion. In this number they anticipated the class-act teams to come, and it earned them billing at the Palace Theater in New York City.

Few Negro dance acts ever reached the Palace, but when they did, they often encountered a frustrating problem. *Covan and Ruffin* were one of the first. Hired because they were outstanding, they found that their talent worked against them. Nobody wanted to follow them, because the audience liked *Covan and Ruffin* so much they booed any attempt to go on with the next act.

So for three days the act was switched around among six or seven other acts. "We never knew until the last minute when we were supposed to go on," [9] says Covan. Each act objected strenuously when it had to follow *Covan and Ruffin.* They were fired by the Palace, promptly hired by the competing Hippodrome, and fired again after a few days—for the same reason. To the management it was the easiest solution.

Other solo dancers helped prepare the way for the class acts by stressing elegance. In the early twenties Maxie McCree had made the knee-drop an aesthetic delight. Another fine dancer, Aaron Palmer, who worked on T.O.B.A. with *The Whitman Sisters* (he married Alice Whitman), danced with an impressively erect posture and tapped with easy elegance. "He could sing, strut, and tap beautifully," [10] says Alice proudly.

A star long before the swing era, Palmer had no use for big band accompaniments. His instructions to the conductor were simple: "Play it so soft I can't hear it." "He dressed even better than Eddie Rector," [11] adds Ida Forsyne.

Of all soft-shoe dancers, Eddie Rector was unquestionably the greatest soloist and the major influence on the class-act teams. Born in Orange, New Jersey, on Christmas Day—he could not remember the year, but it must have been in the late 1890's—Rector came up the hard way, starting as a pick in Mayme Remington's act. "I was fifteen years old, and they dressed me as a girl with a wig and curls, and I danced with one of the boys."[12] In 1914 he played the role of "Red Cap Sam" in an edition of *The Darktown Follies.* Then he and his partner Toots Davis appeared for a time on T.O.B.A. and in carnivals. Later he and his wife, Grace, had an act in vaudeville. "They had real class," says Frank Condos, who remembers seeing them in the early 1920's at Philadelphia's Standard Theater, "and Eddie traveled across the stage like nobody else in the world."[13]

Rector developed his own style, dancing the Cakewalk at Coney Island and the Charleston at Roseland Ballroom in New York (George Raft was one of the champions). Some say Rector invented the Slap step. In those days many tap dancers were proud of the title "hoofer," which meant emphasis on footwork. Rector helped to modify this notion: "I used my hands and arms, loosened up my whole body, and traveled." He impressed Pete Nugent particularly by the way in which he "dovetailed" one step into another. He introduced what became known as stage dancing.

Rector was famous for his Sand dance (his version was one of the few hits in the 1952 revival of *Shuffle Along*) and for his Waltz Clog. "His Clog was better than Pat Rooney's,"[14] says Shorty Snowden—high praise indeed. Billed as "The Boy in Gray," Rector's specialty was a routine he worked out to the song "Bambalina." "At first I wore a bandanna and a full-sleeved white blouse with high-rise pants," says Rector. "Then I switched to top hat and tails—everything pearl gray, even spats. I'd start with a waltz clog and then go into my routine all the way across the stage and back."

Although accounts vary as to when Rector first danced his Bambalina routine, Pete Nugent, who idolized him, says he saw it in *Dixie to Broadway* (1924), which starred Florence Mills. Will Vodery's band occupied one corner at the rear of the stage, while the other corner presented the columns of an old plantation, fronted by a picket fence. In the center a group of stylish ladies sat at tables, drinking tea. Rector entered silently from the side, dressed from top to toe in gray—including a flowing cape. "He looked unbelievably sophisticated," says Nugent.

In strict pantomime Rector requested each of the ladies to dance with him, one by one. They all refused. "It made you want to laugh and cry at the same time," says Nugent. Undismayed, Rector doffed his top hat with a sweeping gesture, as a signal for the orchestra to begin, and went into his Bambalina routine *with an imaginary partner*. "Everybody watched him silently," says Nugent, "and the audience was really moved."

As he traveled, Rector tapped a delicate Time Step—technically, half a triple Time Step on one foot—which he reversed on his return. "He leaned all the way," says Cholly Atkins, "as if he was tilted."[15] The floating—almost shy—grace with which he moved gave it a memorable poignancy.

One of the great teachers of dance routines, Buddy Bradley got his first job in the chorus of a revue at Connie's Inn around 1927, when Rector was the star. "At that time, Eddie was drinking heavily, and we'd have to hold him up and dress him before he went on stage," Bradley recalls, "but the moment he began to dance, he was as straight as anybody. What's more, he did a solid routine that lasted for six full minutes." [16] Rector was Bradley's idol, too.

Rector's routine with his partner Ralph Cooper made an unforgettable impression on Bradley: "They opened together, and then Eddie did his beautiful waltz solo to the tune of 'Wildflower'—no stop-time, just a pretty, flowing clog. After that a military precision-drill to the tune of 'Parade of the Wooden Soldiers,' and finally the Bantam Twist and out." The high point was an exchange of tattoos, a rhythmic counterpoint between the dancers. "No flash stuff," adds Bradley, "just pure and beautiful rhythms." "With Rector the sound of his feet was all-important," says Nick Castle, "and in his spins and turns you could always hear taps." [17]

A few years later, when Bill Robinson was offered $1,000 a week at the Palace, Rector took his place on a tour abroad with *Blackbirds of 1928.* "They kept after me to do the Stair Dance, since I was filling Bo's spot," says Rector, "but I didn't bother, although it was easy enough, and I could do all of Robinson's steps anyway." When the show reached Paris, Rector finally agreed to do it, one of the few times that he copied anyone else's routine.

On his return Rector worked with Duke Ellington at the Cotton Club. "I originated tapping on top of a big drum," he says. Cotton Club producer Dan Healy remembers Rector with admiration: "Eddie worked for me just before he cracked up. He was a great dancer and a dreamer, too. It took me a long time to discover he couldn't read or write." [18] Around 1930, at the Sebastian Club in Los Angeles, Rector played trumpet and led the band just before Louis Armstrong took over. His next jobs, back in New York, were with inferior and short-lived Negro shows including *Hot Rhythm* (1930) and *Yeah Man* (1932), before he was confined to an institution for a number of years. Just why he was locked up is still something of a mystery.

After his recovery he teamed with Ralph Cooper again during the late 1940's and early 1950's. Unfortunately, they were too late—the class acts were dying, and Rector's dancing had lost some of its easy grace. In 1960 Cooper was a disc jockey on a Harlem radio station and too busy to discuss his former partner. Eddie Rector was working as a night watchman. His feet were in bad shape, and he looked tired, but his spirits were high. "I want to do a movie short telling the story of the Buck and Wing, the Soft Shoe, and the Waltz Clog," he told us. "Do you suppose anybody would be interested?" Eddie Rector, a gentle man, died in 1962, unaware that his elegant style of dancing was the greatest single influence on the class acts and had contributed a visual dimension to the aspirations of the Negro.

36 The First Class-Act Team: *Greenlee and Drayton*

BEGINNING IN THE teens and developing rapidly from the early twenties to the late forties, the class acts came to constitute the cream of tap dancing. Unlike flash or acrobatic, Russian or legomania, comedy or Buck dancing—although elements from all these styles were sometimes incorporated—the class acts added a specific quality: grace and elegance.

The true class act consists of two or more dancers—very often three—who perform *precision* dancing (among other things), that is, they execute identical steps together. Dancing in formation, of course, is not rare, but the class acts made it a thing of beauty, combining the unison perfection of the Radio City *Rockettes* with the smoothness of ballroom specialists, and lacing it with taps.

In spite of their acknowledged preeminence within show business, Negro class acts seldom or never played the best white night clubs (Broadway shows hired them occasionally), and by the time they might have gained general recognition and worked their way to the top, nobody wanted tap dancers. They were too much and too early.

The pioneering team in this field was *Greenlee and Drayton.* Rufus Greenlee and Thaddeus Drayton were both born in the South in 1893, came to New York as children of well-to-do families, and decided to be dancers after viewing the same two acts: *Williams and Walker,* and *Coates and Grundy* (*The Watermelon Trust*). They particularly admired the acrobatics of Sherman Coates and the strutting of George Walker.

"We met at Hallie Anderson's dancing school on 53rd Street in New York City," says Teddy Drayton quietly. "Green was already the life of the party, attracting attention as a ballroom dancer." [1] They were taught the Schottische, Waltz, and Two Step, and after class, they learned the rudiments of tap on the sidewalks of 42nd Street. "All the kids wore knickerbockers," says Greenlee, "and met outside and swapped steps." [2]

At that time, Negroes still lived downtown, and the Lafayette Theater did not exist. "When I started dancing in 1906, tap dancing hadn't yet become the rage," says Drayton. "We were doing Russian stuff and eccentric dancing, while that shuffling step they called the Sand was going out of favor because the stagehands got tired of cleaning up the dirt after the dancers."

They were performing in public before they knew it. "We followed Buddy Gilmore and his fife-and-drum corps around," says Greenlee, gesturing with his cigar and forgetting to mention that the corps was composed of girls. "They had dances and cakewalks with real cakes for prizes," explains Drayton, "and to be with the girls we would enter the contests with different partners." Here, their imitation of George Walker's strutting became a social asset.

With a push from gifted parents, Teddy Drayton graduated from choirboy to professional dancer at the age of twelve. "My mother was a fine ballroom dancer, and my father played guitar and tuba with Chris Smith's Quartet—he showed me the first soft-shoe dance I ever saw." Wearing a wig and dressed as a girl, Drayton worked (until his voice began to change) as a pick in a long series of white acts from Gertie Le Clair to Josephine Saxon. When asked whether Gertie Le Clair sang or danced, Drayton smiled: "She just walked across the stage and recited—us kids did all the singing and dancing."

Rufus Greenlee started comparatively late but caught up by sheer determination. His family had reached New York City by way of New Haven, where Yale University is located, and Greenlee, because of his collegiate attire, earned the nickname "Rah! Rah!" At the age of seventeen he worked with Moore's *New Orleans Minstrels* at the 14th Street Theater in New York ("I started as end man"), joined the trio *Rastus Rufus and Apes* at Huber's Museum (King Rastus Brown was one of the trio), and went on tour with a company, *The Georgia Campers.*

Greenlee wanted experience. Between jobs he worked in Greenwald's Beer Tavern at Coney Island earning $22.50 a week. "Two companies, one white and one colored, alternated, each for one hour, and it wasn't minstrel stuff, either," says Greenlee. "They tried the same thing on Broadway in the 1920's." This was in 1909, and Greenlee's greatest admiration was for a lady Buck dancer named Etta Gross. "She was the champion and just as good as Alice Whitman," he declares. "I ought to know because I almost married Alice." He also worked on the same bill with Charlie Chaplin, who was playing his first engagement in the United States. "He wasn't doing that walk then, he saw some colored fellow later and copied him."

Greenlee decided he needed a partner and fastened upon young Teddy Drayton. Drayton was not so sure: "I had been in show business for five years and didn't want to get stuck with an amateur. Then Green went out and landed a job for us, a tour of Europe with a famous act—*Johnson and Dean*—and I changed my mind." It was the beginning of the first class-act *team.*

Working with the well-dressed *Johnson and Dean* act, Greenlee and Drayton had an inspiration—why not dress up, too? "Before we left, we each had a hand-tailored full-dress suit—white tie, tails, and all—made by a tailor on Sixth Avenue for $11.95 apiece," says Drayton. "We also had a monocle, a white flower, white gloves, white socks, and a cane." "Of course," he adds with a sigh, "we couldn't wear spats with a full-dress suit."

The result was a new style. "Before we formed our act, colored teams always consisted of a blackface comedian and a straight man, like *Williams and Walker*," says Greenlee, "but we saw how fine Charlie Johnson dressed, and how well he was received in Europe, and decided right away we wanted a *neat* act—both of us." Unlike Johnson and Dean, Greenlee and Drayton were accomplished dancers; their formal dress went well with their elegant dancing, and indeed, helped to make their dancing even more impressive.

The tour with *Johnson and Dean* lasted well over a year. "Dora and Charlie were married but they never got along too well," says Greenlee, "and when the Archduke was assassinated in 1914 and business slowed down, they separated and went back home to Minneapolis. We stayed in Paris." Greenlee was sure they could take Paris by storm, war or no war. Luckily they had met Ida Forsyne a few months before in St. Petersburg (see Chapter 31). She was at the height of her career as a Russian dancer, and she took care of them.

"I think," says Drayton carefully, "that Ida was a little sweet on Greenlee." When we asked Ida about it, a few days after her eighty-first birthday, she whooped with delight at the memory: "They were so refined and polite and they dressed so well—they just looked wonderful to me." [3] So she got an agent, bought music-books or arrangements, and lent them money until their job at the Moulin Rouge was supposed to start. "Of course," she added reflectively, "Greenlee was money crazy." France declared war before their act opened, and in accordance with government regulations, they sailed sadly for home.

Back in New York, Greenlee took over the publicity. "We spent days walking up and down Broadway, all dressed up and twirling our canes," says Drayton, "and Green asking me questions loudly in different foreign languages." They were rehearsing just as loudly in a centrally located studio when Al Jolson happened to hear them singing "You Great Big Bashful Doll," and, told that they had just arrived from Europe—were they famous foreigners?—sent them to Shapiro and Bernstein, who had them booked by Hugo Morris and Murray File.

"We didn't have our act together, but we said sure we were ready," says

Greenlee. "We rehearsed all night in the basement of the house where we roomed." On the following evening in August 1914 they opened at the Riviera Theater on 97th Street and scored an immediate hit before a white audience. "For nineteen years," states Greenlee complacently, "we never looked back."

The appeal of *Greenlee and Drayton* was new and immense, their upward climb swift and sure. For fourteen consecutive Sunday evenings they played the Winter Garden, where the best white acts appeared, and then went on to Loew's vaudeville circuit. "We ran Vincent Lopez right off the stage at one theater," says Greenlee. E. F. Albee saw them at a police benefit (benefits were carefully covered by talent scouts) and put them on the Keith circuit. Booked solidly thereafter, they commuted between the United States and Europe.

"We played the Palace in New York two or three times a year," says Drayton. "During World War I, Bert Williams, Bill Robinson, and *Greenlee and Drayton* were the only colored dancers to appear there." As the showplace of the Keith circuit, the Palace was the undisputed tops in vaudeville. "When you played the Palace, everybody knew you were the greatest," adds Greenlee. "We were sensational."

They soon put their knowledge of foreign languages to good use. "One night at the Colonial Theater, as we were dancing, Greenlee said to me in German: 'Look at that fellow out there with a bald head' and some of the German musicians in the pit started to laugh." So they tried out their languages at each performance until they found someone in the audience with whom they could carry on a conversation. "We spoke French, German, Russian, Hungarian, Italian, Gaelic, and Yiddish," says Drayton, "and it impressed a lot of people—they thought we had real class."

Their linguistic abilities paid off, too. Every now and then a theater manager called them in to cross-examine them about their languages—especially the Yiddish—and to ask them if it was necessary. Talking acts, it turned out, were paid $100 as a starter, while plain dancing acts were paid from $40 to $80 tops. "Agents were always trying to get us to cut out the talking," says Drayton, "so Greenlee added a lot more and started singing, too."

Greenlee and Drayton were the first real class act I ever saw," says dancer Dewey Weinglass. "It was at the Odeon Theater on 145th Street in 1922, and I was so impressed I just hung around until I could see Drayton and ask him how to do a cartwheel." [4] Drayton was not giving away any secrets: "You learn to do it your own way," he said and Weinglass left, vowing revenge.

He did not have long to wait. A year or so later, Weinglass was on the same bill with *Greenlee and Drayton:* "I went on just ahead of Drayton, and without planning to, it just came to me: I did every one of his steps—

one, two, three, bang—in exact order, and when he came on stage he sure looked worried."

Drayton remembers it well. "I had to change my whole routine on the spur of the moment and do some steps he couldn't do—I was angry at the time, but we're good friends now."

Greenlee and Drayton's act lasted seven minutes and consisted of four numbers. Dressed immaculately, they strolled on stage singing "You Great Big Bashful Doll," promenaded up and down, and concluded on one side of the stage with a sweeping bow, doffing their top hats. ("They were so dicty!" says Ida Forsyne.)

Their first was probably their most famous number: the Virginia Essence (later known as the Soft Shoe) performed in stop time. "We had a special accompaniment, a sort of 'creepy' music to go with our Soft Shoe and give it suspense," says Drayton, "the kind they play in old movies when the villain is creeping up on the heroine."

Just as George Primrose had excelled at a graceful soft-shoe and helped it become known as Picture Dancing, Greenlee and Drayton gave the dance a new impact by performing it together with the utmost precision, while filling the breaks with conversation in various foreign languages.

With the partial exception of Charles Johnson, it was probably the first occasion that any pair of Negroes *not* clad in overalls performed the Soft Shoe on the American stage. It was at this time—and chiefly to describe *Greenlee and Drayton*—that the phrase *class act* came into general use among Negro dancers.

The second number consisted of a song—"The Shiek of Alabam" or "Big Boy"—and an attention-getting trick. While singing, Greenlee nudged Drayton importantly and nodded toward someone in the audience (the lyrics of "Big Boy" lent themselves to this gag), so that soon everyone was turning around to see who it might be. Actually, nobody of importance was in the audience. "They never caught on," says Greenlee.

The third number was a challenge dance, or competition, in which the partners did their various specialties. "I did fast dancing," says Greenlee, "you know: running from one side of the stage to the other and leaping up the walls." He never went in for tapping.

"In his specialties," says Drayton slowly, "I guess you'd call Green a jive dancer—but a good one." (In this context, "jive" usually means *fake.*) Drayton tapped and executed acrobatics.

One of Drayton's specialties, in addition to spins, flips, and splits, was a forward cartwheel—first one hand, then the other, then one foot, then the other—crossing the stage swiftly. ("The Arabs call it a 'tensica' "[5] says acrobat Archie Ware of *The Crackerjacks.*) "Green would run over and grab my hand, just when it looked as if I was going to somersault into the pit," says Drayton.

The act built to a whirlwind climax. "For the fourth and last number we went into our Russian dance—all kinds of Russian steps—at a fast tempo," says Greenlee grandly. "We astounded the Russians with their own steps." At the end they both dropped into Double Around the Worlds at the same instant and finished off with precision kazotskys, kicking their legs out alternately in front of them.

The act was at its peak during the twenties. When *Shuffle Along* opened in 1921, the producers wanted *Greenlee and Drayton* but could not afford them—vaudeville paid more. They starred in another Broadway show, *Liza*, in 1922, however, singing "Lovin' Sam from Alabam" and dancing. They took a cut in salary, but reached a new and influential audience. And in 1923 they helped open the first Cotton Club show uptown.

On their frequent tours abroad Greenlee and Drayton had trouble with orchestral accompaniments. In London they were forced to dance without any music whatever. "The orchestra couldn't get the rhythm right, so we just clapped and patted for each other." (In the forties the Lindy Hoppers faced the same problem at Radio City Music Hall [see Chapter 41].) "You should have heard an Italian orchestra trying to play our special arrangement of 'The Carioca,'" adds Drayton grimly.

When they were on the same program with Bill Robinson at the Holburn Empire Theater, he was having similar trouble. "We had to take him into the dressing room and talk to him like a child," says Drayton. "I told him: 'You were here last night, and you heard how they played *our* music—that's all the better they can do—so don't pull out your gun over here, because even the cops don't carry guns.'"

Greenlee was definitely impatient with the publicity attending Benny Goodman's trip to Russia in 1962. "Why, in 1926 we were in Russia with Sam Wooding's band and played and danced for Stalin." Both Greenlee and Drayton have another grievance: "Even with the prejudice in the old days, there wasn't a vaudeville bill without colored entertainers," Drayton said in 1962, "but now they have disappeared in talkies and television." (With each increase in the coverage of the mass media, it seems that the battle for Negro participation has to be fought all over again.)

As the Depression was setting in around 1930, *Greenlee and Drayton* broke up. "I wanted to come home," says Greenlee, "and Drayton wanted to stay in Paris." By that time the act was no longer imitated by the younger generation in the United States, which had concluded that the parade of foreign languages was corny and the emphasis on Russian dancing old-fashioned. A new style of acrobatics had come in. "We never did flips into splits or knee-drops," says Greenlee.

For six more years Greenlee worked with his wife and then retired to New Haven, where he opened the Monterey Cafe on Dixwell Avenue. He died in New Haven in the summer of 1963. "You'd have thought they were burying the mayor of the city," says Drayton, who went to the funeral. "You know, I really miss Green. He was my best friend for fifty years."

"After we got started," Greenlee once declared, "everybody washed off the burnt cork and tried to do a *neat* act—we paved the way for the class acts." They did more. By combining true elegance with precision dancing, they created a new *genre* and became the first class-act team. In the process, they attained a new degree of acceptance for Negro performers.

37 Pete Nugent and the Class Acts

PETE NUGENT TRAVELS across the stage as if airborne. When he reaches the center, he executes a Tango Twist—a floating half-turn with heel and toe taps—and continues toward the wings. Although performed mainly on tiptoe, the sequence is indisputably manly in appearance and evokes exclamations of delight from the audience. To connoisseurs of tap dance, it is a high point in the performance of one of the greatest class acts: *Pete Peaches and Duke*, "Society's Sepia Sons."

"I used a lot of Eddie Rector's Bambalina routine along with Jack Wiggins's Tango Twist," says Nugent gruffly. "Wiggins was dead and Rector in the hospital, so I got a lot of undeserved credit from younger dancers who had never seen them." [1]

Nugent was in a great tradition. When Big Boy Williams, the actor, first saw him dance in the 1943 production of *This Is the Army*, Williams actually broke down and cried. "Why, this Pete," he sobbed happily, "he dances just as pretty as Georgie Primrose." [2] Williams had seen Primrose in his prime—before Nugent was old enough to walk, let alone dance. The line of descent is clear: Primrose to Wiggins to Rector to Nugent. And that, generally speaking, was the end of that particular line and style.

With personnels changing as frequently as in the jazz orchestras with which they worked, the class acts flourished from the late twenties to the late forties—twenty or more years. They started slowly as the decline of vaudeville became a collapse. In 1919 eighty theaters presented big-time, two-a-day shows; in 1929, only five. [3] Dance acts turned to stage shows and night clubs.

The effect of the Depression, however, was not as bad as might be expected. "Some of us," says Noble Sissle, "did better during the Depression." [4] Many white acts refused to work at reduced pay and quit, whereupon Negro acts, which were paid less anyway, took the jobs. By the mid-thirties show business was pulling out of the Depression, and big bands, which often hired class acts, were becoming popular from coast to coast.

Among the best class acts—to skim the cream—were *Wells Mordecai and Taylor, The Lathrop Brothers and Virginia, The Three Dukes, The Dunhills, Rutledge and Taylor, Ford Buoy and Dailey, The Lucky Seven Trio, The Cotton Club Boys,* and *The Rockets.* Each act had its own specialty (and imitators of that specialty) and its claim to fame, and each made a contribution to the tradition.

Organized in the late twenties, *Wells Mordecai and Taylor*, "The Three Klassy Kids" (every act had a sub-title), became famous for a routine performed in a Cotton Club show to Harold Arlen's tune, "Hittin' the Bottle." The idea came from a folk dance that Ernest Taylor had seen in Charleston. (In his autobiography jazzman Sidney Bechet mentions a similar dance he witnessed earlier in New Orleans.) [5]

Each dancer performs a bewildering variety of steps around a bottle placed on the stage, coming closer and closer without knocking it over. "Our trio had class," says Jimmy Mordecai, who also appears in the film *St. Louis Blues*, dancing the Slow Drag with Bessie Smith, "we had six changes of costume." [6] When the team broke up, Dickie Wells opened a soon-to-be-famous night club. "*Wells Mordecai and Taylor* was one team that didn't copy us," says Nugent. "They didn't need to."

The oncoming swing era helped to make the class acts a success. With the consolidation of earlier jazz into special arrangements for big bands, closer integration between music and dance became possible. "Before the thirties, when we played colored theaters, the pit band could fake the accents we needed," says Al Williams of *The Four Step Brothers*, but the bands in white theaters didn't know how to do it. Eventually, we had to hire arrangers and hand out our own charts." [7]

Dance routines were soon created that not only dovetailed with the melody but also included special accents reinforced in the accompaniment. "Finding an arranger who knew what we wanted was tough," says Honi Coles. "One of the best was Chappy Willett. We'd hum the crazy accents, along with the tune, and he put them in big-band arrangements." [8] (Chick Webb's recording of "Liza" was arranged for *The Miller Brothers*, Jimmie Lunceford's "For Dancers Only" for the chorus line at the Apollo Theater.) The integration of music and dance gave the class acts new distinction.

A white act, *The Lathrop Brothers and Virginia*, was one of the top teams. "As far back as I can remember—and I go back to the early twenties—the colored dancers originated most of the steps," says Nugent, "but there were always a few ofay cats who were right on top, too." This trio performed a soft-shoe in a masterfully understated style, and their exit step was unique.

"Getting off stage is a problem for a class act," says Nugent. "With the accompaniment *fortissimo*, it's a terrible temptation to let go with some flash steps." *The Lathrop Brothers and Virginia* (coached by Nick Castle) tapped quietly and tastefully into the wings amid cheers. "In those days of loud fast finalés," says Cholly Atkins, "it was a relief to watch them." [9]

By the late thirties the number of class acts, near class acts, and would-be class acts ran into the hundreds, and a new finale became the fashion. Everybody used it. Skidding forward together on the right foot, knees and body in a crouch, each member of the act went into a kind of breast-stroke with one hand extended, palm down, as if demanding applause or reaching for a sandwich. "Sam Craig had been auditioning all the dance acts for the Lafayette Theater," says Pete Nugent, "and one day he cracked up and screamed: 'The next guy who sticks his hand out at me for a finish, I'll break his arm!'"

Two other class acts achieved success by following in the footprints of *Pete Peaches and Duke*. *The Three Dukes*, a Negro act organized by Nat Nazzaro, copied the entire routine. "They stole everything but our tap mat," says Nugent furiously.

On the other hand, *The Dunhills* were formed after *Pete Peaches and Duke* broke up, and Nugent helped coach them. (This was not stealing.) *The Dunhills* were a white group, and one of the more durable dance acts. With the addition of ballet-inspired flash steps they were still working in the mid-sixties.

The One Man routine was perfected by *Rutledge and Taylor*, one dancer in front of the other, executing identical foot, body, and hand movements. One of their specialties was "Me and My Shadow," aided by the fact that Rutledge was very fair and Taylor quite dark. The idea was adopted by as many as five dancers, performing in a kind of Indian file. Imitating *Ford Buoy and Dailey* was not as simple: Brother Ford tossed off taps from a toe-stand, ballet style, and walked off stage on his toes. Then *The Lucky Seven Trio* came up with a Dice Dance—not unlike Hittin' the Bottle—in which they danced around and on top of three-foot-square dice. "Honi Coles was with this act for a while," says Nugent, "they even did situation things, things that told a story."

All the class acts, of course, were well-dressed, graceful, and elegant. Neatness was important. (In describing *The Three Eddies*, an early flash act, Pete Nugent once quipped: "Maybe you should call them a class act, because they worked in blackface and kept their collars clean.") The class acts consciously refuted the stereotype of the shiftless comedian.

By 1940 *The Cotton Club Boys* (six—originally ten—tall and handsome dancers) were executing precision tap in *The Hot Mikado* at the New York

World's Fair. This was the group that Cholly Atkins joined and helped coach. "They were doing chorus-boy steps together," says Cholly.

"They were great at drill formations," adds Nugent. "The ladies ran after them in drill formation, too." Precision work was brought to a peak by *The Rockets*—"The Sophisticates of Rhythm"—whose dancing seemed to duplicate the unison choruses heard framing bop solos in jazz. "They took *Rutledge and Taylor* as a model," says Atkins, "and expanded it to three men."

To many dancers, however, *Pete Peaches and Duke* remain unsurpassed, the classic class act. The trio's success was due in large part to its leader, Pete Nugent. Running away from a sheltered home at the age of sixteen—his father was a Howard University graduate and ran an elevator in the White House—Nugent blasted his way up and out of a $25-a-week job on T.O.B.A. to the 1926 Broadway production of *Honeymoon Lane* with Kate Smith. ("And don't think *she* couldn't do the Charleston.") He formed a team with Irving "Peaches" Beaman in Chicago in 1928, and seeing the trend to trios, added Duke Miller in 1931. "Peaches was the balance wheel, Duke was the ladies' man," says Nugent, "and I was hard to handle." For six years *Pete Peaches and Duke* set the pace.

Nugent does his blasphemous best to conceal all traces of his protected childhood. "In spite of coming from one of the best families in Washington, D.C.," says a contemporary, "Pete has the fastest mouth in show business—and I don't mean the sweetest." Once billed as "Public Tapper, Number One" at the Club De Lisa in Chicago, Nugent wound up with the nickname "Tapper."

His influence was great. "Nugent was always ready with some helpful advice," says Cholly Atkins. "He was interested in other dancers."

"A lot of performers even copied the way he walks," says dancer Norma Miller, "a double bounce to his step, a nonchalant hunch to his shoulders, and a hip nodding of his head." [10]

Honi Coles adds thoughtfully, "I'd call it an arrogant swagger—until he starts to dance, and then he moves like an angel." Nugent's response to such comments is pleased but unprintable.

Pete Nugent prides himself on being more than a hoofer. Although he insists on clean, clear taps—"Good dancers lay those rhythms right in your lap"—Nugent is primarily concerned with making full use of the stage. "I'm a tap dancer, of course, first, last, and always, but if you have to make a choice, I prefer all body motion and no tap to all tap and no body motion. Any hoofer can execute all the steps, but the way a man handles his body and travels is what gives it class."

In choreographing the act, Nugent increased the tempo as he built to a calculated climax. "We decided on our closing step first," he says, "and then worked up to it." Opening with a military drill in yachting costumes, and tapping as if glued together, *Pete Peaches and Duke* then soloed in turn, each speeding up the tempo as he came on. Thus, Peaches tapped to a slow four-to-a-bar, Pete to a moderate two-to-a-bar, and Duke to a fast two-to-a-bar—in that order.

During each man's solo, the other two joined in for the middle third of his performance, adding a passage of unison work to the specialty of each dancer. Thus they established a new kind of continuity, interweaving rather than episodic. The act closed with a One Man exit, all three dancers in single file facing the audience and doing a tricky step together. They disappeared into the wings like a man with three pairs of legs. Nugent's insistence on perfection—every move was synchronized—made the teamwork outstanding.

The act broke up suddenly in 1937, when Duke Miller died of pneumonia. "A week later," says Nugent savagely, "they marketed a wonder drug that could have saved him."

Pete Peaches and Duke were tall, light, and handsome—Nugent could easily pass for white—a fact that complicated their existence. "The first ten minutes of our act at a night club was a total loss," says Nugent. "Our taps were drowned out by the buzz of people asking each other if we were white or colored." Being Negroes made a crucial difference—they never played a white hotel or night club.

Nugent never claimed to be the best dancer in the act, although Baby Laurence states flatly that he was.[11] "Duke Miller had a bag of steps he never used," says Nugent. "Wherever we went, acts coming up tried to cut us down, and Duke was our ace in the hole."

One night, after the show at a Detroit night club, a local trio billed as *The Three Esquires* challenged *Pete Peaches and Duke*. "They kept choosing us—you know, stopping in front of our table and making cracks," says Nugent, "so we finally had it out."

With a few patrons left in the club as an audience, *The Three Esquires* trotted out their best steps, noticeably improving upon what *Pete Peaches and Duke* had already done in the floor show. "So I sent Peachie out to match the new stuff," says Nugent. "Then I followed with a couple of things they'd never seen, just to keep them honest." *The Three Esquires* came back with more of the same, until Pete decided to send in Duke. "Duke took off his coat and tie and proceeded to scare those cotton-pickin' mothers to death," says Nugent. "He did steps I'd never seen him or anybody else even attempt, including an impossible Stumble Wing—he danced like a hungry Nijinsky—it was a massacre."

Battles of tap took place anywhere. One afternoon, when Nugent was visiting LeTang's Dance Studio in the Mayfair Theater Building in New York, he ran into Marvin Lollar, a fine young dancer who had just been hired by the *Follies*. "Lollar was feeling no pain," says Nugent. "He thought the time had come to put me in my place."

No gauntlet was thrown down. In fact, to an outsider nothing happened. Lollar spoke first:

"I hear you're a pretty good dancer."

"Thanks," said Nugent.

"Would you like to dance?"

"What for?"

"Well, I thought maybe you wanted to dance a little."

"Not particularly."

"Well, I'd like to show you some things." This succeeded in getting the desired response from Nugent.

"Okay, let's see them." The two dancers adjourned to a practice room, followed by a small crowd, and the fireworks started.

Lollar tossed off a few easy steps to get Nugent started, and Nugent just barely topped them. Bit by bit, as the dancers warmed up, the competition got keener, the steps more intricate.

In twenty minutes the battle was over. Nugent had more experience, he was in good form, and he notes a crucial detail: "My mind was really clicking. I soon discovered that Lollar didn't know too many Wings, so I shot him down. When you start choosing people, you should get yourself together—we'd never let anybody outdance us. We'd die first. Why, we'd even make up new steps."

Tapping to bop posed a problem. In 1944 Nugent was hired to dance with Billy Eckstine's pioneering band, which included Dizzy Gillespie, Art Blakey, and Charlie Parker. As he waited to go on, Nugent's nerves were not soothed by the band opener, "Oo-Bop-Sh-Bam." He followed it, tapping gracefully to "Hickory Stick," which he had introduced in Duke Ellington's short-lived musical, *Jump For Joy*.

Nugent's second solo was his elegant specialty in the Eddie Rector style, with clarinets murmuring low while the piano inserted gentle chimes. "As the second chorus began," says Nugent furiously, "that bop drummer Art Blakey let go with some real bombs—nothing simple, just a long press roll, louder and louder until I couldn't tell which way my feet were pointing, and then an ear-splitting clatter, while he clobbered the cymbal, followed by an earthshaking *boom* on the mother-loving bass drum—I nearly broke a leg."

After the show Nugent told Eckstine exactly how he felt about it. "Billy gave me that faraway look and said, 'But, man, you gotta get with the new sounds.'" Nugent limped away muttering to himself.

The worm was turning: For the first time, drummers were beginning to set the pace for tappers, and rhythms were getting incredibly complicated. "Why, I was on the subway once," says modern tapper Howard Sims, who is billed as "Sandman," "and I had to get off because that simple rhythm of the wheels was interfering with the rhythms I happened to be feeling." [12]

By the mid-forties the class acts were fading. Big bands, which once employed them were disappearing, with the advent of small-group bop. Jazz was no longer played in ballrooms, but in "lounges," where there was no room to dance. In any case the federal tax on dance floors made it impossible. And the trend to a mixture of modern dance and ballet on Broadway and television was increasing. "All I see on TV," snorts Nugent, "is armpits and bulging butts."

Pete Nugent quit dancing in 1952, the year the Dance Masters of America first added a jazz category to their annual convention demonstrations.[13] "I was getting paid a little more than the average single," he says, "but you should see the places I had to work—they were worse than the old Minsky burlesque houses—and I got paid in the dark, I never knew whether I'd get my money or how much of it. If I was just starting, maybe I could enjoy it, but I'm not taking that kind of crap anymore." Asked in the mid-sixties what he does for a living, Nugent ducks his head and replies, "Soldier, I do the best I can." By 1966 he had a job traveling as business manager with a Motown Records rock-and-roll group from Detroit.

38 Coles and Atkins: The Last of the Class Acts

NOBODY CAN DANCE that slowly and well. As Coles and Atkins move into their celebrated Soft Shoe, the music seems to stop. The orchestra is playing "Taking a Chance on Love" as if it will never reach the second note of the melody. The dancers walk, wheel, and tap with leisurely elegance, as the tune gradually emerges. Their dancing holds it together and at the same time makes it flow.

The audience at Harlem's Apollo Theater is transfixed. One graceless motion could shatter the poise and hover, but it never occurs. Relaxed and smiling, Coles and Atkins toss off gliding turns, leaning pull-ups, casual slides, and crystal-clear taps. The suspense is continuous, the execution flawless.

This is not the traditional Soft Shoe. Generations of dancers have used the rhythm: "bippety, bippety, bippety, bop," but here it has been transformed by additional accents into new rhythmic patterns. At the same time, the movement has been expanded, although the mood of grace and elegance remains. Coles and Atkins have choreographed the dance all over again—at a perilously slow tempo.

They execute the same steps together like identical twins, but their contrasting personalities add an invisible spark, more felt than seen. Offstage, Coles is as articulate and forceful as Atkins is quiet and thoughtful, and each has contributed to the routine.[1]

Perhaps the attention of the audience is first attracted to Coles, surprised that a dancer with such a lean and lanky physique—the usual build of a gangling clown—can move with such fierce precision. "Honi was the creator of high-speed rhythm tap," says Atkins. "He could do all of Bubbles's steps but faster."

Then the attention shifts to Atkins, as the audience is delighted by his light-footed aplomb. "Cholly was more modern than the rest of us," says Coles. "He worked out a new blend." Thereafter, the audience watches both, enchanted by the combination.

Coles excels at transitional steps. Most tap dancers slow down and quit tapping on turns, but he pivots fast and adds taps at the same time. "Honi thinks ahead as he dances, setting up steps in advance," says Leroy Myers. "He choreographs his most difficult steps intuitively." [2]

Atkins, on the other hand, has an affinity for modern dance and ballet, blending it miraculously with tap. "The Soft Shoe of *Coles and Atkins*," says Pete Nugent in one of his more reverent moments, "is a classic." [3]

Charles "Honi" Coles (he could never shake the nickname his mother gave him) grew up in the twenties in Philadelphia, where tappers were plentiful and competition keen. "We bore down on the Time Step," he says, "and everybody invented his own variations." Cutting contests exploded on sidewalks, in alleys, or wherever there was enough space to lift a foot. While still at home, Coles had arrived at the astonishing point where he tapped six, seven, and sometimes eight full choruses of a thirty-two-bar tune without repeating a step.

As one of *The Three Millers*, he went to New York in 1931, where the act opened at the Lafayette Theater with a special dance on narrow planks five feet above the stage. The Depression was in full swing, however, and at the end of the engagement they could not find another job. "We were an artistic but not a financial success," he says dryly. Coles went back to Philadelphia, and the two Millers went off on their own.

That was the turning point in Coles's career. Broke but determined, he locked himself in his room at home and practiced. "When Honi makes up his mind to do anything," says Chink Collins, "it's as good as done." [4]

Most tap dancers at that time were chopping up tunes into eight-bar units with a solo break in the last two bars of each unit. In addition to speeding things up—especially on turns—and using more taps, Coles complicated the pattern by extending the duration of steps. "I tried to put together longer, sixteen-bar units," he says, "crossing bar lines to build more sustained combinations." In so doing, he anticipated the extended cadences of the great jazzman, Lester Young, who played tenor sax with Count Basie.

"Centipede steps" is Pete Nugent's term for some of Honi Coles's inventions, and his admiration is unbounded: "Why, Honi has a reverse Wing that seems to go against the laws of nature—his legs and feet pull in opposite directions—I tried it once and nearly broke in two." At the same time Coles concentrates on the qualities that made the class acts famous—grace and elegance—and travels across the stage with every motion making the traditional picture.

When he returned to New York in 1932, Coles became one of the kings of the Hoofers Club and had no trouble finding jobs: a little while with *The Lucky Seven Trio*, a comedy act with Bert Howell, various others gigs, and then a solo spot with Cab Calloway. "The good jobs were with big swing bands," he says, "and somebody spoke to Cab." While traveling with the band from 1940 to 1943, he met Cholly Atkins, and they became fast friends. Atkins and his wife had a song-and-dance act with Calloway. Both Coles and Atkins joined the Army in 1943.

Atkins grew up in Buffalo, where he won a Charleston contest at the age of ten. Later, when he saw *The Chocolate Steppers* at the local theater—two boys and a girl in Cab Calloway's stage show—he knew he was going to be a dancer. "*The Chocolate Steppers* were doing a great mixture of jazz steps," says Atkins. "I copied everything I saw, practicing at home with Teddy Wilson's records."

He was one of *The Rhythm Pals* in 1935, a team that got as far as Hollywood before it was dissolved. "I was in eleven major films," he grins, "always type-cast. For example, I played a Mongolian extra in 'The Charge of the Light Brigade'—it took half an hour to put on the make-up and two hours to take it off." He was paid $12 a day and considered himself lucky.

"I used to take my food in a cardboard box—a sandwich, a bottle of milk, and an apple—and visit other sets during lunch hour," says Atkins. "Nobody ever chased me away, and I saw a lot of choreographers at work." He was fascinated with the ballet movements which various chorus lines were being taught, and he had the good fortune to see the Nicholas brothers rehearsing with dance-director Nick Castle for the "Chattanooga Choo Choo" number in *Sun Valley Serenade*.

On the side Atkins watched and learned. He and a group of friends did sound tracks of tap sequences for white dancers. By the time he returned to New York around 1940, he was offered a job with the popular *Cotton Club Boys* because of his ability to help choreograph the act.

After the war, Honi Coles and Cholly Atkins formed a team. "The original idea was to make enough money to open a studio," says Atkins, "but we never got that far ahead." Nevertheless, their first engagement set a record: they were hired by the Apollo Theater before they ever danced together professionally—an unprecedented vote of confidence by Mr. Frank Schiffman, manager of the theater, who remained one of their most enthusiastic fans.

Their act lasts six or seven minutes, beginning with a fast "attention getter" including patter, a precision "swing dance," and then the famous Soft Shoe. "We had three things in mind when we put together the Soft Shoe," says Atkins. "It had to be slower than anybody else's; at the same time, it had to be really interesting; and finally, it had to be so lyrical that it could stand by itself, that is it had to *sound* just as good with or without accompaniment, so we could do it without music."

The Soft Shoe is followed by a challenge dance, in which each in turn performs his own specialty. "In our solos we work almost entirely with the drummer," says Coles, "and ignore the melody." At that point swinging rhythmic complexity is the goal. They end with some tight precision steps and walk off together.

Coles and Atkins danced with a series of big bands from 1945 to 1949: Cab Calloway, Louis Armstrong, Charlie Barnet, Lionel Hampton, Billy Eckstine, and Count Basie. In 1948, they toured England with great success.

In the course of their travels Coles and Atkins became connoisseurs of stages and audiences. The Stanley in Pittsburgh and Shea's in Buffalo tie for last place. "At the Stanley, it feels as if you're up to your knees in mud," says Atkins, "and Shea's is so big you can't hear the orchestra or yourself." Another grievance is the "raked" stages in England, which slope downward toward the footlights and make things miserable for dancers. "Just keeping out of the orchestra pit," says Coles, "takes all your energy."

Honi Coles feels most strongly about the Regal Theater in Chicago. "They never think of the dancers—this time they had just painted the stage black and shellacked it," he recalls. "I slipped and fell on my face in the middle of the act, and when Cholly looked around I was on my stomach doing a breast stroke—I couldn't think of anything else to do." Atkins helped him up at the end of the number.

Both dancers agree (and other dancers agree with them) that Baltimore has the worst audiences. "At the Royale Theater, patrons walk down to the front row during your act," says Atkins, "and never even take off their hats—it's unnerving." Nobody ever applauds, and ushers patrol the aisles with police dogs. "Once, Cholly and I had just finished a beautiful step together," says Coles, "when a guy in the balcony yells—and I'm censoring it—'Shhhhheeeeeucks, I can do that!' and somebody else answers, 'So can your mother!' "

During the late forties Coles and Atkins began to add comedy to the act. They were dancing at the Lookout House, a gambling casino in Covington, Kentucky, and the audience was not interested in tap. "It was like dancing in a morgue," says Atkins. "Everybody looked as if he had lost his last nickel in the slot machine and was about to put a bullet in his head." In desperation, they began to talk as they danced—anything to break the stony silence.

Coles hit upon the idea of playing the showboat, pointing to himself behind Atkins's back, while Atkins pretended to be annoyed by such foolishness. The audience began to wake up. Crazed with success, Coles broke out of the routine and threw in a syncopated flamenco stamp around Atkins, pantomiming his defiance openly. The audience applauded. To other dancers the comedy gets in the way of the dancing, but regular audiences love it.

They joined the cast of *Gentlemen Prefer Blondes* in 1949, the Broadway musical that made Carol Channing a star, and stayed with it during its run of over two years. "Those were the best times," says Atkins. "We had a steady job, and we could live at home." Coles and Atkins were featured in the second act, singing and dancing to "Mamie Is Mimi."

They ran into a snag at the start. "During rehearsals Agnes de Mille didn't know what to do with us," says Coles, "so finally Julie Styne, who hired us, took us aside and said, 'Look, why don't you fellows work up something, and I'll get her to look at it.'" They located arranger Benny Payne, who knew how to write for tap-dance acts, and the three of them worked out a routine. "One afternoon, Miss de Mille took time off to look at it," says Atkins. "She liked it and told us to keep it in."

On went the show with the Coles-Atkins-Payne routine a hit, and Agnes de Mille listed as choreographer in the program. "Later on we had to get her permission to use our routine on Jack Haley's *Ford Hour*," says Coles. "She was very nice about it." In her autobiography Miss de Mille writes that the "Mamie Is Mimi" number, along with several others, was devised "in a single short rehearsal," [5] presumably by Miss de Mille. This was the standard practice.

When *Gentlemen Prefer Blondes* closed in 1951, Coles and Atkins found jobs were becoming scarce. They played summer stock for a while, appearing in revivals of musical comedies in Dallas, Kansas City, and St. Louis. "For *Kiss Me Kate* we just rehearsed in our hotel room," says Atkins. "We knew the routine by heart." They also appeared occasionally on the television shows of Kate Smith, Garry Moore, and Milton Berle.

In a sense they had classed themselves right out of the market for Negro dancers. Night club operators wanted more of the latest fad: comedy, acrobatics, and flash dancing. The influential booker, Joe Glaser, liked the act but could not manufacture work. "When top Broadway jobs come along," he said, "they'll hire you—maybe four months of the year—but meanwhile you'll starve." [6] Broadway drew the most flexible color line of all.

In an effort to stay with the dancing they loved, *Coles and Atkins* broke up. Atkins went to work as a coach for Katherine Dunham's school of dance, and Coles opened a dance studio of his own with Pete Nugent. But times had changed—even the fondest stage mother saw no reason to have her infant prodigy taught tap. "We'd be sitting around waiting for a customer," says Nugent, "and Honi would jump up and go into a spasm of unholy leaps and waves, right in front of the window—finally I realized that he was trying to con some passerby into taking a lesson."

In 1955 Coles and Atkins went back to work together, joining Tony Martin's act in Las Vegas. "That was a ball," says Atkins. "We really enjoyed it." They never knew why they were suddenly dropped. Martin seemed genuinely happy with them. Later they heard a rumor that his manager was afraid their suave manner detracted from Martin's appeal. "I still don't believe it," says Coles, but at the time the story was no boost to their morale.

During the Las Vegas job Atkins's blend of ballet and tap did not go unchallenged. One evening after the show at the Flamingo, Cholly overheard a group of dancers joking about his use of ballet movements. They were highly versatile chorus boys—"gypsies"—who had been trained in ballet and modern dance, and the idea of adding tap to anything seemed ridiculous to them.

Atkins walked over quietly and said: "Okay, let's see who can dance—I'll bet I can do your ballet movements better than you can do my tapping." Surprised and delighted by the challenge, the dancers agreed, swarmed up on the empty stage, and unlimbered their most complicated balletic maneuvers. Atkins proceeded to duplicate their movements, one after another, with surprising competence. When his turn came, he tossed off a tap step—"one of his Very Special Reserve combinations," says Coles—and the gypsies quit. "We all went out and had a friendly drink afterwards," says Atkins.

For a year and a half, Coles and Atkins worked with Pearl Bailey, thus avoiding unhealthy comparisons with a leading man. Then they found themselves out of work. "We even tried hoking it up in the corniest way imaginable," says Coles, "but I guess our hearts weren't in it." Atkins went back to coaching, and Coles took the job of production manager at the Apollo Theater.

In 1962, when Coles and Atkins dusted off their Soft Shoe to illustrate the history of tap dance at the Newport Jazz Festival, the critics were astonished and enthusiastic. Whitney Balliett wrote in the *New Yorker:* [7]

> At a slow, slow tempo, they slid across, around, and up and down the stage, mixing in off-hand gull turns, polite double toe-taps, hip wiggles, and arm movements, ranging from cold-engine propeller motions to weighty pumping.
>
> It was that rarity—an intensely serious performance that never takes itself seriously for a moment.

Lifted from the act and presented sympathetically by itself, the Soft Shoe came into its own.

Coles and Atkins still dance once a year, or at least have the opportunity to do so. For well over a decade they have had a date—usually in August—with the Billy Eckstine show at the Apollo Theater. The job will last as long as the Apollo books Eckstine, for he has a special clause in his contract specifying that Coles and Atkins must join him. Wherever they are, Coles and Atkins rush into rehearsal and try to get back into shape.

The reunion at the Apollo in August 1962 was a great success. Accompanied by the Quincy Jones band, which included Budd Johnson and Phil Woods, Coles and Atkins presented their act impeccably and then returned for a finale with Eckstine—all three doing a bit of the Soft Shoe together. After the 1964 reunion they announced privately that "this is the last time," but in July 1965, at the respective ages of fifty-four and fifty-two, Coles and Atkins played a week with Billy Eckstine at the Club Harlem in Atlantic City and loved it.

Coles and Atkins got a chance to do their own material at their own pace and in their own way on CBS television's *Camera 3.* In January 1965 they appeared (with one of the present writers as commentator) demonstrating and explaining a variety of Time Steps, Wings, and pioneering styles. Best of all, they presented their Soft Shoe under ideal conditions: a tap mat, a special arrangement, and a fine trio led by pianist Hank Jones. The response from coast to coast was phenomenal.

Almost a year later Honi Coles appeared briefly in the opening of a series entitled *U.S.A. Dance* on National Educational Television. He was supposed to illustrate the influence of jazz (*via* tap) *before American dance really got started.* "Quite possibly the hit of the half hour, however," wrote Jack Gould in *The New York Times,* "was a gentleman named Honi Coles . . . he was superb last night." [8]

Coles and Atkins never made it big where it counted—in films or on television—like Gene Kelly or Fred Astaire or even Bill Robinson. ("Coles could have been a great single," [9] says Bill Bailey. "I tried that, too," answers Coles when asked about it.) Yet they seemed to have everything: singing, comedy, and of course, superb dancing. They were tall, well dressed, and handsome. In fact, unlike many show-biz characters, they were also soft-spoken and gentlemanly. This led to the comment that they lacked punch, and no doubt they might have gone further if they had been unscrupulous and aggressive. "Coles and Atkins," says Billy Eckstine, "are two of the nicest guys in show business."

A few solo dancers tapped off and on into the sixties, while most of the teams disappeared. Broadway musicals—with honorable exceptions—employed modern dance and ballet, and television tagged along timidly. By the mid-sixties, Cholly Atkins was employed by Motown Records in Detroit as choreographer for singing groups, and Honi Coles was president of the Negro Actors Guild and was working as production manager at the Apollo Theater. The decline of *Coles and Atkins* coincided with the passing of the class acts and the disappearance of tap.

PART TEN

The Jitterbug

39 Harlem Background

ON JUNE 17, 1928, the Manhattan Casino, a huge ballroom in New York City, was jammed to the balconies with cheering spectators, watching some eighty couples perform on the dance floor. The occasion was a new craze: dance marathons. A marathon for white dancers had just ended at Madison Square Garden, but this was nonsegregated—which proved to be a sound financial decision, for it mushroomed into a marathon to end all marathons.

The contestants danced an hour and then rested fifteen minutes (you couldn't really sleep, because you would never wake up) day and night, for eighteen days, until the marathon was closed by the Board of Health at 4 A.M. on the Fourth of July. On that morning, four couples were still on their feet; George "Shorty" Snowden, the all-time champion dancer of the Savoy Ballroom in Harlem, and his partner were one of them. They received a fourth of the $5,000 prize money.

While the contestants danced to a phonograph during the day and a real band at night, publicity snow-balled. Shorty Snowden had NUMBER 7 stitched to the back of his shirt, and soon Walter Winchell and Ed Sullivan, who were working on the old New York *Graphic*, got in the habit of announcing that they were going to watch Number 7 again on such and such a night.

Crowds jammed the dance hall, especially in the evening, and by arrangement with the emcee, anyone could offer a prize of five or ten dollars for a short contest among the surviving couples. During one of these contests—as he remembers it—Snowden decided to do a breakaway, that is, fling his partner out and improvise a few solo steps of his own. In the midst of the monotony of the marathon, the effect was electric, and even the musicians came to life. Shorty had started something.

At one point Fox Movietone News arrived to cover the marathon and decided to take a close-up of Shorty's feet. The general impression that Shorty was out of his mind and his dancing a kind of inspired confusion was gaining currency. "What are you doing with your feet," asked the interviewer, and Shorty, without stopping, replied, "The Lindy." [1] Later, they called it the Jitterbug.

As Shorty explained later, trying to recall just how it happened: "I was really doing the regular steps, just like we did them at the Savoy, several of us, only maybe a little faster. That's why they called me a flash dancer, because of my speed. I used to dance seven complete choruses of 'Bugle Blues' or 'Tiger Rag' in a minute and three quarters, which was considered sensational. . . . It was just the speed that confused them maybe, but of course most people had never seen anything like it, fast or slow. It was new to them, and I was sure having a ball, doing whatever came into my head." With increasing frequency, spectators were offering prizes for short contests, just to see Shorty dance, and he won them all. Unlike the other dancers, he began to gain weight.

The effect of Snowden's triumph was decisive on his own home ground, the Savoy Ballroom. Two years earlier, on March 12, 1926, the Savoy had opened its doors with two orchestras: Fess Williams's and Duncan Mayer's Savoy Bearcats. The atmosphere was one of enforced dignity and decorum. The business manager, Charles Buchanan, insisted upon it and hired a bunch of burly bouncers to back him.

The Charleston, for example, was still popular, but no one was permitted to enjoy it. (This rule helped to create a fast-traveling step known as the Run, later incorporated into the Lindy, which left the bouncers behind.) It took two years and the marathon craze to teach Buchanan which side of his terpsichorean bread was buttered.

Before entering the marathon, Shorty had asked Mr. Charles Buchanan if he could represent the Savoy, and the answer had been a firm *No.* At the close of the marathon Charlie presented Mr. George Snowden with a gilt lifetime pass to the Savoy—a good investment for the ballroom. It represented a substantial saving to Shorty, too, although he never would have thought of dancing anywhere else. Thereafter the Savoy Ballroom found its true destiny. Billed as "The Home of Happy Feet," (regular patrons called it "The Track," perhaps because dog races were featured at one time) it proceeded to make musical as well as dance history.

Some 250 big bands played the Savoy during its thirty-three year existence, from Rudy Vallee to Bennie Moten and from Paul Whiteman to Duke Ellington. Even Guy Lombardo "made the scene," as Shorty observes, establishing an all-time attendance record, although "you couldn't do a real Lindy to Lombardo." In more than one sense there seemed to be no discrimination at the Savoy, and that policy paid off.

Of more importance, the Savoy was home base for two extraordinary bands: Chick Webb's Orchestra, and a little later, Al Cooper's Savoy Sultans. Unlike other orchestras of the period, these were less notable for their pitch and precision than for their power and drive. "They were the *swingingest* bands," says Count Basie, who having played opposite them many times, has reason to know. Above all, the two bands were a constant inspiration to the dancers, and their propulsive rhythms set the pace at the Savoy.

Further, the Savoy capitalized on the popularity of battles of music, and the competition among bands was at its keenest on the double bandstand. Bookings were often completed at the last minute, since Buchanan could pick up any big band that happened to be in New York that night without a job at bargain prices. The word would spread around Harlem like wildfire. On one occasion the Chick Webb band, which resolutely took on all comers, is credited with driving Benny Goodman off the stand in good-natured despair, while outside the jam-packed ballroom 25,000 more customers clamored for admission. Other ballrooms existed in Harlem—the New Star Casino and the Alhambra—but the Savoy was the undisputed tops.

The environment from which the Lindy developed had much to do with the nature of the dance. Harlem, from the late twenties to the early forties, was a society in transition. The Irish, German, and Jewish people had already begun to move out as Negroes moved in, and the old-world authority of church and family was crumbling. Bit by bit the newly arrived Negroes began to work out a social equilibrium of their own.

A key role in the establishment of this new equilibrium, and incidentally, the evolution and diffusion of the Lindy, was played by a legendary character named Herbert White. As dancer Al Minns remembers: [2] "Whitey was sort of a fringe hood, a semi-gangster with ideals. He had been a prizefighter, a sergeant in the 369th Division in World War I, and bouncer at the Alhambra Ballroom in Harlem. He was much older than we were, and he knew more angles than a geometrician. He could squeeze money from a stone.

"I think Whitey loved dancing," adds Minns, "although he wasn't much good on the floor, and he was great as a choreographer. 'I have an idea for a step,' he would say, after watching a team of acrobats at the Palace. 'It starts something like this, and it should end like this.' And it would be great. I always had the feeling that Whitey was born too soon, that it was a shame he didn't get an education. He could con anybody, talk the shirt off their back, and he was no slouch in a brawl. I've seen him take on seven guys at once without blinking, and knock their heads together."

In 1923 Herbert White organized the Jolly Fellows,[3] one of many secret gangs in Harlem like the Meteors (a friendly group), the True Pals, the Buffaloes, the Harlem Habits, and the Forty Thieves (one of the roughest), which took up the slack in a disintegrating neighborhood. Whitey was a combination of a penny-pinching Robin Hood and a hip Father Flanagan.

The Jolly Fellows had a clubhouse with their own pool table at 211 West 134th Street—their territory included 134th and 135th Streets—and a membership that grew in the thirties from about one hundred to over six hundred. The minimum age for admission was eighteen. One step in the initiation of new members indicates the underlying intensity of the club's atmosphere: You must walk into a store quietly, hang an uppercut on the jaw of the astonished proprietor, and stand there without running. The results varied.

The Jolly Fellows also had a junior club: the Jolly Friends, and a ladies' auxiliary, the Jolly Flapperettes. Spurred by the interests of its founder and the accomplishments of its members, the Jolly Fellows became the club for dancers. Among them were Shorty Snowden, Leon James, Ralph Henry, Leroy Jones, Sugar Cook, and Little Jerome—all stars of the Savoy, while Whitey became head bouncer. Between them, organized into flying squadrons, they unofficially but literally ran the ballroom.

"I couldn't wait to join the Jolly Fellows," says a former member. "The kids were beating me up every day, and it was the only way to survive." Shorty Snowden, one of the charter members, thought of the Jolly Fellows as a refuge in a crumbling world: "I went to Episcopalian Church every Sunday at eleven A.M., Sunday school at two P.M., and Christian Endeavor at night—the storefront churches came later. I was lucky. My mother had the hardest left hand for spanking you ever felt in your life. She used her right hand to hold me.

"In those days one cop could chase forty kids because all the parents stuck together, and one would tell the others what they saw you doing. But it didn't last. We could see that things were falling apart—buildings, streets, people, everything. It really meant something to belong to the Jolly Fellows."

Whitey demanded unquestioning obedience from the Jolly Fellows, and in return, gave them protection and a place in the sun.

The club was outside the law, a precursor of the street gangs to come. There was plenty of violence in those days, but the papers never gave it much space—it was expected of Harlem, and nobody was interested in what later became known as juvenile delinquency.

The club had its own code, which compared to rules of later gangs, came from the days when knighthood was in flower: All women, for example, must be treated at all times with unfailing courtesy. Members must fight "fair." This simply meant that adversaries should be equal in number and weapons. If an armed gang from one club beat up an unarmed member of another club, the retribution, as one member still insists, "*had* to be death for the leader of the gang that beat him up." Without swift retaliation a club lost face and could no longer protect its members.

The revenge was carried out in a highly formal manner, with the club's emissaries wearing gloves, tight Chesterfields, and derbies in the approved style popularized by Edward G. Robinson in gangster movies. In the brief dialogue with the enemy the leader always used the polite, carefully enunciated, and slightly inane understatement, which real gangsters were supposed to use. ("We truly do not like the way that you gentlemen have treated our friend.")

On one occasion a member of the Jolly Fellows went dancing at the Renaissance Ballroom. It was the territory of the Buffaloes, and he knew he should not be there. Even so if he had worn his Jolly Fellows initials on his jacket—as was the custom—he might have been safe. Noticing a stranger who could dance making a hit with their girls, the local club reduced him to a mass of unseeing pulp. He was fortunate enough to be recognized when he was dumped into the street, and some friends carried him to Whitey's house.

Within an hour a wrecking crew of Jolly Fellows, lugging their semi-conscious member as evidence, descended on the Renaissance Ballroom. They were all wearing their gangster uniforms. In a matter of seconds they had all the doors and windows on the balcony and ground floor locked and guarded. Then Whitey, mincing like a wary panther, walked up to the head bouncer, followed by two members carrying the victim, and asked very quietly why this friend of his, and a Jolly Fellow, too, had been treated in this manner.

Everybody in the ballroom froze. The head bouncer did not know who had done it and said so, but Whitey waited silently as the seconds ticked by. Suddenly, somebody in the balcony made a dash for the exit. (It was a mistake, for the victim had been so badly mauled that he couldn't have recognized his assailant.) Before the culprit reached the door, a Jolly Fellow hit him so hard that he was lifted over the railing and fell with a thud to the ballroom floor. While he lay there, the Jolly Fellows "walked him," that is, formed a circle and kicked him to pieces.

Then the injured Jolly Fellow was given his own knife and told to finish him off, which he did very badly because his eyes were puffed shut. The man was dead before they could get him to a hospital. When the police, in the line of duty, called him in for a routine interview, Whitey chided them softly, and the police were glad to forget the whole affair.

Members of the club had been known to dispose of cops for less reason. Another time, because he was a little drunk and felt irritable, a Jolly Fellow rabbit-punched an unsuspecting policeman while he was standing on the sidewalk, removed his cap, badge, and night stick, and dumped him into a garbage can. He then delivered the insignia without a word of explanation to the local precinct station by way of demonstrating the cop's inadequacy, on the theory that no retribution should follow such a disgraceful exhibition of blue-coated carelessness.

A leader of the tough rival club, the Forty Thieves, was standing nearby and witnessed the carnage, his arms crossed on his chest and a deadpan expression on his face. (Imperturbability was considered the correct attitude toward all violence.) But a look of wonder gradually pierced the mask, and he permitted himself to ask "Whatcha do that for?" adding, to hide his astonishment, "I'll tell the cops."

The reply was "If the cops find out, I'll know who told them." The police never found out.

Such incidents, of course, were not too frequent, but they indicate the tensions of the time and the premium placed upon force and recklessness. Harlem had become a fiercely competitive jungle, and the Savoy Ballroom syphoned off much of the nervous energy this constant pressure generated among the lucky few who became deeply interested in dancing. In turn, this emotional climate was reflected in the tireless vigor and daring invention of the Lindy, or Jitterbug.

The Jolly Fellows, however, could be a force for stability and even creativity. Whitey insisted on personal cleanliness and kept a curry comb, rubbing alcohol, and Fels Naptha soap handy, which he personally applied to any boy, dancer or not, who had the slightest trace of body odor. The club had two mottoes which suggest the range of its activities. The first was practical: "Never fall down in a fight, and don't run unless you have a good exit all picked out." The second was esthetic: "Use Mum, Hush, Be Quiet, Keep Still, and Shut Up." The result, combined with their interest in dancing, was a sweet-smelling, formidable organization that captured all the prizes for jitterbugging in and around New York City.

40 The Savoy Ballroom

UPON ENTERING THE SAVOY BALLROOM, you descended one floor to check your hat and coat at one of several ornate counters staffed by a small army of attendants. Then you climbed two mirrored flights of marble steps until you found yourself in a teeming crowd at the middle of a block-long dance floor. Directly opposite, a raised double bandstand gleamed with instruments, and one of two bands was up there in full swing.

When he first walked up those two flights of stairs, dancer Leon James was genuinely awed: "My first impression was that I had stepped into a different world. I had been to other ballrooms, but this was different—much bigger, more glamor, real *class*. . . ."[1] A completely new floor was installed every three years, and in 1936, when business reached a peak, the Savoy was redecorated at a cost of $50,000.

In the early days the price of admission varied: thirty cents before 6 P.M., sixty cents before 8 P.M., and eighty-five cents thereafter. The number of poor but devoted dancers who attended every night was almost unbelievable. If your heart was really in it, you arrived before six and saved a couple of dollars a week. Hostesses were available as partners, three dances for a quarter. Later, when Prohibition was repealed, bars were erected at one end of the ballroom, and still later, the hostesses disappeared.

The weekly routine of the star dancers at the Savoy became pretty well set. The most hectic of all night's was Saturday, known even then as Square's Night, because everybody squeezed into the ballroom, and there was no room for great dancing. (Squares could be easily identified because they usually accented the first syllable of the word Savoy.) Then

Wednesday and Friday nights were out because they were reserved for social clubs and fraternal organizations. Monday ("Ladies' Night") and Thursday ("Kitchen Mechanics' Night," monopolized by people in domestic service) were not too crowded, however, and perfectly good for practicing.

Tuesday ("400 Club"), reserved for dancers only, at reduced prices, was a fine night for Harlemites—no crowds, plenty of floor space, and all the fine dancers to watch. (At the time, "Killer Joe" Piro was one of the lesser-known members of the club.) But the best night of all was Sunday, when celebrities and movie stars arrived (frequently conducted by the Savoy's publicity agent). "We picked up a lot of cash on Sundays," says Shorty Snowden. "For example, Peggy Hopkins Joyce always told her escorts—and they were never the same—to tip me. I danced from the opening bars of music until the last note was played, and when I went home my shoes were wringing wet." [2] The "Opportunity Contest" was also staged on Sundays: first prize $10, second prize $5, and Shorty won it so many times that they asked him to keep out of it.

To Shorty and his colleagues, dancing was a way of life: "We started getting ready for Sunday on Saturday. The deal was to get our one sharp suit to the tailor to be pressed Saturday afternoon. Then we'd meet at the poolroom and brag about what we were going to do on the dance floor the next night . . ."

"On Saturday night we'd get dressed up and walk over to the front of the Savoy and stand on the sidewalk and wisecrack and watch the squares trip over each other trying to get in where they wouldn't see any real dancing or hear any good music either, because the bands played their best for us. Then sometimes Mister Charles Buchanan would come running down, three stairs at a time, yelling 'Why don't you boys come on up and do a dance for the crowd?' When he finally offered to pay us, we went on up and had a ball. All we wanted to do was dance anyway." Shorty danced at the Savoy at least five out of seven nights a week.

Once inside the ballroom, the dancers followed a strict code of their own. Early in 1928 Snowden and George "Twist Mouth" Ganaway selected the northeast corner of the Savoy as their bailiwick and named it the Cats' Corner. Only the elect were allowed to sit or dance there. If you were one of the regulars, you were permitted to bring over a new girl in order to impress her, and if she knew her way around, she would appreciate the honor bestowed on her. The ways of ejecting an intruder were many, but the most effective was—as he danced by—to break his shins with gracefully executed Charleston kicks.

An iron-clad law existed among the Savoy elite: Nobody was permitted to copy anybody else's steps—exactly. Speaking of the year 1933, Leon James recalls: "When I went up there, Shorty Snowden was the all-time greatest. One thing: Nobody copied anybody else or did somebody else's specialty, because he'd get whipped up, tromped in the middle of the crowd by all the others. I never could do steps like the other guys anyway. I'd just wiggle my legs and it came out different—Clock Clock they called it or sometimes legomania—so they accepted me in the Cats' Corner.

"You also had to be able to dance to very fast tempos. The bands seemed to be swinging faster every night, and all the best dancers could follow them, in new and different ways." The dancers were creating new styles to fit the rapidly evolving big-band jazz to which they danced.

The Savoy was successfully invaded once. A short, hump-backed dancer known as Little Shirley from Jersey (Shirley Jordan, nicknamed "Snowball") walked in one night while Chick Webb's band was playing and took the prize away from Snowden in the Opportunity Contest. (Snowden was five-feet-two and this man was even shorter.) So Snowden went to the ballroom in Newark the next week—a very short trip—and took the prize away from Shirley. "The audiences just cheered for the new talent," says Shorty. By 1931 they were dancing in the same show together.

The Lindy became a recognized part of the American scene in 1936, but what were its origins? One of the main sources of the Lindy was the Texas Tommy. "It was like the Lindy," says Ethel Williams, who with Johnny Peters, introduced the dance in the 1913 *Darktown Follies* (see Chapter 17), "but there was a basic step—a kick and hop three times on each foot." [3]

The Lindy has a basic step of its own—a syncopated two-step or box step—accenting the offbeat. After these basic steps, however, both the Texas Tommy and the Lindy go into an identical breakaway, which is the creative part of these dances: "You add whatever you want there," says Ethel Williams. Thus, both dances constitute a frame into which almost any movement can be inserted before the dancers return to each other.

Shorty Snowden describes it this way: "We used to call the basic step the Hop long before Lindbergh did *his* hop across the Atlantic." (In 1964, on the TV show *Today*, Ray Bolger described at great length how *he* invented the Lindy Hop in 1927—with taps—at the Hotel Coronado in St. Louis.[4]) "It had been around a long time and some people began to call it the Lindbergh Hop after 1927, although it didn't last. Then, during the marathon at Manhattan Casino, I got tired of the same old steps and cut loose with a breakaway. Anything you could dream up was okay for the breakaway, you tried all kinds of things. Everybody did the same starting step, but after that, look out, everybody for himself. For example, the

Shorty George, a step which was well known in Harlem, I just made it up during a breakaway in the Lindy. They also called it the Sabu, from that elephant-boy movie, because it can be made to look kind of Oriental.

"I've put together new steps in the breakaway by slipping and almost falling. I was always looking for anyone dancing in the street or just walking or doing anything that suggests a step. If I could see it, I could do it." The Lindy—by way of the breakaway—incorporated many other dance steps (including a basic amount of the Charleston) and created a host of new ones.

Shorty Snowden once met the fine white dancer Paul Draper, who came backstage after the Lindy Hop show in Washington to congratulate him. "I wish I could do the kind of dancing you do,"[5] said Draper. Invited to see him dance, Shorty was thrilled by some of Draper's ballet-influenced steps and promptly adapted them to his own purposes. "I got a few things from Draper," Shorty recalls, "especially a running floor slide combined with a knee lock." Almost anything was grist for the Lindy mill.

Snowden's mild conviction that he invented the breakaway and thereby the essence of the Lindy is probably true for his time and place. It might be more accurate, however, to say that he rediscovered it, for the breakaway is a time-honored method of eliminating the European custom of dancing in couples, and returning to solo dancing—the universal way of dancing, for example, in Africa—a style that surfaced in the United States with rock-and-roll.

Long before most white musicians were aware of it, the formula for the swing orchestra was being worked out at the Savoy. Unlike the collective improvisation of the earlier and smaller Dixieland bands, written arrangements made it possible for thirteen or more jazzmen to play together effectively. Fletcher Henderson, although he was more or less a fixture downtown at the Roseland Ballroom, played the Savoy off and on from its earliest days, and by 1926 when the Savoy opened, Henderson, with the help of arranger Don Redman, was well on his way toward perfecting big-band jazz.

Other Negro bands, like McKinney's Cotton Pickers and those of Earl Hines, Cecil Scott, Alphonse Trent, Charlie Johnson, Bennie Moten, Luis Russell, and of course, Duke Ellington, had learned the same lesson by the late twenties. In the early thirties, before Benny Goodman adopted the formula (and Fletcher Henderson's arrangements) and became a hit from coast to coast, Cab Calloway, Jimmie Lunceford, Teddy Hill, Les Hite, Don Redman, and Andy Kirk had big, swinging bands of their own. At one time or another, each of them played the Savoy Ballroom, whose patrons constituted the "hippest" dance audience in the world. It was the acid test of a true *dance* band.

One event in the development of big-band jazz and its effect on the dance can be dated by the appearance at the Savoy in 1932 of the Bennie Moten band from Kansas City. This band—with Lips Page on trumpet, Ben Webster on tenor, and Count Basie at the piano—ignited a musical revolution by the sheer power and drive of its playing. Substituting a guitar for the banjo and a string-bass for the tuba, Moten's band generated a more flowing, lifting momentum. The effect on the dancers was to increase the energy and speed of execution, a necessary preliminary for the acrobatics to come.

In a sense, the Lindy is choreographed swing music. Unlike earlier Dixieland jazz, and the Toddle, which was danced to it—a bouncy, up-and-down style of dancing—swing music and the Lindy flowed more horizontally and smoothly. There was more rhythmic continuity. Again, swing music and the Lindy were more complicated, for while a Lindy team often danced together during the opening ensembles of a big band, they tended to go into a breakaway and improvise individual steps when the band arrangement led into a solo.

The similarity is conscious and intentional, for jazz dancers follow the music closely. Describing an incident at the Savoy in 1937, Leon James remarks: "Dizzy Gillespie was featured in the brass section of Teddy Hill's screaming band. A lot of people had him pegged as a clown, but we loved him. Every time he played a crazy lick, we cut a crazy step to go with it. And he dug us and blew even crazier stuff to see if we could dance to it, a kind of game, with the musicians and dancers challenging each other."

Great musicians inspire great dancers—and vice versa—until the combination pyramids into the greatest performances of both. "I wish jazz was played more often for dancing," said Lester "Prez" Young during his last years with the Count Basie band. "The rhythm of the dancers comes back to you when you're playing." [6] One of the reasons for the early development of great big-band jazz at the Savoy was the presence of great dancers.

A crucial point in the evolution of the Lindy at the Savoy took place in the middle and late thirties, splitting the dancers into two groups: those who used floor steps and those who used air steps. The big attraction had been two couples: Shorty Snowden and Big Bea, and Stretch Jones and Little Bea. Big Bea was about a foot taller than Shorty and a leaning tower of strength around which Shorty cut some of his wildest capers. Little Bea was at least a foot shorter than Stretch, so-named because he was excessively tall, and she always seemed to be on the verge of getting lost. Between them, breathtakingly and hilariously, this quartet exhausted themselves and every combination of floor steps that could be put to the Lindy.

A few air steps had been popping up in 1936, however—the Hip to Hip, Side Flip, and Over the Back (phrases describing the trajectory of the girl in the air)—but the old guard, Leon James, Leroy Jones, and Shorty Snowden disapproved. In fact, when Shorty danced with Big Bea, air steps were out of the question, unless she threw Shorty around, because she was so much heavier.

It took a group of younger dancers fresh out of high school: Al Minns, Joe Daniels, Russell Williams, and Pepsi Bethel, to work out the Back Flip, Over the Head, the Snatch, and to get the Lindy off the ground. They learned later that some of these steps were basic ju-jitsu. Beneath it all was the supporting music of great swing bands.

The date of a transitional phase can be fixed with some certainty. In June 1937 two great dancers Leon James and Albert Minns met for the first time. In those days James was King of the Savoy and winner of the Harvest Moon Ball jitterbug contest. (A few years later Minns was to win the same contest.) He had just returned from Hollywood where he had been featured with a group of Lindy Hoppers and the Marx Brothers in *A Day at the Races*. Minns was a seventeen-year-old scrub.

A few months before, Minns had had a stroke of luck. One of the Savoy regulars, Chick Hogan, who knew all the steps, had been teaching them secretly to one of the younger girls by way of demonstrating his all-around charm and versatility. Minns happened to know her well and soon pried the latest routines out of her, which he proceeded to master in his own energetic style. His knowledge of these steps was to cause just enough confusion to save him from a beating on the evening when he blew Savoy protocol sky high.

"King" Leon James arrived in New York on a Saturday, and of course, planned to make his triumphant appearance at the Savoy that night. The Chick Webb band was swinging, and the ballroom was jammed, but the hallowed Cats' Corner—as custom decreed—remained clear and empty, awaiting the performance of the King. By ten o'clock, two of the dancers who had made the Hollywood trip with James arrived—one twirling a long key chain, like Cab Calloway, the other flipping a coin with his thumb, in the manner of George Raft.

It was the tradition for everybody to wait until the King appeared, and then, starting with the scrubs and working up to the King, each couple was supposed to perform in turn. After the King danced, a respectful intermission took place.

At the stroke of twelve, Leon James materialized. He was wearing a riding habit with gleaming knee-high boots. The pants were champagne, the blouse iridescent burgundy, and the ascot powder blue. His right hand flicked a riding crop against his leg. As Al Minns recalls: "Leon waited until everybody had noticed him and then sauntered disdainfully across the floor to the Cats' Corner. He was so nonchalant that he could hardly see where he was going. I had already seen him in *A Day at the Races,* including that corny closeup of him grinning, and all I could think was: 'Why, the *big ham!*'" Minns was wearing a dark business suit and a white shirt with a starched collar.

Minns watched with mounting dissatisfaction, while some sixteen couples did their stuff, until at last, the King condescended to climax the evening. When Leon James finished, an invisible rope sprang up around the Cats' Corner, although the band was still playing and ordinary dancers were crowding the rest of the floor. Everyone of any importance stood respectfully still.

This was the moment that the kid chose to grab a partner and sail out into the Cats' Corner, performing the latest Savoy routines plus a few brand new air steps. The effect was so shocking that everybody continued to stand respectfully still—but this time because they were unable to move. After a few minutes, however, the group rallied, and several of the men crowded around the King, waiting for the word to tear Minns apart. But James hesitated. "This cat is doing our steps. Maybe he knows something." And Minns continued to dance, unmolested, until he had finished.

"I just felt like dancing," Minns insists to this day, although he was fully aware that he was shattering tradition and rather liked the idea. "When I was through, I walked up to James and said: 'Gee, Mr. Leon, I hope someday I can dance as great as you'—thinking *how big-headed can you get!* And James replied: 'Well, boy, you keep on practicing, and maybe someday you will'—thinking *what is this B.S. he's giving me?*" For a year an armed truce existed between them. In 1939, working together on the same team, they became fast friends. By then the Lindy was airborne.

41 From Coast to Coast

FOR NEARLY A DECADE the Lindy—more widely known as the Jitterbug—remained the sole possession of a small group, a kind of folk *avant-garde,* consisting of amateur dancers in a few big cities. As far as the general public was concerned, the dance arrived out of nowhere around 1936 to go with a new music called swing that was played by a man named Benny Goodman.

There were youngsters "jitterbugging in the aisles," as Benny Goodman played the Paramount Theater in New York City and made headlines from coast to coast. (The fire department was called in, and the balconies were checked for safety.) Commentators treated the event as another in a series of inexplicable phenomena produced by somebody else's teen-agers. The swing era, with its own music and dance, had officially begun.

Simultaneously, the public began to see—in the movies, in vaudeville, at night clubs, in ballrooms, and in Broadway musicals—groups of dancers tossing each other around with what appeared to be fatal abandon. To the uninitiated it looked like mass suicide. And yet, no matter how high a dancer soared, he hit the deck right on the beat and swung along into the next step. These were teams of newly professional Lindy Hoppers.

When the average teen-ager who liked to dance looked carefully, he saw that these couples were doing a step together—when they were on the ground—which was not too difficult, and which some of the older, more worldly kids in his own neighborhood were already doing in a comparatively mild fashion. So he tried it. The girls quickly evolved their own uniforms—saddle shoes, full skirts, and sloppy sweaters—while across the land, at high school proms, young ladies in evening gowns began to jitterbug, presenting a happily incongruous spectacle.

Writers have referred to the Lindy as "the only true American folk dance," but it is more than that. The Lindy is a fundamental approach, not an isolated step, used in later dances from the Afro-Cuban Mambo to the rock-and-rollers' Chicken. The Lindy caused a general revolution in the popular dance of the United States.

The decisive nature of this revolution is partly explained by a member of an older generation, George Wendler, who recalls sadly how the Lindy hit Detroit: [1] "The Lindy Hop reached here about 1929 as the Jitterbug. . . . It became the foundation for all sorts of eccentricities from my old-fashioned point of view. It seemed to gobble up and incorporate every novelty that followed it."

"Looking back at it, though, it did eventually open up dancing for white people. The sophisticated mask was discarded, you were permitted to get with it and be carried away. The girls' pleated skirts, billowing and whisking this way and that as they reversed their pivots, added a new beauty. Then when partners became separated, they would 'truck' or strut or maybe improvise something of their own.

"We old-timers had what I might call a bread-and-butter style, always dancing close to our partners, and performing variations on the Waltz and Fox Trot, sometimes with real style and grace. We could do a few novelties like the Charleston, but not, of course, as a steady diet. We just went back to our bread-and-butter steps. We felt this way about the Lindy—a novelty that wouldn't last.

"But then the Lindy became the bread-and-butter style of all the following generations, and we died on the vine, replaced everywhere by some kind of Lindy Hoppers. I don't recall any conservative style of dancing making a hit since the Lindy revolution." The Lindy became the first step youngsters learned, and it remained the foundation of most of their dancing.

The influence of the Lindy, and the more flowing style of dancing that was a part of it, spread swiftly and surely. It went deep as well as far. For example, a youngster named Ernie Smith, who later became a top executive in a New York advertising firm, lived in a white middle-class suburb of Pittsburgh and felt the tremors in 1939 when he was fifteen years old. The girls at high school had taught him to dance, and his interest in jazz was awakened. But there was something missing.

Smith went to hear the big white bands at the Westview Ballroom and the big Negro bands at the Stanley Theater. As his appreciation grew, he found himself irresistibly attracted to a ballroom in Hill City, the Negro section of Pittsburgh: "I lived a kind of Jekyll-Hyde existence. In the daytime I went to high school and got along fine with my friends there. At night I'd sneak over to Hill City and study the dancers from the balcony of the ballroom. I found what I'd been missing." [2] Smith imported his own version of Hill City dancing at the next high school prom, shocking and impressing his friends in a very satisfying fashion.

The fundamental lesson of Hill City was to dance smoothly. Hopping and bouncing around the dance floor, while pumping your partner's arm—the hitherto approved style—was corny: "The hardest thing to learn is the pelvic motion. I suppose I always felt that these motions are somehow obscene. You have to sway, forwards and backwards, with a controlled hip movement, while your shoulders stay level and your feet glide along the floor. Your right hand is held low on the girl's back, and your left hand down at your side, enclosing her hand. At this time, the girls at high school wouldn't or couldn't dance that way."

Smith soon mastered the Lindy, which was known in Hill City as the Jitterbug, and perfected his own versions of the breakaway, improvising variations on the Boogie Woogie, Suzie-Q, Shorty George, and Camel Walk, in a manner mildly reminiscent of Snake Hips Tucker. The response at high school became more and more gratifying, but he realized that he could no longer attend such childish dances.

Instead, Smith became a member of a pretty rough gang of white kids, who went dancing to jukeboxes at nearby mill towns, picking up partners on location. These boys had never attended high school, and they wore their hair cut long and one-button, rolled-lapel suits with peg-trousers. They even walked alike—a sort of catlike bounce, shoulders hunched and head bobbing up and down, with arms held close in front of the body and fiingers snapping. In those days they thought of themselves as "hep" (later "hip").

On these excursions, Smith found girls who could dance. They were the first white girls who could move in the authentic, flowing style: "I suppose you'd call those mill-town girls lower class. They were poorer and less educated than my high-school friends, but they could really dance. In fact, at that time it seemed that the lower class a girl was, the better dancer she was, too. I never brought any of them home."

Because they had more opportunities to see Negro dancers, or because they were simply less inhibited—or both—these mill-town girls were the first white girls in that area to dance the Lindy. It was one stage in a process taking place here and there across the country.

Meanwhile, the Savoy Ballroom set the pace. Bands, vaudeville, night club performers, and dance acts were booked in New York; phonograph recordings, musical shows, and radio programs originated there. Although other parts of the country favored other steps at other times, the Savoy's influence was all pervasive and conclusive. Harlem, with its rapidly increasing population from the deep South, had the talent and the tap-root connections with a dance tradition that could nourish a fine art.

John Martin, writing about the Savoy Ballroom in *The New York Times*, was one of the few dance critics to realize—later—the importance of what had happened:

> The white jitterbug is oftener than not uncouth to look at . . . but his Negro original is quite another matter. His movements are never so exaggerated that they lack control, and there is an unmistakable dignity about his most violent figures . . . there is a remarkable amount of improvisation . . . mixed in with . . . Lindy Hop figures.
>
> Of all the ballroom dancing these prying eyes have seen, this is unquestionably the finest.[3]

The point at which a Lindy dancer became a real professional is difficult to determine, because the stars of the Savoy danced for the fun of it without a thought of turning pro. By the late thirties, however, contests were frequent, and a good dancer could make a little pocket money. Members of the Savoy group went downtown to enter contests at the Roseland Ballroom, giving their hometowns as Detroit, Chicago, or Toronto, and danced off with the prizes. (The champion Lindy Hopper at Roseland was a white boy named Lou Levy, who later married one of the Andrews Sisters.)

With swing music the rage and jitterbugging the dance to go with it, Herbert White, still head bouncer at the Savoy, became the agent of all the Lindy groups who proceeded to appear in vaudeville, night clubs, Broadway musicals, and the movies. (Shorty Snowden was the first and last dancer to defy Whitey openly and leave the group to tour with the Paul Whiteman orchestra—a decision that took considerable courage.) Whitey employed around seventy-two dancers—the equivalent of a dozen troupes—under such names as *The Savoy Hoppers, The Jive-A-Dears,* and *Whitey's Lindy Hoppers.*[4]

He also managed to turn a pretty penny every step of the way. When the contract called for transportation by train, Whitey sent the dancers by bus and pocketed the difference. No matter how much the act earned, they continued to be paid the small amount Whitey had offered in the beginning. The dancers never objected. They knew nothing about show business, and they were being paid, however poorly, for doing what they loved to do.

"Those Lindy Hoppers made it tough for everybody," says Pete Nugent grimly. "With their speed and air steps they made all the other dancers look like they were standing still. They never made any money, and Whitey treated them like slaves, and they dressed like a little-league baseball team, but they stopped the show wherever they appeared."[5]

Whitey had a monopoly. In 1939 Mike Todd hired seven teams of Lindy dancers to perform in *The Hot Mikado* at the New York World's Fair. (Six teams were needed, but Whitey persuaded Todd that an extra couple should stand by.) When a backstage argument arose—for the dancers were an undisciplined and clamorous group—Todd fired them. He then discovered that no other dancers were "available"—Whitey had them all booked. Todd flew all the way to Chicago in search of Lindy Hoppers and could find none good enough for the show. On his return he decided he had never fired the original group, and the show continued.

Making the best of an old stereotype, the male dancers in the troupe, who wore tight jersey trousers, padded their supporters with handkerchiefs (a trick that has been known to happen in ballet) and executed an occasional slow, stretching step facing the audience. It was a private joke. Eventually even Mike Todd noticed it with horror. "If this isn't stopped, I'll never be able to put another show on Broadway." He ran to the wardrobe mistress to ask whether the dancers were wearing supporters. When assured that they were, he decreed that thenceforth each must wear *two* supporters.

Whether or not they knew show business, the Lindy Hoppers proved to be a big draw. When rehearsals for *The Hot Mikado* began, nobody spoke to them, and the star of the show, the great Bill Robinson, took it upon himself to refer to "that raggedy bunch of crazy kids." In their ignorance they sassed Bojangles and got in bad with everybody.

When the show opened, however, all was forgiven and they became the darlings of the cast. Even Bojangles changed his mind and announced at a backstage party in Pittsburgh: "Nobody had better mess with me or the Lindy Hoppers—*they* take care of the first act and *I* take care of the second."

Some kind of a climax in the diffusion of the Lindy occurred during the late thirties at Radio City Music Hall. The Music Hall, of course, prides itself on the dignity of its stage shows and takes great pains to make its mammoth productions impressive. During the swing craze, however, somebody at the Music Hall lost his head and hired a troupe of Whitey's Lindy Hoppers.

The widely advertised film at Radio City was *Jezebel*, featuring Bette Davis and George Brent, while the management dreamed up the complementary theme, *The World of Tomorrow*, for the stage show. Toward the end of a long and involved stage presentation, six Lindy Hoppers—three boys and their partners—danced resolutely all the way to the center of the great stage. Al Minns remembers it with horror: "Everybody backstage was so polite, too polite, and then going out on that great expanse was terrifying. Why, dancing there is like dancing inside an enormous cave, you can't see the audience at all, it's just solid black out there, but you can hear a quiet restlessness or breathing." The Music Hall was a far cry from the Cats' Corner at the Savoy Ballroom.

Supporting the dancers with what the management considered much better than the real thing, Erno Rapee stood solemnly upon the podium, conducting a very square symphony orchestra. A hundred-voice male choir costumed like jolly tars lined the back of the stage, performing a stationary Truck, with one finger pointing limply skyward. The entire aggregation was plodding through a nonrhythmic version—amplified beyond endurance—of "I'm Just a Jitterbug."

At the end of exactly three minutes of dancing, precisely planned by the director, the Lindy Hoppers quietly withdrew and giants emerged on both sides of the stage and hammered two big gongs. They were stripped to the waist as if they were introducing a J. Arthur Rank movie. At this moment, right on cue, ballet dancer Patricia Bowman ascended briskly on a rising platform through a trap-door in the center of the stage, posed like a butterfly, ready to swoop about.

After several days and nights of this careful routine, the Lindy Hoppers rebelled. One evening without warning they reverted to form, ignoring the accompaniment and clapping their hands and stomping their feet to give themselves some kind of beat. They even screamed and hollered encouragement to each other. In fact, they forgot where they were, and their dancing improved astonishingly. Whereupon the huge audience forgot where it was, too, and began to clap, stomp, scream, and holler, but more loudly.

The dancing seemed to be over before it started, and at the correct moment, the giants strode out to hammer the gongs and Patricia Bowman started rising. But nobody could hear the gongs and everybody was yelling "More! More! More!" demanding an encore and wondering for a moment, who is that woman coming through the floor and messing things up? When the audience showed no signs of stopping, Miss Bowman descended slowly out of sight.

Backstage, as the Lindy Hoppers were returning to their dressing rooms on the fourth floor, the intercom started to bellow "Lindy Hoppers back onstage to take a bow! Lindy Hoppers back onstage to take a bow!" and they ran back five times to bow and cool off the audience so the show could continue. Each time, meanwhile, the giants had been wearing out the gongs, and Patricia Bowman was bobbing up and down without being permitted to swoop about.

As they ran back onstage for the last time the Lindy Hoppers heard a Rockette exclaim: "At last, show biz comes to the Music Hall!" The foundations of Radio City trembled, and the next day the group received a check and a polite note saying their particular type of act was not the kind needed at that precise moment. No real Lindy dancers appeared there again.

(Tap dancer Bill Bailey reports similar difficulties at Radio City. "Those violins gave me a hard time, swooping and sliding all over the place," he says, "but I finally got them to quit playing until I finished, and then I told them they could play whatever they wanted." [6])

Herbert White died wealthy in the forties. The Savoy Ballroom was torn down in 1959 to make way for a housing development. In the same year, *Ballets Africaines*, "direct from Africa" (via Europe) was playing to sellout crowds on Broadway, with a finale composed, according to critic Douglass Watt, of "a thoroughly expert Lindy Hop." [7] Perhaps the Lindy had come full circle and influenced one of its sources.

Like other old-timers—the doctor made him quit dancing in 1938 because his feet had been pounded shapeless—Shorty Snowden has his reservations about what is happening today: "Lindy Hopping today seems to be mostly acrobatic tricks. The kids don't stop to learn the fundamentals first—they just start throwing each other around. To be done right, the Lindy is mostly footwork, and now there's no real footwork anymore. And they can't do it fast, they have to dance half-time." [8] By 1950 Al Minns and Leon James were working in factories.

Today, a mild version of the Lindy has penetrated the length and breadth of the land. The director of a coast-to-coast chain of dance studios describes the Lindy as "our national dance" and is prepared to teach an emasculated version of it to anyone in a very short time. (The youngsters adopted a watered-down sample of it in the late fifties for a rock-and-roll dance called the Chicken.) In a small number of ballrooms, in a limited number of big cities, we are told that a few young dancers are still capable of an inspired Lindy.

PART ELEVEN

Requiem

42 Baby Laurence and the Hoofers Club

IN THE FALL OF 1961 dancer Laurence Jackson, known professionally as Baby Laurence, visited a class on the history of jazz at the New School in New York City. He wore a dark business suit, carried himself with great dignity, and with prematurely gray hair at the age of forty, looked rather distinguished. Suddenly his nickname seemed disturbingly inappropriate.

He was eager to demonstrate how tap dance offers a new and visual dimension to jazz. "Tap dancing is very much like jazz music," he announced. "The dancer improvises his own solo and expresses himself." He then illustrated how tap evolved: King Rastus Brown started with flat-footed hoofing, Bill Robinson brought it up on the toes, Eddie Rector gave it body motion and elegance, and John Bubbles added rhythmic complexity.

"As a finale," he said formally, "I should like to improvise a 'Concerto in Percussion.'" For about five minutes he tossed off a variety of alternately light and heavy taps, scrapes, and stamps in the course of a series of hops, jumps, and spins. They were all executed on an area of about three square feet, and the emphasis was upon footwork—plus new and complex rhythms. The class was on its feet, cheering—the calm of the coolest hipster was shattered—and several members of the class found themselves enjoying the jazz of the accompaniment for the first time. Watching Baby gave it meaning.

The dancer who led tap into its last creative phase, Baby Laurence participated also in the last days of the Hoofers Club, the Harlem headquarters for tap dancers. He was eleven years old and singing with Don Redman's band in 1932, when he first visited New York. "Don discouraged my dancing," says Baby, "but when we hit town my first stop was the Hoofers Club—it was the biggest thrill of my life." [1]

While on Loew's circuit with Don Redman, Baby had studied two acts: *Pete Peaches and Duke,* and *Bill Bailey and Derby Wilson.* "I had to develop a liking for it," he says, "but after I saw them, I knew I wanted to dance." In those late days the stars of the Hoofers Club came from a new generation: "Honi Coles, Raymond Winfield, Roland Holder, and Harold Mablin were the kings then, and each had his own style."

Home in Baltimore after the Redman tour, Baby Laurence ran headlong into a numbing personal tragedy: Both his parents had died in a fire. "I don't think I ever got used to the idea," he says quietly. "They always took such good care of me." It was decided that he should go back to school and live with an aunt.

As soon as he could pull himself together, Baby ran away to New York. "I was lucky, I got a job at Dickie Wells's night club right away," he says. "Business was so fine that sometimes I made as much as two hundred dollars a night in tips—more money than was good for me." It was Wells, the retired dancer who had worked with *Wells Mordecai and Taylor,* who gave Baby his nickname and tried to take care of him. "I bought bicycles for my friends, and we rode all over Harlem." He also wrote a little poetry, but spent most of his time at the Hoofers Club, where he concentrated on tap and did his best to forget.

Protocol at the Hoofers Club fostered the invention of new steps. "Thou Shalt Not Copy Another's Steps—Exactly" was the unwritten law. You could imitate anybody inside the club, and it was taken as a compliment. But you must not do so professionally, that is in public and for pay. If and when your act appeared on the stage of the Lincoln, or even better, the Lafayette Theater in Harlem, your routine must be notably different.

Once word got around that an act was booked at these theaters, other dancers lined up, and as soon as the doors opened, rushed down to the front rows. "They watched you like hawks," says Baby, "and if you used any of their pet steps, they just stood right up in the theater and told everybody about it at the top of their voices."

The best dancers would not copy steps exactly anyway. "One of the fellows who was trying to help me got sore when I didn't do his step the way he did it," says Baby mildly. "I just didn't feel it his way." But many of the big shots refused to help the youngsters. "Bubbles came in to gamble, and Bojangles, to shoot pool." Eddie Rector and Harold Mablin helped Baby. Unlike most of the others Rector was not possessive about his steps. "Shuck, if you could copyright a step," he once said, "nobody could lift a foot." [2]

Baby Laurence watched and learned quickly at the Hoofers Club. "We told him he'd never be a dancer," says Warren Berry of *The Berry Brothers,* "and then one day he was better than any of us." [3]

From the mid-thirties, Baby worked with several acts. He started with *The Four Buds*, singing, dancing, and playing the tipple (a stringed instrument). When they joined *The Three Gobs* in 1937, one man quit, and the new act was billed as "The Six Merry Scotchmen." They all wore kilts. Later the name was changed to *The Harlem Highlanders*, and they danced and sang Jimmie Lunceford arrangements—in six parts—at Kelly's Stables. "We sure were international," says Baby.

In Cleveland Baby met dancer-choreographer Leonard Reed, who helped him put an act together and during the forties he was employed steadily, dancing with such big bands as Count Basie, Woody Herman, and Duke Ellington. "Those were the days," says Baby wistfully. "I was making more money than I knew what to do with, and every day was a ball—you just can't imagine how great it is to have the Ellington band backing you up."

Baby's fame was spreading rapidly. Around 1938 he was egged into a battle of taps with Freddie James on the corner of Harlem's 126th Street and Lenox Avenue. "Fans would start arguments," John Bubbles explains. "Then the dancer would come along and have to prove himself." [4] Other dancers agree that Freddie James, the star of *The Four Step Brothers* for several years, was one of the very best.

After the police broke up the crowd on the sidewalk, the contest adjourned to a nearby night club. They fired steps at each other from 11 P.M. to 4 A.M.—while Bill Bailey accompanied them on piano—and Freddie James finished with his feet in the air, tapping with his hands. "I think we were even," says Baby softly, but several eye-witnesses claim that he won.

From the first, Baby Laurence was primarily interested in the sounds he could make. "There was Baby Laurence, a man who did a tap dance as purely acoustic as a drum solo," wrote Edwin Denby in 1942. "It was interesting how he ignored the 'elegant' style in shoulders and hips, sacrificing this Broadway convention to the sound he made." [5]

"By 1945, when the small bop bands became popular," says Baby Laurence, "my style of dancing had begun to change." Bop drumming had evolved radically and, since most tappers thought of themselves as drummers, the dancers were crucially affected. Before bop, a good drummer like Jo Jones or Sidney Catlett—unless he was taking a solo—maintained a steady beat in the background, more felt than heard. After bop, the drummer participated as another solo voice on the cymbal, as well as adding eccentric explosions on the bass drum.

For the first time in the parallel histories of jazz music and dance, the drumming often became more complicated than the tapping. To the calculated complexity of such drummers as Kenny Clarke, Art Blakey, and Max Roach—who had learned from tappers at the start of their careers—tap dancers in 1945 could add little, and what they might add often conflicted with the drumming.

In those years Baby was singing with Art Tatum's group at the Onyx Club on 52nd Street. "Every time I heard Tatum play the piano, I had a crazy impulse to move my feet as fast as he moved his fingers," says Baby. Next door Charlie Parker was playing a new style of jazz, and Baby studied his rhythms. "I think my style of dancing was influenced more by Tatum and Parker than by other dancers," he says. "While I danced, I hummed Parker's solos to myself and tried to fit rhythmic patterns to them with my feet—those solos have subtle new accents that some musicians haven't heard yet."

The noisy ferocity of bop drumming persisted well into the sixties, but Baby had no trouble. Other dancers who adjusted to it are still not enthusiastic. The mildest of them all, Bunny Briggs, observes gently: "Some drummers nowadays think they're helping you when they drop bombs, but that's when I begin to worry." [6] Like James Barton years earlier, Briggs says "*Sh-Sh-Sh*" to the drummer before he even picks up his sticks. "Sometimes it works," he adds drily.

The fundamentals of tap were changing, too. By the fifties nobody used the Time Step any more. Four basic steps were combined with endless ingenuity: the Slap, the Slide, the Cramp Roll, and the Pull Up. In the Slap the foot is thrown out and down, usually for two short beats; the Slide gives a melodic quality to the sound and is of even shorter duration; the Cramp Roll consists of four fast beats, toe-heel, toe-heel—usually leading into or finishing up a step; and the Pull Up is a brush out, back, and hop, which lasts less than a measure. The outstanding characteristic of all these steps is their transitional nature and brevity, which allows them to be endlessly combined to fit the complex rhythms of bop.

"When I began, Bubbles was hitting a step for eight bars, and then Honi Coles extended the line to sixteen bars or more with variations," says Baby. "I went the other way and broke it down into single bars or even ran my steps together, to go with the new sounds." Baby knew all the standard steps, but they emerged in fragments and quickly changing combinations. "He has no routine, and he seldom 'buck-and-winged,' " says his friend and admirer Bunny Briggs. "He is an *ad lib* dancer, improvising as he goes along."

Baby likes to practice before a mirror, warming up with an energetic Shag step and clapping a Charleston beat—"Then you've got two rhythms going for you as a starter." Once he has warmed up, he takes some bop tune that he likes, and working with his accurate memory of the recording —as he did with Charlie Parker's "Billie's Bounce" at the Newport Jazz Festival—reconstructs and embellishes the melodic accents with his feet.

Paradoxically, Baby Laurence is more like a traditional hoofer than a stage dancer. Although he has a flair for ballet turns, he does not travel across the stage like the great dancers of the class acts. Nor is he concerned with presenting a pretty picture. He stays in one spot, concentrates on his footwork, and builds up a cascading complexity of sound. "Baby would be a regular hoofer," says Cholly Atkins, "if his taps weren't so complex and clear." [7] He achieves, according to Whitney Balliett, "what celebrated workers like Fred Astaire and Gene Kelly have only dreamed of these many years." [8]

Baby has given the matter of dancing to jazz serious thought. "I'd classify it three ways," he says, "*tap, interpretive,* and *choreographic.*" "Tap" emphasizes hoofing, represents the mainstream, and includes such dancers as Bill Robinson, John Bubbles, and Baby himself. "Interpretive" stresses body motion and traveling, and includes such dancers as Eddie Rector and Pete Nugent. "Choreographic" attaches special importance to the dance director or coach and includes dancing influenced by "modern" dance and ballet.

Baby has strong reservations about choreographic dancing to jazz. "From my point of view, having a choreographer tell me what to do would ruin everything," he says. "I wouldn't be able to improvise or interpret the music, and I couldn't express myself." He also has his doubts about the influence of ballet. "The moment you start to learn ballet, you become so conscious of poise and how you look that it limits what you can do with your feet, and worst of all, *you stop swinging.*"

In 1961, after a lengthy illness, Baby Laurence played an engagement at the Apollo Theater in Harlem with Count Basie. He looked tired and wan, but his feet possessed their old magic. In the middle of an impossibly difficult combination, which Baby put together on the spur of the moment, some unimpressed youngster in the audience jeered: "Show off!" Baby smiled for the first time, and in a voice barely audible in the front of the theater, replied, "You're just saying that because it's true."

A year later Baby made a comeback at the jazz festival, *Newport '62.* In fact, he was discovered by the jazz critics, who had heard about him for some time but never seen him. The new generation of musicians seem to appreciate Baby Laurence, too, even more than the critics. Pianist Bill Rubenstein, who accompanied Baby at the festival, voiced their feelings: "Now I've seen everything."

Years before John Bubbles had told Baby that he did not know the fundamentals of tap. Later on Bubbles changed his mind: "Why, Baby's the toughest dancer I ever battled with—he's in sort of a dream world and can dance like nobody else."

Since 1965 Baby Laurence has been back home in Baltimore, dancing occasionally. "Of all the dancers who came up in those last years," says Pete Nugent, "Baby was the most original." [9]

43 Groundhog

"GROUNDHOG?" said Mr. Wilhelm Smithe, President of Local 814 of the A.F.M. in Cincinnati. "A good dancer. Last time I saw him was around 1950 at the old Cotton Club they tore down—don't know where he went." [1] This trip, too, was a failure, and we still had not located the man behind a puzzling legend. Groundhog had disappeared.

Few tap dancers volunteer praise of Groundhog—in fact they seldom mention and never flock to see him—but if you ask them point blank about him, they all rate him at the very top. "He is short and not very good looking," says Baby Laurence, who first saw him in Detroit, "but he's a fine drummer, he knows all the acrobatic flash steps, and he has two of the greatest dancing feet in the world." [2]

Pinned down, other dancers agree. "Forget about carriage, because he doesn't have it," says Conrad Buckner. "He's strictly a hoofer, a dancer's dancer, a carny type." [3]

Louis Williams, who worked with him, adds: "He's a great jazz and eccentric dancer, too," [4] and Honi Coles once admitted: "He's just about the best dancer I've ever seen." [5] Even Pete Nugent, to whom style is all-important, admits that "Groundhog can *really* dance." [6]

We first heard of Groundhog from Alice Whitman. *The Whitman Sisters* had been tops on T.O.B.A. during most of the circuit's existence in the teens, twenties, and thirties. "Oh, yes, Pops had many dancers who worked with him," said Alice, reminiscing about her famous son. "One of them was Groundhog, a boy who was always disappearing." [7] The nickname alone was unforgettable, and persistent inquiry only clouded a paradoxical legend.

In October 1964 guitarist-raconteur Danny Barker walked into the Copper Rail Bar and Grill in New York, between sets at the Metropole, and announced, "Groundhog's in town." According to Danny, a group of dancers had locked him up in a Harlem cellar and were making him show them his steps. "They're feeding him liquor," he said, "while they steal his stuff." [8]

Another rumor concerned Groundhog's buddy, Rhythm Red. Red was supposed to be working as a night watchman at a building under construction on Eighth Avenue and 52nd Street while he and Groundhog practiced together among the cement mixers. A midnight tour, yelling "Hey, Red!" as inconspicuously as possible, brought no results and made us feel foolish. Rhythm Red must have disappeared, too.

We finally caught up with Groundhog at the Village Vanguard, where he had gone to hear his old friend, Max Roach. We were telling Mrs. Roach—singer Abbey Lincoln—about our search for Groundhog, when she motioned to the man at her side: "This is Groundhog." He was wearing a rumpled business suit and scuffed Oxfords. Putting his drink down carefully, he gave us a gap-toothed smile offset by a slight cast in one eye and offered a rough, work-worn hand.

For the next two hours, we alternated between listening to the Max Roach group with Abbey singing, and trying to interview Groundhog along with Rhythm Red, a giant of a man who loomed up at his side. Groundhog spoke so thickly that we could hardly understand him: "My name is Earl Basie," [9] he said gruffly. With that he became silent, while Rhythm Red talked pleasantly.

Groundhog did not want to be interviewed. From bits and scraps of conversation during the next two weeks, however, we pieced together something of his career. Born in Birmingham in 1922, he grew up with a local spasm band. "I used to dance in the streets with a tin-can band, along with Slick and Slack who tapped with bottle caps between their toes. Then I saw Rastus Murray at the Frolic Theater and decided to be a real dancer."

His mother was a chorus girl, and his father, a comedian known as Showboy Holland. "When I was six years old, *The Whitman Sisters* came through town. They saw me dancing in the streets and May Whitman talked my father into letting me go with them; I was billed as 'Showboy Holland, Jr.'" Groundhog and the young dancing star of the show, Pops Whitman, who was three years older, lived, worked, and played together.

"Pops and I used to shoot marbles," says Groundhog, "and several times I've kept him from falling over the footlights. As a matter of fact, I saved his life once in Birmingham—Pops accidentally tripped a man with his jump-rope, and the man knocked Pops down and was going to kill him, but I talked the man out of it."

Dancing with Pops Whitman, who was one of the first and greatest flash, or acrobatic, dancers, gave Groundhog inspiration. "When I saw

Pops dance, I knew I had to do better." Groundhog worked in the same style, and some say, soon surpassed his model. "I think they fired Groundhog because he learned to dance so much better than Pops," says Baby Laurence, "and it made Pops look bad."

For a six-year-old, life with *The Whitman Sisters* troupe was no bed of roses. May Whitman ran the company with an iron hand, and her husband, "Uncle" Dave Peyton, conducted a school with compulsory classes. Groundhog solved the problem by running away—in both directions—to and from home. "When I was twelve, my mother came and snatched me home, but I ran back to *The Whitman Sisters*." Another dancer who worked with *The Whitman Sisters*, Louis Williams, remembers the day when the troupe boarded a train in New Orleans for New York City. "Groundhog took a train for Los Angeles," says Williams. "They had a terrible time finding him."

Groundhog worked with *The Whitman Sisters* off and on for eight years, from 1928 to 1936. At first he danced as Pops Whitman's "shadow," taps and all. "Everything he did, I did right behind him at the same time," says Groundhog. "I didn't really get interested in tap dancing until I saw Fayard Nicholas." After leaving *The Whitman Sisters*, he had an act with his sister billed as "Showboy and Annie."

Then came years abroad. "I've been to Europe about seven times," says Groundhog, "spent three years in Paris—the French don't appreciate tap, so I used jazz, flash, and eccentric." In 1950, when Pops Whitman died at the age of thirty-nine in Athens, Groundhog was dancing at a nearby night club in the same city.

Groundhog also worked briefly in Hollywood, appearing in *The Big Store* with the Marx Brothers. "I did a no-hand flip onto a truck," he says. "They had to run three takes because I wasn't too sober." In 1951, he says, he helped Nick Castle choreograph a number for the chorus in *Skirts Ahoy* with Billy Eckstine. "Nick Castle is a beautiful guy to work with," he adds.

"He would never stay in New York City and *compete*," says Rhythm Red indignantly. "That's why Groundhog never got the credit he deserves." [10] Rhythm Red, whose name is John Chivers, resembles a kindly Mr. Clean and is a loyal friend. "I'm a midwestern boy," Groundhog growls, "I hang around Detroit mostly."

"You should have been in Chicago around 1942 when I first met Groundhog," says Rhythm Red, his eyes shining. "The South Side was jumping with great dancers: Groundhog, *Pops and Louis*, Jack Williams, and *The Rhythm Maniacs* were all on the same bill at the Rhumboogie; Baby Laurence and *Nip and Tuck* at the Club DeLisa; and me and Leon Collins at White's Emporium, with lots of other dancers—Red Simmons, Derby Hicks, and Monte Blue—passing through town."

An old tradition had been revived on the South Side. Around five o'clock in the morning after the night clubs closed, the entertainers swarmed out to relax on the benches along Garfield Boulevard. "One morning I was just sitting there watching several dancers trying to carve each other when this little cat"—Rhythm Red points at Groundhog—"saw his chance and cut loose. He started with Cramp Rolls on the concrete and built up fast to knee-drops, flips, and splits. It was all over in a minute, and after a stunned silence, we all cheered loud and long—and that was the end of the dancing. Nobody dared follow him."

At the Village Vanguard, watching Max Roach take a drum solo, Groundhog seemed to mellow. "Drumming and dancing are the same," he observed. "Max taught me how to drum paradiddles when he was working with Benny Carter. I lie in bed and listen to a metronome for two hours every night, inventing new combinations. I don't like to repeat a step unless it's necessary to help the audience catch on—dancing is about twenty years ahead of its time, and people don't understand it." Of all the dancers he has seen, Groundhog prefers Aaron Palmer (Pops Whitman's father), Eddie Rector, John Bubbles, and Paul Draper.

With the help of Max Roach, we planned an appearance for Groundhog. "I learned a lot just listening to Hog's feet," [11] says Max. The Village Gate had a fine floor, specially constructed for Carmen Amaya, and proprietor Art D'Lugoff offered to sandwich our act in between folk-singer Buffy Sainte-Marie and the Swingle Singers. He also generously agreed to furnish the Jo Jones Trio as accompaniment and to pay the dancers.

Rhythm Red got together three more unemployed dancers to furnish a build-up for Groundhog: Gentleman Peppy (Ernest Cathy), Tommy Powell, and Isaiah "Lon" Chaney. We had one rehearsal supervised by Max Roach. For the opening all the dancers lined up to "Tea for Two" and went through the Shim-Sham routine. Then each dancer selected the tune for his number and ran through three choruses. The pianist Jo Jones brought along had trouble with the standard tunes, but we assumed he would learn them in time for the performance.

The high point of the rehearsal—and indeed of the entire project—occurred toward the end, when Jo Jones and Groundhog started to trade fours, or alternate four bar solos. Jones soon gave up and Max Roach took over the drums. Roach tossed off complex rhythmic patterns of multiple tones (including bass-drum explosions) and Groundhog, with similar variations in pitch achieved by dropping his heels, stamping and slapping, repeated, commented upon, and answered them. For almost a quarter of an hour they seemed equally matched.

We all agreed that this should be the climax of the act, with Max planted in the audience and invited to come on stage and participate in a "spontaneous and unrehearsed" duet. The performance was to take place the next evening at ten-thirty before a specially invited audience of critics and promoters.

As an afterthought we asked Lon Chaney if he could find his friend,

Chuck Green, and bring him along. Four years older than Groundhog, Chuck was one of the original team of *Chuck and Chuckles*, which had danced with big bands all over the country. He was also the protégé of John Bubbles, and many said that he now excelled his master. Despite a serious illness some years ago, Chuck still danced beautifully and seemed to be in another—and more peaceful—world.

Groundhog's debut was a shambles. The bass player arrived without his instrument, and while everybody waited, some misguided patron of the dance circulated a bottle backstage. With the exception of Chuck Green, the dancers were understandably nervous. They had seen Groundhog dance at rehearsal and knew they were about to be cut to pieces. Further, reporters from the *Village Voice*, the *Times*, and the *New Yorker* were in the audience. Most nerve-racking of all, Negro comedian Nipsey Russell, whose recommendation might mean a job, was talking loudly at a front table.

Suddenly it became clear that Groundhog was the most nervous of all. During the delay he sat down with us and said hoarsely: "I've been waiting to battle Chuck Green for twenty years. Dancing is like a gang war and tonight I'm up against one of the best." He looked almost frightened. "Every dancer," he added, "is my enemy."

When the act was finally announced, all the dancers came on for the opening ensemble—except Groundhog. Then each dancer, with an eye on Nipsey Russell, who commented enthusiastically during each number, made a speech about what he was going to do and proceeded to run overtime. Concluding blasts on the drums by Jo Jones, who shouted "Goin' home!" at the dancers, had no effect. The efforts of the emcee to keep the program as planned were ignored. Only Rhythm Red announced briefly that he would do the best he could and did it. By then it was clear that the pianist would never know any of the tunes.

When his turn came, Chuck Green went on without a word and brought forth cheers for his effortless dancing. "It's like a continuous melody of taps," said a fellow dancer in the audience. Here was a great dancer.

At last Groundhog was announced—and nothing happened. He was fussing with his shoelaces just offstage and took an interminable two minutes to mount the platform. Then, to one unrecognizable chorus of "Ladybird," he burst into a wild assortment of tap, eccentric, jazz, and acrobatic steps. It was over and Groundhog was bowing almost before it started.

To fill the astonished pause, Max Roach was invited onstage and sat down at the drums. Instead of trading fours with Max, Groundhog called Chuck Green back and signaled for him to dance and keep on dancing. "I'm gonna put something on you," Groundhog shouted as Chuck obliged with a tap Charleston.

As time went on, it looked as if Groundhog was trying to wear Chuck down. "You can do better than that," he continued, and then, as Chuck went into a graceful tapping turn, Groundhog cried, "Oh, show biz?" Groundhog proceeded to execute an incredibly fast series of syncopated staccato taps, including a bit of flamenco, ending with a knee-drop—down and up in a split second—which left the audience gasping.

Chuck merely looked puzzled while Max Roach went back to his seat. There was no more music. "I never lost a case!" Groundhog yelled, interrupting Chuck's elegant rhythm tap whenever he saw a chance. Max had disappeared and the emcee quit in despair.

Groundhog knew what he was doing. By way of contrast to Chuck Green's relaxed, fluid, and almost dreamlike grace, he exploded into combinations fused at white heat. He simply swept the audience off its feet with his hard-hitting and dramatic dancing.

It was not exactly a battle between a dancer with one great style and another with an endless bag of tricks. Groundhog was by no means ragged, for each of his combinations had a style of its own. He was improvising, combining styles in a new way. The show ended when Groundhog decided that he had won. "Bewildering," said the *New Yorker*.[12] "Groundhog stratospherized us," said the *Village Voice*, "King of the Gate." [13]

We saw Groundhog for the last time at the Copper Rail, where Rhythm Red had been installed as bouncer. Groundhog's walk was unsteady. When we told him how much we enjoyed his dancing, he murmured something about always trying to do his best. His speech was hard to understand, but his modesty rang true. "I hate that name Groundhog. I think my old man gave it to me when I was too young to argue." We tried to cheer him.

Suddenly he was talking about his mother and his wife, the tears rolling down his cheeks. "My wife's a good dancer, but I'd rather go out and dig ditches than have her work for some of those promoters—look at these hands." They were covered with thick callouses from some kind of manual labor. "A dancer gets no credit for being an artist. Instead, he's persecuted—all my life I could never earn enough money to live like a man."

Groundhog promised solemnly to come down to visit us the following afternoon. "I'll tell you the *inside* story of tap." The next day he did not appear. At last report, the undisputed King of the Gate was still out of a job.

44 The Dying Breed

DANCERS KNOW THEIR JAZZ, especially the music of their own times, better than most jazz critics. They have to. The musicians furnish the accompaniment that can often make or break them. They live and work with jazzmen, tailoring their dancing to the most subtle nuances of the music. Frequently they help to put together the very arrangements to which they dance. Their activities and attitudes are consequently bound up closely with the jazz world.

By the mid-forties and the emergence of jazz with more complex rhythms, the few dancers who survived were forced into a subordinate role. No longer the innovators who led drummers toward more flowing rhythms, they dwindled to dependent followers, who, to get along, adopted jazz fashions and often found it expedient or exciting to emulate the activities of such pioneers as Charlie Parker and others, who seemed bent on self-destruction.

Dancers, perhaps because of the three-dimensional nature of their art, are traditionally more eccentric than musicians—they had their "cool cats," like Dynamite Hooker and Red, of *Red and Struggy,* before the jazzmen took up the phrase—but by the forties their eccentricities, anticipating the excesses of jazzmen, became more tragic than comic. The process was hastened by the fact that they were trying to make a living in a dying art.

Back in the thirties, for example, young Freddie James had astonished other dancers with his versatility. Star of his father's tab show on T.O.B.A. he had been featured in five spots on the program with his singing, comedy, and dancing. He played both guitar and trumpet expertly. "In my book," says Cholly Atkins, "Freddie had as much talent as Sammy Davis—and I love Sammy." [1]

In 1939 members of *The Four Step Brothers,* a durable favorite among dance teams, saw Freddie James practicing at the Hoofers Club. "He was sensational," says Maceo Anderson.[2]

Freddie could do everything including acrobatics—spins, knee-drops, flips, and splits—he could even dance on his hands. "He was so talented that the discipline of working with us and taking his turn," says Al Williams, "made him perform even better." [3]

For four years, from 1939 to 1943, James was the star of *The Four Step Brothers.* "On one occasion I saw him play trumpet," says Buddy Bradley, "and then dance rings around Bill Robinson!" [4] Another time, he and Baby Laurence battled to a draw. Again, one evening while Freddie James was dancing at a club named Chicken Charlie's in Washington, D.C., Pete Nugent left to perform at the Howard Theater and returned forty-five minutes later to find Freddie still dancing. "He wasn't repeating any steps either," says Nugent. "He had so much stuff he didn't know what to do with it." [5]

In 1943, having tried to keep up with the habits of some of the jazzmen of the day, Freddie James became ill and a new and chilling legend was born. "Once when he was sick," says a contemporary, "they say he took off his clothes, shinnied up a stoplight and said 'Turn green *now* you S.O.B.' " Again they said he stopped in the middle of his act, ran down to a seat in the audience, and looking back at the stage, shrieked "Look at that cat dance!" This was a decade before James Dean, Dylan Thomas, and Charlie Parker succeeded in killing themselves.

Perhaps the career of Teddy Hale is more tragic. Five years old in 1931, "Little Hale" was dancing with Ted Lewis in vaudeville and receiving rave reviews. By the age of ten he had worked with Luckey Roberts, appeared in a show at Connie's Inn, and was singing and dancing with an Ethel Waters troupe. At fifteen he was a successful single and had made movie shorts, dancing with various bands.

In the middle forties Pete Nugent saw twenty-year-old Teddy Hale solo at the New York Paramount. He was so staggered that he went back, dragging with him dancer Derby Wilson, whose ticket he paid for, just to have a witness. "Hale opened with three terrific choruses of a waltz before anybody realized what was happening," says Nugent. A routine to "Begin the Beguine" followed—it became Hale's trademark—making an immediate hit with the audience. "Then he threw in five lightning choruses of tap," Nugent remembers, "using transitional steps that only another dancer could appreciate."

As a finale Hale sat down in a chair and danced to an up-tempo two-to-a-bar—a very difficult feat—and then closed the act with a breathtaking assortment of spins, flips, and splits. "Derby Wilson's only comment," says Nugent, "was a reverent 'Sweet Jesus!' "

Teddy Hale came up at about the same time as Baby Laurence, and they were sometimes pitted against each other. Recalling a battle of tap in the early fifties at the Club Harlem, trumpeter Ray Nance says "It was the hottest night of the year, and Baby Laurence and Teddy Hale, the sweat pouring off them, fought to a draw." [6] Nance, a former dancer, could not decide who was better.

In 1954 Laurence and Hale met again at Minton's Playhouse with the same verdict. "I never realized how good Teddy was," says Baby Laurence, "until he got out of the army." [7] It was rumored that Hale had been rehearsing with Groundhog.

"There never was no clearer taps than Teddy Hale—easy and beautiful," says Bill Bailey, "and when he was off the dope, he was better than Baby Laurence." [8] There is general agreement, however, that Baby was more inventive. Some say Hale died of a brain hemorrhage; others say an overdose of narcotics. He had been dancing off and on at a seedy night club in Washington, D.C., where he had also been employed off and on as a kind of janitor. When he died, Teddy Hale was in his early thirties.

Other dancers had other problems. Paul Draper pioneered by tapping triumphantly to classical music on the concert stage. A liberal in the Joe McCarthy era, he soon found himself unemployed. "Paul Draper combines ballet steps and gestures as well as suggestions of Spanish and 'modern' with tap dancing," wrote Edwin Denby in 1944, adding "I wish he had more rhythmic freedom in his tap rhythms." [9]

Dancers express it differently: "His steps are kind of intellectual," says Pete Nugent. "They miss that swinging feeling."

In blending two or more diverse styles, Draper is bound to lose something. Perhaps a loss of rhythm was inevitable, for although the music of Bach moves—and merrily—it does not swing in the jazz sense. On the other hand, he may yet put together a winning combination, for that is the way vernacular dance evolved in the past. By the 1960's Draper was giving occasional concerts with harmonica-player Larry Adler.

Although his art has fallen upon evil times, Bunny Briggs is a cheerful exception to the tragedies that accompanied the decline of tap dance. In the 1960's he was the only Negro dancer of whom many white dancers had heard, probably because he was consistently employed. Much of his good fortune is due to his mother, a capable woman of strong character who had the courage to turn down Bill Robinson when he wanted to take young Bunny on as his protégé. Bunny was already doing well on his own, thank you.

In 1931, at the age of eight, Briggs made the improbable leap from the sidewalks of Harlem to the homes of society's Four Hundred—the Wanamakers, the Hitchcocks, and the Vincent Astors—when he joined Charles "Luckey" Roberts and his society orchestra as a singer and dancer. Roberts was a kind of Negro Meyer Davis, who played superb stride piano. In the summers, Briggs went on cruises in private yachts to Halifax and Bermuda. "Luckey taught me my manners," [10] says Bunny.

As the Depression deepened, society jobs folded, and Bunny finally found a job singing with Lucky Millinder's band. When that came to an end, he became the featured dancer with Erskine Hawkins and the 'Bama State Collegians at the Ubangi Club in Harlem. "I was just doing regular tap then," he says, "plus the Buck and Wing."

One night the band's manager told Briggs that he was adding another dancer. Briggs was not pleased. "The next evening Baby Laurence appeared and started to take over. I said, 'I'm dancing last,' and Baby said, 'No, I'm dancing last,' and I pretended to agree." In short order, Laurence worked out a routine to the tune "It's Off Time." Bunny sang first, they danced together, Bunny soloed, and Baby finished it. "When Baby was through there wasn't anything left to do," says Bunny. "I went home and told my mother 'I saw a fellow dance, and his feet never touched the floor.'" It was the beginning of a close friendship.

Bunny learned a great deal from Baby Laurence, and dancing with Earl Hines's band at Kellys Stables, made the transition to modern jazz—bop variety—with flying colors. "Both Dizzy Gillespie and Charlie Parker were in that band," says Bunny, "and it helped me work out my own style of Paddle and Roll."

East Coast dancers think that Paddle and Roll originated in the Midwest by way of an answer to New York styles. Buddy Bradley says it owes something to flamenco dancing. Although John Bubbles and Willie Bryant used elements of it earlier, Paddle and Roll hit New York full-blown around 1937, when Walter Green arrived from Chicago. Green placed a large sign in front of the Elks Rendezvous, where he was working, announcing in capital letters that all dancers were invited to drop in and be shot down by his unique footwork. "That was his big mistake," says Leroy Meyers. "Ralph Brown, Freddie James, Albert Gibson, and Chuck Green went over one night and clobbered him." [11]

Technically, the "Roll" in Paddle and Roll consists of staccato taps with the toe and heel in a rocking motion, usually of one foot (the other leg stiff) held to the beat by sheer tension. The "Paddle" consists of intermittent accents varying the steady roll. Some call it the Tommy Gun. Groundhog insists that he uses it when he wants to rest.[12] "Once you get the hang of it," says Honi Coles, who uses it as a sort of flavoring, "it's not so difficult." [13]

Short and slim, Bunny Briggs twinkles with an elfin charm that captivates audiences. He adapted Paddle and Roll to endless bits of pantomime —skating across the stage, pretending to have a backache, imitating a galloping horse, doing a pansy walk, or lifting his feet out of the snow. At the same time the *diddle, diddle, diddle,* with eccentric accents of Paddle and Roll, augmented by jingles in his shoes, reverberates throughout the theater. To this he adds jazz steps such as the Suzie-Q, the Mess Around, and the Applejack, and at the climax, throws himself down and up in a split.

When Bunny Briggs and Baby Laurence danced alternately and then together with Duke Ellington's band at the 1963 Newport Jazz Festival—they had agreed not to try to outdo each other—the jazz critics seemed to prefer Bunny, who was new to most of them (they had seen Baby the year before), while the modern musicians had eyes only for Baby. Baby's rhythmic patterns were more complex, but Bunny was the better showman.

By the fall of 1965 Briggs was dancing frequently with Duke Ellington. He had a fine solo entitled "David Danced before the Lord with All His Might" in a series of religious concerts given by Ellington at home and abroad (including Grace Cathedral in San Francisco and Coventry Cathedral in England). The accompaniment was Duke's "Come Sunday" theme from *Black Brown and Beige*. Briggs's tap solo can be heard on Duke Ellington's *Concert of Sacred Music*, Victor LPM 3582, recorded at Fifth Avenue Presbyterian Church in New York, and on an album *My People*, Contact LP CM1, recorded from a show written by Ellington and produced in Chicago.

"Working with Duke is an inspiration," says Bunny. "You have to create, and sometimes I feel as if I'm dancing on a cloud."

Vernacular dance died hard as one dancer after another quit, got sick, or simply disappeared. Freddie James, Teddy Hale, Baby Laurence, and Bunny Briggs (who survived in good health) are outstanding among many good but forgotten dancers, like Bobby Ephraim, Tommy Conine, Ralph Brown, Howard Sims, Jack Ackerman, Paul White, and Taps Miller. One fact was established, however, by two revivals at the Newport Jazz Festival (with Pete Nugent, Cholly Atkins, Honi Coles, Baby Laurence, Bunny Briggs, Chuck Green, Charles Cook, Ernest Brown and one of the present authors as commentator). Although American vernacular dance is unknown to young, middle-class Americans, once they see it performed, they are ecstatic. To the knowledgeable jazz fan its appeal is immediate and powerful; to others it presents an exciting visual dimension to jazz itself, as well as a new art.

"If they can beat this lecture-demonstration on tap dance plus jazz for knock-out entertainment," wrote Walter Terry in the New York *Herald Tribune*, "they are going some." [14]

"Five Negroes stepped out onto the stage," added George Frazier in the Boston *Herald*, "and suddenly their Shim Sham sanctified the sunlight, so that if you had never seen this before, you could hardly believe that creativeness could seem so casual. And then, for more than an hour, these men—this dying breed—made a lithe litany." [15]

Excited by their reception at Newport, the dancers nevertheless had to turn to their everyday jobs, which meant no more dancing. Like everyone else, they could only watch the chief retailer of dancing today—television—and the experience is bewildering and frequently depressing to any performer who loves to dance to jazz. "Where did the real thing go?" they ask.

"Most dance productions on television don't swing," says Honi Coles. "A good dancer feels the music and moves his body *between* the taps he is making."

Cholly Atkins insists on a fundamental point: "Remember, with taps you have to *sound* good as well as *look* good. It's twice as *hard*." On the other hand, old-timer Willie Covan is critical of ballet and choreography in general. "All those movements are regulated and set," he says, "so how can you express your *own* self?" [16] (Balanchine, who states frankly that to him dancers are "obedient animals," [17] might say you should *not* express yourself.)

Many years ago Eddie Rector, the idol of countless dancers, saw Fred and Adele Astaire in a Broadway show, *Dancing in the Dark*, and loved their combined grace of movement. "Nowadays everybody's doing nothin' but them leaps, like goosin' butterflies," he said in 1960. "Why, to come from dancing like I used to dance and then break out into them leaps! I couldn't get a job noways, and I wouldn't give that dancing nohow." [18]

45 Epilogue

AMERICAN VERNACULAR DANCE seems to embrace an emerging tradition with a usable past that, judging by what has gone before, may guarantee its eventual survival, for the Afro-American tint in the terpsichorean tapestry has become an increasingly dominant color. It has yet to become fully visible in the over-all pattern.

By the mid-sixties the vernacular tradition hit a new low. The old skills and know-how were disappearing while ballet was booming. "The world's most famous [ballet] companies tour the country competing for eager audiences with each other," wrote *Life* in a lyrical piece on George Balanchine, "and with over 200 regional companies."[1] Hundreds of less-publicized groups gave recitals in modern and "jazz" dance (which had little to do with jazz) from coast to coast, while the chains of dance studios as well as individual dance instructors did a thriving business teaching dilute ballroom dancing.

Dancers and dance critics—especially of ballet—seem to be concerned about one aspect of the dance: Is dancing for sissies? "The ballet is a purely female thing; it is a woman," says America's most famous choreographer, George Balanchine, "a garden of beautiful flowers, and man is the gardener."[2] This is hardly reassuring, for Balanchine clearly thinks of himself as the gardener and apparently leaves no place for male dancers. (Elsewhere he asserts, however, that ballet can make a dancer manly.)

The ladies meanwhile are developing an unflowerlike aggressiveness. "But all the girls, athletically piston-legged Furies," writes Clive Barnes reviewing a performance of Jerome Robbins's *The Cage* by the New York City Ballet, "[were] pouncing upon Stravinsky's rhythms like tigers." To Barnes, the ballet seemed "fiercely and sadly antifeminist" and perhaps he felt unduly threatened. With unshakeable conviction, nevertheless, he concludes that "women are here to stay." [3]

Gene Kelly is not so sure about the men. In 1966 he told an interviewer that he is deeply concerned about "the paucity of men entering the dance field, for a reason no one wants to talk about—the feeling that the field is dominated by homosexuals." [4] Several years before, Kelly had put on a TV program defiantly entitled "Dancing Is A Man's Game" and won an award from *Dance* magazine.

Kelly does not think of himself as a gardener, but rather as a sort of Olympic decathlon champion—an attitude reflected by his energetic style of dancing. "Dancing is a form of athletics," he declares, "and I'd like to see it attract strong young men who can experience the value and the sheer joy of it." There are many on both sides who would second this wish.

Whenever introduced to someone, "I see in their eyes the nagging question: 'Is he a man?'" Jacques d'Amboise of the New York City Ballet told *Time* magazine, which adds, "many male dancers are not." [5] Another dancer, commenting on the performance of Rudolf Nureyev and Margot Fonteyn in *Giselle* is quoted as saying "I couldn't tell which was the ballerina." Analyzing the state of the dance, *Time* observes: "Even today, if a boy hints that he might like to be a dancer, he becomes the playground freak, and Daddy goes rushing off to consult the family psychiatrist."

Time insists nevertheless—and again and again—that "the men are coming back." (Kelly's optimism is limited to the belief that "we're growing up, not putting labels on things as much as we used to.") "But times are changing," *Time* repeats, "and where once the ratio of girls to boys taking up the dance was 50 to 1, it is now about 15 to 1." Meanwhile, modern dance has moved out of "dingy halls and one-night stands in Manhattan's 92nd Street Y.M.H.A. into engagements at the glittering New York State Theater and Philharmonic Hall."

Perhaps it is enough to add that the question of whether or not dancers were sissies *never arose in the native American tradition of vernacular dance.*

In Broadway musicals elements of vernacular dance continued to appear without much approval from either the jazz-oriented dancers or the established dance critics. The dancing on Broadway in 1966, according to Clive Barnes "is not so much second rate as second grade . . . a style of dancing for people who don't like dancing." After complimenting *Golden Boy* as "the best dancing as dancing" (Sammy Davis actually tapped in this, but he is not the greatest of tap dancers), he selects *Fiddler on the Roof* and *Man of La Mancha* as the flawed best because they have "dance feeling but no specific dances." Most of the dancing gives "the impression of having been created by the same man," he concludes, "and most of all, designed so it will appeal to average Mr. Theatergoer. . . ." [6]

Logically enough, the greatest amount of all kinds of dancing during the sixties appeared on television, a medium that can make very effective use of it. In addition to special performances by celebrated ballet and modern dance companies, every program that might possibly need them—and many that did not—employed a line of professional (and not always virile) dancers, from the fading rock-and-roll programs to such variety shows as Jackie Gleason's. Opening with a big dance production hardened into a rigid formula.

The most lavish productions were devoted to such companies as the Bolshoi Ballet, Jerome Robbins's *N.Y. Export: Opus Jazz,* and various groups of exotic or ethnic dancers from almost anywhere outside the United States. Smaller presentations of American groups performing modern dance occurred less frequently on educational television, and rarely, on the networks.

Along with reruns of old film musicals, snippets of real vernacular dance appeared on television during the sixties: the unique Fred Astaire and Gene Kelly programs, Eleanor Powell on the Perry Como show, *The Four Step Brothers* and *The Dunhills* on Ed Sullivan's program, Gower Champion and Ray Bolger on *Today*, Hal Leroy on *Tonight*, *The Nicholas Brothers* and Ann Miller on *Hollywood Palace* (which had Fred Astaire as dancing host several times), the *Copasetics* on Sammy Davis's short-lived series, and the pioneer John Bubbles on *Tonight*, Bob Hope's show, and the little-known *American Musical Theater* programs. Most of these performances were brief, one-shot appearances.

For a weekly and straightforward presentation of tap and other vernacular dance, the viewer has one unexpected source: Lawrence Welk's Saturday night show. Three men (at least two of them double on instruments), Bobby Burgess, Jack Imel, and Arthur Duncan, are usually featured in one or more creditable dances. They may not be the all-time greatest in the field, but they are talented, and they have come by their dancing honestly. Thus, Duncan has taken lessons from Nick Castle among others, Burgess from Willie Covan. "Artie Duncan wanted me to teach him a routine by Bill Robinson which only I know," confides Willie Covan, "but I'm keeping it for later." [7]

Perhaps because the Lawrence Welk show has commercials with Ted Mack selling Geritol to balding citizens who have "low" blood, the network executives permit tap dance to be presented without apology, along with nostalgic tunes at a businessman's bounce and occasional up-tempo Dixieland numbers featuring the trumpet of Dick Cathcart and a swinging small combo. Tap dance has been relegated to entertainment of a harmless old-timey nature.

In general, however, most dancing on TV, as Jerome Robbins concludes, is "second rate and shot poorly . . . the dances all become clichés." He considers the *possibilities* for imaginative choreography on TV "fantastic," and one can only agree sadly.[8]

Again, critical confusion seems to have contributed to the decay of vernacular dance. Dance critics are a relatively recent addition to American journalism, and they naturally tend to keep close to the tried and true, which usually means ballet. In the process—as is so often the case—the native product is neglected, and if mentioned at all, praised or blamed for the wrong reasons.

Conflicting opinions of *N.Y. Export: Opus Jazz*, choreographed by the highly successful Jerome Robbins, illustrate the confusion. The esteemed critic John Martin thought it "contaminated by acceptance of the jazz techniques," [9] while professional jazz dancer Leon James could find little or no jazz movement in it.

To be specific: James noted a parody of the Jig Walk, a nonswinging version of the Pimp's Walk (employed years ago by "Sportin' Life" in *Porgy and Bess*), a clumsy Suzie-Q, "without the slide which makes it smooth," a rudimentary Charleston, and a gyration in which the dancers bend over backwards, protrude their stomachs and bounce—"we used to call it the Belly Rock," says James, "and ostracized any cornball who did it." [10]

Watching *Opus Jazz* was a disillusioning experience for Leon James. "Why it's just a bunch of girl-boys doing stretches, bumps, slides, and calisthenics."

John Martin agrees, in part, referring to "skirtless girls scarcely identifiable from the boys." [11]

The truth is that Robbins, who has been acclaimed "the first jazz choreographer," [12] employs movements that are *derived* from the vernacular, changed and molded—quite properly—to fit his own notions. That they are not particularly authentic is of little importance; that they lack the rhythmic propulsion which is at the heart of jazz is less fortunate, since it could create additional force and flavor.

In the past, praise of vernacular dance has generally been limited to a few jazz critics who have a feeling for swinging movement. When Allen Hughes commended a "Jazz Ballet" by Lee Becker—a fine modern dancer who shows little sensitivity to jazz rhythms—Whitney Balliett in the *New Yorker* was highly critical: "The ballet . . . consisted largely of decorous bumps-and-grinds, writhing, and push-ups."

Meanwhile any understanding of vernacular dance seems to be disappearing. "Trying to show that tap dancing is an art," announced Ann Barzel, *Dance* magazine's TV critic, "is like trying to make a silk purse out of a sow's ear." [13] Back in 1941 dance critic Walter Terry had a more favorable view: [14]

> Serious dance lovers rate tap pretty low in the dance scale, for although they may enjoy individual performers such as Bill Robinson or Fred Astaire, the actual technique of tap is generally considered superficial and limited in scope.
>
> An overdose of slam-bang tapping, of posture that resembles that of an anthropoid ape and of accompanying music that is cheap in quality has set tap at a low level . . . about the only human quality it can project is good spirits.
>
> Yet with the exception of Indian dance, tap is America's only indigenous dance form . . . with proper and knowing guidance there is no reason why tap dance should not expand into a richer dance art.

Nowadays the accompanying music of jazz needs no apology, the "anthropoid posture" lends flexibility and may be used to advantage, and the wide emotional range of vernacular dance can be documented on film.[15]

In 1962 Walter Terry was thrilled by tap dancing at the Newport Jazz Festival [16]—a program that helped to justify his twenty-year-old estimate of the potential of tap. That program, however, was a lecture-recital of vernacular dance history, while a sustained ballet, opera, or musical incorporating the true vernacular dance has yet to be created.

Will vernacular dance survive, and if so, how? Perhaps it disappeared only to be reborn, transformed into something at present too fresh and strange. The most highly developed dancing of the past—tap dance—is the most completely lost, partly because it is so difficult, but also because a revolution in mass culture apparently needs to begin all over again with something new and relatively simple.

With the appearance of rock-and-roll dancing (see Chapter 1), a revolution in popular taste took place from coast to coast, adding a flexible stance further liberated from European rigidity and accompanied by a more swinging—although rudimentary—music. Accordingly, it may evolve more rapidly than ever before.

The vernacular tradition, with its usable past, can never be scrapped entirely, for the moment anyone, amateur or professional, attempts to create a new dance—in Nashville, Hollywood, New York, or elsewhere—he inevitably falls back upon some previous movement (there are only so many), embellished perhaps by some minor gestures. To the youngsters of the day, however, it will be thrillingly new and a welcome addition to whatever rebellion is going on at the time.

Moreover, the manner of survival may be documented. Thus we can illustrate one of the processes by which dances originating among the folk and elsewhere survived in the rock-and-roll repertory. At Harlem's Apollo Theater in the early fifties, five ill-matched teen-agers scramble on stage dressed in rainbow-colored suits, manicured and marcelled to a fare-thee-well, and so heavily plastered with makeup that their faces resemble gargoyles. One of thousands of similar Negro groups, these youngsters represent the more immediate precursors of the Beatles.

The one who appears to win the race to stage center tilts the microphone at a forty-five degree angle and erupts into agonized song about the awful fact of adolescent infidelity. The others huddle around a second microphone and hum and burp accompaniment, each jerking and jouncing to his own separate rhythm. The group, like many others before and after, has just recorded a smash hit on a hitherto-unknown label and rocketed to fame—for a month or so.

These teams vanished long before the promoters who invested in them received what they thought they were entitled to get. The youngsters were at a serious disadvantage, because in a live performance on stage, all the flattering gimmicks of the recording studio—where the original "sound" was manufactured—were impossible. Furthermore, the kids had no idea how to handle themselves in public.

Polishing the act was the first step toward increasing profits. This led directly to choreography and Cholly Atkins, who had a reputation as a fine teacher.[17] Starting with a group called *The Cadillacs* in 1953, he improved the act so drastically that he was subsequently hired to coach the *Cleftones, Moonglows, Heartbeats, Solitaires, Bow Ties, Turbans, Dominoes, Satins, Teen-Agers*, and other groups that became popular in the fifties and later.

In the process Atkins became the number one babysitter and scout master for a series of rock-and-roll acts, hammering stage etiquette and specially tailored dance routines into their heads. They were often pathetically grateful when he suggested that the soloist should stand forward or that bowing with the legs wide apart left room for improvement. "When they were rehearsing, and the band leader asked them what tempo or key they wanted," says Cholly, "those kids didn't know what he was talking about. Slow-spoken and even-tempered, Atkins somehow found the patience and endurance for the job.

"The kids were real characters," he recalls, "very cocky, making big money, while the girls swooned over them. Some of those fourteen-year-olds went around with a wad of hundred-dollar bills in their pockets as spending money. I was supposed to keep them in line, too."

So Atkins flattered them: "You'll be even *more* popular if you put a little *class* into the act—do a few steps together." He scared them: "If you don't come to rehearsals and learn the routines together, the girls will forget you and flip over some *new* group" (which happened anyway). And he kept after them eternally to master the special series of steps he had worked out for each number.

Whenever he could get their attention, Atkins taught them bits of ballroom, jazz, or even tap steps—the Charleston, Trucking, Jig Walk, Applejack, Boogie Woogie, Suzie-Q, Slow Drag, Camel Walk, and so on—anything from the vernacular tradition that fit the lyrics they were supposed to be singing. A few learned a simple version of the Time Step. Little Frankie Lyman, star of the Teen-Agers at the age of thirteen, studied further with Pete Nugent and Baby Laurence and became a good tap dancer.

The major problem was getting a group to sustain a routine. "I wore them and myself out rehearsing," says Atkins, "making them remember cues for steps by the lyrics and the music.

The result was usually successful and often hilarious, for the youngsters did pretty much as they pleased on stage. For a while one of their most treasured gestures, which they inserted no matter what was rehearsed, consisted of pointing a finger and firing an imaginary pistol at the emcee as they went off stage. By 1965 Atkins was in Detroit, coaching the highly successful Motown groups, including *The Supremes.*

Something of vernacular dance was bound to survive: In whatever shape and form Atkins's steps materialized on stage, they became immediately enshrined in the hearts of adoring teen-age audiences. Thus, these vernacular movements, simplified and reinterpreted, took on a new and widespread life, sooner or later popping up on such TV programs as Dick Clark's *American Bandstand* and circulating from coast to coast.

Another less conspicuous but perhaps more potent bridge from old to new dances was furnished by Latin, or more accurately, Afro-Cuban dancing. By the late forties and well into the fifties, dancers at New York City's Palladium Ballroom on Broadway and 53rd Street, reinforced by jazz dancers from the Savoy, were incorporating a variety of vernacular steps into the Mambo, Cha Cha Cha, and other Latin dances.

"You can dance whatever you feel at the Palladium," [18] says Andy Bascus, who introduced his version of taps and legomania with great success during the Wednesday night competitions. A youngster named Teddy Hill incorporated an around-the-back Lindy and a through-the-legs Charleston into the Mambo.

"Sure I use tap in the Mambo," adds Cuban Pete (Pedro Aguilar), who was brought to New York from Puerto Rico at the age of three and enrolled in a tap class, "along with jazz steps, acrobatics, and even rock-and-roll dances." [19] He put together a much-imitated routine in which he kicks forward, draws back, and adds two heel taps with one foot.

By 1953—the year rock-and-roll groups began crowding the Apollo Theater in Harlem—the Palladium team of Charles Arroyo and Michael Ramos, billed as "The Cha Cha Taps," was employing buck-and-wings, brushes, and slaps, and blending ballet arm and hand gestures with Afro-Cuban body movement and tap footwork. They managed to combine just about everything and make it swing. A big hit at the Palladium, although the Mambo was "going cool" around 1957, they were several light years ahead of the general public.

Perhaps the best-known link between old and new *via* Afro-Cuban dancing is the durable Frank "Killer Joe" Piro. A star of the Savoy in the thirties, by 1940 he had won the jitterbug title in the famous Harvest Moon Ball competitions. After World War II he became the master of ceremonies and instructor at the Palladium, where he taught Afro-Cuban dances. "I used a lot of ideas from the Savoy at the Palladium," he says.[20]

When the Twist came along in 1960, Piro was more than ready and proceeded to compose new steps, drawing inevitably upon the wealth of older dances he had known, jitterbugging at the Savoy, and teaching the Mambo at the Palladium. Then he spread them far and wide through his studio lessons and highly publicized exhibitions. Sitting in Shepheard's discotheque and watching the dancers in 1965, Piro commented: "All that hip movement . . . it's got new names but you know they were doing that at the Savoy Ballroom in Harlem when I was seventeen."[21] Piro is a one-man bridge over thirty years of popular dance.

The long-range influence *via* Afro-Cuban on vernacular dance is easier to estimate than its immediate impact. Certainly the many charadelike hand and body gestures of such rock-and-roll dances as the Swim, Hitchhike, Monkey, Woodpecker, and so on owe a great deal to Afro-Cuban dancing, which thrives on pantomime. Judging by the past, we may expect the Afro-American, and perhaps to a lesser extent, the Afro-Cuban traditions to become more and more dominant.

Finally, it seems certain that art dance and vernacular dance will combine more and more effectively as time passes. They have already blended in theatrical dancing. The merging has progressed for some time—like the blending of classical music and jazz—and the extent of the mixture is a matter of degree, for neither tradition can assimilate the other completely, and for the same reason, the resulting blend will always be new, different, and perhaps fine art.

The fluid spine and flexed knees of tap dancing, for example, wreck ballet posture, just as pointing the feet at a forty-five-degree angle in the ballet tradition makes tapping impossible. But different approaches of the two traditions, such as strict or casual displacement in person and on the stage, traditional or improvised movement, and contrasting or repeated gestures, have merged to varying degrees.

Perhaps rhythm is the key to future mixtures. Employing the free meter of art dance in the over-all structure, with insertions of the strict vernacular beat as contrast, might unite the best of both. The problem is to find dancers (and musicians) who are expert in both idioms and can modulate back and forth between them.

Nevertheless, we are witnessing increasingly successful borrowings and blends from both the art and the vernacular dance traditions by such choreographers as Donald MacKayle, Jerome Robbins, Jack Cole, Peter

Gennaro, Alvin Ailey, Robert Fosse, Michael Kidd, and Gower Champion—to name a few of the best. The blending has been going on for years, and although no one blend pleases everybody, the process is time-honored and the result—at any moment—may be truly great.

The sixties, then, were a transitional era in which the old was dying and the new struggling to be born. There is little reason to believe that the great tradition of American vernacular dance has vanished forever, and much evidence to support the belief that a new and perhaps more remarkable age of highly rhythmic native dance will arrive in the not too distant future. Not the least of our problems is to recognize it when it appears.

Notes

Much of the material in the following chapters is taken from interviews rather than from printed sources. Accordingly, where most of the material in a chapter comes from numerous interviews with one dancer, we have simply footnoted the first quotation in the chapter.

INTRODUCTION

1. Introduction to *Ballet in Britain,* ed. Peter Brinson (London: Oxford University Press, 1962), p. 3.
2. Agnes de Mille, *The Book of the Dance* (New York: Golden Press, 1963), p. 65.
3. "Jazz Dance, Mambo Dance," *Jazz Review* (November, 1959), p. 63.

CHAPTER 1

1. See Paul Ackerman, *High Fidelity* (June, 1958), *passim.*
2. *Life* (21 May 1965), p. 97.
3. Morris Goldberg, "It Ain't No Sin to Sing," New York *Enquirer* (9 July 1956).
4. 18 June 1956.
5. 16 September 1956.
6. Goldberg, "It Ain't No Sin."
7. James and Annette Baxter, "The Man in the Blue Suede Shoes," *Harper's* (January, 1958).
8. *Ibid.*
9. Charles Gruenberg, "The Rock and Roll Story," New York *Post* (4 October 1956).
10. New York *World Telegram* (26 October 1961).
11. New York *Herald Tribune* (29 November 1961).
12. *The New York Times* (17 August 1965).
13. Earl Wilson, New York *Post* (23 November 1965).
14. *Life* (21 May 1965), pp. 83-5.
15. New York *Herald Tribune* (29 November 1961).

CHAPTER 2

1. Leopold Sedar Senghor, "African-Negro Aesthetics," *Diogenes* #16 (Winter, 1956), p. 33.

2. Melville J. Herskovits, *The Myth of the Negro Past* (New York: Harper & Brothers, 1941), p. 76.
3. *Dance* (March, 1958), p. 91.
4. Herskovits, *The Myth of the Negro Past,* p. 146.
5. A. N. Tucker, *Tribal Music and Dancing in the Southern Sudan* (London: Wm. Reeves Ltd., n.d.), p. 36.
6. Frederick Kaigh, *Witchcraft and Magic in Africa* (London: Richard Lesley & Co. Ltd., 1947), p. 21.
7. From a lecture at the Philadelphia meeting of the Ethnomusicological Society, 1961.
8. In conversation, New York: 1959.
9. From numerous interviews, New York: 1962-1965.
10. Herskovits, *The Myth of the Negro Past,* p. 76.
11. We are grateful to Professor Thompson for his thoughts on many subjects in the course of numerous lectures, correspondence, and conversations, over the past decade.
12. See *supra* note #7.
13. Geoffrey Gorer, *Africa Dances* (London: John Lehmann, 1949), p. 213.
14. John Martin, *The Dance* (New York: Tudor Publishing Company, 1963), p. 179.
15. From manuscript for *Grolier Encyclopedia.*
16. Martin, *The Dance, Ibid.*
17. *Ibid.* p. 178.
18. Reprinted in Edwin Denby, *Looking at the Dance* (New York: Pellegrini & Cudahy, 1949), p. 364.
19. *Ibid.* p. 361.
20. Harold Courlander, *The Drum and the Hoe* (Berkeley: University of California Press, 1960), p. 130.
21. A. M. Jones, *Studies in African Music,* Vol. I (London: Oxford University Press, 1959), pp. 256, 274-5.
22. Lisa Lekis, *Dancing Gods* (New York: Scarecrow Press, 1960), p. 37.
23. Lisa Lekis, *Folk Dances of Latin America* (New York: Scarecrow Press, 1958), p. 226.
24. *Ibid.* p. 277.
25. Katherine Dunham, *Journey to Accompong* (New York: Henry Holt & Co., 1946), pp. 24, 26.
26. Lisa Lekis, *Folk Dances of Latin America,* p. 275.
27. Katherine Dunham, *Journey to Accompong,* p. 135.
28. Lisa Lekis, *Folk Dances of Latin America,* p. 229.
29. "Behind the Mask of Africa," *The New York Times Magazine* (15 May 1966), p. 30.
30. Lisa Lekis, *Folk Dances of Latin America,* p. 196.

CHAPTER 3

1. "New Orleans Marching Bands: Choreographer's Delight," *Dance* (January, 1958), p. 34.
2. "The Dance in Place Congo," *Century Magazine,* Vol. XXXI (February, 1886), p. 522.
3. *Impressions Respecting New Orleans,* ed. Samuel Wilson, Jr. (New York: Columbia University Press, 1951), p. 51.
4. Quoted by Rudi Blesh and Harriet Janis, *They All Played Ragtime* (New York: Alfred A. Knopf, Inc., 1950), pp. 82-3, from a biography of Louis Gottschalk by Henry Didimus (Henry Edward Durell).

5. "Creole Slave Songs," *Century Magazine,* Vol. XXXI (April, 1886), p. 818.
6. "The Dance in Place Congo," p. 520.
7. Quoted and translated from *Nouveau Voyage aux Isles de l'Amerique* (Hague, 1724) in *Dance Index,* Vol. V, No. 10 (October, 1946), p. 254.
8. Quoted and translated from *Nouveau Voyage etc.* in Gilbert Chase, *America's Music* (New York: McGraw Hill Book Company, Inc., 1955), p. 314.
9. See Moore in *Dance Index, supra* note #7, p. 255.
10. In conversation and from his *Music in New Orleans, the Formative Years 1791-1841* (Baton Rouge, La., Louisiana State University Press, 1966), pp. 45-47 *et passim.*
11. From an interview, New Orleans: 1959.
12. From an interview, New Orleans: 1959.
13. Dena J. Epstein, "Slave Music in the United States before 1860," *Notes* (Spring, 1963), p. 198.
14. *Journal of Nicholas Cresswell, 1774-1777* (New York: L. MacVeagh, The Dial Press, Inc., 1924), pp. 17-19. Quoted in Epstein, *Ibid.* p. 201.
15. *Richmond in By-Gone Days* (Richmond: George M. West, 1856), pp. 179-180.
16. *America's Music,* p. 77.
17. From numerous interviews, New York: 1959-1966.
18. Quoted in Blesh and Janis, *They All Played Ragtime,* p. 96.
19. Paul Oliver, *Conversation with the Blues* (New York: Horizon Press, 1965), p. 44.
20. "Levee Life," (17 March 1876).
21. From an interview, New York: 1959.
22. From numerous interviews, New York: 1959-1966.
23. From interviews, New York: 1960-1964.
24. Paul Oliver, *Conversation,* p. 61.
25. From interviews with Mrs. Leola Wilson (Coot Grant), Whitesboro, New Jersey: 1959-1960.
26. Tom Davin, "Conversations with James P. Johnson," *Jazz Review* (July, 1959), pp. 11-12.

CHAPTER 4

1. Melville J. and Frances S. Herskovits, *Rebel Destiny* (New York: Whittlesey House, 1934), p. 330.
2. Lydia Parrish, *Slave Songs of the Georgia Sea Islands* (New York: Creative Age Press, 1949), p. 111 *et passim.*
3. Savannah Unit, Georgia writers' project, W.P.A., *Drums and Shadows* (Athens: University of Georgia Press, 1940), p. 115.
4. From interviews with Mrs. Leola Wilson (Coot Grant), Whitesboro, New Jersey: 1959-1960.
5. From an interview, New Orleans: 1959.
6. From an interview, New York: 1959.
7. Melville J. and Frances S. Herskovits, *Suriname Folk-Lore* (New York: Columbia University Press, 1936), p. 93.
8. From an interview with Mr. and Mrs. Jodie Edwards (Butterbeans and Susie), Chicago: 1960.
9. *The Dance* (January, 1928), p. 41.
10. "Creole Slave Songs," *Century Magazine,* Vol. XXXI (April, 1886), p. 808.
11. "Juba and American Minstrelsy," *Chronicles of the American Dance,* ed. Paul Magriel (New York: Henry Holt & Co., 1948), p. 40.
12. Lisa Lekis, *Folk Dances of Latin America* (New York: Scarecrow Press, 1958), p. 226.

13. *Ibid.* p. 240.
14. Harold Courlander, *Haiti Singing* (Chapel Hill: University of North Carolina Press, 1939), p. 161.
15. Thomas W. Talley, *Negro Folk Rhymes* (New York: The Macmillan Company, 1922), pp. 296-7.
16. "Levee Life," Cincinnati *Commercial* (17 March 1876).
17. Mark Twain, *Life on the Mississippi* (Boston: J. R. Osgood, 1883), p. 49. This "raft passage" was part of an 1876 draft of *Huckleberry Finn* that purports to describe customs "forty to fifty years ago."
18. Douglas Gilbert, *American Vaudeville* (New York: Whittlesey House, 1940), p. 171.
19. June, 1952.
20. John A. and Alan Lomax, *Folk Song, U.S.A.* (New York: Duell, Sloan & Pearce, 1947), p. 335.
21. "Under the Palmetto," *Continental Monthly*, Vol. IV (August, 1863), p. 197.
22. From the *Nation* (30 May 1867) as quoted in *Slave Songs of the United States,* ed. William Francis Allen, Charles P. Ware, and Lucy McKim Garrison (New York: A. Simpson Co., 1867), p. iv.
23. Lydia Parrish, *Slave Songs of the Georgia Sea Islands,* p. 55.
24. Frances A. Kemble, *Journal of a Residence on a Georgia Plantation in 1838-1839* (New York: Harper & Brothers, 1864), p. 97.
25. Herbert Ravenel Sass, *A Carolina Rice Plantation of the Fifties* (New York: William Morrow and Company, 1936), p. 76.
26. Quoted by Rudi Blesh and Harriet Janis, *They All Played Ragtime* (New York: Alfred A. Knopf, Inc., 1950), p. 190.
27. Curt Sachs, *World History of the Dance* (New York: Seven Arts Publishers, 1952), p. 350.

CHAPTER 5

1. Cited by Hans Nathan in *Dan Emmett and the Rise of Early Negro Minstrelsy* (Norman: University of Oklahoma Press, 1962), p. 70 and note.
2. Benjamin A. Botkin, *Lay My Burden Down* (Chicago: University of Chicago Press, 1945), pp. 56-7.
3. From an interview, Philadelphia: 1963.
4. Lincoln Kirstein, *The Book of the Dance* (Garden City, N.Y.: Garden City Publishing Co., 1942), p. 342.
5. Charles Durang, *The Ball-room Bijou, and Art of Dancing* (Philadelphia: Fischer and Brother, n.d.), p. 158.
6. Henry Tucker, *Clog Dancing Made Easy* (New York: The DeWitt Publishing Co., 1874), p. 4.
7. From numerous interviews, conversations, and correspondence (see Chapter 37), New York, Newport, R.I.: 1959-1966.
8. "John Durang the First American Dancer," *Chronicles of the American Dance,* ed. Paul Magriel (New York: Henry Holt and Co., 1948), p. 21.
9. Quoted by Moore, *Chronicles of the American Dance,* p. 25.
10. Paul Magriel, ed., *Chronicles of the American Dance,* p. 40.
11. 5 June 1881.
12. Magriel, ed., *Chronicles of the American Dance, Ibid.*
13. George C. D. Odell, *Annals of the New York Stage,* Vol. IV (New York: Columbia University Press, 1927), p. 372.
14. Quoted in Hans Nathan, *Dan Emmett and the Rise of Early Negro Minstrelsy,* p. 52, note #2.

15. Thomas W. Talley, *Negro Folk Rhymes* (New York: The Macmillan Company, 1922), p. 13.
16. Carl Wittke, *Tambo and Bones* (Durham, N. Carolina: Duke University Press, 1930), pp. 27, 29.
17. 13 April 1878.

CHAPTER 6

1. Carl Wittke, *Tambo and Bones* (Durham, N. Carolina: Duke University Press, 1930), p. 27.
2. Gilbert Chase, *America's Music* (New York: McGraw Hill Co., 1955), p. 260.
3. Constance Rourke, *American Humor* (New York: Harcourt, Brace and Co., 1931), pp. 98-9.
4. New York *Clipper* (6 November 1858).
5. Edw. LeRoy Rice, *Monarchs of Minstrelsy* (New York: Kenny Publishing Co., 1911), p. 48.
6. Michael B. Leavitt, *Fifty Years in Theatrical Management* (New York: Broadway Publishing Co., 1912), pp. 33-4.
7. "Juba and American Minstrelsy," *Chronicles of the American Dance*, ed. Paul Magriel (New York: Henry Holt and Co., 1948), p. 42.
8. Herbert Asbury, *The Gangs of New York* (New York: Alfred A. Knopf, 1927), pp. 5-9.
9. Ladies of the Mission, *The Old Brewery and the New Mission House at the Five Points* (New York: Stringer & Townsend, 1854), initialed B.M.A., p. 197.
10. Rourke, *American Humor*, p. 92.
11. "100 Years of Tap," *Dance* (November, 1937).
12. Cited by Winter in *Chronicles of the American Dance*, p. 42.
13. *Ibid.* pp. 43-5.
14. *Ibid.* p. 47.
15. Rice, *Monarchs of Minstrelsy*, p. 40.
16. Leavitt, *Fifty Years in Theatrical Management*, p. 34.
17. Charles Dickens, *American Notes*, Vol. I (London: Chapman and Hall, 1842), p. 218.
18. Quoted by Winter in *Chronicles of the American Dance*, p. 50.
19. *Ibid.* p. 52.
20. *Ibid.* p. 50.
21. *Ibid.* p. 42.
22. "Three Years As a Negro Minstrel," *Atlantic Monthly*, XXIV (July, 1869), p. 72.
23. *Chronicles of the American Dance*, p. 53.
24. *Ibid.*
25. Rourke, *American Humor*, pp. 88, 95.
26. Hans Nathan, *Dan Emmett and the Rise of Early Negro Minstrelsy* (Norman: University of Oklahoma Press, 1962), p. 151.
27. Carl Wittke, *Tambo and Bones*, p. 57.

CHAPTER 7

1. Edward B. Marks as told to A. J. Liebling, *They All Sang* (New York: The Viking Press, Inc., 1935), p. 65.
2. Douglas Gilbert, *American Vaudeville* (New York: Whittlesey House, 1940), p. 24.
3. McIntyre interview with Helen Ormsbee, New York *Herald Tribune* (10 November 1935).
4. Fagan's obituary, New York *Herald Tribune* (13 January 1937).

5. Barrett interview with A. J. Liebling, New York *World Telegram* (9 November 1932).
6. See *supra* note #3.
7. "Juba and American Minstrelsy," *Chronicles of the American Dance,* ed. Paul Magriel (New York: Henry Holt and Co., 1948), p. 55.
8. New York *Clipper* (22 May 1858).
9. Carl Wittke, *Tambo and Bones* (Durham, N. Carolina: Duke University Press, 1930), p. 223.
10. Gilbert, *American Vaudeville,* p. 130.
11. From unpublished notes by Rudi Blesh and Harriet Janis, *They All Played Ragtime.*
12. See *supra* note #11.
13. From interviews and correspondence with Miller, Los Angeles: 1960, 1965, 1966.
14. This and all further quotes by him in this chapter are from numerous interviews, conversations, and correspondence, New York: 1962-1966.
15. From an interview, Chicago: 1959.
16. From interviews, Los Angeles: 1960, 1965.
17. "Hoofing," *Saturday Evening Post* (Sept. 14, 1929).
18. From interviews, New York: 1960-1961.
19. Edw. LeRoy Rice, *Monarchs of Minstrelsy* (New York: Kenny Publishing Co., 1911), p. 236.
20. Harlowe Hoyt, *Town Hall Tonight* (Englewood Cliffs, New Jersey: Prentice-Hall, Inc., 1955), p. 163.
21. Marks, *They All Sang,* p. 67.
22. From Harland Dixon interviews.
23. Marks, *They All Sang,* p. 60.

CHAPTER 8

1. Gilbert Chase, *America's Music* (New York: McGraw Hill Co., 1955), p. 268, footnote #4.
2. Carl Wittke, *Tambo and Bones* (Durham, N. Carolina: Duke University Press, 1930), p. 121.
3. Frances A. Kemble, *Journal of a Residence on a Georgia Plantation in 1838-1839* (New York: Harper & Brothers, 1864), p. 96.
4. Edward B. Marks, *They All Sang* (New York: The Viking Press, Inc., 1935), p. 70.
5. *Ibid.* pp. 62-3.
6. *Ibid.* p. 66.
7. *Ibid.* pp. 69-70.
8. William C. Handy, *Father of the Blues* (New York: The Macmillan Company, 1941), p. 34.
9. "Juba and American Minstrelsy," *Chronicles of the American Dance,* ed. Paul Magriel (New York: Henry Holt & Co., 1948), p. 57.
10. James Weldon Johnson, *Black Manhattan* (New York: Alfred A. Knopf, Inc., 1930), p. 89.
11. Magriel, ed., *Chronicles of the American Dance,* p. 55.
12. "The Real Coon on the American Stage," *The Theatre* (August, 1906).
13. *Ibid.*
14. See James Weldon Johnson, *Black Manhattan,* pp. 90-93.
15. Handy, *Father of the Blues,* p. 33.
16. *Ibid.* p. 44.
17. *Ibid.* pp. 50-51.

18. Marks, *They All Sang*, p. 69.
19. Magriel, ed., *Chronicles of the American Dance*, pp. 57-8.
20. In conversation, Hyannis, Mass.: 1966.

CHAPTER 9

1. This and all further quotes by him in this chapter are from interviews, New York: 1959-1963.
2. This and all further quotes by him in this chapter are from interviews, New York: 1961-1966.
3. This and all further quotes by him in this chapter are from interviews, New York: 1959-1962.
4. From an interview, Chicago: 1959.
5. Paul Oliver, *Conversation with the Blues* (New York: Horizon Press, 1965), p. 127.
6. *Ibid.* p. 125.

CHAPTER 10

1. Ethel Waters, *His Eye Is on the Sparrow* (Garden City, N.Y.: Doubleday & Company, Inc., 1951), pp. 82, 93, 47.
2. This and all further quotes by him in this chapter are from interviews, New York: 1961-1966.
3. This and all further quotes by him in this chapter are from interviews, New York: 1959-1963.
4. This and all further quotes by him in this chapter are from interviews, New York: 1959.
5. This and all further quotes by him in this chapter are from interviews, New York: 1959-1962.
6. From an interview with Mrs. Glover Compton (Nettie Compton), Chicago: 1960.
7. From interviews, New York: 1960-1964.
8. From an interview with Mrs. Paul Howard (Susie Beavers), Los Angeles: 1960.
9. Paul Oliver, *Conversation with the Blues* (New York: Horizon Press, 1965), p. 123.
10. Abel Green and Joe Laurie, Jr., *Show Biz* (New York: Henry Holt & Co., 1951), p. 323.

CHAPTER 11

1. This and all further quotes by him in this chapter are from interviews, New York: 1962.
2. Tom Fletcher, *100 Years of the Negro in Show Business* (New York: Burdge & Co., Ltd., 1954), p. 20.
3. This and all further quotes by him in this chapter are from numerous interviews and conversation, New York, Lenox, Mass., Chicago: 1952-1966.
4. From numerous interviews, New York: 1963-1965.
5. From interviews, Los Angeles: 1960, 1965.
6. This and all further quotes by him in this chapter are from interviews: New York: 1960-1964.
7. From numerous interviews and conversation, New York, Lenox, Mass., Newport, R.I., Falmouth, Mass.: 1952-1966.
8. This and all further quotes by her in this chapter are from numerous interviews, conversations, and correspondence with Ida Forsyne Hubbard, New York: 1960-1966.

9. 29 May 1897.
10. Clarence Muse and David Arlen, *Way Down South* (Hollywood, Calif.: David Graham Fischer, 1932), manuscript in scrapbook form, n.p.
11. From numerous interviews, conversations, and correspondence, New York; Newport, R.I.: 1959-1966.
12. This and all further quotes by him in this chapter are from interviews, New York: 1960-1961.
13. In conversation, New York: 1964.
14. Paul Oliver, *Conversation with the Blues* (New York: Horizon Press, 1965), pp. 128-9.
15. *Ibid.* p. 135.
16. C. A. Leonard in New York *Herald Tribune* (7 May 1929); New York *Age* (14 May 1932), quoting from *Billboard.*
17. *Ebony* (September, 1954).
18. Joe Laurie, Jr., *Vaudeville* (New York: Henry Holt & Co., 1953), pp. 56, 203.
19. From interviews with Mrs. Leola Wilson (Coot Grant), Whitesboro, New Jersey: 1959-1960.
20. From an interview with Mrs. Paul Howard (Susie Beavers), Los Angeles: 1960.
21. This and all further quotes by him in this chapter are from numerous interviews and conversations, New York: 1960-1966.
22. From interviews, New York: 1959.

CHAPTER 12

1. The material in this chapter is taken largely from numerous interviews and correspondence with Essie, Alberta, and Alice Whitman, Chicago: 1960-1965.
2. Muse and Arlen, *Way Down South* (Hollywood, Calif.: David Graham Fischer, 1932), manuscript in scrapbook form, n.p.
3. From an interview with Mrs. Paul Howard (Susie Beavers), Los Angeles: 1960.
4. This and all further quotes by him in this chapter are from numerous interviews and conversations, New York: 1959-1966.
5. From interviews, New York: 1960-1964.
6. Quoted by Rudi Blesh and Harriet Janis, *They All Played Ragtime* (New York: Alfred A. Knopf, Inc., 1950), pp. 172-3.
7. This and all further quotes by him in this chapter are from interviews, New York: 1962-1963.
8. This and all further quotes by him in this chapter are from interviews, New York: 1962.
9. From an interview, Philadelphia: 1963.
10. This and all further quotes by him in this chapter are from numerous interviews, conversations, and correspondence, New York, Newport, R.I.: 1959-1966.
11. This and all further quotes by her in this chapter are from an interview with Mrs. Count Basie (Catherine Basie), New York: 1962.
12. Muse and Arlen, *Way Down South, op. cit.* n.p.
13. From interviews, New York: 1960.
14. From interviews, New York: 1961-1965.
15. From an interview, New York: 1961.

CHAPTER 13

1. Sigmund Spaeth, *A History of Popular Music in America* (New York: Random House, Inc., 1948), p. 369.

2. *Ibid.*
3. Sylvia G. L. Dannett and Frank R. Rachel, *Down Memory Lane* (New York: Greenberg Publishers, 1954), p. 76.
4. Tom Fletcher, *100 Years of the Negro in Show Business* (New York: Burdge & Co. Ltd., 1954), p. 193.
5. Dannett and Rachel, *Down Memory Lane,* p. 75.
6. Stated by Max Morath in a television series *Ragtime Years,* KRMA-TV, Denver, Colorado (National Educational Television), April, 1961.
7. Quoted in New York *News* (1 February 1956).
8. Cecil Smith, *Musical Comedy in America* (New York: Theatre Arts Books, 1950), p. 155.
9. *Ibid.* p. 166.
10. Dannett and Rachel, *Down Memory Lane,* p. 80.
11. Spaeth, *A History of Popular Music in America,* p. 388.
12. Mr. and Mrs. Vernon Castle, *Modern Dancing* (New York: Harper & Bros., 1914), p. 177.
13. From interviews, New York: 1961-1966.
14. William C. Handy, *Father of the Blues* (New York: The Macmillan Company, 1941), p. 226.
15. "Swing Music and Popular Dance," *Dance Herald* (February, 1938).
16. Edward B. Marks, *They All Sang* (New York: The Viking Press, Inc., 1935), p. 177.
17. From numerous interviews and conversations, New York, Lenox, Mass., Newport, R.I., Falmouth, Mass.: 1952-1966.
18. From an interview, New York: 1960.
19. From an interview, New York: 1960.
20. Lydia Parrish, *Slave Songs of the Georgia Sea Islands* (New York: Creative Age Press, 1949), p. 14 in footnote #15; p. 117.
21. From an interview, Los Angeles: 1960.
22. Thomas W. Talley, *Negro Folk Rhymes* (New York: The Macmillan Company, 1922), p. 258.
23. *Ibid.* p. 1.
24. Isaac Goldberg, *Tin Pan Alley* (New York: John Day Co., 1930), pp. 159-160.
25. From interviews, New York: 1960-1964.
26. From numerous interviews, New York: 1959-1966.
27. In conversation, New Orleans: 1959.
28. From numerous interviews, conversations, and correspondence with Ida Forsyne Hubbard, New York: 1960-1965.

CHAPTER 14

1. The material in this chapter is taken largely from numerous interviews and conversations with Perry Bradford, New York: 1959-1966. A book of his own reminiscences *Born with the Blues* was issued in 1965 by Oak Publishing Co., New York.
2. Mae West, *Goodness Had Nothing to Do with It* (Englewood Cliffs, New Jersey: Prentice-Hall Inc., 1959), p. 65.
3. Quoted in Gilda Gray's obituary, *The New York Times* (23 December 1959).
4. *Ibid.*
5. 4 January 1960, p. 43.
6. May, 1927.
7. The phrase "Shake it and break it" is identified by James T. Maher as circus slang around 1890 (in correspondence with Maher, 1966).

8. From an interview with Mrs. Glover Compton (Nettie Compton), Chicago: 1960.
9. Ethel Waters, *His Eye Is on the Sparrow* (Garden City, N.Y.: Doubleday & Company, Inc., 1951), pp. 108-9.
10. January, 1928, p. 41.
11. From an interview with Ethel Williams, New York: 1961.

CHAPTER 15

1. The material in this chapter is taken largely from numerous interviews and conversations with Perry Bradford, New York: 1959-1966.
2. From numerous interviews, conversations, and correspondence with Ida Forsyne Hubbard, New York: 1960-1966.
3. January, 1928, p. 41.
4. This and all further quotes by him in this chapter are from interviews, New York: 1959.
5. From an interview, Chicago: 1959.
6. Sylvia G. L. Dannett and Frank R. Rachel, *Down Memory Lane* (New York: Greenberg Publishers, 1954), p. 110.
7. LeRoi Jones, *Blues People* (New York: William Morrow and Company, Inc., 1963), p. 17.
8. From numerous interviews, New York: 1962-1965.
9. From numerous interviews and conversations, New York, Lenox, Mass.: 1952-1966.
10. From interviews with Mrs. Leola Wilson (Coot Grant), Whitesboro, New Jersey: 1959-1960.
11. Tom Davin, "Conversations with James P. Johnson," *Jazz Review* (July, 1959), p. 125.
12. From interviews with Maxey, New York: 1960, 1961.
13. Fred Astaire, *Steps in Time* (New York: Harper and Brothers, 1959), p. 125.
14. From an interview with Herbert Harper quoting Jordan, Upper Montclair, New Jersey: 1964.
15. Abel Green and Joe Laurie, Jr., *Show Biz* (New York: Henry Holt & Co., 1951), p. 228.
16. "Jazz Dance, Mambo Dance," *Jazz Review* (November, 1959), p. 62.
17. From numerous interviews and conversations, New York: 1952-1964.
18. 8 July 1922. This dispatch was unearthed by the New Orleans surgeon and musician, Dr. Edmond Souchon.

CHAPTER 16

1. 13 May 1909.
2. Rennold Wolf, "Greatest Comedian on the American Stage," June, 1912.
3. From an interview, New York: 1960.
4. Cecil Smith, *Musical Comedy in America* (New York: Theatre Arts Books, 1950), p. 121.
5. "Juba and American Minstrelsy," *Chronicles of the American Dance*, ed. Paul Magriel (New York: Henry Holt and Co., 1948), p. 62.
6. James Weldon Johnson, *Black Manhattan* (New York: Alfred A. Knopf, Inc., 1930), pp. 95-6.
7. *Ibid.* p. 96.
8. *Ibid.*
9. *Ibid.* p. 97.
10. *Ibid.* p. 102.

11. *Ibid.* p. 109.
12. *Ibid.* p. 102.
13. From interviews and correspondence, Los Angeles: 1960, 1965, 1966.
14. Johnson, *Black Manhattan,* pp. 102-3.
15. From numerous interviews and conversations with Charles Luckeyth ("Luckey") Roberts, New York: 1952-1966.
16. Edward B. Marks, *They All Sang* (New York: The Viking Press, Inc., 1935), p. 91.
17. Tom Fletcher, *100 Years of the Negro in Show Business* (New York: Burdge & Co., Ltd., 1954), pp. 138-141.
18. Quoted by Cecil Smith, *Musical Comedy in America,* p. 128.
19. *Ibid.*
20. "The Real Coon on the American Stage," *The Theatre* (August, 1906).
21. Johnson, *Black Manhattan,* 106.
22. Marks, *They All Sang,* p. 94.
23. "Hoofing," *Saturday Evening Post* (14 September 1929).
24. From interviews, New York: 1960-1964.
25. From an interview, New York: 1959.
26. Joe Laurie, Jr., *Vaudeville* (New York: Henry Holt & Co., 1953), p. 42.
27. This and all further quotes by him in this chapter are from interviews, New York: 1960-1965.
28. James Weldon Johnson, *Black Manhattan,* p. 105.
29. Tom Fletcher, *100 Years of the Negro in Show Business,* p. 108.
30. Magriel, ed., *Chronicles of the American Dance,* p. 61.
31. *Ibid.* p. 62.

CHAPTER 17

1. This and all further quotes by her in this chapter are from an interview, New York: 1961.
2. James Weldon Johnson, *Black Manhattan* (New York: Alfred A. Knopf, Inc., 1930), p. 174.
3. This and all further quotes by him in this chapter are from numerous interviews, New York: 1959-1966.
4. This and all further quotes by her in this chapter are from numerous interviews, conversations, and correspondence with Ida Forsyne Hubbard, New York: 1960-1966.
5. From interviews and correspondence, Los Angeles: 1960, 1965, 1966.
6. 30 April 1911.
7. Johnson, *Black Manhattan,* p. 170.
8. *Ibid.* p. 174.
9. From an interview, New York: 1962.
10. From an interview, Chicago: 1959.
11. From an interview with Mrs. Glover Compton (Nettie Compton), Chicago: 1960.
12. From an interview with Mrs. Paul Howard (Susie Beavers), Los Angeles: 1960.
13. From an interview, New York: 1963.
14. From interviews, Los Angeles: 1960, 1965.
15. From interviews, New York: 1960-1965.
16. Caroline and Charles Caffin, *Dancing and Dancers of Today* (New York: Dodd, Mead & Co., 1912), pp. 269-271.
17. 9 November 1913.
18. 12 December 1913.

19. From numerous interviews and conversations, New York, Lenox, Mass.: 1952-1966.
20. Tom Fletcher, *100 Years of the Negro in Show Business* (New York: Burdge & Co., Ltd., 1954), p. 108.
21. April, 1914.
22. 12 November 1913.
23. From numerous interviews and conversations with Charles Luckeyth ("Luckey") Roberts, New York: 1952-1966.
24. Cecil Smith, *Musical Comedy in America* (New York: Theatre Arts Books, 1950), p. 188.
25. 5 March 1927.

CHAPTER 18

1. From interviews, New York: 1961-1965.
2. From *Vanity Fair* (Summer, 1922). Published in *The 7 Lively Arts* (New York: Sagamore Press, 1957), p. 150.
3. This and all further quotes by him in this chapter are from interviews and correspondence, Los Angeles: 1960, 1965, 1966.
4. This and all further quotes by him in this chapter are from numerous interviews and conversations, New York, Lenox, Mass.: 1952-1966.
5. James Weldon Johnson, *Black Manhattan* (New York: Alfred A. Knopf, Inc., 1930), p. 199.
6. This and all further quotes by him in this chapter are from numerous interviews and conversations, New York, Lenox, Mass., Chicago: 1952-1966.
7. From interviews, New York: 1961-1962.
8. From interviews, New York: 1961-1966.
9. New York *American* (25 May 1921).
10. 24 May 1921.
11. 24 May 1921.
12. New York *Mail*, n.d. (from clipping file in Theater Collection, New York Public Library).
13. 28 November 1922.
14. *Zits* (5 September 1924).
15. 13 July 1927.
16. Reprinted in Gilbert Seldes, *The 7 Lively Arts* (1957), p. 236.

CHAPTER 19

1. 13 June 1925.
2. Frank W. Wilstack, New York *World* (3 September 1922), quoting from *Billboard.*
3. This and all further quotes by him in this chapter are from an interview, New Haven, Conn.: 1962.
4. Ethel Waters, *His Eye Is on the Sparrow* (Garden City, N.Y.: Doubleday & Company, Inc., 1951), p. 217.
5. From numerous interviews, New York: 1959-1966.
6. "It's Getting Dark on Old Broadway," by Louis A. Hirsch, Dave Stamper, Gene Buck; published by Harms Inc.
7. New York *Dramatic Mirror* and *Theatre World* (27 August 1921).
8. 24 August 1921 (review signed "Q. L. M.").
9. 24 August 1921 (review signed "P. Mc.N.").
10. New York *Tribune* (20 June 1922).
11. This and all further quotes by him in this chapter are from interviews, New York: 1961-1966.

12. This and all further quotes by him in this chapter are from numerous interviews and conversations, New York, Lenox, Mass.: 1952-1966.
13. From interviews, New York: 1962-1963.
14. 18 July 1922 (review signed "L. M. R.").
15. 18 July 1922 (review signed "C. P. S.").
16. 18 July 1922.
17. 18 July 1922.
18. 18 July 1922.
19. This and all further quotes by him in this chapter are from numerous interviews and conversations, New York, Lenox, Mass., Chicago: 1952-1966.
20. This and all further quotes by him in this chapter are from numerous interviews, New York: 1962-1965.
21. New York *World* (28 November 1922).
22. New York *Herald* (28 November 1922).
23. 28 November 1922.
24. From interviews, New York: 1961-1965.
25. From interviews and correspondence with Clarence ("Buddy") Bradley, London: 1963-1966.
26. This and all further quotes by him in this chapter are from interviews, New York: 1961-1962.
27. 17 April 1923.
28. 17 April 1923.
29. New York *News* (18 April 1923).
30. New York *World* (18 April 1923).
31. This and all further quotes by him in this chapter are from numerous interviews, conversations, and correspondence, New York: 1962-1966.
32. Atlantic City *Union* (6 March 1923).
33. 30 October 1923.
34. James Weldon Johnson, *Black Manhattan* (New York: Alfred A. Knopf, Inc., 1930), p. 190.
35. This and all further quotes by him in this chapter are from interviews and correspondence, Los Angeles: 1960, 1965, 1966.
36. From interviews, Los Angeles: 1960, 1965.
37. 3 September 1924.
38. 30 October 1924.
39. 30 October 1924 (name of paper torn—from clipping file, Theater collection, New York Public Library).
40. New York *World* (30 October 1924).
41. New York *American* (30 October 1924).
42. New York *Herald Tribune* (30 October 1924).

CHAPTER 20

1. "The Art of Jazz," *Dance Lovers* (July, 1925), pp. 10-11, 61.
2. 6 April 1926.
3. 28 June 1927.
4. Ethel Waters, *His Eye Is on the Sparrow* (Garden City, N.Y.: Doubleday & Company, Inc., 1951), p. 189.
5. New York *Herald Tribune* (12 July 1927).
6. 12 July 1927.
7. Waters, *His Eye Is on the Sparrow,* p. 71.
8. *Ibid.* p. 91.

9. Martin Dickstein, 13 July 1927.
10. 13 July 1927.
11. New York *Herald Tribune* (13 July 1927).
12. Dickstein, *Ibid.*
13. Alison Smith, 13 July 1927.
14. 22 November 1927.
15. Perriton Maxwell, January, 1928.
16. Percy Hammond, 10 May 1928.
17. New York *World* (10 May 1928).
18. Charles Brackett, 10 March 1928.
19. Robert Littell, New York *Post* (28 February 1928); Alan Dale, New York *American* (28 February 1928).
20. Willard Keefe, 9 January 1929.
21. Henry Hazlitt, 8 January 1929.
22. Wilella Waldorf, 8 January 1929.
23. Hazlitt, *Ibid.*
24. From interviews, New York: 1959-1962.
25. This and all further quotes by him in this chapter are from numerous interviews and conversations, New York, Lenox, Mass.: 1952-1966.
26. 22 February 1929.
27. 21 February 1929.
28. 21 February 1929.
29. 21 February 1929.
30. Charles Brackett, 4 May 1929.
31. Perriton Maxwell, July, 1929.
32. Percy Hammond, 15 May 1929.
33. *Ibid.*
34. Wilella Waldorf, 21 June 1929.
35. F. P. Dunne, Jr., 21 June 1929.
36. Stephen Rathbun, 21 June 1929.
37. Wilella Waldorf, 21 June 1929.
38. From interviews, New York: 1961-1966.
39. From a playbill, Hudson Theatre (14 October 1929).
40. From numerous interviews, conversations, and correspondence, New York: 1962-1966.
41. From numerous interviews, conversations, and correspondence, New York, Newport, R.I.: 1959-1966.
42. Arthur Pollack, 21 June 1929.
43. Bide Dudley, New York *Evening World* (21 June 1929).
44. 27 June 1929 (review signed "W. A. U.").
45. Richard Dana Skinner, 24 July 1929.
46. Richard Lockridge, 22 August 1930.
47. 22 August 1930.
48. Robert Littell, 22 August 1930.
49. 22 August 1930.
50. Percy Hammond, 8 October 1930.
51. Robert Littell, 8 October 1930.
52. Percy Hammond, *Ibid.*
53. 8 October 1930.
54. 22 October 1930.
55. 18 October 1930.
56. 8 October 1930.

57. Arthur Pollack, 8 October 1930.
58. New York *Evening Post* (8 October 1930).
59. Bennie Butler, 17 October 1930.
60. 1 November 1930.
61. *Ibid.*
62. *The New York Times* (29 April 1962).
63. Richard Lockridge, 7 June 1930.
64. Percy Hammond, New York *Herald Tribune* (23 October 1930).
65. *The New Yorker* (1 November 1930).
66. Robert Garland, 23 October 1930.
67. 10 September 1930 (review signed "E. F. M.").
68. Arthur Pollack, 4 September 1930.
69. *Judge* (15 November 1930).
70. *The New Yorker* (16 May 1931).
71. New York *Evening Post* (17 September 1931).
72. New York *World Telegram* (26 December 1931).
73. *The New York Times* (26 December 1931), review signed "J. H."
74. New York *American* (16 September 1931).
75. Ibee, 28 July 1937.
76. *Time* (16 April 1965), p. 51.

CHAPTER 21

1. Whitney Bolton, 2 May 1929.
2. Eudora Garrett, 1 May 1929.
3. October, 1929.
4. Webb interview by Mary Morris, 11 November 1945, name of paper torn (from clipping file in Theater collection New York Public Library).
5. This and all further quotes by him in this chapter are from interviews and correspondence with Clarence ("Buddy") Bradley, London: 1963-1966.
6. This and all further quotes by him in this chapter are from numerous interviews, conversations, and correspondence, New York, Newport, R.I.: 1959-1966.
7. This and all further quotes by him in this chapter are from numerous interviews, New York: 1962-1965.
8. This and all further quotes by him in this chapter are from an interview, Upper Montclair, New Jersey: 1964.
9. Cecil Beaton, *The Wandering Years, Diaries: 1922-1939* (Boston: Little, Brown and Company, 1961), pp. 215-6.
10. From an interview, Philadelphia: 1963.
11. Quoted in "Agnes de Mille's Repertory of Americana," by Walter Terry, New York *Herald Tribune Magazine* (21 March 1965), p. 47.
12. Quoted by Bradley in interviews.

CHAPTER 22

1. This and all further quotes by him in this chapter are from numerous interviews, conversations, and correspondence, New York, Newport, R.I.: 1959-1966.
2. From interviews, Chicago, New York: 1959-1963.
3. This and all further quotes by him in this chapter are from interviews, Chicago, New York: 1959-1963.
4. From an interview, New York, 1960.
5. From an interview, New Haven, Conn.: 1962.

6. This and all further quotes by him in this chapter are from interviews, New York: 1960-1965.
7. From interviews, New York: 1959-1963.
8. This and all further quotes by him in this chapter are from interviews, Los Angeles: 1960, 1965.
9. From an interview, New York: 1960.
10. "Hoofing," *Saturday Evening Post* (14 September 1929).
11. Beale Fletcher, *How to Improve Your Tap Dancing* (New York: A. S. Barnes & Co., 1957), p. 81.
12. Ned Wayburn, *The Art of Stage Dancing* (New York: The Ned Wayburn Studios of Stage Dancing Inc., 1925), p. 177.
13. "Hoofing," *Saturday Evening Post, Ibid.*
14. From interviews, New York: 1961-1966.

CHAPTER 23

1. From interviews, Chicago, New York: 1959-1963.
2. 8 October 1930.
3. This and all further quotes by him in this chapter are from an interview, New York: 1960.
4. O'Connor, 13 August 1921.
5. 10 May 1928.
6. 10 May 1928.
7. 10 May 1928.
8. 10 May 1928.
9. 10 May 1928.
10. *The Dance* (July, 1928).
11. 24 August 1929.
12. *Ibid.*
13. 23 May 1931.
14. *The Dance* (May, 1929).
15. New York *Daily News* (30 November 1949).
16. From interviews and correspondence, Los Angeles: 1965-6.
17. From interviews, Los Angeles: 1960, 1965.
18. *The Dance* (May, 1929).
19. *Vanity Fair* (August, 1929).
20. 4 December 1933.
21. From an interview, New York: 1960.
22. Ethel Waters, *His Eye Is on the Sparrow* (Garden City, N. Y.: Doubleday & Company, Inc., 1951), p. 157.
23. This and all further quotes by him in this chapter are from numerous interviews, conversations, and correspondence, New York, Newport, R.I.: 1959-1966.
24. *Down Beat* (7 October 1965), pp. 22-3.
25. Tom Fletcher, *100 Years of the Negro in Show Business* (New York: Burdge & Co., Ltd., 1954), p. 291.
26. From numerous interviews and conversations, New York, Lenox, Mass., Newport, R. I., Falmouth, Mass.: 1952-1966.
27. George Jessell, *Elegy in Manhattan* (New York: Holt, Rinehart & Winston, 1961), pp. 48-9.
28. Most of the anecdotes about Robinson are from conversations with various members of the Copasetics Club: Charles Atkins, Pete Nugent, Honi Coles, Leroy

Myers, Phace Roberts, Eddie West, Charles Cook, Ernest Brown, Emory Evans, Paul Black, Johnny Thomas, Chink Collins, New York: 1959-1966.

29. From an interview, Maywood, New Jersey: 1961.
30. From numerous interviews, New York: 1959-1966.
31. From an interview, Philadelphia: 1963.
32. From numerous interviews, conversations, and lecture-demonstrations, New York, Lenox, Mass., Newport, R.I., Chicago, Philadelphia, Cooperstown, N.Y.: 1952-1966.
33. From interviews, Los Angeles: 1965.
34. Ethel Waters, *His Eye Is on the Sparrow,* p. 141.

CHAPTER 24

1. This and all further quotes by him in this chapter are from interviews, New York: 1960-1964.
2. This and all further quotes by him in this chapter are from numerous interviews, conversations, and correspondence, New York, Newport, R.I.: 1959-1966.
3. This and all further quotes by him in this chapter are from numerous interviews, conversations, and lecture-demonstrations, New York, Newport, R.I., Wilmington, Del., Chicago, Cooperstown, N.Y.: 1959-1966.
4. From an interview, New York: 1960.
5. From interviews, New York: 1960-1965.
6. From numerous interviews, conversations, and lecture-demonstrations, New York, Newport, R.I., Wilmington, Del., Chicago, Cooperstown, N.Y.: 1959-1966.
7. 16 November 1927.
8. 16 November 1927.
9. 16 November 1927.
10. 23 November 1927.
11. 16 November 1927.
12. From an interview, Chicago: 1959.
13. From an interview, Chicago: 1959.
14. From interviews, New York: 1959-1962.
15. From interviews, New York: 1960.
16. From interviews, New York: 1962.
17. Quoted in an interview with Kelly by Phyllis Battelle, "The Manly Art of Dancing," New York *Journal-American* (17 May 1964).

CHAPTER 25

1. This and all further quotes by him in this chapter are from an interview, New York: 1960.
2. 18 May 1923. Name of paper torn (from clipping file in Theater Collection, New York Public Library.)
3. 18 May 1923.
4. Con, 24 May 1923.
5. Burns Mantle, 18 May 1923.
6. James Craig, 18 May 1923.
7. Charles Darnton, 18 May 1923.
8. Arthur Hornblow, July, 1923.
9. Clipping torn (from clipping file in Theater Collection, New York Public Library).
10. *Ibid.*
11. Clipping torn (from clipping file in Theater Collection, New York Public Library).
12. 18 May 1923.

13. James Craig, 18 May 1923.
14. 20 November 1923. Name of paper torn (from clipping file in Theater Collection, New York Public Library).
15. 18 May 1923. Name of paper torn (from clipping file in Theater Collection, New York Public Library).
16. New York *World* (17 May 1923).
17. 18 May 1923.
18. From numerous interviews, conversations, and correspondence, New York, Newport, R.I.: 1959-1966.
19. From interviews, Los Angeles: 1965.
20. Skig, 30 June 1926.
21. Stephen Rathbun, 25 June 1926.
22. Ethel Waters, *His Eye Is on the Sparrow* (Garden City, N.Y.: Doubleday & Company, Inc., 1951), p. 179.
23. From interviews, New York: 1961.
24. *Variety*, 21 February 1962.
25. "Ziegfeldiana," in *25 Years of American Dance*, ed. Doris Hering (New York: Rudolf Orthwine, n.d. ca. 1954), p. 73. Reprinted from *Dance* (September, 1947).
26. *Variety*, 21 February 1962.

CHAPTER 26

1. Most of the material in this chapter is from numerous interviews, conversations, and correspondence, New York: 1962-1966.
2. From interviews, New York: 1961.
3. Joe Laurie, Jr., *Vaudeville* (New York: Henry Holt & Co., 1953), p. 46.
4. Bernard Sobel lists dancing acts as "Dutch, Irish, Plantation, Rough, Blackface, Neat, Whiteface, Grotesque, and Acrobatic"–the labels used by booking agents. From his article "Vaudeville, the Last Days of a Glorious Profession," *25 Years of American Dance*, ed. Doris Hering (New York: Rudolph Orthwine, n.d., ca. 1954), p. 50.
5. 3 November 1921. Name of paper torn (from clipping file in Theater Collection, New York Public Library).
6. Philadelphia *Ledger* (13 January 1924).
7. 12 January 1924.
8. Clipping torn (from clipping file in Theater Collection, New York Public Library).
9. Clipping torn (from clipping file in Theater Collection, New York Public Library).
10. "Hoofing," *Saturday Evening Post* (14 September 1929).
11. From interviews, Los Angeles: 1965.
12. Laurie, *Vaudeville*, pp. 43-7.
13. From interviews and correspondence, London: 1963-1966.
14. *Theatre Arts* (August, 1927).
15. Abel Green and Joe Laurie, Jr., *Show Biz* (New York: Henry Holt & Co., 1951), p. 434.
16. 26 January 1963, p. 26.

CHAPTER 27

1. Much of the material in this chapter is from interviews with John Sublett (John W. Bubbles), New York: 1960-1963.
2. Quoted by Sobel in "Comedy Dancing," *25 Years of American Dance*, ed. Doris Hering (New York: Rudolf Orthwine, n.d., ca. 1954), pp. 126-7. Reprinted from *Dance* (March, 1947).

3. From interviews, New York: 1961.
4. From interviews, New York: 1960-1964.
5. From interviews, Los Angeles: 1965.
6. From interviews and correspondence, London: 1963-1966.
7. From interviews and correspondence with Laurence Jackson (Baby Laurence), New York, Newport, R.I.: 1960-1964.
8. Quoted in Dave E. Dexter, Jr., album notes, *Kansas City Jazz*, Decca Records, Album A-214, p. 2.
9. From numerous interviews, conversations, and lecture-demonstrations, New York: Newport, R.I., Wilmington, Del., Chicago, Cooperstown, N.Y.: 1959-1966.
10. From interviews, New York: 1961.
11. From numerous interviews, conversations, and correspondence, New York, Newport, R.I.: 1959-1966.
12. "Hoofing," *Saturday Evening Post* (14 September 1929).
13. From an interview, Maywood, New Jersey: 1961.
14. In conversation with Leonard Feather, New York: 1961.
15. "Bubbles Bounces Back," January, 1965, p. 50.

CHAPTER 28

1. "Astaire," *Show* (October, 1962).
2. This and all further quotes by Astaire in this chapter are from his book, *Steps in Time* (New York: Harper and Brothers, 1959), and from correspondence and telephone conversation.
3. 25 August 1941.
4. Astaire, *Steps in Time,* p. 57.
5. *Ibid.* p. 79.
6. From an interview, New York: 1965.
7. From an interview with Ann Miller by Philip K. Scheuer, *Dance* (January, 1947).
8. *Life* (25 August 1941).
9. From interviews and correspondence, London: 1963-1966.
10. Astaire, *Steps in Time,* p. 32. Quoted from a letter Wayburn wrote to Mrs. Astaire, 8 June 1911.
11. This and all further quotes by him in this chapter are from numerous interviews, conversations, and lecture-demonstrations, New York, Newport, R.I., Wilmington, Del., Chicago, Cooperstown, N.Y.: 1959-1966.
12. From an interview, New York: 1960.
13. From an interview, Maywood, New Jersey: 1961.
14. This and all further quotes by him in this chapter are from interviews, Los Angeles: 1965.
15. From interviews and correspondence, Los Angeles: 1965, 1966.
16. From numerous interviews, conversations, and lecture-demonstrations, New York, Newport, R.I., Wilmington, Del., Chicago, Cooperstown, N.Y.: 1959-1966.

CHAPTER 29

1. 16 February 1938.
2. From numerous interviews, conversations, and lecture-demonstrations, New York, Newport, R.I., Wilmington, Del., Chicago, Cooperstown, N.Y.: 1959-1966.
3. This and all other quotes by him in this chapter are from an interview, Philadelphia: 1963.
4. Descriptions of Dotson's act are from numerous interviews, conversations, and correspondence, New York, Newport, R.I.: 1959-1966.

5. From interviews, New York: 1959.
6. From interviews, New York: 1960.
7. From interviews with Ulysses S. ("Slow Kid") Thompson, New York: 1961-1966.
8. From interviews with William ("Chink") Collins, New York: 1960-1965.
9. From interviews and correspondence, New York: 1959-1962.
10. In conversation, New York: 1961.
11. From an interview, Chicago: 1959.
12. In conversation, Hyannis, Mass.: 1966.
13. From interviews, New York: 1961-1965.
14. From numerous interviews, conversations, and lecture-demonstrations, New York, Lenox, Mass., Newport, R.I., Chicago, Philadelphia: 1952-1966.
15. 10 May 1928.
16. 18 May 1928.
17. July, 1928.
18. 4 July 1931.
19. From an interview, Chicago: 1959.
20. From an interview with Mr. and Mrs. Jodie Edwards (Butterbeans and Susie), Chicago: 1960.
21. From interviews with Dewey ("Pigmeat") Markham, New York: 1959-1963.
22. From interviews, Los Angeles: 1960, 1965.
23. From numerous interviews and conversations, New York, Lenox, Mass., Chicago: 1952-1966.

CHAPTER 30

1. Material on Stringbeans and Sweetie May is from numerous interviews, conversations, and correspondence with Professor Willis L. James (Spelman College, Atlanta), New York, Lenox, Mass., Newport, R.I., Falmouth, Mass.: 1952-1966.
2. Lyrics as recalled by Professor James.
3. Ethel Waters, *His Eye Is on the Sparrow* (Garden City, N.Y.: Doubleday & Company, Inc., 1951), p. 179.
4. From an interview with Mr. and Mrs. Edwards, Chicago: 1960.
5. From an interview, New York: 1960.
6. From *Butterbeans and Susie*, Festival album M-7000.
7. *Ibid.*
8. Two-Story Tom act described by Professor Willis L. James.
9. This and all further quotes by him in this chapter are from interviews and conversations, New York, Newport, R.I.: 1960-1966.
10. From interviews, New York, Newport, R.I.: 1960-1965.
11. See also Marshall W. Stearns, *The Story of Jazz* (New York: Oxford University Press, 1956), pp. 314-5.
12. LeRoi Jones, *Blues People* (New York: William Morrow and Company, 1963), p. 84.

CHAPTER 31

1. From an interview, New Haven, Conn.: 1962.
2. Much of the material in this chapter is from numerous interviews, conversations, and correspondence with Ida Forsyne Hubbard, New York: 1960-1966.
3. This and all further quotes by him in this chapter are from numerous interviews, New York: 1962-1965.
4. From interviews, New York: 1961-1966.

5. From interviews, Los Angeles: 1960, 1965.
6. This and all further quotes by him in this chapter are from numerous interviews, New York: 1960-1966.
7. From interviews, New York: 1960-1963.
8. From interviews, New York: 1960-1965.
9. From program of Palace Theater, London, 1906.
10. James Weldon Johnson, *Black Manhattan* (New York: Alfred A. Knopf, Inc., 1930), p. 170.

CHAPTER 32

1. Joe Laurie, Jr., *Vaudeville* (New York: Henry Holt & Co., 1953), p. 28.
2. From interviews, New York: 1960-1961.
3. From interviews, Los Angeles: 1960, 1965.
4. From an interview, Chicago: 1959.
5. Laurie, *Vaudeville, Ibid.*
6. From numerous interviews, New York: 1962-1965.
7. From numerous interviews, conversations, and correspondence, New York: 1962-1966.
8. This and all further quotes by him in this chapter are from interviews, New York: 1963-1965.
9. This and all further quotes by him in this chapter are from an interview, New York: 1963.
10. From interviews with William ("Chink") Collins, New York: 1960-1965.

CHAPTER 33

1. From interviews with Earle Basie (Groundhog), New York: 1964.
2. This and all further quotes by him in this chapter are from numerous interviews, New York: 1960-1966.
3. From interviews, New York: 1960-1963.
4. Lait, 26 August 1921.
5. This and all further quotes by her in this chapter are from an interview, Los Angeles: 1965.
6. This and all further quotes by him in this chapter are from numerous interviews, conversations, and correspondence, New York, Newport, R.I.: 1959-1966.
7. This and all further quotes by him in this chapter are from interviews, Los Angeles: 1960, 1965.
8. From interviews, New York: 1961-1966.
9. This and all further quotes by him in this chapter are from numerous interviews, conversations, and lecture-demonstrations with Charles ("Cholly") Atkins, New York, Newport, R.I., Wilmington, Del., Chicago, Cooperstown, N.Y.: 1959-1966.
10. Joe Laurie, Jr., *Vaudeville* (New York: Henry Holt & Co., 1953), p. 40.
11. From an interview, Chicago: 1959.
12. This and all further quotes by him in this chapter are from interviews, New York: 1960.
13. From numerous interviews, conversations, and lecture-demonstrations with Charles ("Honi") Coles, New York, Newport, R.I., Wilmington, Del., Chicago, Cooperstown, N.Y.: 1959-1966.
14. From an interview, Chicago: 1960.
15. This and all further quotes by him in this chapter are from interviews, Chicago, New York: 1959-1963.

16. In conversation, Hyannis, Mass.: 1966.
17. This and all further quotes by him in this chapter are from interviews, Chicago, New York: 1959-1963.
18. From interviews and correspondence, Los Angeles: 1965-1966.
19. This and all further quotes by him in this chapter are from an interview, New York: 1961.
20. From interviews, New York: 1960-1965.
21. From interviews and correspondence with Laurence Jackson (Baby Laurence), New York, Newport, R.I.: 1960-1964.

CHAPTER 34

1. Much of the material in this chapter is from interviews, New York: 1960, 1966.
2. This and all further quotes by him in this chapter are from interviews and correspondence, Los Angeles: 1965-1966.
3. From numerous interviews, conversations, and lecture-demonstrations, New York, Lenox, Mass., Chicago, Cooperstown, N.Y., Philadelphia, Newport, R.I.: 1952-1966.
4. From numerous interviews, conversations, and correspondence, New York, Newport, R.I.: 1959-1966.
5. From interviews, Los Angeles: 1965.
6. Clipping torn (from Schomburg Branch, New York Public Library).
7. Cp. Duke Ellington's recording of the same name, released under Joe Turner and His Memphis Men, Columbia 1813D.
8. From numerous interviews, conversations, and lecture-demonstrations with Charles ("Honi") Coles, New York, Newport, R.I., Wilmington, Del., Chicago, Cooperstown, N.Y.: 1959-1966.
9. "Jazz Dance, Mambo Dance," *Jazz Review* (November, 1959), p. 63.
10. This and all further quotes by him in this chapter are from numerous interviews, conversations, and lecture-demonstrations with Charles ("Cholly") Atkins, New York, Newport, R.I., Wilmington, Del., Chicago, Cooperstown, N.Y.: 1959-1966.
11. From numerous interviews, conversations, and lecture-demonstrations, New York, Lenox, Mass., Newport, R.I., Philadelphia, Chicago, Cooperstown, N.Y.: 1952-1966.
12. In conversation, New York: 1964.
13. From an interview, Los Angeles: 1965.
14. From interviews and correspondence with Clarence ("Buddy") Bradley, London: 1963-1966.
15. From interviews, Chicago, New York: 1959-1963.

CHAPTER 35

1. Joe Laurie, Jr., *Vaudeville* (New York: Henry Holt & Co., 1953), p. 42.
2. February, 1953.
3. From an interview, New Haven, Conn.: 1962.
4. From numerous interviews, New York: 1962-1965.
5. In conversation, Minneapolis, Minn.: 1953-1954.
6. In conversation, New York: 1964.
7. From interviews, New York: 1959-1963.
8. This and all further quotes by him in this chapter are from numerous interviews, conversations, and correspondence, New York, Newport, R.I.: 1959-1966.
9. From interviews, Los Angeles: 1960, 1965.
10. From numerous interviews and correspondence, Chicago: 1960-1965.
11. From numerous interviews and correspondence with Ida Forsyne Hubbard, New York: 1960-1966.

12. This and all further quotes by him in this chapter are from an interview, New York: 1960.
13. From interviews, New York: 1960-1964.
14. From an interview with George ("Shorty") Snowden, New York: 1959.
15. From numerous interviews, conversations, and lecture-demonstrations with Charles ("Cholly") Atkins, New York, Newport, R.I., Wilmington, Del., Chicago, Cooperstown, N.Y.: 1959-1966.
16. From interviews and correspondence with Clarence ("Buddy") Bradley, London: 1963-1966.
17. From interviews, Los Angeles: 1965.
18. From interviews, New York: 1961.

CHAPTER 36

1. This and all further quotes by him in this chapter are from numerous interviews, New York: 1962-1965.
2. This and all further quotes by him in this chapter are from an interview, New Haven, Conn.: 1962.
3. This and all further quotes by her in this chapter are from numerous interviews, conversations, and correspondence with Ida Forsyne Hubbard, New York: 1960-1966.
4. From numerous interviews, New York: 1960-1966.
5. From interviews, New York: 1963-1965.

CHAPTER 37

1. This and all further quotes by him in this chapter are from numerous interviews, conversations, and correspondence, New York, Newport, R.I.: 1959-1966.
2. This anecdote occurs in several versions, including Nugent's.
3. Bernard Sobel, "Vaudeville, the Last Days of a Glorious Profession," *25 Years of American Dance,* ed. Doris Hering (New York: Rudolf Orthwine, n.d., ca. 1954), p. 49.
4. From numerous interviews and conversations, New York, Lenox, Mass.: 1952-1966.
5. Sidney Bechet, *Treat It Gentle* (New York: Hill & Wang, 1960), p. 52.
6. In conversation, New York: 1962.
7. From interviews, Chicago, New York: 1959-1963.
8. This and all further quotes by him in this chapter are from numerous interviews, conversations, and lecture-demonstrations with Charles ("Honi") Coles, New York, Newport, R.I., Wilmington, Del., Chicago, Cooperstown, N.Y.: 1959-1966.
9. This and all further quotes by him in this chapter are from numerous interviews, conversations, and lecture-demonstrations with Charles ("Cholly") Atkins, New York, Newport, R.I., Wilmington, Del., Chicago, Cooperstown, N.Y.: 1959-1966.
10. In conversation, New York: 1964.
11. From interviews and correspondence with Laurence Jackson (Baby Laurence), New York, Newport, R.I.: 1960-1964.
12. From interviews, New York: 1963.
13. From interviews with acrobatic teacher Joe Price, New York: 1959-1962. One of his pupils, Charles Morrison, demonstrated the Boogie Woogie in 1952.

CHAPTER 38

1. Most of the material in this chapter is from numerous interviews, conversations, and lecture-demonstrations with Coles and Atkins, New York, Newport, R.I., Wilmington, Del., Chicago, Cooperstown, N.Y.: 1959-1966.

2. From interviews, New York: 1960-1965.
3. This and all further quotes by him in this chapter are from numerous interviews, conversations, and correspondence, New York, Newport, R.I.: 1959-1966.
4. From interviews with William ("Chink") Collins, New York: 1960-1965.
5. Agnes de Mille, *And Promenade Home* (Boston: Little, Brown and Company, 1956), p. 174.
6. As reported by Coles and Atkins.
7. 21 July 1962.
8. 15 December 1965.
9. From an interview, Philadelphia: 1963.

CHAPTER 39

1. This and all further quotes by him in this chapter are from an interview, New York: 1959.
2. This and all further quotes by him in this chapter are from numerous interviews, conversations, and lecture-demonstrations, New York, Lenox, Mass., Newport, R.I., Philadelphia, Chicago, Cooperstown, N.Y.: 1952-1966.
3. Much of the material on the Jolly Fellows club is from numerous interviews, conversations, and lecture-demonstrations with Leon James, New York; Lenox, Mass., Newport, R.I., Philadelphia, Chicago, Cooperstown, N.Y.: 1952-1966.

CHAPTER 40

1. Much of the material in this chapter is from numerous interviews, conversations, and lecture-demonstrations with Leon James and Albert Minns, New York, Lenox, Mass., Newport, R.I., Philadelphia, Chicago, Cooperstown, N.Y.: 1952-1966.
2. This and all further quotes by him in this chapter are from an interview with George ("Shorty") Snowden, New York: 1959.
3. From an interview, New York: 1961.
4. "World of the Dance," *Today* show, NBC-TV (24 September 1964). It is conceivable but unlikely that the step known as "The Hop" at the Savoy Ballroom before 1927 is the same step that Mr. Bolger put together in St. Louis.
5. As reported by Shorty Snowden.
6. Quoted in "Lester Young," by Nat Hentoff, *The Jazz Makers,* ed. Nat Shapiro and Nat Hentoff (New York: Rinehart & Co., 1957), p. 267.

CHAPTER 41

1. The following quotes are excerpted from correspondence with Mr. Wendler, Detroit: 1959.
2. This and all further quotes by him in this chapter are from numerous interviews, conversations, correspondence, and lecture-demonstrations with Ernest R. Smith, New York, Cooperstown, N.Y.: 1956-1966.
3. 10 January 1943.
4. Anecdotes about Herbert White and the Lindy Hoppers are from numerous interviews, conversations, and lecture-demonstrations with Leon James and Albert Minns, New York, Lenox, Mass., Newport, R.I., Philadelphia, Chicago, Cooperstown, N.Y.: 1952-1966.
5. From numerous interviews, conversations, and correspondence, New York, Newport, R.I.: 1959-1966.
6. From an interview, Philadelphia: 1963.
7. New York *Daily News* (18 February 1959).

8. From an interview with George ("Shorty") Snowden, New York: 1959.

CHAPTER 42

1. This and all further quotes by him in this chapter are from interviews and correspondence, New York, Newport, R.I.: 1960-1964.
2. From an interview, New York: 1960.
3. From interviews, New York: 1960, 1966.
4. From interviews, New York: 1960-1963.
5. Reprinted in Edwin Denby, *Looking at the Dance* (New York: Pellegrini & Cudahy, 1949), p. 360.
6. This and all further quotes by him in this chapter are from interviews, New York: 1961-1965.
7. From numerous interviews, conversations, and lecture-demonstrations with Charles ("Cholly") Atkins, New York, Newport, R.I., Wilmington, Del., Chicago, Cooperstown, N.Y.: 1959-1966.
8. *The New Yorker* (20 February 1960), p. 146.
9. From numerous interviews, conversations, and correspondence, New York, Newport, R.I.: 1959-1966.

CHAPTER 43

1. In conversation, Cincinnati: 1962.
2. This and all further quotes by him in this chapter are from interviews and correspondence with Laurence Jackson (Baby Laurence), New York, Newport, R.I.: 1960-1964.
3. From an interview, New York: 1961.
4. This and all further quotes by him in this chapter are from an interview, New York: 1961.
5. From numerous interviews, conversations, and lecture-demonstrations with Charles ("Honi") Coles, New York, Newport, R.I., Wilmington, Del., Chicago, Cooperstown, N.Y.: 1959-1966.
6. From numerous interviews, conversations, and correspondence, New York, Newport, R.I.: 1959-1966.
7. From numerous interviews and correspondence, Chicago: 1960-1965.
8. In conversation, New York: 1964.
9. This and all further quotes by him in this chapter are from interviews, New York: 1964.
10. From interviews, New York: 1964.
11. In conversation, New York: 1964.
12. Whitney Balliett, 12 December 1964, pp. 47-9.
13. J. R. Goddard, "The Night Groundhog Was King of the Gate," 26 November 1964.

CHAPTER 44

1. This and all further quotes by him in this chapter are from numerous interviews, conversations, correspondence, and lecture-demonstrations with Charles ("Cholly") Atkins, New York, Newport, R.I., Wilmington, Del., Chicago, Cooperstown, N.Y.: 1959-1966.
2. From interviews, Chicago, New York: 1959-1963.
3. From interviews, Chicago, New York: 1959-1963.
4. From interviews and correspondence with Clarence ("Buddy") Bradley, London: 1963-1966.

5. This and all further quotes by him in this chapter are from numerous interviews, conversations, and correspondence, New York, Newport, R.I.: 1959-1966.
6. In conversation, New York: 1961.
7. From interviews and correspondence with Laurence Jackson (Baby Laurence), New York, Newport, R.I.: 1960-1964.
8. From an interview, Philadelphia: 1963.
9. Reprinted in Edwin Denby, *Looking at the Dance* (New York: Pellegrini & Cudahy, 1949), p. 384.
10. This and all further quotes by him in this chapter are from interviews, New York, Newport, R.I.: 1961-1965.
11. From interviews, New York: 1960-1965.
12. From interviews with Earl Basie ("Groundhog"), New York: 1964.
13. This and all further quotes by him in this chapter are from numerous interviews conversations, and lecture-demonstrations with Charles ("Honi") Coles, New York, Newport, R.I., Wilmington, Del., Chicago, Cooperstown, N.Y.: 1959-1966.
14. 9 July 1962.
15. 8 July 1962.
16. From interviews, Los Angeles: 1960, 1965.
17. "Mr. B. Talks about Ballet," *Life* (11 June 1965).
18. From an interview, New York: 1960.

CHAPTER 45

1. "Mr. B. Talks about Ballet," *Life* (11 June 1965).
2. *Ibid.*
3. *The New York Times* (30 March 1966).
4. Quoted by Joseph N. Bell, "Imagine That–Dr. Kelly, the Old Hoofer," *National Cbserver* (20 June 1966).
5. This and other quotes from *Time* (16 April 1965).
6. *The New York Times* (25 February 1966).
7. From interviews, Los Angeles: 1960, 1965.
8. *The New York Times* (10 January 1960).
9. *The New York Times* (29 October 1961).
10. In conversation, New York: 1961.
11. *The New York Times* (29 October 1961).
12. Robert Kotlowitz, "Corsets, Corned Beef, and Choreography," *Show* (December, 1964), p. 91.
13. *Dance* (February, 1965), pp. 66, 68.
14. New York *Herald Tribune* (31 August 1941).
15. See appendix pp. 395-419 for a list of films in which dancing appears.
16. See Chapter 44, "The Dying Breed."
17. The following material is taken from numerous interviews, conversations, correspondence, and lecture-demonstrations with Charles ("Cholly") Atkins, New York, Newport, R.I., Wilmington, Del., Chicago, Cooperstown, N.Y.: 1959-1966.
18. In conversation, New York: 1960.
19. In conversation, New York: 1960.
20. In conversation, New York: 1960.
21. Quoted by Norman Poirier, "Discotheque," *Saturday Evening Post* (27 March 1965), p. 26.

Selected Bibliography

(A number of key articles on the dance published in magazines are not listed here but are cited in the footnotes.)

Allen, William F., Ware, Charles P., and Garrison, Lucy M., editors. *Slave Songs of the United States.* New York, A. Simpson Co., 1867.

Asbury, Herbert. *The Barbary Coast.* New York, Alfred A. Knopf, Inc., 1933.

———. *The Gangs of New York.* New York, Alfred A. Knopf, Inc., 1927.

Astaire, Fred. *Steps in Time.* New York, Harper & Bros., 1959.

Balliett, Whitney. *Such Sweet Thunder.* New York, The Bobbs-Merrill Company, Inc., 1966.

Baral, Robert. *Revue.* New York, Fleet Publishing Co., 1962.

Barber, Rowland. *The Night They Raided Minskys.* New York, Simon & Schuster, 1960.

Beaton, Cecil. *The Wandering Years, Diaries: 1922-1939.* Boston, Little, Brown and Company, 1961.

Bechet, Sidney. *Treat It Gentle.* New York, Hill & Wang, 1960.

Blesh, Rudi and Janis, Harriet. *They All Played Ragtime.* New York, Alfred A. Knopf, Inc., 1950.

Blum, Daniel. *A Pictorial History of the American Theatre, 1900-1950.* New York, Greenberg Publisher, 1950.

Bond, Frederick W. *The Negro and the Drama.* Washington, D.C., Associated Publishers, 1940.

Botkin, Benjamin A. *Lay My Burden Down.* Chicago, University of Chicago Press, 1945.

Bremer, Fredrika. *Homes of the New World,* Vol. II, New York, Harper & Brothers, 1853.

Brinson, Peter, editor. *Ballet in Britain.* London, Oxford University Press, 1962.

Burton, Jack. *Blue Book of Broadway Musicals.* New York, Century House, 1952.

———. *Blue Book of Hollywood Musicals.* New York, Century House, 1953.

Butcher, Margaret J. *The Negro in American Culture.* New York, Alfred A. Knopf, Inc., 1956.

Cable, George W. *Creoles and Cajuns.* Garden City, New York, Doubleday & Company, Inc., 1959.

Caffin, Caroline. *Vaudeville*. New York, Mitchell Kennerley, 1914.
Caffin, Caroline and Charles. *Dancing and Dancers of Today*. New York, Dodd, Mead & Company. 1912.
Cantor, Eddie and Freedman, David. *Ziegfeld*. New York, Alfred H. King, 1934.
Carpozi, George Jr. *Let's Twist*. New York, Pyramid Books, 1962 (paperback).
Castle, Irene. *Castles in the Air*. Garden City, New York, Doubleday & Company, Inc., 1958.
Castle, Mr. and Mrs. Vernon. *Modern Dancing*. New York, Harper & Bros., 1914.
Charters, Samuel B. and Kunstadt, Leonard. *Jazz: A History of the New York Scene*, Garden City, New York, Doubleday & Company, 1962.
Chase, Gilbert. *America's Music*. New York, McGraw-Hill Book Company, Inc., 1955.
Clark, Mary. *Presenting People Who Dance*. London, Paul Hamlyn, 1961.
Clemens, Samuel (Mark Twain). *Life on the Mississippi*. Boston, J. R. Osgood, 1883.
Cochran, Charles B. *Secrets of a Showman*. New York, Holt & Co. 1926.
Courlander, Harold. *The Drum and the Hoe*. Berkeley, University of California Press, 1960.
———. *Haiti Singing*. Chapel Hill, University of North Carolina, 1939.
Crowe, Eyre. *With Thackeray in America*. London, Cassell & Co., 1893.
Cunard, Nancy, editor. *Negro*. London, Wishart & Co., 1934.
Dadswell, Jack E. *Hey There Sucker*. Boston, Bruce Humphries, Inc., 1946.
Daly, J. J. *A Song in His Heart*. Philadelphia, John C. Winston Co., 1951.
Dannett, Sylvia G. L. and Rachel, Frank R. *Down Memory Lane*. New York, Greenberg Publishers, 1954.
Darbois, Dominique. *African Dance*. Prague, Artia, 1962. (Photographs with text by V. Vasut).
Davis, Sammy, Jr., Boyar, Jane and Burt. *Yes I Can*. New York, Farrar, Straus & Giroux, 1965.
De Mille, Agnes. *And Promenade Home*. Boston, Little, Brown & Co., 1956.
———. *The Book of the Dance*. New York, Golden Press, 1963.
———. *Dance to the Piper*. New York, Little, Brown & Co., 1952.
Denby, Edwin. *Looking at the Dance*. New York, Pellegrini & Cudahy, 1949.
Deren, Maya. *Divine Horseman*. New York, Thames & Hudson, 1953.
Dickens, Charles. *American Notes*, Vol. I., London, Chapman and Hall, 1842.
Donahue, Jack. *Letters of a Hoofer to His Ma*. New York, Cosmopolitan Book Corp., 1930-1931.
Dunham, Katherine. *The Dances of Haiti*. A pamphlet. Mexico, D.F., Acta Anthropoligica II: 4. Translated into Spanish by Javier Romero, November, 1947.
———. *Journey to Accompong*. New York, Henry Holt & Co., 1946.
Durang, Charles. *The Ball-room Bijou, and Art of Dancing*. Philadelphia, Fischer and Brother, n.d.
Ewen, David. *The Story of America's Musical Theater*. New York, Chilton Co., 1961.
Farnsworth, Marjorie. *The Ziegfeld Follies*. New York, Bonanza Books, 1956.
Flanders, Ralph Betts. *Plantation Slavery in Georgia*. Chapel Hill, University of North Carolina Press, 1933.

Fletcher, Beale. *How to Improve Your Tap Dancing*. New York, A. S. Barnes & Co., 1957.
Fletcher, Tom. *100 Years of the Negro in Show Business*. New York, Burdge & Co., 1954.
Fortier, Alice. *Louisiana Studies*. New Orleans, F. F. Hansel & Bro., 1894.
Franks, Arthur H. *Social Dance*. London, Routledge and Kegan Paul, 1963.
Georgia Writers Project. Works Projects Administration. Savannah Unit. *Drums and Shadows; Survival Studies among the Georgia Coastal Negroes*. Athens, University of Georgia Press, 1940.
Gilbert, Douglas. *American Vaudeville*. New York, Whittlesey House, 1940.
———. *Lost Chords*. New York, Doubleday, Doran & Co., 1942.
Goldberg, Isaac. *Tin Pan Alley*. New York, John Day Co., 1930.
Gorer, Geoffrey. *Africa Dances*. New York, John Lehmann, 1949.
Green, Abel and Laurie, Joe Jr., *Show Biz*. New York, Henry Holt & Co., 1951.
Green, Stanley. *The World of Musical Comedy*. New York, Grosset & Dunlap, 1960.
Greenwood, Isaac John. *The Circus*. New York, The Dunlop Society, 1898.
Gresham, William Lindsay. *Monster Midway*. New York, Rinehart & Co., 1948.
Handy, William C. *Father of the Blues*. New York, The Macmillan Company, 1941.
Hearn, Lafcadio. *Children of the Levee*, ed. O. W. Frost. Lexington, University of Kentucky Press, 1957.
Hering, Doris, editor. *25 Years of American Dance*. New York, Rudolf Orthwine Pub., ca. 1954. Anthology of articles from *Dance* magazine.
Herskovits, Melville J. *The Myth of the Negro Past*. New York, Harper & Brothers, 1941.
Herskovits, Melville J. and Frances S. *Rebel Destiny*. New York, Whittlesey House, 1934.
———. *Suriname Folk-Lore*. New York, Columbia University Press, 1936.
Holbrook, Stewart H. *The Golden Age of Quackery*. New York, The Macmillan Company, 1959.
Hoyt, Harlowe. *Town Hall Tonight*. Englewood Cliffs, New Jersey, Prentice-Hall Inc., 1955.
Huet, Michel and Fodeba, Keita. *Les Hommes de la Danse*. Lausanne, La Guilde du Livre, 1954.
Hungerford, Mary Jane. *History of Tap Dancing*. New York, Prentice Hall, Inc., 1939.
Hurston, Zora Neale. *Mules and Men*. Philadelphia, J. B. Lippincott Co., 1935.
Jessell, George. *Elegy in Manhattan*. New York, Holt, Rinehart and Winston, Inc., 1961.
Johnson, James Weldon. *Black Manhattan*. New York, Alfred A. Knopf, Inc., 1930.
Jones, A. M. *Studies in African Music*, Vol. I. London, Oxford University Press, 1959.
Jones, LeRoi. *Blues People*. New York, William Morrow and Company, 1963.
Kaigh, Frederick. *Witchcraft and Magic in Africa*. London, Richard Lesley & Co., Ltd., 1947.
Kemble, Frances A. *Journal of a Residence on a Georgia Plantation in 1838-1839*. New York, Harper & Brothers, 1864.

Kennedy, Stetson. *Palmetto Country.* New York, Duell, Sloan & Pearce, 1942.

Kirstein, Lincoln. *The Book of the Dance.* Garden City, N.Y., Garden City Pub. Co., 1942.

Kmen, Henry. *Music in New Orleans, The Formative Years* 1791-1841. Baton Rouge, Louisiana State University Press, 1966.

Krehbiel, H. E. *Afro-American Folksongs.* New York, G. Schirmer Inc., 1914.

Ladies of the Mission. *The Old Brewery and the New Mission House at the Five Points.* New York, Stringer & Townsend, 1854.

Latrobe, Benjamin H. B. *Impressions Respecting New Orleans,* ed. Samuel Wilson, Jr. New York, Columbia University Press, 1951.

Laurie, Joe Jr. *Vaudeville.* New York, Henry Holt & Co., 1953.

Leaf, Munro. *Isles of Rhythm.* New York, A. S. Barnes & Co., 1948.

Leavitt, Michael B. *Fifty Years in Theatrical Management.* New York, Broadway Publishing Co., 1912.

Lee, George W. *Beale Street.* New York, Robert O. Ballou, 1934.

Lekis, Lisa. *Dancing Gods.* New York, Scarecrow Press, 1960.

———. *Folk Dances of Latin America.* New York, Scarecrow Press, 1958.

Lomax, John A. and Alan. *Folk Song U.S.A.* New York, Duell, Sloan & Pearce, 1947.

Lucchese, John A. *Joey Dee and the Story of the Twist.* New York, MacFadden Books, 1962 (paperback).

———. *Pachanga.* New York, Avon Books, 1961 (paperback).

Magriel, Paul, editor. *Chronicles of the American Dance.* New York, Henry Holt & Co., 1948. This anthology contains "Juba and American Minstrelsy" by Marian Hannah Winter and "John Durang the First American Dancer" by Lillian Moore.

Marcosson, Isaac F. *Charles Frohman Manager and Man.* New York, Harpers, 1916.

Marks, Edward B. as told to Liebling, A. J. *They All Sang.* New York, The Viking Press, Inc., 1935.

Marks, Joseph E. III. *America Learns to Dance.* New York, Exposition Press, 1957.

Martin, David. *The Films of Busby Berkeley.* San Francisco, David Martin, 1964 (monograph).

Martin, John. *The Dance.* New York, Tudor Publishing Co., 1963.

Mates, Julian. *The American Musical Stage before 1800.* New Brunswick, New Jersey, Rutgers University Press, 1962.

McLean, Albert F. Jr., *American Vaudeville As Ritual.* Lexington, University of Kentucky Press, 1965.

Moody, Richard. *America Takes the Stage.* Bloomington, Indiana University Press, 1955.

Murray, Kathryn. *My Husband, Arthur Murray.* New York, Simon and Schuster, Inc., 1960.

Murray, Marion. *Circus!* New York, Appleton-Century-Crofts, 1956.

Muse, Clarence and Arlen, David. *Way Down South.* Hollywood, Calif., David Graham Fischer, 1932.

Nathan, Hans. *Dan Emmett and the Rise of Early Negro Minstrelsy.* Norman, University of Oklahoma Press, 1962.

Nettl, Paul. *The Story of Dance Music.* New York, Philosophical Library Inc., 1947.

Noble, Peter. *The Negro in Films.* London, British Yearbooks Ltd., n.d. ca. 1949.

Odell, George C. D. *Annals of the New York Stage,* Vol. IV. New York, Columbia University Press, 1927.

Oliver, Paul. *Conversation with the Blues.* New York, Horizon Press, 1965.

Osofsky, Gilbert. *Harlem: The Making of a Ghetto.* New York, Harper & Row, 1965.

Parrish, Lydia. *Slave Songs of the Georgia Sea Islands.* New York, Creative Age Press, 1949.

Paskman, Dailey and Spaeth, Sigmund. *Gentlemen Be Seated.* Garden City, N.Y., Doubleday, Doran & Co., 1928.

Ramsey, Fred Jr. *Been Here and Gone.* New Brunswick, New Jersey, Rutgers University Press, 1960.

Rice, Edw. LeRoy. *Monarchs of Minstrelsy.* New York, Kenny Pub. Co., 1911.

Riis, Jacob A. *How the Other Half Lives.* New York, Charles Scribners Sons, 1890.

Robinson, Solon. *Hot Corn: Life Scenes in New York.* New York, DeWitt & Davenport, 1854.

Rothberg, Gerald. *Let's All Twist.* New York, Esquire, Inc. 1962 (paperback). 16 pages on How to Twist by Arthur Murray, pp. 45-60.

Rourke, Constance. *American Humor.* New York, Harcourt, Brace & Co., 1931.

Rowland, Mabel, ed. *Bert Williams, Son of Laughter.* New York, The English Crafters, 1923.

Sachs, Curt. *World History of the Dance.* New York, Seven Arts Publishers, 1952.

Sass, Herbert Ravenel. *A Carolina Rice Plantation of the Fifties.* New York, William Morrow and Company, 1936.

Saxon, Lyle, Dreyer, Edward, and Tallant, Robert, compilers. *Gumbo Ya-Ya.* Boston, Houghton Mifflin Co., 1945. Louisiana Writers' Project, W.P.A.

Seabrook, W. B. *The Magic Mountain.* New York, The Literary Guild of America, 1929.

Seldes, Gilbert. *The 7 Lively Arts.* New York, Sagamore Press, 1957.

Shapiro, Nat and Hentoff, Nat, editors. *The Jazz Makers.* New York, Rinehart & Co., 1957.

Shaw, Charles G. *Night Life.* New York, John Day, 1931.

Slonimsky, Nicolas. *Music of Latin America.* New York, Thomas Y. Crowell Co., 1945.

Smith, Cecil. *Musical Comedy in America.* New York, Theatre Arts Books, 1950.

Smith, Kate. *Living in a Great Big Way.* New York, Blue Ribbon Books, 1938.

Sobel, Bernard. *A Pictorial History of Burlesque.* New York, G. P. Putnam's Sons, 1956.

Sobel, Bernard. *A Pictorial History of Vaudeville.* New York, The Citadel Press, 1961.

Spaeth, Sigmund. *A History of Popular Music in America.* New York, Random House, Inc., 1948.

Stearns, Marshall W. *The Story of Jazz.* New York, Oxford University Press, 1956.

Stone, Fred. *Rolling Stone.* New York, Whittlesey House, 1945.

Talley, Thomas W. *Negro Folk Rhymes*. New York, The Macmillan Company, 1922.

Terry, Walter. *The Dance in America*. New York, Harper & Bros., 1956.

Trotter, James M. *Music and Some Highly Musical People*. Boston, Lee & Shepard, 1879.

Tucker, A. N. *Tribal Music and Dancing in the Southern Sudan*. London, Wm. Reeves, Ltd., n.d., ca. 1933.

Tucker, Henry. *Clog Dancing Made Easy*. New York, The DeWitt Publishing Co., 1874.

Tucker, Sophie. *Some of These Days*. Garden City, N.Y., Doubleday, Doran & Co., 1945.

Waters, Ethel with Samuels, Charles. *His Eye Is on the Sparrow*. Garden City, N.Y., Doubleday & Company, Inc., 1951.

Wayburn, Ned. *The Art of Stage Dancing*. New York, The Ned Wayburn Studios of Stage Dancing, Inc., 1925.

West, Mae. *Goodness Had Nothing to Do with It*. Englewood Cliffs, New Jersey, Prentice-Hall, Inc., 1959.

Wilkinson, W. C. *The Dance of Modern Society*. New York, Funk & Wagnalls, 1884.

Wittke, Carl. *Tambo and Bones*. Durham, N. Carolina, Duke University Press, 1930.

Writers' Program of the Work Projects Administration, unpublished works, 1936-1940. *Negroes of New York*. "The Dance," 15 numbers, 1 volume. "Music and Musicians," 36 numbers, 2 volumes.

Yarborough, L. W. *Haiti-Dance*. Frankfort, Bronners Druckerei, n.d. ca. 1959.

A Selected List of Films and Kinescopes

An enormous amount of film footage has passed into cinema history. Faced with the general unavailability of a great deal of motion picture material, I have had to rely on private collections, cinema societies, motion picture theaters with rerun policies, publicity sheets, trade publications, *Film Daily Yearbooks,* early movie magazines, old film reviews, the memory of dancers and film buffs, the generosity of film libraries, and gallons of black coffee during those long hours of viewing vintage movies on late-night television.

Then, too, dancers have occasionally appeared in films that did not showcase their major talent. Rather than exclude such material and take a chance on missing something important, I decided in most cases to include any titles likely to be of value.

For dates, titles, distributors, cast, etc., I have relied upon three publications: *The Film Daily Yearbook of Motion Pictures, The International Motion Picture Almanac,* and *The Catalog of Copyright Entries: Motion Pictures,* (1894-1959, published by the Copyright Office of The Library of Congress).

I decided, where possible, that the copyright date should be utilized. This will explain why the dates in this listing frequently differ from the theatrical release dates.

Many of the Negro cast films produced down through the years apparently were never submitted for copyright nor listed in the *Film Daily Yearbooks.* In such cases, an "educated guess" is employed to establish a motion picture's vintage.

To aid the future researcher and historian I am employing an alphabetical code.

FL – Feature Length Film
SS – Short Subject
Nws. – Newsreel
Ctn. – Cartoon
Doc. – Documentary
Sd. – Sound Film (Titles not so noted indicate that they are either silent or the sound component cannot be determined.)

Scr. – Screened (Titles so designated have been reviewed by either myself or a colleague. Omission of this code indicates that the footage has not been screened.)

Where possible, a brief description of the dance content has been given.

In another important area, I have found that keeping track of all significant television material is impossible. A short listing of television titles, however, has been included.

Every effort has been made to make this list as complete and accurate as possible. Any such list is inevitably out-of-date however, almost from the moment it is published. Fresh material is continually being uncovered. This list is only a beginning.

Ernest R. Smith
1364 Lexington Avenue
New York City

PRE-1900

BUCK DANCE
Feb. 24, 1898, Thomas A. Edison

DANCING DARKEY BOY
Oct. 25, 1897, Thomas A. Edison

DANCING DARKIES
Jan. 7, 1897, American Mutoscope Co.

ELSIE JONES, NO. 1
"The Little Magnet"
1894, Edison Kinetoscope Co.
Buck Dance.

GRUNDY AND FRINT
1894, Edison Kinetoscope Co.
Breakdown, from *South Before The War.*
(A Tab Show)

JAMES GRUNDY
1894, Edison Kinetoscope Co.
Buck and Wing dance.

JAMES GRUNDY
1894, Edison Kinetoscope Co.
Cake Walk

PICKANINNIES (3), THE
Dance from *The Passing Show*
1894, Edison Kinetoscope Co.
From a revue presented May 12, 1894 at the Casino Theater in New York City.

1900 to 1919

BALLY-HOO CAKE WALK
May 21, 1903, American Mutoscope & Biograph Co.

CAKE WALK
May 11, 1903, American Mutoscope & Biograph Co.

CAKE WALK ON THE BEACH AT CONEY ISLAND, A
July 28, 1908, American Mutoscope & Biograph Co.

CHILDREN'S CAKE WALK (KINOPLASTIKUM)
Aug. 8, 1914, Commercial Biophone Co.

COMEDY CAKE WALK
May 11, 1903, American Mutoscope & Biograph Co.

DANCING LESSONS
1913, 3 reels, Kalem
Tango and Turkey Trot demonstrated by members of the Ziegfeld Follies.

DARKTOWN JUBILEE
1914
Bert Williams

I RATHER TWO STEP THAN WALTZ
Jan. 11, 1908, S. Lubin

JAMAICA NEGROES DOING A TWO-STEP
Apr. 12, 1907, Thomas A. Edison

MR. AND MRS. VERNON CASTLE BEFORE THE CAMERA
Apr. 15, 1914, Mortimer Henry Singer

UNCLE REMUS VISIT TO NEW YORK
1914, 2 reels, Hunter C. Haynes Photo Play Co.
Mr. and Mrs. Charles H. Anderson, the Negro exponents of the latest society dances appear in a portion of this film.

UNCLE TOM'S CABIN
1903, Thomas A. Edison, (Scr.)
(Directed by Edwin S. Porter)
Early examples of the time step, breaks, the Strut, and Cake Walk.

WHIRL OF LIFE, THE
1914, (Scr.)
Vernon and Irene Castle demonstrate the Castle Maxixe and Tango steps. Filmed at their Long Beach Casino *Castles by the Sea.*

1920 to 1928

ALOMA OF THE SOUTH SEAS
Aug. 3, 1926, Paramount (FL)
Gilda Gray

CHARLESTON IN SIX LESSONS, THE
Mar. 2, 1926, J. S. Grauman, Inc., 6 reels

CHARLESTON QUEEN, THE
Sept. 17, 1926, Pathe Exchange, Inc., (Paul Terry, author)

DANCING COLLEENS, THE
cir. 1928, Rayart Pictures Corp.
Erin's Famous Tap Dancers

DEVIL DANCER, THE
Dec. 29, 1927, Sam Goldwyn, (FL)
Gilda Gray

MILDRED UNGER DANCES CHARLESTON
1926, Pathe, (Nws.)
Mildred Unger dances the Charleston atop an airplane two thousand feet up in the air.

OUR DANCING DAUGHTERS
Sept. 1, 1928, MGM (FL, Sd.)
Joan Crawford does the Charleston

REB SPIKES' BAND
(Reb Spikes and his Follies Entertainers)
Oct. 17, 1927, 1 reel, Vitaphone Corp. (SS, Sd.)
Four unknown Negro tap dancers.

RUBY KEELER
June 4, 1928, 1 reel, Movietone Number, Fox Case Corp. (SS, Sd.)
Tap dance, two minutes.

SO THIS IS PARIS
July 2, 1926, Warner Bros. (FL, Scr.)
Charleston sequence.

1929

AFTER SEBEN
May 17, 1929, 2 reels, Paramount (SS, Scr. Sd.)
James Barton performs a solo eccentric dance. Three pairs of Lindy dancers from Savoy Ballroom, including George "Shorty" Snowden, perform early Lindy. Steps include examples of Charleston, the Breakaway, and Cakewalk. Music furnished by the Chick Webb Orchestra.

BLACK AND TAN FANTASY
Dec. 8, 1929, 2 reels, RKO Productions, Inc. (SS, Scr. Sd.)
Recreation of a Cotton Club floor show with Duke Ellington and his Orchestra, Fredi Washington in a specialty dance number, and The Five Hot Shots performing a unison tap dance.

BLACK NARCISSUS
Aug. 17, 1929, 2 reels, Pathe (SS)
Buck and Bubbles

FOWL PLAY
Nov. 16, 1929, 2 reels, Pathe (SS)
Buck and Bubbles

GOLD DIGGERS OF BROADWAY
Sept. 12, 1929, Warner Bros. (FL, Sd.)
Ann Pennington

HALLELUJAH
Sept. 3, 1929, MGM (FL, Scr. Sd.)
Couple perform Cake Walk and Strut during wedding scene.

HAPPY DAYS
Dec. 23, 1929, Fox (FL)
Ann Pennington

IN AND OUT
Oct. 8, 1929, 2 reels, Pathe Exchange, Inc. (SS)
Buck and Bubbles

IS EVERYBODY HAPPY?
Oct. 6, 1929, Warner Bros. (FL)
Ann Pennington

LADY FARE, THE
Sept. 27, 1929, Paramount, 2 reels (SS)
Cotton Club-like chorus line.

MARKING TIME
Oct. 3, 1929, 2 reels, Universal (SS)
Rooney Family with Pat Rooney, Sr., performing a clog and soft shoe. Pat Rooney II performs a buck and tap.

NIGHT PARADE
Oct. 27, 1929, RKO Radio (FL)
Ann Pennington

ON WITH THE SHOW
June 19, 1929, Warner Bros. (FL, Scr. Sd.)
The Four Covans

PICCADILLY
July 29, 1929, British International Picture (FL)
Gilda Gray

ST. LOUIS BLUES
Sept. 8, 1929, 2 reels, Radio Pictures (SS, Scr. Sd.)
(RKO Productions, Inc.)
Starring famed blues singer Bessie Smith and dancer Jimmy Mordecai (of Wells, Mordecai, and Taylor). Jimmy Mordecai performs specialty tap number. A brief bit of slow-drag dancing is seen during cabaret scene.

SUNSHINE SAMMY AND HIS BROTHERS in STEPPIN' ALONG
Feb. 4, 1929, 1 reel, MGM (SS, Sd.) (Movietone Act)
Stairway buck dance.

TANNED LEGS
Nov. 10, 1929, RKO Radio (FL, Sd.)
Ann Pennington

1930

DARKTOWN FOLLIES
Feb. 4, 1930, 2 reels, Pathe (SS, Sd.)
Buck and Bubbles

DIXIANA
Aug. 16, 1930, RKO Productions (FL, Sd.)
Bill Robinson

GOING PLACES (Shaw and Lee in *Going Places*)
June 9, 1930, Vitaphone Corp. (SS)
Shaw and Lee, loose-jointed eccentric dancing.

HELLO BABY
June 9, 1930, 2 reels, Vitaphone Corp. (SS, Sd.)
Ann Pennington

HIGH TONED
Jan. 18, 1930, 2 reels, Pathe (SS)
Buck and Bubbles

HONEST CROOKS
Feb. 8, 1930, 2 reels, Pathe (SS)
Buck and Bubbles

LEGACY, THE (Betty Compton in "The Legacy")
cir. 1930, Warner Bros. (SS, Sd.)
Betty Compton, tap dance.

MANHATTAN SERANADE
Nov. 20, 1930, 2 reels, MGM Colortone Revue (SS, Sd.)

Connie's Inn Chorus line. (There is reason to believe that Earl "Snake Hips" Tucker appears in this film.)

NEGROES ENTERTAIN SAILORS ON U.S.S. TEXAS
1930, Issue 81, Paramount (Nws.)
Tap dance to music made on a tin can.

SONG PLUGGER, THE
June 9, 1930, 2 reels, Vitaphone (SS, Sd.)
Joe Frisco

UNDERDOG, THE
Jan. 15, 1930, 2 reels, Vitaphone (SS, Sd.)
James Barton

1931

BLUE RHYTHM
Aug. 25, 1931, Walt Disney Productions, Ltd. (Ctn. Sd.)
Mickey and Minnie Mouse perform animated tap dance to St. Louis Blues.

EXILE, THE
May 16, 1931, Oscar Micheaux Pictures, (FL, Sd.)
Leonard Harper Chorus

GAY COLORED STAR STEPS OUT IN PARIS
1931, #18, Pathe, (Nws., Sd.)
Josephine Baker performs at French Charity Fete.

IT TAKES "HOT DOGS" TO WIN THE LINDY HOP
1931, #23, Pathe (Nws. Sd.)
New York City–Harlem Dance Hall.

1932

HARLEM IS HEAVEN
1932, Lincoln Pictures Inc. (FL, Scr. Sd.)
Bill Robinson performs tap routines with chorus line to the music of Eubie Blake and his Orchestra. He also performs his famous Stair Dance to the tune of Swanee River.

PHANTOM PRESIDENT, THE
Oct. 6, 1932, Paramount (FL, Scr. Sd.)
George M. Cohan dances.

PIE, PIE BLACKBIRD
1932, 1 reel, Warner Bros. (SS, Scr. Sd.)
Nicholas Brothers dance to music of Eubie Blake and his Orchestra.

1933

BARBER SHOP BLUES
Sept. 23, 1933, 1 reel, Vitaphone Corp. (SS, Sd.)
The Four Step Brothers with Claude Hopkins Orchestra

BUNDLE OF BLUES
Sept. 1, 1933, 1 reel, Paramount (SS, Scr. Sd.)
Florence Hill and Bessie Dudley perform a fast, acrobatic tap to Bugle Call Rag played by Duke Ellington Orchestra.

DANCING LADY
Nov. 27, 1933, MGM (FL, Sd.)
Fred Astaire

FOOTLIGHT PARADE
Nov. 21, 1933, Warner Bros. (FL, Scr. Sd.)
Ruby Keeler

FORTY-SECOND STREET
Mar. 29, 1933, Warner Bros. (FL, Scr. Sd.)
Ruby Keeler

FLYING DOWN TO RIO
Dec. 29, 1933, RKO Radio (FL, Scr. Sd.)
Fred Astaire, Ginger Rogers

GOLD DIGGERS OF 1933
June 17, 1933, Warner Bros. (FL, Scr. Sd.)
Ruby Keeler

MR. BROADWAY
1933, Broadway-Hollywood Productions (FL, Sd.)
Hal LeRoy, Joe Frisco.

SMASH YOUR BAGGAGE
Mar. 22, 1933, 1 reel, Vitaphone Corp. (SS, Scr. Sd.)
"Rubber Legs" Williams and the Connie's Inn Chorus with the Elmer Snowden Orchestra.

THAT'S THE SPIRIT
Mar. 13, 1933, 1 reel, Vitaphone Corp. (FL, Scr. Sd.)
Cora La Redd, tap dance to music of Noble Sissle Orchestra.

USE YOUR IMAGINATION
Sept. 12, 1933, 2 reels, Vitaphone Corp. (SS, Sd.)
Hal LeRoy, Mitzi Mayfair

WAY OF ALL FRESHMEN, THE
Apr. 18, 1933, 2 reels, Vitaphone Corp. (SS, Sd.)
Hal LeRoy

1934

DAMES
Oct. 3, 1934, Warner Bros. (FL, Scr. Sd.)
Ruby Keeler

DON REDMAN AND HIS ORCHESTRA
Dec. 30, 1934, 1 reel, Vitaphone
Red and Struggy, comic dance.

FLIRTATION WALK
Nov. 16, 1934, First National Pictures, Inc. (FL, Scr. Sd.)
Ruby Keeler

GAY DIVORCEE, THE
Oct. 11, 1934, RKO Radio, (FL, Scr. Sd.)
Fred Astaire and Ginger Rogers

GEORGE WHITE'S SCANDALS
Mar. 16, 1934, Fox Film Corp. (FL, Sd.)
Dixie Dunbar

HARLEM AFTER MIDNIGHT
cir. 1934-35, Micheaux Pictures Corp.
Ralph Brown, tap dance.

KID MILLIONS
Dec. 8, 1934, United Artists (FL, Scr. Sd.)
Nicholas Brothers

KING FOR A DAY
June 28, 1934, 2 reels, Vitaphone Corp. (SS, Scr., Sd.)
Bill Robinson

"THE MARCH OF TIME"
Cir. 1934, MGM (An MGM Revue) (SS, Sd.)
Barney Fagan, King of the Soft Shoe Dancers

PICTURE PALACE
Jan. 29, 1934, 2 reels, Vitaphone Corp. (SS, Sd.)
Hal LeRoy

PRIVATE LESSONS
Apr. 18, 1934, 2 reels, Vitaphone Corp. (SS, Sd.)
Hal LeRoy

SYNCOPATED CITY
Oct. 20, 1934, 2 reels, Vitaphone (SS, Sd.)
Hal LeRoy

WHOLE SHOW, THE
Dec. 17, 1934, 2 reels, Universal (SS, Sd.)
(Mentone Musical)
James Barton

WONDER BAR
Feb. 23, 1934, First National (FL, Sd.)
Hal LeRoy

1935

ALL-COLORED VAUDEVILLE SHOW
Sept. 6, 1935, Vitaphone Corp. (SS, Sd.)
Nicholas Brothers

BIG BROADCAST OF 1936
Sept. 26, 1935, Paramount (FL, Scr. Sd.)
Bill Robinson, Nicholas Brothers

BROADWAY HIGHLIGHTS No. 4
Sept. 27, 1935, 1 reel, Paramount SS, Scr. Sd.)
Cora La Redd and a Cotton Club rehearsal.

BROADWAY MELODY OF 1936
Sept. 16, 1935, MGM (FL, Scr. Sd.)
Eleanor Powell, Buddy Ebsen

GO INTO YOUR DANCE
June 5, 1935, First National Pictures (FL, Scr. Sd.)
Ruby Keeler

HOORAY FOR LOVE
June 14, 1935, RKO Radio (FL, Sd.)
Bill Robinson, Jeni Le Gon

IN OLD KENTUCKY
Sept. 6, 1935, 20th Century-Fox (FL, Sd.)
Bill Robinson

LITTLE COLONEL, THE
Feb. 22, 1935, Fox Film Corp. (FL, Scr. Sd.)
Bill Robinson, Shirley Temple

LITTLEST REBEL, THE
Dec. 27, 1935, 20th Century-Fox (FL, Scr. Sd.)
Bill Robinson, Shirley Temple

MAIN STREET FOLLIES
July 6, 1935, 2 reels, Vitaphone Corp. (SS, Sd.)
Hal LeRoy

MUSICAL MEMORIES
Nov. 14, 1935, Paramount (SS, Sd.)
Hal LeRoy, Ruby Keeler

ROBERTA
Feb. 26, 1935, RKO Radio (FL, Sd.)
Fred Astaire and Ginger Rogers

SHIPMATES FOREVER
Oct. 16, 1935, First National (FL, Sd.)
Ruby Keeler

SYMPHONY IN BLACK
Sept. 12, 1935, 1 reel, Paramount (SS, Scr. Sd.)
Earl "Snake Hips" Tucker with Duke Ellington Orchestra.

TOP HAT
Aug. 29, 1935, RKO Radio (FL, Scr. Sd.)
Fred Astaire and Ginger Rogers

VAUDEVILLE REEL No. 4
1935, Vitaphone (SS, Sd.)
Pat Rooney, Sr., Pat Rooney, Jr.

1936

BIG BROADCAST OF 1937
Oct. 9, 1936, Paramount (FL, Scr. Sd.)
Louis DaPron

BLACK NETWORK
May 5, 1936, 2 reels, Vitaphone Corp. (SS, Sd.)
Nicholas Brothers

BORN TO DANCE
Nov. 23, 1936, MGM (FL, Scr. Sd.)
Eleanor Powell

BY REQUEST
Mar. 2, 1936, 1 reel, Vitaphone Corp. (SS, Scr. Sd.)
Tip, Tap and Toe with Claude Hopkins Orchestra

COLLEEN
Mar. 26, 1936, Warner Bros. (FL, Sd.)
Ruby Keeler, Paul Draper

COLLEGE HOLIDAY
Dec. 25, 1936, Paramount, (FL, Sd.)
Johnny Downs, Louis DaPron

DANCING FEET
Feb. 28, 1936, Republic (FL, Sd.)
Nick Condos

DEEP SOUTH
Dec. 11, 1936, 2 reels, RKO Radio (SS, Scr. Sd.)
(Radio Musical No. 2)

Cakewalk is performed during rural wedding sequence.

FIRST BABY, THE
May 15, 1936, 20th Century-Fox (FL, Sd.)
Dixie Dunbar, Johnny Downs

FOLLOW THE FLEET
Feb. 20, 1936, RKO Radio (FL, Scr. Sd.)
Fred Astaire and Ginger Rogers

GOLD DIGGERS OF 1937
Dec. 31, 1936, Warner Bros. (FL, Sd. Scr.)
Lee Dixon, tap dancer.

GREAT ZIEGFELD, THE
Apr. 19, 1936, MGM, (FL, Scr. Sd.)
Ray Bolger

HIDEAWAY GIRL
Nov. 20, 1936, Paramount (FL, Sd.)
Louis DaPron

KING OF BURLESQUE
Jan. 3, 1936, 20th Century-Fox (FL, Scr. Sd.)
Dixie Dunbar with Fats Waller and his Rhythm.

MUSIC GOES 'ROUND, THE
Feb. 25, 1936, Columbia (FL, Scr. Sd.)
Eddie "Rochester' Anderson and Johnny Taylor do an eccentric dance. Nyas Berry, acrobatic tap. Les Hite Orchestra.

OH, EVALINE
Feb. 17, 1936, 2 reels, Vitaphone (SS, Sd.)
Hal LeRoy

PIGSKIN PARADE
Oct. 23, 1936, 20th Century-Fox (FL, Sd.)
Dixie Dunbar, Johnny Downs

RED NICHOLS AND HIS WORLD FAMOUS PENNIES
Apr. 21, 1936, Warner Bros. (SS, Scr. Sd.)
Negro (2) tap dancers perform in farmer costumes.

RHYTHMITIS
Aug. 10, 1936, 2 reels, Vitaphone Corp. (SS, Sd.)
Hal LeRoy

SAN FRANCISCO
June 22, 1936, MGM (FL, Scr. Sd.)
Cakewalk production number.

SING, BABY, SING
Aug. 21, 1936, 20th Century-Fox (FL, Scr. Sd.)
Dixie Dunbar

SWING TIME
Sept. 27, 1936, RKO Radio (FL, Scr. Sd.)
Fred Astaire and Ginger Rogers

THREE CHEERS FOR LOVE
June 26, 1936, Paramount (FL, Sd.)
Louis DaPron

WATCH YOUR STEP
Mar. 30, 1936, Vitaphone Corp. (SS, Sd.)
(Broadway Brevity)
Hal LeRoy

1937

BIG APPLE
Aug. 1937, Paramount (Nws.)
New dance "sweeping up" from South. Demonstration of the Shag, Trucking, Suzie-Q, Charleston, and Shine.

BROADWAY MELODY OF 1938
Aug. 16, 1937, MGM (FL, Scr. Sd.)
Eleanor Powell, George Murphy, Buddy Ebsen

CALLING ALL STARS
1937, British Lion (England) (FL, Sd.)
Nicholas Brothers, Buck and Bubbles

DAMSEL IN DISTRESS
Nov. 19, 1937, RKO Radio (FL, Scr. Sd.)
Fred Astaire

DATES AND NUTS
Dec. 31, 1937, 2 reels, Educational Films (SS, Sd.)
Arthur Murray Shag Dancers.

DAY AT THE RACES
June 10, 1937, MGM (FL, Scr. Sd.)
During Ivie Anderson's "All God's Chillun Got Rhythm" number, numerous Lindy dancers perform, including Leon James.

52ND STREET
Oct. 18, 1937, United Artists (FL, Sd.)
Cook and Brown, Rocco and Saulter, Ella Logan

HOW TO DANCE THE SHAG
Dec. 17, 1937, Skibo Productions Inc. (SS, Scr. Sd.)
Arthur Murray Instructional Film.

JIMMIE LUNCEFORD AND HIS DANCE ORCHESTRA
Feb. 18, 1937, 1 reel, Vitaphone (SS, Scr. Sd.)
The Three Brown Jacks, acrobatic tap.

LIFE OF THE PARTY, THE
Sept. 3, 1937, RKO Radio (FL, Sd.)
Ann Miller

LONDON BY NIGHT
July 29, 1937, MGM (FL, Sd.)
George Murphy

MELODY FOR TWO
Mar. 18, 1937, Warner Bros. (FL, Sd.)
Jack and Donald O'Connor

NEW FACES OF 1937
July 1, 1937, RKO Radio (FL, Sd.)
Ann Miller, Three Chocolateers (Peckin')

ONE IN A MILLION
Jan. 1, 1937, 20th Century-Fox (FL, Sd.)
Dixie Dunbar

ONE MILE FROM HEAVEN
Aug. 13, 1937, 20th Century-Fox (FL, Sd.)
Bill Robinson

PHONY BOY
Nov. 19, 1937, 1 reel, RKO Radio (SS, Sd.)
(Nu-Atlas Musical)
Shag Dance winners from Harvest Moon Ball

READY, WILLING AND ABLE
Feb. 5, 1937, Warner Bros. (FL, Sd.)
Ruby Keeler, Shaw and Lee

ROSALIE
Dec. 20, 1937, MGM (FL, Sd.)
Eleanor Powell, Ray Bolger

SHALL WE DANCE?
May 7, 1937, RKO Radio (FL, Scr. Sd.)
Fred Astaire and Ginger Rogers

SOMETHING TO SING ABOUT
Sept. 1, 1937, Grand National (FL, Sd.)
James Cagney

SWEET SHOE
Dec. 31, 1937, 1 reel, RKO Radio (SS, Sd.)
(Nu-Atlas Musical)
The Four Specs, tap dancers.

SWING
cir. 1937, Micheaux Pictures (FL, Sd.)
The Tyler Twins, tap dancers.

SWING FOR SALE
May 3, 1937, 2 reels, Vitaphone (SS, Sd.)
Hal LeRoy

TOP OF THE TOWN
Apr. 6, 1937, Universal (FL, Sd.)
George Murphy, Peggy Ryan, Ella Logan

UNDERWORLD
cir. 1937, Sack Amusement Enterprises (FL, Scr. Sd.)

Dorothy Salters, rhythm tap, and Raymond Collins, rope dancer.

UPS AND DOWNS
Oct. 18, 1937, 2 reels, Vitaphone (SS, Sd.)
Hal LeRoy

VARSITY SHOW
July 14, 1937, Warner Bros. (FL, Scr. Sd.)
Buck and Bubbles

VOGUES OF 1938 (Walter Wanger's Vogues of 1938)
Sept. 7, 1937, United Artists (FL, Scr. Sd.)
Dorothy Salters, The Four Hot Shots with Maurice Rocco Orchestra

WAKE UP AND LIVE
Apr. 23, 1937, 20th Century-Fox (FL, Scr. Sd.)
Condos Brothers

WOODY HERMAN AND ORCHESTRA
1937, 1 reel, Vitaphone (SS, Scr. Sd.)
Shag Dancing.

YOU CAN'T HAVE EVERYTHING
Aug. 6, 1937, 20th Century-Fox (FL, Sd.)
Tip, Tap and Toe, tap dancers.

YOU'RE A SWEETHEART
Dec. 17, 1937, Universal (FL, Sd.)
George Murphy

1938

ALEXANDER'S RAGTIME BAND
Aug. 11, 1938, 20th Century-Fox (FL, Scr. Sd.)
Dixie Dunbar, Wally Vernon

'ALLIGATORS' PLUS 'CATS' PLUS 'JIVE' EQUALS MORE SWING!
June 1938, 101 ft., Paramount (Nws.)
Shag Contests; Trucking, Lindy Hop

CAFE RENDEZVOUS
Dec. 28, 1938, 1 reel, RKO Radio (SS, Sd.)
(Nu Atlas Musical)
Samuels Brothers and Edith Fleming, tap dancers

CAREFREE
Sept. 2, 1938, RKO Radio (FL, Sd.)
Fred Astaire and Ginger Rogers

CARNIVAL SHOW
June 24, 1938, 1 reel, RKO Radio (SS, Sd.)
(Nu Atlas Musical)
Three De Loveliers, tap dance trio

CARL "DEACON" MOORE AND HIS BAND
Aug. 10, 1938, Vitaphone Corp. (SS, Sd.)
Dancers perform the Big Apple

COLLEGE SWING
Apr. 29, 1938, Paramount (FL, Sd.)
Slate Brothers

EVERYBODY SING
Jan. 28, 1938, MGM (FL, Sd.)
Whitey's Lindy Hoppers

HARLEM HOOFERS FRY THEIR CORNS
Aug. 1938, Paramount (Nws.)
Lindy dancing

HOCKSHOP BLUES
July 11, 1938, 1 reel, RKO Radio (SS, Sd.)
Wally and Ver'dyn Stapleton, rhythm tap

HOLD THAT CO-ED
Sept. 16, 1938, 20th Century-Fox (FL, Sd.)
George Murphy, Johnny Downs

JITTERBUG JAMBOREE
1938, Vitaphone (SS, Sd.)
(Broadway Brevity)
Shag dancers from the Harvest Moon Ball Competition.

JITTERBUGS JIVE AT SWINGEROO
June, 1938, 126 ft., Paramount (Nws.)
Randall's Island Jazz Festival with candid shots of couples doing the Lindy Hop and Shag.

JUST AROUND THE CORNER
Nov. 11, 1938, 20th Century-Fox (FL, Sd.)
Bill Robinson, Shirley Temple

KNIGHT IS YOUNG, THE
Dec. 5, 1938, 2 reels, Vitaphone Corp. (SS, Sd.)
Hal LeRoy

LITTLE MISS BROADWAY
July 29, 1938, 20th Century-Fox (FL, Sd.)
Shirley Temple, George Murphy

LOVE ON A BUDGET
Feb. 25, 1938, 20th Century-Fox (FL, Sd.)
Dixie Dunbar

OLD BOSTON A-JIVE WITH JITTERBUGS
Oct. 1938, 116 ft., Paramount (Nws.)
Jitterbugging couples at Charity Fund Drive.

PRISONER OF SWING, THE
June 11, 1938, Vitaphone (SS, Sd.)
(Broadway Brevity)
Hal LeRoy

RADIO CITY REVELS
Feb. 11, 1938, RKO Radio (FL, Sd.)
Ann Miller

RADIO HOOK-UP
Jan. 28, 1938, 1 reel, RKO Radio (SS, Sd.)
(Nu Atlas Musical)
Charles Collins, tap dancer

REBECCA OF SUNNYBROOK FARM
Mar. 18, 1938, 20th Century-Fox (FL, Sd.)
Bill Robinson, Shirley Temple, Dixie Dunbar

ROOM SERVICE
1938, RKO Radio (FL, Scr. Sd.)
Ann Miller

SKYLINE REVUE
Apr. 1, 1938, 1 reel, RKO Radio (SS, Sd.)
(Nu Atlast Musical)
Billy and Milly with Sugar Nichols (six-year-old tap dancer)

START CHEERING
Dec. 31, 1937, Columbia (FL, Sd.)
Hal LeRoy

SWING, SISTER, SWING
Dec. 20, 1938, Universal (FL, Sd.)
Johnny Downs

THRILL OF A LIFETIME
Jan. 21, 1938, Paramount (FL, Sd.)
Big Apple

TWO SHADOWS
Dec. 20, 1938, Vitaphone (SS, Sd.)
Jean and her Big Apple Dancers

UP IN LIGHTS
Aug. 13, 1938, 2 reels, Vitaphone Corp. (SS, Sd.)
(Broadway Brevity)
Pat Rooney

UP THE RIVER
Dec. 9, 1938, 20th Century-Fox (FL, Sd.)
Bill Robinson

WALKING DOWN BROADWAY
Mar. 11, 1938, 20th Century-Fox (FL, Sd.)
Dixie Dunbar

WOODY HERMAN AND HIS ORCHESTRA
Dec. 27, 1938, Vitaphone Corp. (SS, Scr. Sd.)
Hal and Honey Abbott, jitterbug specialists

'WORLD SERIES' DANCE HAS NEW YORK SWINGING
Sept. 1938, Paramount, (Nws.)
At Harvest Moon Ball, competing couples perform Shag and Lindy Hop.

1939

BROADWAY BUCKAROO, THE
June 3, 1939, Vitaphone Corp. (SS, Sd.)

(Broadway Brevities)
The Condos Brothers

HARVEST MOON BALL
Aug. 30, 1939, Paramount (Nws.)
Couples do the Shag, and Lindy Hop.

HONOLULU
Jan. 31, 1939, MGM (FL, Sd.)
Eleanor Powell

I'M JUST A JITTERBUG
Jan. 16, 1939, A Walter Lanz Cartune, Universal (Ctn.)
Mother Goose characters do the Shag and Lindy Hop.

IT'S SWING HO—COME TO THE FAIR!
Oct. 1939, 96 ft., Paramount (Nws.)
Jitterbugging crowds in front of City Hall in New York City. Bill Robinson dances on the street as a promotional stunt.

READIN', 'RITIN', AND RHYTHM
Feb. 16, 1939, RKO Radio (SS, Scr. Sd.)
Eight Raggle Taggles, winners of New Jersey jitterbug contest.

SOPHOMORE SWING
June 21, 1939, Vitaphone Corp. (SS, Sd.)
(Broadway Brevity)
New York Harvest Moon Dancers in jitterbug sequence.

STORY OF VERNON AND IRENE CASTLE, THE
Mar. 30, 1939, RKO Radio (FL, Scr. Sd.)
Fred Astaire and Ginger Rogers

'THE MIKADO' GOES SWING
Mar. 1939, 151 ft., Paramount (Nws.)
Federal Theater version of Gilbert and Sullivan Operetta. Leading dance couple perform.

1940

BROADWAY MELODY OF 1940
Feb. 9, 1940, MGM (FL, Scr. Sd.)
Fred Astaire, Eleanor Powell, George Murphy

DOWN ARGENTINE WAY
Oct. 11, 1940, 20th Century-Fox (FL, Scr. Sd.)
Nicholas Brothers

HIT PARADE OF 1941, THE
Oct. 15, 1940, Republic (FL, Scr. Sd.)
Ann Miller

I CAN'T GIVE YOU ANYTHING BUT LOVE, BABY
May 20, 1940, Universal (FL, Sd.)
Johnny Downs

JITTERBUG JAMBOREE
Sept. 1940, Hearst-Paramount-Pathe (Nws.)
Jitterbugs at New York World's Fair

SING, DANCE, PLENTY HOT
Aug. 10, 1940, Republic (FL, Sd.)
Johnny Downs

TIN PAN ALLEY
Nov. 29, 1940, 20th Century-Fox (FL, Scr. Sd.)
Nicholas Brothers

TOO MANY GIRLS
Nov. 1, 1940, RKO Radio (FL, Sd.)
Ann Miller, Hal LeRoy

1941

AIR MAIL SPECIAL
Dec. 8, 1941, Soundies Dist. Corp. of America, (SS, Scr. Sd.)
Lindy dancing to Count Basie Orchestra.

ALL-AMERICAN CO-ED
Oct. 30, 1941, United Artists (FL, Sd.)
Johnny Downs

BALLET DANCERS' NIGHTMARE
Aug. 4, 1941, Soundies Dist. Corp. of America (SS, Sd.)
Eccentric dancing, Slate Brothers

FOUR JACKS AND A JILL
Dec. 18, 1941, RKO Radio (FL, Sd.)
Ray Bolger

GO WEST, YOUNG LADY
Nov. 22, 1941, Columbia (FL, Sd.)
Ann Miller

GREAT AMERICAN BROADCAST, THE
May 9, 1941, 20th Century-Fox (FL, Scr. Sd.)
Nicholas Brothers

HARVEST MOON BALL
Aug. 29, 1941, Paramount (Nws.)
Pick dance champs. Couple do Lindy Hop.

HELLZAPOPPIN'
Dec. 24, 1941, Universal (FL, Scr. Sd.)
Lindy Hop dancers

HOT CHOCOLATE
Dec. 31, 1941, Soundies Dist. Corp. of America (SS, Sd.)
Whitey's Lindy Hoppers with Duke Ellington Orchestra

JAZZ ETUDE
Jan. 31, 1941, Soundies Dist. Corp. of America (SS, Sd.)
Novelty tap dancing by Billy Burt

KISS THE BOYS GOODBYE
Aug. 1, 1941, Paramount (FL, Scr. Sd.)
Eddie "Rochester" Anderson, slide and shuffle dancing

LADY BE GOOD
July 2, 1941, MGM (FL, Scr. Sd.)
Eleanor Powell, Dan Dailey, The Berry Brothers

MANHATTAN
May 19, 1941, Soundies Dist. Corp. of America (SS, Sd.)
Grace McDonald, tap dance.

MOONLIGHT IN HAWAII
Aug. 1, 1941, Universal (FL, Sd.)
Johnny Downs

RIDE 'EM COWBOY
Dec. 4, 1941, Universal (FL, Sd.)
Three Congeroos

RISE AND SHINE
Nov. 21, 1941, 20th Century-Fox (FL, Sd.)
George Murphy

ROOKIES ON PARADE
Apr. 17, 1941, Republic (FL, Sd.)
Louis DaPron

SHADOWS IN SWING
May 5, 1941, 2 reels, Universal (SS, Sd.)
Louis DaPron

SUN VALLEY SERENADE
Aug. 29, 1941, 20th Century-Fox, (FL, Scr. Sd.)
Nicholas Brothers and Dorothy Dandridge with the Glenn Miller Orchestra.

SUNNY
May 30, 1941, RKO Radio (FL, Sd.)
Ray Bolger

SWEETHEART OF THE CAMPUS
June 26, 1941, Columbia (FL, Sd.)
Ruby Keeler

SECOND CHORUS
Jan. 3, 1941, Paramount (FL, Scr. Sd.)
Fred Astaire

TIME OUT FOR RHYTHM
June 20, 1941, Columbia (FL, Sd.)
Ann Miller

TOOT THAT TRUMPET
Dec. 22, 1941, Soundies Dist. Corp. of America (SS, Sd.)
Cook and Brown

WITH A TWIST OF THE WRIST
July 7, 1941, Soundies Dist. Corp. of America (SS, Sd.)
Rhythm tap dance, Grace McDonald.

YOU'LL NEVER GET RICH
Sept. 25, 1941, Columbia (FL, Scr. Sd.)
Fred Astaire

1942

BEHIND THE EIGHT BALL
Sept. 28, 1942, Universal (FL, Sd.)
Johnny Downs

BLI-BLIP
Jan. 5, 1942, Soundies Dist. Corp. of America (SS, Sd.)
Marie Bryant and Paul White, "Jive" Dancing.

BY AN OLD SOUTHERN RIVER
Jan. 12, 1942, Soundies Dist. Corp. of America (SS, Scr. Sd.)
Bill Robinson, song and tap.

CUBAN EPISODE
July 20, 1942, Soundies Dist. Corp. of America (SS, Sd.)
Katherine Dunham Dancers

FLAMINGO
Jan. 5, 1942, Soundies Dist. Corp. of America (SS, Sd.)
Katherine Dunham Dancers with Duke Ellington Orchestra

FOR ME AND MY GAL
Sept. 11, 1942, MGM (FL, Scr. Sd.)
Gene Kelly, George Murphy

FUZZY-WUZZY
Dec. 31, 1942, Soundies Dist. Corp. of America (SS, Sd.)
Ruby Richards

GET HEP TO LOVE
Aug. 25, 1942, Universal (FL, Sd.)
Donald O'Connor, Jivin' Jacks & Jills.

GIVE OUT, SISTERS
July 27, 1942, Universal (FL, Sd.)
Dan Dailey, Jivin' Jacks & Jills.

HARLEM RHUMBA
Dec. 21, 1942, Soundies Dist. Corp. of America (SS, Sd.)
The Chocolateers

HOLIDAY INN
June 12, 1942, Paramount (FL, Scr. Sd.)
Fred Astaire

IT COMES UP LOVE
Sept. 21, 1942, Universal (FL, Sd.)
Donald O'Connor

JIVIN' JAM SESSION
July 20, 1942, 2 reels, Universal (SS, Sd.)
Louis DaPron, tap dance.

LET'S SCUFFLE
Jan. 12, 1942, Soundies Dist. Corp. of America (SS, Scr. Sd.)
Bill Robinson, song and tap.

MOONLIGHT MASQUERADE
June 10, 1942, Republic (FL, Sd.)
Three Chocolateers

ORCHESTRA WIVES
Sept. 4, 1942, 20th Century-Fox (FL, Scr. Sd.)
Nicholas Brothers with Glenn Miller Orchestra

OUTLINE OF JITTERBUG HISTORY
Mar. 23, 1942, Soundies Dist. Corp. of America (SS, Sd.)
Whitey's Lindy Hoppers

PANAMA HATTIE
July 21, 1942, MGM (FL, Scr. Sd.)
Dan Dailey, Berry Brothers

PARDON MY SARONG
July 21, 1942, Universal (FL, Sd.)
Tip, Tap and Toe, Katherine Dunham Dancers

PECKIN'
Nov. 9, 1942, Soundies Dist. Corp. of America (SS, Scr. Sd.)
The Chocolateers, comic dance.

PRIORITIES ON PARADE
July 22, 1942, Paramount (FL, Scr. Sd.)
Ann Miller

PRIVATE BUCKAROO
May 29, 1942, Universal (FL, Sd.)
Donald O'Connor, Jivin' Jacks & Jills.

SHIP AHOY
Apr. 23, 1942, MGM (FL, Scr. Sd.)
Eleanor Powell, Stump and Stumpy

SING YOUR WORRIES AWAY
Jan. 30, 1942, RKO Radio (FL, Sd.)
Buddy Ebsen

SIX HITS AND A MISS
Nov. 9, 1942, Warner Bros. (SS, Sd.)
Ruby Keeler, Paul Draper

SPIRIT OF BOOGIE WOOGIE
Aug. 17, 1942, Soundies Dist. Corp.

of America (SS, Sd.)
Katherine Dunham and her Dancers.

STAR SPANGLED RHYTHM
Dec. 29, 1942, Paramount (FL, Scr. Sd.)
Katherine Dunham

SUGAR HILL MASQUERADE
Nov. 23, 1942, Soundies Dist. Corp. of America (SS, Sd.)
Whitey's Lindy Hoppers

SWING FROLIC
Feb. 24, 1942, 2 reels, Universal (SS, Sd.)
Peggy Ryan tap dance.

TRUE TO THE ARMY
June 18, 1942, 2 reels, Universal (SS, Scr. Sd.)
Grace MacDonald, tap dance; Jivin' Jacks & Jills and Harry James Orchestra.

TRUE TO THE ARMY
Mar. 17, 1942, Paramount (FL, Sd.)
Ann Miller

TRUMPET SERENADE
June 18, 1942, 2 reels, Universal (SS, Scr. Sd.)
Grace MacDonald, tap dance; Jivin' Jacks and Jills, and Harry James Orchestra

TUXEDO JUNCTION
Dec. 31, 1942, Soundies Dist. Corp. of America (SS, Scr. Sd.)
The Lenox Hoppers

TWEED ME
Dec. 31, 1942, Soundies Dist. Corp. of America (SS, Sd.)
The Chocolateers

YOU WERE NEVER LOVELIER
Oct. 19, 1942, Columbia (FL, Scr. Sd.)
Fred Astaire

WHAT'S COOKIN'
Feb. 24, 1942, Universal (FL, Sd.)
Jivin' Jacks and Jills

WHEN JOHNNY COMES MARCHING HOME
Nov. 24, 1942, Universal (FL, Sd.)
Donald O'Connor, Four Step Brothers

1943

ALL BY MYSELF
Apr. 30, 1943, Universal (FL, Sd.)
Tip, Tap and Toe

BREAKFAST IN RHYTHM
Oct. 29, 1943, Soundies Dist. Corp. of America (SS, Sd.)
The Three Chefs

CABIN IN THE SKY
Feb, 9, 1943, MGM (FL, Scr. Sd.)
Lindy dancers (Leon James)

CHATTER
Nov. 29, 1943, Soundies Dist. Corp. of America (SS, Sd.)
Cook and Brown

CHOO CHOO SWING
Nov. 12, 1943, 2 reels, Universal (SS, Sd.)
Nicholas Brothers

DANCEMANIA
Oct. 29, 1943, Soundies Dist. Corp. of America (SS, Sd.)
Harris and Hunt, dance team.

DANCE REVUE
Mar. 1, 1943, Soundies Dist. Corp. of America (SS, Sd.)
Pat Rooney III

DU BARRY WAS A LADY
May 6, 1943, MGM (FL, Scr. Sd.)
Gene Kelly

FOOLIN' AROUND
Nov. 1, 1943, Soundies Dist. Corp. of America (SS, Sd.)
Harris and Hunt, dance team.

FLYING FEET
June 28, 1943, Soundies Dist. Corp. of America (SS, Sd.)
Rita Rio, tap dance.

HARLEM HOTCHA
Dec. 21, 1943, Soundies Dist. Corp. of America (SS, Sd.)
Tops and Wilder, tap dancers.

HEAT'S ON AGAIN, THE
Mar. 16, 1943, Soundies Dist. Corp. of America
Slapstick jitterbug routine with the Three Heat Waves.

HE'S MY GUY
Mar. 15, 1943, Universal (FL, Sd.)
Louis DaPron

HEY, ROOKIE
Dec. 31, 1943, Columbia (FL, Sd.)
Ann Miller

HI, BUDDY!
Jan. 4, 1943, Universal (FL, Sd.)
The Step Brothers

HIT PARADE OF 1943
Mar. 16, 1943, Republic (FL, Sd.)
Jack Williams (The Harlem Sandman), Pops and Louie.

HIYA SAILOR
Nov. 2, 1943, Universal (FL, Sd.)
Pops and Louie

HONEYMOON LODGE
July 28, 1943, Universal (FL, Sd.)
Tip, Tap and Toe, tap dancers.

HOW'S ABOUT IT?
Feb. 3, 1943, Universal
Louis DaPron

I DOOD IT
July 27, 1943, MGM (FL, Scr. Sd.)
Eleanor Powell

IT AIN'T HAY
Mar. 25, 1943, Universal (FL, Sd.)
Step Brothers

JIVEROO
June 28, 1943, Soundies Dist. Corp. of America (SS, Sd.)
Harry Day and Della, eccentric dancing.

JUMPIN' JACK FROM HACKENSACK
Oct. 25, 1943, Soundies Dist. Corp. of America (SS, Sd.)
Tommy Thompson, specialty dancer.

MAHARAJA
June 7, 1943, Soundies Dist. Corp. of America (SS, Sd.)
Hal and Betty Takier, jitterbug dancing.

PARDON ME, BUT YOU LOOK JUST LIKE MARGIE
June 28, 1943, Soundies Dist. Corp. of America
The Three Chefs

REVEILLE WITH BEVERLY
Feb. 4, 1943, Columbia (FL, Scr. Sd.)
Ann Miller

RHYTHM OF THE ISLANDS
Apr. 7, 1943, Universal (FL, Sd.)
Step Brothers

POPPIN' THE CORK
June 21, 1943, Soundies Dist. Corp. of America (SS, Sd.)
Billy and Ann, dance team.

RHYTHMANIA
Oct. 29, 1943, Soundies Dist. Corp. of America (SS, Sd.)
Harris and Hunt, Dance Team.

SHE'S FOR ME
Nov. 12, 1943, Universal (FL, Sd.)
Louis DaPron

SKY'S THE LIMIT, THE
Aug. 21, 1943, RKO Radio (FL, Scr. Sd.)
Fred Astaire

SONG AND DANCE MAN, A
Nov. 22, 1943, Soundies Dist. Corp. of America
Taps Miller

STORMY WEATHER
July 16, 1943, 20th Century-Fox (FL, Scr. Sd.)
Bill Robinson, Nicholas Brothers, Katherine Dunham

SWEET JAM
Sept. 27, 1943, 2 reels, Universal (SS, Sd.)
Louis DaPron, burlesque on ballroom dancing.

TAP HAPPY
Dec. 31, 1943, Soundies Dist. Corp.

of America (SS, Sd.)
Slim and Sweets, tap dancers.

THOUSANDS CHEER
Sept. 22, 1943, MGM (FL, Scr. Sd.)
Eleanor Powell, Gene Kelly

TOP MAN
Sept. 24, 1943, Universal (FL, Sd.)
Donald O'Connor and Count Basie Orchestra.

WHAT'S BUZZIN' COUSIN?
July 8, 1943, Columbia (FL, Sd.)
Ann Miller

YANKEE DOODLE DANDY
Jan. 2, 1943, Warner Bros. (FL, Scr. Sd.)
James Cagney in the role of George M. Cohan.

1944

ATLANTIC CITY
Aug. 16, 1944, Republic (FL, Scr. Sd.)
Buck and Bubbles

AUSTRALIAN JITTERBUGS JITTER
Feb. 8, 1944, 83 ft. Paramount (Australian news via Fox) (Nws.)
Australian Lindy dancing.

BOWERY TO BROADWAY
Oct. 26, 1944, Universal (FL, Sd.)
Donald O'Connor

BROADWAY RHYTHM
Jan. 4, 1944, MGM (FL, Sd.)
George Murphy

CAROLINA BLUES
Dec. 11, 1944, Columbia (FL, Scr. Sd.)
Ann Miller, The Four Step Brothers, Marie Bryant, Harold Nicholas

CAVALCADE OF DANCE
May 29, 1944, Warner Bros., (SS, Sd.)
(Melody Masters)
Veloz and Yolanda review of the dance crazes.

COVER GIRL
Apr. 6, 1944, Columbia
Gene Kelly

DANCE IMPRESSIONS
Nov. 20, 1944, Soundies Dist. Corp. of America (SS, Sd.)
Eccentric dancing by Bobby Davis and dance impressions of Pat Rooney, Bill Robinson and Ray Bolger

FOLLOW THE BOYS
Mar. 31, 1944, Universal (FL, Scr. Sd.)
Donald O'Connor

GREENWICH VILLAGE
Aug 3, 1944, 20th Century-Fox (FL, Scr. Sd.)
Four Step Brothers

GROOVIE MOVIE
Apr. 6, 1944, MGM (SS, Sd.)
(A Pete Smith Specialty)
Traces origin of modern jitterbug dancing with amusing commentary by Pete Smith

HEY, ROOKIE
Dec. 31, 1943, Columbia (FL, Sd.)
Ann Miller, Condos Brothers

HI, GOOD LOOKIN'
Mar. 17, 1944, Universal (FL, Sd.)
Tip, Tap and Toe

JAM SESSION
Mar. 22, 1944, Columbia (FL, Scr. Sd.)
Ann Miller

JAMMIN' THE BLUES
Dec. 18, 1944, Vitaphone Corp. (SS, Scr. Sd.)
Archie Savage and Marie Bryant dance the Lindy Hop to the music of Lester Young and an All-Star Group.

MERRY MONAHANS, THE
July 28, 1944, Universal (FL, Sd.)
Donald O'Connor

PENTHOUSE RHYTHM
Nov. 20, 1944, Universal (FL, Sd.)
Louis DaPron

PIN-UP GIRL
May 10, 1944, 20th Century-Fox (FL, Scr. Sd.)
Condos Brothers

RECKLESS AGE
Oct. 26, 1944, Universal (FL, Sd.)
Harold Nicholas

SENSATIONS OF 1945
June 30, 1944, United Artists (FL, Scr. Sd.)
Eleanor Powell

SHINE ON, HARVEST MOON
Apr. 8, 1944, Warners (FL, Sd.)
Four Step Brothers

SINGING SHERIFF, THE
Sept. 15, 1944, Universal (FL, Sd.)
Louis DaPron

SONG OF THE OPEN ROAD
June 2, 1944, United Artists (FL, Sd.)
Condos Brothers

STEP LIVELY
June 26, 1944, RKO Radio (FL, Sd.)
George Murphy

STEPPING FAST
Nov. 13, 1944, Soundies Dist. Corp. of America (SS, Sd.)
Tap dancing routine by Burch Mann Dancers.

THIS IS THE LIFE
Nov. 17, 1943, Universal (FL, Sd.)
Donald O'Connor

1945

ANCHORS AWEIGH
July 9, 1945, MGM (FL, Scr. Sd.)
Gene Kelly

EADIE WAS A LADY
Jan. 23, 1945, Columbia (FL, Sd.)
Ann Miller

EAGER BEAVER
Dec. 30, 1945, Soundies Dist. Corp. of America (SS, Sd.)
Jean Ivory, tap dance.

ON STAGE, EVERYBODY
July 27, 1945, Universal (FL, Sd.)
Johnny Coy

SANDIN' JOE
Sept. 10, 1945, Soundies Dist. Corp. of America (SS, Sd.)
Two tap dancers.

TONIGHT AND EVERY NIGHT
Feb. 22, 1945, Columbia (FL, Scr. Sd.)
Marc Platt

YOLANDA AND THE THIEF
Nov. 15, 1945, MGM (FL, Scr. Sd.)
Fred Astaire

1946

BEALE ST. MAMA
cir. 1946, Sack Amusement Enterprises (FL, Scr. Sd.)
July Jones, tap dance.

BLUE SKIES
Dec. 27, 1946, MGM (FL, Scr. Sd.)
Fred Astaire

BOOGIEMANIA
Apr. 29, 1946, Soundies Dist. Corp. of America (SS, Sd.)
Helen Bangs and Albert Reese Jones, incidental jitterbug dancing.

DIXIELAND JAMBOREE
Apr. 24, 1946, Vitaphone (SS, Scr. Sd.)
Whippets, Nicholas Brothers
(Although copyright date is 1946, footage is of an earlier vintage, cir. 1934.)

LOVE IN SYNCOPATION
cir. 1946, Astor Picture Corp. (Distributor)
Associated Producers of Negro Motion Pictures Corp. (FL, Scr. Sd.)
Tops and Wilda, Ronnell and Edna

LYING LIPS
cir. 1946, Sack Amusement Enterprises (FL, Scr. Sd.)
Clyde "Slim" Thompson, Teddy Hall

MOVIETONE NEWS
Sept. 6, 1946, Vol. 3, MGM (Nws.)
Jitterbug Frolic at Harvest Moon Ball in New York.

NEWS OF THE DAY
Sept. 11, 1946, Vol. 201, MGM (Nws.)
Harvest Moon Dance Champs

SOLID JIVE
Aug. 19, 1946, Soundies Dist. Corp. of America (SS, Scr. Sd.)
Charles Whitty, Jr., novelty dancing.

SOLID SENDERS
cir. 1946, Sack Amusement Enterprises (FL, Scr. Sd.)
"Rubberneck" Holmes, eccentric dance; Clyde "Slim" Thompson, tap dance.

TARS AND SPARS
Jan. 11, 1946, Columbia (FL, Sd.)
Marc Platt

THRILL OF BRAZIL, THE
Sept. 30, 1946, Columbia (FL, Sd.)
Ann Miller

'WORLD SERIES' OF THE DANCE
Sept. 6, 1946, 168 ft., Paramount (Nws.)
Jitterbugging contestants at the Harvest Moon Ball in Madison Square Garden, N.Y.C.

1947

DOWN TO EARTH
July 17, 1947, Columbia (FL, Sd.)
Marc Platt

HI-DE-HO
1947, All-American Pictures (FL, Sd.)
Miller Brothers and Lois, tap dancers.

JUKE JOINT
1947, Sack Amusement Enterprises (FL, Sd.)
The Jitterbug Johnnies; Mae and Ace; Kit and Kat

SOMETHING IN THE WIND
Aug. 12, 1947, Universal-International (FL, Sd.)
Donald O'Connor

SONG IS BORN, A
Dec. 31, 1947, (Samuel Goldwyn Productions, Inc.) RKO Radio (FL, Sd.)
Buck and Bubbles

SWEET AND LOW
Mar. 28, 1947, Paramount (SS, Sd.)
Sammy Davis, Jr., with the Will Mastin Trio.

THAT'S MY GAL
May 7, 1947, Republic (FL, Sd.)
Four Step Brothers

ZIEGFELD FOLLIES
Jan. 15, 1946, MGM (FL, Scr. Sd.)
Fred Astaire

1948

ARE YOU WITH IT?
June 8, 1948, Universal-International (FL, Sd.)
Donald O'Connor

BOARDING HOUSE BLUES
cir. 1948, All-American Pictures (FL, Sd.)
Berry Brothers, Stump and Stumpy

BUDDY RICH AND HIS ORCHESTRA
Nov. 23, 1948, Universal-International (SS, Scr, Sd.)
Louis DaPron, tap dance.

EASTER PARADE
May 26, 1948, MGM (FL, Scr. Sd.)
Fred Astaire, Ann Miller

GIVE MY REGARDS TO BROADWAY
June 8, 1948, 20th Century-Fox (FL, Sd.)
Dan Dailey

JIVIN' IN BE-BOP
cir. 1948, Alexander Distributing Corp. (FL, Sd.)
Ralph Brown, rhythm dancer with Dizzy Gillespie Orchestra.

JUNCTION 88
1948, Sack Amusement Enterprises (FL, Sd.)
"Pigmeat" Markham

KILLER DILLER
cir. 1948, All-American Pictures (FL, Sd.)
The Four Congaroos; The Clark Brothers; Patterson and Jackson

PIRATE, THE
Mar. 16, 1948, MGM (FL, Scr. Sd.)
Gene Kelly, Nicholas Brothers

ROMANCE ON THE HIGH SEAS
June 26, 1948, Warner Bros. (FL, Sd.)
Avon Long

SPIRIT OF THE DANCE
Sept. 8, 1948, Paramount (Nws.)
"Amateur Hoofers Wow Crowds at Harvest Moon Ball."
Jitterbugging couples at Madison Square Garden.

WHEN MY BABY SMILES AT ME
Nov. 5, 1948, 20th Century-Fox (FL, Sd.)
Dan Dailey

WORDS AND MUSIC
Dec. 7, 1948, MGM (FL, Scr. Sd.)
Gene Kelly

YOU WERE MEANT FOR ME
Jan. 16, 1948, 20th Century-Fox (FL, Sd.)
Dan Dailey

1949

BARKLEYS OF BROADWAY, THE
Mar. 15, 1949, MGM (FL, Scr. Sd.)
Fred Astaire and Ginger Rogers

BE BOP
Jan. 1949, 86 ft., Paramount (Nws. Scr. Sd.)
Actualites Francaise (French Newsreel)
Paris in the swing. Jitterbugging couples in night club.

HARVEST MOON BALL
Sept. 19, 1949, Pathe (Nws.)
Jitterbug contestants at New York City's Madison Square Garden.

ON THE TOWN
Dec. 1, 1949, MGM (FL, Scr. Sd.)
Gene Kelly, Ann Miller

TAKE ME OUT TO THE BALL GAME
Mar. 1, 1949, MGM (FL, Scr. Sd.)
Gene Kelly

"WORLD SERIES" OF THE DANCE
Sept. 14, 1949, 142 ft., Paramount (Nws.)
Harvest Moon Ball at Madison Square Garden.
Harlem jitterbugging couples.

YES SIR, THAT'S MY BABY
Sept. 8, 1949, Universal-International (FL, Sd.)
Donald O'Connor

YOU'RE MY EVERYTHING
July 16, 1949, 20th Century-Fox (FL, Sd.)
Dan Dailey, Ananias, and Warren Berry

1950

HARVEST MOON BALL
Sept. 18, 1950, Pathe (Nws.)
Madison Square Garden, couples in Charleston Contest. Also Jitterbugging couples.

KING COLE TRIO WITH BENNY CARTER AND HIS ORCHESTRA
June 9, 1950, 2 reels, Universal-International (SS, Sd.)
Bunny Briggs

LET'S DANCE
Nov. 24, 1950, Paramount (FL, Sd.)
Fred Astaire

MILKMAN, THE
Aug. 31, 1950, Universal-International (FL, Sd.)
Donald O'Connor

MY BLUE HEAVEN
Aug. 23, 1950, 20th Century-Fox (FL, Sd.)
Dan Dailey

SUMMER STOCK
Aug. 7, 1950, MGM (FL, Scr. Sd.)
Gene Kelly

THREE LITTLE WORDS
July 6, 1950, MGM (FL, Sd.)
Fred Astaire

WEST POINT STORY, THE
Nov. 18, 1950, Warner Bros. (FL, Sd.)
James Cagney

1951

AN AMERICAN IN PARIS
Sept. 5, 1951, MGM (FL, Scr. Sd.)
Gene Kelly

CALL ME MISTER
Jan. 31, 1951, 20th Century-Fox (FL, Sd.)
Dan Dailey

HARVEST MOON BALL
Sept. 12, 1951, 85 ft., Paramount (Nws.)
Couples jitterbugging at New York's Madison Square Garden.

HARVEST BALL IN MANHATTAN
Sept. 12, 1951, 85′, Paramount (Nws.)
Jitterbugging couples vie for prizes at Madison Square Garden.

HARVEST MOON MADNESS
Sept. 17, 1951, Pathe (Nws.)
Jitterbugs at Seventeenth Annual Harvest Moon Ball at Madison Square Garden.

MEET ME AFTER THE SHOW
Aug. 15, 1951, 20th Century-Fox (FL, Sd.)
Steve Condos

ROYAL WEDDING
Feb. 5, 1951, MGM (FL, Sd.)
Fred Astaire

TEXAS CARNIVAL
Sept. 10, 1951, MGM (FL, Sd.)
Ann Miller

TWO TICKETS TO BROADWAY
Nov. 5, 1951, RKO Radio (FL, Sd.)
Ann Miller

1952

BELLE OF NEW YORK, THE
Feb. 12, 1952, MGM (FL, Sd.)
Fred Astaire

HAMBURG GETS THE "JITTERS"
Nov. 1952, 135 ft., Paramount (Nws.)
German International Jitterbug Competition

LOVELY TO LOOK AT
June 2, 1952, MGM (FL, Sd.)
Ann Miller

MEET ME AT THE FAIR
Nov. 3, 1952, Universal (FL, Sd.)
Dan Dailey

ROCK 'N ROLL REVUE
cir. 1952, Studio Films (Sd.)
Coles and Atkins perform their tap routine from *Gentlemen Prefer Blondes*. Conrad "Little Buck" Buckner, tap routine.

SINGIN' IN THE RAIN
Mar. 11, 1952, MGM (FL, Scr. Sd.)
Gene Kelly, Donald O'Connor

1953

BAND WAGON, THE
July 3, 1953, MGM (FL, Scr. Sd.)
Fred Astaire

CALL ME MADAM
Mar. 5, 1953, 20th Century-Fox (FL, Sd.)
Donald O'Connor

GIRL NEXT DOOR, THE
May 13, 1953, 20th Century-Fox (FL, Sd.)
Dan Dailey

GLENN MILLER STORY, THE
Dec. 9, 1953, Universal (FL, Scr. Sd.)
The Archie Savage Dancers

HERE COME THE GIRLS
Dec. 1, 1953, Paramount (FL, Sd.)
Four Step Brothers

WALKING MY BABY BACK HOME
Dec. 2, 1953, Universal (FL, Sd.)
Donald O'Connor

"WORLD SERIES" OF THE DANCE
Sept. 9, 1953, 106 ft., Paramount (Nws.)
Harvest Moon Ball at Madison Square Garden.
Jitterbugging contestants.

1954

BRIGADOON
Sept. 2, 1954, MGM (FL, Sd.)
Gene Kelly

JAZZ DANCE
June 22, 1954, Roger Tilton (SS, Scr. Sd.)
Jazz dancing at the Central Plaza, New York City.
Al Minns and Leon James.

"WORLD SERIES" OF THE DANCE
Sept. 8, 1954, Paramount (Nws.)
Harvest Moon Ball. Jitterbugging contestants.

1955

ARTISTS AND MODELS
Dec. 21, 1955, Paramount (FL, Sd.)
Nick Castle

DADDY LONG LEGS
May 5, 1955, 20th Century-Fox (FL, Sd.)
Fred Astaire

HARVEST MOON BALL
Sept. 6 and 7, 1955, Paramount (Nws.)
Jitterbugs dancing at Madison Square Garden.

HIT THE DECK
Feb. 24, 1955, MGM (FL, Sd.)
Ann Miller

IT'S ALWAYS FAIR WEATHER
Aug. 8, 1955, MGM (FL, Scr. Sd.)
Gene Kelly, Dan Dailey

1956

ANYTHING GOES
Mar. 21, 1956, Paramount (FL, Sd.)
Donald O'Connor

BEST THINGS IN LIFE ARE FREE
Sept. 26, 1956, 20th Century-Fox (FL, Sd.)
Dan Dailey

HARVEST MOON BALL
Sept. 11, 1956, 101 ft., Paramount (Nws.)
Jovada and Jimmy Ballard and others dancing Rock 'n' Roll.

INVITATION TO THE DANCE
May 17, 1956, MGM (FL, Sd.)
Gene Kelly

MEET ME IN LAS VEGAS
Feb. 6, 1956, MGM (FL, Sd.)
Dan Dailey, The Slate Brothers

1957

LES GIRLS
Sept. 3, 1957, MGM (FL, Scr. Sd.)
Gene Kelly

SILK STOCKINGS
May 13, 1957, MGM (FL, Sd.)
Fred Astaire

1958

DANCE BEAT
Nov. 2, 1958, 20th Century-Fox (SS, Sd.)
Rod Alexander discusses dance as based on rhythm, beginning with early ritual dance.

1959

None

1960

None

1961

HEY, LET'S TWIST!
1961, Paramount (FL, Sd.)
Peppermint Loungers.

NEGRO FOLK DANCE: HAMBONE
Philadelphia Dance Academy, University of Pennsylvania
Apr. 17, 1961, 100 ft., (Instructional film)
Madison, Pony, Slop, Cha-Cha.

TWIST AROUND THE CLOCK
1961, Columbia (FL, Sd.)
Chubby Checker

1962

DON'T KNOCK THE TWIST
1962, Columbia (FL, Sd.)
Chubby Checker

TWIST ALL NIGHT
1962, American-International (FL, Sd.)
Twist dancers.

1963

JAZZ-DERIVED SOCIAL DANCE STEPS
1963, 300 ft., silent film (Analytical/instructional film)
Philadelphia Dance Academy, University of Pennsylvania
The steps demonstrated include Mashed Potato, Pony, Fly, Fish, Hucklebuck, Stirrup, Crossfire, Monkey, Heat Wave. Portions of the film are in slow motion for analytical purposes.

JAZZ DANCE, DETROIT STYLE
May 26, 1960, 150 feet, silent film (Analytical/instructional film)
Philadelphia Dance Academy, University of Philadelphia
Jazz-derived social dance steps including Hully Gully, Madison, and others as demonstrated by teenagers.

JAMES BERRY
Apr. 29, 1960, silent film (Analytical/instructional film)
Philadelphia Dance Academy, University of Pennsylvania
Demonstration of Break-a-leg, Palmer House, Tac Annie, Eagle Rock, Jig Walk, Strut, and jazz pantomimes.

1964

JAZZ-DERIVED SOCIAL DANCE AND LATIN AMERICAN INFLUENCE
1964, 100 feet, silent film (analytical/instructional film)
Philadelphia Dance Academy, University of Pennsylvania
Dances: Bugaloo, Jerk, Meringue, Guarache.

PRE-JAZZ SOCIAL DANCE, Dorothea Duryea Ohl
1964, 100 feet, silent film (analytical/instructional film)
Dances: Cake Walk, Maxixe, Varsouvienne, Pasadoble.

SOCIAL DANCES—PHILADELPHIA
Sept. 1964, 100 feet, silent film (analytical/instructional film)
Teen-agers demonstrating Pony, Jerk, Twist, Shimmy, Fly, Sloopy, Frug, Mashed Potato.

TELEVISION

(Note: All dates and stations are for New York City)

1959

PLAYBOY CLUB, THE
(Variety show in an informal setting with Hugh Hefner, publisher of Playboy magazine, as host.)
Dec. 1959
Marshall Stearns discusses various styles of jazz dancing. Al Minns and Leon James demonstrate the Charleston, Shimmy, Big Apple, and Lindy Hop.

1960

AMERICAN MUSICAL THEATER
"American Jazz Dances"
Dec. 3, 1960, WCBS-TV
Al Minns and Leon James with Marshall Stearns.

AMERICAN MUSICAL THEATER
Feb. 13, 1960, WCBS-TV
John Bubbles with Bibi Osterwald

ASTAIRE TIME
Oct. 5, 1960, NBC-TV
Fred Astaire and Barrie Chase with Count Basie and his Orchestra.

1961

CHICAGO AND ALL THAT JAZZ
(DuPont Show of the Month)
Nov. 26, 1961, NBC-TV
Al Minns and Leon James dance a specialty number that includes examples of the Charleston, Snake Hips, Shimmy, and Lindy Hop.

PM EAST, PM WEST
Dec. 4, 1961, ABC-TV
Mike Wallace and Joyce Davidson investigate dance crazes from the Black Bottom to the Twist.

THOSE RAGTIME YEARS
(DuPont Show of the Month)
1961, NBC-TV
Al Minns and Leon James demonstrate the various styles of steps associated with "The Ragtime Dance."

1962

AMERICAN MUSICAL THEATER
"Vaudeville Days"
Jan. 28, 1962, WCBS-TV
Sammy Lee, Smith and Dale, Ray Block Orchestra

AMERICAN MUSICAL THEATER
May 27, 1962, WCBS-TV
Ray Bolger

JAZZ IN NEW ORLEANS
Narration by David Brinkley.
Jan. 10, 1962, NBC-TV
Pork Chops and Kidney Stew, two New Orleans dancers.

JOHNNY CARSON
Late-night variety show with Johnny Carson, host.
Dec. 31, 1962, NBC-TV
John Bubbles, guest.

PM EAST, PM WEST
Mar. 1, 1962, ABC-TV
John Bubbles, guest.

TAP DANCE
Whitney Balliett, host and narrator.
(National Educational TV)
Nov. 7, 1962, NET-TV, Channel 13, N.Y.C.
Bunny Briggs, tap dancer.

1963

PERRY COMO
Variety Show
Mar. 6, 1963, NBC-TV
Four Step Brothers

1964

ABC SCOPE
"The Wild World of the Discotheque"
Dec. 30, 1964, ABC-TV
Sybil Burton and "Killer Joe" Piro tour New York City's discotheque night spots.

AMERICAN MUSICAL THEATER
July 19, 1964, WCBS-TV
Earl Wrightson, host with guest John Bubbles, song and dance man.

AMERICAN MUSICAL THEATER
Jan. 25, 1964, WCBS-TV
John Bubbles, Sissle and Blake, Hank Jones

BOB HOPE
Musical—"Think Pretty"
Oct. 2, 1964, NBC-TC
Fred Astaire and Barrie Chase

HOLLYWOOD PALACE
Variety Show
Nov. 14, 1964, WABC-TV
Nicholas Brothers

STEVE ALLEN
Variety Show
Oct. 12, 1964, WPIX-TV
John Bubbles, guest.

1965

BOB HOPE CHRISTMAS SPECIAL
Jan. 15, 1965, WNBC-TV
Ninety minute show composed of film clips of the Bob Hope tour of Vietnam, Korea, Thailand, and the Philippines.
John Bubbles, song and dance.

CAMERA THREE
"Over the Top to Be-Bop"
Jan. 3, 1965, WCBS-TV
James MacAndrew, host. Marshall Stearns discusses evolution of tap dancing. Honi Coles and Cholly Atkins demonstrate various steps including "Through The Trenches," Wings, and Time Steps.

DEAN MARTIN
Variety Show
Sept. 30, 1965, WNBC-TV
John Bubbles, guest.

DIAL M FOR MUSIC
"From Dollars to Disc to Discotheque"
Sept. 25, 1965, WCBS-TV
Program traces the different styles of dancing popular in the United States.

JOHNNY CARSON
Late-night variety show with Johnny Carson, host.
Aug. 30, 1965, WNBC-TV
John Bubbles, guest.

JOHNNY CARSON
Late-night variety show with Johnny Carson, host.
Sept. 11, 1965, WNBC-TV
John Bubbles, guest.

HOLLYWOOD PALACE
Variety Show
Feb. 27, 1965, WABC-TV
Nicholas Brothers, guests.

1966

ED SULLIVAN SHOW
Variety Show
Oct. 23, 1966, WCBS-TV
Bunny Briggs with Duke Ellington Orchestra, guests.

JOHNNY CARSON
Late-night variety show with Johnny Carson, host.
Feb. 12, 1966, WNBC-TV
John Bubbles, guest.

LAWRENCE WELK
WABC-TV
Weekly music show with Lawrence Welk and his Orchestra.
Tap dancers Bobby Burgess, Jack Imel, and Arthur Duncan appear frequently on this Saturday night show.

Analysis and Notation of Basic Afro-American Movements

THE DANCE EXAMPLES IN THIS BOOK have been selected because they present those characteristic elements that determine the form of jazz dancing. These elements reflect a strong African derivation. The unique "indigenous" traits radiate also through the kinetic borrowings from European ballet, Spanish dance, Irish clogging, and French quadrilles. These aspects of theatricalized jazz dance have for the most part not been included in the plates.

Basic shapes of the dance design have been recorded faithfully. Where it seemed important to do so, one or more significant variants of a step were included. Regional variants of all jazz steps are in prolific abundance, and a popular predilection for improvisation has added much distinctive embroidery to the main movement patterns. Such embellishments have been notated, however, only where they were essential to the basic features of a step. The subtle details of personal styles and that special rhythmic ingredient that induces an infectious bounce or swing are implied rather than expressly stated in the scores.

In jazz dance the harmony of body movement is exceedingly complex. Each impulse appears to germinate somewhere in the lower trunk long before it motivates a visible movement. When the action of a step is about to be completed, a new impulse generates a recurrence of the original action. The result is perceived as a continuous stream of overlapping sequences subtly woven into the gross design. Although the flow of design lacks the fluency of many African dances, it is the torso rather than the feet that provides the distinctive folkloric expression.

The dances have been recorded in Labanotation, a system of movement writing originated by Rudolf Laban during the first quarter of the twentieth century. This system has been developed and refined by Albrecht Knust and his associates at the Kurt Joos School in Essen, Germany, the Dance Notation Bureau in New York City, and the International Council for Kinetography Laban. The membership of this Council consists of notators in more than twenty-five countries. These specialists meet biennially to exchange ideas and further the use of movement notation.

A key and full explanation of Labanotation has been published in various sources (see References). Laban has based his notational system on an earlier one published in France and England at the start of the eighteenth century. Like its ancestor, the Feuillet-Beauchamp notation, Laban employed a vertical staff of three parallel lines, the center line serving to divide left and right sides of the body. Along the center line, tiny horizontal marks identify counts or basic units of time. Longer horizontal lines are drawn across the vertical staff to indicate measures. It is therefore possible to verify rapidly the jazz dance steps that occur in two-, four-, or six-count groupings. For purposes of simplification only eight symbols have been used in addition to their qualifying signs (pre-signs). These symbols indicate direction (by their shape), level -high, middle, low- (by their shading), duration (by their length), and the part of the body that moves (by their location on the staff).

Diagrams 1–6 group together dances that share a particular essential trait. Since an up and down vibration occurs in most jazz dance as a vital ingredient, it is not shown on these diagrams but has been included in the notated scores of dances that emphasize this trait.

REFERENCES

Berry, James. Demonstrations, interviews, filming session at Philadelphia Dance Academy, 1960.

Chilkovsky, Nadia. *Three R's for Dancing*. Books I–III. New York: M. Witmark, 1955–1956.

———. *American Bandstand Dances in Labanotation*. New York: M. Witmark, 1959.

Hutchinson, Ann. *Labanotation*. New York: New Directions, 1954.

Knust, Albrecht. *Handbook of Kinetography Laban*. Essen-Werden: A. Knust, 1958.

Laban, Rudolf. *Principles of Dance and Movement Notation*. London: Macdonald and Evans, 1956.

Nicholas Nahumck executed all plates and diagrams. Vernacular-dance specialists and notation students helped to verify and analyze the steps. These include Joseph Alston, Ronnie Arnold, Rose Dickerson, Joseph Garcia, Dyane Gray, Eugene Harris, Alice Lattimore, Janie Lowe, Ann McKinley, Nora Winokur.

NADIA CHILKOVSKY

Philadelphia, 1968

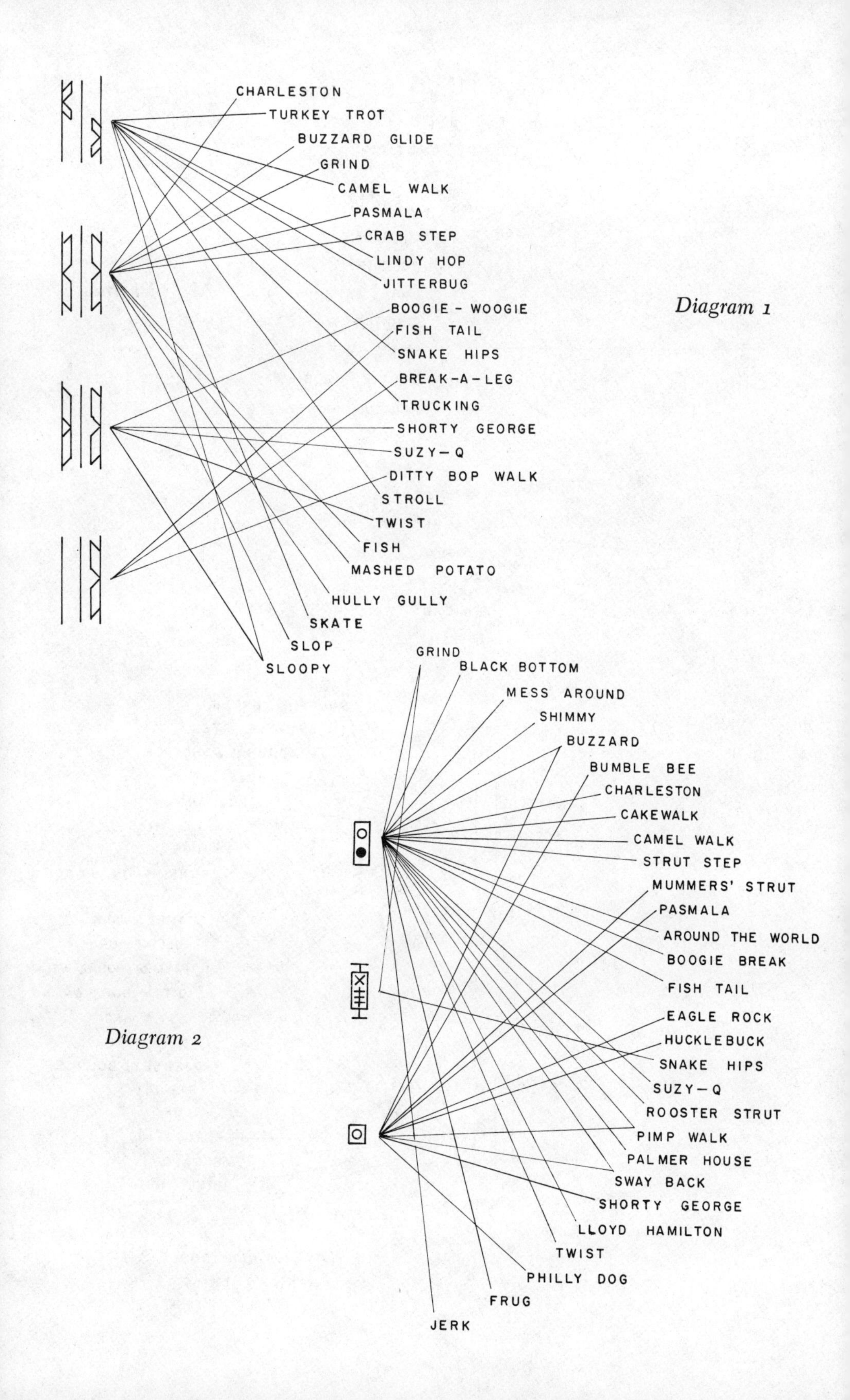
CHARLESTON
TURKEY TROT
BUZZARD GLIDE
GRIND
CAMEL WALK
PASMALA
CRAB STEP
LINDY HOP
JITTERBUG
BOOGIE - WOOGIE
FISH TAIL
SNAKE HIPS
BREAK-A-LEG
TRUCKING
SHORTY GEORGE
SUZY-Q
DITTY BOP WALK
STROLL
TWIST
FISH
MASHED POTATO
HULLY GULLY
SKATE
SLOP
SLOOPY
Diagram 1
GRIND
BLACK BOTTOM
MESS AROUND
SHIMMY
BUZZARD
BUMBLE BEE
CHARLESTON
CAKEWALK
CAMEL WALK
STRUT STEP
MUMMERS' STRUT
PASMALA
AROUND THE WORLD
BOOGIE BREAK
FISH TAIL
EAGLE ROCK
HUCKLEBUCK
SNAKE HIPS
SUZY-Q
ROOSTER STRUT
PIMP WALK
PALMER HOUSE
SWAY BACK
SHORTY GEORGE
LLOYD HAMILTON
TWIST
PHILLY DOG
FRUG
JERK
Diagram 2

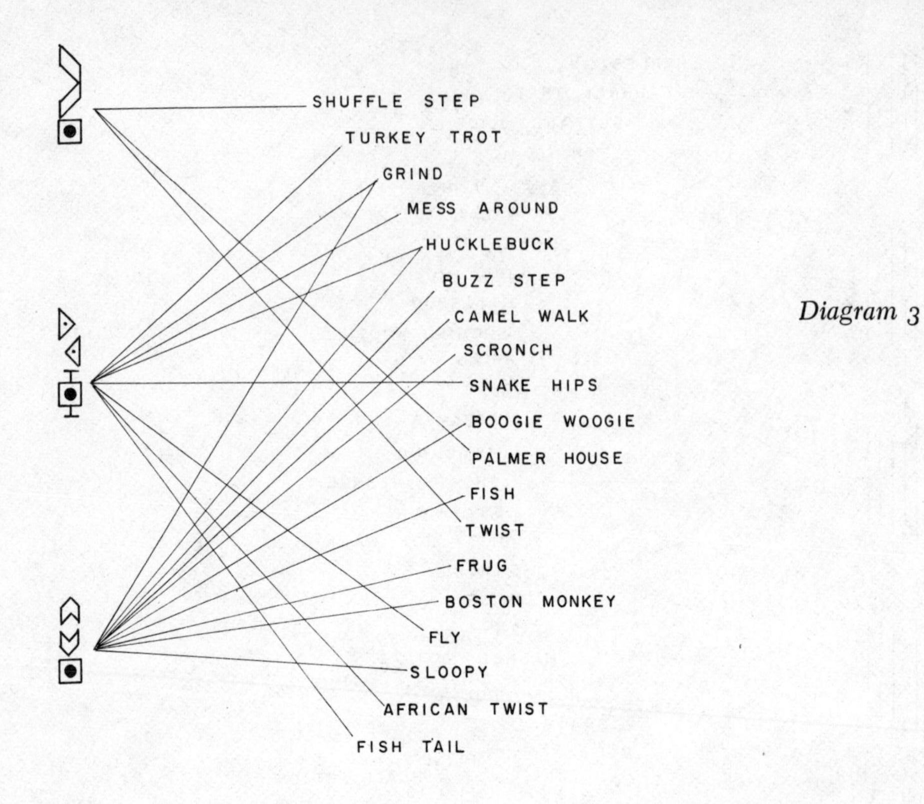

Diagram 3

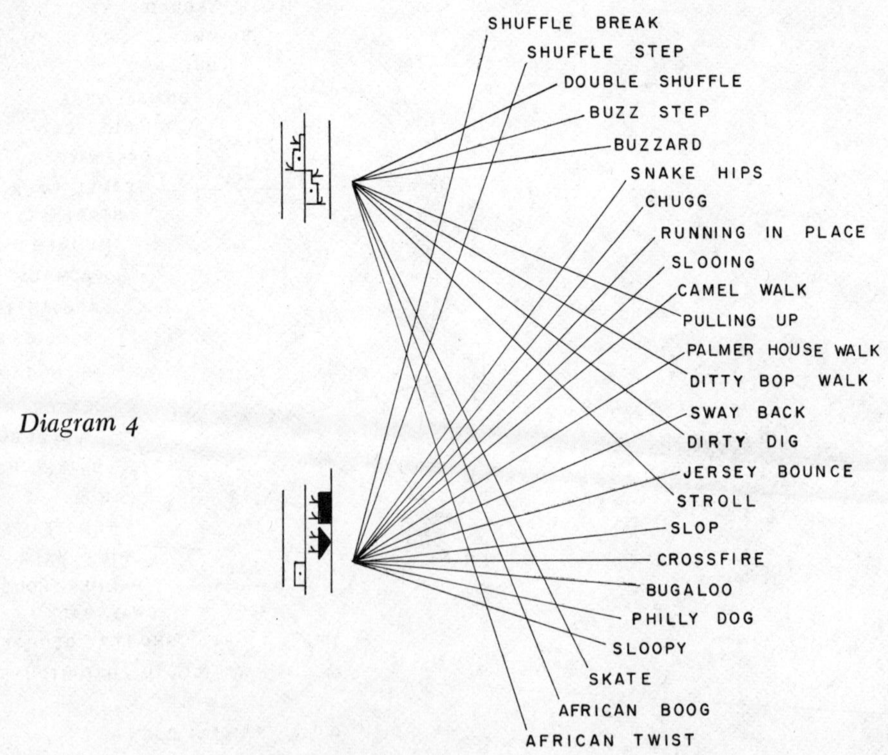

Diagram 4

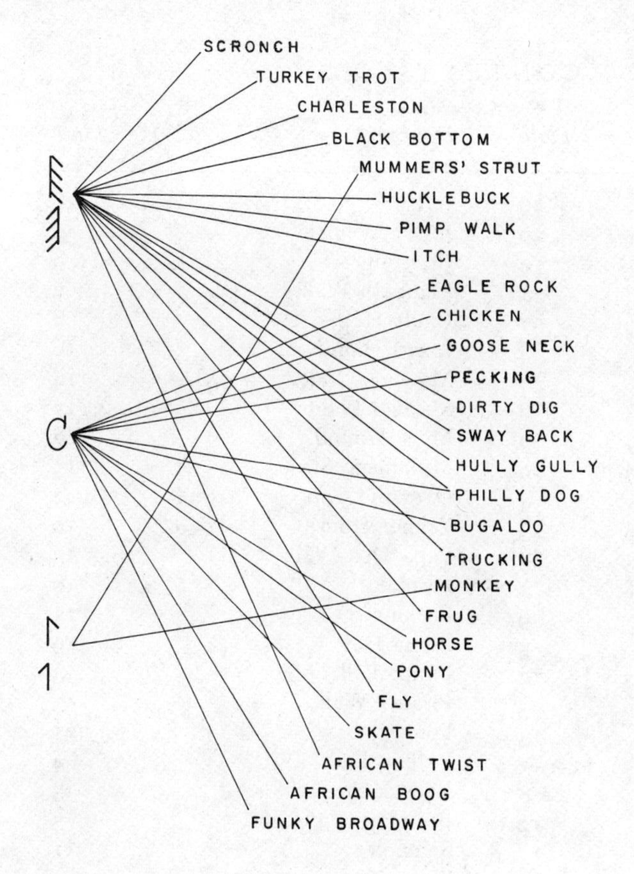

Diagram 5

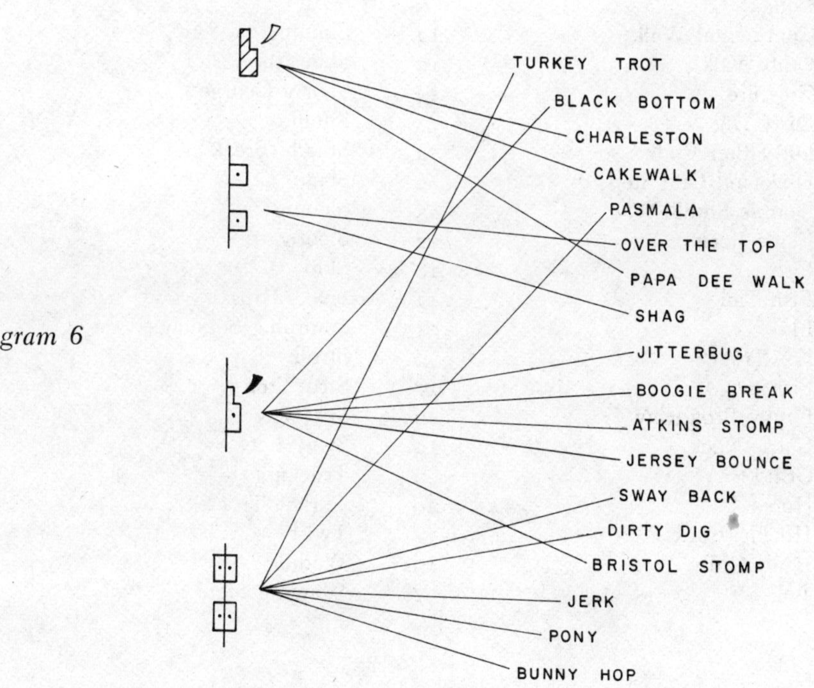

Diagram 6

CONTENTS

GLOSSARY

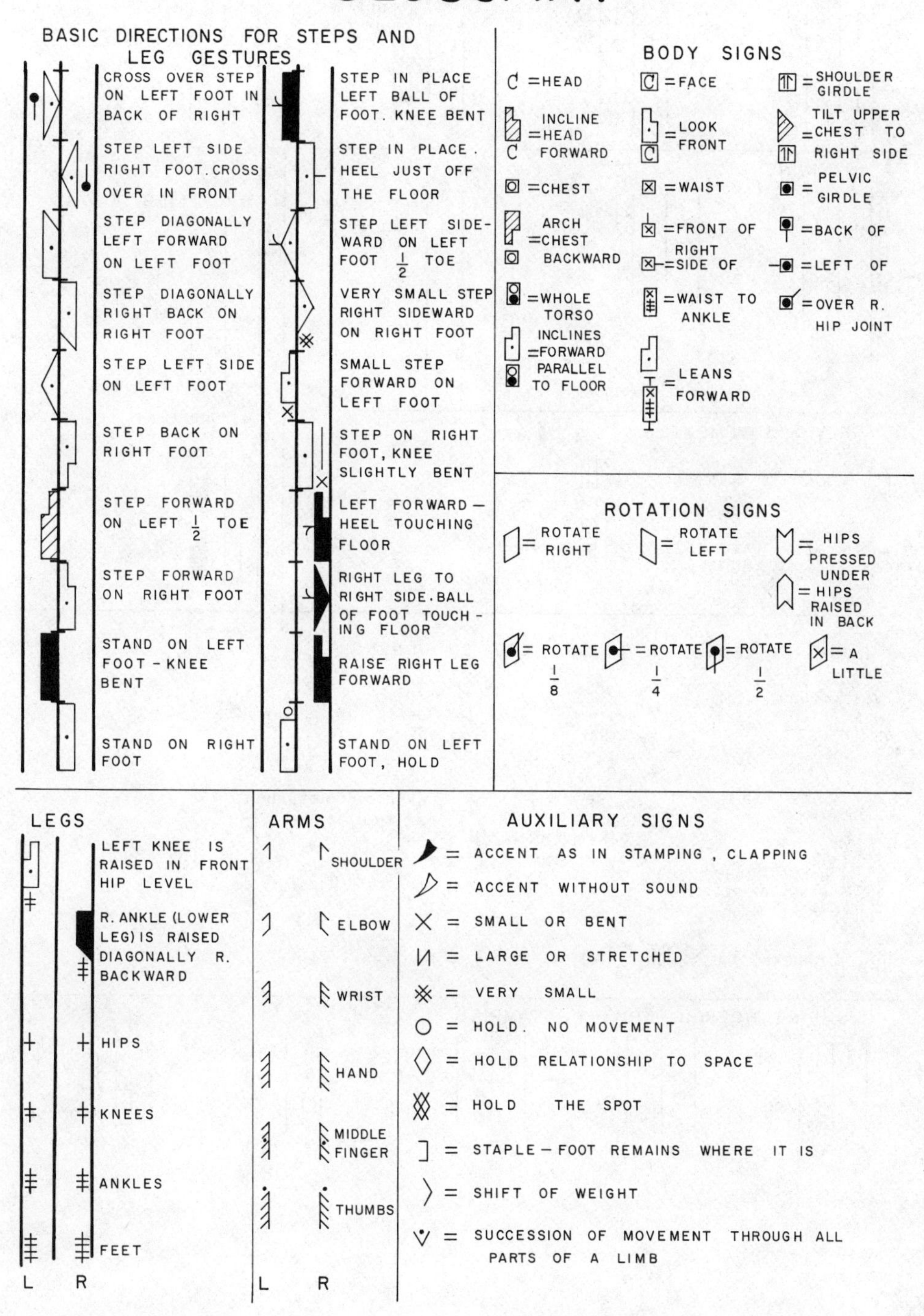
BASIC DIRECTIONS FOR STEPS AND LEG GESTURES
CROSS OVER STEP ON LEFT FOOT IN BACK OF RIGHT
STEP LEFT SIDE RIGHT FOOT. CROSS OVER IN FRONT
STEP DIAGONALLY LEFT FORWARD ON LEFT FOOT
STEP DIAGONALLY RIGHT BACK ON RIGHT FOOT
STEP LEFT SIDE ON LEFT FOOT
STEP BACK ON RIGHT FOOT
STEP FORWARD ON LEFT 1/2 TOE
STEP FORWARD ON RIGHT FOOT
STAND ON LEFT FOOT - KNEE BENT
STAND ON RIGHT FOOT
STEP IN PLACE LEFT BALL OF FOOT. KNEE BENT
STEP IN PLACE. HEEL JUST OFF THE FLOOR
STEP LEFT SIDEWARD ON LEFT FOOT 1/2 TOE
VERY SMALL STEP RIGHT SIDEWARD ON RIGHT FOOT
SMALL STEP FORWARD ON LEFT FOOT
STEP ON RIGHT FOOT, KNEE SLIGHTLY BENT
LEFT FORWARD — HEEL TOUCHING FLOOR
RIGHT LEG TO RIGHT SIDE. BALL OF FOOT TOUCHING FLOOR
RAISE RIGHT LEG FORWARD
STAND ON LEFT FOOT, HOLD
BODY SIGNS
=HEAD
=FACE
=SHOULDER GIRDLE
=INCLINE HEAD FORWARD
=LOOK FRONT
=TILT UPPER CHEST TO RIGHT SIDE
=CHEST
=WAIST
=PELVIC GIRDLE
=ARCH CHEST BACKWARD
=FRONT OF
=BACK OF
RIGHT
=SIDE OF
=LEFT OF
=WHOLE TORSO
=WAIST TO ANKLE
=OVER R. HIP JOINT
INCLINES =FORWARD PARALLEL TO FLOOR
=LEANS FORWARD
ROTATION SIGNS
= ROTATE RIGHT
= ROTATE LEFT
= HIPS PRESSED UNDER
= HIPS RAISED IN BACK
= ROTATE 1/8
= ROTATE 1/4
= ROTATE 1/2
= A LITTLE
LEGS
LEFT KNEE IS RAISED IN FRONT HIP LEVEL
R. ANKLE (LOWER LEG) IS RAISED DIAGONALLY R. BACKWARD
HIPS
KNEES
ANKLES
FEET
L
R
ARMS
SHOULDER
ELBOW
WRIST
HAND
MIDDLE FINGER
THUMBS
L
R
AUXILIARY SIGNS
= ACCENT AS IN STAMPING, CLAPPING
= ACCENT WITHOUT SOUND
= SMALL OR BENT
= LARGE OR STRETCHED
= VERY SMALL
= HOLD. NO MOVEMENT
= HOLD RELATIONSHIP TO SPACE
= HOLD THE SPOT
= STAPLE — FOOT REMAINS WHERE IT IS
= SHIFT OF WEIGHT
= SUCCESSION OF MOVEMENT THROUGH ALL PARTS OF A LIMB

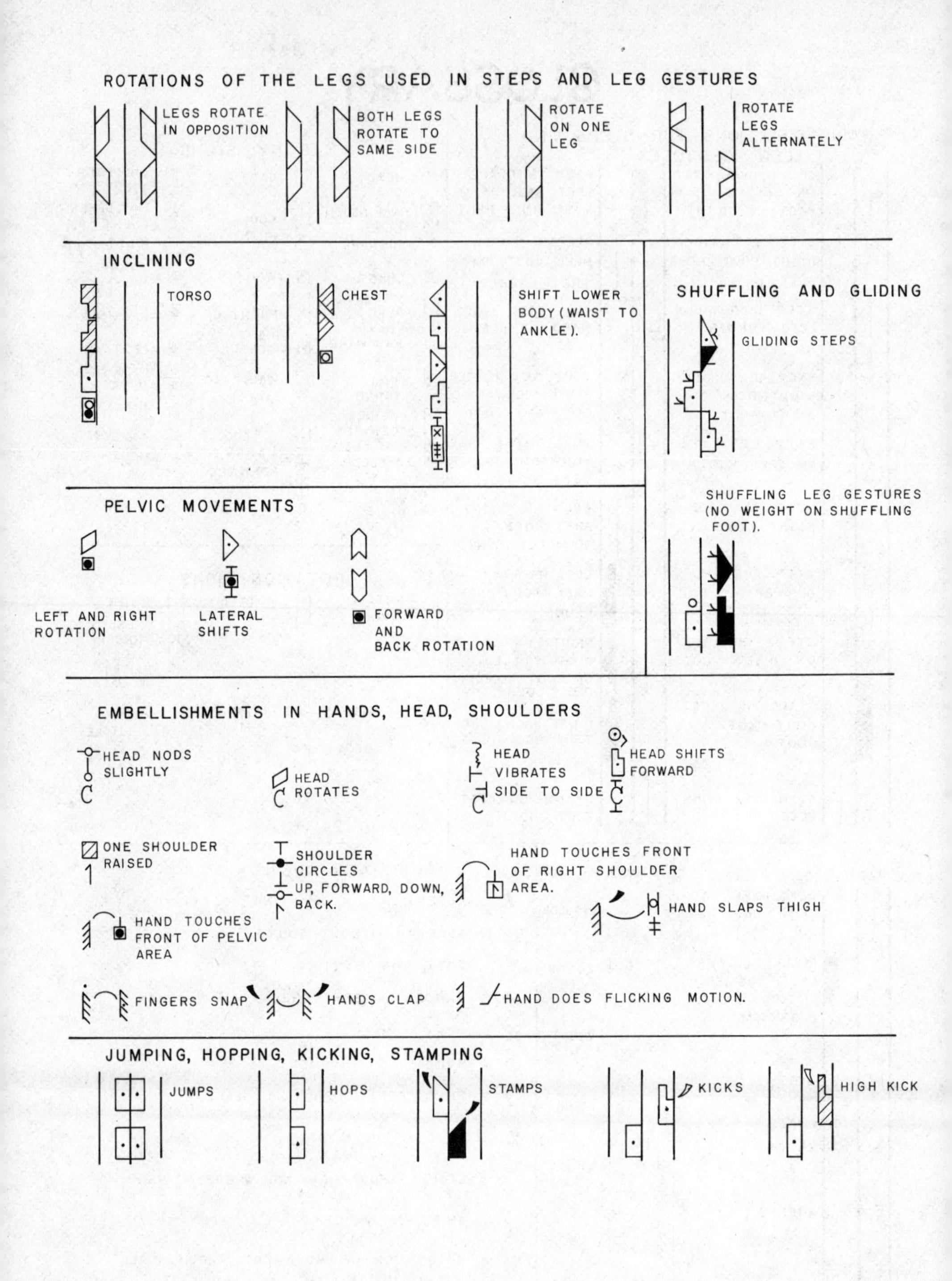
ROTATIONS OF THE LEGS USED IN STEPS AND LEG GESTURES
LEGS ROTATE IN OPPOSITION
BOTH LEGS ROTATE TO SAME SIDE
ROTATE ON ONE LEG
ROTATE LEGS ALTERNATELY
INCLINING
TORSO
CHEST
SHIFT LOWER BODY (WAIST TO ANKLE).
SHUFFLING AND GLIDING
GLIDING STEPS
SHUFFLING LEG GESTURES (NO WEIGHT ON SHUFFLING FOOT).
PELVIC MOVEMENTS
LEFT AND RIGHT ROTATION
LATERAL SHIFTS
FORWARD AND BACK ROTATION
EMBELLISHMENTS IN HANDS, HEAD, SHOULDERS
HEAD NODS SLIGHTLY
HEAD ROTATES
HEAD VIBRATES SIDE TO SIDE
HEAD SHIFTS FORWARD
ONE SHOULDER RAISED
SHOULDER CIRCLES UP, FORWARD, DOWN, BACK.
HAND TOUCHES FRONT OF RIGHT SHOULDER AREA.
HAND SLAPS THIGH
HAND TOUCHES FRONT OF PELVIC AREA
FINGERS SNAP
HANDS CLAP
HAND DOES FLICKING MOTION.
JUMPING, HOPPING, KICKING, STAMPING
JUMPS
HOPS
STAMPS
KICKS
HIGH KICK

JAZZ DANCE STEPS

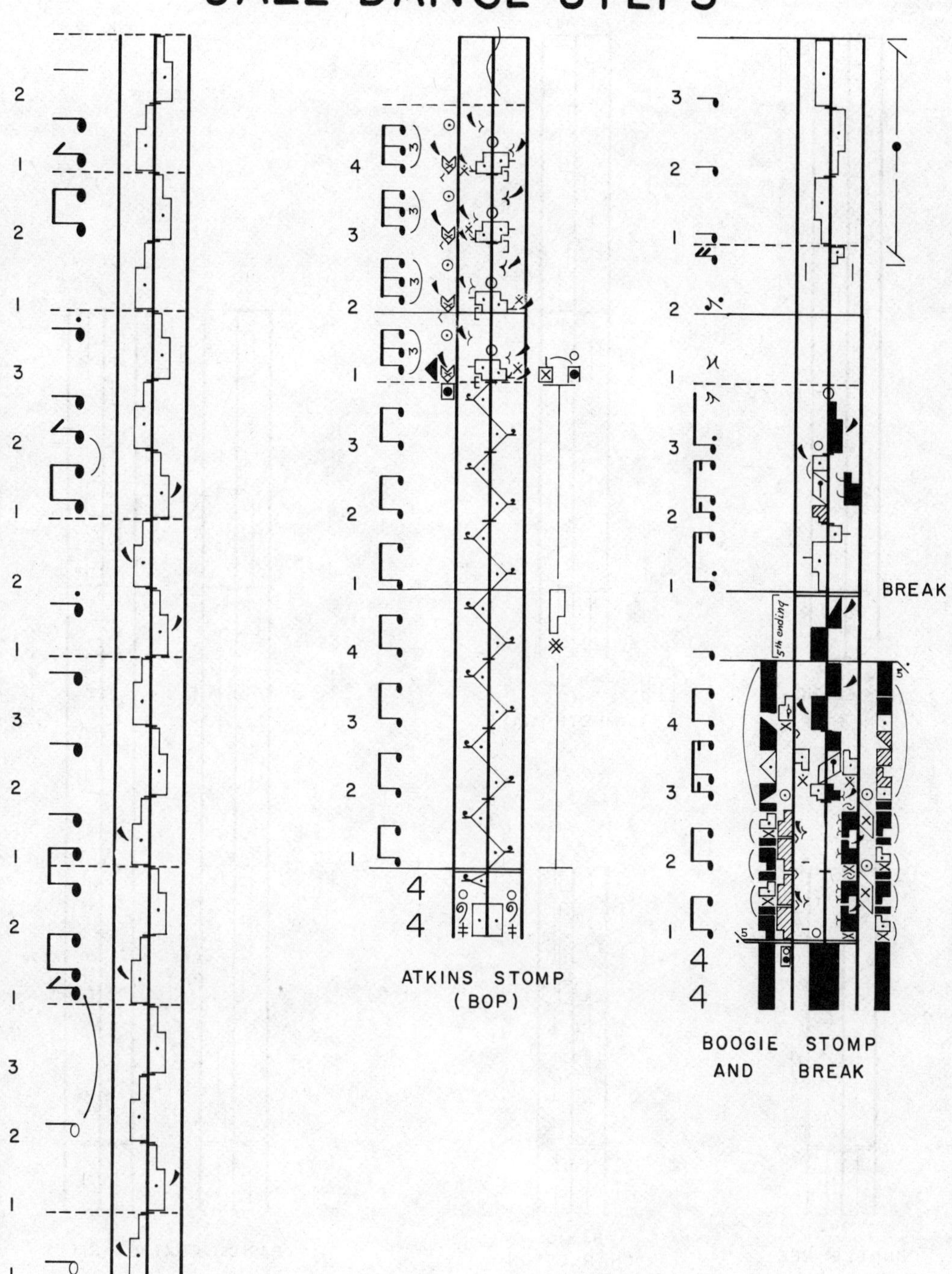

Plate 1

PRE-JAZZ POPULAR DANCES

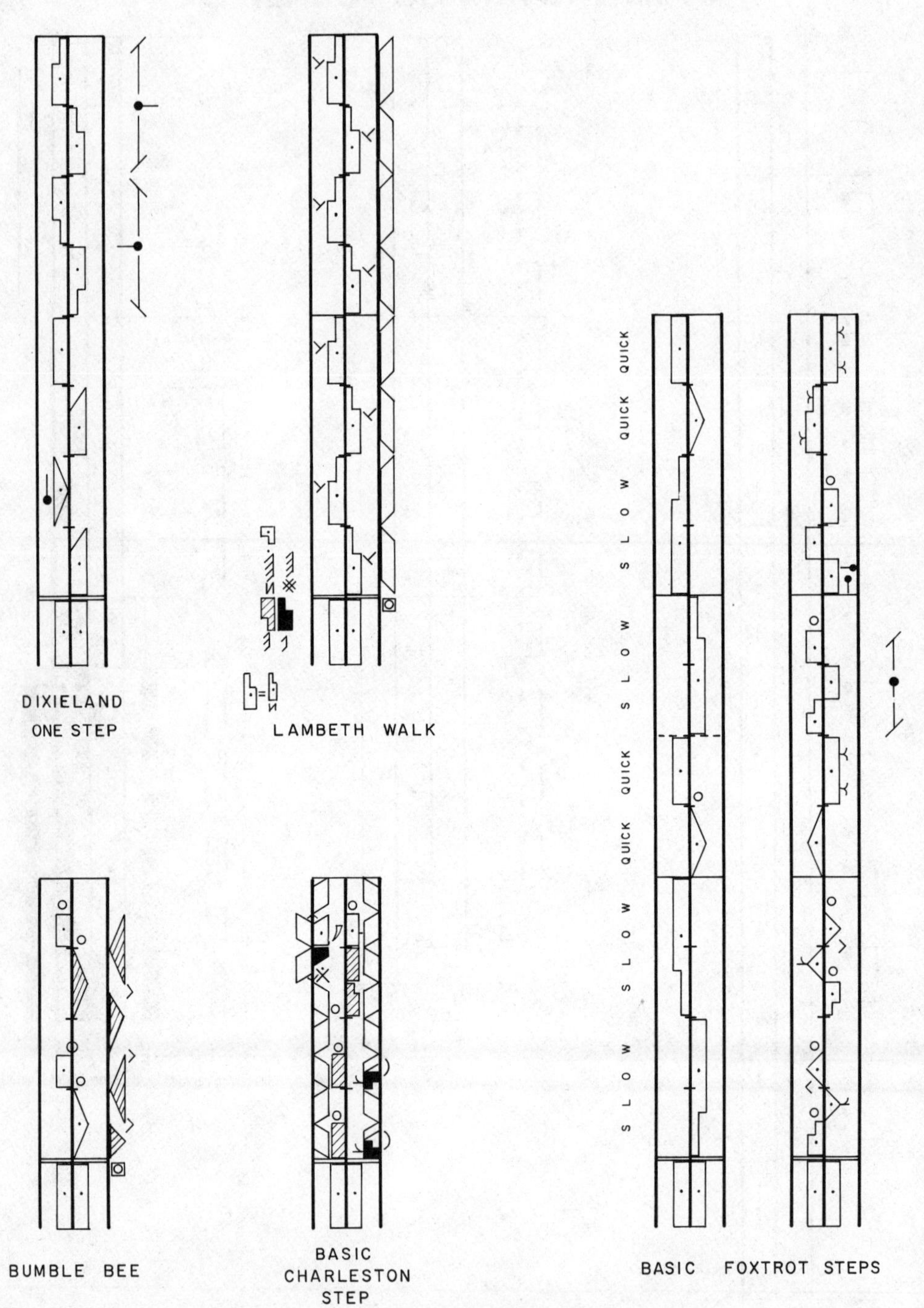

Plate 2

TURKEY TROT

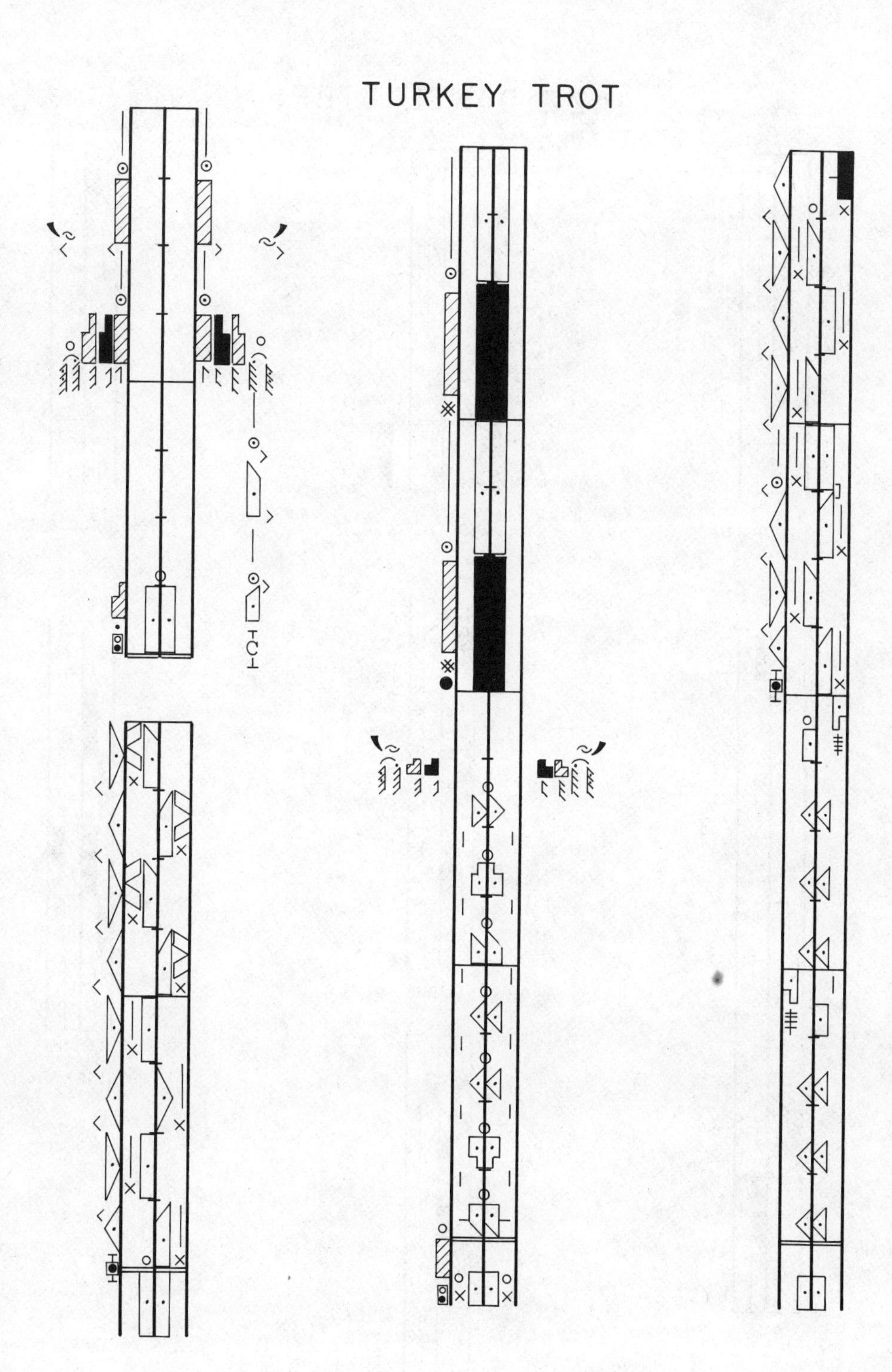

JAZZ DANCE STEPS

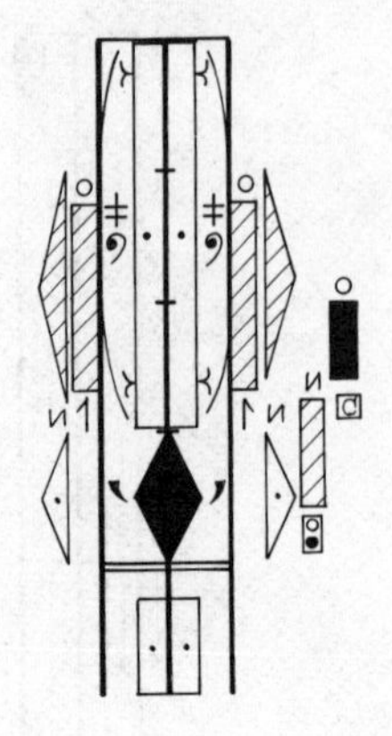

PULLING UP

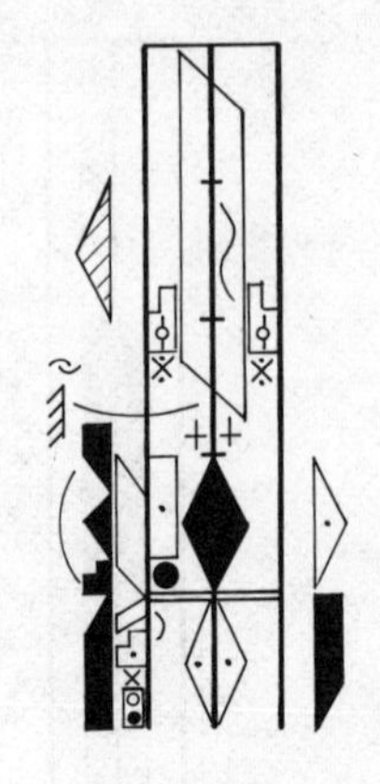

AROUND THE WORLD

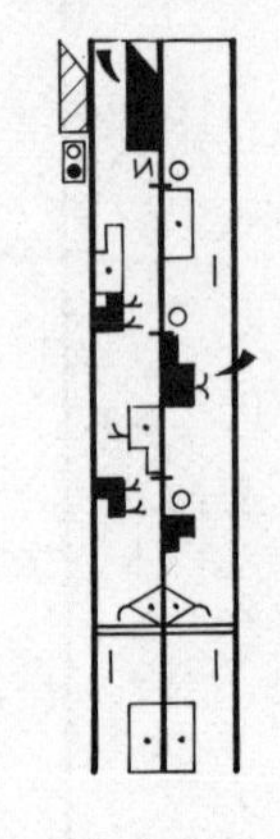

SHUFFLE BREAK

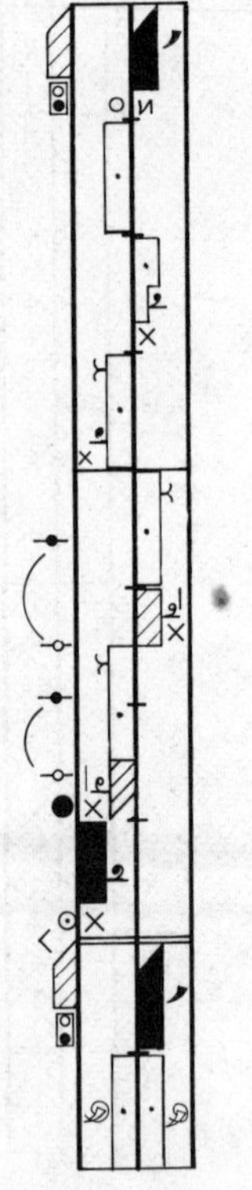

BOOGIE BREAK

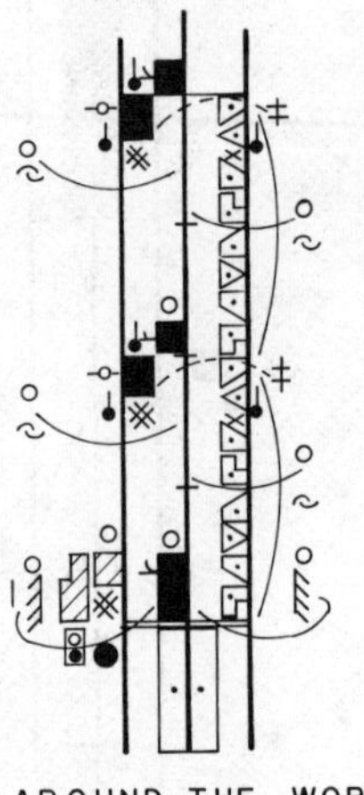

AROUND THE WORLD

WINGING-BASIC

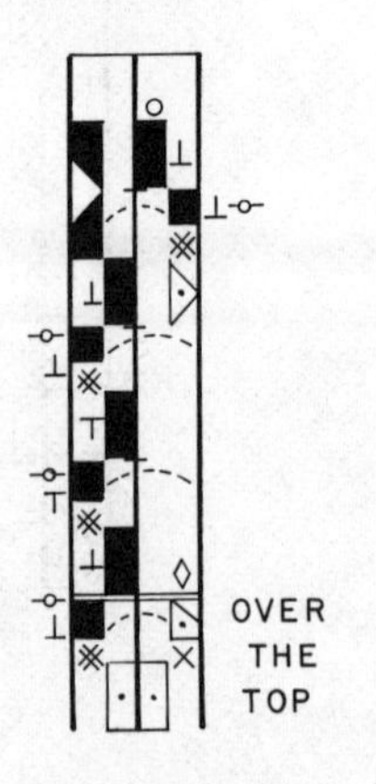

OVER THE TOP

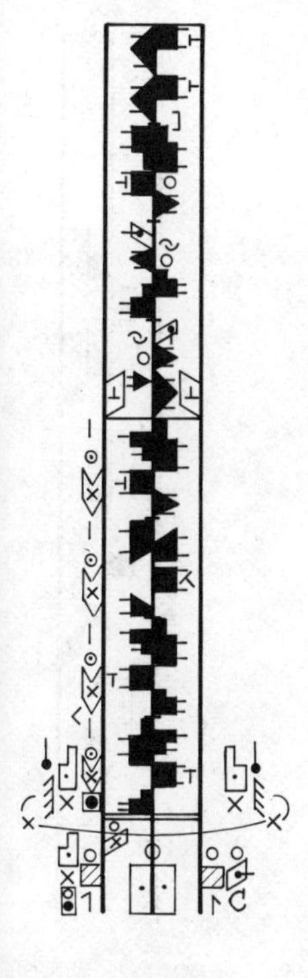

BUZZ STEP

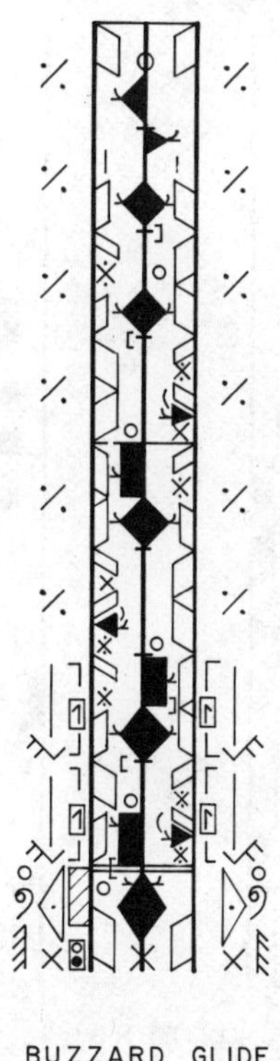

BUZZARD GLIDE

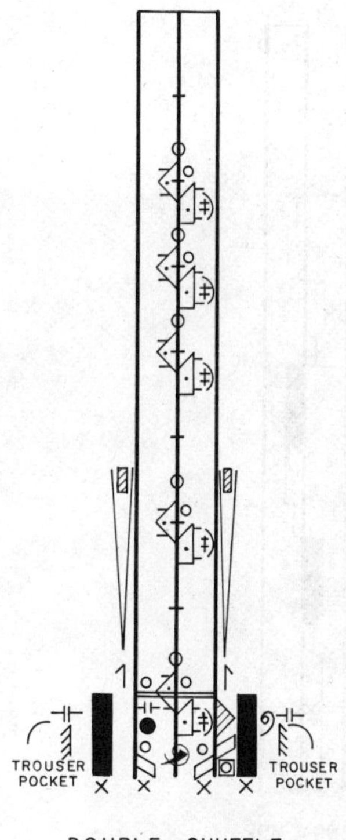

DOUBLE SHUFFLE

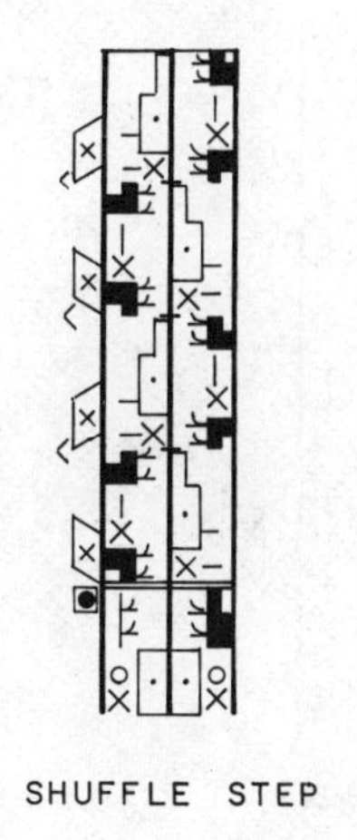

SHUFFLE STEP

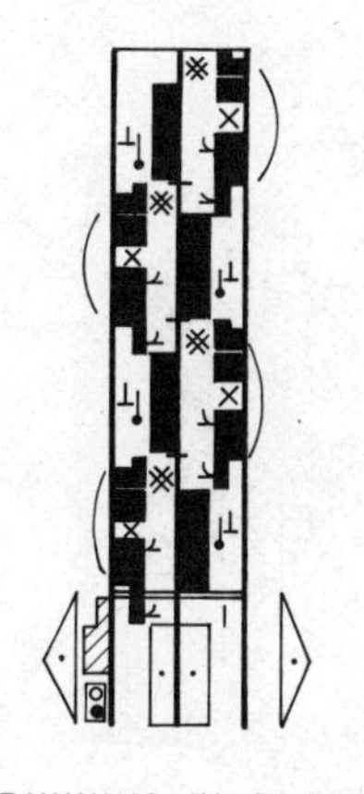

RUNNING IN PLACE

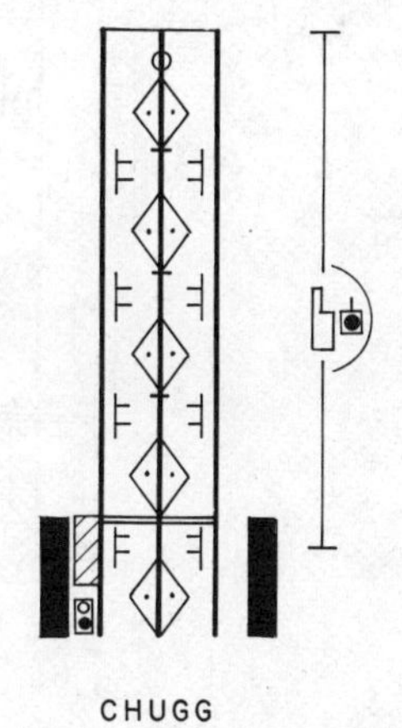

CHUGG

Plate 5

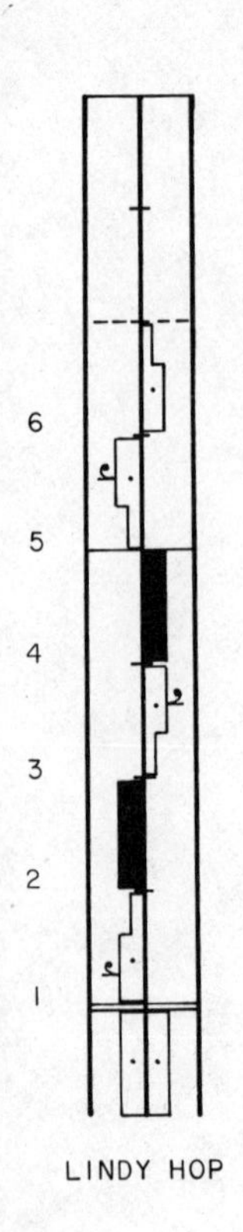

6
5
4
3
2
1
LINDY HOP

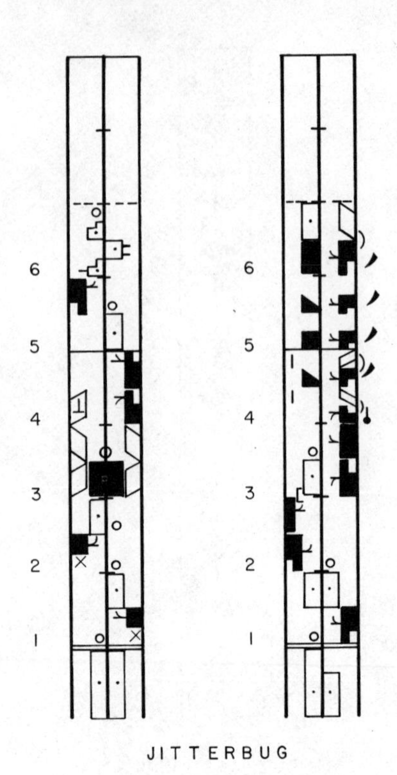

6
5
4
3
2
1
6
5
4
3
2
1
JITTERBUG

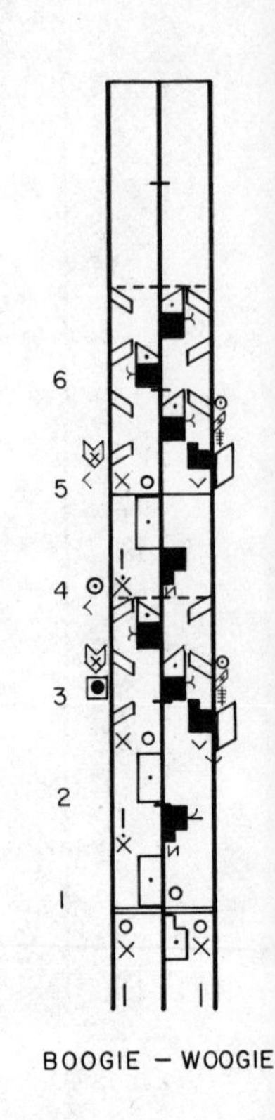

6
5
4
3
2
1
BOOGIE – WOOGIE

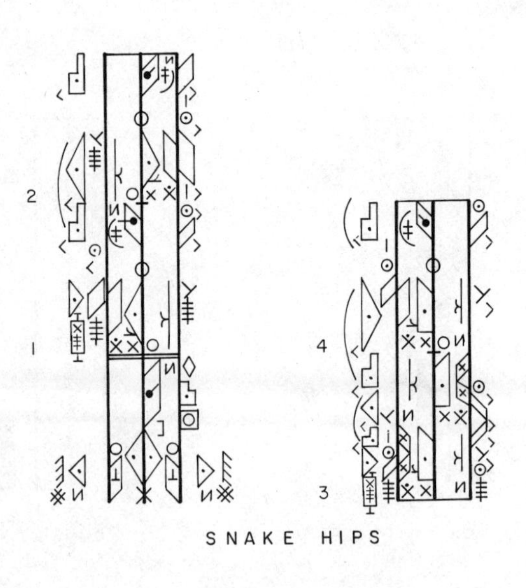

2
1
4
3
SNAKE HIPS

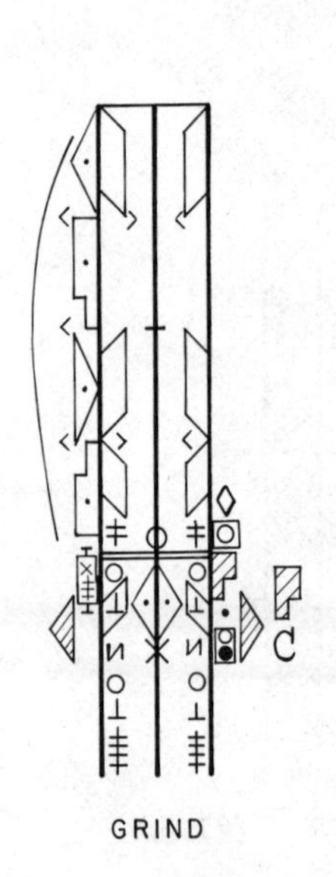

GRIND

Plate 6

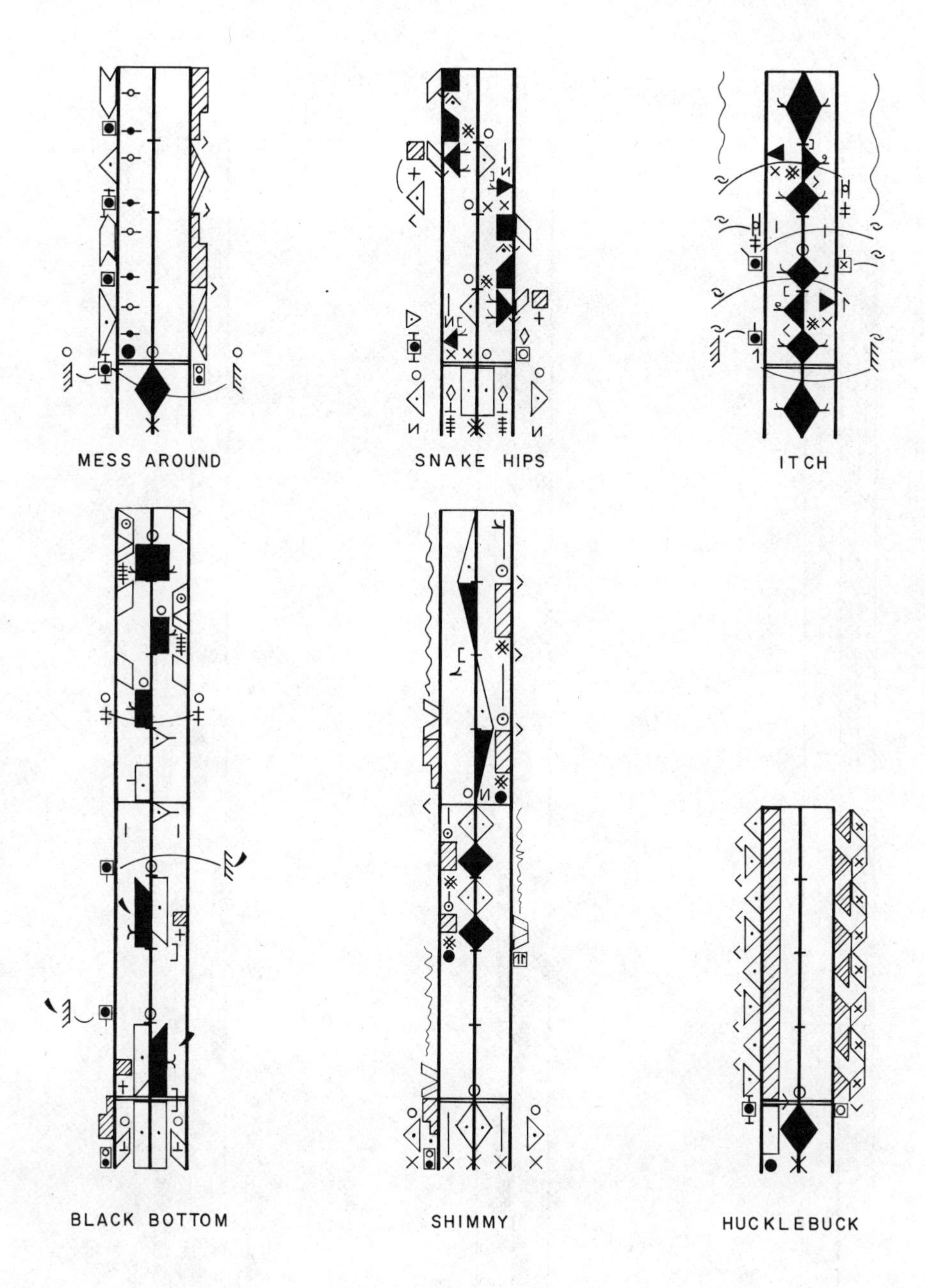
MESS AROUND
SNAKE HIPS
ITCH
BLACK BOTTOM
SHIMMY
HUCKLEBUCK

Plate 7

CHARLESTON STEPS

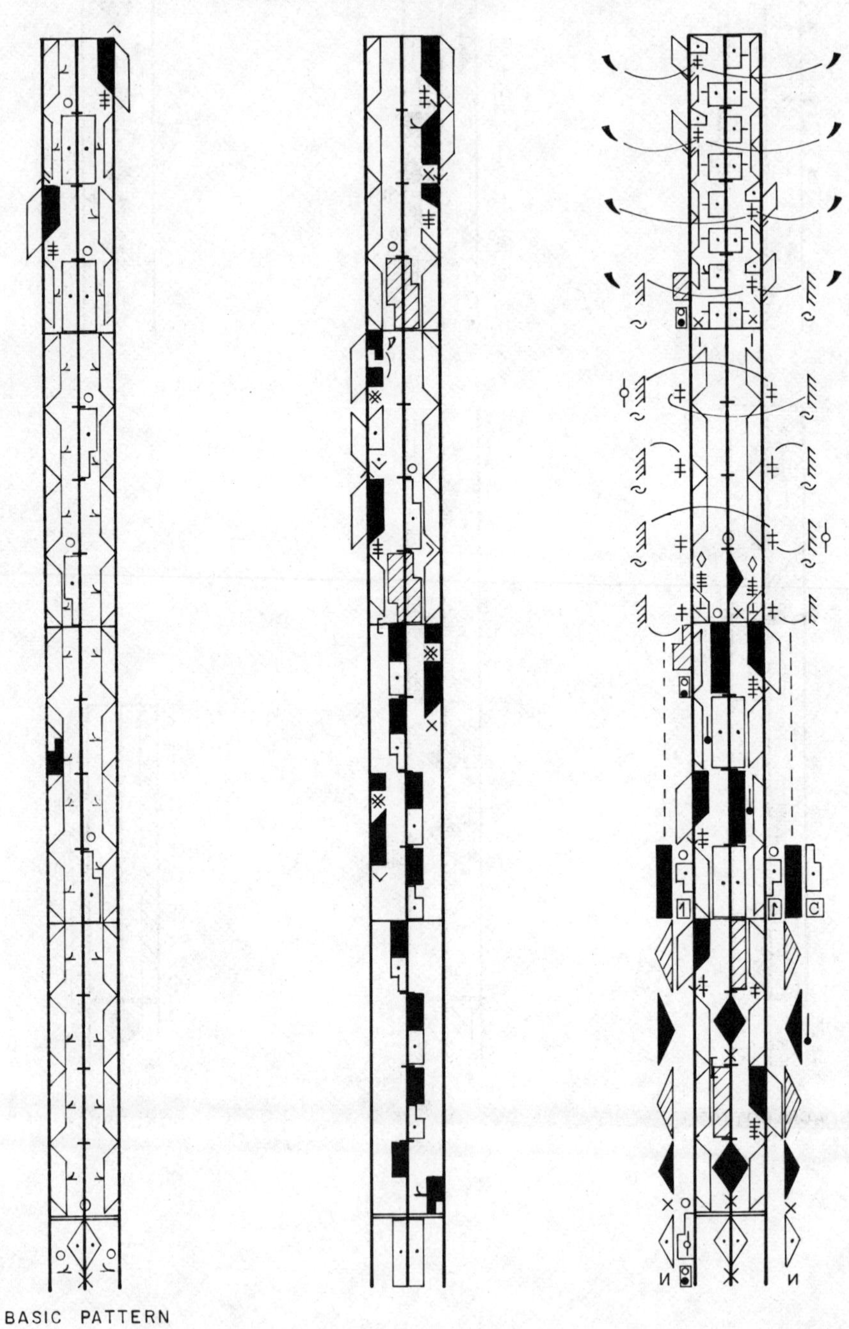

Plate 8

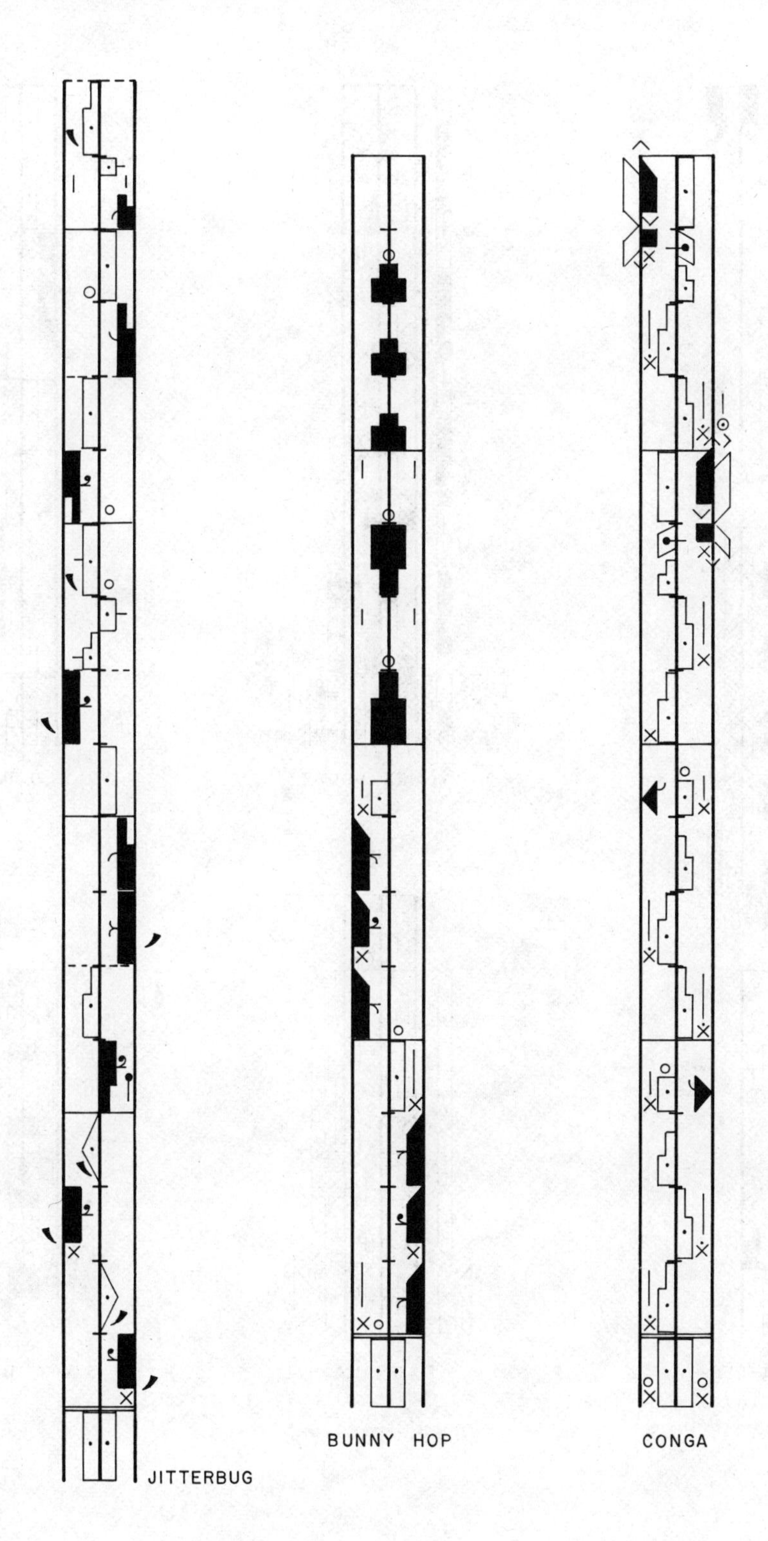

Plate 9

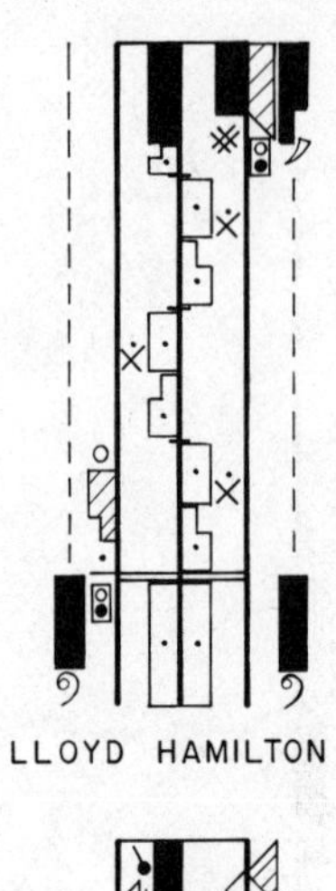

LLOYD HAMILTON

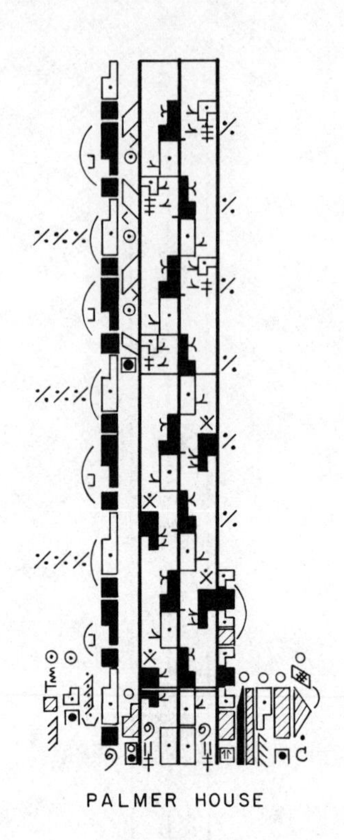

PALMER HOUSE

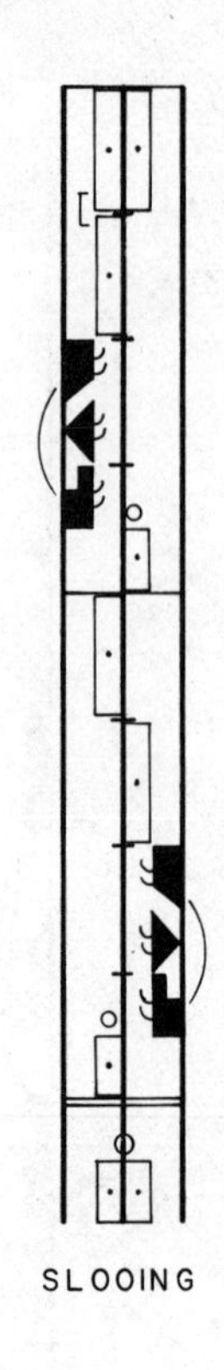

SLOOING

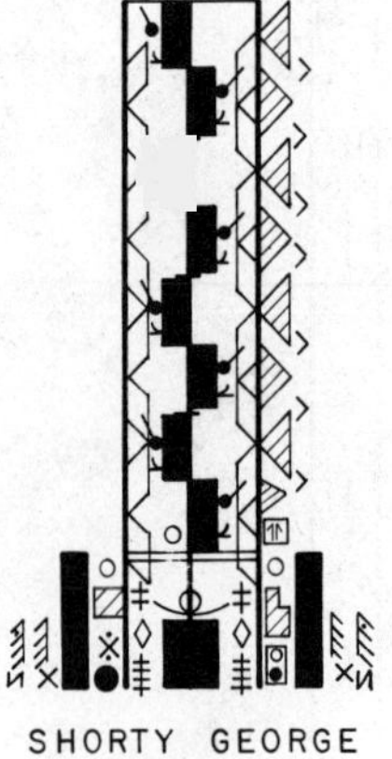

SHORTY GEORGE

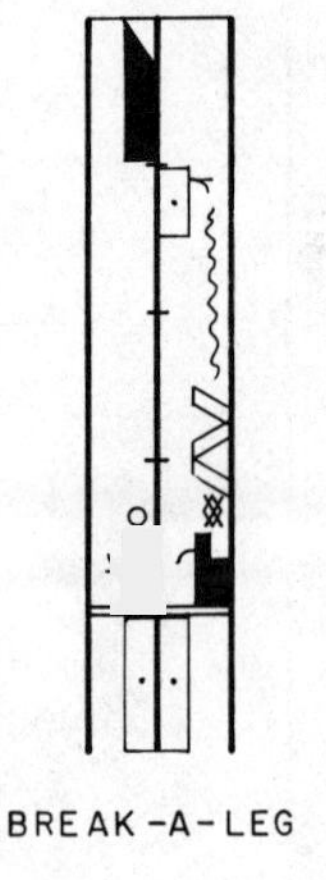

BREAK-A-LEG

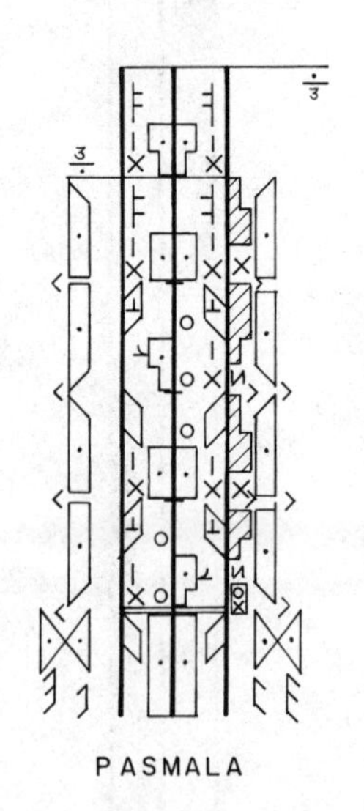

PASMALA

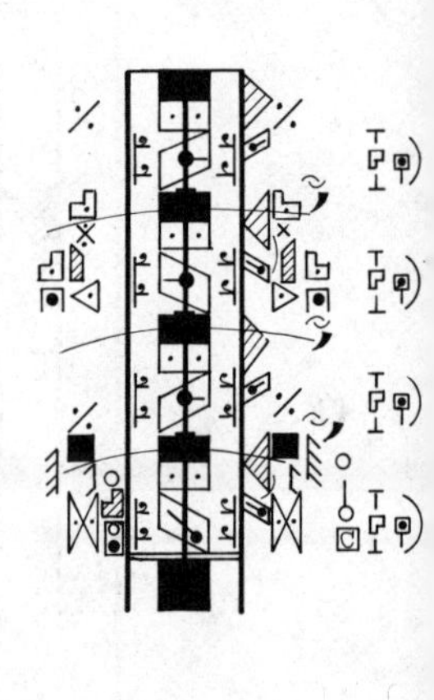

SWAY BACK

Plate 10

TYPICAL JAZZ DANCE STEPS

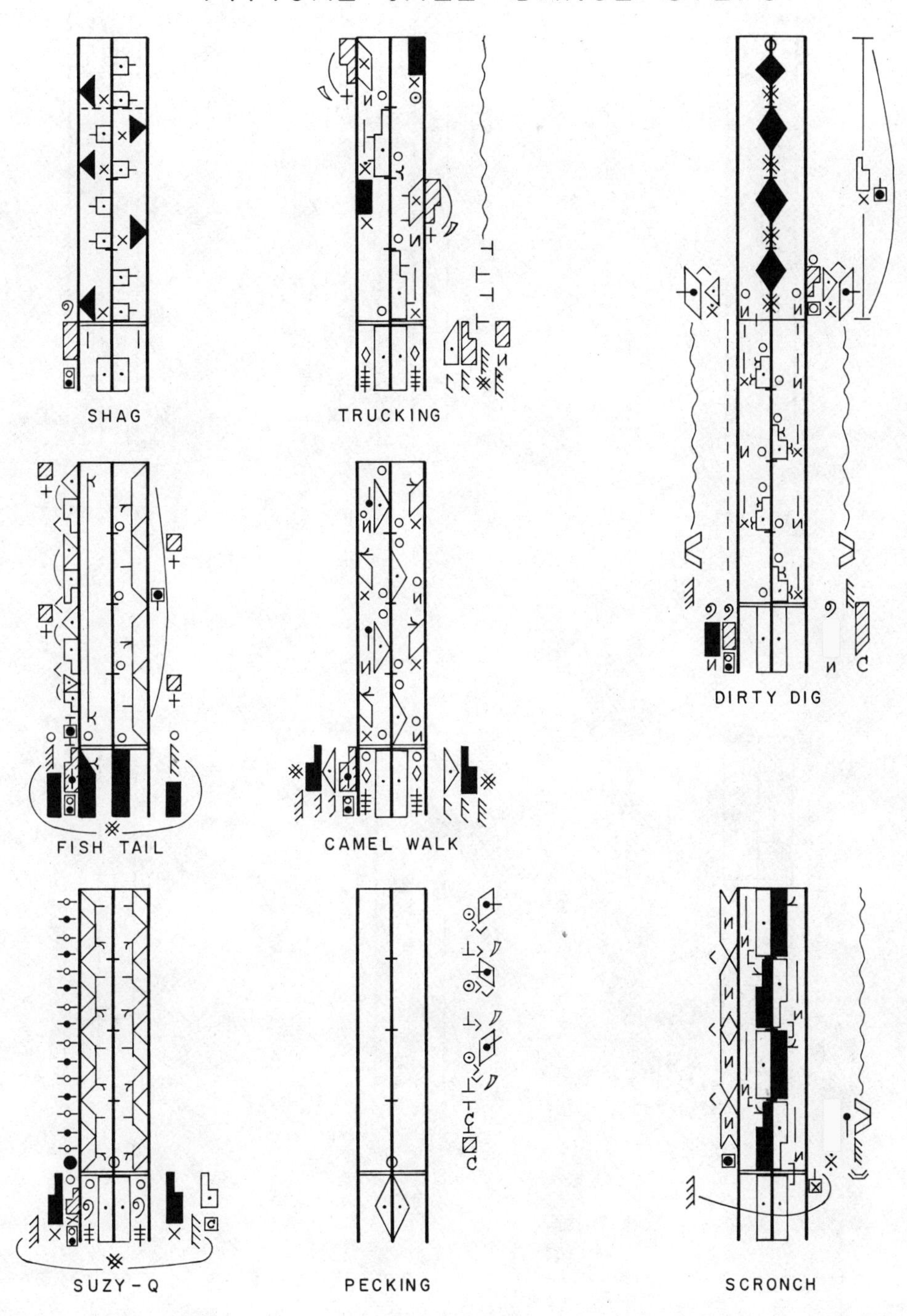

Plate 11

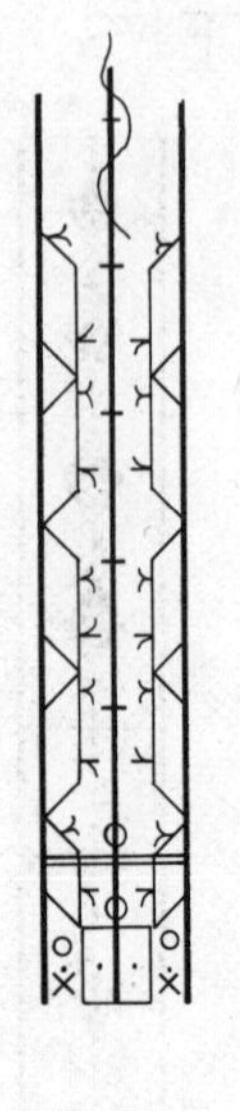

CRAB WALK

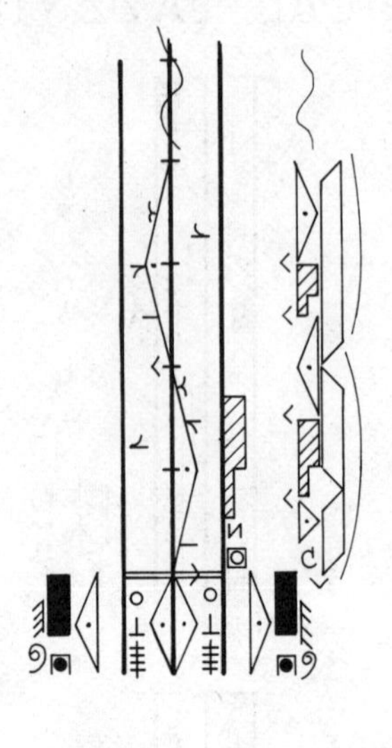

EAGLE ROCK

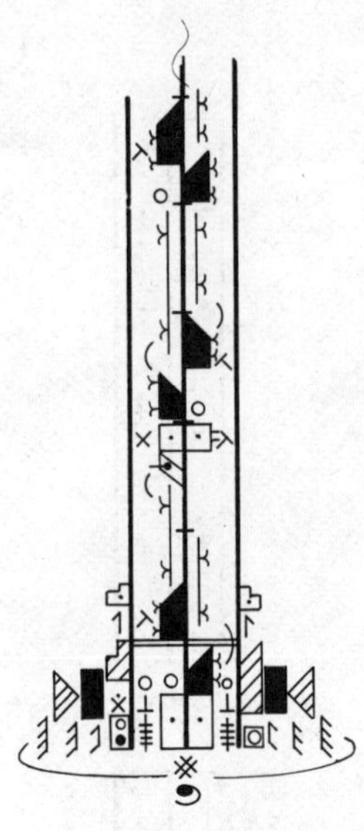

BUZZARD

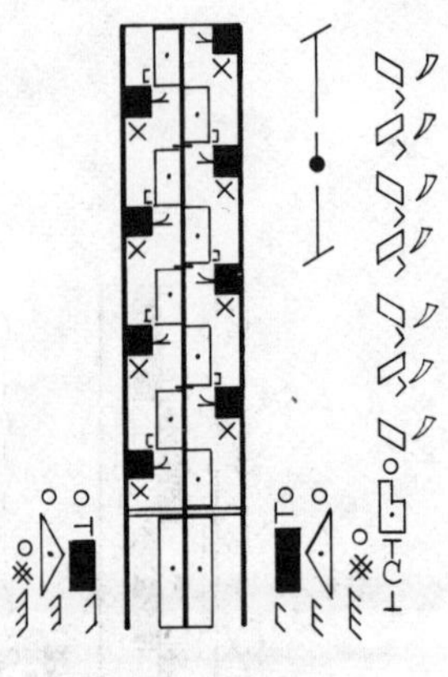

CHICKEN

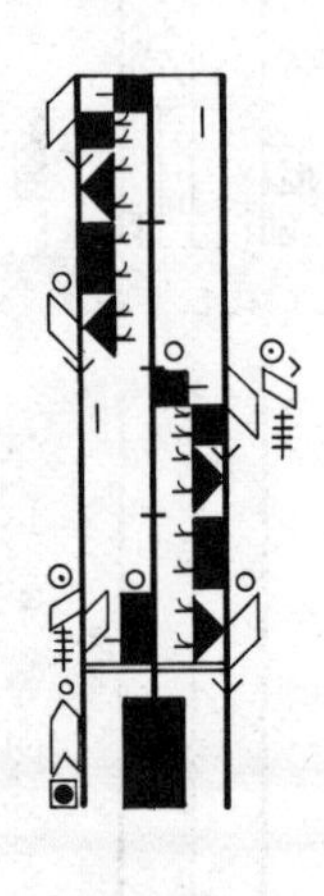

CAMEL WALK

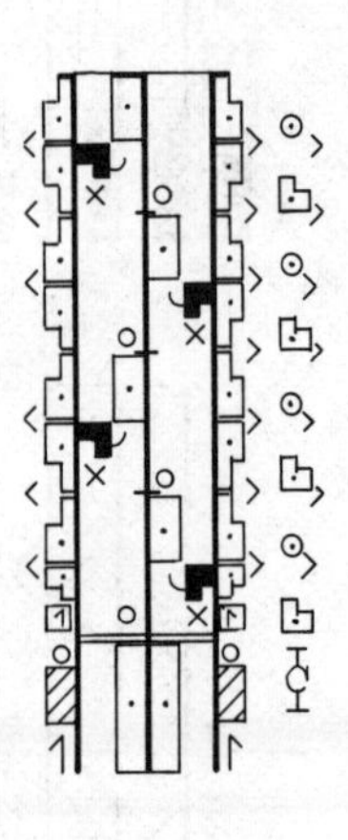

GOOSE NECK

Plate 12

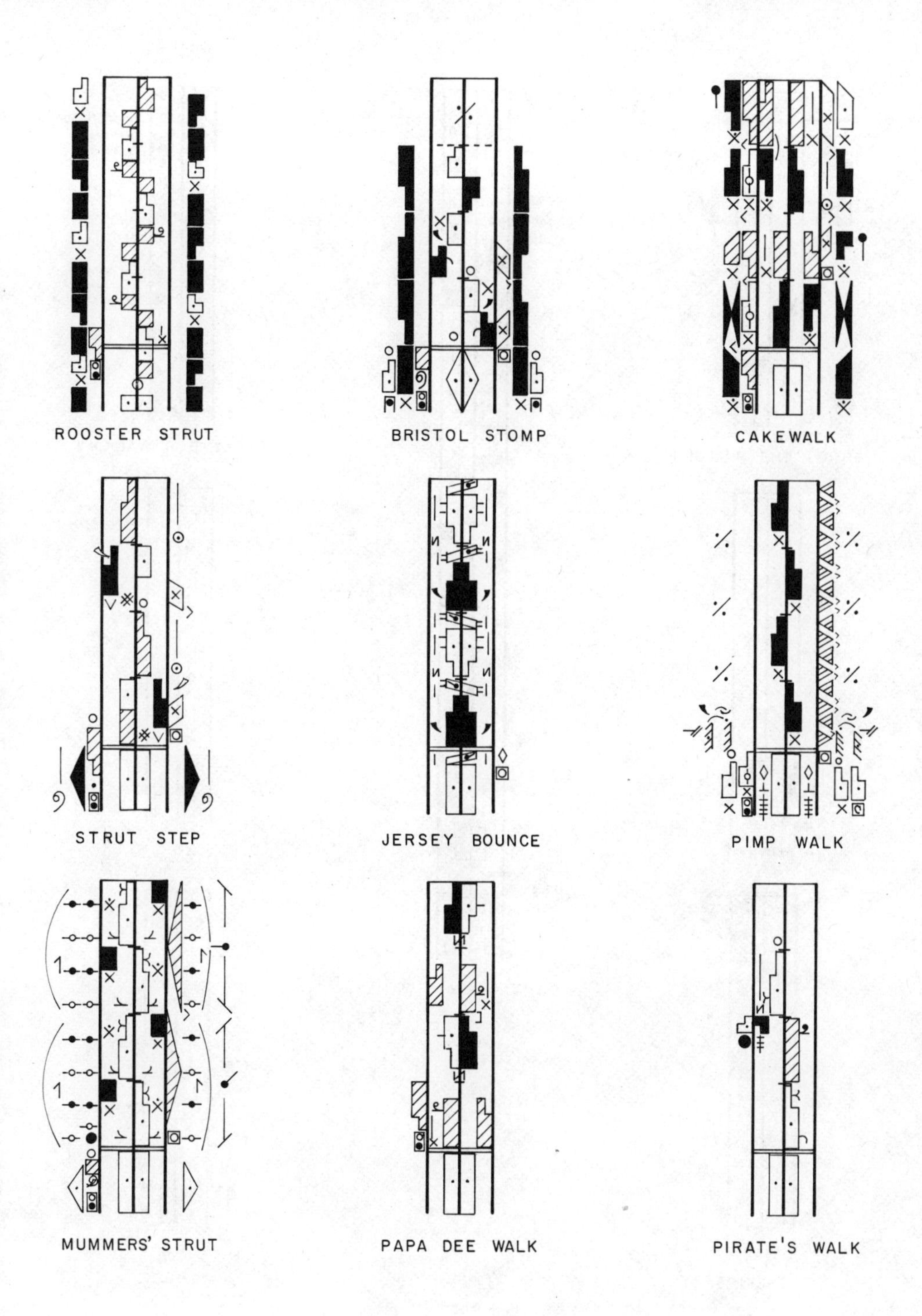
ROOSTER STRUT
BRISTOL STOMP
CAKEWALK
STRUT STEP
JERSEY BOUNCE
PIMP WALK
MUMMERS' STRUT
PAPA DEE WALK
PIRATE'S WALK

Plate 13

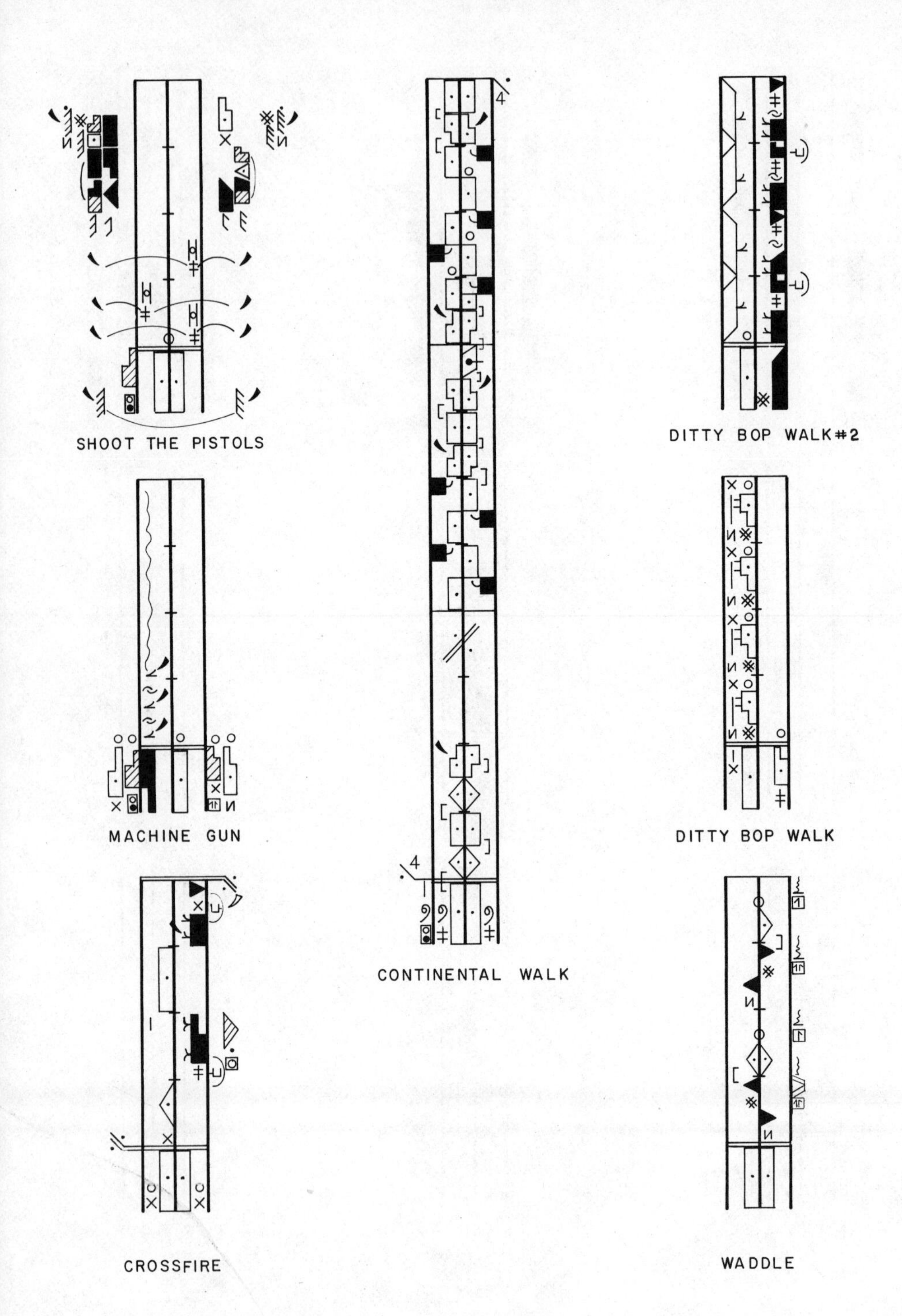
SHOOT THE PISTOLS
4
4
DITTY BOP WALK #2
MACHINE GUN
DITTY BOP WALK
CONTINENTAL WALK
CROSSFIRE
WADDLE

Plate 14

STROLL

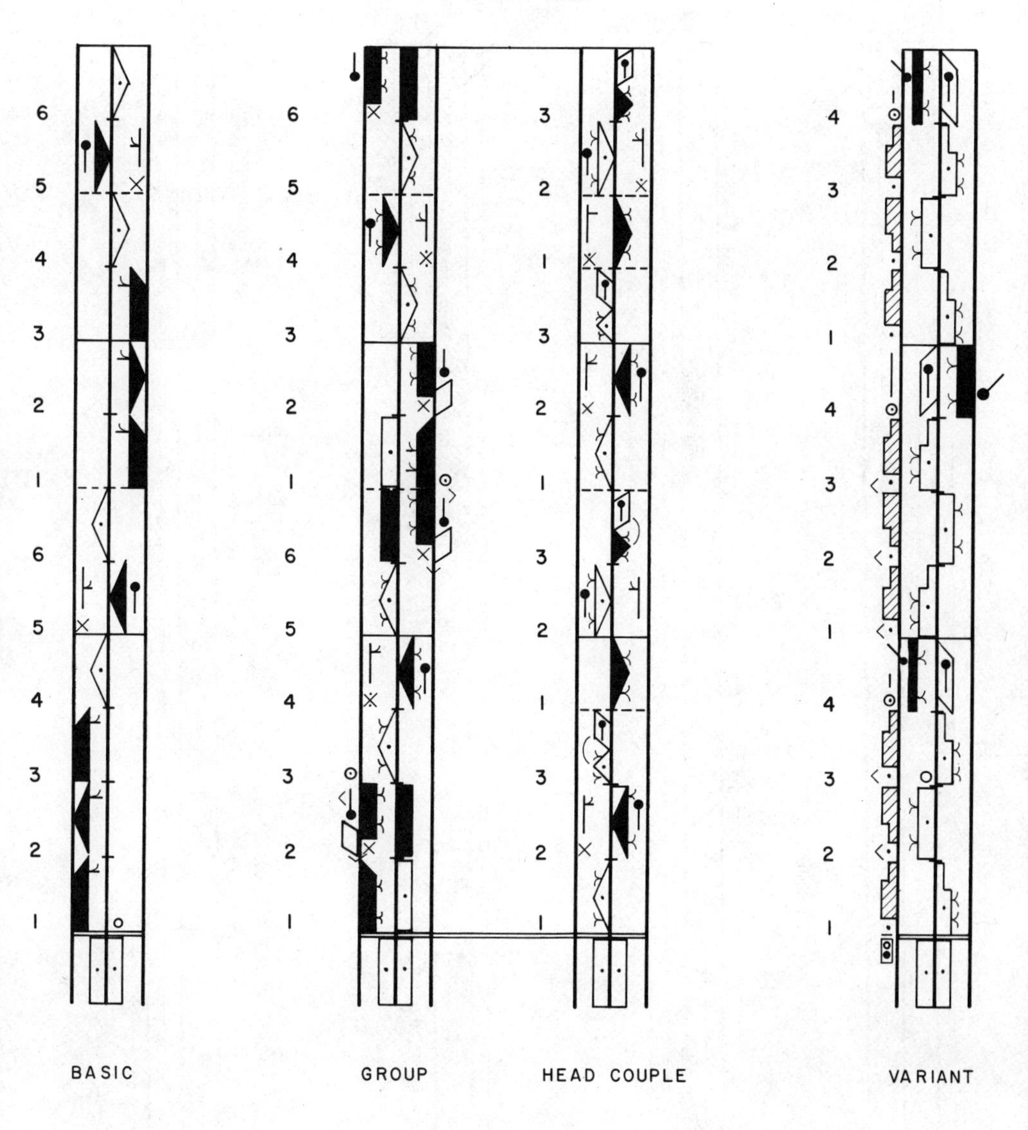

Plate 15

TWIST

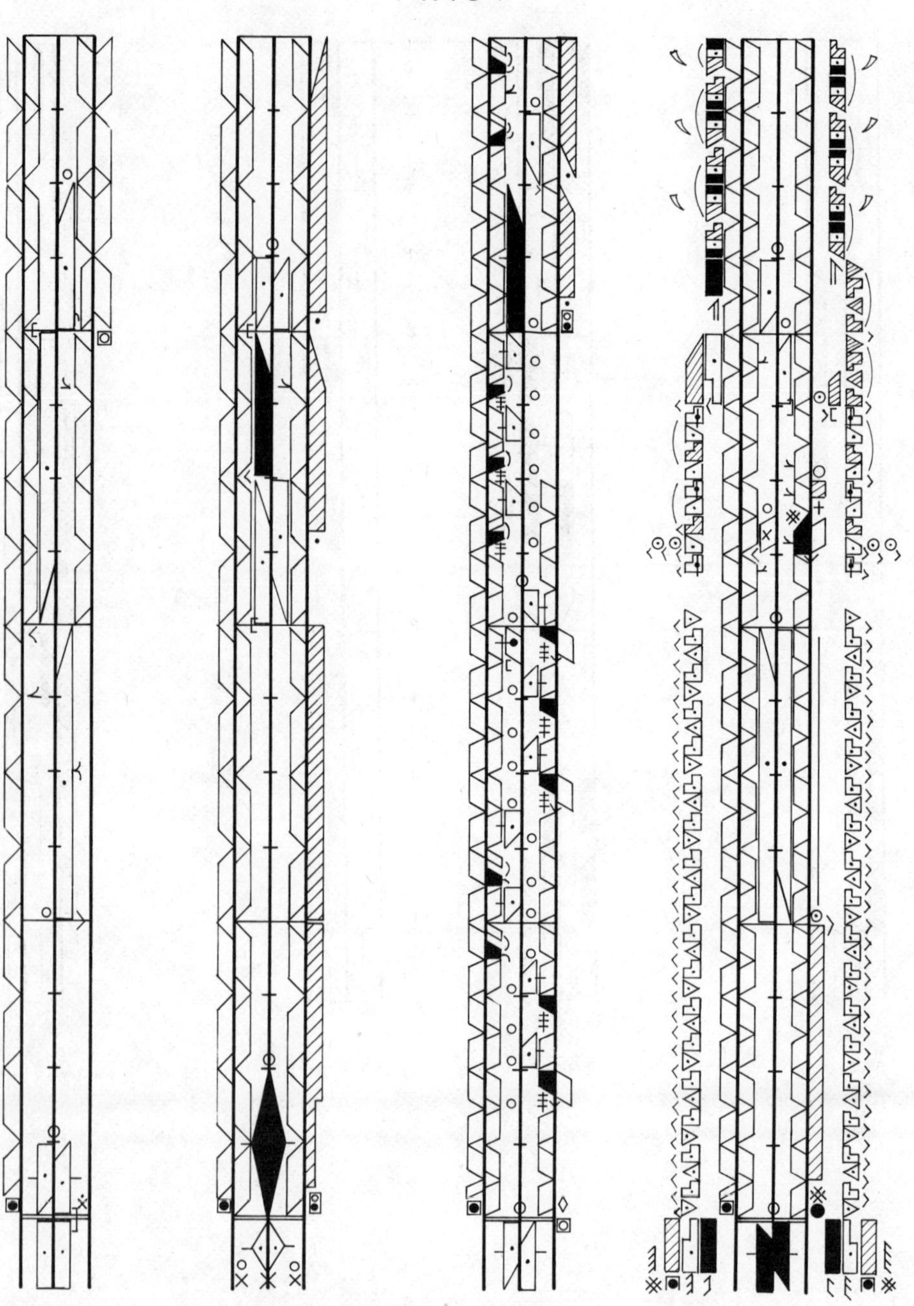

Plate 16

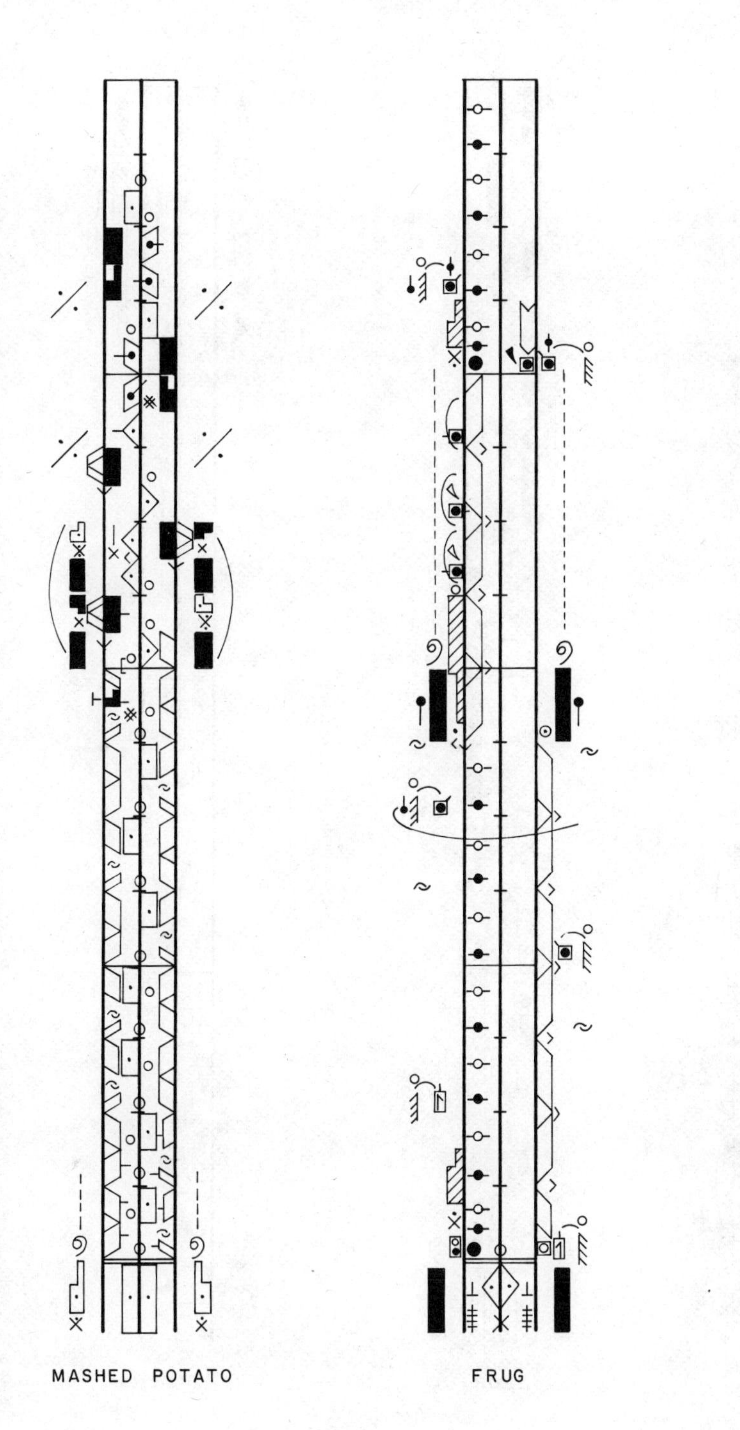

Plate 17

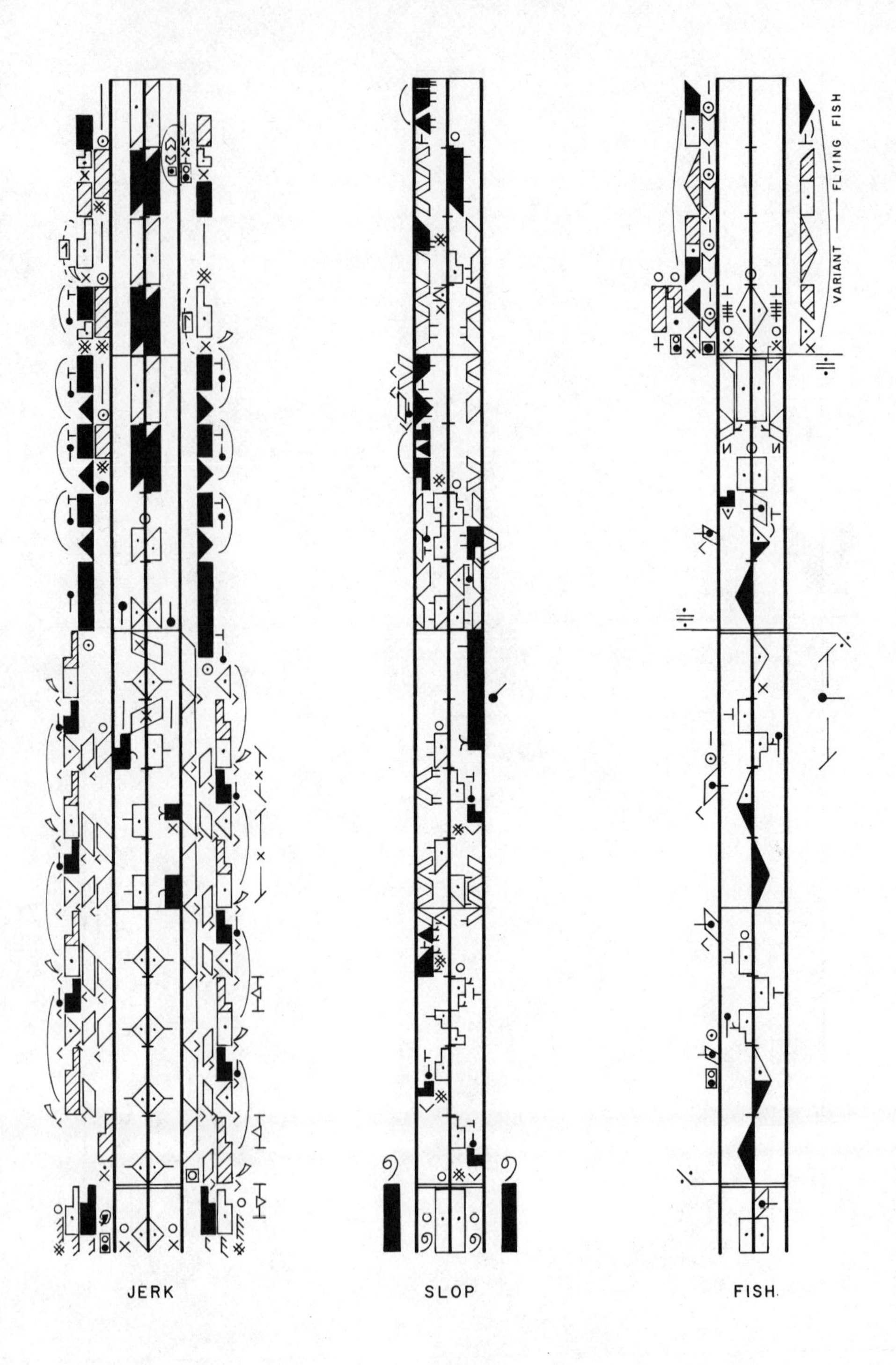

Plate 18

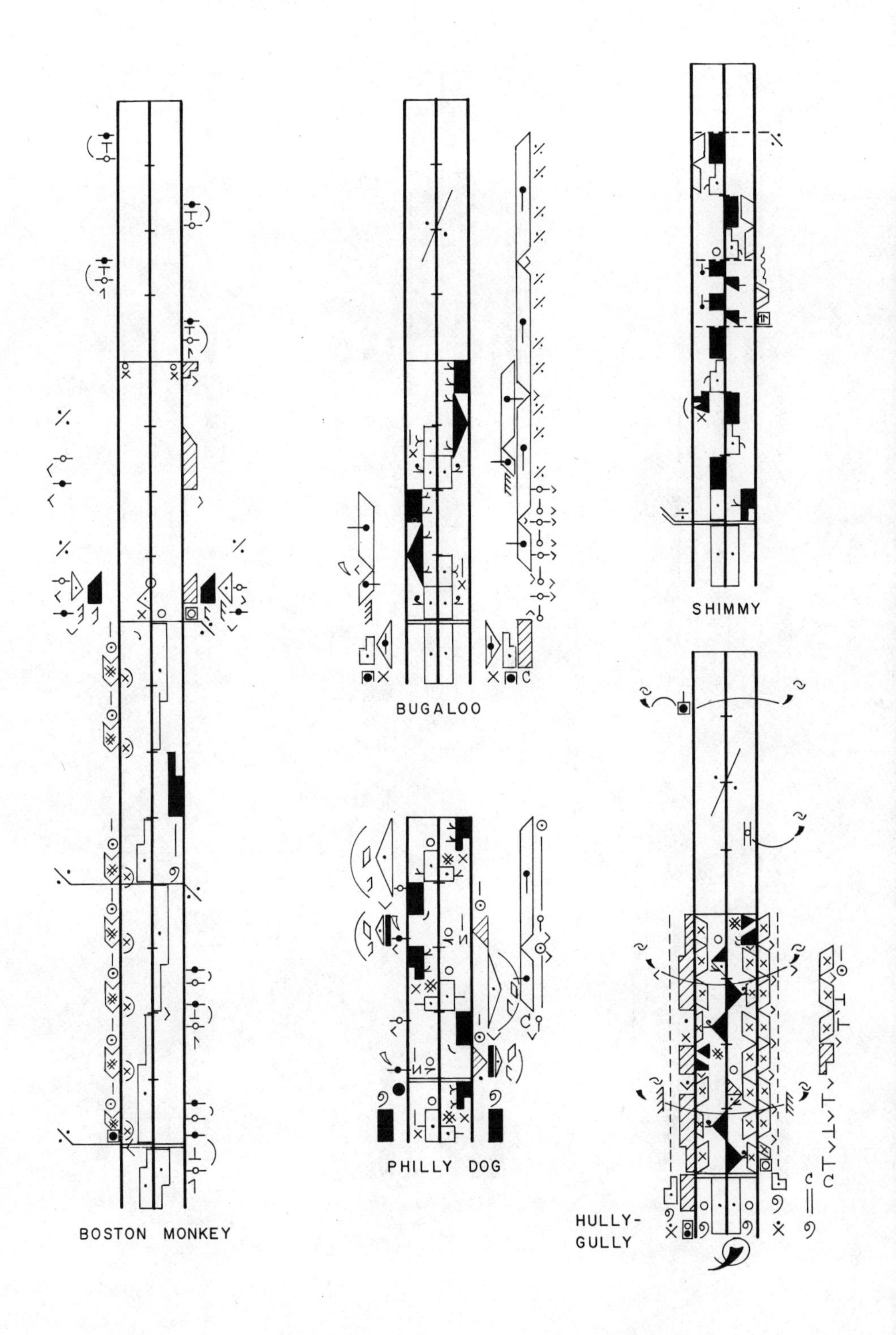

Plate 19

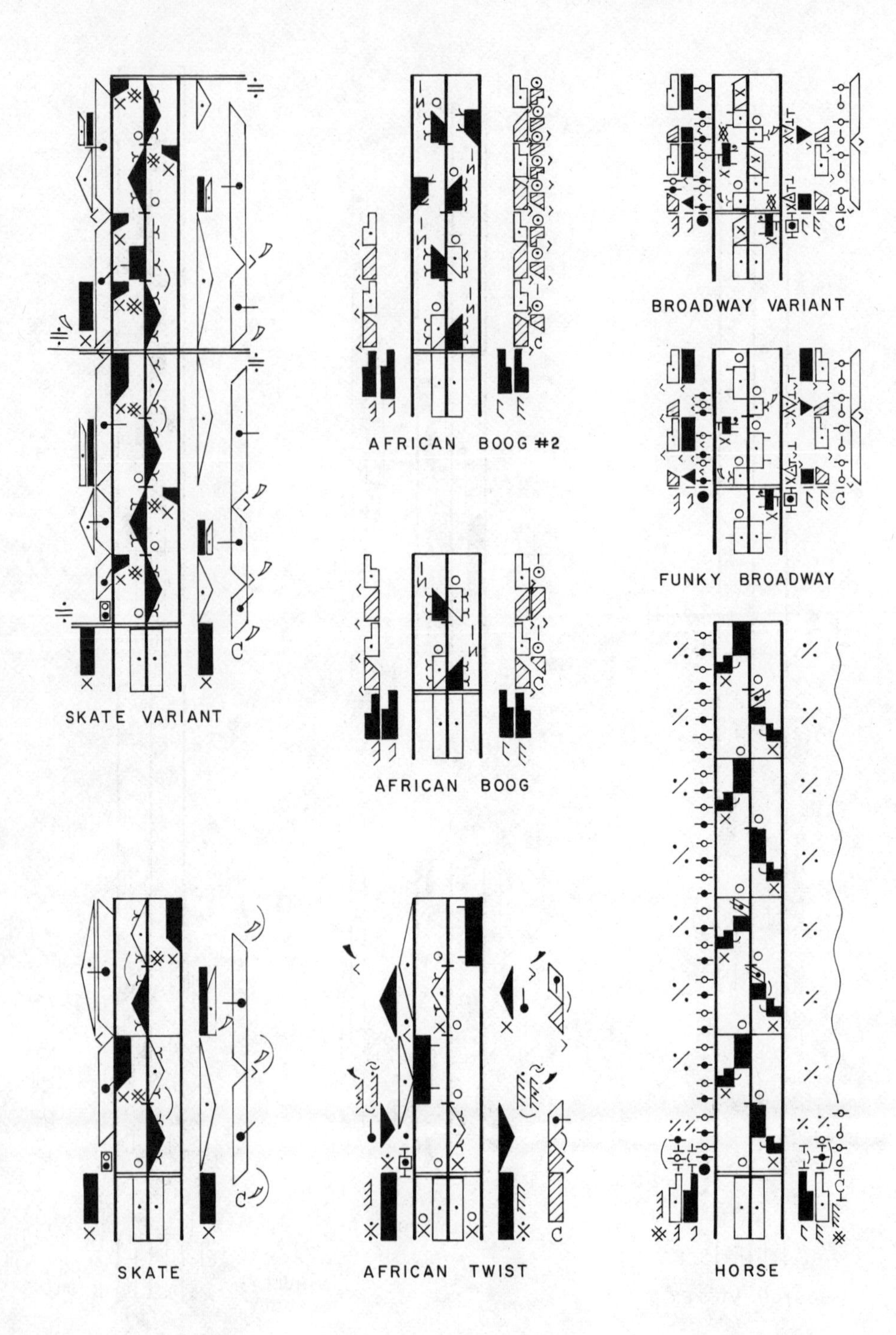
SKATE VARIANT
AFRICAN BOOG #2
AFRICAN BOOG
BROADWAY VARIANT
FUNKY BROADWAY
HORSE
SKATE
AFRICAN TWIST

Plate 20

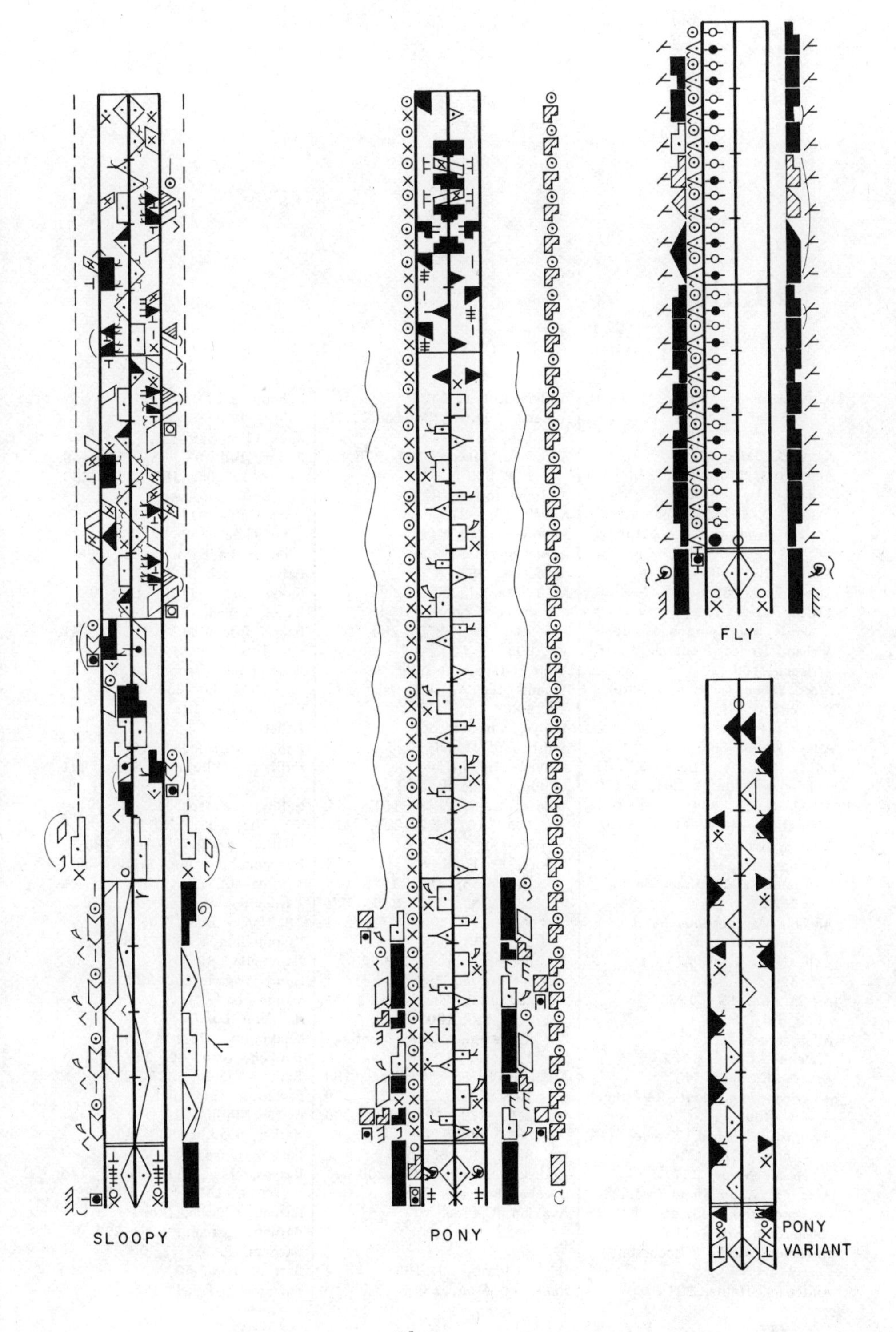

Plate 21

Index